Maureen O'Sullivan

"No Average Jane"

By the same author:
The Cinema History of Burt Lancaster
Kings of the Jungle: A History of the Tarzan Movies
Chuck Connors "The Man Behind the Rifle"
Johnny Weissmuller "Twice the Hero"
Coming in 2008:
Burt Lancaster "In Light and Shadow"

Maureen O'Sullivan

"No Average Jane"

David A. Fury
Artist's Press
MINNEAPOLIS, MINNESOTA

Copyright © 2006 by David A. Fury
All rights reserved under International and Pan-American
Copyright Conventions. Published in the United States
by **Artist's Press,** Minneapolis, Minnesota

Artist's Press is a registered trademark

Library of Congress Cataloging-in-Publication Data
Fury, David A.
Maureen O'Sullivan: "No Average Jane"/by David A. Fury
p.   cm.
Includes bibliographical references and index.
ISBN: 0-924556-06-4 / 978-0-924556-06-7
(Smythe Sewn case : 60# acid-free paper)

1. O'Sullivan, Maureen Paula (1911-1998)
2. Actors — United States — Biography
I. Title.
791.43'028'092 — dc20
(B)   2005-931445   CIP
Printed in the United States of America
10 9 8 7 6 5 4 3 2 1
First Edition

Contents

Author's Introduction vii

1. "Diamond in the Rough Discovered in Dublin" 11
2. "A Child is Born Amongst the Leprechauns" 15
3. "Trite but True ... A Star Is Born" 29
4. "Adventures in La-La Land" 35
5. "Stardom Beckons: The MGM Lion Roars" 51
6. "Woman in Demand: On and Off Screen" 67
7. "The Love Affairs of a Young Actress" 85
8. "Jungle Jane Proves Mighty Courageous" 103
9. "Outta the Jungle, Maureen Still A Big Star" 117
10. "At Last ... A Dying Scene" 135
11. "Accused of Murder ... Woman on the Lam" 151
12. "Back to the Jungle ... Another Tarzan Picture" 165
13. "Marriage and the Madcap Marx Brothers" 185
14. "Maureen and Robert Taylor ... a Fine Romantic Pairing" 209
15. "Maureen Becomes a Mother... On-Screen and Real Life" 235
16. "The Big War Changes Everything" 249
17. "John Farrow Goes to War ... Maureen Carries On" 261
18. "The War Years ... 1940 - 1945" 277
19. "The Big Clock ... tick, tick, tick ... " 295

20. "The 1950s ... Baby Boom Generation" 311
21. "The Redoubtable Mr. Farrow" 325
22. "Aftermath of a Tragedy" 341
23. "The Affairs of an Older Actress" 353
24. "Maureen Meets Her Match: James Cushing" 377
25. "Busy Actress, Happy Lady" 397

Motion Picture Filmography 425
Television Films 436
Radio Appearances 437
Television Appearances 441
Stage Appearances 443
Acknowledgments 447
Bibliography 449
Index 451

Photo section One ... Early Life in Ireland .... 8 pages
Photo section Two ... Stardom in Hollywood, 1930s .... 12 pages
Photo section Three ... Movie Scenes, 1930s - 1950s .... 12 pages
Photo section Four ... Behind the Scenes of the Tarzan Set .... 16 pages
Photo section Five ... John Farrow and Seven Children .... 8 pages
Photo section Six ... Stage, Screen, and Jim Cushing .... 8 pages

Total Pages including Photo Sections 520

Author's Introduction

One glorious summer day in June of 1992 my telephone rang and I was delighted to discover that Maureen O'Sullivan, one of the great actresses of yesteryear, was calling for me.

I had written Maureen a letter a few weeks prior, concerning the possibility of her authoring a foreword for a new Tarzan history and filmography that I was researching for McFarland publishers.

"Good afternoon Mr. Fury. My name is Jim Cushing — I'm Maureen's husband. She would like to speak with you about your request." My heart was racing euphorically when, moments later, our conversation began:

"Hello David, this is Maureen O'Sullivan. I'm flattered that you would consider me to write a foreword for your book. I'm not quite sure where I would begin?" she mused. "I still clearly remember my early beginnings with MGM, and meeting Johnny Weissmuller and the great fun we had making the Tarzan pictures. I was also making dozens of other films for Metro in those years, and many of them went on to be classic films as well."

Her voice was as I remembered — lyrical, gentle and with her inimitable Irish accent. This was the voice that immediately connected me with the beautiful actress I had seen in so many motion pictures.

Over the next several minutes Maureen and I amiably discussed my ideas about the foreword. I asked her to recall her memories of the Tarzan films, and working with Johnny Weissmuller and little John Sheffield over the period of ten years when she filmed six Tarzan adventures. I suggested that she compose a page or two, and to feel free to talk about her career in general. Of course the Tarzan pictures were just a small percentage of her body of work during an amazing 60-year career in the entertainment business.

When the conversation ended, I was exuberant with the results: Maureen had agreed to write the foreword, pending her review of my manuscript. I was filled with pride that my name would be linked with the illustrious name of Maureen O'Sullivan, if only by this small matter of a literary work.

True to her word, the foreword authored by Maureen arrived a few weeks later. Eventually, I sent her a lengthy written interview which she dutifully answered, each and every one of her replies handwritten in her very clear script. She answered questions about her early life in Ireland and her career with MGM, and fondly recalled some of her favorite films, actors, and actresses.

During the ten-year period of 1932 to 1942, Maureen starred in a total of 41 motion pictures for MGM, many of them classics. The six Tarzan films from this era and her role of Jane made her an international sex symbol and a household name. However, Maureen was also Louis B. Mayer's favorite "second lead" female star, and the studio kept her working in one picture after another. Many of her motion pictures were romances where she assumed the female lead opposite several of the Hollywood greats of the Golden Age.

In the ensuing decades, she became a bonafide star. She added radio to her repertoire in the mid-1930s and proceeded to television drama around 1950. Maureen then graduated to the legitimate stage beginning in 1962 with the Broadway hit, *Never Too Late*. After a thirty-year career as a film star, she was a top-drawer stage actress for another twenty-five years, from 1961 to 1986.

Maureen was the girl-next-door that every man adored. Average Joe daydreamed about being the hero who came to her rescue, and then carried her off to the lofty tree-house for a night of jungle passion. Of course every young woman that took in the movies or read the fan magazines would have gladly taken her place in her life of fame and glamour.

In the Tarzan films she oozed sensuality clothed only in the skimpy little jungle outfits that complemented Weissmuller's Tarzan loin cloth. Johnny and Maureen were the sexiest screen couple in America during the 1930s, each individual idolized and adulated by men and women everywhere. They both had a rare combination of personal beauty, perfectly-crafted physiques, and charismatic personalities — the heroic nature of the Tarzan and Jane screen characters made them super-heroes of the era.

Off-screen both Maureen and Johnny were wholesome, all-American types. Weissmuller was a former Olympic swimming champion, and he was equally admired for his past athletic achievements as for his screen heroics in his role of Tarzan. The public would have loved nothing more than to see a real-life romance between Maureen and Johnny, but they were the best of friends and nothing more.

In 1992 Maureen revealed to me their relationship that went beyond the ten years they spent in MGM's imaginary jungle world: "We were dear friends. He was simple, unpretentious, without conceit — a wonderful big kid." Johnny called her "Maggie," because he thought the name Maureen was too sophisticated. He played a myriad assortment of innocent gags on her over the years, including an exploding birthday cake that covered her face with sweet sticky frosting. Sometimes Maureen would reciprocate with her own simple jokes.

After my original Tarzan history was published in 1993, I would send a letter or card to Maureen from time to time, updating her on my projects including a new biography of Johnny Weissmuller (published in 2000). I would always receive a card or short note back from her, but sometimes it would take several weeks for a reply. She told me that she was almost three years behind on her correspondence, so not to fret if her replies to me were somewhat delayed.

The actress did invest a lot of her free time answering mail from her adoring fans, still in vast numbers despite the passing years. She would always sign a photo or autograph whenever possible, never considering it an imposition but rather a privilege.

Maureen had a basic philosophy that you got out of life what you put into it. If you were a kind person, you received kindness back. She caught a break and was brought to Hollywood because she was beautiful, emoted sensuality, and could read lines well enough to pass her initial screen test. But she stayed in Hollywood for decades because she was loved by everyone, from the top man at MGM, Louis B. Mayer, to her fellow actors, her millions of fans, and even the support staff that are part of every Hollywood production.

Life for the most part was kind to Maureen, although she suffered her share of tough blows along the way. She lost her son Michael in a plane crash in 1958, and she raised her children without a partner after husband John Farrow succumbed to a heart attack in 1963.

When Maureen O'Sullivan died in 1998 in Phoenix with her husband James Cushing by her bedside, she was mourned by movie fans around the world. I too was saddened by the loss of this beautiful lady from Ireland, who made America her home and had achieved great success in the tough business of the Hollywood movie factory. She was a marvelous actress, and if you examine her roles from 1930 to 1994, she almost always played heroines, sweethearts, the girl-next-door, and sometimes a victim or jilted lover.

While her most famous character was Jane of the Jungle, she also made a wonderful career out of playing women of courage, character, and heart. Maureen rarely portrayed the bad seed, the nasty-girl roles that instead went to Bette Davis, Joan Crawford, and Barbara Stanwyck.

So this is her story, as true and accurate as the gathered facts portray. Like the other giants of the Golden Age of Hollywood, she was larger than life. Maureen was lucky enough to be born with beauty and grace, and therefore lived a charmed life. She indeed was a kind and wonderful person and deserved the admiration of her fans, and that love and adulation was not in vain. It was appreciated and returned by Maureen O'Sullivan, one of the true heroines of the Silver Screen.

Signed photographs from Maureen O'Sullivan to your author David Fury

CHAPTER ONE
"Diamond in the Rough Discovered in Dublin"

The defining moment in the life of Maureen O'Sullivan, that exact instant in time when fate intervened, came about when a Hollywood film director spotted her at a dance in late summer, 1929. The evening dances were part of the Dublin Horse Show, which was the social event of the season. Young men and women brought in their horses to compete in various equestrian events, and the dances were an opportunity to relax and socialize.

"Horse Show week in Dublin was always a wonderful time for us girls," recalled Maureen fondly. "You'd see all the great horses from all over the world competing. There was a dance every night and I had lots of beaux, eager to be my partner. On the last night I was frightfully tired and ought not to have gone out at all, but I was in a very high-spirited mood, and since my father was away in London at a regimental dinner, I managed to persuade my mother to let me go. I don't know why, but it seemed so terribly important that I should go."

Maureen had been asked to the dance by a handsome young man from Trinity College, so without a doubt she wouldn't have missed it for the world. Perhaps it was the hand of fate giving her a push toward her date with destiny. She waltzed the night away with her escort and other young men who found the courage to ask for a dance.

As the end of the evening approached, Maureen noticed a group of people who didn't seem to fit in with the locals. One man had dark, curly hair and his female companion was a platinum blonde. This table of outsiders had a "Hollywood" look about them, and everyone knew exactly who they were. It was widely reported in the newspapers that an American director and his entourage were in Dublin making a film starring the legendary Irish tenor John McCormack. The curly-headed man was Frank Borzage, one of the most highly-regarded directors and twice a winner of the Oscar (1927 and later in 1931). The blonde beauty at his table was his wife, the former silent picture actress Rena Rogers.

This particular night was a social night for Borzage and his party, but he still kept a sharp lookout for talent among the many attractive young women at the dance. The director had come to Ireland in hopes of casting two important juvenile roles in his production of *Song O' My Heart*. This was to be one of the first talking motion pictures and would feature the beautiful tenor voice of McCormack, a legend in Ireland and America as well.

One of the roles had already been cast: Borzage had located ten-year-old Tommy Clifford through his auditions. The search for a teenage ingenue had proved fruitless thus far, and it had all but been decided that they would use a Hollywood actress rather than a genuine Irish lass. Even the most beautiful girl in Dublin, Grace McLaughlin, had been passed over for the role. The ship would be sailing in a few days, returning Borzage and his company back to America. Several of her friends had auditioned for the part, but Maureen hadn't even considered auditioning for the role of the young girl, because as she admitted later, "I didn't think I was pretty enough."

Frank Borzage that evening had his sharp eye for talent on Maureen, who was eighteen, beautiful, wholesome, and very Irish. As luck would have it, there was the perfect young woman for the role of Eileen O'Brien, only a few feet away at the next table over. Maureen was dancing and laughing, and having the time of her life — and perhaps casting a smile in the direction of the American movie people.

As the evening wound down, and despite exhaustion, Maureen talked her partner into the final dance of the night. "Eventually my escort wanted to go home, but I had a feeling something was going to happen, and I said, 'No, let's stay and have one more dance.' That dance sealed my fate."

In a June 1930 interview with Ted LeBerthon of the *L.A. Record*, Maureen's memory was fresh when she recalled that wondrous night in September 1929:

"Everything happened all of a sudden. To be precise, it was the night of September 11, and I am quite certain it was a Thursday night.

"I was at dinner with a boy. And — I might as well explain to you — we have professional dancing persons in Dublin, 'pros' we call them, who will dance with patrons for six-pence a dance.

"A chap at another table had been dancing with one of the 'pros.' At the conclusion of the dance, the 'pro' brought him over to where I was seated, and said, 'This gentleman is from the Fox Film company, and, while you must pardon us for this intrusion, he wants to know if you would be interested in acting in a picture.'

"My heart was in my mouth. I must confess I was quite overjoyed. For, was I interested? Would a duck swim? But I managed to stammer: 'Oh, of course —' or some such thing. Then the girl 'pro' introduced me to the chap and he turned out to be Chet Lyons, the Fox cameraman. He introduced me, in turn, to Mr. Borzage."

When she returned to her table after the last dance, the head waiter brought her a card with the name *Frank Borzage* identifying the bearer. The short message written on the back of the card stated, "If you are interested in films, will you come to my office tomorrow at eleven?"

Maureen read the card, tired and unsure of what exactly this meant. Was this a real opportunity? She stuck the card into her bag and left for home, and by the next morning she thought she had dreamed the whole thing. But she once again read the note on the card, and realized the whole magical night had been true and the invitation from Mr. Borzage was real. She became wildly excited, and begged her mother for permission to attend the audition that morning. The way that Maureen recalled the moment, she was practically down on hands and knees.

After much pleading from her daughter, Mrs. O'Sullivan agreed on the condition that the family governess would accompany her to the audition. Maureen later noted it was indeed fortunate that her father was in London, as he probably would have quashed the whole deal. "He would have been horrified," she admitted. "He didn't much care for motion picture people."

That morning Maureen went to the office of Frank Borzage, whereupon they exchanged the customary cordialities. He then asked her to come to the light of the window, where he scrutinized her face with a director's eye. Maureen said she had half-expected him to say, "Open wide," like on her visit to the dentist. Instead, he posed the question, "Do you want to be in the movies?"

This was a chance of a lifetime, and she responded to the affirmative without hesitation. Borzage's eyes brightened and Maureen smiled in return. A deal was quickly struck whereby Maureen would be paid three pounds for the next few days to take part in shooting some exterior scenes. In U.S. currency this was about fifteen dollars, and really the first money that the teenager had ever earned.

The exposure of working with other actors, the cameraman, and director Borzage was quite an experience for a teenager: "They took me around the Irish countryside into villages and whenever they needed an Irish girl coming out of a store or something, they used me." On the third day she was asked to learn some lines, and to do a scene with the young boy, Tommy Clifford.

Maureen said she always recalled the concluding line to the scene like it was yesterday, when she spoke the words, "I'll be going far, far away and I don't know when I'll be coming back." By this moment there were tears rolling down her cheeks, because she knew that it was true that she would be leaving her homeland and family. She noted that this was the only time there were genuine tears, even later when the scene was filmed in Hollywood before the cameras.

After finishing this short scene with young Tommy, there was a moment's silence. At this point the author, who had also been in the room, suddenly shouted out, "This girl's a genius!" The vote of approval meant that Maureen had passed the audition, and her life was about to change and never again be the same.

"It was at this point that I realized I'd got the part," said Maureen, "even though it had nothing to do with being a genius. The only important things were that I was young, pretty, and knew how to learn lines."

By this time Maureen's father had returned to the family after his business trip. He was quite perturbed by what had been happening in his absence, and as Maureen had stated, he didn't care at all for motion picture people. Charles O'Sullivan had in fact made up his mind that he wasn't going to allow his eldest daughter to go to America and become an actress.

In a 1989 interview with *Irish America*, Maureen noted that her career almost never happened: "Frank asked if he could take me [to America] for the film. My father said no, and he was never going to tell me that he had turned it down. Frank said, 'I understand that you don't want your daughter to go. If she were my daughter, I'd probably feel the same way. I understand perfectly. But I won't tell her that it was your wish. I'll tell Maureen that her test wasn't as good as I expected it to be. She'll never know you said she couldn't go.' That was pretty nice, wasn't it?"

Later that evening, Charles walked by the room of Maureen's sisters and heard them praying: "Please God, let Maureen's test be successful." The family patriarch, a deeply religious man, took this as a sign from God that he should let his daughter follow her dream. He gave his approval and the rest, as they say, is history.

A chaperone would be required for the trip to Hollywood, and it was decided that her mother would accompany Maureen. Mary O'Sullivan had often been in poor health in her adult life, but she was well enough to make this wonderful journey across the ocean to America. The next few days seemed to be a frantic whirlwind for Maureen to get her things packed and her affairs in order for the trip. At last she was ready, and all of her clothes and possessions were neatly packed in a large green steamer trunk.

This was quite an exciting happening for friends and family of the young woman, and they all came to see her off. At the time of departure from the Dublin dock, there was a band playing and people were throwing streamers. Maureen later recalled this turning point in her life, when she left home at the tender age of eighteen: "It was all highly emotional and I was completely overwhelmed. Then, as we pulled away and my father's figure receded into the distance, I caught sight of my big green trunk standing beside him on the quay."

And thus Maureen began her adventure this autumn day in 1929 to become a motion picture star. But before we can set sail for America to follow the course of Maureen's life, we must first go back to the beginning — to the day of her birth in Ireland.

CHAPTER TWO
"A Child is Born Amongst the Leprechauns"

Maureen Paula O'Sullivan made her entrance on a beautiful spring day in the year 1911, a Wednesday it was, in the historic town of Boyle in the western Irish countryside. The birth of the child took place above a draper's shop on Main Street, a narrow avenue that curves through the downtown area. The draper was a merchant who sold cloth and some clothing.

"I was born in Boyle, Ireland, on May 17, 1911," Maureen noted in 1930 to the Los Angeles press. "I just happened to be there because my father's regiment, the Connaught Rangers, were there. In fact, 'Mummy' didn't know where I was going to be born, I am told. Nearly every room in the town was occupied on account of the troops being in town.

"My 'mater' finally had me in a little room over a draper's shop. There was a big dance in the town, and the gay music accompanied my arrival into the world, I have been told."

Boyle is located towards the north of County Roscommon, the lake country of Ireland, and the population of the town in 1901 was approximately 2,500 people. The Boyle River cuts right through the town and parallels the main street, and there are bridges that span the few cross streets. The town square is called "The Crescent," and in olden days this was the marketplace for the local farmers to bring the fruits of their labors. The ancient Cistercian Abbey in Boyle dates back to the end of the 12th century.

The architecture along Main Street is some of the finest in the town, and the majestic Bank of Ireland is on the corner opposite Maureen's birth place. Many of the buildings that were built around 1900 are still standing like weathered oak trees as time marches along in the present day.

Maureen fondly remembered that this area of her birth was "the land of the leprechauns, the Little People, and the land of the black turf that once supplied Ireland with its heat." The actress felt deeply about her homeland: "Ireland, above all, is the land of my earliest memories and dreams. If I have any magic in my soul, it comes from Ireland."

When Maureen mentioned leprechauns, you must understand that as a child she really believed in them, and according to her, so did most of the other Irish children, as she explained in a 1930 interview: "Elves and pixies and leprechauns, or what we term more broadly the little people," said Maureen with conviction, "are seen and known to almost every Irish child under twelve.

"They not only think they see them — they actually see them," she continued with emphasis. "I saw the little people standing in flowers, walking in the grass, and performing all manner of antics, until but a very few years ago. Now I don't see them any more."

When the interviewer asked if this was merely a childhood illusion, stimulated by nursery tales, 19-year-old Maureen denied it most emphatically. "Oh, no, no, no. Of course, both my 'mummy' and my 'nanny' told me such tales. But I really saw, and knew the little people. It's nothing unique. It's just that the children are somehow able to see them, and grown-ups aren't. It's all very simple to grasp."

Maureen was the first child for the former Mary Lovatt Fraser and her husband Charles Joseph O'Sullivan, a military man who was a major of the Connaught Rangers. According to a 1973 "Playbill" for Maureen's Broadway play, *No Sex Please, We're British*, her family had stemmed from Cork, and her grandfather was Lord Mayor of that city.

Directly across from the draper's shop was a military barracks where Major O'Sullivan was assigned; the Rangers used this facility from 1788 until 1922. This building is now a landmark in Boyle and is called King House, a restored Georgian Mansion built by wealthy aristocrat Sir Henry King around 1730.

Her parents first met at a tennis club. After a spirited match, Mary Fraser walked to the net and shook hands with her opponent, the dashing and handsome Charles O'Sullivan. Mary shocked Charles by informing him of her future plans: "Thank you. Did you know that I was going to marry you?"

Maureen asked her mother years later if she was in love with her father on that day at the tennis club when they first met. "Oh, it was nothing like that," she replied. "I just knew it was inevitable."

Indeed, after a short engagement Charles and Mary were married, and in the words of Maureen, "They lived unhappily ever after." It seems that Mary had never learned to cook and had no domestic skills whatsoever. When Charles told his wife that he liked lamb, Mary bought a whole side of sheep and hung it over the bathtub — where it dripped blood for days.

Mary O'Sullivan also wasn't really prepared for motherhood, and at one point misplaced her baby when they were packing to move to a different house. Maureen was nowhere to be found, and Charles was frantic after searching the entire house for the missing infant. Finally, Mary recalled that mother and child had been together in the cellar, where she was storing some wine. A headlong rush to the wine cellar by Charles found the baby Maureen asleep, without a care, amongst the wine bottles.

The baby girl would eventually have a brother Jackie, three years younger, with whom she was very close. They shared the same nursery and the twosome had wonderful times together as children. Another brother, Daniel, died as an infant of a childhood disease. Maureen recalled that she was racked with guilt for years over the death of her baby brother, because he was taken away shortly after she had accidentally bumped his head. It was just a coincidence, but it was a traumatic memory that haunted the child for a long time.

Maureen also had three younger sisters with whom she wasn't really close because of a substantial age difference. The eldest was born when Maureen was ten, and by that time she had been sent off to boarding school and thus rarely saw her young sisters. The three female siblings were named Elizabeth, born 1921; Patricia, born 1925; and Sheila, born 1928.

During these early years before the war, the family lived in a house in Knockvicar, a small rural village in the Parish of Ardcarne situated about five miles east of neighboring Boyle. This village is also located on the Boyle River, before it joins up with the River Shannon. The old O'Sullivan home in modern times is a guest house for travelers, who are afforded the opportunity to spend a night in the home of Maureen's early childhood.

Maureen was very close to her father, and truly adored him her entire life. Her relations with her mother, however, were strained, and Maureen blamed her for much of her childhood unhappiness. "My mother was a very beautiful and amusing woman, but clearly not a happy one, and her attitude towards us children was extremely negative," said Maureen in a 1994 memoir published in *Hello* magazine. "She was particularly good at undermining me, and, as a result, it shattered my confidence and made me very self-conscious."

Maureen's childhood years, by her own account, were far from idyllic. Assuredly, there were some happy times spent with her parents and siblings, but the atmosphere of her youth was marred by severe health problems affecting both her father and her mother. Perhaps it can all be blamed on the war, which crippled her father and left her mother an emotional wreck, with psychological problems that often required long stretches in nursing homes.

Shortly after World War I began in 1914, Major O'Sullivan of the Irish Connaught Rangers left his family to fight the German forces of Kaiser Wilhelm, who had declared war on France, a close ally of England. The British government was also enraged that the German armies had marched through Belgium on their way to France, damaging much of the country and killing many Belgian citizens who dared to fight back against the German invaders. On August 4, 1914, Britain declared war against Germany in support of France. Subsequently, on September 20, 1914, John Redmond of the Parliamentary Party in Ireland pledged 170,000 Irish National Volunteers to fight alongside the British troops in the trenches in France.

John Redmond was motivated to send volunteers to the war effort in 1914 by the belief that showing solidarity to Britain might appease them somewhat to the Irish situation, as well as in sympathy with Catholic Belgium.

There was also a bitter struggle looming in Ireland at this time for independence from England. However, the fight for home rule was put aside when an agreement was reached with Britain in September, 1914, that Irish independence would be implemented in one year or at the end of the World War, whichever time frame was longer. The greater urgency of the battle against the Germans temporarily brought an uneasy peace between Ireland and Britain, and the contentious transition to home rule would be dealt with at a later date.

The war came particularly close to Ireland on May 7, 1915, when the Lusitania was torpedoed without warning by the German U-boat, U-20, and sank within 18 minutes. The British ocean liner was heading east off the Old Head of Kinsale along the southern coast of Ireland, on its voyage from New York to Liverpool. Of the passengers and crew on board, 761 were rescued, while 1,198 men, women, and children perished in the disaster.

A few months after the beginning of the war, Major O'Sullivan was wounded in action, and his right arm was so severely damaged that the doctors recommended amputation. Charles adamantly refused the removal of his arm, but he was forced to accept a medical discharge from the army.

One of Maureen's earliest memories of her father was visiting him in the hospital, where he lay in his bed alongside rows of other wounded soldiers. "When he came home I'd sit in front of his wheelchair like a little puppy dog," recalled Maureen fondly. "I adored my father."

Throughout his life he endured great pain and numerous shock treatments in attempts to restore the life to his damaged limb, but his arm was virtually useless. (You may notice in photographs that Charles O'Sullivan holds his damaged right arm up with his left hand, making for a more natural pose.)

There was also a change of the political climate after the war, when southern Ireland became the Irish Free State, and Northern Ireland continued as a separate state aligned with Great Britain. This had come about, in part, because of the events of Easter Monday, 1916, at the General Post Office on O'Connell Street in Dublin. The war was still raging in Europe, and British and Irish soldiers were fighting side-by-side in the trenches against the German enemies. Nevertheless, back home in Ireland, a separate war was being waged for freedom.

Independence for Ireland had been promised when the war concluded. However, since the promised home rule had not come about, an armed uprising was staged against the British the week beginning Easter Monday, 1916. Two small military groups, the Republican Brotherhood led by Pádraig Pearse, and the Citizens' Army led by James Connolly, seized several key locations in Dublin.

By this time the goal was no longer home rule for Ireland, but had rather evolved into a quest for a Republic totally independent from Britain. The Irish Home Rule Bill dictated that Ireland be required to swear allegiance to the King of England and would still be considered part of Britain.

From the front steps of the post office, Pearse, a poet and teacher, proclaimed Irish independence with his partisans cheering him on to greater glory. The strength of their force was barely 1,000 men and women, including Countess Markievicz, who was one of the leaders of the revolution. Shortly after the battle began, the Countess shot two British soldiers who were attacking their position.

The glory of the coup was short-lived, however, as the revolt was quickly crushed by a superior British military force of 6,500 troops. The bloody battle lasted six days, with a casualty count that included 60 rebels, 130 British troops, and 300 civilians. This famous rebellion was the longest stretch of fighting in Ireland since 1798.

Irish history records this as the first step towards independence, but there was a terrible price to pay. Martial law was ordered, and some 2,000 Irish patriots were taken to Britain and jailed. The sternest penalty was applied to 15 of the leaders of the revolt, including Pearse and Connolly, who were executed after brief courts-martial. Within a few years, the sought-after independence was gained for southern Ireland, but true peace would be decades away. The Countess, who also was condemned to die, had her sentence commuted to life imprisonment. (Countess Markievicz, born Constance Gore-Booth, was a family friend of the Irish poet William Butler Yeats, and her family and home at Lissadell was a favorite topic of his writings.)

In a few short years the republican movement had gathered significant momentum as a result of this short-lived rebellion. The executions by the British of the leaders of the revolt ironically brought the struggle to the attention of the Irish public, and the sympathies expressed at their execution led to a larger national interest in obtaining outright independence.

There were ten million men killed during World War I, along with 20 million additional men who were physically or psychologically damaged — many beyond repair. Back at home, the women had manned the factories that supplied the munitions to the armies, with most able-bodied men off fighting the war. The women suffered their own severe maladies from this dangerous work of constantly handling chemicals and gun powder over a period of four years.

Undoubtedly the events of the world war and the Irish fight for independence affected the O'Sullivan family, as it affected most people in Ireland. Their recovery as a family was only partial, and indeed, Europe as a whole took years to bury the memories of this terrible war that finally ended in 1918.

The toll on Mary O'Sullivan was especially harsh; she had a series of nervous breakdowns as a result of seeing her husband in the physical and emotional pain that accompanied his crippled state. Maureen later recalled her difficult childhood years, rarely seeing her mother and most often being raised by nannies. "She spent most of my childhood in nursing homes and when she did come home, I didn't particularly like her. She was strange and eccentric, and I felt she didn't like me very much either. That lack of maternal love still bears its scars but I don't blame her for how she treated me. It was just the way she was."

As a child, Maureen never really understood what exactly was wrong with her mother. She would be told that her mother was ill, and then she would be gone for long periods during her stays at nursing homes. Sometimes one of her aunts would stay with Maureen and her brother, temporarily, as she recalled: "The aunts never lasted long because we were far too much trouble for them," said Maureen. "After that we had a great time, but it meant that I never liked my mother coming home because she interfered with our freedom."

Her father was a completely different story, and Maureen simply adored the kindly gentleman who was the one constant in her life. She also felt that since she was the first-born, her father loved her more than her siblings. He wasn't overly demonstrative with his affection, but it was the little things that he did for Maureen, the warmth and kindness he displayed, that caused his oldest child to feel she was the special one in his heart. Maureen reciprocated her father's love and devotion. She said she fell in love with her father at age six and remained so all her life.

"Although I was always sure that my father loved me," said Maureen, "somehow it didn't seem to compensate for the coldness my mother showed towards me. She would make careless remarks about me and tell jokes at my expense which often made my cry. Then she'd try and hug me which I didn't like either, and even when my father stepped in to try and show me affection it didn't make it any better because it would embarrass me."

One day when she was a young child, Maureen had a friend over for tea, and she showed her friend around the beautiful garden, doing her best to be a proper hostess. Maureen overheard her mother say to her father, "Oh look at the poor young thing trying to entertain. Isn't she pathetic?"

And thus Maureen developed as a child into somewhat of a loner, as she noted in a succinct statement that described her youth: "I was always a very independent child and I didn't like people getting too close to me. I wanted to be loved from afar."

There was certainly no love afforded Maureen and her siblings by the various nannies that were hired to care for them. According to Maureen, they were all sweet and friendly around her father, but when he was out of sight they treated the children with considerable menace.

"One cold night when I was three years old," she recalled, "and had done nothing naughty at all, Nanny put me in a cold bath, holding me under the water until I turned blue from cold and was in such a state of shock that I couldn't even cry."

There was one particular nanny that Maureen remembered, and after coming across some old photographs, she recalled her as "a pretty girl in her early twenties with a beguiling smile." Apparently the smile beguiled her father, who thought she was as sweet as her appearance.

The young woman, Nurse Ranger, forced Maureen, about age seven, to steal from her father's desk, including stamps, fine writing paper, and an expensive pen. Then she blamed Maureen as the thief. She also called Maureen all kinds of names at every opportunity, and the words that hurt the most were, "You're ugly! Everyone hates you except your father!"

It never really occurred to the child that Nurse Ranger was just being spiteful, that she wasn't really ugly. She later recalled, "I was almost eight by then and Nurse Ranger had damaged me to an extent that I would not recover," said Maureen. "Things eventually got so bad that I went to my father crying hysterically, and thank God this time he did believe me."

The next day her father fired the woman, and to Maureen's astonishment, Nurse Ranger gave her a beautiful doll as some sort of atonement for all the meanness she had heaped on her seven-year-old charge.

Nevertheless, Maureen hated the woman so much that she took the gift to her room and pulled out the doll's eyes, and then took it to the seashore, which was right at the edge of their property. In uncharacteristic fashion, the young girl took out her anger towards Nurse Ranger on the doll, as she later recalled. "I held her [the doll] under the water until I was sure she was so water-logged that she could not float, and watched happily as a wave carried her out to sea."

Eventually, Maureen's character became stronger, and to prove to the world that she didn't care, the young girl developed a tough attitude towards anyone who attempted to discipline her in any way. "To prove that it did not matter that I was ugly and unloved, I became a rebel," said Maureen of her stand of independence.

Sometime around the end of the World War, the O'Sullivan family moved from Boyle to Saintsbury, Killiney, in County Dublin, a few miles to the south of the city of Dublin. They owned a lovely home right on the coast along Strand Road, where the waves from the ocean would lap against the rocks during high tide, shooting ocean spray into the air. There were beautiful gardens, and plenty of bedrooms for the five children, the parents, and the various nannies that worked for the family during those years. Later in life

Maureen described her childhood home as "an elegant castellated mansion overlooking the sea."

Before Maureen reached the age of ten, her discipline problems caused her to be sent to a convent school in Dublin, where, in her own words, "I broke every rule possible. I would not study, and I hated the nuns — the fusty smell of their black habits, the sinister clank of their rosary beads, and the way they peered at me through keyholes of white frills. But because I admired my father more than anything in the world and wanted to be like him, I was determined to be brave and daring."

Maureen had the spunk to stand up to the nuns, and to do outrageous things the other girls would not even dream of doing. Her combination of bravado and mischief-making earned her the mantle of most-popular girl in the school, but it also bought her a one-way ticket out the door. She was expelled from this school and at least one other convent school, whilst she was still at the tender age of eleven.

It was during the holidays from school that Maureen took her First Holy Communion back in Dublin at age ten. Maureen was the only one scheduled for the ceremony on this date, so she had to spend the night in an empty, and apparently bitterly cold, dormitory. She was awakened by the nuns the next morning, and dressed in her Holy Communion dress and white veil, also stiff and cold. She was ready but scared to death, as she remembered in her 1994 *Hello* memoir.

"I was absolutely petrified receiving my First Holy Communion in case I bit the host in half and committed a mortal sin, then and there," said Maureen. "My mother — who had come to watch me — seemed rather bemused by the whole thing. Afterwards, we all had breakfast with the priest, and, in the middle of it, he turned to me and said, 'Maureen, I want you to promise me that you'll pray for me every day of your life.'

"I didn't know quite what to make of this, but my mother, who was in a very jolly mood that day, was incredulous and told the priest she thought he was being quite ridiculous. 'Come now, Father,' she said. 'She'll do no such thing. Pray for yourself.'

"I may have prayed for him once or twice after that but I soon lost interest. I'm sure he got on fine without me."

Maureen's father did not attend Maureen's First Holy Communion that day, which might seem somewhat strange because he was the Roman Catholic of the family. But Maureen noted that her father was a very private man who always attended mass on Sundays and holy days by himself, while the children would travel to church separately accompanied by their nanny. Her mother chose a different religious path in her lifetime, trying out several faiths before settling on Christian Science.

In the summer of 1922, Maureen's wealthy great-uncle took an active interest in her future and paid for her to attend the very upscale Convent of the Sacred Heart in Roehampton, on the outskirts of London.

An entry in the school register at Roehampton indicates that Maureen's First Communion had taken place in 1921 and that she received her Confirmation in 1922 at the age of eleven. A second entry records her date of entrance as September of 1922, and the date she left school as October of 1926.

PROVINCIAL ARCHIVES
SOCIETY OF THE SACRED HEART
ROEHAMPTON LANE
LONDON SW15 5PH

A photocopy of the original school record for Maureen O'Sullivan at Roehampton

It was on Maureen's second day at her new school that she noticed an extremely pretty young girl standing in the corridor. This young lady, two years younger than Maureen, was Vivian Hartley. A decade later, she would make her motion picture debut as Vivien Leigh, and eventually she would marry another fine actor, Laurence Olivier. On this date she was just another youngster trying to fit in with everyone else.

Only a few days after Maureen arrived at Roehampton, the girls held a competition to determine the prettiest girl in the school. Vivien won with the most votes, but Maureen, to her great shock, came in second place. "I cried all day when I heard the result," she said, "not because Vivian won, but because someone thought I was pretty."

Maureen also had a vivid memory that Vivian, of all girls at the school, was the only one who knew at this young age what she truly wanted from life. Vivian had a burning desire to be a great actress, and indeed she eventually became just that. Who could ever forget her marvelous role as Scarlett O'Hara in *Gone with the Wind* with Clark Gable, who delivered to her the famous closing line, "Frankly, my dear, I don't give a damn."

While Vivian had her dreams to become a renowned actress, most of the other girls just wanted to achieve social success. Maureen's dream of having an exciting future was marrying someone in the foreign service and traveling the world. When they would share their dreams, Maureen admitted that becoming a pilot would be her ultimate goal when she reached adulthood. In reality, they both would become famous actresses, with Maureen making her motion picture debut in 1930, while Vivian acted in her first film in 1934.

Maureen quickly became one of the most popular girls at the school. At first she was teased about her Irish accent, but eventually it disappeared. Her classmates thought of her as the bold and daring Irish girl, who was rebellious and unafraid of the potential discipline from the nuns. Roehampton attracted girls from wealthy families from all over Europe, including France, Austria, Spain, Poland, and of course, Ireland. This gave Maureen an opportunity to become more worldly, more cosmopolitan, by learning about the various cultures from which her classmates had originated.

Eventually, Maureen became a member of a popular quintet of girls, which also included Vivian, Brigit Boland, Dorothy Ward, and Patsy Quinn. To their classmates they were known as "the Exquisites," so crowned because each member was very attractive with long beautiful hair.

"It was a happy time," said Maureen, "but I was happy in the wrong way because I got my kicks out of aggravating the poor nuns. I'd put ink in the holy water and drop peanuts on their heads while in chapel. My biggest regret about that time is that I didn't appreciate the value of learning and didn't take advantage of a good education."

Above: Mary Lovatt O'Sullivan with Maureen (left), age three, and infant brother Jackie
Below: Major Charles Joseph O'Sullivan in the uniform of the Connaught Rangers (1914)

The student body at Roehampton, class photo 1924
Vivien Leigh is in the botton row, fifth from the left

Right: Enlarged photo of Vivien, who knew at an early age that she wanted to be an actress when she grew up. (as a child her name was Vivian Hartley)

Below: Enlarged center section shows Maureen O'Sullivan in second row from bottom, center ... Notice that Maureen is the only girl who is not wearing a white collar and/or sash.

Above: Maureen at age thirteen with a bit of a chip on her shoulder and a mop of hair

Right: About age sixteen, still has the "me-against-the-world" attitude ... she is expelled from Roehampton in October 1926

Above: The Convent of the Sacred Heart, Roehampton, London
(Before it was bombed by the Germans in World War II)
Maureen was educated here from September 1922 until October 1926

Below: The front entrance of the Convent of the Sacred Heart (circa 1925)

Top: The dining hall where the pupils ate their meals at Roehampton
Center: The chapel where religious services were conducted, including mass on Sundays
Below: The study where pupils did their homework, etc.

Director Frank Borzage and his wife Rena Rogers (above) discovered this Irish lass at a Dublin dance in 1929. Maureen at age eighteen, the fresh-faced kid who had never worn any make-up or lipstick her entire life in her homeland of Ireland.

Above: Maureen and Tommy Clifford are right off the boat from Ireland after landing in New York. Ten-year-old Tommy looked at the 1929 New York skyline and, rather unimpressed, said, "Well, is that New York? There's nothing to it!"

Right: After arriving in Hollywood for a major role in *Song O' My Heart*, Fox Film added a touch of make-up and voila: the young woman became a star!

Above: Lobby card for *Song O' My Heart* ... Maureen and Tommy Clifford with John McCormack
Below: A sad moment: Sean is leaving Ireland for America because his heart is broken

Maureen didn't pay much attention to her studies, and instead devoted her thoughts to anything but school, as she daydreamed away the classroom hours. "My head was filled with movies and dances, and once I'd realized I wasn't ugly after all, with young men too. I soon discovered that I was one of the lucky ones who never had trouble getting a partner at a dance."

She was also a very bright young girl, who simply was bored with school. One topic that she did find fascinating was history, and she recalled that she invested considerable hard work and research into her composition on Marie Antoinette, the former queen of France who died on the guillotine in 1793. For the most part, though, she didn't have a great deal of interest in studying the various subjects taught by the nuns, and put forth a minimum effort.

Her classes included English, mathematics, history, and French. Religious studies were stressed emphatically and occupied many hours each week. Optional classes included drama, music, choir, and ballet, which was taught by a nun who had studied classical ballet in her youth. The school also had an orchestra, and lessons were offered in piano, violin, cello, and other orchestral instruments. Maureen did study piano and voice culture, the latter being very helpful when she became an actress a few years down the line.

The drama and music programs at Roehampton were highly regarded, and the only male instructor at the convent was Mr. Britten, a shy young man who taught music. Any class that was taught by Mr. Britten was well-attended, as most of the girls were developing a budding interest in the opposite sex, and he was the only man to be found!

Roehampton was a strict Catholic convent school, and thus sexual awareness was repressed rather than emphasized. The girls could talk about boys only when they were out of earshot of the nuns, and like all good Catholic women they were expected to save themselves — sexually speaking — for the right man that came along with a proposal of marriage.

When Maureen discovered dancing it opened new worlds and new opportunities to meet the opposite sex. She loved to dance and became a very accomplished ballroom dancer who was extremely popular, both for her wholesome beauty as well as her charm and grace on the dance floor.

The entertainment the girls were allowed to enjoy was mostly restricted to playing among themselves and reading; there was no radio or motion pictures, and television was still two decades away. The girls had plenty of make-believe games to play, which were only limited by the bounds of their young imaginations.

The occasional production from the drama department was often a highlight that was looked forward to with much anticipation, including Shakespearean plays such as *A Midsummer Night's Dream* — Maureen was cast in a tiny part as a fairy. Meanwhile, Vivian portrayed Miranda in *The Tempest*.

Life at Roehampton was regimented carefully, and the school was virtually a compound closed away from the outer world. But the grounds were spacious and rather idyllic, with beautiful gardens like the ones Maureen had enjoyed back home in Killiney. There was foliage throughout the grounds, magnificent twisted English oaks, conical Austrian trees, and bushy rhododendrons that offered the perfect hiding place for the oft-played pastime of hide-and-seek. There was also a spacious lawn where croquet was played on Sunday afternoons, and a small lake with a fountain that gushed skyward and offered a cooling bath for the many birds that lived in this sanctuary.

In the summer months the girls played cricket at Middle Field, and ice skating in the chilly winters was a favorite sport on the frozen lake. Calvary Field was surrounded by a walkway lined mostly with acacia trees, providing a path to stroll through the grounds. A pedestrian might enjoy the variety of flora and fauna, including squirrels and pigeons and other tiny creatures.

The convent grew its own vegetables and fruit, and had a small private herd of dairy cows that grazed in a nearby pasture that was known rather lightheartedly as "The South of France." The only outsiders who came on a regular basis were the doctor and the dentist, along with tradesmen who delivered supplies and quickly departed the stern confines of Roehampton.

The girls slept in dormitories, with a double row of beds separated by an aisle down the middle. Each bed had a canopy and curtains that could be lowered for privacy, but they were rarely used. After all, the girls hardly felt the need for seclusion at that young age, and in fact they often talked quietly amongst themselves until they drifted off to sleep each night. The girls would neatly fold their blouses and used underwear and place them on a stool by each bed, where they were collected by a night attendant and taken to the school laundry. Each morning a clean blouse and undergarments awaited on the stool, a fresh start for a new day.

At 6:30 a.m. the Angelus bell was rung three times, while one of the nuns would intone the phrase, "Precious blood of our Lord Jesus Christ." The students gathered at the Great Chapel for early mass at 7:15, followed by a simple morning breakfast of bread with butter and tea. Lunch was in the early afternoon, consisting of fish or mutton, vegetables from the convent's own gardens, and fruit. Milk was readily available at most meals, courtesy of the dairy cows that served the convent. Desserts were considered a real treat, most often a slice of cake or pie baked in the convent kitchen. Cooking and other domestic chores such as laundry and cleaning were performed by lay sisters, who were under vows and wore the habit but were not nuns.

The school was intensely prudish by today's standards, and one of the more inane rules was that when taking a bath each girl had to clothe herself in a long stiff gown and bathe in this extremely modest fashion. Maureen thought this was pure nonsense, and bathed naked as she had always done in her home. When she was finished, she would soak the gown in the tub, pull on the damp garment, and exit the bath area with the nuns none the wiser.

Maureen remained a Catholic all of her life, but found the strict rules difficult to live by, as she recalled. "There are too many don'ts and not enough do's in my opinion," she said. "The convent in Roehampton was full of very holy girls, but I didn't feel like them and wasn't nearly as religious as someone like Vivien Leigh, for example, who later told me that she missed her religion terribly when she divorced and married Laurence Olivier."

Eventually, her outrageous behavior and lack of any real interest in her studies got her thrown out of the Convent of the Sacred Heart in the fall of 1926. Maureen put it succinctly when she said, "I was asked to leave." Her parents were anguished at their daughter's lack of discipline and flippant attitude towards education. Even worse, no other school would consider admitting her after she was rejected by a prestigious school such as Roehampton.

Maureen didn't seem to be overly concerned about this situation, hardly considering it dire. Her parents, however, could not foresee a future for Maureen without an education. The solution to this dilemma was found in France, where a finishing school was located that didn't require academic records or references. A kindly nun who had befriended Maureen located a family in Versailles that boarded English girls attending the local school.

Apparently Maureen enjoyed her schooling in France a great deal, and even managed to stay out of trouble — well, at least she wasn't caught. "I loved France, and best of all, I loved the dances," she recalled fondly. "We had to be heavily chaperoned but, as soon as the chaperones had settled down to a good gossip, we'd sneak off with the French boys who had motorbikes and go up to Paris for the evening. We'd return about midnight, and the chaperones never even knew we'd gone."

Maureen completed her education in France after turning the age of seventeen in May of 1928. She then returned to her family in Dublin, and unprepared for any type of career, basically lived the life of a young socialite. Maureen recalled this as a wonderful time, a carefree period in her life. "I went to dances and met lots of different, interesting people," she said. "Dublin is a very cosmopolitan city, and the best-looking girls used to be invited to dances at the Embassy which was always great fun. But despite all this socializing, I kept feeling that there must be more to life than this. The nuns had trained us to believe in the terrible temptations of the world, but it all seemed so tame. It was a big disappointment."

There were boys in her life of course, starting with a crush on the local policeman when she was a young girl. In her words, "A little later I started to fall in love with my friends' brothers.

"Looking back, I can see that I got really quite depressed around that time because there was nothing to do except enjoy yourself, and that wasn't enough for me."

Her father could see that he had a very bored and unfulfilled young lady on his hands, so he bought her six hens and a rooster. The idea was that Maureen would start a little business selling eggs, and thus would be doing some meaningful work and make some money too. However, she didn't clean out the hen house with regularity, and she simply hated taking care of chickens. "In the end, I'm sorry to say, they all got lice and died," admitted Maureen. "But I was terribly relieved."

Maureen herself thought perhaps helping the poor might keep her busy and be good for her soul as well, and her mother suggested she volunteer to serve food to the indigent and underprivileged. "I'm afraid I didn't last very long at that either," noted Maureen, "because I found the poor such a disagreeable and ungrateful lot. All they did was complain about how badly I served them food. They were right but I didn't want to hear it."

By the summer of 1929, Maureen was searching for some meaning in her life, because deep inside she craved some greater challenges than those offered in her present world. As the summer months faded to autumn, the Dublin Horse Show proved to be the opportunity for a whole new life, and her subsequent "discovery" by film director Frank Borzage.

Meanwhile in New York, unbeknownst to Maureen, she received her first press in the *New York Times* on October 6, 1929, in a movie news column entitled "Projection Jottings":

"Maureen O'Sullivan and Thomas Clifford, two Irish players, will be brought back from Ireland by Frank Borzage for roles in John McCormack's picture. The girl is 18-years-old, a brunette with bobbed hair, and comes from Killiney. The boy is eleven and said to have a good voice for talking pictures."

As she waved good-bye to her family from the deck of a ship bound for New York, there was her green steamer trunk sitting on the dock next to her father. As Maureen remembered about this mischance that might have felt traumatic at the moment: "I had nothing but the clothes I stood up in. It was a small tragedy, but luckily people were kind and I managed to borrow things."

The great ship surged ahead through the ocean waters effortlessly, and soon Ireland faded away in the distance. Maureen really had no idea what the future held for her, but it was surely the beginning of an exciting adventure.

CHAPTER THREE
"Trite but True ... A Star Is Born"

Maureen recalled that the ocean voyage from Dublin to New York lasted five days, and that she had a wonderful experience. Less than a week after leaving Ireland, their small party including her mother and young Tommy Clifford, arrived in New York City.

This was her first trip to the United States, and her heart raced at the anticipation of seeing the renowned New York skyscrapers and the elevated trains that crisscrossed the city. However, when she finally got her first visit to the Big Apple, it seemed to be somewhat of a disappointment.

"When we got there it was a bit of a letdown really and not nearly as magical and weird as we'd been led to believe. Little Tommy Clifford looked at the skyline and in his broad Irish accent said, 'Well, is that New York? There's nothing to it!' "

The New York of 1929 was presided over by Jimmy Walker, a vastly popular mayor who was known as "Beau James" to his constituents. The governor of New York at this time was Franklin Delano Roosevelt, who would be elected as president in 1932 after succeeding current president Herbert Hoover. A week after Maureen left New York, the Stock Market fell precipitously, culminating in the final crash on Black Tuesday, October 29, 1929.

So this was the state of the Union when Maureen first came to America, a nation on the verge of great changes. The Roaring Twenties would soon be replaced by the dark days of the Depression, which would last for most of the decade of the 1930s.

After spending a few days seeing the sights and sounds of New York, they traveled by train to California and their final destination — Hollywood, U.S.A. They arrived on October 26, 1929, and Maureen promptly signed a six-month contract with Fox Films. This was enough time for the production of *Song O' My Heart* and the promotion of the film, and not much more. It was a make-good situation — if the film flopped and she was judged to be lacking as an actress, she would be sent back to Ireland.

Maureen half-expected that all the gossip she had heard would find her in a modern-day Sodom and Gomorrah. "Hollywood has a frightful reputation in England," she said in 1930. "From the stories I heard before I left home, you would have thought I was going to the land of sin itself."

However, when she arrived in Tinseltown she discovered that it was much tamer than all the stories. Maureen was greeted with a big bowl of shamrocks and a shillelagh, which is a cudgel made of hardwood. Maureen later admitted that she had never even seen a shillelagh and didn't have the slightest notion what to do with it! "From the beginning, the Americans thought I was a big fraud because I wasn't nearly Irish enough for them," she noted.

The machinations of the Hollywood publicity people began creating a different girl than the one who came over from Ireland. When the reporters asked her if she spoke Gaelic, she replied: "No, just a few prayers." And of course they wrote down: "She speaks Gaelic." When Maureen described the beautiful castellated mansion that overlooked the sea, where she lived with her family outside Dublin, they romanticized, "She lives in a little thatched cottage."

"All this false information came out in *Fox News*, even saying that I spoke in a charming Irish brogue. I knew that the Americans could only be disappointed in me after that."

Regardless of this somewhat misleading portrait painted by the news media, Maureen was loved by the movie-going public right from the start.

John McCormack signed a contract for $500,000 with the William Fox Corporation in May of 1929, a sum of money which was monumental for the day — especially for an actor making his motion picture debut. Fox Film judged that McCormack would be worth the investment, and that he would be an instant movie star in America. Unfortunately, his great success on the concert stage did not transfer to the motion pictures, and *Song O' My Heart* would be his only full-length feature film.

McCormack was born in 1884 in Athlone, Ireland, a town some 80 miles west of Dublin. He was world-famous in the fields of opera and popular music, and renowned for his flawless diction and superb breath control.

The Irish tenor was an incredible concert artist, and many of his greatest performances were staged in New York, where his popularity soared with every appearance. He sang before an audience of 7,000 fans at the New York Hippodrome on April 28, 1918, and was booked there as many as nine times per season. He could fill Carnegie Hall to capacity up to ten times a year, and also played to record crowds in Richmond, St. Paul, San Francisco, and across America.

The following excerpt from *High Fidelity* magazine (February 1957) by American critic Max de Schauensee reveals some of the reasons for his immense popularity, especially with the ladies, who made up the majority of his audience: "When I think of the word 'singer,' stripped of any extraneous dramatic connotations and in its purest sense, I see John McCormack standing on the concert platform — his head thrown back, his eyes closed, in his hands the little black book he always carried, open, but never glanced at, as he wove a spell over his completely hushed listeners. John McCormack was truly a singer for the people; he was also a singer's singer."

Song O' My Heart began filming in Hollywood on November 25, 1929, and concluded on January 16, 1930. A few background scenes had been filmed in August of 1929 near Moore Abbey, which was McCormack's residence in Ireland at the time. The Borzage company spent five weeks photographing scenes in Ireland, including backgrounds in Galway, West Donegal, Sligo, and Kerry. The cast included John McCormack as Sean O'Carolan, Alice Joyce as Mary O'Brien, with Maureen and Tommy Clifford as her two children, Eileen and Tad.

The story begins in a quaint Irish village where Mary, Eileen, and Tad are forced to vacate their home when her wealthy husband deserts them. Virtually homeless, they move in with an iron-fisted aunt, Elizabeth (Emily Fitzroy). A friend of the family is Sean, a great Irish tenor who has given up his singing career. He still laments his lost love Mary, who was forced by Elizabeth to marry a rich man years before.

Maureen as the lovely innocent Eileen enters seven minutes into the story and says, "Mother darling ... please don't worry so ... at least we'll not be separated." Aunt Elizabeth continues her meddling ways when she drives apart Eileen and her boyfriend Fergus (John Garrick), who leaves for Dublin to seek his fame and fortune as an architect. He vows to return for Eileen, and to claim her hand.

Sean gets an offer to do a concert tour across America, from New York to San Francisco, and realizes this is his opportunity to leave behind old memories. Sean is still close friends with Mary and the children, and loves them like they were his family. He sings them all a goodbye song at his farewell party, and with a heavy heart he departs his homeland and friends.

The concert tour begins triumphantly, but Sean subsequently receives a cable that Mary has died. He knows that he must return to Ireland to take care of Eileen and Tad, and he postpones his tour and leaves immediately for Ireland.

Sean arrives home just in time to stop Aunt Elizabeth from sending Eileen away, and Tad rejoices that his good friend has come back to them. Meanwhile, Fergus returns from Dublin — albeit not the success he had hoped to be. Eileen happily accepts his marriage proposal, and doesn't care at all that he is not a wealthy man. After the wedding, Sean takes Tad with him to America to resume his concert tour.

Song O' My Heart was most assuredly a showcase for the talents of John McCormack, who sang melodies including "Then You'll Remember Me,"

"A Fairy Story by the Fireside," "Just for Today," "Kitty, My Love," "Little Boy Blue," "Ireland, Mother Ireland," and "I Hear You Calling Me."

The plot was simple but engaging, and the three most important roles of Sean, Eileen, and Tad were perfectly cast. Considering that Maureen and Tommy Clifford had never acted in a movie before, they were extremely warm and believable. McCormack's marvelous singing and Maureen's very positive first impression were the highlights of the picture.

Song O' My Heart premiered at the 44th Street Theater in New York City on March 11, 1930, and was lauded by the critics. The film received its western premiere on Saturday, April 19, at Grauman's Chinese Theater in Hollywood. Unfortunately, it was also a financial flop, due in part to the huge salary that had been paid to John McCormack.

Maureen and Tommy Clifford did everything asked of them by Fox Film to make the motion picture a success, and appeared as stage entertainers for a midnight matinee at Grauman's Chinese Theater on May 30, 1930.

"*Song O' My Heart* turned out to be a bomb and fell on its face," recalled Maureen. "Luckily, I wasn't blamed for the film's failure as the studio still felt I had potential."

Maureen with John McCormack

The young actress in fact received some marvelous reviews from critics, including Elizabeth Yeaman of the *Hollywood Daily News*, who heaped praise on April 21, 1930. "It is Maureen O'Sullivan, a newcomer to the screen, who contributes one of the most sympathetic interpretations of romantic innocence that has been seen in a long time. Miss O'Sullivan was recruited in Ireland, and the acting of this beautiful youngster has a freshness and naturalness that is entirely lacking in affectation. The audience would have enjoyed seeing more of her."

Ms. Yeaman also applauded the Irish boy who portrayed Maureen's younger brother. "Tommy Clifford, an engaging little scamp from Ireland, was indispensable to the comedy of the picture. Master Tommy managed to combine naivete and shrewdness in an inimitable manner, and his voice and accent were perfect."

In May of 1930 Maureen did an interview with journalist Edward Stodel of the *L.A. Evening Herald*, which took the form of dinner, dancing, and attending a play sponsored by a college sorority. Stodel's article the next day quoted the Irish actress on her opinion of America, after her first few months in the country:

"When I got here, I was surprised," said Maureen. "The fellows and girls acted normal. They did the same sort of things at affairs that we did at home. The American boy, perhaps, is not as reserved when he meets a girl as is the Britisher, but he is just as nice."

As the evening passed, they walked past Grauman's Chinese Theater, where the crowds were just filing out of a performance of *Song O' My Heart*. Showing off a flair for humor, Maureen joked, "That's an awful picture, I hear, and they say this new Irish girl, O'Sullivan, is terrible!"

This funny, self-deprecating comment brought a smile to Stodel, who noted, "She has an Irish sense of humor, all right, and her laugh — well, it matches her eyes." A final compliment from Stodel concerned her skills on the dance floor, where they spent part of their evening. "She's a good dancer, by the way, and she didn't have to come all the way over here to learn."

Another interview that was published shortly after completion of *Song O' My Heart*, showed the innocence of the young girl who had recently arrived from Ireland:

"All my life I had longed for a stage career," said Maureen, "but the nearest I came to it was when, on one occasion only, I played a fairy in *A Midsummer Night's Dream*. Then one night Frank Borzage, who was directing John McCormack's first all-talking picture, saw me in a Dublin cafe. He decided that I was the exact type for the picture, signed me up a day or two later, and when Mr. McCormack left Ireland for Hollywood, I went with him. For nights I couldn't sleep thinking of the opportunity that had come to me.

"I would like to raise poultry and I play tennis and ride horseback. I studied piano and voice culture in Paris. I have always wanted to fly and hope I will have my pilot's license before I go home to Ireland. I am extremely superstitious, and I like detective stories better than love stories. And what will seem strange to the young girls in this country, I never had a bit of makeup on my face until I started work in the McCormack picture."

Song O' My Heart was long believed to be a lost film, following a warehouse fire in the 1940s. However, a print of the full-dialogue version was discovered and restored in 1974, and presented in New York that October. Subsequently, this version was available on video for a few years in the early 1990s. *Song O' My Heart* is an enjoyable film from a bygone era, highlighted by Maureen's memorable screen debut and the beautiful Irish tenor voice of John McCormack.

Maureen said she'd never worn make-up until coming to Hollywood in 1929 ... an early publicity photo circa 1931

CHAPTER FOUR
"Adventures in La-La Land"

After arriving in Hollywood in October of 1929, Maureen and her mother were provided a house where they lived during production of *Song O' My Heart*. When filming concluded in January 1930, Mary O'Sullivan went back to Ireland, leaving her daughter on her own. Maureen — still only eighteen — was moved to the Studio Club, which was a hostel for young actresses just getting started in the business. She recalled it as a very strict place, with plenty of rules designed to keep the young girls out of trouble.

"Young men could only visit at certain times, and they weren't allowed to venture further than the lobby. It was here that I got really lonely and missed my Irish friends terribly."

Maureen used a little chicanery by telling the head of Fox Films that she was shocked at the lewd behavior at the Club, noting that her roommate was having an affair with a married man. She wasn't really shocked, but the ploy worked and she was moved into a house, along with a chaperone. "All young girls had chaperones in those days," noted Maureen, "and the studio ruled every aspect of your life. They told you who you could and could not mix with and what time you had to be home at night."

One afternoon Maureen went to visit her young Irish friend Tommy Clifford, who had played her brother in *Song O' My Heart*. She discovered that the lad was living with his aunt in downtown Los Angeles, and they were broke after running out of the money Tommy was paid for his acting. He was under contract to Fox for just the one film, and now he was cut adrift.

Maureen was very concerned and once again went to the head of Fox, this time with an axe to grind: "How can you bring this little ten-year-old boy over and then forget about him?"

The head of Fox Film was William Fox, who offered to pay the fare for Tommy to go back to Ireland. However, Mr. Fox warned that if the boy wanted to stay then he would be on his own. Young Tommy did indeed return to his native Ireland, and went on to become a successful businessman. Maureen would visit him whenever she went home to Dublin, and they would talk about the fun they had making the film.

This was a lesson learned by Maureen at an early age, and she began to realize that it was indeed a cold business that she had chosen as a profession:

"It was tough in Hollywood," she recalled, "and I found it hard to understand how callous people could be when I remembered all the fuss that had been made of us when we first arrived."

Maureen's next film was *So This Is London*, a comedy based on the George M. Cohan play, which starred the great American cowboy philosopher, Will Rogers. Maureen was billed fourth, in the role of a charming English girl involved with the son of Texas millionaire Hiram Draper, humorously portrayed by Rogers.

The young actress was traveling with some extremely talented company in her early films. First it was the legendary Irish singer John McCormack. Now she was making her second film with an American icon who is still fondly remembered into the 21st century. Rogers is best known for his beguiling brand of humor, his fancy rope twirling, and a comforting voice to all of America during the Depression until his death in a plane crash in 1935.

Rogers had been a cowboy in his youth and learned an amazing array of rope tricks which he later used in Wild West shows, vaudeville, the Ziegfeld Follies, and in motion pictures.

He was also a journalist for the Saturday Evening Post, and the author of a huge volume of folksy anecdotes entitled: *Rogers-isms: The Cowboy Philosopher on the Peace Conference*.

Maureen with Will Rogers

Will Rogers began starring in films around 1919, and in 1925 produced *The Ropin' Fool*, a hilarious short film that showed off his amazing skills at roping everything including horses, dogs, goats, people, and even a mouse, and sometimes with one, two, or even three ropes at the same time.

Between 1929 and 1935, he made 18 pictures for Fox Film, and his popularity across America as a man of the people was unequaled during this period. So for Maureen to appear in a Will Rogers film and work in numerous scenes with him was a huge boost at this early stage of her career.

So This Is London starred Rogers as wealthy cotton mill owner Hiram Draper, who has a high regard for himself and his Texan way of life. Draper has many flaws including a strong streak of chauvinism, a judgmental nature, and a fairly wicked measure of crudity and vulgarism in his language.

Hiram must make a business trip to London, and of course, he hates anything to do with the British, including the Limey accent. He is accompanied by his wife (Irene Rich) and his son Junior (Frank Albertson), a likable fellow who falls head over heels for the fresh-faced Elinor (Maureen) during the trans-Atlantic crossing from New York to England.

Once in London, Junior is determined to marry Elinor, but his parents strongly disapprove of any such union between their son and a girl who doesn't come from Texas. The young man conspires to have them meet Elinor's parents, Lord and Lady Worthing, at a party. Hiram tries to prove to his son that his judgment is impaired by the girl's beauty, and that he is simply infatuated. The Texan attempts to be worldly and talk international politics, with humorous results. Finally, Hiram enters into a shooting match to prove his cowboy abilities with Lord Worthing — but instead he comes off as an uncouth and uncivilized American.

Beneath his rough exterior, however, Draper actually has a soft heart. After getting to know Elinor and what a wonderful young woman she is, Hiram realizes that he has been completely wrong. He gives his blessing to Junior and Elinor, and does his best to atone for all the stupid things he has done.

Ted LeBerthon of the *Los Angeles Record* was clearly taken with the new girl in town, as he expressed in his column of June 28, 1930: "Maureen O'Sullivan, like Maurice Chevalier, has arrived in the talkies in a needed hour, fulfilling a national necessity. This lovely little Irish girl who is but 18, has touched American hearts so deeply and so immediately, that it is almost as certain as if ordained that she will be not only a great actress of the near future, but a marvelous transforming influence as well ... She already had proven that her acting in *Song O' My Heart* was no fluke by her delicate and amusing comedy in support of Will Rogers in *So This Is London*.

"I say lovely role [in *Song O' My Heart*] because it was she who epitomized Ireland, in a sense, and awakened in the audience a kind of love and delight that had long lain dormant. We who saw her on the screen of Grauman's Chinese theater, surfeited as we are with 'hot mamas' and blondes of the type gentlemen prefer, had always known such a girl in our hearts. But, as we grew older and more skeptical, we had doubted that she could exist in the flesh."

Frank Albertson, Maureen's love interest in *So This Is London* was also mightily impressed with the newcomer, as noted by Jimmy Starr in his *Los Angeles Record* column of May 14, 1930: "Maureen O'Sullivan, pretty little Irish miss who made a distinct hit in *Song O' My Heart,* is causing quite a number of male heart flutterings.

"William Bakewell shakes all over at the mere mention of her name, and Frank Albertson admits his pulse leaps when she's near.

"It seems that Frank introduced Maureen to Billy when they were dining at a cafe. The topper of the gag was that he walked out with Maureen and left Billy with the dinner check."

As Maureen became more acclimated to life in Los Angeles, she also acquired an auto for traveling between the studio and her modest abode in Beverly Hills. It seems that she liked to drive a little too fast and accumulated several citations in the first few weeks after the purchase of her very first automobile. But then insult was added to injury when a young man stole her car one day and took it for a joyride.

Speaking with Kenneth Porter of the *Los Angeles Examiner* in July of 1930, Maureen recalled her misadventures with her vehicle and the subsequent theft:

"I just wasn't acquainted with the ways of Hollywood," said Miss O'Sullivan. "You see, everything is different here. People are all hurrying about so. I had never been so far away from home before and I had few friends when I first arrived. I was a bit afraid of my work, too, for I had never been on the stage or had any theatrical experience.

"I suppose you will laugh when I tell you I am having more fun now, just working. If you think a woman can't keep a secret, just try to find out about my latest picture," she laughed gleefully.

"I felt so sorry for the boy who took my car," she said. "He only drove it around town and left it when the gasoline was gone. I had to go to court when they found the boy and he really looked so sorry I tried to get the judge to let him go. They wouldn't let him go free, so I just didn't tell them about my coat that was missing when my car was found. It only cost me my coat and it might have cost him about three years in prison."

Mr. Porter added the following postscript to his interview: "So Maureen O'Sullivan is not taking Hollywood seriously now. She laughs at the things that seemed serious at first — all but her work, which she claims will always be serious to her."

By this time in 1930, Fox Film had 71 players under contract, many of them raided from the Broadway stage. A majority of these actors and actresses were at the beginning of their careers, including future Hollywood legends John Wayne and Humphrey Bogart.

The complete list of Fox Film actors included John McCormack, Warner Baxter, William Collier, Charles Farrell, Edmund Lowe, Victor McLaglen, Will Rogers, Don Jose Mojica, Milton Sills, Frank Albertson, Robert Ames, Edwin Bartlett, Rex Bell, El Brendel, Robert Burns, Walter Catlett, Thomas Clifford,

John Garrick, George Rossmith, William Harrigan, Mitchell Harris, Ted Healy, Gus Howard, Warren Hymer, Richard Keene, J. M. Kerrigan, Kenneth MacKenna, Paul Muni, J. Harold Murray, George O'Brien, Tom Patricola, Nat Pendleton, Frank Richardson, David Rollins, John Swor, Lee Tracy, Henry Victor, Charles Winninger, Wayne, and Bogart.

The actresses were Janet Gaynor, Lois Moran, Beatrice Lillie, Luana Alcaniz, Lucille Brown, Ilka Chase, Marguerite Churchill, Mae Clark, Joyce Compton, Irene Day, Fifi Dorsay, Noel Francis, Althea Heinly, Rose Hobart, Louise Huntington, Roxanne Curtis, Elizabeth Keating, Helen Keating, Dixie Lee, Claire Luce, Sharon Lynn, Leslie Mae, Mona Maris, Frances McCoy, Goodie Montgomery, Jillian Sand, Marie Saxon, Marjorie White, Ruth Warren, and Maureen O'Sullivan.

There were also seven associate producers, nineteen directors, one stage director, twenty-seven writers, sixteen composers, five dance and ensemble directors, thirty-four dancers, twenty-four singers, two fashion creators, a test director, a music teacher and numerous other officials and technical experts. Of the directors under contract several would eventually make their mark in film history, including Victor Fleming, John Ford, Alexander Korda, and Raoul Walsh.

On November 29, 1930, the *Los Angeles Examiner* noted the following about the young newcomer who was making such an impact in Hollywood: "Maureen O'Sullivan, the little Irish miss who scored such a triumph with John McCormack in *Song O' My Heart*, has one of the leading roles in Will Rogers' comedy, *So This Is London*, at the President. She was educated in Paris. Her slight brogue revealed in *Song O' My Heart* is supplanted by a captivating English accent in the Rogers' picture."

As Maureen became more famous with movie audiences, the cigarette companies started offering her money to endorse their products. The big tobacco manufacturers used every trick in the book to hook young people on cigarettes. A 1932 magazine ad for Lucky Strike featured Maureen's photo and her signature, and the following which was supposedly her endorsement, "My reason for smoking Luckies is that they are so mild and cause no irritation to my throat. Your new Cellophane wrapper is marvelous. Just a pull on the tab and there are the Luckies."

Maureen also did an ad for Camel cigarettes during the 1950s, and the copy boasted the endorsement of the actress: "Camels taste so rich and good — and I'm glad they're so truly mild."

In 1994 Maureen noted her naivete in promoting the cancer sticks: "In between films I also did some advertising for cigarette companies which was something that all the big names did. The money wasn't very good, but part of the remuneration was large supplies of cigarettes. I smoked then like most actresses did. Unfortunately we didn't know any better."

Cigarette cards were also popular, especially in Britain, and a small photo card was included in every pack of cigarettes. Many well-known actors and actresses were featured in the photo cards, including Maureen and Johnny Weissmuller after his film debut in 1932. All these young actors were given free cigarettes and a fee for endorsing them, and a whole generation of young people became addicted.

A few decades later many of the great actors of the 1930s were stricken with lung cancer, including John Wayne, Dick Powell, Gary Cooper, Humphrey Bogart, and too many more to even list. Movie audiences, emulating their screen heroes, also started smoking and they too suffered the same serious health problems as movie stars who smoked.

Maureen's next film for Fox was *Just Imagine*, a screwball romantic comedy that takes place in a futuristic America of 1980. The screwball part came from former vaudeville comic El Brendel, who got top billing as Single O, and performed his role with hilarity as a misplaced 1930s man brought back to life fifty years after suffering a head injury. Brendel was a master of physical comedy, and always spoke in a comedic *faux* Swedish accent in his many films. He fractured the English language in a charming manner, and his numerous pratfalls kept movie audiences laughing.

The romance was between Maureen as LN-18 and her handsome young man, J-21, portrayed by John Garrick (who had also played her love interest in *Song O' My Heart*). The two young lovers have applied for a marriage license, but the tribunal has ruled in favor of a wealthy man, MT-3, who just happens to be a friend of her father's. The girl has no interest in the older man, but the marriage tribunal will have the final say after a waiting period of four months.

In the opening scene, Maureen is flying her personal airplane, which has replaced the automobile as transportation in New York City. She runs into J-21, a pilot for a trans-Atlantic airline, who is also jetting around the city. Later that evening they get together to lament their situation, but lots of kissing seems to make them both feel much better. (At this point of the story John Garrick sings his sweetheart a love song, "I Am the Words, You Are the Melody," and Maureen joins in on the final verse to make it a lovely duet.)

A renowned scientist offers J-21 the opportunity to pilot a rocket-ship to Mars on a dangerous mission, and he realizes that this is his chance to become famous and sway the marriage tribunal in his favor. He is joined on this adventure by his best friend RT-42 (Frank Albertson), as well as Single O (Brendel), a stowaway on the ship with a penchant for goofy behavior.

When they arrive on Mars, it is a crazy world where every good person also has an evil twin counterpart. The two factions are warring between each other, and the three Earth men make friends with the good tribe but later are captured by the evil queen and her warrior women.

Of course this action is all done tongue-in-cheek, as is most of the film. The songs and dialogue by DeSylva, Brown, and Henderson were first-rate, and the dance direction of Seymour Felix provided several musical dance numbers on Mars that were most entertaining.

There is a very touching scene at this point in the story, where J-21 gazes upon Earth through a telescope and visualizes his sweetheart LN-18. (Maureen most often calls him J-darling in the film, and he in turn calls her L-darling.) She speaks the words to the song — their song — "I am the words, you are the melody," in a lovely soliloquy heard only by J-21 in this dream sequence from Mars.

Eventually, the three adventurers manage to escape Mars after a madcap chase and speed back to Earth in their rocket-ship as champions of space exploration. Of course the marriage tribunal is in session and just about to rule in favor of MT-3, who is really a blackheart. But when J-21 bursts into the courtroom with evidence of the successful mission to Mars, he is acclaimed a hero and awarded the marriage certificate that allows the young lovers to marry.

Just Imagine is a combination of the hilarious slapstick of El Brendel along with some very fine acting of Maureen and John Garrick in their romantic scenes together. Maureen has one very touching sequence where she reads a letter from J-21 informing her of his mission, and she becomes overwrought with emotion that her lover will die and never return. It is a beautiful scene in a story that is mostly comedy but has its warm and tender moments.

Maureen later recalled this film in 1994: "During that year, I did my first and only musical, called *Just Imagine*. It was a very humiliating experience because, although I could sing as well as any other 19-year-old girl, when it came to opening my mouth for the camera not a sound came out. The crew kept saying, 'Come on Irish girl, you must be able to sing!' But I couldn't and in the end I had to talk my lines."

An October 11, 1930 review in the *Los Angeles Record* noted Maureen's standout performance in a very positive critique:

> "The cast is excellent, though Maureen O'Sullivan deserves particular praise for her scene with the letter. John Garrick for his reserve in playing. Joyselle for her alluring pair of Martian queens, and Ivan Linow for his twin giants.
>
> "*Just Imagine* ... they hurtle ahead through 50 years to a fantastic 1980. After that there is no time to indulge in independent speculation about the future. Sensational backgrounds counterpoint hilarious laughter so rapidly that a new surprise anticipates any independent imagining on the part of the impressed and convulsed audience.

"DeSylva, Brown and Henderson did some high-powered imagining on this film, but they did not imagine its success ... that's real. This is a film that will be held dear in the hearts of movie audiences for months to come."

Decades later, in the actual 1982, Maureen saw *Just Imagine* and commented that it had not held up well through the years. "Recently, I saw a film that I did called *Just Imagine*. It was one of the first films I ever did. I had such trouble with that film. It was a comedy set in the future — 1982," she noted with a laugh. "My lover was lost on the way to the moon and I receive a letter that he's lost and the news puts me in a terrible state. I'll remember that scene to my dying day. I had to read the letter, look up and count four, clutch it to my bosom, count three and look down, read the letter again and count four, look up with horror on my face, scrunch up the letter and run from the room. I had to do that scene all morning long, while the director was counting with me — one, two, three, four. I thought at the time, well, maybe this is what one has to do. When I saw it recently at a film festival, I realized it was so dated and this director was wrong. If he had only let me do it in my own sincere way rather than like Theda Bara."

After Maureen's excellent reviews in *Just Imagine* and *So This Is London*, Fox Film decided that it was time to give her a starring role opposite Charles Farrell in *The Princess and the Plumber*, a romantic comedy directed by Alexander Korda. Up until this time Farrell was usually teamed with the immensely popular Janet Gaynor.

The studio decided to deviate from this successful formula, and instead handed the female lead of the princess to Maureen in just her fourth film. The story began in the imaginary kingdom of Daritzia, where Princess Louise (Maureen) is being pressured by her father the Prince (H. B. Warner) to marry a wealthy Count (Lucien Prival), because they are literally broke and planning to rent their castle to a wealthy American (Bert Roach).

Maureen with Charles Farrell

Meanwhile, American plumber Charlie Peters (Farrell) comes to the castle to install radiators, and of course when the charming Louise catches his eye, Charlie has more on his mind than the job at hand. As the plot thickens the princess and the plumber fall madly in love and manage to overcome all obstacles including the dastardly Count. It turns out that Charlie actually owns the plumbing company and is wealthy in his own right, and thus the money problems are solved and true love is served in one romantic swoop.

Although this film was deemed a financial flop by Fox, the initial reviews in several publications were quite good. Maureen in particular garnered several comments that extolled her virtues as a rising young actress. *Film Daily* noted on November 30, 1930, "Maureen O'Sullivan steps up another notch with her captivating performance as a sheltered princess, while Charles Farrell is right in his element as the plumber."

Hollywood columnist Louella O. Parsons of the *Los Angeles Examiner* also loved Charles Farrell and Maureen in her December 19, 1930 review of *The Princess and the Plumber*:

> "A farcical edition of good old Graustark with enough sincere comedy to make us forget a few trite situations. Alex Korda has done a deft job of directing.
>
> "The sweet, pure little Princess is played by little Miss O'Sullivan, the Irish girl with the English accent. You will love Maureen, she is so naive in her role of Princess Louise."

Another positive review came from Elizabeth Yeaman of the *Hollywood Daily Citizen*:

> "Maureen O'Sullivan appears as the princess, and Charles Farrell is the plumber. Theirs is a naive romance, and they have endowed it with a light touch of sincerity.
>
> "The acting technique of Miss O'Sullivan improves with each picture, and as she gains experience before the camera she photographs more beautifully.
>
> "Much credit for the success of *The Princess and the Plumber* goes to director Alexander Korda. He has retained a fine balance between comedy and romance, as well as innate good taste. There is no lavish display of royal splendor, but the atmosphere of a proud but decadent little kingdom is firmly established."

The *Los Angeles Record* review of December 19, 1930, lauded the merits of the film:

> "*The Princess and the Plumber* is a rare film. It just leans back with a beautiful 'take it or leave it' attitude and says, 'This is a fairy tale — so there!' knowing very well that nobody's going to leave it. Charles Farrell is seen as the plumber who is sent to one of those delightful mythical kingdoms to install radiators in the castle which is about to be rented to a wealthy American for the good of the royal exchequer.
>
> "Maureen O'Sullivan, quite proud and lovely enough to satisfy anyone's demands of a princess, finds that royal edicts and traditions crumble like the ruins they represent in the face of a plumber's wrench and an American's love."

Hungarian-born director Alexander Korda had begun directing films in Hungary in 1914, moved on to Vienna (1920-1922) and Berlin (1923-1927) before coming to America to work for Fox Film in 1927. *The Princess and the Plumber* was his 10th film during his early Hollywood period, and ultimately his last for Fox; he was unceremoniously fired after the Fox hierarchy decided the film was a distinct failure. A Korda interview with Philip Johnson explained the sudden split between the director and the studio: "Korda made *The Princess and the Plumber*. The big Panjandrums [at Fox] saw it and decided that they wanted 'menace' put into it. Korda didn't think that menace was essential. He thought it would spoil it — if it was good enough to be spoiled. He argued. Next morning he found that he had lost his job."

After completing *The Princess and the Plumber*, Maureen thought the film was going to be a big success, based on the initial reviews. She also finished work on another comedy in January 1931 with Will Rogers called *A Connecticut Yankee*, which looked to be another winner. Having completed four films in barely a year, Maureen decided to go back to Ireland on January 25, 1931, to visit her family for the first time since leaving for America in October of 1929.

Maureen arrived in Dublin to a huge reception from her now-large contingent of fans in Ireland, and she was treated like a major celebrity in her homeland. She felt like she was a big success at this young stage of her career, but she began to have her doubts when she didn't hear from the Fox studio about when she should return for her next assignment. She wired Fox Film and received only a terse reply: "Return whenever you feel like it."

Still confident that she was a star on the rise, Maureen took the next ship to New York. She arrived the first week of April, and was met by the same publicity man who had greeted her upon her initial arrival in the United States in 1929. At that time he had been the perfect sycophant, gushing over her and making her feel immensely welcome.

Now, however, he seemed uneasy and less friendly; he took Maureen to the Fox offices in New York, where the staff looked at her like she was indeed an outsider rather than a rising star. Maureen was instructed to report to the Fox studio in Los Angeles, as she recalled in 1994:

"While I'd been in Ireland, my father had been so impressed by all the publicity I was getting, that he had persuaded me to ask the studio for more money. So, as soon as I got back to Hollywood, I bought myself a beautiful blue hat to match the colour of my eyes and went to see the head of Fox. 'I feel I deserve a pay rise,' I said confidently. There was a moment's silence, during which I saw his jaw visibly drop.

'You what?' he asked. Then came the truth: 'I want to tell you my girl, you're not worth a cent to us. In fact, you're a failure.'

"It transpired that *The Princess and The Plumber* had been a big flop and the critics had been merciless in describing me as poison — which was pretty strong language and very upsetting. But whenever I was upset I used to write things down, so I immediately started to make a list of all the things that were poisonous but beautiful — like the Oleander flower. Having done that I felt much better because I realized it was really quite acceptable to be *poison* after all.

"But it was a great shock and for a while I was extremely miserable. Luckily a very kind Irish producer spotted me looking blue and asked what was wrong. When I told him, he was very dismissive of the studio's attitude. 'I've never heard of anything so ridiculous,' he said. 'Fancy blaming you for the financial woes of the studio.'

"He was right, and I realized that, at the end of the day, what really counted in Hollywood was looks rather than talent. If you were pretty, photogenic, and did what you were told, then you couldn't really fail.

"When I look back at that time, I'm amazed this incident didn't completely crush me. But I think one reason I took it so well was that I had precious little ambition in those days, and so failure didn't seem like such a terrible thing after all. What I was interested in was adventure, and this was just one more ghastly adventure."

Maureen's future at Fox was strictly short-term, after the lambasting she had been subjected to by the executive. She would make only one more film while under contract to Fox Film, a drama called *Skyline*. The proverbial handwriting was on the wall, and her walking papers would be served a few months down the line.

In the meantime, *A Connecticut Yankee* was released in April of 1931 to excellent reviews, and later was chosen as the tenth of the *New York Times* best films of the year. Besides Will Rogers and Maureen, the cast included Myrna Loy as the delightfully wicked sister of King Arthur, played robustly by William Farnum. Within three years, Myrna Loy would become a big star when she teamed with William Powell in *The Thin Man* series, which began in 1934.

A Connecticut Yankee begins in a small Connecticut town where Hank Martin (Rogers) owns and operates a small radio station and a radio parts supply shop. A creepy old mansion on a hill calls with an urgent need for a radio power supply, and Hank Martin makes the delivery himself on a stormy, blustery night. Upon arrival, Hank meets, in order: a strange butler; a distraught young woman (Maureen) who fears for her safety; her boyfriend, who is hiding in a suit of armor; a beautiful woman who warns him not to help the girl or suffer dire consequences; and an eccentric inventor who believes he has developed a radio that can listen back in time to historic events such as Lincoln's Gettysburg Address.

When a blast of wind breaks open a window and knocks a suit of armor upon the head of the radio man, he wakes up in the 6th century in Camelot, the court of King Arthur. Soon thereafter, Hank meets Princess Alisande (Maureen once again), who is pleading for the life of her boyfriend Emile (Frank Albertson). Theirs is a forbidden love because he is a commoner, and Emile has been sentenced to die by burning for his love of the princess.

When the evil Merlin convinces King Arthur that the strange newcomer is some sort of sorcerer, Hank is also sentenced to die by fire. A fortuitous full eclipse of the sun comes along at the moment of the burning at high noon, and Hank convinces the king that this trick is his own powerful magic. Arthur pardons Emile and Hank, who is dubbed Sir Boss and becomes a close confidante of the king.

The king enlists the aid of the brave Sir Boss in rescuing Alisande, who has been kidnapped by his sister, Queen Morgan le Fay (Myrna Loy). Together they ride to the castle of the queen, but they are captured and sentenced to be hanged. Meanwhile, Emile is leading the charge of the king's forces, who are heavily armed and thus win the battle rather handily.

Emile frees Alisande and kisses her passionately, and Sir Boss runs to release all the poor wretched inmates from the dungeon. Suddenly he is surrounded by the Queen, and Merlin, and Sagramor, and he is about to be killed — when Emile sets off a dynamite charge that blows the castle to eternity. Sir Boss is conked on the head once again, as the castle crumbles amidst the explosion.

When he awakens, the former Sir Boss is back to being himself — just a radio man recovering from a knock on the head at the mansion of the goofy inventor. Hank makes a hasty exit to his delivery van, the night still dark and stormy. Moments later he discovers that the girl (Maureen) and her boyfriend Clarence have escaped by stowing away in the back of his van.

The young woman explains that her father is somewhat deranged, and his sister was trying to take her away to stop her from marrying Clarence. Hank is more than happy to help, and loans the two young lovers his van so they can drive to the next town and be married by the justice of the peace. Hank just strolls down the road the short distance to his home, shaking his head and laughing at this strange night that has a most happy ending.

A Connecticut Yankee, which was based on a Mark Twain novel published in 1889, has many humorous situations which are updated from Mr. Twain's original novel. Of course, the radio and the automobile were not yet in everyday use during this era.

One hilarious situation happened midway through the story, when Sir Boss is challenged to a jousting match by Sagramor, the king's unscrupulous knight. In typical Will Rogers' frivolity, halfway through the jousting match Sir Boss drops his lance and produces a rope, and proceeds to lasso and pull his opponent from his horse and drag him across the arena amid wild cheers from the gallery.

Another funny moment came about when King Arthur and Alisande are in chains in the dungeon, and Sir Boss tries to seduce Queen Morgan and sweet-talk her into releasing the king and princess. The queen has a mad crush on Sir Boss and kisses him passionately, at which point the face of Will Rogers' character turns bright red after the seductive kiss! This was a black and white picture and thus each and every print had to be hand-tinted to produce the effect of red cheeks on the flushed and flustered Sir Boss. This was quite a shocker to the audience, which collectively didn't know if this was a small miracle or a figment of their imaginations.

Of her co-star, Will Rogers, whose most famous quote was, "I never met a man I didn't like," Maureen expressed a mild disenchantment. "He didn't particularly like me. I used to wear slacks, and he thought that wasn't feminine. He also thought I was 'fast.' He always said he never met a man he didn't like, but I don't know about women."

A review in the *Los Angeles Examiner* on April 6, 1931, from Louella Parsons spoke of the high level of enjoyment derived from the film:

"Mark Twain stands pre-eminent as America's most beloved humorist. Will Rogers, modern and entirely different in his nonsense slant, is probably our most famous present-day humorist. Combine the two and you just cannot help having a classic.

"This is a strong word, I admit, but after you see *A Connecticut Yankee*, which opened yesterday at the Criterion Theater, there is no doubt that you will agree with me ... I will say, however, that the initial speech made over the radio is typically Rogerian and gets the comedy off to a fine start. Will Rogers, roaming about King Arthur's court, is as funny as anything you can imagine. As the Yankee who, with his twentieth century knowledge, makes chumps out of the sixth century magicians, he is a riot.

"Romance and young love come into the picture in the presence of the youthful Maureen O'Sullivan and the ebullient Frank Albertson. Both are good and villainy is well represented by Brandon Hurst as the jealous Merlin."

Maureen's next project and final film for Fox was *Skyline*, which was based on the 1927 novel by Felix Reisenberg, *East Side, West Side*. The lead role of architect Gordon McClellan was filled by Thomas Meighan, who had been a silent-film star and had successfully made the transition to talkies. Maureen portrayed Kathleen Kearny, and her love interest was Hardie Albright in the role of John Breen, a young man haunted by growing up in the shadow of a brutal stepfather.

Skyline begins when John is told by his dying mother Rose that her husband, a rough barge captain on the East River, is not really his father. When his mother dies, John knocks his stepfather out cold for insulting his mother's memory. Through a series of events, John is befriended by Mike Kearny (Jack Kennedy), an Irish construction worker who takes him home to meet his daughter, Kathleen (Maureen). Lightning strikes, as John and Kathleen almost immediately fall in love.

John manages to get a job working for Gordon McClellan, a famous architect who has built many of New York's skyscrapers. It is John's desire to also become an architect, so they immediately become fast friends in a father-son sort of way, and John calls his new friend "Mac."

The story soon becomes tangled with complications. John tells Mac of his past and shows him a locket with his mother's portrait. McClellan, who was Rose's first husband, realizes that he is actually John's father. Mac does not reveal this to John, who carries an immense amount of anger towards the father he never knew.

John and Kathleen have fallen in love and plan to marry, but a love triangle begins when John becomes infatuated with Paula Lambert (Myrna Loy), who just happens to be Mac's ex-lover. John rages when he discovers Paula and Mac together, and plans to leave town. Mac confronts John, and reveals that he is really his father and that his biggest regret in life was losing track of his former wife Rose and his baby son.

After much soul-searching, John realizes that he has misjudged Mac, and rushes to the construction site where his father has fallen from the third floor. Mac's injuries are not fatal, and John asks his forgiveness and calls him "Dad." Soon thereafter, the new partnership of McClellan and Son celebrates the opening of the towering skyscraper, and John and Kathleen recite their wedding vows.

A September 12, 1931 preview by NEA service writer Dan Thomas had only good things to say:

> "*Skyline,* which stands out as the best of the films previewed this week, is strictly in the entertainment class. There is some beautiful photography of New York's skyline, but that is incidental to the picture. The real value of the production is its simple story told in a straight-forward manner.
>
> "Thomas Meighan, who has entertained a good many people in his day, plays the leading role of the construction engineer. And in doing so, he proves that he is far from through in the picture game. He is a type the public likes, and still is just as good an actor as ever. Hardie Albright, a comparative newcomer, is grand as the boy.
>
> "And that little Irish beauty, Maureen O'Sullivan, furnishes the other half of the romance. Fox officials certainly made no mistake when they brought her over here from Ireland. Myrna Loy, Jack Kennedy and Stanley Fields also give good accounts of themselves."

Other reviews for this little B-picture that had a mix of drama and romance mentioned the excellent acting from the principals. Dick Hunt of the *L.A. Evening Herald* noted of *Skyline* in his column of October 30, 1931:

"The story is one of a father's love for his son and the subsequent misunderstanding before this love is finally realized and returned.

"It's difficult to choose between Thomas Meighan and Albright for stellar honors. Both give impressive, human portrayals. To me, Albright is inclined to be theatrical at the start but he soon warms up to the subject and becomes natural in the part.

"There is a thread of romance, and charming Maureen O'Sullivan gives a capable performance opposite Albright."

Maureen's role of Kathleen Kearny was right up her alley: an Irish girl who falls in love with a troubled Irish boy. In several dramatic situations, Maureen emoted powerfully, in particular the love triangle that involved her young man and the "other woman" — in this case portrayed deliciously by Myrna Loy, who wore a blonde wig for a completely different look.

Maureen O'Sullivan walked the Fox gangplank after completing *Skyline* in June of 1931. She collected her last paycheck and her contract was not renewed; she was, in effect, fired. This was hardly unusual at the time, considering the mounting financial woes of all the major studios.

The studios could no longer afford to pay weekly paychecks to actors who weren't actively working on film projects. In 1930 the Talkie boom led to massive profits for the eight largest studios, to the turnstile-ringing tune of $55 million. By 1931, the Depression had a choke-hold on the movie industry as well as the whole country; profits for the Big Eight would tumble to $6.5 million.

By the following year, 1932, the profit column was blank and the loss column showed a stunning $26 million for the Big Eight. By early 1933, the Fox Film studios, along with Paramount and RKO, all went into bankruptcy or receivership. Myrna Loy, another rising young actress who had appeared with Maureen in both *A Connecticut Yankee* and *Skyline*, also was cut loose from her Fox contract around the same time.

So it is easy to see that Maureen was let go for financial reasons rather than a dissatisfaction with the quality of her work. To the contrary, she had garnered excellent reviews in virtually all of her films and was gaining stature as an actress of considerable talent. Now suddenly she was unemployed, but she was certainly not alone. This was 1931, and the Depression had many proud souls standing in bread lines when their jobs disappeared.

A publicity still for *A Connecticut Yankee*, with Maureen as the Princess Alisande

CHAPTER FIVE
"Stardom Beckons: The MGM Lion Roars"

After having her Fox contract terminated in mid-1931, Maureen was suddenly a free agent and able to sell her services to any studio in Hollywood. Her next screen work was for RKO in a charming romantic comedy, *The Big Shot*, in which she co-starred with Eddie Quillan. Maureen was cast as Doris Thompson, the sweet but feisty girlfriend of Ray Smith (Quillan), a young man with big dreams but a very empty pocketbook.

Ray's various get-rich schemes have all failed, but Doris and her mother Isabel (Belle Bennett) both have faith that Ray will succeed some day. To that end, Doris mortgages her house to finance an "auto camp" for Ray, a resort in the country that rents cabins to weary automobile travelers. The place sounds like a paradise and potential gold mine, but Ray discovers he has been hoodwinked again. The Blue Bird Auto Camp is run down, hasn't had a paying customer in years, and reeks of foul fumes from a small swamp that is also on his property.

Nevertheless, Ray is determined to make a go of the joint, and is helped along by a cranky recluse (Arthur Stone) who lives rent-free in one of the cabins and is known by all as "Old-timer." Despite his hard work, Ray is discouraged because the smell from the swamp chases away all potential customers, with one single exception: a beautiful blonde who decides to hide out there to escape her gangster boyfriend.

The soft-hearted Fay (Mary Nolan) gives Ray a $250 advance, and advises him to pursue Doris more ardently before her heart is captivated by another suitor. That someone else could be her boss at the insurance agency, Jack Spencer (William Eugene), who is lurking in the wings. Jack is hoping that Ray fails with the auto camp and loses the love of Doris in the process. Ray attends the strawberry dance in Pottsville intending to court Doris, but instead gets into a fist fight with Jack that intensifies the bad blood between them.

Jack is an unscrupulous scoundrel, and when he discovers that Ray's swamp is in reality a very valuable warm water sulphur spring, he schemes to buy it before Ray can assay its true value. Doris discovers the plot and frantically races in her automobile to tell Ray. Both drivers — nemesis and heroine — are wildly careening down the back roads to be the first to reach Ray.

At the auto camp, Doris crashes into the swamp and is knocked unconscious, and then Ray gets stuck in the muck trying to rescue her. They both seem doomed, but Old-timer manages to pull them out with a rope, just before they sink into the sticky mud of the swamp.

Naturally, the Blue Bird becomes a huge success as a health resort, as people come from all over to breathe the wondrous sulphur fumes that turned out to be a blessing in disguise.

The Big Shot was filmed between mid-August and early September 1931, and a January 1932 review in the *Film Daily* noted the wonderful fun and laughter of this little film:

> "Eddie Quillan is right in his element as the small town boy with big business ideas ... There is a smooth villain who is the cause of all his grief, and who is also trying to steal his girl. The latter is played well by Maureen O'Sullivan. There is a lot of wholesome small town atmosphere and sentiment nicely combined with the comedy. It gets over nicely as a light bit of entertainment that the whole family can see and enjoy. Eddie Quillan was never better than in this one."

At the end of the summer of 1931, Maureen landed the lead role in *The Silver Lining*, the initial production of the independent company, Atlantic Pictures. The young actress was reportedly paid the paltry sum of $300 for her work in this melodrama, which took only eighteen days to film, October 5-23, 1931. But the old adage "beggars can't be choosers" was never more true than in this instance; Maureen had saved nary a penny during her first two years in Hollywood, and she needed the money for rent and food.

The film was directed by Alan Crosland, who coincidentally had been the director for two of the most important productions of the 1920s: *Don Juan*, the initial film with synchronized music (1926), and *The Jazz Singer* (1927), the historic first film with talking sequences.

It would seem that Maureen's heart was barely in her work in this weak little drama, as she garnered perhaps the only poor review of her career in this 60-minute programmer. She portrayed Joyce Moore, a wealthy and spoiled landlord of several ramshackle tenement buildings on New York's East Side.

Variety noted that she hardly put forth her best effort in this picture, which certainly may have been the case:

> "Maureen O'Sullivan indifferently heads a competent supporting cast in a story that starts off with promising vigor, but which soon peters out ... Miss O'Sullivan displays small acting ability, a rather screechy voice and a weakness in her dramatic moments."

(Ouch. Fortunately for Maureen, negative reviews such as this were few and far between during her long career on screen and stage.)

The Silver Lining begins rather ominously as a small boy falls down three flights of stairs in a rundown tenement, when a rickety bannister collapses in a clear case of negligence. Shortly thereafter, attorney Larry Clark (John Warburton) files suit against the owners of the building, seeking damages for the boy's serious injuries. When slumlord Joyce Moore (Maureen) is informed of the lawsuit by her uncle (Montagu Love), she is furious over what she feels is a petty matter, and storms out to take a walk in the park.

Still fuming as she walks Central Park, Joyce is attacked and robbed of her mink coat by a thug and his moll, and left with someone else's purse. When the police arrive, Joyce is wobbly and disoriented, and is mis-identified as Mary Kane (because of the purse switch). In what might seem to be poetic justice, the police assume the woman is drunk. She is unceremoniously hauled in and sentenced to thirty days in a workhouse for disorderly conduct.

While in jail, Mary (the erstwhile Joyce) is befriended by Kate Flynn (Betty Compson), an angel of mercy who also lives in one of the buildings owned by Joyce Moore. In this case, Kate was jailed herself when she took the blame for a woman who had stolen some food, a woman who just happened to be the mother of the boy injured in the accident. Another regular visitor to the jail is attorney Larry Clark, who finds the person known as Mary Kane to be warm and lovely, and he falls in love with the young woman during their brief encounters. Of course, Larry doesn't realize that Mary is one and the same as Joyce Moore, the very someone he is suing over the matter of the injured boy.

After thirty days Joyce is released and immediately changes her life for the better, abandoning the shallow person she had been before her jail time. She hires workers to implement the repairs and upgrades necessary to make her buildings a decent place to live for her tenants. Without revealing her identity, Joyce invites Larry Clark to her yacht to resolve the legal matter. Larry, of course, is stunned to discover that the girl Mary Kane that he has fallen in love with is in reality Joyce Moore. But in a happy ending, all the differences are resolved and Joyce accepts Larry's proposal of marriage.

The *Motion Picture Guide* said of the film:

> "*Silver Lining* does its best as O'Sullivan does an about-face and ends up marrying Clark. The story is full of implausible situations that haven't aged well. By contemporary standards this is pretty funny stuff. The direction is all right considering the material's inherent shortcomings and performances are fair to middling."

Perhaps Maureen's distracted performance in *The Silver Lining* had something to do with her own brush with the law just a few days before filming began on the picture. The following was reported in the *Evening Herald* on October 3, 1931:

"**ACCUSED OF HIT-RUN DRIVING** — Maureen O'Sullivan, beautiful Irish colleen and film actress, today had a citation of hit-run driving. Officers claim she sideswiped a police car. Drove on and was overtaken after a 15-block run."

Although this appears downright hilarious in retrospect, perhaps Maureen was just plain scared and failed to stop after exchanging paint with a police car in Los Angeles. But it does seem to be a scene right out of a Marx Brothers film: Maureen careening through the streets of Beverly Hills and the police in hot pursuit of a young, wild actress with a tendency to drive a little bit out of control!

If there ever was a low point in Maureen's career, this would be it. She had just received some very weak reviews (and very little pay) for her work on *The Silver Lining*. On the advice of her agent, she invested the last of her ready money in a photographic session that was designed to show a whole different Maureen — a beautiful young woman who had sex appeal as well that certain allure that makes for stardom on the big screen.

This was a critical stage in her career, and if Maureen's gamble in spending her last money on the photo shoot had not paid off, she might have been forced to go back to Ireland. Life in Hollywood was the survival of the fittest, and many young actresses were cast adrift like so much flotsam floating on the sea.

The new publicity photos were taken by Tom Conlon to Metro-Goldwyn-Mayer, and eventually fell into the hands of executive producer Irving Thalberg. Although 32 years old at this time, Thalberg was forever known as the "Boy Wonder" in Hollywood history.

The studio had decided to produce a series of Tarzan pictures, and to that end had acquired the rights from author Edgar Rice Burroughs to bring his legendary jungle character to the big screen. MGM also held an option for two additional films, should this first picture become a big success.

Thalberg looked over the photographs of Maureen, selected his favorite photo and placed it on the center of his desk. Also displayed were publicity stills of various other young starlets who were candidates for the plum role of Jane Parker, the sophisticated English girl who evolves into the jungle mate of an untamed man. One by one Thalberg gathered up the photos and stacked them, until only the photograph of Maureen survived on his desk. He had chosen his Jane.

It has been noted that Thalberg had the final say on the casting of Maureen O'Sullivan as Jane. If this is true, it is further evidence that he most assuredly deserved his nomenclature as a genius in judging talent in the business of producing motion pictures.

The gamble did pay off, perhaps beyond her wildest dreams. The photographs led to her eventual signing with MGM and her subsequent success as Jane in the Tarzan series. This was definitely a turning point in the life of Maureen O'Sullivan, as she recalled to your author David Fury in 1992:

"I shall be ever grateful to Felix Feist, who directed the test that won me the role of Jane in the first of the MGM Tarzan series. I was nineteen at the time, alone in Hollywood. I had exactly two hundred and fifty dollars in the bank, and was a month behind in my rent at the Garden of Allah.

"I was to be the new Janet Gaynor, a threat to the rebellious Janet who was biding her time in Honolulu while the studio threatened not to meet the demands she was making, financial or otherwise. The trouble was that her fans resented this new Janet and when I was cast in a film that had been meant for her, they stayed away in droves. The studio became disgusted with me and dropped me as soon as my contract would allow, while Janet returned to the arms of her loving studio.

"This left me adrift — almost broke, no job and too proud to go home, a failure, to Ireland. So I gambled, got an agent and spent my last money on some very un-Janet like photographs. These photos led me to the test that I have just mentioned — which brings me to Felix Feist.

" 'Take One.' A year at Fox had only taught me my Janet Gaynor act. I was wistful, nauseatingly sweet. 'Cut!' called Felix. 'Stop that! Be strong and straight-forward!' he demanded. (Could I do that? I could and did.) 'It's a wrap!' said Felix, and I went home to wonder whether I had the part or not.

"The next day my agent, a dear Irishman named Tom Conlon, called to tell me I had the role even though the director, Woody Van Dyke, had wanted someone else. After the usual wardrobe and make-up meetings I was taken to the jungle set to meet Johnny Weissmuller, Edgar Rice Burroughs, and Woody Van Dyke.

"Standing well behind the camera I saw a Tarzan that the author could only have dreamed him to be. A golden make-up covered a body that was perfect. The setting sun lit his hair that was touched with gold. One foot was on a (supposedly) wounded lion. His arm was raised and with the most graceful gesture I have ever seen, he drove a spear into the animal's body. I watched in silence.

" 'Cut!' said Van Dyke, who seemed reconciled to the fact that I was to be Jane. 'Come and meet Jane,' called the director to Johnny Weissmuller. 'Hi Maggie!' said Johnny while extending that golden hand. (We had met once before and he thought Maureen too dignified a name.) Edgar Rice Burroughs wanted a picture of us together. 'My perfect Tarzan' he announced, 'and my perfect Jane!' He sent me all of his Tarzan books and in the last book he wrote, 'By now you should know everything there is to know about Tarzan.' "

MGM's slogan was "more stars than there are in heaven," and their stable of stars included: Greta Garbo, Clark Gable, Wallace Beery, Lionel Barrymore, Joan Crawford, John Gilbert, Lon Chaney, William Powell, Jean Harlow, Spencer Tracy, Lewis Stone, Laurel and Hardy, Nelson Eddy, Jeanette MacDonald, and Norma Shearer. James Stewart and the Marx Brothers were signed to the roster in 1935. Later in the decade they would add Mickey Rooney and Judy Garland to this already impressive list of the greatest stars in the movie business.

They were also known widely for the unique trademark, Leo the roaring lion, and its motto, *Ars Gratia Artis* — 'Art for Art's Sake.' The man credited with creating both the trademark and the motto was Howard Dietz, MGM's publicity director.

For the lead role of Tarzan, various Hollywood actors were given the look-see but found lacking in one respect or another and passed over. The jungle man had to have an incredible physique, and Irving Thalberg really wanted someone who was a new face to the American movie-going public. The man eventually chosen was Olympic champion and swimming star Johnny Weissmuller, who had never acted in his life. Johnny's only screen credit was a cameo as Adonis in the 1929 Ziegfeld musical, *Glorifying the American Girl.*

Weissmuller was well-known to the entire nation for his exploits in the swimming world, starting in 1921 as a 17-year-old teenage phenom. Over the next seven years he became a swimming legend and set numerous records in his specialty, the freestyle crawl. When he set the record of 57.4 seconds in the 100-meter freestyle in 1924, the record would last for an amazing ten years before it was broken. The zenith of his career was winning three gold medals at the 1924 Paris Olympics. He also captured two additional gold medals at the 1928 Amsterdam Olympics. Although Weissmuller was a new face to Hollywood, he already had a large base of fans who were excited that the American swimming legend from Chicago had been cast as the jungle man in the new Tarzan picture.

Johnny had a raw, unpolished look about him — he literally looked like he could have spent his days swinging through the trees and his evenings conversing with his friends, the apes and the monkeys. He was also tall, muscular, and lithe like one of the big jungle cats — physically he was perfect for the role of an untamed man living in a savage jungle land. When the friendly young man turned serious before the camera, his deep, brooding countenance and a wild animal expression in his eyes made him extremely believable as Tarzan.

Weissmuller always said that he wasn't an actor and never really tried to act before the camera — he just tried to be himself and do the best he could despite his lack of formal training. He knew his fans would forgive his faults as an actor, because in reality he was an athlete that Hollywood transformed into a hero of the silver screen. It was this basic innocence that made Johnny a fan favorite and resulted in his long career — 25 years — in Hollywood as Tarzan and his subsequent screen character, Jungle Jim.

Maureen O'Sullivan was the final piece of the puzzle in this screen story of a wild jungle man finding his mate, and she was a woman strong enough to handle the physically demanding role. The lead characters of Tarzan and Jane were now finalized in a bit of casting that was so perfect that the couple would be fondly remembered by movie fans many decades later. MGM had also wanted a fresh face for the character of Jane, the adventure-seeking English girl who bravely joins her father's expedition in Africa. Although she had been in Hollywood for almost two years at this point, she had yet to reach stardom in her various roles for Fox Film.

The fact that Maureen had a delightful British accent didn't hurt her chances of landing this role. It also helped that her former studio had stupidly let her go and thus MGM was free to sign her without compensation. The actress had a rare and unique beauty that was now maturing into legendary status, to go along with her ability to emote on screen effectively. When Maureen went into one of her panic modes in the Tarzan pictures or many of her other roles, the audience too clutched their collective bosoms and gasped. She was indeed a fine actress who captured the hearts of movie fans worldwide.

Now they were ready to make a motion picture. Directing this jungle adventure called *Tarzan, The Ape Man* would be W. S. "Woody" Van Dyke, known as "one-take Woody" for his propensity to capture a great scene in a single shot. With this uncommon directorial skill, he was able to bring most of his films in on time and under budget.

Maureen explained to author David Fury in 1992 that "Van Dyke was a strong man, in terms of his character, as well as being lean and handsome in a masculine way." The actress also worked with Van Dyke, who was one of her favorite directors, in *Hide-Out* and *The Thin Man*, both from 1934.

"I got the role of Jane over Van Dyke's dead body, it seems," said the actress. "He never wanted me in the role; he had wanted another actress. And after a good take, he'd say to me 'Kid, I didn't want you in this picture, but that scene was fine.' He always called me Kid," said Maureen with a chuckle, recalling a memory from sixty years in her past.

"Woody was known as 'one-take Van Dyke' and sometimes I'd say 'Van, can I do it again?' And he'd say, 'Why didn't you do it right the first time?' And when I was doing a picture called *Hide-Out* with Robert Montgomery, I had to tie my apron and I got it all tangled up. And I said 'Oh, Van, I got the apron all wrong, can I do it again?' He said no, of course, but when I saw it on screen I knew he was right. It was very natural to get the apron all tied up wrong.

"In *The Thin Man* it was the same thing — do it right, because there was no second chance. There was a certain spontaneity. I liked working with Van Dyke very much."

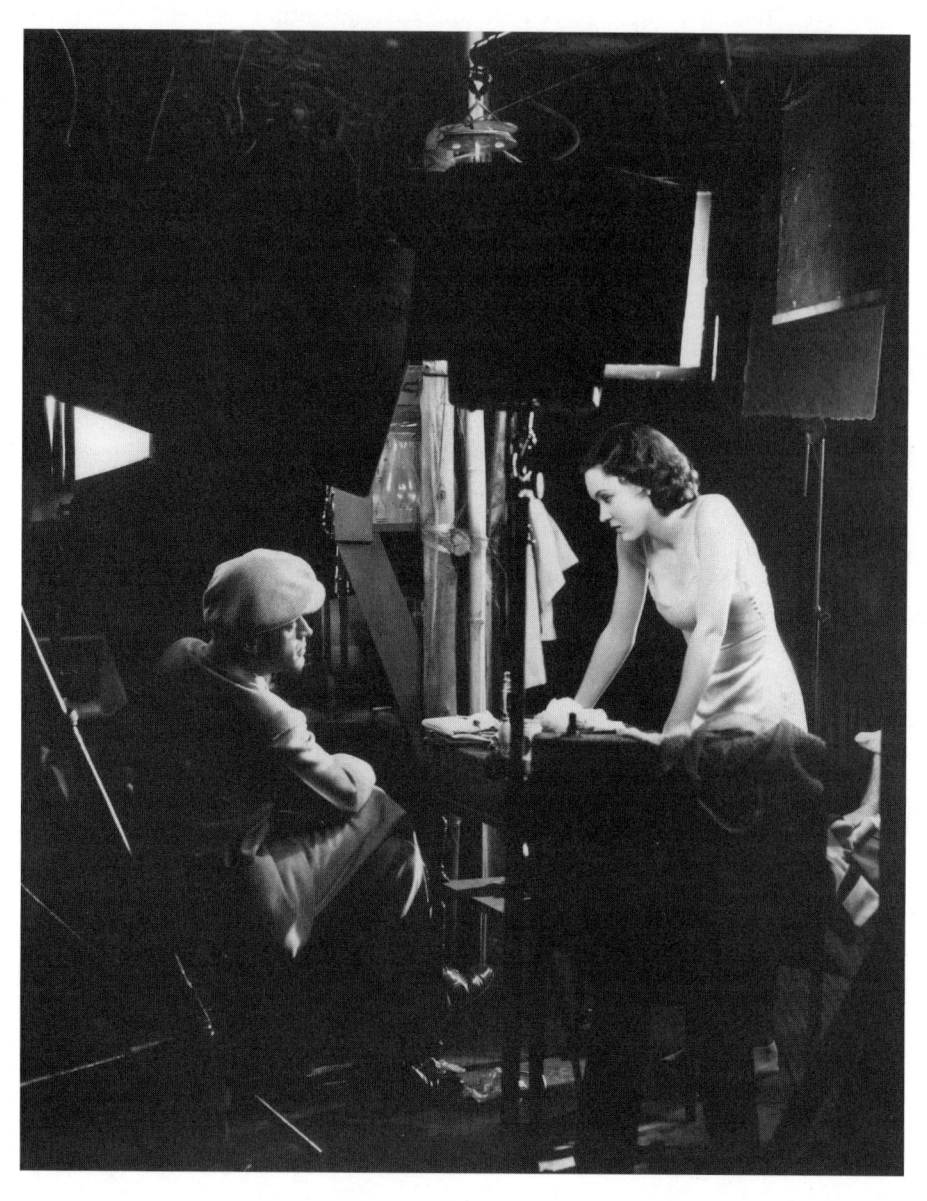

W. S. "Woody" Van Dyke discusses a scene with Maureen ... he always called her "Kid"

Two years before this Tarzan project came about, studio chief Irving Thalberg assigned Van Dyke to direct a jungle picture called *Trader Horn*. The premise was based upon the journals of real-life African adventurer Alfred Aloysius Horn. Van Dyke and his entire MGM crew photographed *Trader Horn* on location in the rugged wilds of Tanganyika, Uganda, Kenya, the Sudan, and the Belgian Congo, under the assumption that they could achieve great realism by filming in Africa without undergoing excessive hardship. That assumption was dead wrong.

There were many dangers in working in the untamed Africa of 1929, and thus a team of professional white hunters escorted the actors and production crew to guard against possible attacks by the wild beasts of the jungles. Of course there are no tigers indigenous to Africa. Author Edgar Rice Burroughs once mistakenly placed a tiger in one of his stories, a *faux pas* that the author later jokingly admitted to not being the only mistake of his writing career.

After weeks of filming wild animals and jungle scenes with star Harry Carey and his supporting cast, Van Dyke was reportedly on the verge of being fired by Thalberg and the picture sent to the scrap heap. The footage sent back to MGM was hardly enough to make the film envisioned, and the numerous problems encountered on a daily basis far outweighed the benefits of filming on location in Africa.

Called back to Hollywood, Van Dyke was allowed to complete his jungle adventure that soon became a box office smash around the world. *Trader Horn*, once almost abandoned, became a classic which was nominated for Best Picture of 1930-31.

Having learned their lessons on the insurmountable difficulties of filming in Africa, the studio decided to film *Tarzan, the Ape Man* entirely in Hollywood, and use the leftover stock footage of wild animals to give this new adventure a genuine feel of the jungle.

Producer Bernard Hyman assembled basically the same crew that worked on *Trader Horn*, including director Van Dyke, scriptwriter Cyril Hume, photographer Clyde de Vinna, editor Ben Lewis, and recording technician Douglas Shearer. Hume is credited with "discovering" Weissmuller at the Hollywood Athletic Club in 1931, and dragging him off to MGM to meet his bosses and to do a screen test for Tarzan.

The MGM jungle was the Toluca Lake region of North Hollywood, which was complete with its own river. An African landscape was created in Hollywood by bringing in truckloads of tropical fruit trees and other lush vegetation, all planted especially for the jungle production. The area west of Hollywood known as Sherwood Forest was also used, and the safari river crossing and the realistic hippo attack were shot at Lake Sherwood.

The hippos were rented from a local zoo and brought in by great trucks straining under the massive weight. The trainer thought it would be safe to let them cavort in the lake, and the whole group promptly went straight down to the bottom of the lake and stayed there for three days, coming up only long enough to gulp some air! Finally, the 800-pound baby came to shore to nibble some succulent plants, then was followed by his mother. The rest of the hippos soon came after the mother, and the company was finally able to shoot one of the most exciting scenes in the film.

The fictional scenario for the MGM Tarzan pictures was beyond a rugged, mountainous barrier — almost a sheer cliff — called the Mutia escarpment located in Cameroon. The African escarpment was represented on the screen by gigantic background matte paintings, some of which were hauntingly realistic and blended smoothly with the jungle sets. Despite the relatively primitive cinematic techniques of 1931, the film succeeded on a technical as well as artistic basis. Rear projections for the wild animal shots were realistic enough to be believable, and the leftover wild animal footage shot by cinematographer Clyde de Vinna in Africa added more realism to the Hollywood shots.

Author Edgar Rice Burroughs was compensated $1,000 per week for five weeks to read the scripts, pointing out any material that conflicted or infringed upon his original stories. Mr. Burroughs became good friends with Maureen during filming, and later asked her to join him in a 1932 book signing to promote his latest novel of adventure.

After the film was previewed in February of 1932, Burroughs sent director Woody Van Dyke a letter thanking him for a screen Tarzan that did justice to his literary creation:

"This is a real Tarzan picture. It breathes the grim mystery of the jungle; the endless, relentless strife for survival; the virility, the cruelty, and the grandeur of Nature in the raw." He described Johnny Weissmuller as a "great Tarzan with youth, a marvelous physique, and a magnetic personality."

An exalted Burroughs also gushed over Maureen O'Sullivan when he called her "... my perfect Jane. I am afraid that I shall never be satisfied with any other heroine for my future pictures ..."

The story of *Tarzan, the Ape Man* began as a young woman, Jane Parker (Maureen), arrives by river boat to a jungle outpost in Cameroon, East Africa. Jane has come to meet her father James Parker (C. Aubrey Smith), who along with his partner Harry Holt (Neil Hamilton) are planning a safari beyond the Mutia escarpment in search of a fabled elephant graveyard, hoping to recover a fortune in ivory tusks. Parker has serious reservations about allowing his daughter to join this dangerous expedition, but she shows off her skills with a rifle and gains the support of Holt, who is infatuated with the young English beauty — and thus Parker relents.

Deep into the jungle they trek, when suddenly a fierce tribe arrives at their camp, blocking their path to the Mutia — they are warned not to continue their journey. The safari natives are superstitious of the Mutia, a sheer mountain of dizzying heights; the narrow trail is perilous as one of the bearers falls to his tragic death. Jane herself slips and falls but is saved from the same fate by her safety rope, and is rescued by Holt and her father.

A treacherous river crossing becomes lethal when they are attacked by a herd of hippopotami and one of their rafts is overturned. The hippos are called off by a strange cry that comes from the jungle, and they get their first glimpse of a savage white man who leaps through the trees — Tarzan the ape-man (Weissmuller).

Maureen with C. Aubrey Smith and Neil Hamilton ... deep in trouble

Jane is the first white woman Tarzan has ever seen, and following a primitive instinct, he abducts her and carries her through the trees to his lofty lair. At first Jane is frightened of Tarzan, who can only mimic her English — but soon she falls in love with the jungle man, who is noble of heart and unafraid of any man or beast.

While Tarzan is away hunting, Parker and Holt discover Jane in the treetops and kill one of the great apes guarding the girl. An enraged Tarzan takes his revenge on the safari, killing them one by one. Later, the ape-man is wounded in the head by a bullet from the rifle of Holt, who jealously covets Jane for himself. Saved by one of his apes, Tarzan is carried to safety by Timba the elephant — the great apes lead Jane through the jungle, and she nurses him back to health.

When Tarzan revives, he and Jane discover romance in their viney "garden of Eden" — their playful fun turns into passionate lovemaking. Tarzan is dejected when Jane rejoins her father, who has been desperately searching for his daughter. The jungle man returns to his world, and Jane reluctantly says farewell. When the safari is captured by a tribe of barbarian pygmies, Cheeta races to warn Tarzan of Jane's precarious plight. With his thundering war cry, Tarzan incites his elephant allies to action and together they charge the pygmy village. The diminutive hostiles begin throwing their captives into a pit containing a giant ape, who crushes his victims like toys.

When Jane is thrown into the pit, both Holt and her father jump in to save her. They all seem doomed until Tarzan arrives in the nick of time to battle the savage brute to the death.

Tarzan's mighty elephants destroy the village and trample the pygmies, while Jane, her father, Holt, and the ape-man escape on the backs of two elephants. One of their huge mounts is wounded and dying, and the noble beast leads them through a waterfall to the secret entrance of the sought-after elephant graveyard. They have found their riches, but their jubilance is short-lived as Parker succumbs to a heart attack.

Jane is heartbroken at her father's death, and sends the dejected Holt back to civilization by himself. Jane remains with Tarzan in the African jungles to share a new life with the man she loves. (A clip of Tchaikovsky's "Overture to Romeo and Juliet" plays in the background as the final scene fades to black.)

Maureen performed her own stunts in riding on the back of elephants in several scenes, along with Johnny Weissmuller. These were dangerous stunts for any actor, and severe injury could easily have occurred if the rider had fallen off the elephant. Weissmuller did many of his own stunts in the Tarzan films, such as climbing trees, swimming and diving, and battling his myriad enemies.

One stunt that he did not perform was the trapeze work flying high through the jungle vines, the ape-man swinging and carrying Jane through the trees. These dangerous tricks were executed by Alfredo Codona, the high-flying aerialist whose greatest fame was the triple somersault that he alone performed during the 1920s.

Codona, who had been worshiped for two decades by circus fans world-wide, committed suicide on July 31, 1937. Codona's beloved wife, Lillian Leitzel, had died in a tragic accident in 1931. He married Vera Bruce in 1932, and the marriage was over by 1937; on that fateful day, the estranged couple were meeting in the office of her lawyer to finalize the divorce. After lighting a cigarette for Vera, he said, "This is the last thing I will be able to do for you." With that epitaph, he pulled a revolver from his coat and shot Vera five times in the chest, saving the last bullet for his own brain. They both were pronounced dead on the scene.

When MGM signed Johnny Weissmuller as Tarzan and Maureen O'Sullivan as Jane, the studio's brilliant bit of casting produced an unbeatable team as the jungle man and his mate. Weissmuller and Ms. O'Sullivan had a very special chemistry for each other that worked remarkably well, giving a warmth and genuineness to their roles as Tarzan and Jane. *Tarzan, the Ape Man* eventually became a classic motion picture because it is a beautiful love story *and* a magnificent adventure in a wild, untamed land.

In 1992, Maureen O'Sullivan appeared on the TNT special, "MGM: As the Lion Roars," and recalled the instinctive relationship formed between Tarzan and the young woman he had found in the jungle.

"He was a man who had never seen a woman before, so it was a fairy tale — and yet it was two real people," analyzed Maureen. "He didn't know what to do with a woman — I guess he found out pretty quick. But he didn't know what it was, when he found her — was it a monkey? She was able to teach him many things that he was unaware of. It was a lovely, innocent concept, and yet very sexy."

A love scene with Maureen and Johnny from *Tarzan, the Ape Man*

Tarzan, the Ape Man succeeded unconditionally as both an exciting adventure and a satisfying romance of the heart. Previewed in February of 1932 and released in late March, fans around the world loved the picture and the excitement created by the electrifying performances of Johnny and Maureen, and rushed to the box offices to make the film one of the top money-makers of the year.

Motion picture critics could find little fault with the film and practically stampeded over each other in praise of Weissmuller, his lovely co-star Maureen, and every aspect of *Tarzan, the Ape Man*. The following review from Thornton Delehanty of the *New York Evening Post* was typical of the fine press garnered by the production:

> "*Tarzan* is a frank and exuberant frolic in the imaginative literature of the screen ... It even has a way now and then of making fun of itself, a ruse so disarming that you are tempted to enjoy the picture most when you are believing it least...
>
> "As the English girl who has gone to Africa with her father in search of treasure, Maureen O'Sullivan gives one of her most charming performances. One can understand why Tarzan swings her around that way in the trees, and why he calls out his elephant friends to save her when she is about to be devoured by a horrible gorilla. She helps to make this infatuation of Tarzan's the most plausible thing in the picture.
>
> "As Tarzan, Mr. Weissmuller makes his bow to the movie-going public, and as Tarzan he will probably remain bowing through a whole series of these pictures ... There is no doubt that he possesses all the attributes, both physical and mental, for the complete realization of this son-of-the-jungle role. With his flowing hair, his magnificently proportioned body, his catlike walk, and his virtuosity in the water, you could hardly ask anything more in the way of perfection. And for the portrayal of Tarzan, nothing short of perfection would be permissible."

There were many outstanding reviews for *Tarzan, the Ape Man*, which turned out to be a hugely successful film and led to stardom and fame for Johnny Weissmuller and Maureen O'Sullivan. Johnny got a large majority of the space in most reviews, and deservedly so. He was magnificent in every respect in his role of Tarzan.

Maureen got her share of good ink too, but was somewhat overshadowed by the huge impression made by Weissmuller in his dramatic debut. However, in retrospect, Maureen was just as important as Johnny in the success of this classic film, as well as the succeeding five MGM Tarzan adventures. *Variety* also loved the picture, and mentioned Maureen first in their review of March 29, 1932:

> "Miss O'Sullivan acquits herself well in a difficult role, while the performance of Weissmuller really makes the picture. Whether the swimming champ will ever find another such outré role to play is the barrier to his career on the screen, but for this production he's a smash.

"The idyllic side of the story has been shrewdly handled and fortified by romantic settings and pictorial beauty that entirely disarm the grotesque situation of a civilized English girl falling in love with a young jungle savage, be he ever so ideal in stature and courage. Sequence of the young people splashing about a forest pool, for instance, has in it enough of visual beauty to discount any feeling of unreasonableness in the romantic situation. Be the situation however implausible, the mere poetic beauty of the backgrounds makes it all charming."

Maureen and Johnny both found instant fame with the release of this 1932 motion picture

Weissmuller supplied the brawn, but Maureen came through with beauty, warmth, sensuality, her own share of courageous moments, and most importantly, some very fine acting that gave a legitimacy to the production. The adventure in these films was spine-tingling, yet the superb dramatic performances from the entire cast, especially Maureen, gave the series an aura of fine picture-making and status as true classics in the adventure genre.

The actress later recalled further memories of her life and the Tarzan movies: "Luckily I was never attracted to my co-stars even though I worked with some of the most glamorous men in the world — Robert Taylor, William Powell, and even Johnny Weissmuller.

"While the whole of America thought I was having an affair with Johnny, nothing could have been further from the truth. Johnny was an amiable piece of beef-cake — a likeable overgrown child who enjoyed childish pranks. There was never a glimmer of a romance between us.

"When we were doing the Tarzan pictures, the MGM publicity department arranged some dates between Johnny Weissmuller and myself, dinner and dancing, because it was nice publicity for the film. It was never done to foster a romance particularly, but to foster a friendship — a nice relationship that would show on screen."

While there was never a romance between Maureen and Johnny, there was instead a great lifelong friendship. During the 1930s, Johnny was a big brother to Maureen, and watched over her in a protective manner. They occasionally socialized together or as couples, Johnny with his wife Lupe Velez, and Maureen with John Farrow. When the MGM Tarzan series ended in 1942, they remained in touch and were always great friends.

Maureen and Johnny Weissmuller — their true friendship showed on the big screen

CHAPTER SIX
"Woman in Demand: On and Off Screen"

After completing *Tarzan, the Ape Man*, Maureen was indeed a "hot commodity," in more ways than one. She signed a new, more lucrative deal with MGM in February of 1932, as her stock at the studio began to rise exponentially. Besides the fact that she was a personal favorite of Irving Thalberg, Ms. O'Sullivan was also highly rated by studio head Louis B. Mayer, who assigned Maureen to the best roles possible and some of the finest MGM films over the next decade. The fact that she was often the second female lead in many of these films had nothing to do with her skills, but rather her youth and innocent looks.

The top roles went to Greta Garbo, Norma Shearer, Joan Crawford, Jean Harlow, and other legendary actresses who all had maturity and experience over Maureen; she would just have to bide her time. But climbing over these many great actresses to reach the top of the heap was nearly impossible. There was a definite pecking order at MGM, and latecomer O'Sullivan, the charming lass from Ireland, would have needed a gun to blast her way past the elite actresses to reach the upper echelon. Nevertheless, she was gaining popularity as a matinee idol, as well as a national following that occurred when the chameleon changed from an unknown to a rising star.

Meanwhile, Maureen was also drawing considerable interest from the male population. In Hollywood, there were plenty of men eager to get acquainted with the young actress right from the day she stepped off the train. She was beautiful, unblemished, with a certain air of innocence and a charming personality. Actors had the best opportunity to get to know Maureen socially, including the various young men she worked with in her films and met through mutual friends.

For a while she was dating Leslie Howard, the distinguished British actor who was 20 years older than Maureen. She called it a "passing relationship," mainly because he was married, and as she noted "he didn't seem to care too much about that." And the Los Angeles press began to take note of her social engagements, around the time that the Tarzan picture was completed. On December 28, 1931, Jimmy Starr of the *Evening Herald Express* reported that Maureen was spotted dining with Russell Gleason, a young actor who was the son of the husband and wife acting team of Lucille and James Gleason.

She was also being invited to the grandest premieres in Hollywood, such as the January 1932 premiere of *Union Depot*, which starred Douglas Fairbanks, Jr. The large theater party hosted by Fairbanks and his wife, Joan Crawford, included the following guests: John Mack Brown, Richard Barthelmess, Paul Bern, Ben Lyon, Bebe Daniels, Clark Gable, Laurence Oliver, Tallulah Bankhead, Douglas Fairbanks, Sr. and Mary Pickford, Jackie Cooper, Harold Lloyd, Marlene Dietrich, and James Cagney, master of ceremonies. These were the biggest names in Hollywood, and now Maureen was traveling in some very select company.

After landing a new long-term contract from MGM, Maureen spoke with Robbin Coons of the *Hollywood Citizen News* in February of 1932 about the changes in her life since she had arrived in Hollywood in 1929:

"People said I was obviously inexperienced in *Song O' My Heart,* and I thought smugly that that was all right — if I could get by without experience and I wouldn't need to study much. And I never had to do anything for myself.

"I was at Fox two years, but I knew long before option time came that they were letting me go. I think that brought me to my senses, made me realize you have to work and get things for yourself in this town if they're going to last. And I made up my mind I would make good on my own.

"Another thing leaving Fox taught me was the value of money. When the salary was coming in every week I never thought about it — just bought anything I wanted. And when the checks stopped coming, I hadn't a thing to show for the two years. Now I'm old lady economy herself."

Robbin Coons noted the following about Maureen, who called herself "old lady economy" at the ripe old age of twenty: "She went about 'making good' by working in an independent picture called *Thirty Days,* which United Artists, incidentally, will release. Then she went out and took a test for the role in *Tarzan*.

"For a little Irish girl who never had her head under water, never had fired a gun, who had a nervous fear of high places such as the Ape Man's tree-top home, that was a tough assignment. But it was her performance as well as trouping courage that won the contract."

The young actress also became a favorite of Louella Parsons about this time, and began showing up in her *Los Angeles Examiner* columns on a regular basis beginning on March 30, 1932, when she reported, "Dorothy Jordan glimpsed in a summer frock at the Brown Derby. That winsome colleen, Maureen O'Sullivan, also there."

Maureen's schedule at MGM was hectic to say the least, sometimes working on several pictures at the same time and also reading future scripts. She did have a month off in January 1932 to rest her weary young bones after the trials and tribulations of making the Tarzan picture, which was a strenuous ordeal indeed. She would get very few breaks over the next decade, and would be perhaps the busiest actress in Hollywood during the 1930s.

Her next film was *Fast Companions*, a comedy for Universal which starred Tom Brown, James Gleason, Mickey Rooney, and Maureen, who was billed third. (This was a loan-out from MGM, and was originally titled *The Information Kid*.)

Mickey Rooney was eleven years old when this picture was made but had been in Hollywood since 1927, when he began starring in a series based on the comic strip, Mickey 'Himself' McGuire. Rooney was born Joe Yule, Jr., and this was the first picture that he began using the name Rooney, rather than the Mickey McGuire moniker he used in the series. Rooney also made a movie with O'Sullivan in 1938 called *Hold That Kiss*, in which he portrayed Maureen's younger brother. By that time Mickey was a rising star in Hollywood at age eighteen, because his lovable Andy Hardy pictures were making the Hardys America's favorite family.

Fast Companions begins as con-men Marty Black (Tom Brown) and his partner Silk Henley (James Gleason) travel from town to town with their race horse, touting the animal as a sure winner. They then make big money by betting against their own horse and forcing him to lose the race.

Marty moves into a boardinghouse run by Sally (Maureen), and the crooked young jockey soon becomes attached to a young orphan boy, Midge (Rooney), who needs a father-figure in his life. They become fast companions, and Sally is friends to both of them.

Marty's horse is entered in the Caliente Stakes and the local town folk have raised $15,000 to bet on the race, assured by Silk that this is a sure thing and that they can't lose. Silk is trusted with the money to place the bet, but plans on skipping town during the race. Meanwhile, the Information Kid (Andy Devine) has tracked Silk into town, and he is convinced that the slippery grifter is up to no good.

Midge gets into a fight with another boy and is reprimanded by Marty, who has great affection for his young friend. When Sally reveals that the boy was fighting to clear his name, Marty confesses that he is really a crook, but pledges to go straight and not steal the money. They hide the cash under Marty's bed, but the Information Kid smells a con and bets the $15,000 on Marty and his horse.

When Marty realizes he must win to save the money for the town folk, he runs his fastest race ever but still might lose. At the last instant, Midge fires a stone at the rump of the horse with his trusty slingshot, and the animal leaps ahead and triumphs by a nose. Marty has redeemed himself and finally wins a race honestly, and also gains the love and affection of Sally and Midge.

Fast Companions was a typical family film of the era, with good guys and bad guys, plenty of excitement, a budding love affair, and of course, a happy ending. *Variety* said of the picture in its review:

"A well made little picture from all angles. Good enough for some of the 'A' houses in a pinch and surefire for any spot below that classification ... Young Rooney, the kid, is outstanding in a set-up part."

The *Hollywood Citizen News* also thought highly of the picture:

"A surefire heart interest angle is introduced in the jockey's befriending a hungry young urchin, who thereafter refuses to leave his side. It is through the kid's idealistic hero worship that the jockey eventually turns straight. Mickey Rooney is splendid as the youngster, and Tom Brown gives an excellent performance as the jockey. James Gleason gives his usual humorous characterization, while Maureen O'Sullivan very prettily contributes the feminine love interest."

With the summer Olympics of 1932 being held in Los Angeles, Maureen was extended a special invitation to take part in a worldwide radio broadcast on May 22, 1932, as reported by Elizabeth Yeaman of the *Hollywood Citizen News*:

"Twelve prominent motion picture stars will make an international radio broadcast this coming Sunday between 12:30 and 1:30 p.m., Pacific Standard Time. The program is being sponsored by the California All Year Club for the purpose of inviting the nations of Europe to attend the Olympic Summer Games in Los Angeles this summer. The program will be broadcast over 35 stations of the Columbia network in this country, and it will be relayed by 105 foreign nations. Will Rogers, probably the best known of the movie stars internationally, will act as master of ceremonies. Elissa Landi, speaking in Italian, will invite the residents of Italy to the games. Marlene Dietrich will extend the invitation to Germans. Claudette Colbert will welcome the French. Bela Lugosi will invite the Hungarians. Tom Mix will talk to Mexico, Dolores Del Rio to Spain, Olga Baclanova to Russia, Maureen O'Sullivan to Ireland, Jean Hersholt to Denmark, and Laurel and Hardy to England. I guess Sweden simply won't get in on the invitation since Garbo, as usual, cannot be persuaded to appear for the broadcast. Each of the stars will speak in the language of the country addressed. This program will be unique in the history of air programs."

Maureen spent some time with the Irish athletes during the Olympics, and of course her friend and co-star Johnny Weissmuller was at the Olympics rooting on the American swim team. (Weissmuller had been a champion at the two previous Olympics, winning five gold medals.) Maureen also celebrated her 21st birthday on May 17th, a rising young star in Hollywood and finally old enough to have her first drink. But of course she couldn't even have that birthday drink, as Prohibition was still in effect until the following year.

Maureen's next role would be in *Strange Interlude*, with two of the greatest stars in Hollywood history, Norma Shearer and Clark Gable. This picture was based on the play by Irish-American playwright Eugene O'Neill, who had sold the screen rights to MGM after a successful run on Broadway. The story covers a time frame of more than forty years, so the actors age rather rapidly over the two-hour length of the movie. (The film also uses the convention of a voice-over track which made the innermost thoughts of each character known to the audience.)

The melodramatic story, so complicated that it took five hours to tell in the stage version (with a dinner break in the middle), revolved around Nina Leeds, who lost her lover Gordon in a plane crash during the war. Nina is so distraught that she goes to work in a sanitarium for wounded soldiers, to ease her guilt over her tragic loss. While there she meets Sam Evans (Alexander Kirkland), an old friend of Gordon's, as well as Dr. Ned Darrell (Gable), who becomes a close friend.

When Nina's father falls gravely ill, she rushes home accompanied by Sam and Ned, both of whom have fallen in love with her. Professor Leeds dies and Nina agrees to marry Sam, even though her true love is Dr. Darrell. Further complicating things is close family friend Charlie Marsden (Ralph Morgan), who although older than Nina, also loves her and longs to marry her himself.

After the marriage, Nina and Sam want to have a baby, a son. Sam's mother tells Nina confidentially that there is mental illness in the family, and it would be better if they never had any children. Bearing this horrible news, Nina has an affair with Ned Darrell, and indeed has the son that her husband coveted — but only Nina and Ned know that the baby is theirs.

Throughout the years Nina is always surrounded by the men she loves — her husband Sam, kindly friend Charlie, her secret true love Dr. Ned, and her son Gordon (Robert Young), who grows to be a fine young man who is devoted to his mother. (Perhaps too devoted, as the son and mother often kiss each other full on the lips to express their affection. Surely, Freud would have called this the Oedipus complex at its clearest example.)

In the conclusion, Sam Evans dies of a stroke, and Gordon tells his mother and Dr. Darrell that they should marry, because he's seen through the years that they are in love. Even though they suspect that Gordon knows the truth, they never confirm it; and they agree to never marry, just stay close friends as they have always been. Gordon of course is free to marry Madaleine (Maureen) and have children, because his true father is Dr. Darrell.

The lead role of Nina Leeds went to Norma Shearer, the wife of Irving Thalberg. When Joan Crawford had asked Thalberg about playing the role, he told her that there was only one MGM star who could possibly pull off the difficult role. "Don't tell me," said Joan. "Let me guess: Marie Dressler," and she stormed out of his office. Crawford's sarcastic retort revealed her anger; she knew the role was going to Norma Shearer, Thalberg's wife.

The male lead of Dr. Ned Darrell was played by Clark Gable, who was fresh off the success of his breakthrough *Red Dust* (1932) with Jean Harlow. *Strange Interlude* was highly melodramatic, and at times it seemed that Gable could hardly believe the lines he was speaking. Maureen O'Sullivan portrayed Madaleine, the fiancée to Nina's son Gordon, who was played by Robert Young.

This was a small role for Maureen, and she doesn't enter the story until there are but 25 minutes left in the picture. Her best scene is with Norma and Gable, who are now age 60 by this time in the story. Nina approaches Madaleine, who is watching Gordon compete in a rowing competition, and tells her she must speak with her on an urgent matter.

On the verge of hysteria, Nina pleads with Madaleine and begs her not to marry her son, and she is about to reveal the terrible family secret: that there is madness that runs in the Evans family genes. Before Nina can complete this revelation, Dr. Darrell jumps in between them and says: "Madaleine, as a doctor I feel that it is my duty to tell you that Mrs. Evans isn't herself. She's morbidly jealous of you and subject to queer delusions. So get back to your race, and God bless you."

Maureen later recalled working with these great stars when she was only 21 years old, still just a babe in Hollywood. She remembered Clark Gable to be very likable and unpretentious: "He was nice, and had a certain virility about him. During the filming of *Strange Interlude*, Clark and Norma were both made-up to appear as this elderly couple.

"He was very nice to me, and I just thought he was this old fellow talking to me. And I saw Norma looking at us, talking together. And the assistant director came over and said to Clark, 'Miss Shearer would prefer that you didn't spend so much time talking to Miss O'Sullivan.' So, Clark says, 'Yeah? I'll tell her what she can do!' " (Maureen did her very best Gable impression at this moment.)

Mr. Gable sauntered over to Miss Shearer and let her know that he would do what he pleased, and that included speaking to Maureen. Later that day he invited her to go horseback riding in Griffith Park on Sunday, but she turned him down because she had a date with Leslie Howard. "When he took his make-up off one day, I saw what I had missed!" lamented Maureen. "He wasn't that old fellow at all. But he was awfully nice, he would take his [false] teeth out, he didn't care. He really was very down-to-earth."

Early photos of Maureen O'Sullivan ... circa 1929
Above: At the Fox Studio Club, a hostel for young actresses
Below: Eighteen-year-old charmer

Maureen in her first car ... she once side-swiped a police car and drove fifteen blocks before being stopped. She also racked-up an impressive number of speeding tickets.
Below: An early photo used for an ice cream lid
Below right: British cigarette card (actual size)

Maureen O'Sullivan publicity photos 1930-1932

Two sports Maureen enjoyed in the 1930s: tennis and sailing

James Dunn and Maureen O'Sullivan were going steady in 1931.
Louella Parsons kept tabs on the couple in her column until the romance fizzled.

Four views of Maureen: smiling, off-guard, pensive, and exuberant!

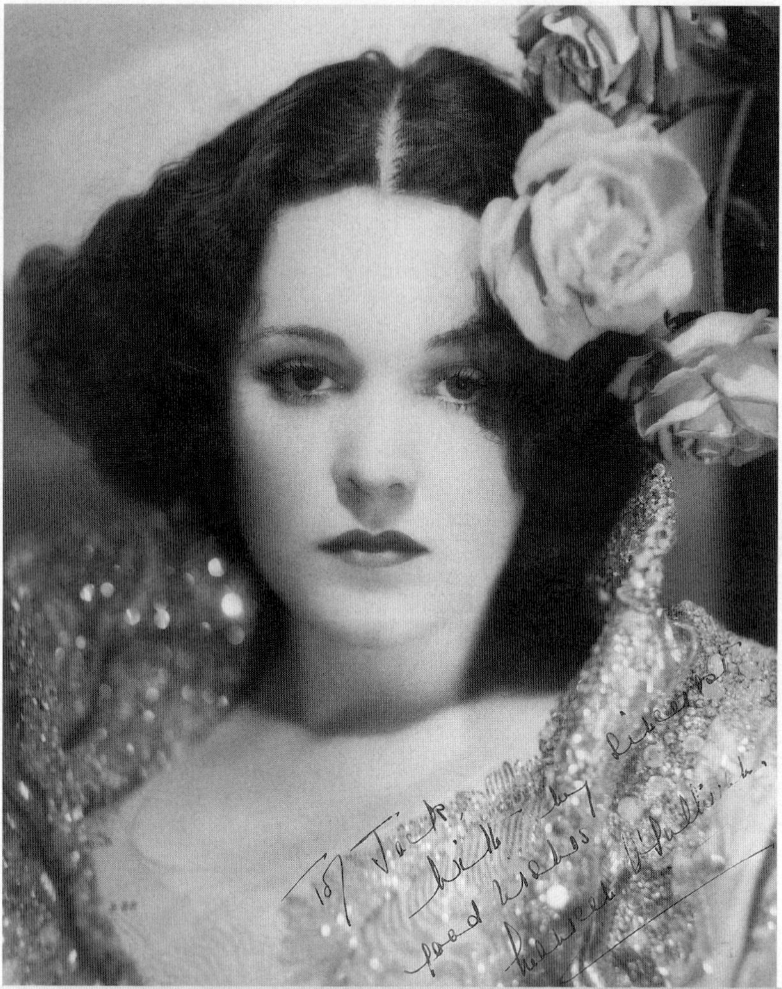
To Jack,
good wishes

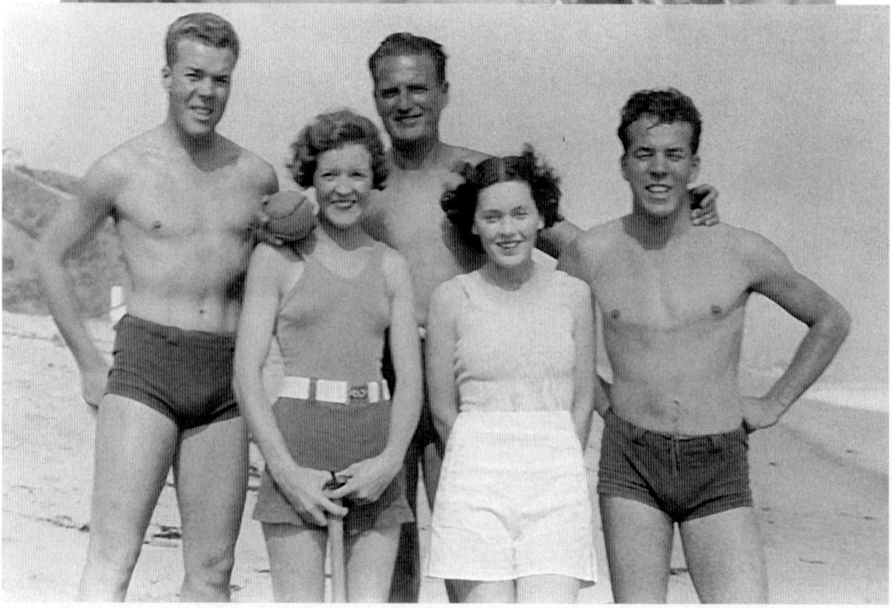

Above: Photograph signed to author Edgar Rice Burroughs ...
Inscription reads: "To Mr. Burroughs, with all my very best regards always ... Maureen"

Opposite top: Signed to Jack Burroughs ...
Inscription reads: "To Jack, with my sincerest and fond wishes ... Maureen"

Opposite lower: Hully Burroughs, Joan Pierce, Jim Pierce, Maureen, and Jack Burroughs. Hully and Jack were the two sons of Edgar Rice Burroughs. A day at the beach arranged by Mr. Burroughs was fruitless in his desire to match Maureen with either of his two sons. Their sister Joan was married to former Tarzan actor Pierce, star of *Tarzan and the Golden Lion* (1927).

Above: Another day at the beach … Maureen brings along her new puppy
Below: 1934 bathing suit modeled by the popular actress

Below: Maureen poses with six squirming puppies, which are quite a handful!

Both pages: Glamour shots, Maureen O'Sullivan, 1930s

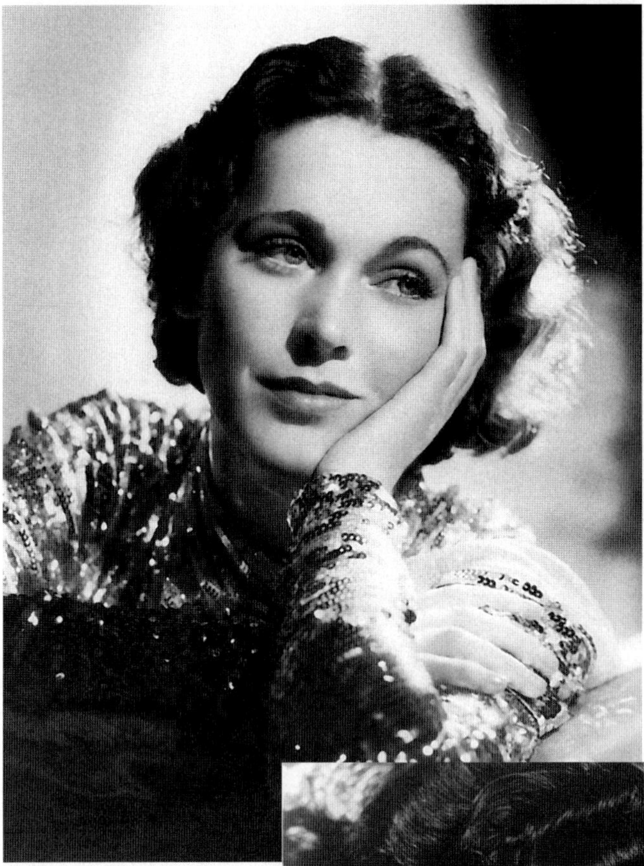

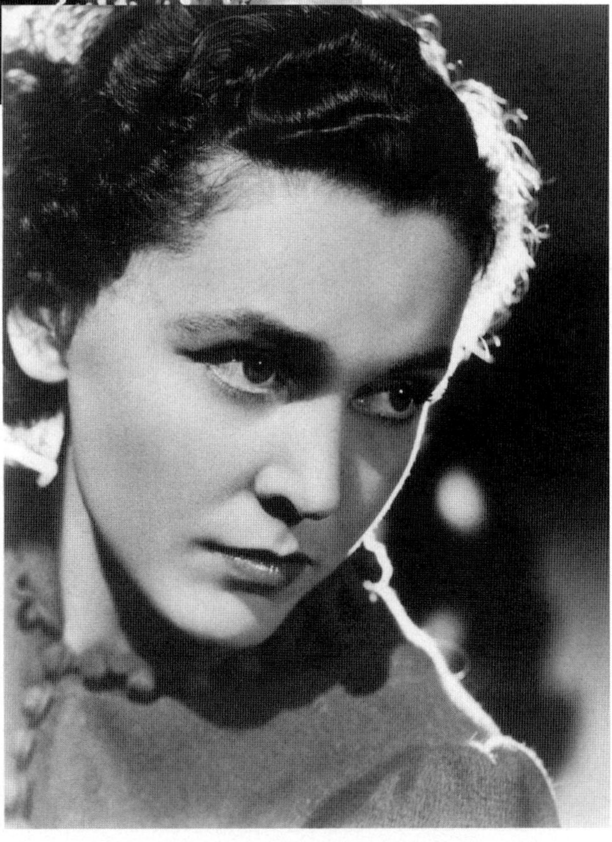

Maureen wore beautiful gowns in many of her films. She also modeled for numerous magazines during the 1930s and 1940s.

About Irving Thalberg, his power at MGM and the fact that he was described as a "genius," Maureen said: "I think he was rather frightening. He was slender, and dark, and rather mysterious. He didn't talk very much, and you didn't know quite what he was thinking. And when he did speak, it had meaning. I found him intimidating.

"He was a remote figure. When he came on the set to visit his wife Norma Shearer, there was silence. I was rather in awe of him."

Maureen and Norma would later appear in one of the finest dramas of the 1930s, *The Barretts of Wimpole Street* (1934), at which point they became close friends. Maureen had first met Miss Shearer at the opening of *An American Tragedy*, in August of 1931. According to Elizabeth Yeaman of the *Hollywood Daily Citizen*, Norma was the hit of the premiere:

"An unusually brilliant parade of stars was on hand last night for the opening of *An American Tragedy*. Street crowds and autograph seekers went wild when Norma Shearer, clad in black satin with a simple and unadorned short wrap of white satin, arrived. Ruth Chatterton arrived at the same time wearing white satin trimmed with narrow sable bands, and other outstanding favorites with the crowd were Sylvia Sidney, Phillips Holmes, June Collyer, Stuart Erwin, Ricardo Cortez, Maureen O'Sullivan, and Regis Toomey."

In July of 1932 *Strange Interlude* was previewed by *Film Daily*:
"A great production of a great story. A class picture finding the talking film in its highest form. For compelling human interest and sheer artistry of performance, here is one of the finest pieces of entertainment yet to reach the screen. It is probably the greatest work of Eugene O'Neill.

"Norma Shearer never gave a better performance and her fans will rave over her. Clark Gable and Ralph Morgan in support are excellent. On the stage the play ran five hours. In cinematic form it runs under two and without slighting the virility of the story a bit. The theme is that of the eternal triangle. Its novelty lies in the bringing to the audience the thoughts of the different characters in audible form. *Strange Interlude* is not fare for the kiddies, but as high-class sophisticated entertainment it reaches the heights."

As the summer months rolled around, Maureen began keeping steady company with James Dunn, a young actor who was in numerous films of the decade as a leading man. His eventual most noteworthy achievement was winning an Academy Award for best supporting actor in the wartime drama, *A Tree Grows in Brooklyn* (1945).

Louella Parsons was keeping tabs on Maureen and her new beau, as she noted in her column of July 2, 1932: "Been so busy watching Maureen O'Sullivan's romance with Jimmy Dunn almost forgot to inquire about her screen engagements. No matter, someone tells me she will play the lead opposite Lew Ayres in *Okay, U.S.A.* It's the story of a columnist, in case you are interested."

Skyscraper Souls was the next assignment for Maureen, a picture one might consider to be a romantic comedy, at least until the stunning ending which included a murder, a suicide, and a thief who dies after being locked in a safe overnight. The story was set up in a similar fashion to *Grand Hotel*, the wonderful MGM classic of 1932. All the players' lives take place in the Dwight Building: their successes, their failures, their love affairs, and even their deaths.

Top-billed was Warren William, the suave leading man who looked a great deal like John Barrymore. Maureen received second billing as Lynn Harding, a young secretary who worked in the magnificent 100-story skyscraper owned by David Dwight (William), a ruthless financial manipulator and president of the Seacoast bank. Also featured was Hedda Hopper as the wife of Dwight, who is a wife in name only but still enjoys the benefits of spending his money. (In a few years Hopper would add journalist to her résumé, and join Louella Parsons as the two most influential and powerful gossip columnists in Hollywood.)

Maureen with Warren William, who seems to be whispering sweet nothings in her ear

The story begins in the Dwight Building, where young bank clerk Tom Shepherd (Norman Foster) develops a serious crush on secretary Lynn Harding (Maureen), and pursues her relentlessly — yet harmlessly — until she agrees to go out with him that evening.

Lynn is the personal secretary to Sarah Dennis (Verree Teasdale), who manages the building for Mr. Dwight and is also having an affair with him. When David Dwight sees Lynn for the first time, he is infatuated with her; he asks her to write a report for him, and deliver it personally that evening to his penthouse apartment in the Dwight Building, where he is having a party.

Sarah is devoted to Dwight and wants to marry him, despite the fact he is a Lothario. Dwight uses his wife Ella (Hopper) as an excuse that he cannot marry, even though he has never even asked her for a divorce. He also decides to "retire" Sarah and give her a parting gift of a house in the country, and replace her with Lynn, who is young and naive and impressed by his money.

When Lynn brings the report to Dwight that evening at his penthouse, she forgets that Tom Shepherd is waiting in the building lobby for her. She joins the party with the other guests, gets tipsy on champagne, and then falls asleep on Dwight's bed. When Lynn awakes, Dwight tries to proposition her, but she turns him down.

Down in the lobby, Tom stews after getting stood up on their date. When he sees her in the building lobby at 3 a.m. with David Dwight, he assumes the worst. The next day, Tom confronts Lynn, and they break up despite the fact that they have great affection for each other.

Meanwhile, Dwight is scheming a financial cozenage to raise the money to pay off the huge bank loan on the Dwight Building, which he financed illegally with the bank's money. After hearing news of a merger, investors rush to buy Seacoast stock and watch in glee as the price soars. They are buying on margin and risking everything they have, but it is a paper fortune. Dwight and a partner artificially inflate the price of the stock, then unexpectedly sell short, ruining all the other investors who lose their money when the stock plummets. Tom Shepherd also has lost his savings of eighteen-hundred dollars, with which he had intended to use for his marriage to Lynn.

The next day Tom and Lynn break up for good, and she decides to go to Europe with Dwight, to enjoy the good life and help him spend his money. But Sarah confronts Dwight just before he is about to sail, and begs him not to ruin Lynn's life as he has ruined hers. Dwight turns to leave, and Sarah shoots him in the back with a pistol.

Dwight is mortally wounded, but claims it is only a superficial wound, and wipes Sarah's prints from the gun. He tells his butler that he dropped the gun and it fired accidentally, and that he should call for a doctor. Moments later Dwight slumps to the floor and dies, and Sarah in her guilt and remorse, runs to the top of the building and jumps to her death. A few months later Ella sells the Dwight Building, the last vestige of David's Dwight's financial empire. Lynn and Tom decide to marry and start a family, after realizing that love — and not money — is the key to happiness.

Released in August of 1932, *Skyscraper Souls* received mostly positive reviews, including *Film Daily*.

"Warren William and his excellent supporting cast, by their consistently interesting performances, are enough to keep this story alive even if it weren't an engrossing and attractively staged romance. The title gives only a part hint of the tale, which revolves around William, an idealist whose career just about runs the gamut of big business and stock market manipulation, with the crooked and the straight both involved in the dealings. Love interest and sex appeal also play their part in the action. General theme of the story — the mad desire of everyone, from bank presidents to the lowest man in the street, to climb up the ladder of fortune — gives the picture a wide appeal. Also, with the present revival of upward activity in the stock market, it has a timeliness angle that should give it much added value. William gives a grand performance, with Maureen O'Sullivan and Verree Teasdale as chief runners-up."

Louella Parsons also thought that *Skyscraper Souls* was excellent, as she noted in her *Los Angeles Examiner* column of August 6, 1932:

"Human emotions, pulsating romance, intrigues of frenzied finance, all hidden within the walls of a towering building. That's the tabloid idea of *Skyscraper Souls*, playing at Loew's State Theater this week.

"The most surprising performance is that of Warren William as the master mind, who first conceived the idea of the skyscraper. An unscrupulous young financier, he worships the high building and does not care how many people lose their fortunes just so he remains in charge of his idol, the huge, towering New York building. In the past I have always thought that Mr. William was self-conscious and prone to tear the scenery. He subdues that tendency in *Skyscraper Souls* and gives a really splendid account of himself.

"Maureen O'Sullivan is likeable as the spirited young stenographer. Norman Foster as the bank teller is well cast."

And while James Crow of the *Hollywood Citizen News* didn't rate the film high, he did credit the acting of Maureen.

"Lack of imagination force, superabundance of dialogue, lack of dramatic cohesion and palpable insincerity are the most marked characteristics of *Skyscraper Souls*... On its credit side, the picture has a splendid cast, headed by Warren William, who wrecks the lives of his friends to realize his dream of owning a great cloud-piercing business structure. William tried hard with only fair success to make something genuine out of an unconvincing role. The best performances were given by Norman Foster and Miss O'Sullivan in a romantic incidental story."

Variety gave a strong nod to the female support in this picture, especially Maureen O'Sullivan.

"Warren William mooches away with the works. On a loan from Warners, he's in good company in this cast. From the stately Verree Teasdale to the dimpled Maureen O'Sullivan, his femme support is extra special, while the underlined men, including Norman Foster, Jean Hersholt and Wallace Ford, are no slouches. The acting they contribute gives the picture all its value, frequently even making for extremely interesting moments."

During these busy months of 1932, Maureen would often work on several pictures at the same time. She might work on one film in the morning, another in the afternoon, and still another in the evening. She had an amazing seven films in release in 1932, and she was literally working night and day.

But that was the MGM movie factory; they pushed the actors to the limits and in the case of the young and naive such as Maureen, pushed until they were nearly exhausted. In August of 1932, Maureen asked for a raise and was given a new contract at MGM. She was making good money now, and earning every penny of it.

She was also having a little fun when she had the time, and the *Los Angeles Examiner* noted that a number of young actresses and actors were spotted dining and dancing at the Cocoanut Grove, including: Maureen O'Sullivan, Ginger Rogers, Alice Joyce, and Sylvia Sydney, among others; and Charlie Chaplin, Mervyn LeRoy, Ricardo Cortez, George O'Brien, George Marshall, and former boxer Jack Dempsey on the male side. Maureen was a fine ballroom dancer, having honed her dancing skills as a young woman on the social circuit in Dublin.

Louella Parsons continued to report in her columns that the romance between Maureen and James Dunn was going strong and that they were becoming seriously involved. They were often seen out and about, having dinner and dancing in the various clubs where stars mingled, such as the Trocadero Café, Ciros (a popular dance club on the Sunset Strip), the Little Club at the Ambassador Hotel, and the Cocoanut Grove.

The *Evening Herald Express* reported on August 6 that "Maureen O'Sullivan is going over big with Ireland's Olympic champions." The summer Olympics of 1932 were offering the Tinseltown elite a worldwide stage, and many of the biggest names attended the premiere events, such as swimming and track and field. When Buster Crabbe won the gold medal for the 100-meter freestyle, Johnny Weissmuller leaped over the railing in his excitement to congratulate his friend and former Olympic teammate.

Maureen's next film was *Okay America*, in which she co-starred with Lew Ayres, the boyish leading man who had made his mark in *All Quiet on the Western Front* (1930). Ayres portrayed Larry Wayne, gossip columnist for the New York *Daily Blade,* and Maureen was his "girl Friday," Sheila Barton. He always calls her plain "Barton" and she wonders aloud why he never makes even the slightest pass at her.

Wayne knows he can't afford to lose her and also that in his business his life expectancy is at best day-to-day. And so they are good friends and partners in tracking down the dirty secrets that permeate the big city where they live.

Wayne has many enemies who want to stay out of his Broadway gossip column, as well as his weekly radio program, "Okay, America." One man even shows up at his office with a gun planning to kill him for smearing his girlfriend. Wayne convinces him he was telling the truth that she was cheating on him, and the troubled soul leaves in peace.

Wayne's boss gives him a legitimate assignment, covering the disappearance of Ruth Drake, the daughter of a wealthy cabinet member. A supposedly retired gangster "Mileaway" Russell (Louis Calhern), gives Wayne a tip that the girl is stashed away, and he can deliver her for $100,000. Wayne arranges for the money from the girl's father, and informs his listeners and the police that he has arranged to bring Miss Drake back home. Wayne and Sheila go to the rendezvous point to pick up the girl, but find only a note: "It can't be done." When it turns out that Wayne has been hoaxed, he loses credibility with the police and his boss at the newspaper.

Wayne is abducted by Mileaway's men, and introduced to the big boss, Duke Morgan (Edward Arnold). Morgan is under federal investigation, and figures by kidnapping the girl he can get the president to reduce the charges in exchange for her freedom. Wayne is unable to negotiate such a deal with the president, but manages to convince Morgan that the deal is set — he thus releases the girl back to her family.

Wayne is so outraged that a gangster like Morgan has attempted to blackmail the President of the United States, that he shoots him three times with a revolver — stone dead. He goes back to his office and tells Sheila that she had better listen to his broadcast that night, as he has a special announcement to make. Wayne kisses her passionately on the mouth, something he has never done — she is worried that something bad is about to happen.

That night at the radio broadcast, Larry Wayne announces that he has rid the world of a notorious killer and gangster, that he has killed Duke Morgan in cold blood. At the same moment, Morgan's mob is waiting in the studio to kill Wayne; when he speaks the words, they shoot him dead. As Sheila hears the whole thing live on the air, her scream breaks the silence.

Much like *Skyscraper Souls*, the conclusion of *Okay America* has a rather shocking ending. First, the mild-mannered character played by Lew Ayres shoots the brutal gangster (well played by Edward Arnold) in cold blood; and then in the final scene, columnist Larry Wayne is also shot dead as retribution by the mob.

Originally the role of a New York gossip journalist was penned for Walter Winchell; in reality the character compared more closely with Mark Hellinger, also a New York columnist who was well-liked by his constituency. (Years later, Winchell was the model for the ruthless Broadway columnist portrayed by Burt Lancaster in *Sweet Smell of Success* [1957].)

Once again Maureen was loaned by MGM to Universal Pictures for this drama. This was a common Hollywood practice, and amounted to "you scratch my back and I'll scratch yours." Whenever MGM wanted to borrow a Universal player, the favor would be returned. Maureen continued to do credible work in each of her films, and once again got good reviews. When the camera did a close up of her incredibly beautiful eyes, the star would swoon (in this case Lew Ayres), the audience would sigh, and a kiss would be inevitable.

Lew Ayres and Maureen made a sweet couple in *Okay America*

James Crow of the *Hollywood Citizen News* wrote highly of the picture when he previewed it in his column of August 16, 1932:

> "*Okay, America*, latest and most ambitious of the newspaper columnist pictures, originally designed to star Walter Winchell, is of credit chiefly to Tay Garnett, the director, and to Lew Ayres, the star, and whatever Monsieur Winchell might have contributed to the opus is not poignantly missed, in view of the good work of these twain.
>
> "The picture tells a fast-moving story which Garnett has saved from the melodramatic by an adroit mingling of the serious and the facetious. A strongly patriotic touch brought the Fairfax Theater's preview audience to its feet at the conclusion of the showing.
>
> "Two outstanding performances are those of Rollo Lloyd and Edward Arnold, the latter in the role of the gang chief. Maureen O'Sullivan is appealing in the role of the columnist's secretary, whose love for him is unrequited."

Maureen's final film of 1932 was *Payment Deferred*, with a fine cast that included Charles Laughton and Ray Milland. The role of the young woman Winnie Marble had been played on stage by Elsa Lanchester, the real-life wife of Laughton. They had performed the roles in the Jeffrey Dell play in London and New York, and they both expected that Elsa would be cast in the same part in the filmed version, as she recalled in her 1983 autobiography, *Herself*:

"Metro-Goldwyn-Mayer planned to film *Payment Deferred* and offered Charles the Willie Marble part. Since the studio was only photographing a play, they thought it would be quick and cheap. Charles was so unquestionably brilliant in the part, it seemed a surefire idea. But for the female part they wanted another big name to bolster the box office. I was shocked when Maureen O'Sullivan was cast in my original role of the daughter, and Charles joined me in my despair. I was said to be so extraordinarily good in the part — why? How could this happen? Iris said, 'That's life, Towser.' I nearly became blind with crying and wanting to scream for England and our bluebell woods. I soon left Hollywood and went home. The train trip alone, and then the boat trip, helped me to forget the pain."

The most obvious reason for not casting Elsa Lanchester for the part was her age; she was only three years younger that Laughton. On the stage, this worked. In a filmed version, selecting her as Laughton's daughter would have been poor casting. And while there might have been some animosity from Laughton towards Maureen because of this situation, they eventually became very close friends. Theirs would become a father-daughter relationship, the same as they had played so superbly in *Payment Deferred*.

The story in brief involves the Marble family of London: William (Laughton), a bank clerk, his wife Annie (Dorothy Peterson), and their daughter Winnie (Maureen). The family is so overwhelmed by debt that Willie Marble is desperate; if he is not able to settle a lawsuit against him within a few days, he will lose his job at the bank and the family literally will be sent to the poor house.

When a nephew drops by whom the family has never met, Marble sees a possible solution to his problems. James Medland (Milland) has recently arrived from Australia, and carries with him a large sum of cash in his wallet. Marble is unable to convince his nephew to invest in a get-rich-quick scheme, and suddenly a very dark plan comes to his mind.

The thought becomes action when he poisons Medland with cyanide placed in a whiskey, and then buries the body in the back yard of their rented flat. With the stolen money, Willie invests in franc speculation through a tip he received from a friend; the result is an amazing windfall of 30,000 pounds, which makes him a wealthy man and able to quit his humble bank job.

Nevertheless, the body in the back yard haunts him, and his guilt over his evil crime begins to cause severe over-reactions to minor events; when the neighbor lad is playing in his back yard, he runs screaming after him and throws him over the fence!

Marble sends his wife and daughter on a vacation, and begins reading books on murder: specifically, cyanide poisoning. Willie also begins an affair with Rita Collins, who owns a local dress shop. Rita sees the possibilities of an involvement with a wealthy married man. When the two women return a day early, Winnie catches her father with the interloper. Winnie doesn't tell her mother, but she is disgusted with her father and leaves to spend time with friends.

Meanwhile, Annie begins to suspect that the money came from foul play. When she finally realizes that her husband has committed murder and buried the nephew in the back yard, she begins to sink into a guilt-ridden depression.

Winnie comes home for a visit with her parents, and she is enraged with her father's cheapness and refusal to buy a new home. (Of course, Marble cannot move from the flat because a body is buried in the back yard!) Winnie storms out of the house in the rain — her mother chases after and later becomes seriously ill from exposure.

Marble is taking good care of his wife at the doctor's orders, and giving her fresh orange juice every day. When Rita Collins drops by the house one day, she demands a payment of 500 pounds from Willie, who realizes this is plain blackmail. Annie hears the conversation from her upstairs room, and assumes they are still having an affair. She is so distraught over her husband's infidelity, she sneaks downstairs and adds cyanide to her glass of orange juice. When the doctor comes to check on Annie's condition, he discovers her death is the result of the cyanide-laced orange juice. His only conclusion is that Willie poisoned her, and Marble is arrested and later condemned to hang for his crime.

When Annie learns of her mother's death, she is guilt-ridden and blames herself. She visits her father in prison, who takes the blame on himself and admits that his current circumstance — his pending execution — is payment deferred for his past sins.

In *Payment Deferred,* Maureen was once again the top-billed actress, in the role of the daughter. Information exists that Neil Hamilton had originally been in several scenes with Maureen as a young professor in love with Winnie Marble, but these scenes must have been deleted in the final cut.

Maureen's character of Winnie undergoes some remarkable changes during the story: from good girl to miscreant and back to good graces. She starts out as a charming young woman attending stenographer school to help out her family, who are behind on all their bills because of the Depression.

When her father makes a great deal of money on the currency exchange market, she gets rather arrogant in her position as a member of the *nouveau riche*, and she leaves home to hang out with her new-found snobby friends. After her mother's death, her love for her father is the last vestige of the happiness they all shared before the unfortunate series of happenings.

This final scene of the picture, at the prison where her father is awaiting death for his crime of murder, is immensely emotional and represents some fine acting from both Maureen and Charles Laughton. Throughout the scene the father clutches his daughter tightly to his bosom, and she sobs as they both express their remorse over the tragic events — all of which came about because of their money problems. This was perhaps Maureen's best acting to date, and showed she could play a serious part in a believable fashion. (This scene is a legitimate tear-jerker. If you have a soft spot in your heart, the tears will be flowing as the picture ends.)

Variety gave Maureen a fine review, saying this final scene was gripping and her best screen work to date:

> "Charles Laughton has the greater advantage here, in that his close-ups and near shots give him a better chance to register emotion. His depiction of a low-grade middle-class Englishman is an achievement. The film story also helps him in the fluidity of its movement ... Maureen O'Sullivan does pleasantly until the close, and then she comes through with a final scene with her doomed father that forms her screen highwater mark. It really grips."

Simon Callow noted the following about *Payment Deferred* in his biography, *Charles Laughton: A Difficult Actor*: "The essential grammar of all Laughton's subsequent performances is there: the heavy lids, the sense of barely contained energy, the sexual voluptuousness a millimetre below the surface, the sudden accelerandos and heart-stopping ritardandos. His mastery of the elusive territory between lower-middle and middle-middle class is as subtle and as striking as it would ever be ... If one of the essential attributes of great acting is to offer value for money, Laughton was already, at the age of 34, a great actor."

Although *Payment Deferred* received mixed reviews and failed financially, the performances from the entire cast were excellent. The only comment *Film Daily* had about the production was: "Unpleasant murder drama revolving around a man's desire for money. Acting is fine."

This film was released at the height of the Depression, and many people were in similarly difficult straits. The general populace wanted to see romances, comedies, and even gangster films. However, a story of murder by cyanide poisoning by a desperate man was also literally poison at the box office. By modern standards, where so many films have dark themes, this story of desperation and murder is a fascinating study.

Laughton was superb as the tortured soul whose fiscal problems are so severe that he poisons his own nephew to gain his cash-laden wallet. In one scene after he is accused of murder, he finally cracks and laughs maniacally for at least 20 seconds — and then in a rather bizarre moment, the screen fades to black except for the head of Laughton, who continues his possessed laughter!

Other excellent performances included Verree Teasdale as the French woman who seduces Marble while his wife is on vacation, and then proceeds to blackmail him, deepening his unstable emotional state; and Dorothy Peterson as Annie Marble, devoted wife and mother who drinks the cyanide poison after discovering her husband has had an affair with the French seductress, Rita Collins.

Charles Laughton, Ray Milland, and Maureen O'Sullivan in a scene from *Payment Deferred*

Ray Milland was cast as the Australian nephew, James Medland, who rather unfortunately comes for a visit with his long-lost British cousins and is poisoned by his uncle. Milland was at the beginning of his long career, and would later co-star with Maureen and Charles Laughton in the 1948 *film noir* thriller, *The Big Clock*, directed by Maureen's husband, John Farrow. In his 1974 autobiography, *Wide-Eyed in Babylon*, Milland recalled working with Maureen and Charles Laughton:

"Early in the new year of 1932, I was assigned to do a picture called *Payment Deferred,* which starred Charles Laughton, newly arrived from England. In it I played a young relative of his from Australia, one with a little money. Laughton was supposed to be a shop clerk very much in debt who, when he saw the roll I was carrying, decided to do away with me by poisoning and then bury me in the garden. I stayed with him for a week, the attraction being his young daughter, who was very pretty, played by Maureen O'Sullivan.

"The director was Hungarian, Lothar Mendes, a man of great charm and a lot of humor and patience. He needed all of it, because he had to contend not only with my lack of talent and inexperience but also with Laughton's outrageous grotesqueries. In the scene where he got the idea of poisoning me Laughton was supposed to walk the length of the little parlor right up into the lens for a huge close-up so that the audience might read in his face the birth of the idea and his decision to go through with it. First his eyes rolled and then they went right up into his head till only the whites showed. Next his upper lip began to twitch and quiver and then, by God, he started to slobber. This went on for over a minute until I really believed he was having an epileptic fit. Suddenly he turned it off, reached into the glass case for the cordial, mixed the lethal concoction, and came back and presented it to me as if it were a piece of the True Cross."

Milland also noted that Mendes was willing to indulge Laughton's histrionics because, as the director, he would simply edit the scene to exactly what he wanted, thus not offending the great actor.

Ray Milland went on to have one of the finest careers in Hollywood, and some of his best films included *Beau Geste* (1939), *The Uninvited* (1944), and *Dial M for Murder* (1954). Perhaps his most famous role was as the alcoholic who desperately wants to quit drinking, but fails, in *The Lost Weekend* (1945). Milland won the Academy Award for Best Actor for this superb role that was the zenith of his motion picture career.

CHAPTER SEVEN
"The Love Affairs of a Young Actress"

Maureen's hectic 1932 was a whirlwind of acting in films, reading scripts, and publicity appearances for MGM to promote newly released movies. Her social life, as a 21-year-old, was quite active and well-reported by the Hollywood news media. Her romance with James Dunn, a young actor who worked for Fox Film, was constantly in the news, as Louella Parsons noted in her *Los Angeles Examiner* column of November 15, 1932:

"The Maureen O'Sullivan-James Dunn romance is one of such long standing, it is perhaps stale news to mention it. Still, both Maureen and Jimmy, since they started 'keeping company,' have had lapses when they parted company, but at this writing the romance is stronger than ever. Jimmy is waiting to slip the engagement ring on Maureen's finger."

Two weeks later, Louella again reported that "Maureen is busy denying that she is to marry Jimmy Dunn, as we announced before ..." And finally, on December 7, the *Hollywood Citizen News* broke the headline and story, "James Dunn and Maureen O'Sullivan today admitted an engagement but denied any plans for a wedding soon."

Maureen spent the Christmas holidays with her boyfriend Dunn, but then the bombshell fell on January 5 of the new year: Louella announced that the couple had broken up.

"This is official, but I wouldn't say final, Maureen O'Sullivan and James Dunn have agreed to disagree. For two days now Maureen hasn't seen Jimmy nor has she telephoned him. 'I suppose,' said she, 'some people just cannot get along and we are among those who aren't meant to be happy together.' Maureen and Jimmy were happy as two turtle doves at Christmas time and over New Year's, but it's all off now, according to Maureen's own words. But there are few lovers' quarrels that are so serious they cannot be patched up. We wouldn't like to believe this battle is final, as Maureen thinks at the moment. There is no one else, she says."

About a week later, Maureen was having lunch with Dunn at Fox Film, where the executives were hoping to team the pair in a romantic comedy — assuming she could be borrowed from MGM for the picture. It appeared that they were back together again, as Louella noted in her "Movie-Go-Round" column of January 18, 1932:

"I might have known when Maureen O'Sullivan called me up and said she had a big story for me — that she and Jimmy Dunn were through forever — that they would make up. When a girl loves a man so much she is as upset as Maureen was over their battle and when a man loves a girl as much as Jimmy admits he loves Maureen, well, a quarrel couldn't be lasting. The two of them, last week, slipped quietly out to the United Airport where they thought they'd be absolutely alone and had their big reconciliation scene. In fact they were so happy that a little bird reports that Maureen leaned across the table and kissed Jimmy right in front of everybody."

Despite this romantic rendezvous, Maureen and Dunn were, well ... done. They stopped being seen in public, and other men began calling on the actress. One admirer in particular was John Farrow, who often would take Maureen horseback riding in the mornings. Farrow was a writer of some success, and had hopes to become a Hollywood director.

Although there were plenty of suitors lined up for Maureen, she was still stinging from her failed romance with James Dunn and was determined to put off marriage for several years. She even considered going back to Ireland for good, she was so miserable over her failed love affair.

In February, Johnny Weissmuller took Maureen out dining and dancing at the Beverly Wilshire, to console her over her loss. They were already close friends, and they also discussed the new picture they were both signed for, *Tarzan and His Mate*. Years later, Maureen noted that she could always count on Johnny for a dinner date and dancing when she was in the dumps over her affairs. This was never a romantic relationship because Weissmuller was head-over-heels in love with Lupe Velez, whom he married in October of 1933.

A few weeks elapsed and Maureen was seen dancing to Gus Arnheim's music with Carl Laemmle, Jr., who was the executive producer at Universal Studios, and the son of Carl Laemmle, who founded Universal in 1912. Carl Jr. had produced Maureen's film *The Information Kid*, and wanted her for another picture. He was also just three years older than the actress, and perhaps had his own romantic notions.

Another of Hollywood's leading men who had more than a passing interest in Maureen was Douglas Fairbanks, Jr., who would eventually divorce Joan Crawford in 1933. "Douglas was calling me — he liked me, and I liked Douglas. He wanted me to have dinner, and I knew they were separating, so I knew it was all right — why not? So I said, 'I'd love to have dinner with you.' But then he said, 'You know we're going to Joan's for dinner.' And I said, 'Oh no we're not, we're not going to Joan's — this is too Noel Coward for me. I really can't take that.

"So then Joan sends me this long telegram, 'My darling Maureen, I would be heartbroken if you don't come and have dinner.' I still didn't go to dinner that time," laughed Maureen.

"I never did understand her. I would get lovely long letters from her, and flowers, and telegrams at Christmas, and I thought she must be my best friend in the world. So when I went to New York and I was playing *Never Too Late* on stage [thirty years later], I had a small cocktail party and I invited Joan over. Joan was the rudest woman possible, why she came at all I don't know. So I said, 'What goes with her ... a friend by mail?' It wasn't a personal relationship with Joan, just one of those interesting things of life."

Despite other suitors, John Farrow was still lurking close by and eventually they began keeping steady company, as Louella noted on March 10. "Where is Maureen O'Sullivan? Her romance with Jimmy Dunn is cold. John Farrow and Maureen dining together."

Maureen continued to make personal appearances for MGM, including the premiere of *Gabriel Over the White House* in April of 1933. Other stars attending included: child-star Jackie Cooper, Franchot Tone, Nils Asther, John Miljan, C. Henry Gordon, May Robson, Elizabeth Allen, Benita Hume, Jean Parker, Mary Carlisle, and Johnny Weissmuller.

Whenever the Hollywood crowd was not making movies, social gatherings were the order of the day. She was invited to various dinner parties at Marian Davies' beach house in Malibu, and also several posh events at San Simeon. "They were weekend affairs at San Simeon, and we'd go overnight on the train," recalled Maureen. "And then we were met by car and driven up to the castle. It was a lovely drive up the road because you could see the castle above the clouds as you drove up to San Simeon, and there were all these wild animals around. There was this big dining room, with flags of all nations. It was very moral at Mr. Hearst's house, very moral. You couldn't do anything. You had one drink before dinner, and if you were caught going to someone's bedroom you'd be thrown out the next morning. Marian had a very amusing nephew, Charlie Lederer, and he used to make me laugh and became a great friend of mine. He used to keep watch in the corridors at night, and he'd tell me who went into who's room after Mr. Hearst went to bed. And we would sit and roar with laughter! We had a good time."

In recalling her personal memories of William Randolph Hearst and Marian Davies, Maureen noted, "I think he was devoted to her, and she was very fond of him. It was a good relationship, and possibly if they could have married, they would have married. Marian was a happy girl, she was a lovely person. The last time I saw Marian was after he had died, and I went to a cocktail party at the Pantages Theater, and Marian was there. She had cancer in her mouth, and she had a painkiller in a wad of absorbent cotton in her mouth, and she told me that she was in the house when he died. And that the boys had taken the body away in the night, so when she woke up he was gone. She was very hurt over that because the boys, the Hearst sons, were always at

San Simeon, and they liked Marian very much. I'm not in a position to judge, but she was very broken up over that. It also hurt her a great deal that a lot of her friends who had been up to the ranch all the time, didn't bother with her anymore after Mr. Hearst died. She didn't have that power anymore — power is a very great weapon you know."

Maureen's first released film of 1933 was *Robbers' Roost*, a western which co-starred George O'Brien as rough-and-tumble cowboy Jim Wall. Westerns were immensely popular during the 1930s, and the novels of Zane Grey were often used as the basis for Hollywood western pictures. This was an extremely well-written story, thanks to the skills of screenwriter Dudley Nichols, who also penned the John Wayne classic, *Stagecoach* (1939), and won an Academy Award for his script for *The Informer* (1935).

Robbers' Roost was a Fox Film production, and Maureen was loaned for future considerations. Fox had basically given her the pink slip when her contract expired in 1931; now just over a year later Maureen O'Sullivan was one of the biggest young stars in the business. The young actress didn't really want to do this B-western, because she knew it would not be a plus-move in her career. But when MGM gave an employee an assignment, they could question but it was unwise to revolt. Independent thinkers had to go visit Mr. Mayer, who could be very intimidating despite his short stature. Mayer had a gigantic office with an adjoining waiting room where you had to sit and think about why the boss had called you in — and what you were going to say in your defense.

Robbers' Roost turned out to be fun after all, and Maureen later noted that she truly enjoyed making westerns. Top-billed was George O'Brien, a greatly-admired cowboy star of the 1930s, who performed all of his own stunts in his movies. O'Brien had started out in Hollywood as a stuntman, so all the riding, roping, and fight scenes were right up his proverbial alley. Ruggedly handsome with a body builder's physique, George got his first starring role in the epic John Ford western, *The Iron Horse* (1924).

Maureen was cast as Helen Herrick, a British lass who comes West for the first time to help manage the ranch that she owns in partnership with her brother. She's rather a haughty gal, and even though she is attracted to cowboy Jim Wall right from the start, she won't admit the attraction even to herself.

The cast also included Reginald Owen in the role of her older brother Cecil, who is stubborn and honest, and has a great deal of love for his sister from back home in England. Owen was a fine character actor, and worked with Maureen in other films such as *Anna Karenina* (1935) and *Tarzan's Secret Treasure* (1941).

The story begins in Arizona, where Jim Wall (O'Brien) gets into a scuffle at a river crossing with Hank Hays (William Pauley), who is the foreman for the Star ranch. Hays likes the shooting ability of Wall, and offers him a job at the ranch. Hays, however, is a crooked scoundrel, and reveals to Wall his scheme to rustle the Star cattle in one month. Wall agrees to join the rustlers, but his conscience is already telling him it's the wrong thing to do.

Back at the Star, Jim Wall is introduced to ranch owner Cecil Herrick (Owen), an Englishman who takes a liking to the amiable Texas cowboy. When Cecil's sister Helen (Maureen) is scheduled to arrive by train, Jim is asked to meet her — a task he rather disdains.

When Jim and Helen meet, they begin a strained relationship. He thinks she is just a stuck-up English girl, and she thinks he is just a run-of-the-mill cowboy. Helen likes to ride horseback, and one day she encounters Jim on the range. She challenges him to jump a chasm and retrieve a white flower on the other side, assuming he would decline. But instead he makes the dangerous jump, brings her the flower, kisses her and rides off. Helen was terrified that Jim would kill himself after her foolish dare, and she begins to realize her affection for the flamboyant cowboy.

That night Jim decides to leave the ranch, and Helen calls him a quitter. She asks him to return something he took from her, and plants a passionate kiss on him. Surprised by the kiss, Jim later admits he has decided to stay. Helen laughs and says she has kissed many men, and the kiss didn't mean anything to her.

When the cattle are rounded up by Hays and his men, a stampede begins and Helen is almost killed by the rampaging herd when she is thrown from her horse. Jim rides hard to save her, and as the cattle rush by, the two huddle behind a fallen steer, barely avoiding being trampled.

Jim has decided he wants no part of the rustling scheme, but when he sends his friend Happy Jack to tell the sheriff, Jack is killed by the rustlers. They also take Jim's gun, and force him to participate under the threat of death.

Helen rides out to locate Jim but is captured by Hays' men, and is taken to their hideout, a place called Robbers' Roost. That night, Cecil Herrick and his riders approach the outlaws' hideaway and are spotted by Jim, who sneaks away and rides to warn them.

When Jim returns, he must scale a cliff and nearly falls to his death when one of the rustlers cuts his rope. Meanwhile, Helen is tussling with Hays, who is trying to seduce her. Jim breaks in just in time, and manages to escape with Helen as the outlaws' bullets are flying all around them. A bullet from Herrick kills Hays, and the rest of the rustlers are subdued.

Jim rides off and Helen is in hot pursuit, telling him if he proposes she will accept. The deal is sealed when he asks for something that she took from him and kisses her passionately.

Robbers' Roost was one of countless B-westerns of the period, and George O'Brien was certainly one of the best B-cowboys to ride the western trail. His ability to perform his own stunts gave his pictures a strong element of reality, and with Maureen O'Sullivan doing all of her own riding, there was plenty of action — and romance. The horseback riding was dangerous of course, and many an actor suffered a serious injury from a fall of this type. (An example would be Audrey Hepburn, who broke her back in a fall from a horse while filming *The Unforgiven* with Burt Lancaster in 1960.)

Although Maureen did her own horseback riding, the dangerous stampede scene where she is trapped in the middle of the rampaging herd was handled by a stuntman wearing a wig. The stuntman was injured performing this thrilling scene, and injury to a stuntman always meant a few broken bones.

It was fortunate, however, that this picture was the only loan-out to Fox during her MGM career. Maureen might have gotten stuck making B-westerns during the 1930s had it not been for the fortuitous happening of signing with the best studio in the business, Metro-Goldwyn-Mayer. When your author David Fury and Maureen's husband Jim Cushing watched this film together in 2006, Jim laughed and wryly added, "That seemed more like a 'C-western,' even if it did star my wife Maureen!"

The critics of the day also had reasonably good things to say about *Robbers' Roost*, including Eleanor Barnes of *Illustrated Daily News* in a review dated February 3, 1933:

"When George O'Brien whips off his 10-gallon sombrero and turns on a dazzling smile, what gal from out west could resist? Nary a one, gol' darn it!

"And when George leaps on a bucking bronco, swoops across the mesquite in a great burst of outdoor enthusiasm, even the usually tearful Maureen O'Sullivan grins lavishly back at him with an 'I-Love-You.'

"In fact, it's been a long time since the writer has seen a star do such thrilling stunts as George leaping from mountain peak to mountain peak in a fashion that would make a Catalina goat seem jumpless, as in *Robbers' Roost*, which is now at the Hollywood Pantages, a Fox picture that is essentially good movie stuff.

"As for dialogue — can you imagine anything more old-fashioned than to have an English heroine, making her first trip out to the American cow country asking if the Indians still scalp the natives? — but, that's Zane Grey for you!

"From a photographic standpoint, it is almost a poem of beauty in certain sequences, thanks to the craftsmanship of George Schneiderman, a cameraman of exceptional artistic ability.

"The cast of *Robbers' Roost* is good, too; particularly well cast is Reginald Owen as the crotchety old Englishman who finds himself victim of a plot to rob him of his honestly-acquired ranch land in America.

"O'Brien is swell. He always is in this type of stuff."

And from *Film Daily* came more sterling words for George and Maureen, playing in her first western and doing a bang-up job as a heroine in the wild west:

> "Grown-up western has unusually strong love interest and plenty of thrills and action. Founded on a Zane Grey story, this western has far more substance to the plot than the routine horse opera. There is also an intelligent and believable love story that will please the femmes, with Maureen O'Sullivan a good popular bet to sell in this connection. Also George O'Brien handles his romantic scenes with almost as much skill as he does his horse and gun. So here is a double-barreled appeal which lifts it out of the rut of the usual drama of the plains. In Robbers' Roost, their mountain hideout, where the girl is held prisoner, O'Brien stages a sensational rescue with some unusual stunt stuff that packs a punch. Above average western."

One of the funniest movie series of the day was "The Cohens and Kellys," about an Irish family and a Jewish family who are neighbors and long-time friends. Starring in the popular series of films was George Sidney as Nate Cohen and Charles Murray as Pat Kelly, who are best buddies and get involved in various misadventures and romantic side-bars to entertain movie audiences. Sidney and Murray were both vaudeville stars who graduated to Hollywood and found success, primarily in this series. There are plenty of the old vaudeville routines used in these films, along with a heavy dose of the slapstick perfected by the great comedy team of Laurel and Hardy.

The last of seven of these comedies was *The Cohens and Kellys in Trouble*, which added Maureen to the cast as Molly Kelly, daughter of her very Irish father, Patrick Kelly. She is a spunky gal who falls in love with a young coast guard officer (Frank Albertson), who just happens to be hassling her father over a matter of illegal liquor. It is still Prohibition, and Captain Kelly likes to drink and often has a bottle on his boat parked in the harbor. Of course this was perfect casting, as Maureen was as Irish as her last name of O'Sullivan would imply.

The very thin plot finds Pat Kelly joined on his tugboat by his old friend Nate Cohen, who after becoming successful as a business man, needs a vacation and a sea voyage is just the ticket. The two men are back together after a separation of several years, and Pat's daughter Molly has grown from a baby to a beautiful young woman. Nate hugs Molly, who is just as happy to see her father's good friend, and she plans a special dinner for the two men. (Molly laughs and says she will be sure to get corned beef that is kosher!)

Pat's boat is docked and is the perfect place to have a drink to celebrate the reunion, but just then arriving on an inspection is Bob Graham (Albertson), an officer with the Coast Guard. The bottle of liquor is passed back and forth in an attempt to keep it hidden from Graham, but when it lands in the hands of Kelly's deck hand Andy Anderson (Andy Devine), the bottle slips and is broken. This puts Graham on the black list of Pat Kelly, who has lost his precious bottle of booze.

When Bob Graham meets Molly, it is love at first sight, despite the fact he had kicked her in the rear when they first met, a case of mistaken identity! Molly agrees to go out with Bob, and when she brings him home to meet her father, the fireworks begin. Kelly refuses to allow Molly to date Bob, the very same Coast Guard officer who had inspected his boat for liquor.

Entering the picture now is Queenie Truelove (Jobyna Howland), who once married Pat Kelly, a union that lasted but a single day. She is now seeking twelve-hundred dollars in alimony, money that the man she calls "the worm" does not have. Pat and Nate hatch a plan to get Queenie married off to Andy Anderson, whom they plan to pass off as a wealthy yacht owner.

At this point things get even crazier, with Nate and Pat involved aboard a runaway speedboat (Pat is pulled along behind like a drunken water skier), and eventually they wind up lost at sea. When their small craft finally sinks, they just happen to come upon an abandoned liquor frigate, and the Coast Guard fires upon them as another wild chase ensues. Molly and Officer Graham are out at sea searching for her father and Nate, and when they find them at last, Molly is greatly relieved.

When Bob Graham offers to drop the bootlegging charge in exchange for his permission to marry Molly, all is peaceful once again in the lives of the Cohens and the Kellys.

This particular edition of "The Cohens and Kellys" was directed by George Stevens, his first feature motion picture after learning the craft helming short films. He eventually directed numerous classics such as *Gunga Din* (1939), *Shane* (1953), *A Place in the Sun* (1951), and *Giant* (1956). For the latter two films Stevens won the Academy Award as Best Director, triumphant moments in a long career that began with this rather silly comedy.

This was certainly a lightweight vehicle for Maureen, in a role in which she and Frank Albertson were the young lovers trying to overcome her strong-willed Irish father who opposes the romance. It was a funny story, as noted in the *Film Daily* review of April 15, 1933:

> "Abundant laughs make this comedy one of the best of the Cohens and Kellys series. Sidney and Murray in top form. If it's plain, home-made laughs that your audiences want, this latest adventure of the Cohens and Kellys should fill the bill in a satisfactory manner. George Sidney and Charlie Murray are in fine form, there is a good supporting cast with Maureen O'Sullivan and Frank Albertson supplying the incidental love interest, and action is more plentiful than in the majority of pictures these days."

Variety called it the one of the best of the series, and a sure money-maker on April 18, 1933:

"In the lives of the Cohens and Kellys, *Trouble* is an exceptionally good chapter. It will make money, because it has good comedy value and sufficient weight to hold its own in all but the most particular 'A' houses.

"Love interest is sketched for Maureen O'Sullivan and Frank Albertson. As the daughter of Kelly, Molly finds it comparatively simple to fall for her father's enemy, Bob, the coast patrol officer."

Eventually, John Farrow would be the regular guy in Maureen's life, although their relationship would be a rocky on-again, off-again affair for the next few years. In 1974, Maureen recalled her first meeting with Farrow, who had a well-deserved reputation as a ladies man around Hollywood:

"I met John when I first came to Fox Studios," said Maureen. "He was a writer then, and I was doing a film called *Just Imagine*, a science-fiction musical set in 1980. I met him because I was looking for my director, David Butler. I was on early call and wanted to look at something in the rushes and I did not know where his office was, and I wandered into John's office. John always thought I did it on purpose, and that was the beginning of our meeting. Fate. So then we made a date on my birthday."

John Villiers Farrow was born in Sydney, Australia, in 1904, the same year as Johnny Weissmuller's birth. He never knew his father, Joseph Farrow, and his mother Lucy died as a result of his birth when she was nineteen years old.

An early portrait of John Villiers Farrow

He was raised by an aunt until age fifteen, at which point he was sent to England to further his education at Winchester College. That was in 1919, and not far away was a young girl named Maureen who lived in Dublin, Ireland. But their initial meeting would come a dozen years later.

The youthful Farrow didn't care for college, and so he lied about his age and joined the merchant marine and later the Royal Canadian Navy. He was also a natural born writer, and by 1927 had landed in Hollywood and was writing screenplays. Some of his early work included *Ladies of the Mob* (1928), *Wolf Song* (1928), *A Dangerous Woman* (1929), *Seven Days Leave* (1930), and *Woman of Experience* (1931). He also completed a novel in 1930, *The Bad One*, that was produced as a motion picture starring Dolores Del Rio and Edmund Lowe that same year. Another novel, *Laughter Ends* (1933), was a story of love and lust set in Tahiti, a favorite hideaway for Farrow. He would later spend almost a year on the island where he wrote his biography of Father Damien, published in 1937 and titled *Damien, the Leper*.

Maureen later admitted that she was quite lonely during her first year or so in Hollywood, and that was before she became part of the MGM "family." Her only steady relationship with James Dunn had failed, and all of her friends and family were back in Ireland. So when she met Farrow, he captured her fancy as a dashing sort who had traveled the world and enjoyed many adventures in his life by the time he was in his early twenties.

"I had only been in Hollywood a little over a year when I first met John Farrow. I was very lonely at the time and I thought he was wonderfully exciting and dangerous. He was twenty-six, and without a doubt the most colorful character in Hollywood, having earned himself the worst reputation in town as far as women were concerned. Sexually, his prowess was legendary, and there was even a rumor that he had brought a new sex cult to America. The women he slept with — and there were many — fell madly in love with him, while the women he didn't sleep with were insulted at being left out of this fascinating experience and had nothing good to say about him. This only added fuel to the legend.

"He had a tattoo on his ankle like a bracelet with the Latin *Semper Fidelis* meaning 'always faithful.' Also, a pretty garter snake tattoo on his thigh made a circle before disappearing inside his bathing suit, coming to rest ... where, I wondered?

"He seemed to do nothing very much to create this image — although he secretly enjoyed it — and was in fact boyish and rather shy. But he was a great raconteur and a young man of infinite charm and good looks."

Besides the snake tattoo on his leg, Farrow also had a tattoo of a shamrock and a black flag and skull on his wrist, souvenirs from his Navy days. A few inches taller than Maureen's five-foot-four, he had a slim build and blonde hair. He didn't have movie star looks, but he did have a worldly suavity that the women apparently went for in a big way.

About their first date, Maureen noted that Farrow paged through his date book and that his first free evening was two weeks later. Maureen was only nineteen years old and had a chaperone at the Fox studio, and they had warned her not to become involved with Farrow because of his reputation.

"We spent our first evening together at a very popular nightclub called the Cocoanut Grove, but the date turned out to be a big disappointment because John hardly spoke to me all evening. Instead we sat in silence listening to Bing Crosby and his band and I thought how strange this all was. He wasn't like other people in the industry — he was a complete mystery to me which was all part of the attraction.

"Despite this rather miserable beginning, we started going out together after that and before very long I was deeply in love with him. But it was rocky from the very beginning. Shortly after he'd started dating me I discovered that he was seeing someone else at the same time. I was very upset and told him as much, hoping he would drop the other girl, but instead he dropped me. The phone just suddenly stopped ringing."

When the phone did start ringing again some months later, Maureen and John attended a big social party at the Little Club, as noted by Harrison Carroll in the *Evening Herald Express* on April 10, 1933:

"They're all talking about that 'Little Club' party of Saturday night. Never so many stars in one dance place before. Carole Lombard and Bill Powell gave a party that took up almost one end of the room. Gloria Swanson and Michael Farmer arrived late, but the Clark Gables were even later. Kay Francis and Ken MacKenna, the Zeppo Marxes, Jessica and Dick Barthelmess, the Clive Brooks, and many other famous ones were guests of Carole and Bill. Almost every other table had its celebrities ... Maureen O'Sullivan and John Farrow seemed devoted; Ruth Selwyn put on a Salvation Army lass's hat and took up a collection."

On May 17, it was a 22nd birthday celebration for Maureen, as Farrow and a few friends raised a glass to the young woman who was the toast of Hollywood. A few days later, reporter Jimmy Starr was keeping a watchful eye and noted that "Maureen O'Sullivan has been selecting some new ties for boyfriend John Farrow." In July, Harrison Carroll reported that Maureen and Mr. Farrow would be taking an ocean voyage near Catalina Island over the 4th of July.

It was also around this time that U. S. immigration officials mounted a campaign to deport illegal aliens who were not gainfully employed. Maureen was interviewed in January, but of course was under contract to MGM so she would have no problems. Australian John Farrow was also questioned, and his status was somewhat shaky before reaching a resolution with the federal government, as detailed by Elizabeth Yeaman in her *Hollywood Citizen News* column of July 6, 1933:

"Johnny Farrow's troubles with immigration officials seem to be definitely over. I don't know just how he ironed out the difficulties which threatened to send him back to Australia as an undesirable alien, but from all indications he seems set to remain in Hollywood. Furthermore, he seems all set to remain at MGM, where he has been on the payroll as a writer for some time, and where his fiancée, Maureen O'Sullivan, is also under contract. Johnny is to branch out in the field of directors. He wins his first directorial opportunity on a two-reel musical short to be filmed in Technicolor. It is titled *Beauty and Truth,* and the story was written by himself. If Johnny proves his ability as a director on this picture, he will be allowed to direct a whole series of shorts."

Later that fall, in October, Farrow was dining with Maureen at the Cocoanut Grove when he had a waiter bring a tray of gifts to his table, whereas he then asked Maureen to select the one she liked best. Louella Parsons would also chip in her two cents worth, when she said, "Maureen O'Sullivan and John Farrow are also cooing."

MGM's biggest money-maker of 1933 was *Tugboat Annie,* a drama that had everything a great motion picture should have — humor, pathos, exciting drama, and heartwarming romance. The humor and pathos were provided by lead actors Marie Dressler and Wallace Beery. The exciting drama came at the end of the picture in the form of a heroic rescue in a blinding rainstorm at sea. And the romance came from Robert Young and Maureen O'Sullivan as the young lovers. Directing the picture was Mervyn LeRoy, who later in the decade would be hired by MGM as their top producer after the untimely death of Irving Thalberg.

Two of MGM's biggest stars of the 1930s were Dressler and Beery, and although neither was even remotely glamorous, they both were box office money in the bank. Marie Dressler was perhaps the most unlikely movie star of them all; she played character roles in silent films until winning an academy award in *Min and Bill* (1930), and in this earlier film her screen partner was also Wallace Beery. She had a string of huge hits after winning her award, including *Emma* (1932), *Prosperity* (1932), *Tugboat Annie* (1933), and *Dinner at Eight* (1933). Unfortunately, at the height of her success and popularity, she died of cancer in 1934 at age 65.

Wallace Beery, meanwhile, was also a huge star and had won his own Academy Award for his marvelous portrayal of a washed-up boxer in *The Champ* (1931), with child actor Jackie Cooper. Some of his best films included *Grand Hotel* (1932), *Treasure Island,* also with Cooper (1934), and *Slave Ship* (1937). A famous quote from Beery was, "Like my dear old friend Marie Dressler, my ugly mug has been my fortune."

The story revolves around Annie Brennan (Dressler), captain of the tugboat *Narcissus,* and her husband Terry (Beery). He is a drunk but Annie loves him despite of all his many faults. Annie always said that when Terry was sober, he was as fine a man as could be found anywhere. They have a son Alec, who as a boy plans to quit school and get a job to help out his beloved mother.

Annie would hear nothing of it, and pushes him to get his education to fulfill his dream of becoming a sea captain.

When Alec is grown (Robert Young) he indeed becomes the youngest ship's master on the Pacific Coast, and he also falls in love with Pat Severn (Maureen), who is the daughter of his employer, Red Severn. In the old days, Annie and Red (Willard Robertson) had been competitors in the tug business, but now they are good friends and soon to be in-laws.

Meanwhile, Terry continues his drunken ways and finally Alec gives his mother an ultimatum — either she leaves her husband and comes to live with him, or he would never see either of them again. Annie cannot bear the thought of leaving her husband, because she knows he would die of loneliness without her. Things get much worse when Terry causes an accident with the tug, that severely damages an excursion vessel. The *Narcissus* has to be sold to pay off the lawsuit, and Annie is retained as skipper; however, the tug is now used to pull garbage scows, to her mortification at having sunk to such a low station.

Pat comes to see Annie in hopes of reconciling Alec and his mother, and Annie admits that the stink of the garbage is practically killing her. Pat would do anything to see Alec and Annie back together, but it is doubtful as long as she refuses to leave her husband.

The four stars of *Tugboat Annie* — Beery, Young, Dressler, O'Sullivan

Some time later, Annie and Terry are hauling garbage when a storm comes up, and they hope to make it back to port in their old tub *Narcissus*, with its leaky steam boilers that should have been replaced years ago. Also on the stormy seas this day is the *Glacier Queen*, the passenger liner that is captained by Alec Brennan.

At the height of the storm the *Glacier Queen* breaks a propeller, and is forced to send up a distress signal. Annie sees the call for help, and heads the *Narcissus* in the direction of her son's ship, which might capsize in the storm. Terry cuts the rope that releases the garbage scows, and they get close enough to the *Glacier Queen* to hook up with a tow rope.

The *Narcissus*, weakened by the leaky boilers, cannot pull the double load in the storm. Terry volunteers to go into the boiler chamber to make the repair, knowing that everything hangs in the balance. The chamber is steaming hot, and by the time Terry has made the repairs, he is severely burned. Annie is able to get both vessels into port, and to get her husband to the hospital for treatment of his burns.

Terry eventually recovers and is called a hero by the steamship company, which buys the *Narcissus* for Annie, and promises that it will be refitted with all new equipment and boilers. Alec and Pat plan to marry, and the whole family is back together again. Terry even promises to quit drinking, but Annie knows that he will never change his ways.

Maureen continued to be cast in films with some of the greatest stars in Hollywood, and in the case of *Tugboat Annie*, she once again was the love interest of Robert Young (as she had been in *Strange Interlude*). Young would have a respectable career in the movies as a leading man, but would find his greatest success after reaching middle age with two vastly popular television series, *Father Knows Best*, and *Marcus Welby, M.D.* Maureen would appear in a total of five films with Young, also including *West Point of the Air* (1935), *The Emperor's Candlesticks* (1937), and *Sporting Blood* (1940).

Tugboat Annie was a superbly-acted motion picture, and a particularly touching scene involved Maureen visiting Annie (Dressler) on her tugboat, the ancient vessel now relegated to work as a garbage tug. Maureen's character of Pat is offering consolation to Annie, mourning the loss of her son, who is estranged because of his anger with his father. Maureen and Dressler are hugging each other, and the emotions are freeing flowing along with the tears. Robert Young also has a very fine scene with Dressler and Beery, where he suspects that his father has hit her, when she had in fact simply tripped. Young was usually cast as amiable types, but in this role he had his intense moments.

About her co-stars, Beery and Dressler, Maureen recalled the negative that went with working with greatness. In this case, Beery made his own rules, and there was very little anyone could do about it:

"Wallace Beery was a tiresome actor," said Maureen, "very tiresome. He always stopped work at four o'clock (for which I didn't blame him). He'd say: 'That's it, that's it!' Anyhow, he had speeches that were miles long, and he'd come in in the morning and say, 'Well, what'll we do today?' When he was given these speeches, they would take him most of the day to learn, and he'd stumble through them. We had all studied them the night before, and we just went on and on and on and on until we were exhausted, but *he* came out looking very good! Mumbling and stumbling along — that was his method of working, and he used to say, 'When I'm finished at the studio, I'm studying *nothing.*'

"Marie Dressler was much more of a professional, although Beery was a fine actor of course, and I don't know how they got on personally but the speeches in *Tugboat Annie* were much shorter and he could learn them much quicker. But this was certainly not the case with *Port of Seven Seas.*" (The latter was a film Maureen made with Beery in 1938.)

Large audiences came to see the teaming of Dressler and Beery, along with young stars Maureen O'Sullivan and Robert Young. Reviewers jumped on-board for *Tugboat Annie*, including Jerry Hoffman of the *Los Angeles Examiner*:

"*Tugboat Annie*, as a picture, has the two best assets of the movies: Marie Dressler and Wally Beery. It is the strength of their personalities, the warm love that Marie inspires, which makes possible the actual entertainment contained in this over-long picture. In the hands of others, most of the slapstick comedy would be so much tripe. Few gags of the old break-away one and two-reel comedies have been omitted in the first four reels of *Tugboat Annie,* even to the drinking of hair-tonic and the slipping of soap into sauerkraut.

"The king, however, can do no wrong, and, in this instance, the queen certainly cannot. So long as Marie Dressler does whatever it is, fans, and myself, will glow with pleasure, thrill with delight — because Marie does it.

"Robert Young makes a convincing and appealing son. Maureen O'Sullivan is a charming ingenue."

Harrison Carroll in the *Evening Herald Express* also applauded the picture and noted the fans approval of *Tugboat Annie:*

"A mixture of broad comedy, melodrama, and thickly spread sentiment, *Tugboat Annie* is a picture after the hearts of Marie Dressler-Wallace Beery fans. They flocked to Loew's State yesterday where they stood in line patiently until other Dressler-Beery fans moved out to make room for them. Once inside, they thoroughly enjoyed the adventures of Annie Brennan, courageous skipper of a Puget Sound tugboat, and of her worthless, blundering husband, whom she refused to cast out.

"Naturally, the lion's share of footage in *Tugboat Annie* goes to the two stars. Among the supporting players, Maureen O'Sullivan and Robert Young do very nicely as the youthful sweethearts.

"Director Mervyn LeRoy kept both eyes on the box office in this picture. It will cash in handsomely for Metro-Goldwyn-Mayer."

Stage Mother was Maureen's final released film for 1933, with Alice Brady in the title role of Kitty Lorraine, and Maureen as her daughter, Shirley. The film was based on the novel by Bradford Ropes, about a woman who pushes her young daughter to reach for the stars on Broadway, seeking the fame that had eluded herself. Maureen's love interest was portrayed by Franchot Tone, who had made his film debut the year before in *The Wiser Sex* (1932). Tone was suave and handsome, and his sincerity in falling in love with Maureen's character in this picture revealed him to be a fine actor as well.

Maureen with Franchot Tone in *Stage Mother*

The story begins on the vaudeville stage, where Kitty Lorraine has received the news that she is pregnant, and thus her husband Fred (Russell Hardie) goes on with their trapeze act on this date by himself, with Kitty watching in the wings. At the conclusion of the act, tragically, Fred falls from the trapeze to his death on the stage below.

After the baby is born, Kitty and daughter Shirley go to live with Fred's in-laws in Boston, strict Puritans who insist that she give up her vaudeville career and get a real job. Kitty has little choice, but still longs for life on the stage from her job in a music store. When a friend from the past, comedian Ralph Martin (Ted Healy) shows up one day, she accepts his invitation of marriage and joins him in his act. The family is outraged, and insists that Shirley stay with them. Once again, Kitty agrees that this is best for the child, but vows to return one day so she can claim her daughter.

Ralph turns out to be nothing but a drunk, and while in a drunken stupor falls dead just minutes before they are supposed to go on stage. Thanks to a friend in the New York talent business, Kitty becomes a success as his office manager. Now financially stable, she sends for her daughter Shirley, who is a fresh-faced sweet-sixteen. Kitty is determined that Shirley will be a big success on the stage, and enrolls the girl in a renowned dancing school. After two years of intense training, Shirley wins the lead role in a touring musical revue, and receives rave reviews. As various men make advances on Shirley, Kitty fends them off like an angry lioness.

Eventually Shirley is booked into the New Amsterdam in New York, and once again she is a huge success and the manager signs her to a long-term contract. When an even better offer comes along from a Broadway-bound revue, Kitty blackmails the manager into releasing the girl from her contract. During the review's Boston tryout, Shirley goes to visit her childhood home, now owned and occupied by Warren Foster (Tone), a promising young artist.

Shirley and Warren soon fall in love, and while Kitty is in the hospital with appendicitis, they spend the night together. Later, when Kitty intercepts one of Warren's letters and finds out that they are lovers, she goes to his parents and blackmails them out of $10,000, payment for his apparent indiscretion. When Warren finds out about the blackmail, he thinks Shirley is in on the scam and breaks off their relationship.

While Shirley continues to rise to stardom, her mother controls the strings of her life and her heart. She directs her daughter to a relationship with a mayoral candidate, then insists on a $25,000 payment from his campaign manager to end the affair. And when a British lord comes along, Kitty once again pushes her daughter into the liaison (while the girl's heart still laments her lost love, Warren).

In the end, the love between mother and daughter overcomes all the mistakes that both have made in the meteoric rise of Shirley Lorraine to the top of the heap. They kiss and make up, and this allows the daughter to also reunite with her true love, the young artist Warren Foster.

Alice Brady was an excellent stage actress who made numerous movies in the 1930s, with a high point of an Academy Award for her supporting role in *In Old Chicago* (1937). The casting was perfect, as Brady was 19 years older than Maureen, and the mother-daughter relationship was sublimely convincing.

The ending of *Stage Mother* was a real tear-jerker, and her fine acting was why Maureen was cast in this and similar roles. When it came to turning on the tears in dramatic moments, she could evoke sympathy from even the toughest audiences.

The reviews were positive when the film made its debut in November 1932, including the *Motion Picture Herald* by R.W. Hickman:

> "*Stage Mother* with Alice Brady and Maureen O'Sullivan. This picture was well liked, and drew a lot of extra business. O'Sullivan perfectly cast, and turns in a fine performance. Don't be afraid of this one. It will stand all the publicity that you can give it."

Variety noted that the film had box office potential, and called Maureen's performance "excellent" on October 3, 1933:

> "*Stage Mother* should get b. o. attention for some nice biz. Alice Brady as the machinating stage mother is not above sacrificing her daughter for mutual gain, but the squarer is towards the end when she reunites Maureen O'Sullivan and Franchot Tone, who was the 'first man' in the ingenue's life.
>
> "Miss O'Sullivan is excellent as the mother-knows-best child. Ditto Miss Brady. Tone and Holmes are virtually sacrificed for bits. Ted Healy as a hambone is the McCoy."

Maureen with Alice Brady in *Stage Mother*

The balance of 1933 was not idle for Maureen, who began work on *Tarzan and His Mate* the first week of August; the film would be in production for seven full months, and finally completed in late February, 1934. This classic motion picture would define her as an actress, and eventually bring her status as an international sex symbol.

Tarzan and His Mate is remembered and is still popular as one of the great screen adventures of all time, and it is also one of the films that defined the 1930s as the Golden Age of Hollywood. Maureen O'Sullivan and Johnny Weissmuller performing heroics in the African jungle remain to this day an indelible image that cannot be forgotten by millions of movie fans.

CHAPTER EIGHT
"Jungle Jane Proves Mighty Courageous"

In the middle of production of *Tarzan and His Mate*, Maureen landed in the Cedars of Lebanon Hospital on November 21, 1933, where she had to undergo a common appendicitis operation. The *Evening Herald Express* made it sound quite ominous the following day, when she was being treated for a subsequent bout of peritonitis.

"Maureen O'Sullivan condition critical, awaits special serum." Twenty-four hours passed and the *Los Angeles Post-Record* issued this startling headline: "Maureen O'Sullivan battling for life after operation for appendicitis."

A news release on November 23 reported that Maureen was "somewhat improved" and that she was being cared for by her physician, Dr. William E. Branch. On the following day, the *Illustrated Daily News* announced that she was now out of danger: "Maureen O'Sullivan, film actress, who has been in serious condition at the Cedars of Lebanon Hospital, last night was reported to be 'greatly improved.'" She would be released from the hospital in a few days, and did have all of December off to recuperate from her surgery.

Maureen missed 45 days of the shooting schedule of *Tarzan and His Mate*, while the rest of the company shot scenes that didn't include the character of Jane. For the Christmas holidays 1933, she hosted a party at Grauman's Chinese Theater for all of her friends, including boyfriend John Farrow. Also partying at Grauman's on the same day were Will Rogers, John and Lionel Barrymore, Dolores Del Rio, Ricardo Cortez, Laura La Plante, Esther Ralston, Frank McHugh, Adolphe Menjou, Charlotte Greenwood, and Greta Garbo.

Reporter Reine Davies of *Los Angeles Examiner* in the "Hollywood Parade" column of New Year's Day, 1934, noted what brings a smile to the faces of various Hollywood stars, including Maureen:

"If any one of the many Hollywood stars were asked, 'How's your sense of humor today?' the answer would be as varied as the personality involved. Things that would send one player into roars of laughter would not get a smile from another and vice versa.

"I have heard that a property man on Joan Crawford's set always makes her laugh by giving insane parodies of the songs in her various pictures.

"That Ed Wynn gets his biggest laugh out of the world's worst puns. John Barrymore converts a mistake in dialogue into some uproarious gag that starts the whole company laughing.

"That Maureen O'Sullivan enjoys Irish dialect stories, and Walter Huston likes to tell laughable stories of Paul Bunyon in the big woods of the Northwest.

"That Jimmy Durante secures many laughs from the memory of his adventures on New York's Lower East Side, and when he smoked his first cigar to appear grown up. And I?" added Reine Davies. "Oh, I see the funny side of almost anything."

Well, now we know what tickled Maureen's funny bone — just a good old story of her home country regaled in an Irish dialect.

It was soon back to work on *Tarzan and His Mate* for Maureen and company, and there were many friends who would visit the set to watch the filming. Two of the guests to visit with Maureen personally were members of the Irish aristocracy, Lord Decles and his daughter Moya, as noted in Louella Parsons column of January 19, 1934:

"The delight that Lord Decles and his daughter, Miss Moya Beresford expressed in their tour of the Hollywood studios was nothing compared to the thrill Maureen O'Sullivan had in meeting them. Born and brought up nine miles from Lord Decles' estate near Dublin, Maureen had known of the family, but she had never met them. The two girls, who look not unlike, each a type of Irish beauty, made plans to meet each other when Maureen goes home. Of all the motion picture fans it has been my privilege to meet, I have never met two people who had seen as many motion pictures and who were greater fans."

Another familiar guest was author Edgar Rice Burroughs, who was paid $45,000 by MGM for the rights to produce *Tarzan and His Mate*. He later wrote a letter to his son Hulbert, and among his observations he noted that "the underwater shot of Weissmuller fighting the croc" was going to be "very thrilling."

Mr. Burroughs was particularly enamored with Maureen O'Sullivan after she had appeared at one of his book signings in 1932, and autographed books and photos for Tarzan fans.

At one point, Maureen was a guest of Burroughs' sons Hully and Jack for a day at the beach in Santa Monica. It seems that Ed Burroughs was playing matchmaker with his two sons, ages 23 and 19, and Maureen, who turned 21 in May of 1932.

Burroughs had already seen his daughter Joan marry Tarzan actor James Pierce in 1928, and now he had hopes that his favorite "Jane" might also become a member of the family.

Didn't happen of course, but you can't blame Mr. Burroughs for trying to arrange a match between Maureen and his bachelor sons. (Note: James Pierce played Tarzan in the 1927 silent film, *Tarzan and the Golden Lion*.)

Maureen with a fan at 1932 book signing with author Edgar Rice Burroughs (at far right)

Woody Van Dyke, director of *Tarzan, the Ape Man,* had been expected to continue his fine work in the sequel, *Tarzan and His Mate,* but was unavailable. (Van Dyke did, however, direct Maureen's next two films, *The Thin Man* and *Hide-Out.*) Assigned to direct the picture was Cedric Gibbons, the brilliant art director for MGM on hundreds of films, including the Tarzan adventures. Gibbons had never directed a motion picture, and for the most part was filling in for Van Dyke, who originally was listed as "co-director." This situation didn't work out at all.

Filming began on the MGM back lots on August 2, 1933, with the primary actors of Johnny Weissmuller, Maureen O'Sullivan, and Neil Hamilton resurrecting their roles from *Tarzan, the Ape Man.* Cast as Martin Arlington, the corrupt partner of Holt, was Rod LaRocque, who was a popular leading man of the silent era.

Apparently there was some friction between Gibbons and LaRocque, and things hardly were going smoothly overall, when a bomb was dropped three weeks into the filming schedule. Jack Conway, a versatile contract director who worked for MGM, was brought in to replace Gibbons as director. Also, LaRocque was fired and replaced by the suave, mustachioed Paul Cavanagh in the second lead role of Arlington. (Gibbons would return to his job as art director and work for MGM for decades, but never again in the role of director. He was, however, listed as director on the credits of all versions of *Tarzan and His Mate*, and Conway was uncredited.)

When asked about the famed art director in 1992, Maureen beamed and said: "Oh, the whole color of MGM was Cedric Gibbons. He set the whole tone of the studio. He was sheer brilliance with his sets — the great mystery and the magic of Metro-Goldwyn-Mayer led to Cedric Gibbons, in my opinion. He was wonderful, and a very handsome man."

When filming resumed in early September, Conway directed the dialogue segments of the film while three assistant directors — James McKay, Errol Taggart and Nick Grinde — worked with the second units. McKay was given primary credit for staging the jungle fights, including the attacks of the lions, and working with the monkeys that save the life of Tarzan. Once again Sherwood Forest and Lake Sherwood were the basic shooting scenarios, along with the swamp lands of Woodland Park, plus Big Tujunga and China Flats.

Approximately 40 lions were used in the climactic lion attack scene, and McKay handled the cats in one large set, adding greatly to the hazard of the shots. One of the most difficult sequences to capture on film was the scene where the monkeys gather about the injured Tarzan, trying to bring him to life. McKay spent a week getting the chimps to do it just right.

After the immense success and worldwide popularity of *Tarzan, the Ape Man*, a series of Tarzan films was inevitable. Movie fans the world over were eagerly awaiting the return of their hero, Johnny Weissmuller, and their heroine, Maureen O'Sullivan, to the silver screen with a new jungle adventure. The long-awaited reunion of Weissmuller and O'Sullivan in *Tarzan and His Mate*, delayed for many months because of production problems, was finally ready for release in the spring of 1934.

Tarzan, the Ape Man concluded with Jane remaining in the jungle with Tarzan, presumably to live their lives together. In this 1934 sequel, *Tarzan and His Mate*, the story once again begins in an African village, where Harry Holt (Neil Hamilton) is planning a return to the elephant burial ground where Jane's father had died. A fortune in ivory tusks lies in the dangerous land guarded by the Mutia Escarpment, waiting for anyone bold enough to steal it.

Holt has enlisted a new partner, Martin Arlington (Paul Cavanagh), and the two men plan a safari to locate the ivory and also return Jane to civilization. Holt remains in love with Jane, and hopes to use a selection of the latest Paris fashions to tempt her to leave Tarzan.

The safari natives are led by Saidi (Nathan Curry), the strong, silent type who reports only to the two white men. Deep into the jungle the safari is besieged by a hostile tribe, a warning that they are getting too close to the Mutia; they lose at least a dozen men. Later they are under attack by fierce gorillas and more men die, but Tarzan and Jane fortuitously arrive to call off the apes.

Jane is excited to see Holt, whom she regards as a good friend. Arlington is introduced to Tarzan, and he accepts the outsiders because they are friends of Jane's. While Tarzan is gone hunting, the two men begin wooing Jane, first with the selection of Paris clothes and then with music from a record player. When Arlington is dancing with Jane, he forces her to kiss him. She rebuffs his advances, and also tells Holt that Tarzan is the only man she will ever want. Tarzan returns and carries Jane to their tree-house in the sky, as Holt and Arlington look on in frustration.

Paul Cavanagh, Neil Hamilton, Johnny, and Maureen in *Tarzan and His Mate*

When the safari resumes the next morning, Tarzan sends a huge elephant along to break a trail through the jungle. There is sorrow when big Cheeta is flattened by a rampaging rhinoceros that has threatened Jane — the rhino is subsequently killed by Tarzan. When Jane finally tells Tarzan that the two men aim to steal the ivory, he refuses to lead them to the burial ground.

Arlington coldly shoots the guide elephant, knowing that the wounded animal will instinctively head for the ancient graveyard to die. When they do arrive at the burial ground, Tarzan sends a herd of elephants to prevent them from removing the ivory, and Jane convinces them to leave the next morning. Holt and Arlington have no intention of departing without the ivory tusks, after risking their lives for the prize. Arlington follows Tarzan into the jungle and shoots him from ambush, leaving him to die when he falls into the river.

Tarzan is saved by a hippo and one of the great apes, while Arlington goes back to tell Jane that her man has been killed by a crocodile. Jane doesn't believe it, but she is later convinced when she finds a bracelet she had given Tarzan — the "always" bracelet — in the river where he presumably met his death.

Jane points the way, while Tarzan distrusts Arlington and Holt

Now her remorse clouds her judgment and Jane agrees to lead them to the burial ground. They locate the ivory and begin the trek back fully loaded, but suddenly the safari is cornered by the fierce Giboni tribe. They manage to escape to a rocky gorge where they are surrounded by a pride of man-eating lions, with little hope of rescue. Little Cheeta has warned Jane that Tarzan is still alive, and escapes the lion trap to seek out the ape-man — now the only hope to save Jane.

The first to die is Saidi, bravely attempting to recover a box of ammunition. Holt dies trying to save Jane, and the cowardly Arlington meets his death in the jaws of a lion. Jane is the last survivor clinging to her life as the lions surround her — only a small fire she has started separates her from sure death. Jane knows that Tarzan is alive, and she repeatedly calls out in hopes he will arrive in time. When she hears Tarzan's return cry, she lies on the ground to pretend she is dead. A lion sniffs at her, but growls and walks away.

Tarzan has recovered from his head wound, nursed back to health by the apes, and leads his elephants on a triumphant charge to crush his enemies, both human and wild beast. After rescuing Jane, Tarzan gathers her in his arms, as she tells her beloved mate, "Tarzan, *always* is just beginning for us." Together they ride one of Tarzan's mighty elephants back to the sanctity of their jungle home.

It is reasonable to say that *Tarzan and His Mate* is the greatest Tarzan picture ever produced. The few possible competitors for this lofty title fall by the wayside because of a lack of a romantic angle, which in this picture is really the center of the story. The treacherous journey to the lost graveyard and the dangerous souls who also covet Jane, are secondary to the love story of Tarzan and Jane. This particular screen collaboration of Johnny Weissmuller and Maureen O'Sullivan is simply the definition of a classic romantic adventure.

Weissmuller's dark-haired, virile image and the perfect symmetry of his physique helped to form the definitive Tarzan. Meanwhile, Maureen was undeniably sexy in virtually every scene of the picture, whether it was her skimpy Jane outfit, the glamorous gown that rips off when she dives for a morning swim, or the close-ups of those beautiful eyes and enchanting smile. (Louella Parsons noted in her column that Maureen had gained some character in her face since her arrival in Hollywood in 1929, and that was true; a few lines gave her a certain maturity beyond her years, and enhanced her desirability.)

In over one-hundred publicity stills photographed for *Tarzan and His Mate* by MGM photographer Clarence Bull, Maureen is pictured in her skimpy antelope-skin two-piece outfit, and Johnny in his loincloth. In many of the photos, Tarzan has Jane slung over his shoulder, ready to carry her off to the treetops for an assumed primitive romantic interlude. There probably have never been a sexier set of photographs taken for any other legitimate film in history. More importantly, the fans were enthralled by this jungle romance between the ape-man and his mate, and the many photographs taken for this picture thoroughly enhanced the beauty of the event.

Once again the catch lines from a massive advertising campaign blared out the return of Tarzan and Jane in an all new jungle thriller, *Tarzan and His Mate*:

"WHITE GODDESS of the JUNGLE! She traded civilization for the love of Tarzan, her mate! While Tarzan's brawny arms held her close ... the jungle's furies meant nothing to the White Goddess of wild Africa."

"HE DARED JUNGLE TERRORS FOR HER LOVE! Ruler of a wild domain, sharing his throne with a White Goddess who defies the laws of society for the thrill of being carried away in the arms of her mate!"

"THE ORIGINAL TARZAN — JOHNNY WEISSMULLER! Primitive lovers in a Paradise of Peril! America's Adam and Eve return to thrill you as the Adonis of the jungle battles man and beast — for his bride — in the greatest romantic adventure of them all!"

The fact that Maureen was called a "White Goddess of the Jungle" pretty much sums up the direction the advertising would take for this Tarzan adventure. In most of Maureen's films she would be known for her convincing portrayals of gentle women, and her own unique beauty made her a legend in an era of unforgettable female movie stars. But the scanty outfit that she wore in *Tarzan and His Mate* also brought her a certain amount of notoriety when the film was released.

A leather halter top and matching loincloth were Jane's basic wardrobe, and for taking a swim with Tarzan she wore nothing at all! Naturally, these scenes caused a furor with the censorship people.

A comment from Elizabeth Yeaman of the *Hollywood Citizen News* further clarifies the skimpiness of Maureen's outfit, which a good wind would have blown away completely: "I might add," said Ms. Yeaman, "that the scantiness of Miss O'Sullivan's costume is so precarious that it may make feminine members of the audience a little nervous."

As screen characters, Johnny and Maureen breathed life into the storybook players of Edgar Rice Burroughs, capturing the essence of a primeval man and his mate. The playfulness between Tarzan and Jane on-screen was often endearing, and ultimately provocative. In one scene Jane receives gifts of an evening gown, stockings, French perfume and dresses to impress Tarzan. He approves of this new look with a gleam in his eye, and scoops up his mate and carries her away to their lofty love-nest, with nary a protest from Jane.

Sol Lesser, who tried in vain to coax Maureen out of retirement when he became producer of the Tarzan series in 1943, offered his retrospective viewpoint of Miss O'Sullivan as Jane:

"Maureen O'Sullivan was an ideal Jane with a figure that is greatly revealed in the second Metro picture — but done so beautifully that it couldn't be criticized. As I recall the situation she is standing on a tree limb with Tarzan. He tugs at her garment, dives in the water and she dives in after him. Then she comes up from the swimming scene with her breast exposed. It was done in such good taste — I think that a kind of snobbishness developed afterwards with Miss O'Sullivan from her role as Jane. Maybe the public kidded her too much — or maybe she thought it wasn't good acting, I don't know. But I do know the movie audiences worshiped her."

The controversial underwater swimming sequence that followed Jane being tossed into the river by Tarzan was, in actuality, Weissmuller and Josephine McKim, a petite Olympic swimmer who doubled for Miss O'Sullivan. This underwater "ballet" is memorable for its graceful choreography and again the playful love between Tarzan and Jane. The ape-man kissing his beloved mate underwater is one of filmdom's most memorable love scenes.

Johnny's Tarzan wears his loincloth during the scene, but Jane (Miss McKim) is *au naturel;* this particular sequence was unacceptable to the Production Code Office which previewed the picture. After getting the thumbs down from the censors, MGM appeased the Code Office by re-shooting the scene with Jane in her basic halter and loincloth. However, three different versions (one included the original nude sequence) were released to different areas of the country, depending on local censorship codes. When the first three MGM Tarzan pictures were released on video in 1991, the nude swimming sequence was included in its entirety. Fortunately for real film fans, this scene — tasteful rather than lewd — was not lost in the previous half-century.

There were many great stunts in *Tarzan and His Mate*, many of them executed by the actors themselves. It is well known that Weissmuller rode on Mary the rhinoceros in one scene, an extremely dangerous stunt. Meanwhile, Maureen and Johnny rode the elephants throughout the picture without using stunt doubles. Jungle Jane rode the elephants numerous times by herself, dismounted as the animal brought its head down, and climbed aboard another mighty pachyderm to converse with Tarzan. Johnny also grappled with Jackie the tame lion, and performed many other dangerous stunts such as leaping from tree to tree, often times carrying his counterpart.

Perhaps the most magnificent scene in this picture is of Johnny and Maureen astride two charging elephants, as the entire herd called by Tarzan surrounds the ancient elephant burial ground. This portrait was both primitive and majestic, watching two wild creatures themselves riding to the rescue on the majestic beasts that were the friends of Tarzan. There were some very genuine risks involved for Johnny and Maureen in working with the many dangerous animals used in the Tarzan pictures. A fall from the back of an elephant, or from a lofty tree branch, would have brought serious injury. As it was, there were plenty of minor injuries and animal bites with which to contend.

Maureen was a central figure in the climactic lion battle — in one scene she hovers on a ledge while an angry lion paws at her and she in turn pokes back with the butt of a rifle. Likely the lion was chained, and it was probably Jackie, but it still looked immensely real. Betty Roth, wife of lion trainer Louis Roth, doubled for Miss O'Sullivan in some of the lion scenes, including the one where Jane lies down and plays possum as a last resort, and then the lion sniffs her over and departs. Maureen's stand-in for many of the Tarzan pictures was Martha Schollander, the mother of future champion swimmer Don Schollander.

Maureen appeared in numerous scenes with the chimps, and she received several bites from the monkeys who seemed to love Tarzan but not so much Jane! She also did a cute scene where a beautiful bird lands in her hand, and she chats with it and then sends it flying away. The lithe actress was square in the middle of every action sequence, firing a rifle, soaring with Tarzan on vines from tree to tree, diving and swimming, and riding on the backs of mighty elephants.

She also later recalled that for this Tarzan picture they decided to make a mechanical rhinoceros, because the live rhino was so dangerous to work with. "A rhinoceros goes straight at you, it can't turn — so they made a mechanical rhino," noted Maureen. "And then they couldn't put a man inside to steer it, or it would have ground him into sausage meat! So they settled for a real rhino."

Alfredo Codona once again doubled for Johnny in the treetops, and the Flying Codonas performed the scene where Tarzan, Jane, and Big Cheeta do their own jungle "trapeze" act. An adagio team executed the stunt of Jane diving from a high branch into Tarzan's waiting arms below.

Johnny and Maureen also did the stunt themselves, but her leap was from a much lower platform; the effect being that it looked very much like they had executed the high dive themselves.

The production of *Tarzan and His Mate* was more than a year in the planning stage, and, it took approximately seven months to complete the filming. The final cost of $1.3 million dollars was an enormous sum for the Depression and almost double the cost of filming *Tarzan, the Ape Man*. In the United

States and abroad, the film was a smashing, resounding success which played to massive audiences (especially in foreign markets, punctuating the international appeal of Tarzan). When the picture opened in New York in mid-April of 1934, it was received with thunderous applause and appreciation by fans who had long anticipated the return of Johnny and Maureen as Tarzan and Jane.

Maureen and Johnny are threatened by this rhino ... undoubtedly "trick" photography

Meanwhile the critics were even more lavish in their praise than they had been for *Tarzan, the Ape Man*. The Los Angeles press, the New York dailies, and numerous national publications almost unanimously said the same thing: that *Tarzan and His Mate* was the crown jewel of the Tarzan adventure series and a great motion picture. A few sample reviews herewith:

Los Angeles Examiner (April 23, 1934) Louella O. Parsons

"Take every exciting mystery story you have read and every bloodcurdling play and put them together and you won't have half the thrill that *Tarzan and His Mate* will offer. You'll forget its improbabilities and the tax on your credulity when you see some of the battles in the jungle. Loew's State, where the picture is playing this week, should really serve heart stimulants for those who faint easily. Of all the animal pictures made, this *Tarzan* number furnishes the most exciting wild animal scenes.

"Johnny Weissmuller swings from tree to tree with an agility that is hardly human. He has only a few words to say, but he makes up in his action what he lacks in dialogue.

"Maureen O'Sullivan, his mate, who lives in the jungles without any of the conveniences we feel are necessary to our peace of mind, swims with a grace almost equal to that of Tarzan. She also does a little tree-swinging on her own."

Evening Herald Express (April 23, 1934) Harrison Carroll

"The biblical plight of Daniel in the lions' den was mere play compared to the hair-raising adventures that beset the characters of *Tarzan and His Mate,* the new jungle thriller which MGM offers for your entertainment this week at Loew's State Theater.

"From the moment that the two Englishmen (Neil Hamilton and Paul Cavanagh) head their safari toward the ivory fortune in the elephants' graveyard, there is a thrill a second. Boa constrictors, lions, crocodiles, rhinoceri, elephants, boulder-tossing apes do their worst. In fact, it's all Tarzan can do to save the lovely Jane. The rest of the party are all wiped out.

"Recent stories about Johnny Weissmuller riding a rhinoceros were no exaggeration. It's Johnny, no mistaking. You can see his face. And here's news. Tarzan yells just as much as ever but he also speaks words and short-sentences in the new film.

"Both Johnny Weissmuller and Maureen O'Sullivan do excellent work as the ape-man and his mate. You melodrama fans must not miss this picture. It's a bit on the gruesome side, but the picture is corking entertainment."

Evening Herald Examiner (April 14, 1934) Jimmy Starr

"A lot of wise guys will probably tell you this is 'kid stuff,' but I happened to be at a preview of *Tarzan and His Mate* and the theater audience was composed almost entirely of adults. Surprisingly enough, the adults went 'kiddish' and yelled, screamed, and literally remained on the edge of their theater chairs until the final fade-out. If one desires more of an adventure-thriller film, I don't happen to know what it could be.

"Maureen and Weissmuller, of course, are tops. If you like wild-animal thrills, see *Tarzan and His Mate.*"

Family Circle (April 1934) Harry Evans

"When a film such as *Tarzan and His Mate* comes along, the writer breathes a sigh of relief. The decision is simple. If you like romance and adventure, and have enough imagination to shut off your analytical mental machinery for a couple of hours, you will have a perfectly swell time watching Tarzan and his animal pals weave the sort of heroic drama that our fondest childhood dreams were made of. What boy hasn't dreamed of himself as the jungle knight created by Johnny Weissmuller — and what girl hasn't imagined herself a Maureen O'Sullivan, being rescued every 15 or 20 minutes by her primitive sweetheart?

"And another thing: Goodness knows there are few enough films that are suitable for children. Even in this one there are one or two scenes and a few lines of dialogue without which the picture would have been more acceptable juvenile entertainment. But taken as a whole, it is an exceptionally fine thing for your youngsters to see, and the best part of it is that you can go along with them and get just as much kick out of it as they do. When a film like that comes along, it's news.

"Mr. Weissmuller, as Tarzan, is more at home before the camera than in his first film. In his athletic activities — such as diving and swimming, and scrapping with the critters — he is everything that could be desired.

"Miss O'Sullivan as Tarzan's wife continues to be one of the most delightfully natural and naive of the screen's young ladies.

"All of which has probably given you the impression that this reporter thinks you should see *Tarzan and His Mate*. And I might add that you should take the children, but the advice would be superfluous. Every youngster in the country will probably want to see it — and I don't blame them."

The incredible sex appeal of Maureen and Johnny ... savage, untamed, beautiful

CHAPTER NINE
"Outta the Jungle, Maureen Still A Big Star"

With the vast success of *Tarzan and His Mate*, Maureen's Hollywood star was rising at a meteoric pace. Metro-Goldwyn-Mayer had numerous projects lined up for her, including some of their grandest motion pictures and many with the top stars in the MGM stable. Maureen was immensely popular with movie fans and they clamored to see her in as many films as possible; the studio gladly obliged.

After the smoke had settled from her recent jungle adventure, Maureen put her clothes back on and was assigned as the young female lead in *The Thin Man*, the first teaming of William Powell and Myrna Loy in the Dashiell Hammett inspired series of detective films. The "thin man" of Hammett's 1932 crime novel was actually the murder victim, but the name stuck to Powell and was used in the five sequels: *After the Thin Man* (1936), *Another Thin Man* (1939), *Shadow of the Thin Man* (1941), *The Thin Man Goes Home* (1944), and *Song of the Thin Man* (1947).

The Thin Man series proved to be a fan favorite, and Powell and Loy were two of the biggest stars of the 1930s and 1940s, in part because of the popularity of these films. William Powell was the picture of debonair: suave, handsome, with an ever-present pencil-thin mustache. His trademarks as detective Nick Charles in *The Thin Man* series were his penchant for drinking martinis, his sarcastic wit, a certain charm with the ladies, and a brilliant ability to solve crimes.

Myrna Loy, thirteen years younger than Powell, portrayed his equally sarcastic wife, who helped him solve the various murder mysteries and never let him get the upper hand in their marital relationship. Nora Charles could drink just as hard as her husband, and she could fire zingers with the best of them. Nora was always charming and alluring, and she knew her spouse better than anyone. If he got too full of himself, she firmly put him back in his place.

It has been noted that Myrna's domestic scenes with Powell in *The Thin Man* were the first time a sophisticated, affectionate marriage had been realistically portrayed on screen. Of course the witty repartee between them was their stock in trade, and provided many humorous and even slapstick scenes in their films — which included the little dog Asta who was always sticking its nose where it didn't belong.

The stories were part comedy but also contained some serious melodrama. When the father of Maureen's character is discovered dead, it was no laughing matter to her. The young actress had several fine scenes in the picture with Edward Ellis, who played her father, and also with Powell. And when a man is murdered in cold-blood, the audience would gasp as the sound of the staccato gunfire echoed and the victim slumped to the ground.

This marvelous classic film took only sixteen days to shoot, which was amazing even in an era of quickie films. It comes as no surprise that W. S. Van Dyke was the man in charge, a confident director who gave his acting crew very few second chances.

Maureen recalled in 1974 that when working with Van Dyke, an actor had to be ready for every scene: "Woody Van Dyke used to get very spontaneous performances out of people," said Maureen, "because he would take it and he'd say, 'Okay, print it.' Consequently there was a great spontaneity in his films — perhaps I was a better actress than I thought I was, or perhaps we all were, because the results were always very fresh.

"*The Thin Man* was obviously going to be good," noted Maureen. "There was a lot of importance attached to it while we were making it; William Powell had great style and it was Myrna Loy's first breakthrough really, I suppose, from being the Oriental vamp. I don't think it was conceived as a series, I doubt it. In most cases, if a film proved to be successful, then they would go on and make another . . . and then another."

Van Dyke was also fortunate to have James Wong Howe behind the camera for this project. Howe was the cinematographer in numerous classic films in a long career that spanned more than 50 years, from 1923 to 1975. Motion picture historian Leslie Halliwell gave kudos to Howe for "the visual sensitivity that is evident in every shot of every one of his films."

Maureen also began a casual relationship with William Powell, as she later recalled: "I enjoyed *The Thin Man* very much. I became friends with William Powell, and between takes and over lunch hours I would go to his house and swim in his pool, and we had a good time together. That was before he got involved with Jean Harlow."

The Thin Man begins as Dorothy Wynant (Maureen) visits her eccentric inventor father, accompanied by her fiancé Tommy (Henry Wadsworth), and they break the news to dear old dad of their pending nuptials. Clyde Wynant (Edward Ellis) gives his stamp of approval, and promises to be back from a mysterious business trip in time for the wedding. Wynant instructs his lawyer MacCauley (Porter Hall) to handle his affairs in his absence.

Wynant is divorced and now keeps a mistress named Julia Wolf (Natalie Moorhead) — who has stolen $50,000 worth of bonds from him. She is also having an illicit affair with an unknown accomplice. Wynant warns her to repay the money immediately, or he will turn her over to the police.

Henry Wadsworth and Maureen in *The Thin Man* with William Powell and Myrna Loy

Wynant fails to return in time for the wedding, which is postponed, setting off a chain of events. Dorothy is concerned for her father, while her mother, Mimi (Minna Gombell), is frantic that her ex-husband is not around to pay her bills. Mimi goes to see the mistress to ask for money, but finds Julia's body on the floor with a fresh bullet hole — her hand is clutching the watch chain of Clyde Wynant, implicating him as the murderer.

Meanwhile, arriving in New York for the Christmas holidays are Nick Charles (Powell) and his charming wife Nora (Loy), who just happens to be wealthy and beautiful. Dorothy asks the help of old family friend Nick, who was formerly a detective, in finding her father. Nora encourages her husband to help Dorothy, and although reluctant, he agrees to look into the matter. When Nick is wounded in a scuffle with a thug, police lieutenant Guild (Nat Pendleton) gets involved in the investigation. A subsequent murder is also blamed on Clyde Wynant, in absentia.

MacCauley continues to get letters from Wynant instructing him to give money to Mimi, and he states that he will return shortly to answer to the murder charges. But Nick finds the skeletal remains of a third body hidden at Wynant's laboratory, and when he notices a piece of shrapnel in the leg, he knows that it is Wynant himself. Dorothy is shattered when she learns of her father's death, and goes into a depression in which she refuses to marry Tommy.

Nick gathers all the suspects together with the help of Lieutenant Guild, and begins to unravel the mystery over dinner. One by one each suspect is eliminated, until it is revealed that MacCauley has been embezzling from Wynant and is also the murderer. Nick Charles has solved another case, in his usual spectacular fashion. In the final scene, Nick and Nora, and Dorothy and Tommy are traveling by train, the latter couple for a belated honeymoon.

The Thin Man was nominated for four Oscars, including Best Picture, Best Adapted Screenplay, Best Director, and Best Actor (Powell). The film was also one of the top-ten money-makers of 1934, and elevated both William Powell and Myrna Loy to star status that would last for decades.

Everyone seemed to love *The Thin Man* when it was released in July 1934, and the critics agreed, beginning with Louella Parsons, the queen of Hollywood reviewers:

"I beg you, please, don't miss seeing *The Thin Man* at Loew's State Theater. It's the greatest entertainment, the most fun and the best mystery drama of the year. Extravagant words, perhaps, but I can only speak as I feel.

"*The Thin Man* will take you right out of yourself. If you have any trouble, real or fancied, you will forget it in the excitement of wondering what happened to the missing inventor. If you feel that a good cry is what you need, you will change your tune and have a good laugh. The dialogue, the situations and the big moments are so amusingly related that you divide the chills down your spine with your laughter.

"William Powell, to whom it has remained to make detectives utterly charming people, is delightful as Nick. Bill is grand and so is Myrna Loy, the rich wife who is the other bright spot in the collection of cops, underworld characters and hardened women.

"Maureen O'Sullivan, to whose lot it falls to play a really dramatic role, is excellent as the thin man's daughter. Again I beseech all those who haven't seen the picture not to miss the opportunity. I won't give you even a hint of the plot, because that would be just too, too unfair."

Maureen continued to grow as an actress, and Harrison Carroll of the *Evening Herald Express* could hardly contain his enthusiasm for the ensemble cast and the superior performances:

"A best-seller as a book, Dashiell Hammett's *The Thin Man* has been splendidly produced by MGM, and will be gobbled up by movie fans who love mystery and laughs. Be prepared to meet an entirely new Bill Powell in *The Thin Man,* and a Myrna Loy who completely reveals, for the first time, her ability as a comedienne. You'll like Nick and Nora better than any two movie characters you've met in a long time. They are crack-brained but exciting and are acted with perfection by Bill Powell and Myrna Loy.

"The supporting players also are swell — Maureen O'Sullivan, as the inventor's daughter; Minna Gombell, as her greedy mother; Edward Ellis, as the missing inventor; Nat Pendleton, as the dumb cop; Porter Hall, as the attorney; Harold Huber, as the stool-pigeon; Edward Brophy, as the nervous gangster; and all the rest.

"Don't, under any circumstance, miss *The Thin Man*."

Elizabeth Yeaman of the *Hollywood Citizen News* noted in her review that Maureen handled the serious acting in *The Thin Man*, and performed her role with excellence:

> "Murder mysteries are not generally laughing matters, but the latest picture of this type, *The Thin Man*, is far more humorous than it is spine-chilling. The picture is beautifully timed, and swings along at a fast comedy pace. William Powell and Myrna Loy are well cast in the two leading roles.
>
> "Minna Gombell gives one of her most effective performances as the slightly mad mother in the story. Maureen O'Sullivan does well with a heavy dramatic role as the daughter. W. S. Van Dyke has directed skillfully."

The relationship between Maureen and John Farrow kept in the news, as Louella Parsons reported in her column the latest gossip: "Maureen O'Sullivan and Johnny Farrow have had all the news hounds on their toes for months waiting for the grand elopement which is said to be planned for a few weeks hence. I even know of one news hound who parked himself at Miss O'Sullivan's front door so as not to miss the scoop for his paper."

Maureen's next film was scheduled to be *Hide-Out*, a drama with Robert Montgomery. When her father became seriously ill, she was replaced by Loretta Young, so that Maureen could go back to Ireland. However, Loretta became quite sick herself before production began, and she was unable to accept the role. In the meantime, Charles O'Sullivan's health improved, and Maureen was once again assigned to co-star in the film.

Robert Montgomery was one of the big stars of the 1930s and 1940s, and there's a long list of classic films to his credit. Two of his most famous roles were in *Here Comes Mr. Jordan* (1941), and as Phillip Marlowe in *The Lady in the Lake* (1946), which he also directed.

Montgomery's role was of racketeer Lucky Wilson, who is a heartless crook and also a notorious womanizer. Wilson is going out with four women at the same time, and he shamelessly flirts with the cigarette girl, the hat-check girl, and the maid of one his girlfriends. The caddish Lucky is attracted to a nightclub singer one evening, and drops his date of the moment without an ounce of remorse.

Hide-Out was directed by Woody Van Dyke, and featured Edward Arnold as the tough cop who is determined to put Wilson and his gang behind bars. Also in the fine cast were Elizabeth Patterson as Ma Miller, Whitford Kane as Pa Miller, and Mickey Rooney as Willie, the little brother to Maureen's character of Pauline Miller.

Maureen was the romantic lead opposite Montgomery, as she was slowly gaining the maturity to do serious love scenes with older actors. She had just turned 23 years old, and had all the attributes of a beautiful woman; in this film she gave a warm, convincing portrayal as an innocent young lady in love.

The story begins when playboy gangster Lucky Wilson (Montgomery) forces his way into a partnership in a nightclub, at the behest of his boss Tony Berrelli (C. Henry Gordon). Tony and Lucky are using their laundry business as a front for an illegal protection racket, forcing several nightclub owners to take them in as partners.

Lieutenant MacCarthy (Edward Arnold) is determined to wipe out crime in his section of New York, and arranges for the club owners to testify against Lucky. Tony gets word that a warrant has been issued for Lucky, and tells him to head for the Catskills to lie low for awhile. Lucky arranges to meet a woman at his hotel, planning to take her with him on his holiday. The police spot the gangster at the hotel, and in a shoot-out he is wounded and barely escapes the city in his automobile.

Lucky manages to get as far as the Connecticut countryside, where his car crashes and he is left unconscious. He is discovered by Pa Miller, who takes him back to his farm to care for his bullet wound. The Miller family, including Ma Miller, young son Willie (Rooney), and 20-year-old daughter Pauline (Maureen) welcome the stranger and nurse him back to health. Pauline is a school teacher, and she also helps on the farm feeding the chickens and milking cows.

A scene from *Hide-Out* ... Rooney behind the wheel with Ma and Pa, Robert, and Maureen

Lucky tells the Millers he was ambushed by racketeers, and has Tony send up his own mob doctor from New York. Lucky is itching to get back to the city, until he sees Pauline and almost instantly falls in love with her. The young woman helps to take care of the wounded stranger, and they spend time doing chores around the farm and having picnics together. Before long, Pauline has fallen for Lucky, whom she thinks is a business consultant. Willie also makes friends with Lucky, who offers to buy him the BB gun that he wants but can't afford.

Eventually Lieutenant MacCarthy gets wind that Lucky is up in the country and arrives to make the arrest of the wanted man, who will be going to prison for racketeering. Lucky tells MacCarthy that he is a changed man and will be going straight, and asks him to go along with his charade. Realizing that the family loves Lucky, the tough cop relents to allow him a few moments alone with Pauline before they must take him away.

Lucky breaks down and tells Pauline that he is a gangster and will be going to prison for 18 months for his crimes. Pauline sees that Lucky is genuine in his feelings for her, and promises to wait until he returns. Lucky leaves with the police, but knows he has a loving woman waiting for him after he pays his debt to society.

Hide-Out was one of those "little" films that no one seems to remember, but it was superbly acted and great family entertainment. Although this is labeled a "B" picture, in reality a "B" drama from MGM was what was called an "A" picture from most of the other studios.

Mickey Rooney was thirteen years old at this time, and the lad was on the verge of stardom. It is easy to see why he would soon become a big star, from his heartfelt acting. In one scene the whole family is having a fancy dinner with their guest Lucky, and Willie suddenly realizes the main course is one of his pet rabbits that Ma Miller has prepared. The kid breaks down and runs from the table sobbing, and the audience must have melted with empathy for the lad. At that point, a very fine scene enfolds with Rooney and Montgomery, who comforts him and tells him he will buy him the BB gun if he quits crying. The boy wipes his tears, and the gesture from the gangster is rather touching.

The romance between Maureen and Montgomery was also superbly played out, and very believable. When former New York hoodlum Lucky sees what he can have in the Connecticut countryside, he is completely willing to give up his life of crime and go straight. The love of a good woman is the only reward that Lucky Wilson needs to change his life-style from gangster to solid citizen. His transformation is so complete, even tough cop Edward Arnold sees that he is a changed man and lets him leave with dignity.

There was excellent screen chemistry between the two lead actors, and Maureen and Montgomery were later reported to be teamed in a subsequent film called *Small Town Girl*, but it never happened for one reason or another.

Film Daily previewed *Hide-Out* on August 18, 1934:

"Dandy entertainment. Nicely handled story of racketeer who is turned straight by country girl. Typical of the 'Turn to the Right' school, this story is a smartly-conceived combination of romance, human interest and racketeering, with the latter employed only as an expedient. Action starts with Robert Montgomery in his glory as a dashing young gangster who also makes the dames fall right and left. Obliged to do a hideaway from the police and being wounded by his pursuers, he lands at a farm run by some kindly folks with a kindly daughter, Maureen O'Sullivan. The rest, though obvious in outcome, is engineered with a shrewd sense of entertainment values, and builds up to a strong sentimental climax where the reformed Robert, being taken away by detectives, vows to come back to Maureen after he has served his time. An ace cast and expert direction help the story considerably."

And three snapshot reviews in the *Motion Picture Herald* from 1934/1935 also noted the merits of this family film that started out like a tough crime drama, but evolved into a warm and endearing melodrama on the farm:

Hideout — Robert Montgomery, Maureen O'Sullivan. — "A very good program picture. Good story and well acted. Gave good satisfaction but did not draw any extra business. But a splendid entertainment and clean." — Bert Silver, Silver Family Theatre, Greenville, Mich. Town and country patronage."

Hideout — "One of the sweetest pictures we have run in a long time. Cleverly directed and excellent story material. Although Montgomery has not been a drawing attraction in the past, he certainly scored in this picture. You can shoot the works on this picture and they will come and go away pleased." — H.M. Johnson, Avon Theatre, Avon Park, Fla. General small town patronage.

Hideout — "Played this late but glad we picked it up. Just the kind of a picture you are glad to present to your patrons and they are glad they came to see. Hottest weather on record played as opposition, but those who did turn out were well repaid and told us so." — M.R. Harrington, Avalon Theatre, Clatskanie, Ore. Small town and rural patronage.

When Maureen was working on *Hide-Out* she took a little break one day and went for a walk. The afternoon turned out to be quite unusual for the actress, as noted by Edwin Marin of the *Hollywood Citizen News* in his "Cinemania" column of July 10, 1934:

"Who said that Hollywood didn't have a heart? Here's a little story that trickled in today ... and not from any studio publicity department, either ... Maureen O'Sullivan was on location with an MGM company at Santa Cruz and had been given the afternoon off ... while wandering along a by-street, she was attracted by a building which had a sign: 'Visitors Welcome'... she entered, and found herself in the midst of 20 or more girls, all happily sewing — and all blind. It was the Braille Institute, operated by blind women.

"Miss O'Sullivan asked if she could join them ... she was introduced and passed the rest of the day sewing dresses with the girls and telling them about

Hollywood ... while the assistants of the company searched frantically for her because she was suddenly needed on the set ..."

About a week later, Maureen did an interview with W. E. Oliver of the *Evening Herald Express*, concerning the new rules and regulations that went hand in hand with the Production Code of 1934:

"DEMURE COLLEEN THINKS CENSORSHIP BIG HELP TO HER":

"Another actress who welcomes the campaign to take searing themes off the screen is Maureen O'Sullivan, although she does for reasons that don't sound logical to me. This young Irish lass whom you are seeing today on Loew's State screen in that gay melodrama, *The Thin Man,* says she is glad censorship has come.

"It will provide more opportunities for the demure type of girl. It will give more chance for actresses to be charming and not merely sexy," said Maureen.

"Now the strange thing to me is that this girl who has for the most part been given the more demure roles since coming to Hollywood is not demure at all. Talked to in person, she has a fascinating manner that would fit any of the sophisticated characters.

"By this I don't mean racy, but the glamour that hovers around a woman who has been places, seen things, knows her mind, has been given a scintillating dash of French schooling, the perfect finish of an English education and who has the natural spirit of the Irish to give all these things zip.

"Maureen does not think she is interesting to men. She actually started off our talk at luncheon with 'I hope I'm not boring you.' As if — ! When I told her, however, that her face showed development of personality and character since coming to Hollywood she was very pleased.

"To my doubts about censorship — that if it succeeds in removing from the screen the more picturesque heroines, replacing them with the kind men marry, the husbands may perhaps stay home, she gave a nice answer.

'Men do go to pictures to be entertained,' noted Ms. O'Sullivan. 'But to say they get most from seeing the sexy types is to say the baser part of their nature is most important. There is always that in people, but we shouldn't give in to it.'

"Maureen, who won't give an answer unless she thinks she knows, believes the golden age of movie art is now coming with the producers, writers and directors put on their mettle by censorship demands.

"We were getting along swimmingly — the English and the Irish, until a suntanned arm, with a shamrock and black-skulled flag tattooed on the wrist was deposited on the table. It belonged to Johnny Farrow. He spoke a few polite words while his looks told her lots of other things, entirely different. When he had gone, for some reason only a young couple would know, it was difficult to get back on the job.

"I did discover, though she leaves for Ireland in a week for her first rest in almost four years, that she hates having innocuous likes, such as sun-bathing, turned into sensational fan magazine articles making her out a nudist. She dislikes being asked questions about marriage by women with children already, that her ideal woman is Mrs. John McCormack (not her own mother?), that she has never felt at home in Hollywood and wants to settle down in southwest England. But she didn't tell me what the tattoo marks on Johnny Farrow's wrist meant."

In the latter part of July 1934, Maureen was finally able to schedule a visit home to Ireland. The engagement to John Farrow, long rumored, was now confirmed, and she was bringing him home to meet her parents and siblings.

There was also one problem to be resolved before they could be married: Farrow had been married before, and since both were Catholic, a special dispensation from the Catholic Church was required in order for the union to take place. They could always marry outside of the church, but that bridge would be crossed later if necessary. Louella Parsons as usual had her spies watching Maureen, and one day she noted in her column that John Farrow and Maureen were seen "lunching on salad and love at the Roosevelt Hotel."

In her *Los Angeles Examiner* column of July 17, 1934, Louella reported:

"Maureen O'Sullivan will not go to Ireland alone. John Farrow will accompany her, traveling with her to get her family's blessing. The wedding probably will take place at Maureen's home, after which she and Johnny will go to England and investigate an offer they have received to make a picture with Farrow as the director and Maureen as the star. There has been much talk that the wedding will take place before they leave Hollywood, but both of them are firm in their reiterations that they will not marry until Maureen's family has a chance to meet her fiancé. They leave next week."

Maureen and Farrow were supposed to leave on July 24 for a month-long vacation, but she was delayed in Hollywood for retakes on her two most recent MGM pictures. On this date Farrow left by train for Seattle, where he would rendezvous with Maureen, who would be flying to meet him.

Louella Parsons kept her fans informed on the ongoing saga of when and where the couple would wed: "Today Maureen O'Sullivan and John Farrow start on their pilgrimage to Ireland. If a special dispensation is obtained they will be married in the Cathedral at Dublin. If not, the marriage will be held up waiting for ecclesiastical leniency. But come what may, they will both be back in Hollywood August 28, Maureen is to play the role of Dora, David Copperfield's wife."

And when Maureen finally did escape the rat race on July 27, the *Los Angeles Examiner* reported on that date: "Will Maureen O'Sullivan's return trip next month from Ireland to Hollywood be a honeymoon tour as the bride of

John Farrow? Or will she return here as Miss O'Sullivan and be married in Hollywood?

"That was what their friends in Hollywood were trying to guess yesterday, with Miss O'Sullivan, MGM screen actress, hurrying toward Canada on the first part of her trip back to her native home in Dublin."

After her vacation to Ireland, Maureen returned to Hollywood and was scheduled to start work on *David Copperfield* in mid-September.

On September 13, 1934, Elizabeth Yeaman reported that the wedding between the couple was off, and perhaps the relationship was over:

"A special dispatch from London indicates that Maureen O'Sullivan did not receive a special dispensation from the Catholic Church permitting her to marry John Farrow, Australian writer. The dispatch reports that Maureen and John have both sailed from London, with Maureen a passenger aboard the Columbus, bound for New York, and John on the passenger list of the Empress of Australia, headed for Quebec. Does that mean that these two have decided to sever their romance for good? Maureen has had an on and off romance with Farrow for over four years now."

There is some question whether John Farrow actually made it to Ireland with Maureen for this particular trip to meet her family. Years later she recalled that a vacation to Ireland was spent touring with her father, with Farrow remaining back in the United States. Maureen said he called her long-distance while they were in a remote village, and she wondered how he had managed to locate her. This was during one of their break-ups, and after the phone call they began seeing each other again.

Maureen also admitted in 1994 that John was hardly the faithful type, but that she nevertheless wanted him in her life despite this glaring character flaw: "During the time that we lived together, John was unfaithful a few times but I never considered leaving him. I accepted him as he was, realizing that he just didn't know any better. I think things would have been easier all round if I'd realized that he really did love me, but I was so insecure that I just couldn't believe it."

The relationship between Maureen and Farrow was on-again, off-again during the several years they knew each other before they actually wed in September of 1936. As Maureen noted later about her feelings toward Farrow: "I couldn't live with him, and I couldn't live without him."

For the time being her work would keep her busy, and Maureen's final released film of 1934 was *The Barretts of Wimpole Street*, a costume piece set in London in 1845 with an all-star cast. This was the classic love story of poets Elizabeth Barrett and Robert Browning, played superbly by Norma Shearer and Fredric March.

Portraying Elizabeth's younger sister Henrietta was Maureen, while Charles Laughton appeared in the role of the father Edward. The estimable Laughton was fresh from winning the Academy Award for *The Private Life of Henry VIII*. The Barrett family was quite large — six actors with similar looks were cast as the younger brothers, and Katharine Alexander was the other sister, Anabel.

The story was based on the play by Rudolf Besier, and begins at the Barrett home on Wimpole Street. Poetess Elizabeth Browning (Shearer) is an invalid, and is dominated by her controlling father Edward (Laughton), who is suffocating his daughter to the point that her illness is probably a consequence of their relationship. Elizabeth is almost forty years old, bedridden most days, and rarely leaves the house. Her poetry is well-known, and her only enjoyment comes from the companionship of her six brothers and two sisters, Anabel and Henrietta (Maureen). The Barrett women are not allowed any sort of romantic entanglement, because the strict father believes that amatory love is a sin.

One of her fans is fellow poet Robert Browning (March), who sends Elizabeth letters admiring her work and requests that he be allowed to meet her. When they finally do meet in person, it is an immediate deep attraction for both parties. The enthusiastic Browning admits that, through her letters and poetry, he has fallen in love with her. Elizabeth is overwhelmed by his proclamation and tries to dismiss it, but permits him to come see her again in one week. After he leaves, she rises from her bed and struggles to the window to see him depart — she herself feeling the euphoria of love.

After three months of seeing Robert, her condition has improved greatly, and her doctors recommend that a winter in Italy would do wonders for her. Robert also plans to go to Italy to be with Elizabeth, and she is so joyous that she descends the staircase by herself for the first time in years. When her father comes home and hears of the Italy plan, he refuses to give his approval. Instead, he deflates her joy by announcing that the doctors are all wrong, and a trip to Italy might kill her. Finally, he humiliates her by forcibly carrying her back up the staircase to her bedroom.

Elizabeth tries to stand up to her father, but she is not strong enough yet — she tells Robert that the Italy trip is off. Robert intends to break her father's cloying hold on Elizabeth, and proposes to her. She initially claims to be too ill to marry, but also admits her love for Robert. She promises to give him an answer within one week.

Meanwhile, Henrietta also has a secret boyfriend, Captain Surtees Cook, a soldier in the service of the Queen. When Edward finds Cook at the house visiting Henrietta, he begins to realize that they are having an affair beneath his nose. Henrietta admits that she loves the officer, and her megalomaniacal father forces her to swear on a Bible that she will never see Captain Cook again, or he will evict her from the house with only the clothes on her back. Henrietta is sobbing uncontrollably, but she chokes out the pledge with fear and loathing in her eyes.

Edward devises a malevolent plan to move the family to Surrey, to force his daughters away from their lovers and back into his total control. The father tells Elizabeth that they will once again be "close" when they are alone in the country, and she suddenly realizes her utter contempt for him. After he retires, she tells Henrietta that she is leaving the house forever to join Robert, or the father will probably kill her. Henrietta is also emboldened, and tells Elizabeth that she will break her pledge to her malignant parent, and continue to see her young suitor.

With the help of the family maid, Wilson (Una O'Connor), Elizabeth is able to sneak from the house with only the clothes on her back and her little dog Flush. She rushes to Robert, who is overjoyed and tells her that they must marry that evening and elope to Italy. Back at the house, Henrietta gleefully hands her father a note informing him of the elopement. Edward is stunned, and his final hateful act is to order one of his sons to have her dog killed in the morning. Henrietta once again is bearer of the grand news that the dog is safely with Elizabeth.

As Edward is choking on the bile of his own hatred, Elizabeth Barrett and Robert Browning are reciting their vows at the church, with Wilson as one of the witnesses. (Robert and Elizabeth were married in September of 1846. They had fifteen beautiful years together, and she died in her husband's arms on June 29, 1861, in Florence, Italy.)

The Barretts of Wimpole Street was nominated for Best Picture and Norma Shearer was nominated for Best Actress, but lost out to Claudette Colbert in *It Happened One Night* (which also won Best Picture). The play had been immensely successful on the London and New York stages, but missing from the screen version was the incestuous element between the rather perverse father Edward and his invalid daughter, Elizabeth. Knowing that the Hays Office would censor this relationship out, it was only hinted in veiled references throughout the picture. But it was obvious Edward Barrett had an unhealthy fixation on Elizabeth, and Laughton, in the scene where he is clutching his daughter to his bosom, crosses the line. As he warns his eldest daughter that they will be "close" like they used to be when the family moves to the country, there is a rather evil look on his face, "They can't censor the gleam in my eye," said Charles Laughton, in his own defiance to the censors.

Maureen's performance was really one of her best, or perhaps the best of her early career. She has several touching scenes with Norma as the two sisters commiserate over their unfortunate lot as the daughters of the vindictive Edward Barrett. In one scene, Maureen as Henrietta dances and spins around the living room filled with her brothers and sisters, and sings a rousing version of "Little Brown Jug." Later, she convinces her sister Elizabeth (Norma) to sit at the piano and sing an enchanting aria that shows off her beautiful voice, greatly appreciated by the family as they all join in on a second chorus.

In 1992, Maureen noted that a great deal of her education in life came simply from her days as an actress at MGM: "It was very interesting to work on films at Metro during that era because everything was authentic. The books on the set were of that period, the silver was correct, the clothes were handmade. You learned a lot about history just from walking around the set. In *The Barretts of Wimpole Street*, Irving Thalberg had his own methods, and we rehearsed it like a play. We had two weeks rehearsal, which was lovely. But in between takes we had time to enjoy the set, and the clothes and the atmosphere — it was really like being there [in early 19th century London]. It was like you were living that particular moment in time. It was wonderful."

Maureen has several intense moments with Charles Laughton, scenes that were important in her development as a dramatic actress; he had just won the Academy Award as Best Actor, and was one of the acknowledged great actors in the business, both on stage and screen. The character of the father was despicable on good days, and downright evil when he was at his worst, and Charles Laughton recalled in *Film Weekly* his model for the role: "As a matter of fact, I based Mr. Barrett on an acquaintance of mine whose sadism, prudery, and long-drawn-out prayers I had often suffered in my youth."

Film critic Louella Parsons said in her *Los Angeles Examiner* review that this was Maureen's best work as an actress:

> "Irving Thalberg has made many pictures. He has given proof innumerable times of his ability as a producer, but *The Barretts of Wimpole Street* must stand out as finest example of his genius. And genius is the word I mean.
>
> "I use that superlative and rarely deserved word because the whole combination is so perfect — the cast, the beauty of the production, the tempo of the story and the flashes of relieving comedy.
>
> "Two impressive portrayals stand out in addition to Miss Shearer's gorgeous Elizabeth. There is Fredric March, dashing, handsome, and excellent as Robert Browning. You are conscious of his strength, his virility, and his power to save the pathetic little poetess. Then Charles Laughton, who gives a magnificent portrait as the tyrannical, selfish father. What a characterization, and one that won't be forgotten for a long time!
>
> "A very close second to these three principals is Maureen O'Sullivan as Henrietta, younger sister of Elizabeth. Thwarted in love, chilled out of her youthful enthusiasm by her father's cruelty, Maureen reveals unexpected talent in this, her very best performance."

Variety noted that the film was sure box office, with the three big stars heading the cast (October 2, 1934):

"*The Barretts of Wimpole Street*, for all its celluloid lethargy, is box office, insured by Shearer, March and Laughton on the marquee and an artistic cinematic translation of the Katharine Cornell stage success.

"The romance between Elizabeth Barrett (Shearer) and Robert Browning (March) is a beautiful exposition in its ethereal and physically rehabilitating effect on the ailing Miss Barrett. The unnatural love of Papa Barrett is graphically depicted by Charles Laughton, in another of his outstanding screen portraits as the psychopathic, hateful character whose twisted affections for his children, especially daughter Elizabeth, almost proves her physical and spiritual undoing.

"Casting throughout is noteworthy. Not the least of the many good performances is the nifty chore turned in by Marion Clayton as the lisping Bella Hadley. Maureen O'Sullivan, Katharine Alexander, Una O'Connor, and Ralph Forbes all register."

Maureen and Norma spent many long days rehearsing together as sisters Elizabeth and Henrietta Barrett, and the first day that Laughton came on the set with his mutton-chop sideburns, they both pretended to faint dead away! Charles didn't quite see the humor in it and walked off the set, but returned later and no harm was done.

About Charles Laughton, who also played her father in *Payment Deferred*, Maureen remarked candidly: "Charles was a pain to work with, he really was. He would charge into his close-ups and miss his marks, and we'd have to do the scenes over and over. And I didn't know at the time that he really hated me, because he had done the play with his wife Elsa Lanchester and he told me afterwards that he really loathed me because she didn't get the part and I did. I was unaware of that and we became good friends.

"And then he started hating me again during *David Copperfield*, because he wanted Elsa to play the role of Dora, and once again that was my role. So in between hating me," Maureen laughed, "we became very good friends."

In many interviews, Maureen loved to reminisce about Norma Shearer, and the friendship that bloomed on this picture: "Norma was such a flirt. I adored Norma. She didn't mean any harm, but she was a born flirt. She flirted with life, she flirted with every man who came on the set. She flirted with Maurice Chevalier, and I'm sure all these men thought she was madly in love with them — so she probably kept Irving on his toes. I don't know what went on privately," giggled Maureen. "I can't answer that."

"Norma would say to me, 'Maureen, let's go visit Maurice [on the next set] and she would flirt with him shamelessly … she was rather naughty. She would say to him, 'Whose perfume do you like best Maurice, mine or Maureen's?' And of course he would say, 'Why yours, Norma. Yours is the best perfume, and you look so lovely.' And Norma would laugh!

Maureen and Norma Shearer ... they became close friends after portraying the Barrett sisters

"So then she invited me to dinner at her beach house, and she had me seated between Irving and Maurice. And Irving said to me, 'Oh Maureen, you are naughty. I hear you have such a crush on Maurice!'

Maureen said she threw a look at her, thinking, "Norma, I'm going to kill ya!") Of course that comment was spoken in jest, and in this instance she laughed and said, "That naughty Norma."

She also described Norma as "very beautiful in an offbeat way. The cast in her eye I personally thought rather attractive — although you couldn't always be sure whether she was looking at you or not.

"As an actress I found her extraordinarily professional. In a way very studied. She hardly ever varied anything. Yet as a person she could be very flirtatious — she flirted like crazy, in fact, but in a charming way. And yet, underneath it — like the acting — there was something else. She was a very passionate woman."

There were other connections between the two women, of course; Norma's husband Irving Thalberg was the producer of this film, and was responsible for signing Maureen to her first MGM contract. He had also personally chosen her to be Jane in the Tarzan movies, which led to her own stardom. Norma Shearer was a huge star, and her marriage to Thalberg was the stuff from which legends were made. They were one of the original power couples of the Golden Age of Hollywood, and it seemed that their storybook life-style was what every person wanted in this world. Unfortunately, it would all end in barely two years, when Irving Thalberg died prematurely at age 37.

Maureen also commented on the death of Irving Thalberg, and what it meant to her career: "When we finished *The Barretts of Wimpole Street*, Mr. Thalberg liked me very much in the film. He really did. And he had plans for me. If Irving had lived, I would have gone on to a lot of good things — for him.

"I had just finished a Tarzan picture and I went on my honeymoon with John Farrow to Ensenada, Mexico, and we got word that Irving had died. So it was all over when we got back. It was a great shock, but he always looked very frail. But when someone is young and they die, it is a great shock."

1934 was a tremendous year for Maureen regarding the quality of her film work and her growth as an actress, and she had lead roles in three of the biggest MGM hits of the year, *Tarzan and His Mate*, *The Thin Man*, and *The Barretts of Wimpole Street*. The motion picture industry as a whole began rebounding from its darkest days of the Depression, and the turnstiles were clicking at a rate of 75 million customers per week. This was not yet up to the pre-Depression levels of 110 million movie-goers per week, but an improvement of 25% over the previous year.

For many people, attending a movie once a week was the only entertainment they could afford, and they chose carefully which films to attend. However, the MGM studio with all its great stars was usually a surefire bet for getting your quarter's worth of excitement, drama, and sheer adventure.

In November of the year, Charles O'Sullivan came to the United States for his first visit to see his daughter, the Hollywood star. The family patriarch was very interested in learning everything he could about film-making, and in meeting as many as possible of the actors and actresses that worked with Maureen in the picture business.

Charles visited the MGM lot and was given the guided tour for V.I.P.'s, and also met several of the studio bigwigs. He was able to watch his daughter act in front of the camera in *West Point of the Air*, a drama that was released a few months later in 1935.

At one point Maureen's younger sister was supposed to come with Mr. O'Sullivan and have her own audition to try out for the movie business, but he overruled before it ever happened: "I put my foot down on it. Elizabeth is only thirteen, she is too young to come to Hollywood." Maureen also had two other young sisters, Sheila and Patricia, who were ages six and nine respectively at this time. To anyone's knowledge, the three youngest O'Sullivan girls never followed in the footsteps of their famous acting sister.

Maureen with her father Charles O'Sullivan during his 1934 visit to Hollywood

CHAPTER TEN
"At Last ... A Dying Scene"

*D*avid Copperfield, based on the Charles Dickens classic tale, was a gigantic hit for MGM in 1935. It cost more than one million dollars, yet grossed nearly three million dollars during an 86-week run that enchanted American moviegoers. The picture also was exceptionally well-received in England, where the story of the waif Copperfield was practically part of their national heritage. The film wound up being one of the top 10 money makers of the year, and earned an Academy Award nomination for Best Picture.

The biggest stars in the picture were W. C. Fields, Lionel Barrymore, and Maureen O'Sullivan, with the rest of the cast an all-star collection of famous character actors including Edna May Oliver, Lewis Stone, Roland Young, Basil Rathbone, Elsa Lanchester, Jessie Ralph, Lennox Pawle, and Una O'Connor. Portraying the boy was Freddie Bartholomew, a ten-year-old child actor discovered by David O. Selznick, with Frank Lawton as the adult Copperfield.

In describing Selznick, Maureen said in 1992: "He was rather like a large teddy bear. He was a personal friend of John Farrow, and so I knew him away from the studio as well. His hair was rumpled, his tie was awry, and he wore thick, horn-rimmed glasses. He didn't give the appearance of being an intellectual, really.

"I was cast to be Dora in *David Copperfield*, and they didn't have the child actor yet for the part. So John Farrow and myself went to Canada and England searching on behalf of Selznick, but we didn't find him. They did discover Freddie Bartholomew in London for the role of the young David Copperfield."

Maureen's memories of W. C. Fields were mostly censored, and tinged with humor: "The only things I know about him I can't repeat. But when I arrived each day on the set of *David Copperfield*, I would pass him on the street and he would say: 'Good morning, my little Chickadee.' " Only Mr. Fields, of course, could make that line work on a consistent basis.

The well-known story begins in England where a child is born, David Copperfield, six months after his father has died. He lives with his mother Clara (Elizabeth Allen) and Nurse Peggotty (Jessie Ralph), who loves David fiercely like he was her own son. A few years later, Clara gets re-married to Mr. Murdstone (Rathbone), who dismisses Peggotty and replaces her with his own old-maid sister Jane. Murdstone and his sister are both cruel-hearted and treat

David like chattel — he often flogs the lad if he forgets his school lesson. David's mother must stand by helplessly, as she too is dominated by her husband and his heartless sister.

When Clara dies in childbirth, David is sent to London to work in a factory even though he is but a boy of ten. The lad makes friends with Micawber (W. C. Fields), who is somewhat of a rascal and suffers perpetually from financial problems. Eventually, Micawber is arrested and sent to debtors prison, and David sets out to traverse 72 miles to join his aunt in Dover, a relative he has never even seen.

David's dangerous journey sees him being robbed of his only money, selling his coat to buy bread, several days of marching along dusty roads, and a terrible rainstorm that soaks him to the bone. When he finally arrives at the house of Aunt Betsey (Edna May Oliver), she thinks he is just a common beggar and starts to chase him away. But when he proclaims that he is her nephew David, she shrieks with disbelief. In conference with her cousin Mr. Dick (Lennox Paule), they decide the best course of action is to bathe and feed the lad!

David eventually becomes very close to his Aunt Betsey, but he must have an education, so he is sent to Canterbury. While in school, he lives with a wealthy family headed by Mr. Wickfield (Lewis Stone) and his daughter Agnes (Madge Evans). David soon comes to distrust a skulking clerk who works for Wickfield's firm named Uriah Heep (Roland Young). After David finishes his schooling, he moves to London intending to become a writer. He also falls madly in love one day with a young woman he sees at the opera — she is beautiful and charming and her name is Dora (Maureen O'Sullivan).

David (Frank Lawton) announces to his Aunt Betsey and Agnes that he is in love and intends to marry Dora; they are shocked because they had assumed that he returned the love of Agnes. The union of David and Dora has its ups and downs, but they are happy nevertheless. Dora's health is fragile and she becomes ill; she weakens and succumbs, leaving David a young widower in great sorrow.

Young Mr. Copperfield turns his attention to his friends Mr. Wickfield and daughter Agnes, and discovers that Uriah Heep has risen in power to become a partner in the family business. Heep is a knave who wants to take over the whole firm by marrying Agnes, who is repulsed by the lecherous fool. David sees through the treacherous Heep, and intends to expose him for the villain that he is — he only lacks the evidence.

Meanwhile, Micawber is working for Heep, and has been secretly keeping track of the fact that he has been stealing a fortune from Wickfield, mostly by forging his name on financial documents. Finding his courage, Micawber exposes Heep and produces a ledger that proves that he has pilfered bonds and cash from Wickfield. David offers him a choice of returning the stolen goods or going to prison, and Heep has no choice — he turns over his ill-gotten gains and skulks away into the night. Agnes confesses to David that she has always loved him, and now he realizes that she is the woman that he will love the rest of his life.

This was a completely different type of role for Maureen. The young woman, often called the child-wife in the picture, is beautiful but fragile, sweet and innocent yet flighty. For the most part she is incapable of common undertakings such as organizing a dinner or even keeping the household expense ledger.

Almost all of Maureen's scenes were done with Frank Lawton, as well as a funny sequence where the dinner she has supervised for David and his Aunt Betsey and Mr. Dick turns out to be a disaster; the mussels are uncooked and the lamb roast is burned to a crisp — everyone goes hungry that evening.

The actress also did a marvelous job with perhaps the most difficult of dramaturgy, a tragic death scene (with Lawton) where she fades and dies. Late in the story, Dora's fragility turns to illness, and her health begins to fail. The doctors are trying to save her, but they have to inform David that his young wife will soon die. On her death bed they have a heartfelt conversation, and she suggests that perhaps he will be better off without her, that she could never be the wonderful wife that he deserved. David of course refuses to even consider this notion, because he loves Dora with all his heart.

As she weakens, Dora requests a private moment with David's longtime friend Agnes (Madge Evans), who since they were children has secretly been in love with David. With her dying words Dora tells Agnes that she should reveal her feelings to David, before it is too late. When she dies, it is Agnes who brings the sad news to David, who is heartbroken.

Frank Lawton with Maureen O'Sullivan

As Maureen was preparing for the role, she wasn't really sure what director George Cukor wanted from her character of Dora, the child-bride: "I didn't quite understand what he wanted, and I felt I wasn't doing it right," she later noted. "I went for hairdressing tests, and I came back to the set to show George my hairdo, which was the same as the one I'd worn in *The Barretts of Wimpole*

Street. I'd rather fancied myself in that and had pictured Dora as being a more fiery character, which was opposed to George's notion. George was very disappointed. 'Oh,' he said, 'I thought you were going to come up with a new hairdo.'

"George told you explicitly what line reading he wanted," she said. "He was very adamant about exactly what he wished you to do, where to stand, how to move. He wasn't really open to suggestions, and I didn't make any because I was in awe of him. George was not dictatorial or fussy; he just knew what he wanted."

Maureen admitted that she learned a great deal from Cukor, including "the intimacy of the camera, what it shows, what it picks up." The actress also explained that he was a patient director, and showed his actors how to reach "a second level of thinking for the camera."

The actress laughed when recalling her dying scene in *David Copperfield*, in which she was supposed to cry: "I couldn't dredge up a tear," admitted Maureen. "Absolutely none. And they had my close-up, and no tears and director George Cukor twisted my feet, off camera, until I was in agony and that's how he got the tears for the scene. Very mechanical process, and it worked. Like I say, a good director like Cukor could get a great performance out of a stone, if you knew how to do it."

Louella Parsons noted that Maureen's Dora was one of several fine performances in this filmed version of the Dickens' classic: "Maureen O'Sullivan, in the difficult characterization of David's child wife, excels."

The role of Micawber was originally assigned to Charles Laughton, but that didn't work out because of an illness that landed the actor in the hospital. Shortly after production began in September of 1934, Laughton was replaced by W. C. Fields, who was borrowed from Paramount and who turned out to be a marvelous choice as the kind-hearted but financially-challenged Micawber. The actor famous for his bumbling characters and his love of the bottle later said of his role in *David Copperfield*: "I've been playing Micawber all my life under a lot of different names, and never knew it. He's the kind of guy who is always expecting something to turn up to help him out of his present difficulties, and is always having difficulties waiting for something to turn up. You know the type. Of course, this is the first time in my life I ever played a character part. At first, I was a little wary about playing Micawber, but as soon as I got into the part, I knew it was made to order."

Director George Cukor later became a close friend of Maureen's, and they exchanged long letters over a period of many years until his death in 1983. Cukor directed many classic films in his career, and he was known for getting fine performances from his actors (especially women); he certainly coaxed superb dramatic performances from his child-actor Freddie Bartholomew, as well as from Maureen O'Sullivan. In writing of the great collaborations of Cukor and producer David O. Selznick, author David Thomson has high praise for this particular film: "... the magnificent *David Copperfield*, still a landmark in literary adaptation because of its fidelity to the spirit and the look of Dickens."

The critics from the day also loved this screen version of Charles Dickens' story, and it was lauded and applauded as a great film. Louella Parsons of the *Los Angeles Examiner* gushed over the film in her review, and also noted that Maureen excelled in her difficult role of Dora (February 9, 1935):

> "The spirit of those beloved characters in *David Copperfield* has been captured in an unbelievably realistic and delightful manner in the screen version now playing at Loew's State and Grauman's Chinese theaters. I dreaded to see my old friend, Micawber, my adored Betsey Trotwood, David himself, Uriah Heep, Agnes Wickfield, little Dora on the screen, because I had a terrific fear that we should see a moviefied edition of Charles Dickens, a thing I couldn't bear. David Selznick, who produced *Copperfield,* and George Cukor, who directed it, have done a beautiful job.
>
> "You cannot single out any one character, each one is so well done. Of course, Freddie Bartholomew is wonderful. He is so sweet, so sincere and such a darling, you feel that you could feed his cruel stepfather rat poison, which only goes to show what a grand performance Basil Rathbone gives.
>
> "Edna May Oliver's Aunt Betsey is a classic. W. C. Fields is Micawber; he is so perfect. Roland Young makes Uriah Heep absolutely loathsome — an accomplishment. Maureen O'Sullivan, in the difficult characterization of David's child wife, excels. Then there is Frank Lawton, as the grown-up David. There isn't one bad or indifferent performance. The beautiful part of *David Copperfield* is that it lives and becomes a reality in the performance of these players, who are all so excellent."

Being a well-known celebrity on at least two continents, Maureen often was called upon to entertain visitors to Hollywood, especially ones who were desirous of meeting her. On January 19, 1935, the *Evening Herald Express* reported her social calendar as having a royal tinge to it: "Maureen O'Sullivan lunching with a princess one day and British Consul Gerney the next day ..."

Another item in the *Los Angeles Examiner* of February 4, 1935 in the "I Cover Hollywood" column by Lloyd Pantages noted that the actress had a soft heart for canines, and they were beginning to overrun her apartment: "Maureen O'Sullivan's menage looks vaguely like the City Pound for she collects all the stray dogs that come her way ..."

On February 20, the *Evening Herald Express* reported that a huge fire at the fashionable Voltaire apartments at 1428 Crescent Heights put several of the residents out on the street, including Maureen and John Farrow, who were photographed in their pajamas, and actor Alan Hale. According to the news item, the fire rose to 150 feet in the air and it took eleven fire companies to put out the blaze.

It was also not surprising that Maureen was subsequently forced to find a new apartment, as noted by Reine Davies in the "Hollywood Parade" column of the LA *Examiner* on March 2, 1935:

"Maureen O'Sullivan entertained as her weekend guests the retiring French consul, Henry Didot, and his wife. Maureen has recently moved into a new apartment, and they were her first guests."

And according to journalist Harrison Carroll of the *Evening Herald Express*, Maureen was taking navigation lessons at the University of Southern California in preparation of co-piloting a yacht that was purchased and being delivered to John Farrow. The couple had been guests of Johnny Weissmuller on his sailing vessel, *The Allure*, a number of times, and they had such a good time that Farrow ordered his own boat.

Speaking of Weissmuller, a year after the release of *Tarzan and His Mate*, the film was still playing to great crowds in small towns across the country. Two capsule reviews from the *Motion Picture Herald* in March of 1935 noted the continued popularity of Johnny and Maureen in the second installment of their jungle adventures:

"*Tarzan and His Mate*: Johnny Weissmuller, Maureen O'Sullivan — "In spite of this being nearly a year old, it drew the best Friday-Saturday business for us that we've had this winter." — A. N. Miles, Eminence Theatre, Eminence, Ky. Small Town Patronage.

"*Tarzan and His Mate:* Johnny Weissmuller, Maureen O'Sullivan — "A wonderful picture. Every minute enjoyed here. Old but that didn't keep them away." Running time, 105 Minutes. Played March 14-15. — J. T. Justice, Jr. Pickfair Theatre, Kernersville, N.C. Small Town Patronage.

When she was growing up in Ireland, Maureen was the daughter of a soldier; her father was a retired major of the Connaught Rangers. She was able to draw on that experience for her role as an Army brat in *West Point of the Air*, an aviation drama about the training of Army Air Corps fighter pilots during a period when there were rumblings of war coming from Europe. Top-billed was Wallace Beery as Sergeant "Big Mike" Stone, a career soldier who trains pilots at Randolph Field in Texas for the Army. The second lead was Robert Young as his son, "Little Mike," who is a top West Point graduate but while training under his father suffers a series of tragic mishaps which force him to the brink of quitting the military.

The tough-yet-wise General Carter was played by venerable Lewis Stone, Maureen co-starred as his daughter Skip, Russell Hardie was her brother Phil, and in one of her earliest roles, Rosalind Russell was tall and seductive as the vampish Dare Marshall. Also in a very minor role as a pilot trainee was Robert Taylor, who would soon become a major star; in this picture he had one short scene and one very brief line to speak.

The story begins at West Point, where Mike Stone (Young) is about to graduate with honors, and he is also a star on the football team. Mike has grown up with Skip Carter (Maureen), who has been in love with him since they were children. Also in the same graduating class is Phil Carter, who is best friends with Little Mike. They both are intent on becoming pilots for the Army.

When Mike Stone leads his team to a victory over Navy in the annual Army-Navy game, Dare asks Big Mike to introduce her to his son, the football star. The sophisticated Dare moves in quickly and gets involved with Mike, squeezing Skip out of the picture and leaving her as "just a friend" in the heart of the man she loves.

When the training starts at Randolph Field, Big Mike is assigned as trainer for both his own son Mike and Phil Carter, the son of the general. On the night before an important training flight, Dare has Mike out partying when he should have been resting at his quarters. The next day, Phil crashes his plane while trying to avoid Mike's auto on the runway, rushing in late after his night of carousing.

The result is that one of Phil's legs has to be amputated, and Mike feels guilty for causing the accident. Both the general and Big Mike absolve him of blame, saying that Phil should have been able to avert the crash. Skip is overcome with grief at the hospital when visiting her brother, whose career as a pilot is over.

On the day of his flying test, Mike causes a mid-air collision which sends his fellow pilot to a fiery crash below. Mike is so distraught over causing the accident, he doesn't notice that his own landing gear is damaged. Big Mike jumps in a plane and flies up to meet his son's plane, then bravely jumps to his son's disabled aircraft and lands safely with a "pancake" landing. He wants his son to take credit for the landing, and in the ensuing argument, the father punches his own son. According to military law, Sergeant Mike is arrested for striking an officer — in this case his own son, Lt. Mike Stone.

At the court martial, General Carter cannot be lenient even for his good friend, and Sergeant Mike Stone is stripped of his rank and kicked out of the service. The younger Mike subsequently decides to quit the Army and goes to see his father, who is working as a mechanic and also hitting the bottle. Mike's father tells him to stick it out, and stand up and "be a man." But Mike has lost his courage, and tells his father he's going to skip his last assignment that evening, a flare drop during flight maneuvers. Big Mike tells him he'll do the flare drop himself in his rickety old plane, but Little Mike doesn't take his drunken father seriously.

Back at the base, Dare has convinced Mike to sign his resignation papers and turn them in immediately. Skip arrives to confront Mike about his decision, lecturing him about duty and honor as Dare stands by with little to say. When Mike hears his father's old plane in the sky, he jumps in his own plane to stop him from killing himself. Big Mike does the flare drop, but indeed his old plane breaks apart and crashes in a lake. Little Mike is right behind him and crash lands in the lake, risking his own life to save his father. He manages to remove Big Mike from the burning wreckage, and pulls him safely to shore.

At the graduation ceremony, Big Mike has been restored to his former rank of sergeant by the Secretary of the Army, and is given the honor of pinning the wings on his son, the Army aviator. Mike has also come to his senses concerning his love life, and is back together with Skip, his true love.

West Point of the Air was an outstanding drama with a superb cast, and really brought home the patriotic theme of the bravery of the American Army pilots. It was a realistic motion picture because it was filmed with the cooperation of the Army Air Corps, and location shooting took place at Randolph Field, Texas. Several planes were crashed by stuntmen; in some of the scenes dozens of planes assemble in various formations, followed by an evacuation of paratroopers that filled the skies majestically in their descent to the earth.

Maureen was now an integral part of the MGM family, and she knew or had worked with many of the great stars employed by Louis B. Mayer and the studio. Wallace Beery was a huge star during the 1930s, and he was fresh from the success of perhaps his most famous role as Long John Silver in *Treasure Island* (1934). Most of Beery's characters were "everyman" types that movie audiences could relate to in their own lives. He was like the guy next door, or a brother or uncle that you knew.

Beery was also a powerful actor who could draw sympathy from a turnip — with a character like Big Mike you couldn't help but root for the guy. The father-son relationship was the crux of this story, and their very genuine emotions made this drama a cut above the average aviation picture. *West Point of the Air* was the second of three films that Maureen would do with Beery, and this was the third time she had been the flame of Robert Young.

Maureen had several fine dramatic scenes in the story. When she is jilted by Young for the "other woman" (Rosalind Russell), she shows her pain yet nonchalantly tries to laugh it off. Another fine moment was when her brother Phil (Hardie) tragically loses a leg in a plane crash. She bravely carries on a conversation with him as he lies in his hospital bed, and hasn't yet realized that his leg has been amputated. And also the scene in which her character of Skip accidentally breaks in on Mike and the flashy Dare, who is prodding him to resign from the Army. She gives him a good lecture on patriotism, bravery, and fighting for just causes rather than taking the easy way out. In the end she wins her man back, giving him a transfusion of her own courage to help him regain his self-respect and the admiration of his father.

Variety described the picture as an average programmer that had its exciting moments and a strong cast (April 10, 1935):

"*West Point of the Air* follows what has become a routine formula for service scripts. Has the benefit of a first-class production plus a commendable cast.

"Effort of an old army sergeant (Wallace Beery) to make both a man and an air ace out of his son (Robert Young) is the highlight of the story. But they are overshadowed, as far as entertainment merit is concerned, by the atmospheric flying stuff. Because there's little or nothing in the flying line that hasn't been done and seen before, this one is apt to be regarded as just another aviation picture.

"As a flying picture from a technical standpoint, this one is aces. For playing support, Beery has lots of help. Lewis Stone makes a good general. Maureen O'Sullivan is fine as the nice girl, and Rosalind Russell shows much promise as the not-so-nice one. Robert Young doesn't stand up at all times as a swell-headed boy, but he's a good enough performer to cover up a natural deficiency in his assignment."

A snapshot review from the *Motion Picture Herald* called the picture a winner and well worth the price of admission (July 20, 1935):

"*West Point of the Air:* Wallace Beery, Robert Young, Maureen O'Sullivan — "Saw this picture in Omaha before our showing and was in a position to tell them all about it. Recommended it to our patrons as a 100 percent entertainment. Grossed our largest three-day business this season. Wallace Beery excels his work in all previous productions. Don't fail to tell your patrons about West Point. Many returned for second night and the neighboring towns came drifting in as reports reach them of the goodness of the picture. Some wonderful scenes and thrilling shots and the story is excellent." — John J. Metzger, Oriental Theatre, Beaver City, Neb. Small Town Patronage.

One of the great British stage actors was George Arliss, who was persuaded to come to Hollywood to make movies at the age of sixty. He promptly won an Academy Award for his stunning portrayal in *Disraeli* (1929). Over the next few years he played kings, statesmen, rajahs, and eccentric millionaires.

In 1935, he was cast as the title character in *Cardinal Richelieu,* a historical drama set in 17th century France. Arliss was magnificent as one of history's arch-politicians, the cleric and advisor to King Louis whose great ambition was to unite France into a European power, rather than a conglomeration of numerous small kingdoms.

Maureen O'Sullivan portrayed his ward Lenore, and Cesar Romero played her young suitor Andre de Pons. Also in the outstanding cast were Edward Arnold as King Louis XIII, Douglas Dumbrille as Baradas, Violet Kemble Cooper as Queen Marie, and Francis Lister as Gaston.

On an interesting side note, Reginald Sheffield was cast as Richelieu's outrider; the British character actor was the father of Johnny Sheffield, who would later be chosen as Boy in the Tarzan pictures, with Maureen as his screen mother, Jane.

The story begins in the year 1630, as a group of feudal lords are locked in a power struggle with Cardinal Richelieu (Arliss), who is the omnipotent minister to King Louis XIII (Arnold). Richelieu has prepared an edict to strip them of their lands, and before the nobles can request that the pope intercede, the king signs the document.

The leader of the nobles is Count Baradas, who convinces the queen mother that Richelieu is insane and power mad. She in turn informs the king that Richelieu has accepted a huge bribe from the Duke of Normandy, and is using the money to build his own palace. She reasons that Richelieu is a disloyal subject whose actions may lead to a civil war.

Entering the palace through a secret door, Richelieu explains to the king that the money is being used to build up the royal army, and that the palace when completed will be turned over to the king as a gift. Richelieu is a brilliant orator, and he convinces King Louis of his loyalty.

Meanwhile, Richelieu's ward Lenore (Maureen) has fallen in love with Andre de Pons (Romero), who is on the cardinal's death list because of his conspiracy with the nobles to resist the edict. When the king meets Lenore he lusts after her, and insists that she be brought to court so that she can be married. Richelieu refuses this request, knowing that this is just an excuse for the king to be able to conveniently seduce Lenore.

Eventually an alliance forms between Andre and Richelieu, who convinces the younger man that France must be unified to defeat England, Austria, and Spain, who are arming against her. Richelieu tests Andre's love of Lenore with a threat of death, and when he passes the test, they are permitted to marry.

With war looming, the king's army is led out of Paris by Richelieu himself, and then turned over to commander Le Moyne in preparation for battle with the Spanish troops. But Baradas and the queen mother have conspired to take a secret treaty to the Spanish forces, and Andre is persuaded by Baradas that he must assassinate Richelieu for the good of France.

Andre later realizes that he has been tricked, and that Richelieu has the best interest of France in his heart. While Andre convinces Baradas that he has strangled Richelieu, the cardinal has confronted the queen mother and gained possession of the treaty. As he is taking the document to the king, Richelieu is surrounded by the king's guard who move to seize him. He then raises a cross and proclaims, as a priest, that he has a circle of sanctuary and must be allowed to approach the king.

Richelieu makes a grand gesture and presents the treaty to the king, revealing the conspiracy that threatened the monarchy. He then declares that France is now united into a great kingdom — therefore, all of its power belongs to Louis XIII, and he, Richelieu, is the king's shadow.

Maureen O'Sullivan was loaned to 20th Century Pictures for a lead role in *Cardinal Richelieu*. Once again she turned in her usual fine performance as the young woman that all men lust after, including Edward Arnold's King Louis and Cesar Romero's dashing French nobleman, Andre de Pons.

Maureen was the love interest in almost every one of her films, and she eventually kissed most of the handsome young leading men of Hollywood. For the lucky male actors it wasn't exactly unpleasant work — many were still hoping that John Farrow might eventually lose his grip on her heart and she would be once again on the open romantic market.

Rather humorously, in the scene where the very tall Cesar Romero must kiss the petite Maureen O'Sullivan, it was necessary for him to stoop to do so. That, of course, was against the basic Hollywood rules for love-making. It was suggested by the studio that an eight-inch stool be placed under her. That was tried but didn't turn out so well. It was finally decided that Romero would have to lift her off the ground every time the script called for a kiss.

When *Cardinal Richelieu* was released in April of 1935 it was given excellent reviews, which were typified by this excerpt from *Film Daily*:

> "This is a class production that will satisfy all the George Arliss fans. As the witty, resourceful uncrowned ruler of France, who outwits his enemies at every turn, Arliss gives an outstanding portrayal. Another praiseworthy characterization is that furnished by Edward Arnold as King Louis. The picture has been ideally cast down to its smallest role, and Rowland V. Lee has turned in a laudable directorial job. Cesar Romero and Maureen O'Sullivan are excellent as the young lovers."

Variety called the picture one of Arliss' best roles, with excellent acting from the cast and an honorable mention going to Maureen (April 24, 1935):

> "*Richelieu* provides George Arliss with one of the most effective vehicles given him since he went in for the historical cycle ... A fine technical production, its appeal becomes perforce limited because of the nature of the subject, and the secular aura emanating from the central character ... Most of the opportunity goes to the star, but Edward Arnold makes a very human Louis and Haliwell Hobbes, as the prelate's secretary, is a quiet yet always efficient foil with the others all rating honorable mention without gaining special distinction. Douglas Dumbrille is effective as Louis' chief aide, Maureen O'Sullivan's ingenue is one of those things. Cesar Romero bespeaks of future promise as her vis-a-vis."

After the success of *Cardinal Richelieu*, Maureen spoke with Reine Davies of the L.A. *Examiner* and admitted that even after five years in Hollywood, she was still awed by the actors and actresses with whom she had worked. She noted that she prepared meticulously for each role so as not to embarrass herself when working with the greats of the screen, including Academy Award winners George Arliss, Charles Laughton, Wallace Beery, and Marie Dressler:

"No one could be more tremulously awed when meeting a great star for the first time. I even collect their pictures on the quiet," said Maureen in April of 1935.

"Working with them doesn't make a bit of difference. Marie Dressler, Norma Shearer, Greta Garbo, George Arliss — Mr. Arliss in particular. When I lived in Ireland, I would go with friends to see him on the stage. We would sit and sigh in unison over his great artistry.

"Then one day to be working with him in *Richelieu* — it was a little too much. Before every scene with him, I had to give myself a 'pep' talk to fortify my waning courage.

"But my hero-worshipping, and the fact that I can't assume the matter-of-fact movieland attitude toward them, oddly enough has been a boon to my career. For, being in awe of them, I find myself driven to exacting preparation for each of my roles, so that I will not blunder in scenes with them.

"Yes, I'm a natural born movie fan."

When Maureen was allowed a brief break in her schedule in May of 1935, she wanted to see one of the natural wonders of the world, the Grand Canyon in Arizona. She flew into the area for a weekend getaway and arrived at the huge natural ravine on Saturday evening, which was experiencing a blinding rainstorm. She was able to stand on the edge of the canyon, but all the beauty and grandeur were obscured.

The weather didn't cooperate on Sunday, and an early Monday morning call at MGM forced her to return before the weather cleared. Maureen was disappointed, and the news report in the *Evening Herald Examiner* said that she was "downright exasperated" that her short vacation was rained out. Despite being there, she still hadn't seen the Grand Canyon.

At Metro-Goldwyn-Mayer, when Mr. Louis B. Mayer called, you answered. In the case of Maureen's next film, *The Flame Within*, she inherited the role of an emotionally disturbed woman that was supposed to go to another actress. When Merle Oberon was unable to accept the part, Maureen was assigned the role of Lillian Belton, a British socialite living in New York.

Top-billed was Ann Harding as psychiatrist Mary White, who is so dedicated to her work that she continually puts off the marriage proposals of Dr. Gordon Phillips (Herbert Marshall), who is devoted to her and is willing to wait forever if necessary.

The writer and director was Edmund Goulding, who had a reputation of coaxing fine performances from actresses in filmed melodrama. This was certainly the case here, as Ann Harding and Maureen had the most important roles and turned in fine dramatic portrayals. Meanwhile, Herbert Marshall, Louis Hayward and Henry Stephenson remained on the periphery as supporting characters. Goulding's most famous work was *Grand Hotel*, and *The Flame*

Within may have had similar intentions in gazing at the inner workings of people's lives. This was a cut above the typical 1930s melodrama, using the themes of love, unrequited love, alcoholism, and suicide to weave its tangled web.

Maureen as the suicidal Lillian Belton in *The Flame Within*

As the story begins, Lillian Belton (Maureen) has just attempted suicide by cutting her wrists. She survives, and later is attended to by her physician Dr. Gordon Phillips (Marshall). He in turn refers the troubled young woman to Dr. White (Harding), hoping that she can discover the emotional trauma that has driven her to such despair.

Mary White is a brilliant psychiatrist, and when her good friend Gordon proposes to her at the annual Hospital Circus Ball, she turns him down once again. He had made the same proposal one year earlier, and although she admits to loving him as well, she cannot take the time away from her work to have a normal life. Their friendship continues, and he will patiently wait for the woman he loves.

When Mary begins treating her patient, she discovers that Lillian feels hopelessly in love with a young man who is an alcoholic, and treats her like she really doesn't matter to him. She is so distraught, in fact, that when the doctor turns away for a moment, Lillian opens a window and steps to the ledge. Dr. White grabs her before she can jump, and tells her that no problem would be answered by this solution.

Dr. White asks to meet Jack Kerry (Hayward), who is the life of the party and drinks from morning until night each day. The moment he arrives at her home, he makes himself a drink to chase away last night's hangover. After their session, Jack comes back that evening while Mary is out, and crashes on her couch in a drunken stupor.

Mary later convinces Jack that he could straighten out his life and perhaps he should appreciate Lillian, who loves him very much. He agrees to go to a clinic for treatment of his alcoholism, and after several months he is showing signs of improvement. Mary and Gordon visit him and he demonstrates a chair he has designed for use in airplanes, that he hopes to market in the near future. Lillian joins them and is amazed at the new sober and industrious Jack, and later she joyfully accepts his proposal of marriage.

After the wedding, the young couple join Mary and Gordon at a dinner dance. Jack asks Mary to dance, and he then tells her privately that he is in love — with the doctor. Dr. White rejects this notion, but she too has developed some feelings for her former patient. When Lillian sees her husband dancing closely with Mary White, and gazing in her eyes, she begins to see the truth. Lillian has a tremendous argument with Jack, and accuses Dr. White of trying to break up her marriage.

Dr. White later consoles Jack that this infatuation between them is just that — and could only destroy both of their lives. She convinces him to return to Lillian and dedicate himself to enjoying his marriage to the beautiful young woman who loves him. Mary also decides that she must now accept the proposal of Gordon, and they plan to marry.

A review in the *Hollywood Citizen News* (May 24, 1935) by Jerry Hoffman called the film "intriguing," and from the standpoint of fine dramatic acting, this was true:

> "It won't be long before movie fans know all about psychiatry. *The Flame Within* is an unusual story headed by as fine a cast of dramatic actors as can be found in Hollywood. Ann Harding and Herbert Marshall are the two central figures. Ann, as a famed woman psychiatrist, is called upon to straighten out a youthful dipsomaniac so that a spoiled wealthy girl won't insist upon killing herself over him. Marshall is an equally famous surgeon, in love with Harding.

In regenerating the boy, the lady doctor finds he has become part of her life. After the young man is cured of his liquor-passion and weds the wealthy girl, he realizes that he has come to love the psychiatrist.

"New is Louis Hayward, who portrays the juvenile sort. He proves an unusually good actor, worthy of being cast in the company of splendid artists such as the lovely Harding and the charming Herbert Marshall. Maureen O'Sullivan is very good as the girl with the suicidal mania and Henry Stephenson rounds out the quintet of brilliant principals. Goulding offers something novel in his treatment and direction."

Variety noted that *The Flame Within* was a well-acted melodrama, and that Maureen was credited with some "splendid trouping" in her role as the unstable Lillian Belton (June 5, 1935):

"Miss Harding combining looks with a doctor-like penetration, holds the pivot position within the story and makes far-fetched possibility seem to have an affinity with everyday realism. Maureen O'Sullivan does some splendid trouping as the girl who loves too well. Marshall's role is a trifle stiff since he is called upon to impersonate a passive pillar of moral strength upon whose shoulder the confused lady doctor may at last rest.

"It would be untrue to say that Louis Hayward, new film recruit from legit, steals the picture but he will probably get most of the written comment because of his newness and his excellent performance. He plays the drunk with plenty of conviction. Not particularly handsome but a good, serious type and the camera and mike both do well by him. And Edmund Goulding has generously allotted him a multiplicity of close-ups."

Ann Harding was a major star of the 1930s, and film historian David Thomson said of the actress: "Elegant, refined, serene, classy, superior, noble, aristocratic — perhaps 'patrician' best suggests the quality Ann Harding conveyed at the height of her starring career, from 1929 through the mid-thirties."

That's a mighty long list of superlatives, but after viewing her fine performance in *The Flame Within*, it doesn't seem to be unjustified. Of her co-star in the picture, Maureen later noted her kindness and professionalism:

"Ann Harding, with whom I had to play a rather difficult scene in a film called *The Flame Within*, was one [who treated her kindly] ... I was not worried about it, but everyone was thinking I was just not able to do it and that made me nervous. She said: 'Remember one thing — that an emotion released is an emotion lost.' In other words, always keep something back for the imagination of your audiences. A couple of little things like that stand out in my mind."

In speaking of Louis B. Mayer some thirty years after leaving MGM, Maureen stated in an interview that the head of the studio was all-powerful but that the portrait painted of him was not always truthful or accurate:

"Many of the tales about Louis B. Mayer were true — to an extent," said Maureen. "He was a very emotional man and did put on quite an act, but I must say that I do hate to hear or read these things about him because I am terribly against them being said about people when they are dead. At the time, Mayer was king of the lot, people trembled in their boots when he came around, and he was treated with great respect, I didn't have any of these strange experiences that these other actresses tell of how awful he was — I found him very polite, very pleasant.

"Most of the books being written now, I suppose, are by young people who have never met their subjects so rumors have grown — so young people like Judy Garland, perhaps an oversensitive girl, come out badly. I was never given any drugs or shots or anything like that.

"In fact, I never heard of it at the time. It is only in later years that I heard these strange things. I was never even chased around a desk — a disappointment to me, I must say. It didn't speak well for my sex appeal! It all seems to have grown larger than life as far as I can tell."

Maureen had plenty of sex appeal, but she had her protectors at MGM, including Mr. Mayer. She was one of his favorites, and to mistreat Maureen in any way would have brought the hammer down on the perpetrator. She had other friends in high places as well, including her co-star in the Tarzan pictures Johnny Weissmuller, so Maureen went about her days unscathed and unscarred by the working environment at MGM. In her own naive way, she was one of the fortunate.

"At Metro-Goldwyn-Mayer, we saw always the best of everybody," noted Maureen. "Happy memories and a golden era — of course it's not very original to say that. I think that MGM brought out the best in everybody. I don't remember mean people, I don't remember unpleasant people, or cruel people. I only remember the best, and that's a wonderful thing to be able to say after all those years. There was something about the studio, something about the people. They were good people — they brought out everything that was good in you. I find it hard to sum it up, except to say that they were years I wish everybody could have had somehow.

"We didn't realize at the time that film is forever. So these people will never really be forgotten. It's an immortality that film has given people. Now it would be nice to be collecting residuals and money and what not," said Maureen with a wistful smile. "But you have to settle for what you get."

CHAPTER ELEVEN
"Accused of Murder ... Woman on the Lam"

In 1935, Maureen O'Sullivan was accused of murder, chased by the police, shot at — and even considered suicide. Of course, this all happened in the MGM crime drama *Woman Wanted*, in which she was top-billed and co-starred with Joel McCrea. The impressive cast included Lewis Stone as the tough district attorney, Louis Calhern as the mob boss who leaves a trail of bodies in his wake, Adrienne Ames as the beauty who has Joel McCrea hog-tied (until he meets Maureen), and a superb portrayal by Robert Grieg as the butler Peedles, whose loyalty to McCrea is complemented by his sublime sense of humor.

It was difficult for a woman to get top billing in Hollywood in the Golden Age, and this was the first time on the top of the marquee for Maureen while under contract to MGM. Joel McCrea was approaching stardom, but he hadn't quite arrived yet — in this picture he showed the qualities that would make him a star for more than two decades. Two fine portrayals, *Foreign Correspondent* (1940) and *Sullivan's Travels* (1941), turned Joel McCrea into a household name, and by the 1950s his forte would be as a weathered cowboy hero.

This was a serious crime drama with a wee bit of comedy, in a similar fashion to the smash hit, *The Thin Man*. There was some subtle humor and also a few scenes that were raucously funny — including one where Maureen and McCrea get the local constable drunk on apple jack to facilitate their escape. They too become inebriated, and Maureen O'Sullivan doing a drunk scene was pretty funny stuff! Besides her hiccuping, she does an imitation of Ma Kettle to fool some hoods who are searching for her. When they do make their getaway, they are weaving down the country roads like a couple of drunken fools.

The story begins as a jury deliberates the fate of Ann Grey (Maureen), who is accused of killing gangster Ted Arnold. While Ann awaits the decision, lawyer Tony Baxter (McCrea) flirts with her from across the building air space, and pantomimes a request for a lunch date. Ann laughs it off, for her fate rests in the hands of the jurors.

After she is found guilty, Ann manages to escape with the help of crime boss Smiley (Calhern), who thinks she is holding a quarter-million in stolen bonds. Smiley's hoods cause an accident to the police transport vehicle, and Ann slips away in the confusion. As fate would have it, Tony Baxter's car is nearby — she hitches a ride and hastily agrees to his offer of lunch.

They go back to his hotel so she can clean the dirt off her clothes, and the hotel dick recognizes Ann from her picture in the newspaper. The detective calls for the police, as the couple ride the elevator to Baxter's suite. Tony finally discovers that she is Ann Grey, and realizes that he has a fugitive on his hands. Things get further complicated when his fiancée Betty (Adrienne Ames) shows up at the hotel, and he has his butler Peedles hide Ann in the bedroom.

The resourceful Peedles manages to keep Ann hidden from the police, who give up the search. Tony tells Betty that he has to go out to help a client, and she warns him that he better show up that evening at their engagement party. Finally alone, Ann explains to Tony that she got mixed up with the wrong crowd when she came to New York, including gangster Monk Shelby, but she proclaims her innocence in the murder ordeal.

When Shelby calls Ann at Tony's apartment, the gangster says the whole mess can be straightened out. Tony agrees to drive her to the meeting place in the country, but it turns out to be a trap set by Joe Metz, one of Smiley's stooges. Beneath a hail of bullets, Tony and Ann escape down a country road, but the gangsters are in close pursuit. Unbeknownst to them, Shelby is just a dupe and is left to die in a ditch with eight bullet wounds.

With the help of some chicanery, Tony and Ann elude the Smiley gang and are then arrested by a local constable for entering Ma Purdy's roadside diner, closed for the evening. They manage to

Maureen and Joel McCrea in *Woman Wanted*

get the amiable officer drunk on apple jack, and make good their escape back to town. Tony is picked up by the police and taken to see District Attorney Martin (Lewis Stone), who prosecuted Ann in the murder trial. Tony claims to know nothing about her whereabouts, but Martin receives a call from Ann saying that she wants to come in and surrender, before anyone else is killed.

Her nerves frazzled, Ann has a gun and considers using it on herself. Just then a hand reaches out and covers her mouth. She is kidnaped by Joe Metz, who puts a bullet in Peedles, as he was attempting to protect Ann. Tony and Martin arrive to call a doctor for Peedles, who will survive his superficial wound.

Meanwhile, in a meeting with Smiley, Ann is threatened if she doesn't turn over the bonds; she is told that Monk Shelby has already been killed. Tony leads Martin and the police to the Show Boat Café, the nightclub owned by Smiley. Tony goes into the club first to find Ann, and is knocked unconscious by Joe Metz. The smooth-talking Smiley tells D. A. Martin that he doesn't have the girl, just as his men have slipped her out the back way and escaped in a speedboat with both Ann and Tony as hostages.

The police have set their own trap, and fire upon the gangsters with a machine gun from a police gunboat. Smiley tries to shoot his way out of the nightclub, but is wounded and arrested by Martin. Monk Shelby has survived his wounds and has implicated Smiley in the death of Arnold, which vindicates Ann. Tony and Ann speed away in the police boat for a romantic getaway, and the deal is sealed with a kiss between them.

Richard Boleslawski, the Polish stage director who came to Hollywood in 1930 and made several outstanding films before his premature death in 1937, began as director of *Woman Wanted*. Plans changed and Boleslawski was assigned to another picture, and eventually was replaced by George B. Seitz, who had a reputation as a no-nonsense director who got the job done quickly and efficiently, as Maureen recalled in 1974:

"*Woman Wanted* was directed by George B. Seitz who worked like a streak! I think he was a very underrated director; he was always handed all the "B" pictures and he would bring them in on an extraordinary schedule in a very few days. I liked working fast. Richard Thorpe was like Seitz — ground them out and brought them in well ahead of schedule."

The acting from the entire cast was superb including stars Maureen and McCrea, Louis Calhern as the gang boss and Noel Madison as his subordinate Joe Metz, Erville Anderson as the easily inebriated constable, Adrienne Ames as the gorgeous dame who has her hooks in McCrea, and also Edgar Kennedy as the exasperated hotel detective.

In one of his finest portrayals, Lewis Stone was the tough district attorney who prosecutes Maureen, and then responds to the press that she will get the death penalty, regardless that she is a woman. Stone was often the fatherly type in many of his roles, but here he was hard-boiled in his dealings with the criminal element, which included Maureen until she was later proven innocent.

The butler Peedles was played with gusto by Robert Grieg, who made a living playing similar characters in many motion pictures. Here he was just plain funny in a very droll manner, and capable of easily outwitting the cops who are pursuing Maureen, and coming up with brilliant remedies to every quagmire in which he becomes entangled. Finally, he is shot trying to protect Maureen from the gangsters, proving to be heroic rather than just comedic.

For the role of Tony Baxter, both Franchot Tone and Wallace Beery were considered but the part went to McCrea, who was the perfect complement to Maureen O'Sullivan. No other actor could have been any better than McCrea as the lawyer who gets involved with the dame on the lam, gets caught in the cross fire of the police and gangsters who are both chasing the purported murderess Ann Grey, and finally and inevitably falls in love with her.

The critics applauded this film when it was released and the audiences raved as noted in several 1935 reviews:

Motion Picture Herald (July 27, 1935)

"This is based on an exciting premise. It's 10, 20 and 30 percent melodrama, making use of the theatrical effects that made that type of legitimate entertainment so popular, but produced on a somewhat higher scale. In idea, *Woman Wanted,* the title being of definite exploitation quality, is a romance with a gangster menace background which is not lacking in comedy or the madcap adventure ingredients that delight the thrill fans.

"Built of the materials that usually interest the masses, its particular appeal being directed to those who enjoy tingling action entertainment, and uses the other romantic, comic and semi-mystery features to intrigue the run-of-the-mill fans, looks to the best selling medium." — McCarthy, Hollywood.

Film Daily (August 10, 1935)

"Thoroughly enjoyable entertainment combining action, suspense and romantic interest. There's plenty doing in this yarn to make it a nicely satisfying affair for audiences at large. Love interest between Miss O'Sullivan and McCrea is pleasing, and there is a good sprinkling of comedy touches among the more melodramatic activities, all nicely paced by director George B. Seitz."

Evening Herald Express, W. E. Oliver (September 29, 1935)

"A high-spirited murder mystery, romantically pairing Maureen O'Sullivan and Joel McCrea, *Woman Wanted* has a lot of *The Thin Man* eclat about it. Miss O'Sullivan is seen as a girl convicted of a gang murder and McCrea is the young attorney whose romantic interest in her starts him on the most exciting and unorthodox case of his life.

"Love enters, of course, but the events are so fast and tense that there is little time for conventional goo-goos. The spine-tingling is done to the accompaniment of comedy, a very acceptable formula for action."

Motion Picture Herald "What the Picture Did For Me"

Woman Wanted: Maureen O'Sullivan, Joel McCrea — "A murder mystery that is different and better than most of the cycle of murder films. Excitement, thrills and romance with a good cast that will please any audience. Hope they star Joel McCrea in another picture soon. He is great. Played September 21-22." — Gladys E. McArdle, Owl Theatre, Lebanon, Kan. Small Town Patronage. (October 5, 1935)

Woman Wanted: Maureen O'Sullivan, Joel McCrea — "A dandy and well-liked. Splendid entertainment." Played November 22-23. — M. W. Mattecheck, Lark Theatre, McMinnville, Ore. Local Patronage (December 14, 1935)

Anna Karenina was Maureen's next work for MGM, with Greta Garbo in the title role and Fredric March as her impassioned lover, the Russian soldier, Vronsky. Maureen was once again the young woman in love, Kitty, and the object of her love — the dashing and well-liked Vronsky — abandons his interest in Kitty when he sees Anna Karenina (Garbo), stepping down from the train in Moscow, her beautiful face like an apparition through the steam from the locomotive.

Greta Garbo was, of course, the great actress of the silent era and the 1930s, and veiled in all of her mystery, she acted with great emotion. She was always given such wonderful lines to say in her films, and it was as if she felt more and at a deeper level than ordinary people.

In 1928, *Life* magazine said of Garbo, "She is the dream princess of eternity, the knockout of the ages." And the *New York Mirror* defined her screen sexuality when it wrote, "Her alluring mouth and volcanic, slumbrous eyes stimulate men to such passion that friendships collapse."

Garbo died in many of her films, as in her suicide in the ending of *Anna Karenina*, but Robert Rubin of MGM later noted that this was acceptable to her fans, and that it only furthered her tragic mystique: "Garbo was the only one we could kill off. The Shearer and Crawford pictures had to end in a church, but the public seemed to enjoy watching Garbo die."

In addition to Garbo, March, and Maureen, the cast included young Freddie Bartholomew as Anna's son, Sergei, and Basil Rathbone as her cold-hearted husband, Alexei. The child actor Bartholomew had made his smashing debut in *David Copperfield*, and now producer David O. Selznick wanted to take advantage of his young prodigy's popularity with the public. And the scenes with Garbo and Freddie as mother and son, when they are reunited after a long absence, are immensely touching and heartfelt. According to dialogue writer S. N. Behrman, the only time he ever saw real tears from Garbo was in this very difficult, emotional scene with eleven-year-old Freddie.

The story, based on the 1876 novel by Leo Tolstoy, is set in the late 19th century, and begins as a train travels from St. Petersburg to Moscow. One passenger, Anna Karenina (Garbo), the wife of Alexei Karenin, arrives at the station and is greeted by her brother, Stiva, who introduces her to his friend, Count Vronsky (March), an officer of the Russian army. Vronsky is immediately drawn to Anna, and he cannot take his eyes off of her. Before leaving the station, Anna and Stiva witness an accident when a railroad inspector is caught under the wheels of a moving train; Anna calls the tragedy "an evil omen."

At the home of her brother, Anna acts as peacemaker between Stiva and his wife Dolly, who considers leaving him because he is having an affair. Anna convinces her to stay with her husband for the good of their three children, and to give him a second chance.

Anna also has great affection for Dolly's sister Kitty (Maureen), who confides in her that she has lost interest in her old boyfriend Levin (Gyles Isham), and now she is secretly in love with Count Vronsky, the dashing soldier who has been paying her a certain amount of attention. At the grand ball, Kitty wants to dance the Mazurka with Vronsky, who instead chooses Anna to be his partner. Kitty is almost in tears, but Levin comes to her rescue and chooses her as his partner for the dance. Even though she has spurned his recent proposal of marriage, Levin remains in love with Kitty.

When Anna departs for her home in St. Petersburg via the train, Vronsky follows despite knowing that she is a married woman with a young son. During the long journey, he professes his love for her, while she attempts to dissuade him from pursuing his fantasy. At the St. Petersburg station, Vronsky disembarks with Anna and is introduced to her husband, Alexei (Rathbone), a distinguished Russian statesman.

Vronsky and Anna begin spending a great deal of time together, and the inevitable happens — they fall in love with each other. When Alexei discovers his wife is having an affair with Vronsky, he warns her that he will never give her a divorce and she will lose her son if she ever leaves him. Anna has a difficult choice to make, as she loves her young son Sergei (Bartholomew) more than life itself.

Finally, Anna gives in and tells Vronsky that she cannot live without him and they elope to Venice, where they spend many happy months together. Meanwhile, Kitty has married Levin and Anna and Vronsky return to Moscow to visit the new bride and her family. Vronsky also discovers that his old regiment is preparing to enter the Serbo-Turkish war, and he is itching to get back in uniform and join his comrades in the battle.

Back in St. Petersburg, Alexei has told his son Sergei that his mother Anna will never return, that she is dead. The boy doesn't believe it, and he hates his father for telling him lies about his beloved mother. Anna returns to see Sergei on his birthday, who is frantic with joy as they embrace. But Alexei catches Anna as she is leaving the house, and warns her never to return.

Anna's despair deepens when she learns Vronsky is planning to join the war, and he refuses to confirm that he still loves her. He says he is sick of love, and now he only wants to go to war with his army comrades. Later, Anna hopes to have a final good-bye with him at the train station, but he is with his mother and a young woman. She fears that the woman is his new lover, and that she has lost Vronsky forever.

Anna can only watch as the train pulls out, and the words she wanted to speak to him are left unspoken in her heart. When the train is out of sight, Anna's desperation reaches a crescendo, and she throws herself under a passing train to a sudden death.

Maureen O'Sullivan's part in *Anna Karenina* was definitely a secondary role, but she did have one splendid scene alone with Miss Garbo, just the two of them conversing as friends. And for a young actress to have this opportunity to act in a scene with Greta Garbo, it would surely have been a great thrill for Maureen. The three-minute scene broke down as follows:

Maureen was cast as the second female lead Kitty, the sister-in-law of Garbo's Anna Karenina, and together they sit and discuss Kitty's obvious joy, a happiness that comes from falling in love. Garbo says: "Oh it's such a happy time in your life. That blissful time when childhood is just ending. And the future is all warm and inviting. I remember ... one swims in a mysterious blue haze ... like the mist on the mountains in Switzerland. That mist covers everything and out of it may rise at any moment the shape of the beloved one ... only half-imagined, half-dreamed." (Only Garbo could deliver lines like that and be taken seriously!)

The incomparable Greta Garbo with Maureen in *Anna Karenina*

When Maureen tells her that the man she has fallen in love with is Count Vronsky (Fredric March), Greta looks troubled for a moment and admits that she met him that morning at the railroad station. She also asks about Levin, the young officer who was pressing her for marriage. Maureen admits Levin is too serious for her, and he lives some distance away.

Maureen asks her what she thinks of Vronsky, and Garbo replies that he is "very charming and very kind ..." Their conversation is interrupted by the brother Stiva (Reginald Owen), who is quite happy that his wife Dolly (Phoebe Foster) has decided to give him another chance.

Later at the ball, Vronsky asks Anna to dance, but she declines. Instead, he dances with Kitty (Maureen), who tells him that he seems strange and appears to have changed. She senses that his attentions are now directed to Anna Karenina, who Kitty calls "the most beautiful woman at the ball."

The ballroom scene from *Anna Karenina* ... Maureen, Greta Garbo, and cast members

While Kitty is surrounded by young admirers including Levin, Anna relents and agrees to dance with Vronsky, who is persistent in his own charming manner. Kitty is immensely disappointed that Vronsky has jilted her, and she does accept the invitation of Levin to dance the mazurka, the climax of the evening. Kitty tells Levin, "I shall never forget your kindness." And of course she doesn't — she later marries the young man.

Maureen had the one long scene and several shorter scenes with Garbo. She really did a marvelous job of portraying the young woman who loses the love of her life, and eventually realizes that she has lost him because he has fallen for Anna Karenina. Kitty doesn't have any animosity towards Anna, because she is kindhearted and a dear friend who doesn't return the advances of Vronsky — until later.

In Garbo's words, from the book *Garbo: Her Story* by Antoni Gronowicz, she recalled the wonderful talent that collaborated in *Anna Karenina*: "I was lucky to work with talented actors like Fredric March as Vronsky, May Robson as his countess, and Maureen O'Sullivan as Kitty. Karenin was created by Basil Rathbone.

"The camera was operated by Bill Daniels, who knew the lights and shadows of my body and my soul. Before we had started to work on the film, Clarence Brown, the director, said to me, 'We have an intimate relationship. I am not afraid of you and you are not afraid of me. You are the best actress in the world to direct. I love your art and love to work with you.'"

Maureen and Greta both did their own dancing in the ball scene, even the long shots. Originally they had planned to use a professional double for Garbo, but she turned out to be a quick study and a natural on the ballroom floor and no double was needed. Maureen, of course, had been dancing since she was a child, and flowed gracefully around the floor during the waltz sequence with Fredric March and throughout the lengthy mazurka finale.

Garbo was famous for her line in *Grand Hotel*, "I want to be alone," but in real life she demanded her privacy as well. Maureen commented in 1974 on her relationship with the mysterious actress, and that Greta loved the Irish soda bread that her young counterpart would bring her each morning:

"I did not have very much contact with Garbo during the making of *Anna Karenina*," said Maureen. "I liked her; she was nice, very beautiful. As an actress, she gave you very little. In other words, it was a love affair between her and the camera. In fact, when working with her, one felt she was doing nothing really, that she wasn't even very good, until you saw the results on the screen. The camera with her was quite extraordinary. I think she was just a natural. And, of course, she always had marvelous cameramen who photographed her divinely. Karl Freund was one who knew just exactly what lights brought out her cheekbones and things like that.

"I got along with her very well. I had a cook who used to make Irish bread, and I used to bring her that every morning. I remember meeting her on the lot one day after we had finished the film, and there was no way of avoiding her because we were on a very narrow street. I had always heard that she did not like to be associated with people when a film was over, so I turned my head away as we passed, thinking, 'I'll do it first.' And she stopped and said, 'Vot is the matter with you?' I explained what I had always heard. 'Vere did you get that idea from?' she said in a very friendly manner. 'You never bring me any Irish bread any more!'"

A humorous incident happened on the set of *Anna Karenina*, involving prankster Fredric March. He handed Maureen an envelope — and when she opened it, a mechanical spider jumped out! The actor and actress had worked together on *The Barretts of Wimpole Street*, and now Mr. March felt he knew Maureen well enough to play practical jokes on her. Perhaps it was Johnny Weissmuller who put him up to it, as the Tarzan actor played similar tricks on her numerous times to while away the idle hours and keep the company amused. Maureen had one of the highest-pitched screams in the business, and after the shriek everyone — including the victim of the prank — broke into laughter.

Anna Karenina was recognized as one of the Top 10 films of 1935, and was also vastly successful in movie houses around the world. Garbo was truly an international star, and the King of Sweden, Gustaf V, crowned her "Garbo the Genius!" after seeing the picture. Of course the critics applauded Miss Garbo, noting that it was a great motion picture but not without its flaws.

Variety kicked off the reviews and described this film as one of Garbo's greatest roles (September 4, 1935):

> "Greta Garbo has never had a part which suited her more comfortably than the one in *Anna Karenina*. David O. Selznick's production has invested the proceedings with what at moments seems an overabundance of somberness and there are those who will be distinctly depressed by the picture. But the acting is of such a superior nature, the photography excellent, the physical production impressive and the name marquee value so definite as to make it cinch b.o. anywhere. In the foreign markets it should come close to establishing modern-day highs.
>
> "An almost perfect choice for the part of Miss Garbo's husband is Basil Rathbone. Reginald Owen handles the only comedy assignment as Stiva and does it beautifully. His wife is played by Phoebe Foster acceptably; it's a thankless role. Freddie Bartholomew as the child handles a few emotional scenes in tip-top form. March as the lover is at all times convincing and believable. Other ace performances, out of a large cast, are handled by May Robson, Maureen O'Sullivan and Guy d'Ennery."

Los Angeles Examiner, Louella O. Parsons (October 11, 1935)

> "Surely *Anna Karenina* must convince MGM that a vivacious Greta Garbo with a chance to be a human being, is much more acceptable than an automaton who seems devoid of feeling. Her magnificent portrayal of Anna Karenina, the Russian wife who falls in love with the dashing officer and is made an outcast by a cruel husband, is proof that what Garbo needed was just this picture.
>
> "Garbo completely dominates each scene with the exception of those in which that delightful child, Freddie Bartholomew, appears. As the son of Anna he is almost uncanny in his precocious, dramatic portrayal of the little boy bereft of the mother he adores and left to the tender mercies of his unrelentingly stern father.
>
> "No one could be more effective than Basil Rathbone as that father, whose love of discipline and rigid regard for the conventions far outweighs

any paternal feeling. Rathbone is a fine actor. Maureen O'Sullivan, Reginald Owen, May Robson, Phoebe Foster, Reginald Denny and Gyles Isham all add to the excellence of the production with their individual performances."

Evening Herald Express, Harrison Carroll (October 11, 1935)

"Finding in *Anna Karenina* something at last worthy of her talents, Greta Garbo renders a performance of emotional intensity and beauty. In this talking version of Tolstoy's novel, the Swedish star may well be said to reach the top point in her career as an artist.

"Garbo finds a new gaiety and fire in the Anna of the earlier episodes. Her scenes with Freddie Bartholomew are as touching as any one recalls. Her melancholy as the drama draws towards its finish is deeply moving. Altogether, it is a performance that belongs on the honor role of the screen.

"Fredric March, as the dashing Vronsky, gives a clear, sympathetic picture of Anna's lover. They are all fine. Freddie Bartholomew is, if anything, more appealing than in David Copperfield. Basil Rathbone's impersonation of the smug Karenin burns like acid. Reginald Owen, as the amiable philanderer, Stiva, is most amusing, and Maureen O'Sullivan, May Robson, Reginald Denny, Joan Marsh and several others score. *Anna Karenina* is one of the fine pictures of the year."

In the fall of 1935, Antoni Gronowicz, then a young poet and years before writing the biography, *Garbo: Her Story*, approached Polish intellectual circles with the idea of organizing a nationwide committee to sponsor an international conference against fascism. The committee sent letters to five hundred outstanding cultural figures. One of the people contacted was Maureen O'Sullivan, who was also one of the people who responded back to the committee, as Gronowicz later recalled:

"Most of those invited sent papers expressing fear about the impending world tragedy or telegrams supporting our cause. Some of the writers were Nobel Prize winners: Romain Rolland, André Gide, and Thomas Mann, as well as Jules Romains, Lion Feuchtwanger, Ernst Toller, and Joseph Roth. Among the many film notables who responded were several who had played in Garbo's films, including Lionel Barrymore, Douglas Fairbanks, Fredric March, Maureen O'Sullivan, and Robert Montgomery. But the Sphinx herself did not send any communication. When, years later, I asked Garbo why she had not responded to our appeal, she replied, characteristically, that she had not received our invitation."

Maureen's final released film of 1935 was *The Bishop Misbehaves*, an MGM comedy with a mostly British cast. Edmund Gwenn made his American debut as the bishop of the title. Maureen portrayed Hester Grantham, a young woman seeking retribution from an unscrupulous man who has cheated her father out of a large sum of money. Hester organizes a gang of misfits to rob the culprit, in a misguided attempt to attain justice.

Gwenn was already sixty years old by the time this film was made, and he would be a star for the next twenty years in many memorable roles. Some of his top films were *Pride and Prejudice* (1940 — also with Maureen); *The Miracle on 34th Street* (1947) — Gwenn won an Academy Award for his performance; *Mister 880* as a bumbling counterfeiter (1950); and Hitchcock's *The Trouble with Harry* (1955). The lovable curmudgeon Gwenn was also in two other films with Maureen: *A Yank at Oxford* (1938) and *Bonzo Goes to College* (1952).

The outstanding cast included several actors with whom Maureen had worked with in past films. Norman Foster portrayed the American who offers to help her with her scheme and immediately falls in love with the charming Hester. Reginald Owen was the delightfully wicked Guy Waller, while Robert Grieg was the roguish Rosalind who runs Lime House, a pub for unemployed criminals. Foster also had played her boyfriend in *Skyscraper Souls*, Owen was cast as her older brother in *Robbers' Roost*, and Grieg was the worldly butler that extricates her from some tough jams in *Woman Wanted*.

The story begins when Donald Meadows (Foster), a young American studying architecture on a walking tour of the English countryside, is captivated by the sight of a distraught young woman, Hester (Maureen), who is praying at the cathedral at Broadminster. He flirts with her long enough to form a friendship, and she confides in him that she is in a desperate situation and is about to undertake a criminal act.

Hester reveals a plan to rob Guy Waller, a scoundrel who has cheated her father out of a valuable patent on one of his inventions. Donald thinks she is joking, but she is serious and has put together a gang that includes: Waller's chauffeur; "Red," the bartender at the Red Lion Inn; and "Frenchy," recruited from Limehouse, run by the disreputable Rosalind.

The scheme goes off perfectly, initiated when Hester places a board with nails across the road to cause a flat tire on Waller's auto. While he and his wife are waiting at the Red Lion Inn for repairs to be made, Donald arrives with his gun and collects her jewels and his wallet, which contains proof that the patent was indeed stolen from Mr. Grantham. The booty is hidden in a beer stein behind the bar, which is to be picked up later by Frenchy.

Things begin to go awry when the Bishop of Broadminster (Gwenn) and his sister Emily (Lucile Watson) arrive at the pub to get out of the night's storm. The bishop discovers the three people tied up in the back room and releases them; he also finds the jewels and wallet, and puts them in his own pocket on the sly.

The bishop is an amateur sleuth who is fascinated by crime novels, and now he has his very own mystery to solve. He leaves his card inside the beer stein, with a hastily scrawled message to come to his home later that evening.

Well past the midnight hour at the home of the bishop, all the principals are gathered in a game of cat and mouse, with the wily old gent as the orchestrator. Finally, with the help of Waller's wife Millie (Lillian Bond), the bishop forces Waller to write Hester a check for ten-thousand pounds, or be publicly exposed as a thief and a liar. Hester and Donald, having fallen in love, retire from the crook business whilst the gang of felons slip away in the wee hours of the night, and no criminal charges are filed. The bishop decides his crime books have caused too much trouble, and with the assistance of Hester, Donald, his sister and his butler, tosses all of his pulp fiction into the furnace.

The Bishop Misbehaves was one of those rare MGM pictures that didn't have a major male star in it, but nevertheless it was a funny, enjoyable comedy that came close to hitting a home run. Jimmy Starr of the *Evening Herald Express* thought the film missed the mark as he reported in his September 1935 preview:

> "Starting out nicely as a breezy combination farce and hokum mystery comedy-melodrama, *The Bishop Misbehaves* just misses being a charming bit of light and amusing comedy. Newcomer Edmund Gwenn is a likeable old chap, who manages rather nicely with his first role in Hollywood cinemas. Norman Foster and Maureen O'Sullivan carry off the romantic department with ease."

Also, a couple of capsule reviews in the *Motion Picture Herald* from late 1935 noted that *The Bishop Misbehaves* was "a pretty fair comedy" and also "a good program that did surprisingly well ..."

Maureen was quite excellent as the feisty English lass who is devoted to her father, and therefore is determined to achieve justice even if it means breaking the law to accomplish her noble cause. Edmund Gwenn was absolutely priceless as the mischievous clergyman who manages to tilt the scales of justice just enough for a happy ending.

Many of the Hollywood parties in the 1930s were big, and some were just plain gigantic — as was the birthday party thrown for 20th Century-Fox kingpin Darryl Zanuck in September 1935. The guest list included many of the biggest names in the film business, including Maureen O'Sullivan and John Farrow, as reported by Reine Davies in his "Hollywood Parade" column in the *Los Angeles Examiner* (September 9, 1935):

> "Friends of Darryl Zanuck not only 'went native' at the Trocadero last Saturday night, but a bit savage as well. But, what with the booths of the Parisian room converted into jungle huts, the bar into an African trading post, the room itself completely blocked out with jungle trees and foliage, and a rumba band gone African for the occasion, it was small wonder.
>
> "All of which was to the complete surprise of Darryl who came to the Trocadero quite oblivious of all the preparations that the William Goetzes

had been making to celebrate his thirty-third birthday and to commemorate the young producer's big-game hunt in Africa a year ago. However, the menus, adorned with a picture of Darryl in hunting costume, announced the piece de resistance as 'lion meat, tracked down by Darryl Zanuck.' The cocktails were served in coconut shells. And great was the conviviality thereof.

"Hollywood-ites who assumed a jungle attitude in celebration of the Twentieth Century-Fox producer's birthday were Virginia Zanuck, Joe Schenck, the Lawrence Tibbetts, Joan Crawford and Franchot Tone, Jessica and Dick Barthelmess, Mrs. Anthony de Rothschild, Claudette Colbert and Dr. Joel Pressman, the Irving Berlins, Carole Lombard and Bob Riskin, the Clarence Browns, the Myron Selznicks, Sally Blane and Norman Foster, the David Selznicks, the David Butlers, Elizabeth Allen, Louis B. Mayer, Harry Joe Brown and Sally Eilers, the John Considines, Christine and Ricardo Cortez, the Merian Coopers, Sandra and Gary Cooper, the Jack Conways, Constance Bennett, the John Cromwells, Marlene Dietrich, the Harry Cohns, Harry Crocker, the Ray Griffiths, Dr. Harry Martin and Louella Parsons, Countess de Maigret, Willis Goldbeck, the Clark Gables, Dolores Del Rio and Cedric Gibbons, the William K. Howards, Katharine Hepburn, the Mark Kellys, the George Jessels, *Maureen O'Sullivan* and *John Farrow*, the Sam Jaffes, Jimmie Amster, the Ernst Lubitsches, Buddy DeSylva, the Bob Leonards, Eddie Lowe, the Louis Lighteons, Bernard Newman, the Adolphe Menjous, Lloyd Pantages, the Eddie Mannixes, Bill Powell, the Gene Markeys, Cesar Romero, the Wells Roots, the Zeppo Marxes, Harry Wardell, the Lewis Milestones, the Lew Schreibers, the Raoul Walshes, the William Seiters, the Walter Wangers, the Sol Wurtzels, the Larry Weingartens, and a host of others."

Maureen was often working on more than one film at a time for MGM, and it was fortunate that she had an extremely good memory, as Lloyd Pantages noted with admiration in his *Los Angeles Examiner* column "I Cover Hollywood" of September 3, 1935:

"I'm afraid Maureen O'Sullivan's head contains one of our better brains. She can memorize a script by merely reading it through two times and if you've ever given a once-over to a script you will realize that THIS is really something."

During the final months of 1935, Maureen was indeed acting in two pictures for MGM, including her third Tarzan picture with co-star Johnny Weissmuller. One of the hardest workers in Hollywood, she did put her foot down and insisted to her bosses that she be allowed to be home in Ireland with her family for the holidays. She had been invited to attend the wedding of an old school chum a few days before Christmas, and she intended to be there come hell or high water. One would assume that Mr. Mayer acquiesced.

CHAPTER TWELVE
"Back to the Jungle ... Another Tarzan Picture"

It was the call of the wild once again for Maureen, as the third in the MGM series of Tarzan adventures began filming in July of 1935 and continued until the end of October. Various titles were contemplated, including *Tarzan Returns, Capture of Tarzan,* and *Tarzan and the Vampires.* They were working from a script written by Karl Brown, with a contribution from John Farrow.

At the end of the four-month production schedule, the film was previewed by a test audience of children who were frightened by gruesome scenes, and outraged mothers who felt the story was way too scary and violent.

Originally filmed was a terrifying sequence with the safari attempting to traverse a creepy, haze-shrouded swamp that was infested with deadly vampire bats and hostile pygmies. This vampire bat scene was one of the objectionable segments that didn't survive the final released version entitled *Tarzan Escapes.*

MGM had forgotten that Tarzan was an adventure for the whole family, and what they had at this point was an adult film that had lost sight of that goal. The boys in the think-tank were unhappy with what they saw in the screening room, and ultimately they decided to start over from scratch. Ultimately, director McKay was relieved of his duties, as was the producer, the screenwriter, and several crew members. The cast was also revised.

Maureen wound up sitting and doing nothing during January and February of 1936, waiting for a new script to be written. This was the beginning of her dissatisfaction with doing the Tarzan pictures; she felt — and rightfully so — that she was missing out on other roles when she was sitting on the sidelines for weeks on end. Up until this time she was perfectly happy with the fame that being Jane had brought her. Now, however, her inactivity was driving her crazy as she lost a few choice roles during this period of limbo. MGM was producing many classic films during the 1930s, and Maureen was one of their star attractions. However, she sometimes had to settle for a lesser film with a short production schedule to accommodate the waiting game.

When her twenty-fifth birthday rolled around on May 17, Maureen had hoped to be home visiting with her family. Instead, Harrison Carroll of the *Evening Herald Express* reported the following: "Since the *Tarzan* picture apparently is going on forever, Maureen O'Sullivan doesn't even talk anymore of that Irish trip, but the star treated herself to a birthday present of a 20-minute telephone conversation with her family in Ireland. Before it was over, her mother, brother Jackie, and three sisters had been on the phone."

Maureen had two other films in release in 1936, *The Voice of Bugle Ann* and *The Devil Doll*, and in both she co-starred with one of the great actors of the silver screen, Lionel Barrymore. Along with brother John and sister Ethel, the Barrymores were the high royalty of Hollywood and the most famous family in the business. Maureen continued to work with actors and actresses who had won the Academy Award; so far Maureen had co-starred with Norma Shearer and Marie Dressler, as well as Fredric March, Wallace Beery, Charles Laughton, and now Lionel Barrymore *(A Free Soul* 1931).

She had also appeared with Clark Gable in *Strange Interlude* (1932), and he had won in 1934 for *It Happened One Night*. Of course Maureen had recently worked with the incomparable Greta Garbo in *Anna Karenina*. Although Miss Garbo never won an Oscar, she was presented a Special Academy Award in 1954 "for her unforgettable screen performances."

Maureen was underrated and never even nominated for an Academy Award; nevertheless, she was one of the better actresses in Hollywood. The simple fact that Garbo never won the Oscar exemplifies the fact that omission does not mean guilt; but there was only one award per year in the Best Actress category, and during Maureen's prime ten years of 1932-1941 she was not taken that seriously because of her continuing role as Jane in the Tarzan pictures.

The Voice of Bugle Ann begins in the Ozark mountains of Missouri, where the local farmers breed special dogs that they use for fox hunting. This was a humane type of fox hunting, where the foxes are treed by the dogs, who then return to their masters when the horn is blown.

Springfield Davis (Barrymore) loves his dogs greatly, and when his favorite dog Molly dies giving birth to a litter of pups, the runt of the litter is dubbed "Miss Ann," and becomes his sentimental favorite. As the dog matures, she becomes a champion hound with a "bugle voice" bark, and the proud Spring dubs her "Bugle Ann."

When neighbor Jacob Terry (Dudley Digges) erects a fence on the property line and warns that he will kill any dogs that trespass onto his sheep ranch, a feud erupts between the two families. This feud is complicated by the fact that Benjy Davis (Eric Linden) is in love with Camden Terry (Maureen O'Sullivan), who just happen to be the respective son and daughter of the warring fathers. One evening, Camden is struck by her father in an argument over her relationship with Benjy, and she drives away in a fit of anger.

The next day Bugle Ann is missing, and Spring suspects that his wretched neighbor Terry is responsible after someone reported hearing a dog yelping from his property. Spring and several of his friends arm themselves and go looking for the dog on Terry's farm, where a confrontation soon escalates between the two principals. Both men are pointing their guns and Terry denies that he had anything to do with the dog's disappearance. Terry takes aim at Spring with his rifle, but before he can fire, Spring shoots him in self-defense.

The body of Bugle Ann is never found — Spring Davis is convicted of manslaughter and sent to prison for twenty years. Within a year, the sound of Ann's voice is heard at night throughout the county, and the local farmers believe it is a ghost. Two years later, the body of Bugle Ann is found strangled in a wire fence in the hills, and everyone realizes that Jacob Terry was telling the truth when he said he had not killed the dog that fateful night.

Maureen was very close to Lionel Barrymore ... with the pooch from *Bugle Ann*

Another year passes and the governor suddenly decides that Spring should be pardoned. He is released from prison and returns to his farm and his beloved dogs. On the night of his first hunt, in the distance he hears a familiar bugle bark and simultaneously Camden comes to his campfire, with a heartfelt confession to make.

On the evening of her argument with her father, she had accidentally hit Bugle Ann with her car when she angrily drove away. She cared for the dog, who later had four pups — one of which was named "Proctor Pride" and inherited the bugle bark that Spring had heard that evening. Ann was killed one day when coming home from a hunt, after she became entangled in the wire fence. Camden also revealed that it was she who had petitioned the governor on the grounds that her father's death was an accident, resulting in Spring's subsequent release.

Camden and Benjy are able to put the whole unfortunate incident behind them, and make plans to marry. Spring is presented with one of Ann's pups, "Little Lady," who has inherited the bugle voice and will fill the void in Spring's heart for his lost Bugle Ann.

Maureen O'Sullivan's love interest in *The Voice of Bugle Ann* was originally planned to be James Stewart, who was just at the beginning of his career and still a virtual unknown. He was replaced by Eric Linden, playing the boy next door who falls in love with the girl next door — Maureen O'Sullivan. Hindsight is 20-20, of course, but a few years later Stewart would be one of the biggest stars in Hollywood, while Linden just faded away into the woodwork.

The rest of the cast were the usual MGM suspects, all of them fine actors that included Dudley Digges as the misguided neighbor Jacob Terry, Spring Byington as Ma Davis, with Charley Grapewin and Henry Wadsworth as members of the Royster clan, local farmers.

Variety noted in its review (March 4, 1936) the difficulties of photographing a story with a limited appeal, rather than being directed at a general audience:

"*Bugle Ann* will be appreciated chiefly by dog lovers, although it's not likely that even the most rabid pooch fancier would condone the murder of a man over a dog which is something attempted in this picture. Its appeal will be very limited. Lionel Barrymore does what he can with the role of Springfield Davis. He kills a mean cuss of a neighbor because he believes he destroyed his favorite foxhound, and he manages to command considerable sympathy for his consequent plight.

"Besides the murder, story concentrates on Barrymore's love of his dogs and a romance between Eric Linden, as the old man's boy, and Maureen O'Sullivan as the murdered man's daughter.

"Fox hunt sequences are well done and interesting, but it's the type of material that needs more and better than has been provided. With this story the novel material fails to make a satisfactory feature. Without it, the chase stuff might have made a good short subject.

"Barrymore receives excellent support from Miss O'Sullivan, Linden, Dudley Digges, Spring Byington, Charley Grapewin and others. But everybody, including director Richard Thorpe, was up against the old, unbeatable literary handicap."

Variety was referring to the fact that *The Voice of Bugle Ann* was based on the 1935 novel by MacKinlay Kantor, and in transferring it to the big screen in a 70-minute version from book-length ... something was lost in the translation.

Above: Marie Dressler, Robert Young and Maureen O'Sullivan starred in *Tugboat Annie* (1933)
Below: Warren William and Maureen co-starred in *Skyscraper Souls* (1932)

Above: *Strange Interlude* (1932) with Ralph Morgan in the foreground, and Alexander Kirkland is standing behind Maureen. This drama also starred Clark Gable and Norma Shearer.
Below: Maureen with Marjorie White, her co-star from *Just Imagine* (1930). She was a talented comedienne, but died tragically in 1935 in an auto accident in Hollywood.

Above: As the child-bride Dora in *David Copperfield* (1935)
Below: Maureen with Frank Lawton as the adult David Copperfield, on their wedding day

Above: Robert Montgomery finds love with Maureen in *Hide-Out* (1934)
Below: Maureen relaxing at home; smartly dressed in *Hold That Kiss* (1938)

Maureen was featured in several costume dramas of the 1930s …
Above: as Maria Orlech in *The Emperor's Candlesticks* (1937)
Below: MGM publicity photo, unknown role; as Lenore in *Cardinal Richelieu* (1935)

Maureen was half-naked in the six Tarzan films in which she starred ... clothed only in skimpy outfits that greatly revealed her figure. In the balance of her sixty motion pictures she wore beautiful clothes and long gowns. One of the men who photographed Maureen for MGM was Clarence Bull, who captured her beauty as Jane of the jungle as well as the belle of the ball.

Two photographs from *The Crowd Roars* (1938) with Maureen and Robert Taylor

Two photographs from *The Big Clock* (1948), with handsome co-star Ray Milland

Maureen and husband John Farrow are dressed up as Native Americans for the gala Photographer's Costume Ball at Ciro's nighclub (October 1948)

The eyes have it ... Maureen O'Sullivan had the most beautiful eyes in Hollywood

A decade goes by and hairstyles change ... *clockwise from upper left:* 1942, 1947, 1952

Above: Rod McKuen riding the horse, Maureen is sharing the wagon seat with Gigi Perreau and Paul Birch in a scene from *Wild Heritage* (1958) *Below:* 1958 portrait of Maureen O'Sullivan

A capsule review in the *Motion Picture Herald* noted that *Bugle Ann* was likeable even if they did describe the film as "homely."

The Voice of Bugle Ann. Lionel Barrymore, Maureen O'Sullivan — "This is a homely little picture with outdoor settings, and a good story. It is a little too talky, but in a fox-hunting country it would go big, I think, and even though we lack the foxes, the picture pleased, and except that it is a little slow tempo-ed, it is good entertainment. Dog lovers will like it and Bugle Ann certainly does her stuff as does the cast." — A. E. Hancock, Columbia Theatre, Columbia City, Ind. General Patronage. (May 30, 1936)

Maureen totally adored Lionel Barrymore, who bore a resemblance to her father both in physical appearance and kindly demeanor. They were in four pictures together, including *David Copperfield, The Voice of Bugle Ann, A Yank at Oxford* (1938), and their next picture together, the rather creepy chiller, *The Devil Doll*, in which Barrymore did indeed portray her father.

Harrison Carroll of the *Evening Herald Express* was on the set of *The Devil Doll* one day in May of 1936, when he observed the following sequence of events:

"Lionel Barrymore, wearing his disguise of an old woman, has to take Maureen O'Sullivan into his arms and comfort her. She is crying because of the injustice she has done for her father. The scene will have a double kick for the audience because it will know that Lionel IS the father.

"Director Tod Browning summons a maid to help Barrymore with his costume. 'All right,' he says, 'hook up this old war-horse and we'll get going.'

"They take the scene one, two, three times. Maureen pats Lionel on the shoulder. 'That was a nice one,' she says.

"As they are changing the setup a few minutes later, she comes over to me. 'Isn't he wonderful?' she exclaims. 'If it wasn't for Johnny Farrow, I'd be in love with him.' "

The story of *The Devil-Doll* begins on Devil's Island, where Paul Lavond (Barrymore) is serving a life sentence for robbing his own Parisian bank, a crime in which a guard was killed. In reality, Lavond was framed by his three partners and now his every thought is upon vengeance. Imprisoned for seventeen years, Lavond and fellow inmate Marcel (Henry Walthall) escape and are able to reach the secluded home of Marcel's wife Malita (Rafaela Ottiano), who has continued her husband's experiments.

Marcel shows Lavond his life's work, a scientific formula that shrinks house pets to miniature size. The tiny dogs appear to be dead, but Marcel is able to bring them to life with his own thought-waves that control their actions. Experimenting on the servant Lachna (Grace Ford), the girl is reduced to a doll-like size and Lavond sees a way to use this formula to exact revenge on his former partners — Radin, Coulvet, and Matin.

Marcel is old and dies of a heart attack, but Lavond and Malita agree to work together and set up a toy shop in Paris as a front, with Paul disguising himself as a kindly old woman, Mme. Mandalip. The police are searching for Lavond, so he wears his disguise when he goes to visit his mother (Lucy Beaumont), who tells her son that his daughter Lorraine (Maureen) is working as a laundress in a wash house. Lorraine hates her father intensely for his criminal acts, which caused such pain for her mother that she committed suicide. The girl works two jobs to help support her grandmother who is blind, and is also engaged to a cab driver, Toto (Frank Lawton).

When Lorraine comes to visit her grandmother, Paul Lavond is also there in his disguise as Mme. Mandalip, and is able to visit with his daughter for the first time in seventeen years. Lorrane doesn't realize, of course, that the kindly old woman who owns the toy shop is in reality her father, the falsely accused murderer.

Lavond puts his plan into play, and tricks Victor Radin into visiting the toy shop, drugs him, and subsequently reduces him to miniature size. Coulvet is next in line for revenge, and Mme. Mandalip sells one of the dolls to Coulvet's wife; the doll is actually Lachna who steals the family jewels and tosses them off the balcony to Lavond, waiting there in his disguise. The tiny Lachna then injects the terrified Coulvet with a drug that permanently paralyzes him, and makes good her escape with Lavond.

By now the third partner Matin is so terrified that he seeks police protection, fearing that Lavond will somehow get him too. Lavond sneaks his tiny soldier Radin into Matin's house, despite the presence of the police. Every noise causes Matin's nerves to jump, and just as the pint-sized Radin is about to stab his leg with poison, Matin screams out that he is guilty and that Paul Lavond was framed.

Back at the doll shop, the vindicated Lavond tells Malita that he is quitting and leaving Paris forever. She is outraged and wants to continue the experiments, but he only wanted his revenge and nothing more. Malita accidentally knocks over some of the chemicals in the shop and it explodes; she dies but Lavond is able to escape. Now the police will think that Mme. Mandalip was responsible for all the wrongdoings, and his name will remain clear.

The newspapers report that Paul Lavond's fortune will now go to his mother and daughter Lorraine, and that his partners will be sent to prison in his stead. Lavond must see Lorraine one more time, and arranges through Toto to see her on the top of the Eiffel Tower; this time he tells her that he is an old friend of her father's from prison. Lorraine feels that she knows the old man, and is comforted by his kindness and his kiss on her forehead. Lavond doesn't reveal his true identity, but departs knowing that his daughter will now have a good life and has a decent man in Toto to share the future.

The Devil Doll was based on the 1933 novel by Abraham Merritt called *Burn, Witch, Burn!* Director Tod Browning was famous for numerous horror films he had made in the silent era starring Lon Chaney, as well as other fright classics such as *Dracula* (1931) and *Freaks* (1932). Browning also wrote the story, and collaborated with Eric von Stroheim in writing the screenplay (along with Garrett Fort and Guy Endore). The producer was Eddie Mannix, who previously had pulled the financial strings at MGM, as well as being the troubleshooter who handled problems at the studio.

A scene from *The Devil Doll* ... Mr. Barrymore in disguise, Maureen, and Frank Lawton

A few weeks before the premiere of *The Devil Doll* in June of 1936, Lionel Barrymore and Maureen O'Sullivan were guests of Louella Parsons on her radio show "Hollywood Hotel," along with Frank Lawton and Rafaela Ottiano. The actors performed excerpts from *The Devil Doll* during the hour-long broadcast and also chatted with Louella about the movie.

One of the fascinating things about *The Devil Doll* was the use of special effects, then known as trick photography. This was one of the earliest uses of miniatures, which were superimposed to make it appear that the tiny dogs and little doll-people were real — and for the most part these were very credible special effects. Director Tod Browning was a master at scaring people, and these tiny dolls that crept into people's bedrooms — then stabbed them with poison — were chillingly effective. Adding to the creepiness of the film was a haunting musical score by Franz Waxman, one of the great Hollywood composers who later won Academy Awards for his music in *Sunset Boulevard* (1950) and *A Place in the Sun* (1951).

Browning's casting was also superb, especially the character of Malita, a strange witch-woman with a silver streak in her hair and a glint of madness in her eyes. Rafaela Ottiano portrayed Malita and other sinister roles in films of the 1930s. Frank Lawton was cast as the cabbie Toto, and he was excellent as the sympathetic boyfriend. Once again Robert Greig popped up in another of Maureen's films, this time as one of the unscrupulous partners who framed Paul Lavond. Greig was a fine character actor who was equally at home playing kindly butlers or dastardly scoundrels.

Louella O. Parsons loved this motion picture, as she noted in her *Los Angeles Examiner* column (July 30, 1936):

> "Eerie and creepy, *The Devil Doll* will intrigue any audience with its sheer novelty. Tod Browning, who has written and directed more horror films than any living person, has saved his best and most effective moments for this MGM thriller.
>
> "Technically, Tod and Eddie Mannix, the very able producer, make history by presenting doll-sized figures which actually move. The whole idea of the story is so unusual that it would be unfair to go into detail and spoil the enjoyment of everyone who will want to see this macabre spree. Sufficient to say, the dolls take part in jewel robberies and are instrumental in helping the leading character, played by Lionel Barrymore, get revenge for an unjust imprisonment.
>
> "Lionel Barrymore gives an amazing impersonation as an old lady, the pseudo manufacturer of these dolls. The change in his voice and his appearance is incredible. When I first saw the picture I thought that the voice probably had been dubbed, but when Mr. Barrymore played this same role on the 'Hollywood Hotel' radio program he proved that he had no assistance.
>
> "Maureen O'Sullivan as the unhappy daughter does a fine piece of dramatic acting. Frank Lawton, who has very little to do, manages to register in

spite of his limited opportunities. Rafaela Ottiano as the mad accomplice gives a surprising and great performance in the difficult role of a crazed woman.

"If Eddie Mannix can turn out pictures of this caliber, then our advice to him is to make pictures and leave the business end of MGM to someone else!"

Variety (August 12, 1936)

"The premise is a scientist's discovery of a process by which all living things, including humans, can be reduced to one-sixth their normal size. As an imaginative piece of business, that's quite intriguing, offering wide scope for development. The director, cameraman and art department make the most of it, but the writers' contribution is lacking in originality and seldom is equal to the 'idea' in back of it.

"For Barrymore the leading part is a field day. Rafaela Ottiano, with a white streak in her hair and hobbling on a crutch, is convincing as the scientist's wacky widow. Capable ingenue that she is, Maureen O'Sullivan had no trouble as Barrymore's daughter, but Frank Lawton, her opposite in the romantic secondary theme, is much too British and refined for a cab driver assignment."

Fifty-five years later, Maureen still had fond memories of working with the venerable older Barrymore brother: "Oh I loved him," she laughed and said, "I was devoted to Lionel Barrymore! He was a gruff character. We did *The Devil Doll*, and he played this old woman part of the time. He was so virile, but at that time he was not well. He was crippled with arthritis, so he was in his wheel chair and sleeping, comatose, on the set. But when they said 'Action!' he would jump to his feet, and he was a real man. Off went the wig, and he was just great.

"And he gave me some records, he wrote music and poetry. We had a nice friendship, we really did. He lived in the valley alone, and he lived with the memory of his dead wife. I liked him very much."

By the summer of 1936, the Tarzan picture that had originally gone into production exactly one year prior was now finally ready to start over once again with the new title, *Tarzan Escapes*. Richard Thorpe took over as director, and worked from a script written by Cyril Hume, the writer who had penned the original classic, *Tarzan, the Ape Man* (1932). Thorpe was one of Maureen's favorite directors; they had just completed *The Voice of Bugle Ann* together. Significant cast changes included Darby Jones replacing Everett Brown as Bomba, and Herbert Mundin added as Rawlins, the kindhearted sad sack. By the time filming concluded in September, the budget was obliterated and the final cost ballooned in excess of one million dollars.

Poor Maureen was bitten by a bird just when they were ready to roll and wound up in the hospital, as reported by Lloyd Pantages in his "I Cover Hollywood" column (July 25, 1936):

"*Tarzan Escapes,* one year in the making so far and already having cost some six hundred thousand dollars, is being completely reshot, with the exception of the Swamp Sequence, and as though that weren't headache enough, Maureen O'Sullivan has just been bitten by a cockatoo. They were afraid of Psittacosis setting in, so she is hospitalized for the time being."

Psittacosis is an infectious disease of birds which is transmissible to humans, and often results in pneumonia accompanied by a high fever. Taking all precautions, the studio put her in the hospital until she was pronounced in the clear. Maureen was often bitten by monkeys, and now she could add the cockatoo to her list of animal bites.

Tarzan Escapes begins with Tarzan and Jane once again living in the wilds of Africa, but now they have set up housekeeping and have built a real jungle home. The ape-man has constructed a tree-house for his better-half, that is complete with running water, ceiling fans, and even an elevator. Jane's cousins Rita (Benita Hume) and Eric (William Henry) have traveled to the Dark Continent to inform her of a one-million dollar inheritance that has been bequeathed to Jane by a rich uncle.

Rita and Eric hire a safari guide, Captain Fry (John Buckler), who secretly devises a scheme to capture Tarzan and to take him back to England and display him like a sideshow attraction. Fry's assistant is the bumbling Rawlins (Herbert Mundin), and the leader of the safari natives is Bomba (Darby Jones), who takes his orders from the self-avowed great white hunter.

As they arrive at the Mutia escarpment, Fry has his men capture and cage several of Tarzan's ape friends, including Cheeta, to draw in the man described by the natives as a "great white ape." Fry has brought along a tall metal cage that is big enough for his prize, and he hopes to trap the ape-man by using one of the small chimps as bait. Tarzan of course is too smart for this folly, releases all the apes in the night, and takes a silk scarf owned by Rita back to the tree-house to show Jane.

Jane is excited that her cousins from London have come for a visit, and she tells Tarzan that Rita and Eric are friends, along with Rawlins. Tarzan instinctively rejects Fry as a friend, and smashes his rifle against a tree. Nevertheless, they are all invited to the tree-house for a sumptuous feast prepared by Jane.

Rita and Eric tell Jane that they have invested their entire savings to inform her of the inheritance. Jane offers the money to Eric and Rita, but they insist that she must return with them to sign the documents — she reluctantly agrees. When Tarzan learns that Jane is leaving him, albeit temporarily, he bolts for the jungle to be alone. She later reassures her mate that she loves him and will return in three months, but she knows this is a terrible blow to Tarzan.

Jane and Tarzan restrain Captain Fry, portrayed with duplicity by John Buckler

When the safari departs, Fry and Bomba double-back and plan to capture the ape-man in the metal cage. Rawlins gets wind of the trap, and confronts his nefarious employer. Before he can inform Tarzan, Fry shoots the little man in the back. The duplicitous Fry manages to trick Tarzan into his cage, and then rejoins the safari.

Suddenly they are surrounded and captured by the fierce Hymandi tribe, who begin making human sacrifices one by one. Tarzan, still caged, hears Jane's cry for help and, with the aid of his elephant friends, escapes from the steel bars. As the elephants stampede through the hostile village, Tarzan leads his friends to safety by bringing them through a smoky cave filled with prehistoric lizards and beasts.

Safe at last on the far side, Tarzan sends Fry back into the cave-swamp where a sure death awaits — his cries from the interior signal his demise. Tarzan is aware that Fry had shot Rawlins in the back, and this was the justice of the jungle. Jane vows to her mate that she will never leave him, and instead signs the documents for Rita and Eric thus giving them the inheritance.

Maureen O'Sullivan was guilty of some very fine acting in *Tarzan Escapes*, in particular a scene where she explains to Tarzan that she must return to England to sign the documents for her cousins, but she realizes that her mate doesn't understand — it is all Greek to him. Her Garbo-esque dialogue with the ape-man, who can only gaze at her with his sad eyes all welled up with tears, is stunningly beautiful:

"How shall I tell you darling? I love Tarzan. Tarzan is Jane's love ... like the stars in the night. Like the air to breathe, Tarzan makes me alive. But Eric and Rita are my friends ... friends ... like rain at the end of the summer ... like wind moving in the tops of the jungle ... I am yours and you are mine, my darling ... But I must help Rita, she is my friend. Like Tarzan is Cheeta's friend, to help her when she was in the trap."

Jane explains that this trap is the money trap, which she says can be just as deadly, just as devastating. Tarzan asks her, "Jane want to go?"

"Tarzan, believe me ... when the moon has made safari three times, three times ... and when she comes out of the river and looks in on us here ... she'll find us as we are now ... together ... and my safari will be over forever ... and I will never go away again ... Tarzan and Jane ... (she speaks some words of love in African Swahili ...) Understand?"

Tarzan hugs her close, as tears glide down his cheeks, and says, "Understand ..." He says he understands, but of course, he really doesn't. He does know she must go and is devastated.

Maureen seems to be in a spot of trouble here in a scene from *Tarzan Escapes*

Maureen had learned so much about the acting craft from appearing in numerous films with Greta Garbo, Norma Shearer, Marie Dressler, and other fine actresses, that now she was shining herself in the dramatic moments of her screen roles. Especially in the Tarzan pictures, where she was definitely Queen of the Show, Maureen was worthy of Oscar consideration. But the simple fact that these were Tarzan pictures — adventure for the adults and fun for the kids — made the possible consideration for an award an unlikely event. Any motion picture that had chimpanzees for comic relief would never be considered at Oscar time.

Weissmuller himself did an excellent job of portraying desolation at the thought of Jane leaving him to return to England. The former swimmer never claimed to be a great actor, and the restrictions put on his character didn't give him much latitude for artistic expression. Nevertheless, you could always feel genuine heartfelt emotion coming from his character of Tarzan. The love scenes of Johnny and Maureen were tender and touching, giving the story clearly a memorable romantic theme as well as being a thrilling jungle escapade.

Maureen noted in 1992 that she was misquoted when it was published that she was consistently sick when making the Tarzan films. "I would say that was a misquote. I got sick once, in *Tarzan Escapes*. I loved making the first Tarzan film, and also the second. The third film stretched over sixteen months, and I began to tire of it. I was perpetually, up until the day I left, making a Tarzan. So I got awfully tired of them.

"My husband John Farrow directed part of *Tarzan Escapes*, and it was just awful. He directed the scene in a swamp with these devil bats. It's a wonder we even got married at all. He was up there on the boom, nice and dry — and we were in a swamp. The stage was a swamp, and we were up to our chests in this filthy water. We were in there with the actors, and safari natives, and it was the most disgusting thing that ever happened. And all day long we were in this swamp, and excuse me for saying, I don't think anyone could possibly get out to go to the bathroom. I got very sick after that. That's the time I was sick, yes. And then they cut the scene from the picture as being too frightening for the children."

To pacify the censors and the rigid Production Code of 1934, Maureen O'Sullivan's revealing outfit from *Tarzan and His Mate* was replaced in *Tarzan Escapes* with a ragged jungle shift that displayed a lot less "skin" and toned down her sexuality. She also had a gorgeous mop of curly brown hair, longer that she had ever worn it. Slightly more conservative in dress, Jane of the jungle was nevertheless more lovely than she had ever been.

Maureen had been working out in a gym with a personal trainer the past few years, and her figure had that perfect blend of youth and tone. At age twenty-five she had lost her "baby fat" and was one of the most stunning women in the world. She also photographed beautifully.

Herbert Mundin as Rawlins makes friends with Tarzan and Jane ... Tarzan Escapes

There was a lot of playful fun in this picture between Johnny and Maureen; in one scene he is wheeling her around like a wheel barrow, and then after hiding in a tree, he reaches down and pulls her right up to his branch, like she is as light as a feather. They then both begin poking in the chest area and almost knocking each other off the branch, and Jane says, "I wouldn't scream if this was the tallest tree in Africa and there were 10,000 lions below!" Johnny speaks some words of love to her in the Swahili language, and Maureen professes her true love forever in return as they embrace closely. It was a beautiful moment.

An underwater swimming "ballet" similar to the one in the previous film was used, but this time they kept the basic jungle attire on the couple. After their playful swim which includes an underwater kiss, Jane responds in kind to Tarzan's "look of love." Her expression melts into submissive sensuality, and she releases the orchid in her hand into the slow river current. The scene fades to black, with the obvious implication that Tarzan and his mate will consummate their love for each other. Back in the 1930s, they knew how to do a love scene with class. This was an era of romance, rather than blatant sex in the cinema.

In one scene Maureen is conversing with Rawlins, portrayed superbly by Herbert Mundin, who provided comic relief as a nervous, jumpy, bumbling lieutenant to Captain Fry. When he first meets Tarzan, he is so frightened he faints dead away. Later, he gains respect and also develops a genuine affection for the ape-man. "Miss Jane, Tarzan is the finest gentleman I've ever known, trousers or no trousers," confides Rawlins to Jane. Later, he risks his own life to warn Tarzan of the treachery of Fry, who coldly shoots him in the back before he can act on his heroic intentions.

John Buckler was excellent as the so-called white hunter with a streak of villainy, and was on the verge of stardom in Hollywood. He'd had a major part in *David Copperfield*, was suave, good-looking, and bore a resemblance to John Barrymore. On October 31, 1936, one week before the premiere of *Tarzan Escapes*, Buckler and his father Hugh Buckler were both killed after an auto accident. Their vehicle skidded into Malibu Lake in the middle of the night, and was not found until the following morning. The bodies of both men were still in the auto, a grim scene that bore an eery similarity to Buckler's death in *Tarzan Escapes*, where he stumbles into the swamp and drowns in grisly fashion. Sadly, this was real life.

Maureen, the ill-fated Buckler, and Benita Hume hitch a ride on this camera truck

Although not a true classic as were the first two films of the series, *Tarzan Escapes* succeeded as a first-rate adventure that held audiences spellbound in the United States and around the world. MGM literally made two motion pictures to get it right, but the result was well worth the extra effort. The story was rich with excitement, the romance of Tarzan and Jane, the splendor of wild animal photography, the comic humor of Herbert Mundin and of course, the monkeys.

The *New York Times* concluded that *Tarzan Escapes* was good entertainment, and that Maureen was more than holding up her end of the bargain:

> "The interesting question is no longer whether Tarzan is going to escape from his enemies — that much we may take for granted — but whether his enemies will ever be able to escape from Tarzan. It seems very unlikely, too, so long as the handsome pithecanthrope continues to be surrounded by such rich and leisurely productions as Metro has draped about his handsome shoulders in *Tarzan Escapes*, at the Capitol.
>
> "The flavor and the monstrous spell, the strange and horrifying beauty of the Dark Continent are all there, carefully processed and sound-tracked, to offset the comical ululations of the ape-man or such delightful spectacles as the elephant-operated lift by which Maureen O'Sullivan, showing surprisingly few signs of exposure after all these years in the bush, elegantly ascends to her arboreal love nest."

Meanwhile W. E. Oliver of the *Evening Herald Express* thought highly of the production in his review (December 12, 1936):

> "These new Tarzan wonders are being shown at the Four Star under the title of *Tarzan Escapes*. Conveniently retarding Tarzan's education in English, the plot has the wondrous ape-man victim of an adventure's scheme to cage him for carnival sideshow purposes when a party of English folk comes in the jungle supposedly to get his wife's signature to an important document, but secretly to get her back to England.
>
> "Tarzan cannot understand enough English to get this and believing Jane wants to leave him, falls prey to the would-be showman's skulduggery. But with usual skill and that ululating howl that has become part of the play lore of American kids, he effects his own rescue and that of the party when it falls victim to the treachery of an African tribe.
>
> "More comedy has been put into this current film. The amusing friendship between Tarzan and Cheeta, the female ape, is retained, along with his astounding alliance with elephants and other good-natured jungle folk.
>
> "Weissmuller easily retains his title as No. 1 ape-man in the film and Maureen O'Sullivan is so attractive as his mate that the fans will likely want to keep her at it."

There were many rewards in being a famed actress, but the most tangible was getting paid each week by the studio cashier. Most of the stars would have an authorized agent collect their paychecks, but some of the biggest names would show up at the pay window each week. Fred Astaire would always be at the pay window bright and early on Wednesday mornings to collect in person from Harry Peale, the RKO cashier. Peale noted in 1936 that you always knew when Katharine Hepburn was coming to collect: "You can hear her laughing and joking a block away — but she's mighty nice."

At MGM, Maureen O'Sullivan was one of the few who called for her weekly pay in person, along with Mary Carlisle, Cecilia Parker, and Henry Wadsworth. She would line up with the extras, bit players, carpenters, electricians and property men, and joke and kid around just like one of the boys. Her first two years in Hollywood she wasted money like it was water, and wound up broke and unemployed in mid-1931. Ever since those difficult days she placed a higher value on money. Collecting that check each week was her way of reminding herself that this was still the Depression, and a lot of people were standing in bread lines, not payroll lines.

The Garden of Allah hotel on Sunset Boulevard was home to numerous celebrities between 1927 and 1959, when it was demolished by the wrecking ball. Maureen O'Sullivan called the Garden home in the early years of her career, and the list of movie stars that resided there during its 32-year existence simply reads like a "Who's Who" of Hollywood.

The famous hotel opened on January 9, 1927, and there were twenty-five villas that surrounded the lotus-shaped pool. Hollywood columnist Sheila Graham said of the Garden, "In the thirty-two-year span of its life, the Garden would witness robbery, murder, drunkenness, despair, divorce, marriage, orgies, pranks, fights, suicides, frustration, and hope. Yet intellectuals and celebrities from all over the world were to find it a convenient haven and a fascinating home."

Greta Garbo lived at the Garden in the early days, and 1930s residents included F. Scott Fitzgerald, Somerset Maugham, Ernest Hemingway, Robert Benchley, Dorothy Parker, John O'Hara, violinist Mischa Elman, pianist-composer Rachmaninoff, Katharine Hepburn, John Barrymore, and Errol Flynn. All of the Marx Brothers lived at the Garden in the early 1930s, and Sam Marx, patriarch of the Marx family, lived and died there in his old age. As the years passed new residents included Frank Sinatra, Artie Shaw and his wife Ava Gardner, John Carradine, Humphrey Bogart, Lauren Bacall, David Niven, Jackie Gleason, and musicians Woody Herman, Jascha Heifetz, Benny Goodman, and Frankie Laine, a passionate young singer who was working in a shipyard and was known at that time as Frankie Lo Vecchio.

If you didn't live there, you could still do your drinking at the popular Garden bar, as did W. C. Fields, Jimmy Durante, and Fred Allen. Some of the wildest Hollywood parties ever were held at the Garden of Allah, and the guest lists included many of the biggest names in Hollywood. On any given day you might find Clark Gable, Gary Cooper, Wallace Beery, Joan Crawford, Claudette Colbert, William Powell, Carole Lombard, Janet Gaynor and Charlie

Farrell. If they didn't come to party, then they came to swim in the pool and enjoy the scenery of beautiful young starlets in bathing suits.

After one of the parties had extended until five a.m. the next morning, Tallulah Bankhead proceeded to the top diving board, and dived in wearing a heavy beaded evening gown. The dress quickly became waterlogged and Tallulah shed the garment at the bottom of the pool, came to the surface crying for help. The actress couldn't swim a stroke.

One of the guests was Johnny Weissmuller, the Olympic champion who starred in water shows in-between Tarzan pictures, and also gave swimming and diving lessons to celebrity friends. Johnny immediately dived in and rescued the floundering Bankhead, who when she was pulled from the pool — buck naked — scampered briskly back to her cottage. Meanwhile, the few remaining guests laughed at the outrageous sight of the streaking actress.

Sheila Graham interviewed many former residents when she was writing a book about the Garden of Allah in 1970, and Maureen recalled the following story: "An actress who had made a name for herself on the British stage came to stay at the Garden. She called late one afternoon and said, 'I'm sorry to ask you so late. But I'm giving a big party tonight. Joan Crawford and Clark Gable are coming, and I wasn't sure there would be room for you and Johnny [Farrow]. But you're my neighbor, and I suddenly felt awful that I had not invited you.'"

Maureen said she understood and accepted the belated invitation. "I arrived early with Johnny. There were thousands of hors d'oeuvre and dozens of bottles of liquor with hundreds of glasses. And nobody came, except Eddie Goulding and us, and all the press and all the photographers. We stayed for hours because we were sorry for her. It was so ghastly and embarrassing. The press had a marvelous time, eating and drinking and not having to work."

About John Farrow, Ms. Graham recalled, "There was a court at the Ronda Apartments on the side street where Johnny Farrow lived when Maureen O'Sullivan was at the Garden.

"Mr. Farrow had a snake tattooed on the upper part of the inside of his left thigh. He posed for long periods at the end of the Garden's diving board wearing short swimming trunks, and the snake appeared to be emerging from his reproductive organs. Later he married Maureen."

In one of several interviews Gladys Hall conducted with Maureen during the 1930s, a February 1936 chat resulted in the actress admitting that her indomitable spirit came mostly from her Irish heritage: "I don't think I'll ever commit suicide," said Maureen with a laugh. "I don't think I'll ever have melancholia or die of a broken heart or be hauled off to a psychopathic ward or go under for the third time. Perhaps I might for love, but for nothing else.

"To go back, I'll never do anything desperate about anything else that may befall me because when I have most reason to be depressed, then I am most do-and-daring. When I'm down, I'm up. I'm also like my native Ireland in this respect. I parallel the history of my country — I'm at my best when I'm cornered and have to fight. I've always been like this.

"When I was a tiny youngster at home in Ireland, if I happened to be on the outs with my family and was being ignored and sent to Coventry, my back was up right away. I'd do drastic things to recall attention to myself. I'd work like a demon in school so that my report card would be better than the reports of my sisters and brother. Or I'd give away all of my clothes to the poor so that I could pass as a poor little martyr, stripped to the skin. Or I'd deliberately fall downstairs, injure myself in some carefully minor way so that I would be in the limelight, entitled to sympathy. It usually worked — and once I was reinstated I promptly lapsed again.

"When I was sent to the convent in London to school I did very well at first, I got good marks, both in my work and in my conduct. There seemed to be nothing to strive for then. So I just did nothing. I muffed my studies. I didn't so much disobey rules as disregard them. I let inertia go to such an extent that I was — and I've never told of this blot on my record before — I was expelled!

"My people were sent for, from Ireland, to come and take me home. I knew that I had a battle on my hands. I knew that I would have to face the music and that the music would be plenty martial. I was down in the slough of despond and defeat and — my spirits rose and soared! I prepared for the fray! I wore my prettiest dresses. I decided not to eat too much so that I would lose weight and look pale and interesting. I adopted the martyr pose as the one best suited to my needs. I played my part excellently. I posed as a Free Soul who could not be subjected to English rule, or something. The result was excellent for me, for I was sent to Fontainbleau [south of Paris] to live for several months. And it did me some good. I got more out of that experience than I could ever have got of remaining in school. I learned to speak a very decent French. I met some interesting people. It really did things for me ..."

Maureen also admitted that success really didn't motivate her, and that she still had somewhat of an inferiority complex that lingered from her childhood. She never really thought she was pretty (let alone beautiful), she never thought she was a particularly talented actress, and she felt that success would come her way only with difficulty: "You see, I have a peculiar battle to fight — with myself. One part of it is that success doesn't stimulate me as it would most people. It sort of lulls me to sleep. And when I wasn't successful and about as far down as one can get, I begin to gnash my teeth and thrash about."

Now she raised her voice and said with conviction, "But you can't keep on being down, you know — for one of the times the count will be down and

OUT! But I think that underlying even this truth about myself is my feeling that I will never be a really big star. My feeling that I am not 'star material.' I'm not *different* enough ..."

When the young actress had finished spilling her guts to Gladys Hall, the journalist took over the narrative to inform Maureen that she did indeed have 'the right stuff' to be a big star: "I interrupted at this point to say, with honesty and not flattery, that that's just what I think Maureen is — different. She is the one screen personality I can think of who is utterly unspoiled and completely natural, fresh, honest, and un-bedaubed with glamour."

At this point in time Maureen had been in Hollywood about five years, she was still only twenty-five, and she continued with her self-deprecation: "That's nice of you to say, but I'm not different in the right way, you see. I haven't the mystery of Garbo. I haven't the seductiveness of Jean Harlow. I haven't the glamour of Crawford. I haven't the enigmatic beauty of Dietrich nor the extraordinariness of a Hepburn. It's just *me* — and that's not star-stuff.

"I don't do anything to myself. I've never touched up my hair. I don't use makeup. I don't dress in an unusual way. I don't swank about in opulent cars. I don't play the game at all. And what's worse, I don't want to. I don't go to parties and meet the 'right people.' I don't entertain the 'right people.'

"I don't think what I am is an actress at all. I'm really just a little Irish girl who *happened* to come to Hollywood — and who doesn't belong here. I'll give it all up one day," she waxed nostalgic, "if it doesn't give me up first. I'll say good-bye to Hollywood, a last good-bye. We'll travel, John and I, when we can be married. We'll do interesting things together and settle in England and have our own home and our children.

"For one thing I never 'lie down' about is being in love. There are some girls who, when the man they care about is the most devoted, the most tender, sort of get careless and take-it-for-granted. I don't. I never do. Perhaps I've grown suspicious. But I sometimes feel, 'I wonder, now, why all the devotion? Why this attack of attentiveness?' And so, when things are going most beautifully between John and me I'm always most on my toes.

"I'd like to make good in pictures, of course. For it's in line with what I've been saying. I'll feel down until I can prove to myself that I'm really up. And I can prove that only by doing at least one picture that really satisfies me — only by getting some parts that are really big and important. I've got to fight until I'm as 'up' as possible. And I will.

"I may not be an actress. *I'm sure I'm not.* But, I am an 'Irishman' and you can't keep a good Irishman down — not a *fighting* Irishman!"

Maureen's career would continue on for over sixty years, and eventually she would come to realize that she was indeed born to be an actress. She would never attempt any other kind of work with her life, and history would record that she was truly regarded as a very fine actress.

CHAPTER THIRTEEN
"Marriage and the Madcap Marx Brothers"

On August 12, 1936, Charles O'Sullivan announced from Ireland that his daughter Maureen was now officially engaged to John Farrow, and that the wedding would take place in Dublin on a date yet to be announced. He stated that a special dispensation for the marriage had been granted by the Vatican, after the couple had waited two years for it. Farrow had previously been married to Felice Lewin, who was the daughter of Arthur Lewin, a millionaire mining tycoon from San Francisco.

With the final impediment to their marriage dissolved, the wedding plans began to take shape and September 12 was chosen as the date. Maureen would be starring in the Marx Brothers movie *A Day at the Races*, so an extended honeymoon would have to wait until later in the fall.

A few days before the wedding a prenuptial party was held in Maureen's honor in Beverly Hills, and attended by many of her female friends that included Norma Shearer and Jean Harlow. Covering the event for the *Evening Herald Express* was columnist Sally Moore:

"All the world loves a lover, so goes an old saying. The world loves romance, too. And Hollywood is no exception. All of which was decidedly apparent when the popular Carmelita Geraghty (Mrs. Carey) Wilson entertained at her Beverly Glen home Thursday in honor of Miss Maureen O'Sullivan, soon to become the bride of John Villiers 'Johnny' Farrow, writer and director.

"One of the most popular members of Hollywood's younger set, Maureen has been much feted since the announcement of her engagement.

"And Carmelita's party was one of the loveliest pre-nuptials, a clever green and white color scheme, honoring Maureen's Irish birthright, and a huge cake in the form of a shamrock, with a bride and bridegroom atop it, adding further to the decorative note. A shower of lovely gifts for the bride-elect was a feature of the afternoon.

"Among the guests bidden to the party were Louella O. Parsons, Norma Shearer, Jean Harlow, Mrs. Sam Katz, Benita Hume, Paulette Goddard, Betty Hill, Sheila Geraghty, Mrs. Ernst Lubitsch, Mrs. Mervyn LeRoy, Virginia Bruce Gilbert, Mrs. Larry Gray, Sally Blane, Kay English, Mrs. John W. Considine Jr., Mrs. Sam Marx, Nathalie Bucknall, Mrs. Clarence Brown, Alice Moore Knight, Una Merkel, Mrs. Harold Lloyd, and Virginia Valli."

Following an old Irish tradition, Maureen did not have any contact with her fiancé for the entire week before the wedding. Irish custom says that it would be an ill omen to do so, and the actress carried out the tradition strictly, even though the MGM press department was pleading for advance pictures of the bride and groom.

Maureen even requested that the news photographers refrain from taking pictures at the church until the conclusion of the one hour and fifteen minute ceremony. Although the couple had hoped to be married in Ireland, the ceremony was performed in Santa Monica to accommodate the many Hollywood friends who could only attend a local wedding.

On the morning of September 12th, 1936, Maureen Paula O'Sullivan decided to break a lot of hearts and officially end her status as one of Hollywood's most desirable bachelorettes, as reported in the *Evening Herald Express*:

"With many film celebrities as guests and a crowd of several hundred fans girdling St. Monica's church at Santa Monica, pretty Maureen O'Sullivan, Irish film star, and John Villiers Farrow, Australian-born film writer, were married just before noon today.

"The bride arrived at the church in a big tan limousine exactly at the appointed hour, alighted and walked into the church, dressed in her flowing white satin wedding gown, with lace veil and a beautiful bouquet of lilies of the valley and gardenias.

"Other members of the wedding party had proceeded her. Farrow arrived almost unnoticed, according to the custom which in Miss O'Sullivan's country also had dictated that she do not see her husband-to-be until they meet at the altar.

"Rev. Monsignor Conneally celebrated the nuptial high mass. Mrs. Norman Foster attended the bride as matron of honor and Hon. Michael Tandy, British consul in Los Angeles, was best man.

"After the ceremony, the couple went to the home of Loretta Young for a wedding breakfast and reception, and then departed on a wedding tour that is necessarily short because both principals must resume their film work soon."

By Monday, September 14, the new bride was on her honeymoon with John Farrow down Mexico way. She was due back in a few days to begin work on *A Day at the Races*, which starred Groucho, Chico, and Harpo along with Maureen and Alan Jones as the romantic couple. Also featured was the very talented comedienne Margaret Dumont as Groucho's foil. The following day, tragic news spread throughout the rank and file of the studio that Irving Thalberg, the MGM "Boy Wonder" and husband of Norma Shearer, had died at age thirty-seven the previous evening. The cause of death was listed as pneumonia; ever since a 1933 bout of pneumonia had weakened his heart,

Thalberg had lived in a state of less than perfect health. Director Sam Wood broke the news to cast members, who along with all MGM employees were sent home and the studio was closed indefinitely. The funeral service would be conducted on Thursday, September 17.

At the time of his death Thalberg was producing the Marx Brothers comedy *A Day at the Races*, and also *Camille* starring Greta Garbo, *Maytime* starring Nelson Eddy, and *The Good Earth*, which was completed. He was the executive producer for many of MGM's greatest pictures up until his death, including *The Barretts of Wimpole Street*, which had starred his wife Norma Shearer, Fredric March, Charles Laughton, and Maureen O'Sullivan.

Maureen and Norma were two of the many talents that were developed by Thalberg for MGM; others included Greta Garbo, John Gilbert, Clark Gable, Robert Young, Joan Crawford, Myrna Loy, Jean Harlow, and Marie Dressler.

Tributes and condolences poured in from the heads of all the major studios: Nicholas Schenk, president of MGM and Loew's, Inc.; M. H. Aylesworth, chairman of RKO Pictures; Sidney R. Kent, president of Twentieth Century-Fox; Jack Cohn, vice-president of Columbia Pictures; Adolph Zukor, chairman of Paramount Pictures; and Harry Warner, president of Warner Brothers.

A representative tribute came from Samuel Goldwyn, the dean of Hollywood producers, who said after the premature death of the MGM mogul: "I cannot express the terrible grief I feel at the passing of my dearest friend, Irving Thalberg. We, his close friends, have suffered an irreparable loss, but my heart goes out to Mrs. Thalberg and her children. They have lost a great husband and father. Not only was he the foremost figure in the motion-picture industry, but beyond that he was a man of great character and personal integrity and an inspiration to all of us who have had contact with him."

This was truly one of the shocking events during the Golden Age of Hollywood, because Thalberg was so brilliant and still very much in the prime of his life. On the day of his funeral, September 17, Metro remained closed and all the other Hollywood studios observed a five-minute silence in memoriam at 10 a.m. The service was held at the Wilshire Boulevard Temple in Los Angeles, and in attendance were bigwigs Louis B. Mayer, Eddie Mannix, the Warner brothers, Adolph Zukor, Nick Schenk, and Howard Hawkes, who escorted Norma Shearer into the temple.

Every MGM contract player of note was there to pay tribute, including Greta Garbo, Jean Harlow, the Marx brothers, Mary Pickford and Douglas Fairbanks, Sr., Freddie Bartholomew, Mickey Rooney, Johnny Weissmuller, John Farrow, Maureen O'Sullivan, and many others. The ushers who escorted them to their seats were Fredric March, Clark Gable, and the playwright Moss Hart. After the service, Thalberg was buried at Forest Lawn Memorial Park, in a grandiose marble pavilion in the Sanctuary of the Benediction.

In 1936, Maureen added dramatic radio to her repertoire of talents and made her first of many appearances on the "Lux Radio Theatre," which was hosted by famed producer/director Cecil B. DeMille. This one-hour radio drama was entitled *Captain Applejack*, and was presented on the CBS radio network on October 19, 1936. The cast featured Maureen O'Sullivan, and several outstanding supporting players: Frank Morgan, Akim Tamiroff and Zita Johann.

Each program would open with the bold pronouncement, "Lux ... presents Hollywood!" The "Lux Radio Theatre" made its debut in 1934, offering radio dramas of Broadway plays from New York. The show moved to California in June, 1936, where the greatest names in the business were available to star in radio versions of hit motion pictures. The big stars increased their popularity with fans who couldn't get enough of their favorite actors and actresses, and pocketed huge fees up to $5,000 per show. And when host Cecil B. DeMille called — you better believe the actors all came running. Nobody turned down Mr. DeMille.

The show was on the airways for two decades, and when it departed the air in 1955 it left a legacy of being the most successful dramatic radio program in history. Maureen made numerous appearances on the "Lux Radio Theatre" over the course of her career, and her distinctive British/Irish accent was easily recognizable with radio fans.

When the tragedy of Irving Thalberg's death began to fade, everyday life gradually went back to normal at Metro-Goldwyn-Mayer. *A Day at the Races* was shut down indefinitely, pending the selection of a new producer to replace Thalberg. This was an extremely difficult time for Groucho Marx, who later admitted his personal sadness at the unexpected death of his close friend: "After Thalberg's death, my interest in the movies waned. I continued to appear in them but my heart was in the Highlands. The fun had gone out of picture making. I was like an old pug, still going through the motions, but now doing it solely for money."

Maureen was finally able to schedule a visit from her entire family from Ireland in the fall of 1936. Charles O'Sullivan was so excited to be coming to America that he wired his eldest daughter: "Arriving Saturday by train," but neglected to let her know which train. And thus Maureen cabled every train on the line until her family was located, at a cost of $23.70.

The long-awaited visit from the O'Sullivan clan happened in late October, and Harrison Carroll of the *Evening Herald Express* noted the following in his column of October 26, 1936:

"If Maureen O'Sullivan's handsome brother, Jack, would say the word, he'd get a screen test in a minute. Billy Grady, MGM's casting director, thinks he has definite possibilities. Chances of anything developing along this line, however, are pretty slim. I ran into Johnny Farrow, Maureen, and the family last night at the Beverly Brown Derby and Farrow says that Lieutenant O'Sullivan has only two months leave from his regiment and is wrapped up in his army career."

The first week of December, Maureen and John Farrow hosted a huge Hollywood dinner party with an African theme for all of their friends, as a sort of late celebration of their September betrothal. The actress had received permission from the MGM brass to use one of the back-lot sets from *Tarzan Escapes*, and her guests ate African food out of native plates to the accompaniment of booming tom-toms.

The new couple also settled on a place to live, a house that was very near and dear to Maureen's heart, as she described it: "After we married," said the actress, "we moved into a lovely house on a hill in Bel-Air which we built ourselves. It was our first proper marital home and we loved it. What is now the Bel-Air Hotel was then riding stables nearby and John built a trough for the horses to drink out of as they came past the house. Riding was very much the thing in those days and I even went as far as to buy John a horse as a present, not realizing it was a stallion. I'm sorry to say that it very nearly killed him because every time it saw a female it would go into a mad frenzy and try to throw him off."

Maureen later described the house in an interview with journalist Gladys Hall, and her life with John after their marriage: "I have a lovely home," said the bride, "all the lovelier because it is *our* home. We dreamed it and planned it and built it together, and it's built right out of our hearts. It's not a large house, you know, it's fairly small. It's a house we could run very well if neither of us were working and so had to economize.

"It's a California-American type of house, I'd say, which means that it is a little bit of everything. There are some old English pieces in the house, there are Spanish tiles in the patio, there are old pieces that John and I brought over from my parents' home in Dublin when we were there last year — and we live in our home exactly as it pleases us to live.

"Almost always, when we are alone, we have dinner in front of the fire, on a card-table. Sometimes, when I have been working and come home tired I go to bed and have a tray brought to me. John has his dinner on a tray in my room too, and we have a fire going — we have a fireplace in every room in the house — and we talk and play records and it's so lovely.

"We seldom give big parties because we like a few people, our close friends around us — now and then we give small dinner parties, never for more than eight. Our best friends are the John McCormack's and the P. G. Wodehouse's, also Ronald Colman and Michael Brook and a few others who come occasionally. We seldom play games at dinner. I'm no good at games at all. We like to get people over who talk well and enjoy talking and that's what we do — talk."

Maureen also noted that John had a certain amount of freedom, if he wanted a night out: "As husband and wife, John and I are what used to be called old-fashioned which now means we are really ultra-modern. But as individuals, on the other hand, as careerists we are completely free to do as we choose, when we choose. For instance, John has a separate entrance at home. So that when I am tired and want to go to bed early, he can if he feels like it, go out with the boys and come in again without disturbing me. That's perfectly all right with me. If I want to go out for an evening with the girls, that's all right too. We don't ask each other more than each wants to give."

The actress also acknowledged her own vanity to Gladys Hall, and that she didn't want to be lost in the shadow of her director husband, John Farrow: "You see," explained Maureen, "I am very vain. I don't want to be overshadowed by John too completely. For John is the kind of man who immediately attracts attention and compels interest. Now I don't compel interest at all. I'm not the type."

Ms. Hall contradicted Maureen's self-assessment and gave her own unbiased opinion of the young actress in the looks department: "The dark beauty of the dark Maureen, so much more vivid than the best photography has yet revealed — would cause the Sphinx to break into a shag [a dance]. I didn't interrupt her to tell her so, she wouldn't have believed me anyway. Maureen's modest estimate of herself is in her very roots, and is unassailable."

When the interview was concluding, Maureen revealed her true feelings about her life in Hollywood, the land of make believe: "I am the luckiest girl in the world. I'm all the luckier because I *know* how lucky I am. I have everything. It's like a fairy tale. And like the best of all fairy tales I hope that after my story will be written, 'and they lived happily forever after.'

"Forever after," repeated Maureen. "But even if those words are never written, I'll still thank my fairy godmother. I'll still," said Maureen under her breath, almost to herself, "I'll still thank — God."

Eventually, after a delay of three months, *A Day at the Races* went back into production on December 21, 1936. Replacing the late Irving Thalberg as executive producer on the project was Lawrence Weingarten, who was the brother-in-law of Thalberg. Directing was Sam Wood, who had also helmed the vastly successful *A Night at the Opera*, a film in which Allan Jones had brought his marvelous voice to the big screen — a tenor voice that rivaled Nelson Eddy in quality.

Maureen had certain trepidations about appearing in a Marx Brothers film — she was wary of ending up as a foil to the brothers' cockamamie antics. After she read through the script and learned that she had the romantic lead, two fine co-stars in Margaret Dumont and singing star Allan Jones, and a sub-plot that would allow her to do some legitimate acting, she acquiesced to accepting the role.

A Day at the Races begins with sanitarium owner Judy Standish (Maureen) and her driver Tony (Chico Marx), discussing ways to save her hospital before it is taken over by crooked banker Morgan (Douglas Dumbrille) in one month. They propose to ask wealthy patient Mrs. Upjohn (Dumont) to become an investor, but back at the sanitarium she is threatening to leave and return to her old physician in Florida, Dr. Hugo Z. Hackenbush (Groucho).

Tony deceives Mrs. Upjohn and tells her that Hackenbush has just been hired as chief of surgery, and immediately wires him to come and take the job. (Hackenbush, unbeknownst to anyone, is really just a veterinarian who previously treated Mrs. Upjohn, a hypochondriac, with sugar pills.)

Maureen O'Sullivan with Allan Jones and the Marx Brothers in *A Day at the Races*

Judy's boyfriend Gil (Allan Jones) has purchased a racehorse, Hi-Hat, with his last fifteen-hundred dollars, and also inherits light-fingered jockey Stuffy (Harpo) as the horse's rider. Gil hopes to win the money to help Judy, who scoffs at the idea. She calls it a long shot, and warns him not to quit his day job as a singer at a local nightclub.

Dr. Hackenbush arrives amidst great fanfare, but of course he has no references to show Judy's business manager Whitmore (Leonard Ceeley), who is in cahoots with Morgan. Mrs. Upjohn is delighted that Hackenbush is now in charge of her care, and also has romantic designs on the charming Hugo. Later, Tony and Stuffy discover that Hackenbush is really a horse doctor, and together they work to keep that information out of the hands of Morgan and Whitmore.

Meanwhile, Judy has forgiven Gil for buying Hi-Hat, and attends a concert he is giving at a grand water carnival. The sexy blonde Cokey (Esther Muir) is trying to seduce Hackenbush, and spoil his relationship with Mrs. Upjohn. To the rescue are Tony and Stuffy, who manage to warn him that Cokey is working for Morgan.

The sheriff is trying to take possession of the horse because the boys haven't paid the feed bill, and they lead the local law on a merry chase to avoid arrest. They also discover that Hi-Hat is a jumper and not a race horse, and plan to enter him in the annual steeplechase event.

On the day of the big race the boys manage to elude the law, and the race is on with Stuffy in the jockey seat. Judy, Gil, Tony, and Hackenbush are all rooting for Hi-Hat to win, and Stuffy motivates the horse by showing him a picture of Morgan, who abused the horse in the past. Hi-Hat wins the race, and the money is used to pay off the mortgage on the sanitarium. Gil sings Judy a beautiful love song — he has won his sweetheart back. Hackenbush recruits Mrs. Upjohn, Tony, Stuffy, and Hi-Hat to join in the big celebration.

There was everything to like about *A Day at the Races*, and literally nothing to not like about the film. The comedy of the Marx Brothers was falling-down hilarious throughout the picture, especially the classic "Tutsi-Frutsi" ice cream routine. In this bit, Chico cons Groucho out of enough money to place a bet on his favorite nag by selling him a stack of horse racing books. With each worthless volume that he sells to Hackenbush, he walks around and announces, "Getta your Tutsi-Frutsi ice cream ..."

Margaret Dumont was simply marvelous as Mrs. Upjohn, who's not really sick but is convinced the medically dysfunctional Dr. Hackenbush is the only person keeping her alive. There were so many wacky goings-on in this picture that the action is literally nonstop.

Then there was Maureen as the sympathetic young woman who needs all the help she can get from the Marxes and Allan Jones to keep the dastardly banker, Douglas Dumbrille, from stealing the valuable property and turning it into a casino.

The opening scene sets the stage, and you know that you are going to like her character of Judy Standish right from the start. She laments that with business so bad at the sanitarium she won't be able to pay her driver Tony

(Chico) a salary anymore. He smiles warmly and responds, "That's okay, Judy. You don't have to pay me, but that don't mean you're gonna get rid of me ..."

Maureen gives Tony her million-dollar smile in gratitude for his loyalty, and the merry mayhem of this wild adventure is underway. Later, Allan Jones sings two beautiful love songs to Maureen, and the romantic sub-plot gives one a chance to catch the breath in between all the hilarity of Groucho, Chico, Harpo and the divine Ms. Dumont.

The breathtaking music and dancing is worth the price of admission alone, because this picture is really a musical romantic comedy. The water carnival sequence is the big production number, with a stunning dance routine featuring dancer Vivien Fay doing an unbelievable number of consecutive spins; and a wondrous rendition of "All God's Children Got Rhythm" that featured an entire troupe of African-American singers and dancers, which was so spectacular that Dave Gould was nominated for an Academy Award for his direction of the number.

Maureen got in on the action of the wild fight scene, and clobbered one of the deputies with a horse collar, while the Marx Brothers wreaked mayhem in trying to escape the clutches of the sheriff and his merry men. And the music of Chico and his brother Harpo was always special in a Marx Brothers film; as usual Chico performed one of his marvelous piano renditions, and Harpo subsequently demolished the piano and turned it into his instrument of choice, the harp. Both brothers were amazingly talented musicians, and when Harpo was playing his harp, he suddenly became a serious artist. The clowning was kept to occasional eye flutters, but Harpo could break your heart with his beautiful harp performances.

A Day at the Races was the number fourteen film at the box-office and grossed $5 million dollars, more than five times the cost to produce the feature. It was the most profitable of all Marx Brothers films, and certainly the most popular comedy of the year. As the 21st century arrived it was earning even bigger bucks in video rentals and DVD sales. The movie critics loved this film back in 1937, and many decades later it is still one of the funniest comedies of any era. A few sample reviews:

Los Angeles Examiner (June 11, 1937)

"Months in the making, the Marx Brothers hilarious new comedy, *A Day At the Races,* was previewed at the Alexandria Theater last night and proved a worthy successor to the madcap comedians' previous successes.

"Screamingly funny, the picture has Groucho as a horse doctor posing as a real physician and giving a sanitarium's patients his horse pills; Chico as a race track tout, and the inimitable Harpo as a jockey.

"Unusually original 'gags' abound in a plot that includes saving a race horse from the sheriff, holding up a race until the horse can be brought to the track, and through the horse, saving the sanitarium in lieu of the old homestead.

"The music also is unusually good, with several excellent numbers sung by Allan Jones, who with Maureen O'Sullivan, provides the young romantic element. Margaret Dumont is excellent as a socialite in love with Groucho, and the brothers have their own musical feature, with Groucho singing with Chico's piano and Harpo's harp.

"The comedy is splendidly directed by Sam Wood, and MGM has not spared expense in its production."

Los Angeles Examiner Louella O. Parsons (June 17, 1937)

"The mad Marxes live up to their reputation and even exceed it as top gagsters in *A Day at the Races*. I don't know when I ever have seen one picture so crammed full of original bits of nonsense and hilariously funny gags. Usually a comedy of this caliber offers two or three outstanding comedy situations, but this newest Marx opus is replete with side-splitting moments, one funnier than the other.

"There is really everything in this picture that makes for entertainment — great variety — grand music — superb comedy, and a story which lends itself primarily to fun without any forced situations. Robert Pirosh, George Seaton and George Oppenheimer, the authors, have provided an unusually good story structure that actually has a plot and which, even in the face of the broad farce, carries suspense and interest throughout.

"Really, *A Day at the Races* is a three-ring circus with something doing every second. Groucho bursting into song and dance; Harpo playing the harp and Chico at the piano. Credit goes to Sam Woods for his fine direction of comedy which, I can promise, will make you forget your income tax, the rent, your relatives or any other annoyance.

"The three Marxes have excellent support in Maureen O'Sullivan, who is charming as the owner of the sanitarium; Margaret Dumont as the wealthy patient is also very good, for last but by no means least, there is Allan Jones, owner of the race horse and the possessor of a singing voice that gets better all the time."

In 1994, Maureen admitted that if she hadn't been involved with John Farrow, she could have easily been swayed romantically by Mr. Marx:

"Actually, there was one man I could quite easily have had a romance with, and that was Groucho Marx. He was a well-read, considerate man and I liked him enormously. I even found him rather sexy, although he wasn't at all good-looking. I first met him in 1934 just after I'd finished in *The Barretts of Wimpole Street*. Because this was supposed to be an important film, I was feeling rather grand at the time and didn't want to do just any old second-rate movie. So when I was asked to be in a film with the Marx brothers, I wasn't in the least bit enthusiastic.

"'I really don't think I want to get mixed up with those monkeys,' I told the director bluntly. But despite my resistance he tried to persuade me by giving me a detailed description of the plot. Apparently it was to be about a girl's struggle to prevent a ranch from being closed.

"Okay," I said, "that's fine, but what about the Marx brothers? 'Oh, they'll be around,' said the director rather ominously. In the end I agreed to do the film and in the course of shooting I became very close to the Marx brothers, especially with Groucho."

Maureen reiterated these feelings of friendship and possibly more for Groucho, in a 1996 video interview: "Now Groucho, every morning — we worked at the Santa Anita racetrack, and I had a portable dressing room — he would come over and try out his jokes on me. At like seven in the morning he would try to be funny. Finally, I said 'Groucho, look — I really don't like funny men. So let's not be funny anymore, let's just try to be friends if we can.'

"And we became great friends, and I was devoted to him — and he was to me, I think. I really think so. I could have been in love with him. Now that sounds very strange. Maybe comedy and romance are close. I don't know. I've tried to analyze that. You know like tears and laughter.

"But he was very idealistic, a very intelligent man. Very kind, very nice. And no more jokes! Unless they were really funny, he couldn't help it. But that was all right.

"I thought he was sexy. He was very considerate of others, even Margaret Dumont. Off-screen he was very nice to her."

Groucho Marx biographer Stefan Kanfer said that he had "an unrequited crush on O'Sullivan," and that a friend had said of the matter: "Groucho couldn't keep his eyes off her. She was a beautiful shicksa with doe eyes and soft hair, and given his home situation she couldn't have come along at a more opportune time. Alas, she was never anything other than sweet to him."

Maureen and Groucho Marx became devoted friends

In a 1971 interview that was published in a book authored by Groucho Marx, *The Marx Brothers Scrapbook*, he accused John Farrow of being physically abusive of Maureen:

"My dad [Sam Marx] was a hot sport," noted Groucho. "All you have to do is look at a picture of him to know that. He died in the Garden of Allah. It was a hotel on Sunset Boulevard. A very famous place that was named after Valentino's wife, Allah Nazimova. He died there. I lived there, too.

"You know who else lived there? Mia's mother, Maureen O'Sullivan. She played with us in *A Day at the Races*. Once she came in with a black eye. Her husband had beat her up. She couldn't work that day.

"He was a Catholic and later wrote some books on leprosy. He was a talented man but he liked to hit his wife.

"I never hit my wives except in self-defense."

Maureen was one of MGM's most valuable stars and any type of physical abuse, spousal or otherwise, would have been greeted with anything but indifference. The bosses at MGM had warned her in the past about dating John Farrow, as she confided in an August 21, 1994 interview with the *Chicago Tribune*:

"They told me he was a dangerous ladies' man," recalled Maureen, "so I immediately went after him. I looked innocent, so people didn't suspect me of too much."

If Groucho's charges were indeed the truth, there would have been an immediate reaction from the MGM hierarchy. Louis B. Mayer would have ordered his chief lieutenant, Eddie Mannix, to handle the problem. A couple of decades in the past Mannix had been a bouncer for the Schenck brothers when they were in the amusement park business, a tough guy who could handle the most problematic situations. Irving Thalberg biographer Roland Flamini described Mannix as "... the rugged, foul-mouthed Irish general manager."

Eddie Mannix was an imposing Irish strongman who was very fond of MGM's prize Irish talent, Ms. O'Sullivan. His most notable motion picture as the occasional producer was *The Devil Doll* (1936), which had starred Maureen along with Lionel Barrymore.

The truth of the matter is that John Farrow never worked for MGM after this time, with one single exception* almost two decades later. Although he had been employed by Metro for several years as a writer and assistant director, and was being groomed for directorial duties, the latter never happened. They immediately parted ways with no true explanation offered by either party. (*Ride Vaquero!*, a 1953 MGM western that starred Ava Gardner and Robert Taylor, was directed by Farrow.)

While Maureen was filming *A Day at the Races*, Farrow began directing Warner Brothers B-pictures such as *West of Shanghai* (1937) with Boris Karloff. He later worked for RKO, Paramount, and other studios.

A week before *A Day at the Races* was released, the nation was rocked once again by the death of one of its most beloved Hollywood stars, Jean Harlow, who died in the Good Samaritan Hospital on June 7, 1937. Miss Harlow was admitted to the hospital with a severe case of uremic poisoning, which is a toxic condition of the blood and can result in kidney shutdown. At her bedside at the time of her death was close friend William Powell, her mother and stepfather, and a cousin.

Miss Harlow was known as a "wise-cracking platinum blonde" and had made her mark in several classic films after arriving in Hollywood at the age of seventeen in 1928. She appeared with Jimmy Cagney in *Public Enemy* (1931), and some of her other memorable roles included *Red Headed Woman* (1932), *Red Dust* (1932), *Dinner at Eight* (1933), *Bombshell* (1933), *China Seas* (1935), and *Libeled Lady* (1936). Her famous line from the Howard Hughes produced *Hell's Angels* (1930) was: "Excuse me — while I slip into something more comfortable."

Of the many tributes that were published after her death, Louis B. Mayer eulogized, "This is the end of a rich personal friendship. This girl, whom so many millions adored, was one of the loveliest, sweetest persons I have known in thirty years of theatrical business. I have lost a friend, the world has lost a ray of sunlight."

Maureen and Jean Harlow were both twenty-six years old, both women were born in 1911, and they were good friends that traveled in the same social circles. Harlow came to Maureen's 1936 prenuptial party and also attended her wedding to John Farrow. They never worked in the same film together, but at the Metro studio it was one big family; you ate lunch together in the commissary, you were invited to the same parties, and the girls danced at the same nightclubs. Because they were the same age, they had a lot in common.

The funeral was held on June 9 and was attended by the many friends Ms. Harlow had made during her career, including Maureen and John Farrow. A description of the service was published in the *New York Times*:

"A brief and simple funeral service was held today for Jean Harlow in a suburban chapel overflowing with flowers. The service in the Wee Kirk o' the Heather lasted only twenty minutes. At the outset Jeanette MacDonald sang 'The Indian Love Call.' Nelson Eddy sang another of Miss Harlow's favorite songs, 'Ah, Sweet Mystery of Life.'

"Barely 250 persons, most of them Hollywood stars and studio executives, were admitted to the service. William Powell was there early. Warner Baxter also was an early arrival. Clark Gable, who was both an usher and pallbearer, came with Carole Lombard. Spencer Tracy, his face deeply lined, was without a hat.

"Myrna Loy wore a dark gown with a black veil attached to her hat. Una Merkel and Madge Evans came together. Mr. and Mrs. Robert Montgomery and Maureen O'Sullivan and her husband sat near each other.

"The pallbearers escorting the coffin to the mausoleum were those with whom Miss Harlow had worked — Mr. Gable; Edward J. Mannix, MGM executive; Hunt Stromberg, producer; Jack Conway and W. S. Van Dyke, directors; and Ray June, cameraman."

Decades later in 1992, Maureen recalled her brief friendship with Harlow: "I didn't know Jean that well, but with Jean — what you saw, was what you got. There didn't seem to be any subterfuge or subtlety about Jean. I was spending the weekend with Myron Selznick, David's brother at Lake Arrowhead. And Jean and I had one room, and John Farrow was sharing a room with William Powell — things were more circumspect in those days.

"So Jean and I were sharing one room, and she used to open the window at night and it was freezing. It was Christmas, I think, and the icicles were hanging outside the window. Jean loved the windows open, but she would get up in the morning and close them so that I wouldn't be cold. She never wore a nightgown at all, she slept in the raw. The brave girl would get up and close the windows, and she was very sweet like that.

"And then she'd say, 'The maid might be embarrassed,' and she'd take her nightgown and rumple it up and throw it on the bed to make it look like she's slept in it. And she didn't wear any underwear at all. And she'd step into her white slacks and white sweater and a 'swoosh' of her perfume... you know the bottles that they had with a long handle in those days. And off she'd go to breakfast. And that was Jean Harlow.

"The last time I saw Jean she was doing *Saratoga*, and for some unknown reason she took me to the studio. And she was wearing a big star sapphire ring that William Powell had given her. The ring was so big, and she looked so frail. I said, 'Jean, how do you feel?' And she said, 'I'm not well.' I said, 'Oh well, we all have those days. You'll be all right,' but she didn't look well. And she died pretty soon after that. I didn't know her that well, but what I saw of her I liked. I had also been at her wedding to Hal Rosson. She was a nice girl."

Maureen noted that despite this tragedy and many others in Hollywood, it was mostly kept within the family: "At the studio, and it's the same on stage, there's surprisingly little gossip. We don't gossip about each other, we don't even talk about each other really, except in a nice way. It's hard to believe but that's a fact. We didn't gossip, that would be outside the studio domain. As I've said, we were a family — we didn't destroy each other."

Maureen O'Sullivan next appeared in the entertaining spy drama, *The Emperor's Candlesticks* (1937), with two of MGM's top names, William Powell and Luise Rainer, in the lead roles. Powell was the Polish spy Baron Wolensky, and Rainer portrayed the sultry Russian agent Countess Mironova.

This was a serious drama with a subtle touch of humor, and two romantic subplots that build suspense as the story unfolds: the two spies fall for each other on a train that speeds through Europe; and back in Vienna a brave young woman (Maureen) falls for the prince that she has betrayed and lured into a trap that may mean his death.

Maureen was cast as Maria Orlech, the daughter of a man being held hostage as a political prisoner in Russia, while the handsome Robert Young once again was her love interest, the Grand Duke Peter. Other members of the cast included the wonderful character actor Frank Morgan, who would later earn his fame as the wizard in *The Wizard of Oz* (1939); Douglas Dumbrille, often the unconscionable villain in countless films of the era (such as his Baradas in *Cardinal Richelieu*); and Henry Stephenson, who played in several of Maureen's films, usually as the distinguished, fatherly type.

Luise Rainer was an Austrian actress who made her Hollywood debut in *Escapade* (1935), co-starring William Powell, and then shocked the motion picture world by winning the Oscar for Best Actress in her next two films: *The Great Ziegfeld* (1936), and *The Good Earth* (1937). This was her third film in two years with William Powell, and they certainly made an exciting romantic lead team: he with his worldly charm and dashing looks, she with her haunting beauty and exotic Austrian accent.

Maureen O'Sullivan as Maria Orlech

The story begins in Vienna in the early part of the 20th century, at a costume ball attended by many of the social elite. Arriving without fanfare, Peter (Robert Young), the son of the Russian czar, is dressed as Romeo and accompanied by Baron Suroff (Frank Morgan). When he sees a beautiful girl dressed as Juliet, it is love at first sight and the flirting turns into a passionate kiss. The young woman is Maria Orlech (Maureen), who leads her unsuspecting suitor into a trap, where he is thus confined and held for ransom. The price is the life of Thaddeus Orlech, who will die in 15 days as a political prisoner unless the czar — Peter's father — pardons the man.

His captors, Polish nationalists, instruct him to write a letter to the czar and ask for the release of Orlech in exchange for his own life. The young duke refuses, until he learns that the condemned man is the father of his "Juliet" — Maria Orlech — and then he immediately complies and writes the letter to his father.

The man entrusted to deliver the letter is Baron Wolensky (William Powell), who appears to be a suave playboy but is in reality a trusted spy for the Polish nationalists. Wolensky visits his friend Johan (Stephenson), who asks him to take a pair of ornate candlesticks to a lady friend on his planned visit to St. Petersburg. Each of the candlesticks has a secret compartment, so Wolensky hides the valued letter in one and is told the package would be delivered to him at the station that evening.

Countess Miranova also visits Johan, and she convinces him to let her deliver the candlesticks; he hesitates, but acquiesces. The countess puts her own document in the matching candlestick; this letter contains damning evidence that Wolensky is a spy and should be arrested immediately upon his arrival in Russia. Later, the baron discovers that the countess has possession of the candlesticks and has left for St. Petersburg on an earlier train.

Eventually Wolensky catches up with the countess, and despite the fact they are on opposite sides, they begin to fall in love with each other. When the candlesticks are stolen and later sold to an art dealer, they begin a cross-continent chase together that takes them to Paris and finally London, where the candlesticks are about to be sold at auction. The final bid is £3000, a sum they raise by pooling their money; they complete the transaction and each takes one of the candlesticks. Both are mistaken when they assume they have the candlestick with their own important document, when in fact they have been switched.

Meanwhile, back in Vienna, Peter remains a political prisoner and his captors are threatening to execute him if necessary. Maria rallies to his cause, and warns them that she will go to the police if they do not wait for word from Wolensky. After all it is her father's life that is at stake, so she has the final say. Peter remains grateful to Maria, and she asks his forgiveness for betraying him — they both realize they are falling in love.

Back in Russia, Wolensky discovers the documents that the countess has been carrying would condemn him to death. He confronts the countess, and promises to return to her his death warrant — after his letter is delivered to the czar. As the letter travels through underground channels, Colonel Radoff of the Russian Secret Service arrests Countess Mironova for collaborating with the enemy. He also accuses her of falling in love with Wolensky, at which she scoffs but throws the evidence against him into the fire, destroying it.

William Powell and Luise Ranier as spies in *The Emperor's Candlesticks*

When the czar receives his son's letter, he immediately signs the pardon papers for Maria's father, who is released from prison. Subsequently Peter is also granted his freedom, and, blindfolded, is only able to sense the presence of his lover Maria nearby as they part ways. Back in St. Petersburg, the czar warns Wolensky and Countess Mironova that he could have them both executed for treason. However, he is so impressed with their loyalty to each other and that both had risked death, he grants them immunity and allows them to leave Russia. As they travel on the night train, a passionate kiss seals their new partnership.

Luise Rainer's career faded and was ordinary after her meteoric beginning, and she later lamented that her good fortune had really been a curse:

"For my second and third pictures I won Academy Awards," observed Rainer. "Nothing worse could have happened to me."

For Maureen O'Sullivan, *The Emperor's Candlesticks* was an opportunity to work in a film with exceptional actors Robert Young, Frank Morgan, and Douglas Dumbrille, and also observe from the sidelines the superb interplay between Rainer and William Powell, himself twice nominated for Best Actor in *The Thin Man* (1934), and *My Man Godfrey* (1936).

Several reviews noted the appeal of this picture and the excellent acting of the principals, especially the Irish actress. Meanwhile, Rialtan of the *Evening Herald Express* noted that Maureen was simply "gorgeous."

Hollywood Citizen News (June 24, 1937)

"*The Emperor's Candlesticks* is the one about the two spies, male and female, who are instructed by unromantic superiors to put the kibosh on each other, and who eventually fall in love. It is Miss Rainer's picture. She has, I believe, what the dictionary calls 'elan.' She exercises her charms somewhat too extravagantly, I thought, in view of the demands of her role, but the charms are such that it is really a welcome fault.

"There is a very pretty and appealing minor romance enacted expertly by Maureen O'Sullivan, as the Polish girl whose patriot father is held by the Russians, and by Robert Young, as the Russian crown prince who is held by Polish nationalists until the Polish patriot is freed."

Evening Herald Express by the Rialtan (July 1, 1937)

"Just chock full of political intrigue, romance and suspense is *Emperor's Candlesticks*, which stars the debonair William Powell and the beautiful Luise Rainer. The superb acting of this pair in this tale of a pair of candlesticks with secret compartments that figure in an international intrigue raise what would ordinarily be a common film into one that is quite entertaining.

"The supporting cast comes in for a good part of praise, for it is they who help the picture to run along smoothly and make one imagine he is actually present at the events and not sitting in a movie house.

"They include gorgeous Maureen O'Sullivan, inimitable Frank Morgan, who, always good, adds a small share of comedy to the film, and Robert Young as the czar's son."

Between Two Women (1937) was a hospital soap opera with stars Maureen O'Sullivan, Franchot Tone, and Virginia Bruce in a romantic triangle that also involved a series of personal tragedies for the principals. Maureen and Tone had been the young lovers in *Stage Mother*, and he was often cast as a man of strong character; this melodrama was a typical role for him, a brilliant doctor who gets caught in the middle between two women who fall in love with him for different reasons. Virginia Bruce had that "society glamor" look about her, and in this picture she was excellent as the pampered rich girl who gets whatever she wants, including the handsome young doctor.

There's a modicum of humor in between the onslaught of crises, in the form of wisecracking hospital telephone operator Sally (Helen Troy), and a nosy newspaper guy named Snoopy (Cliff Edwards). Sally is Claire's friend and they do a lot of joking around with the doctors in the waiting room, and every other comment is a wisecrack. Snoopy, meanwhile, has a crush on Claire and repeatedly asks her for a date for "next Tuesday" — she knows he's kidding and always responds, "Sure, but not next Tuesday — let's make it two years from next 4th of July."

Set in New York City, *Between Two Women* was based on an original story by Erich von Stroheim, the writer-director-actor who is perhaps most famous for his role in *Sunset Boulevard* (1950) as Max, the chauffeur and former husband to Gloria Swanson's mesmerizing Norma Desmond. Directing was the competent George B. Seitz, who helmed many of Maureen's films in the late 1930s and churned them out at MGM quickly and efficiently.

The story begins when Dr. Allen Meighan (Tone) is called to the scene of a life-and-death situation, where a man is pinned in a construction accident. In order to save his life the doctor amputates one arm, using a bottle of liquor as an anaesthetic. Back at General Hospital he is congratulated by all of the other doctors and also his nurse, Claire Donahue (Maureen). Allen and Claire are good friends and have a certain attraction for each other, but she is married and thus their flirting is platonic. Her husband Tom (Anthony Mace) is an unemployed alcoholic who strikes his wife on occasion when in one of his drunken moods. He is a big-time loser and Claire unfortunately is stuck in a loveless marriage.

Meanwhile, wealthy socialite Patricia Sloan (Bruce) is admitted after an accident, and through the diligent care of Dr. Allen Meighan she recovers completely after a three-week stay in the hospital. The spoiled Patricia has her sights aligned on Allen, and traps the good doctor into a proposal of marriage. Although he is in love with Claire, Allen realizes this is hopeless and instead ties the knot with Patricia.

Meighan's work as a doctor comes first in his life, and he repeatedly must break social engagements with Patricia to be at the hospital for surgery. Of course, Nurse Claire is always by his side, which angers his wife and pushes them farther apart. Her confidante is wealthy young doctor Tony Wolcott (Leonard Penn), who is only in the medical field to appease his father.

When Tom Donahue is injured in a car accident, he is rushed to the hospital where Dr. Wolcott is called in to perform an amputation of one leg. Claire is hysterical and realizes that Wolcott has been drinking and might kill her husband with his incompetence — she frantically contacts Dr. Meighan to come in and take over the operation. Allen abruptly leaves his wife Patricia at a party, which angers her, and rushes to the hospital. When he arrives, he is forced to slug Wolcott, who is in his own maniacal rage. Dr. Meighan tries to save the life of Tom Donahue, but he is too late and Claire's husband dies on the operating table.

After a hearing, Wolcott loses his medical license and goes to see Patricia for consolation — he also talks her into going to Paris with him for a "vacation." When Allen comes home, he has a terrible argument with Patricia and they both agree to a divorce. He storms out into the rainy night, and heads for the hospital to see Claire. She is understanding and takes him out for dinner to let him talk out his frustrations. They both readily admit they made mistakes in marrying the wrong people.

That evening, Patricia and Tony Wolcott board a train out of town, planning to travel to Paris together. Before the train is ten miles out of town, it derails and both of them are severely injured — he with mangled legs and she badly disfigured on one side of her face. Transported to General Hospital, Wolcott asks Dr. Meighan to try and repair his legs rather than amputate; Allen performs a magnificent surgery that lasts for hours and saves both legs.

A team of doctors and plastic surgeons are working on Patricia, and when Allen sees her with half her face bandaged, he takes her home and promises to take care of her forever. A few weeks later at a coming-out party, Patricia reveals her face and is as beautiful as ever — she has healed completely without scars. She also tells Allen she is going to set him up with a fancy Park Avenue medical practice, and they can forever live the life of the rich and the elite.

Allen finally realizes that they are a complete mismatch, and informs her he is returning to the hospital to be a surgeon. They both now admit that the marriage is over, and it is best that they part ways. Back at the hospital, Dr. Meighan and Nurse Claire are reunited where they belong — and now they are free to fall in love and have the happiness they deserve.

The reviews were generally kind, and hospital dramas of the day were quite popular with the film-going crowd:

Hollywood Citizen News James Francis Crow (June 25, 1937)

"*Between Two Women,* albeit unpretentiously produced, is an adornment of the current cycle of doctor films. It brings along with it a quantity of overly familiar material — (not to say hokum) — and it follows the line of least resistance to an easy and obvious happy ending. But, thanks to clean-cut acting and sound direction, it will keep you fooled for at least the duration of your stay in the theater, and its total impression is that of an unusually solid and entertaining little photoplay.

"The locale is a general hospital. The theme is that of the love and self-sacrifice of the residents therein. Franchot Tone is the doctor. Maureen O'Sullivan is the nurse with whom he is really in love, but Virginia Bruce is the beautiful and wealthy patient.

"The film-play finds easy answers and excuses for all concerned, but so skillfully and ingratiatingly do the principals play their roles that the outcome, far from appearing forced, seems natural and inevitable. There is a fourth good performance by Leonard Penn as the handsome young heavy. Neatly interpolated comedy helps keep the audience in good humor, and Director Seitz handles effectively the several dramatic highlights of surgical room action."

Variety (August 11, 1937)

"Story has Franchot Tone as the earnest young surgeon in love with the nurse, Maureen O'Sullivan. She also loves him, but is married to a failure whom she sticks to out of loyal pity. Beauteous young heiress, Virginia Bruce, comes to the hospital for an appendectomy, takes to the doc and works out on him. He tumbles and there's a wedding.

"Tone is noble enough, self-sacrificing enough and understanding enough to inspire mayhem or all the femininely tender yearnings. Maureen O'Sullivan is properly small and loyal, truly the brave little woman. Virginia Bruce, looking not quite so lovely as she has in previous films, is one of those rich, spoiled, selfish — er, ladies out of a Hollywood script. All three play the parts so easily they might be doing it all from memory, which wouldn't be surprising, either.

"George B. Seitz's direction clearly demonstrates that he knows exactly what to do with a stereotype yarn like this one."

Comedy is something that is perhaps overlooked in the repertoire of Maureen O'Sullivan, but the actress was an exceptional comedienne when given the opportunity — which came along in *My Dear Miss Aldrich* (1937), with co-stars Walter Pidgeon and Edna May Oliver. This was definitely Maureen's starring role, although she accepted second billing to the divine Ms. Oliver, who was one of the superb comic actresses in the picture business.

Pidgeon, meanwhile, played the tough newspaper boss who feels that women have no place as reporters in the news game — until the feisty Miss Aldrich (Maureen) comes along to show him otherwise. Walter Pidgeon usually portrayed gentlemen with class, but in this case he was an old-school chauvinist who becomes rattled by the beauty and charm of his new boss. She in turn is determined to open his eyes that women belong in the newspaper business as reporters, and can do the job as well as any man.

The story begins when a wealthy newspaper magnate dies without an heir and ownership of the *New York Globe-Leader* reverts to his niece, Nebraska school teacher Martha Aldrich (Maureen). The managing editor is Ken Morley (Pidgeon), who strongly believes that a woman's place is — well, anyplace other than working at his newspaper. When he learns that a woman is the new owner, he is expecting her to be a crabby old spinster; instead, it turns out to be the charming Martha and the crabby old spinster is in fact her aunt, Mrs. Lou Atherton (Edna May Oliver), a puzzle fanatic who tags along to watchdog her niece in the big city.

A huge story is in the works when the Queen of England is visiting New York and rumors persist that she is pregnant. However, none of the papers are able to confirm or even get a comment from the monarch. Martha takes it upon herself to phone the queen at her hotel, who takes a liking to her country charm. The monarch kindly informs her that she is indeed pregnant and even schedules an interview for the *Globe-Leader*.

With this success as a wedge, Martha asks Morley for a job as a reporter; since she owns the paper he can hardly turn her down and tells her the standard pay is $30 a week. The tough managing-editor is getting weak-kneed whenever he is around Martha, and gets tongue-tied when he tries to buy her lunch but she insists on paying her own bill. He's falling in love, but she is as cool as a cucumber.

While buying a hat, Martha gets a hunch that labor leaders Mr. and Mrs. Sinclair are holding confidential meetings to try to avert a strike against a major industrialist, Mr. Talbot. Martha visits Mrs. Sinclair (Janet Beecher) to see if she can get the exclusive story, but the talks are secret — she is unceremoniously shown the door. The nosy reporter follows the Sinclairs to the Red Apple Inn, where they and Talbot are ratifying a new labor agreement.

Martha is trying to get the scoop by hiding in a dumbwaiter, but when her subterfuge is discovered she is bound with ropes. Morley and Mrs. Atherton are worried about Martha and track her to the Red Apple, wherefore he boldly brandishes Martha's unloaded gun while demanding answers and the story for the *Globe-Leader*. The bouncer (Guinn Williams) shows up and knocks Morley out with one punch — they too are tied up and locked in a room. It looks as though the scoop will go to the *Chronicle*, but Martha uses her broken compact mirror to cut the ropes and they are free.

A plan is hatched that Aunt Lou will pretend to have small pox, and when Morley's reporters arrive dressed as medical examiners, the whole hotel is quarantined. Somehow the crazy scheme works, and the *Globe-Leader* gets the exclusive story about the labor settlement. Ken is now convinced that a woman can do the job, and offers her a dual full-time position — as a reporter and also as his wife. She accepts the former and promises to consider the latter proposal!

Maureen and Edna May Oliver made a delightful one-two comedy punch in *My Dear Miss Aldrich*, a charming change-of-pace role for the Irish actress. And with the likeable Walter Pidgeon as the object of most of her shenanigans, the picture had plenty of laughs and sticky situations that resolved only when he finally realized that she had the upper hand.

Nebraska school teacher Martha Aldrich showed that she was no country bumpkin, and the weaker sex handily won all of the battles with her editor

Ken Morley; using wit, charm and brains, she easily out-matched his clumsy machismo and old-fashioned ideas. In the end he does win the girl, but it appears she will be wearing the pants in the family. A corny ending indeed, but all MGM comedies of the era concluded this way — the guy gets the girl, and a kiss seals the deal.

The reviews for *My Dear Miss Aldrich* were positive, noting that it was an enjoyable comedy with the class that comes from an MGM production:

Film Daily (October 13, 1937)

"Good entertainment for everybody with laughs, punch, and action. A newspaper story written from the comedy angle. Miss O'Sullivan as the attractive Nebraska school teacher, who falls heir to the biggest paper in New York, and Miss Oliver as her crotchety aunt who is suspicious of everybody in the big city, make a good team. Walter Pidgeon as the smooth managing editor, who is a confirmed woman hater, plays his part for all it's worth and gets the girl in the end. Miss Oliver is funny and draws laughs throughout with her niece and editor at odds until the final clinch. The story is rapidly paced throughout and moves to a swift climax with laughs and a happy ending."

Variety (October 6, 1937)

"When Metro goes out to make a Class B picture, they give it plenty of production, steady direction and, a certain amount of class. It may not have big draw stars and the situation may be overdone, but it certainly will stand up on the second picture shelf in the theatres for which it was designed. *My Dear Miss Aldrich* apparently fits into this category. It makes no pretense at being more than a light, fluffy comedy. And that's what it is.

"Edna May Oliver, yet legit trouper, comes through with one of the funniest performances as the aunt of the youthful newspaper boss. Maureen O'Sullivan is pert and enjoyable as new head of the Manhattan daily, who decides the managing editor should change his ideas on femme scribblers. Walter Pidgeon makes a fairly genuine managing editor."

With four pictures in release for 1937, Maureen continued to be immensely busy and one of the most popular actresses in Hollywood. On July 6, Elizabeth Yeaman of the *Hollywood Citizen News* noted the following about her next assignment for the studio:

"It will be Maureen O'Sullivan who will be in the romantic spotlight with Robert Taylor in the first picture that MGM is to produce in England, under the title of *A Yank at Oxford*. Sam Wood will go over to direct the picture, and Louis B. Mayer and his retinue leave Hollywood on Thursday for London, to inaugurate the MGM production unit there. The unit is being created partially to meet film quota regulations in England.

"With the two principals and the director being exported for the picture, perhaps the studio thought it advisable to have one of those principals a British subject. Maureen, you will recall, was imported from Ireland by Fox about seven years ago, to play with John McCormack in *Song O' My Heart*."

It was also reported by Ms. Yeaman a couple of weeks later that John Farrow had landed his first directing job for Warner Brothers, in a film tentatively titled *Without Warning,* starring Boris Karloff. What had appeared to be a working vacation in England for Maureen and her husband now meant that she would make the trip on her own.

On the positive side of the ledger she would be able to spend some of her free time with her family. It would be just a short hop over to Dublin from her location shooting in England. In a November 1937 letter back to the States, Maureen noted that the fog was so bad at times in London that she was living in her dressing-room to escape the drive to her cottage.

With a million-dollar smile and a sparkling personality, Maureen made an excellent comedienne

CHAPTER FOURTEEN
"Maureen and Robert Taylor ... a Fine Romantic Pairing"

Maureen co-starred with Robert Taylor in two films released in 1938, *A Yank At Oxford*, a romantic comedy, and also *The Crowd Roars*, a boxing drama. The immensely popular Taylor was one of the most handsome actors during the Golden Age of Hollywood, along with Clark Gable, Gary Cooper, Errol Flynn, and James Stewart.

Mr. Taylor had dark wavy hair, a perfect athletic physique, drop-dead smile, a glib personality and the animal magnetism to charm his female co-stars. Like many actors, Taylor chose a new moniker when he became an actor — he had been born in Nebraska as Spangler Arlington Brugh, which in itself explains the name change. Robert Taylor went on to marry actress Barbara Stanwyck in 1939, a marriage that made them two of Hollywood's most beautiful people during the decade of the 1940s.

A Yank At Oxford, filmed in England, had an exceptional cast that included Maureen and Taylor, along with Lionel Barrymore, Edmund Gwenn, and also Vivien Leigh, her former school chum from Roehampton. Vivien, at this time, had not yet achieved any degree of success in the movies, while Maureen was a big star in America and in England as well. Vivien's fame would come later and she would be remembered for two Oscar-winning roles — as Scarlett O'Hara in *Gone with the Wind* (1939), and later as Blanche Du Bois in *A Streetcar Named Desire* (1951).

Louis B. Mayer was upset that a virtual "unknown" — Vivien Leigh — was cast as the second female lead; however, she was chosen by Michael Balcon, the British producer who was in charge of the production. Since Vivien had a secondary role as the flirty, adulterous wife of an older man, she was naturally billed behind Maureen. The actual order of billing was Robert Taylor, Lionel Barrymore, Maureen, Vivien, and then Edmund Gwenn.

The actress later remembered that her old classmate had her claws out in their first meeting since school days, and Leigh snubbed her in the most hurtful manner she could muster:

"I felt fine about that [the casting order] but unfortunately Vivien held it against me," said Maureen. "And when she had a party for the cast on our arrival in London I was the only one who wasn't invited. I don't entirely blame her, but I can't say I cared for her much after that."

In the picture, Maureen portrayed the charming Oxford upper-grad Molly Beaumont who later lands the handsome American import, Lee Sheridan (Taylor). Leigh, meanwhile, was the catty town tramp who cheats on her pale, bookish husband at every opportunity. When Vivien's Elsa Craddock begins an illicit affair with Molly's brother Paul, there is quite a row between the two females during a face-to-face encounter at the bookstore. This was their only scene together, and considering the off-screen tension between them, it was probably not a difficult moment to enact.

As the sequence progresses, Molly sees Lee hunting for a book in the upper shelves, and when she too climbs a ladder in search of a particular volume, they begin flirting and discussing a kiss that he had forced upon her the previous day. The following conversation takes place across a bookshelf:

"I've had quite enough of your amateurish kisses, thank you," says Molly with a coy smile. "Why don't you practice on Mrs. Craddock? I'm sure you'd find her most cooperative."

"I wouldn't take her home if I won her in a raffle," warns the American. "These college widows are about as dangerous to play with as a stick of dynamite!"

The lovely Molly admits that for once they agreed upon something, and he asks her for a dinner date. She says no — but they do wind up at an ice skating rink where he falls unceremoniously on his tail end, and brings the girl down with him. Suffice to say, the laughter soon turns into a full-blown romance.

The story begins at Lakedale State College, where Lee Sheridan (Taylor) is the best athlete on campus, and also a top student. His father Dan (Barrymore) is his biggest supporter and runs the town newspaper; he often holds up editions to make sure that Lee's latest athletic exploits make it to the public hot off the press. The Dean at Lakedale arranges a Rhodes scholarship for Lee to attend Cardinal College at Oxford University, and Dan Sheridan takes out a loan from the bank to make sure his son has the money to go to England.

Lee arrives and is bound for Oxford aboard the train, where he meets three of his new classmates, Paul Beaumont (Griffith Jones), Wavertree, and Ramsey. They surmise that the American is rather full of himself, and trick him into leaving the train ten miles before Oxford to avoid a nonexistent reception committee. He also is introduced to Beaumont's sister Molly (Maureen), and the sparks begin to fly right from the start.

Once off the train, Lee realizes that the joke is on him — but he takes it in good nature. When he finally arrives at Oxford, a second hazing gag has him being introduced to a fake Dean, which in reality was Wavertree in disguise. Lee chases him across the campus, then boots him in the derriere. However, by this time it was the genuine Dean of Cardinal (Edmund Gwenn) and now he is in real trouble thirty minutes after his arrival at Oxford.

The Dean has a sense of fairness, but warns Sheridan that he will be "sent-down" (expelled) if there are any further shenanigans. By now Lee is fed up with anything British, and is tempted to quit; he is talked out of leaving by his "scout," Scatters, who enlightens Lee to all the great history at Oxford down through the ages.

Lee makes a stop at a bookstore run by Elsa Craddock (Vivien), a married woman who flirts shamelessly with all the college boys and is having an affair with Paul Beaumont. Molly arrives at the shop and has an angry exchange with Elsa, arguing that her brother is jeopardizing his Oxford education by involving himself with the disreputable Mrs. Craddock.

Maureen and Robert Taylor are making eyes for each other as Vivien Leigh waits her turn

Lee and Molly, after a rough start, become mad for each other and he often writes to his father Dan back home about his wonderful new English girlfriend. The American also becomes a star on the track team, but gets into a fight with Paul when Lee grabs his position in the relay and is subsequently shunned for his unsportsmanlike act. That evening, the student body forcibly "de-pants" Lee — which is just a joke, but escalates into a fist fight at the tavern between the two men.

Coming in late one evening, Elsa is quizzed by her husband. She races to the college to warn Paul that he will be looking for him. When Craddock arrives at

Cardinal, Lee hides Elsa in his dorm room but is caught red-handed by the Dean. Although she is involved with Paul, Lee covers up for him and as a result the American is sent-down and asked to leave school.

This is bad timing for Lee, because his father is arriving to watch him row in the crew races against Cambridge the coming weekend. He explains to his father why he was expelled, but continues the lie that he was having an affair with Elsa Craddock. Lee's father cannot fathom this, considering his letters regarding his affection for Molly.

Dan goes to see Molly, who says she doesn't believe a word of the charges against Lee. Dan also visits Elsa at the bookstore, who admits that Lee was just covering up for Paul so he wouldn't get into trouble. Her heart is in the right place, so Elsa goes to see the Dean and explains the situation; she also names Wavertree as her lover because he actually wants to be sent-down to follow in the footsteps of his wealthy uncle.

The Dean reinstates the flamboyant Sheridan, but refuses to expel Wavertree because of his good record at Oxford. With all his worries behind him, Lee gets back together with Molly and his team wins the rowing championship as Dan Sheridan cheers his son on to victory.

A Yank At Oxford was one of the very best romantic comedies that MGM produced in the late 1930s, and really it had a lot more going for it than just humor. There was the warm relationship between the father and son (Taylor and Barrymore), and the lovely romance that develops between the upstart American and the bright and witty English girl (Maureen).

The mostly British cast was superb, including Edmund Gwenn as the tough but fair Dean of Cardinal. In one scene he sorely wishes to kick young Sheridan squarely in the butt, at the moment the young man is bending over to pick up a stack of fallen papers. He can barely restrain himself from returning the indignity that Sheridan had bestowed upon him.

Maureen did a very tender scene with Lionel Barrymore, her co-star from *The Devil Doll* (1936). As Lee's father, he sits down with her and tries to learn the truth why his son was expelled; the English girl who is in love with the young man admits that she really believes that he is covering up for someone. It was obvious that Maureen and Lionel liked each other a great deal, and really enjoyed working together.

The contract players at MGM were like one big family: Barrymore was a father-figure to Maureen, Weissmuller was like a brother, and all the young actors such as Mickey Rooney, Judy Garland, and Freddie Bartholomew — well, they were the children, running around the studio lot. Robert Taylor became part of that family, and two decades later said, "For seventeen years it was Mr. Mayer that guided me, and I never turned down a picture that he personally asked me to do."

This picture was a stepping-stone for Vivien Leigh, and shortly thereafter she landed the plum role of Scarlett in *Gone With the Wind*. When Vivien married Laurence Olivier, it appeared to be one of the great story book romances. Sadly, her life would be far from happy, and she was childless with Olivier during their marriage.

Vivien was troubled by years of poor physical health and eventually mental illness; when she died she was only fifty-four years old and had made just three films over the final sixteen years of her life. Hers was a story of tragedy rather than triumph, but she will always be remembered for her wonderful characters of Scarlett O'Hara and Blanche Du Bois.

Louella O. Parsons of the *Los Angeles Examiner* really loved *A Yank At Oxford*, as she noted in her column of February 17, 1938. Her comment about Maureen was simply that she was getting better and better with every picture in which she appeared:

> "Maureen O'Sullivan seems to this reviewer to become a better actress with each step in the progress of her histrionic career. She is very charming as the English girl with whom the American falls in love.
>
> "Robert Taylor's role is that of a typical American youth, doted on by his father, a country publisher. After winning all the athletic honors possible in a small western university, Bob wins a scholarship and goes to Oxford to show the British what an American can do. He takes some pretty hard bumps in doing it, and while he nearly always comes out on top he by no means has things all his own way. There is no pretty boy suggestion in this robust character, and again we are reminded that Bob, when all is said and done, is a good actor.
>
> "Lionel Barrymore's portrayal of the adoring father, a grand character, will not soon be forgotten. Vivien Leigh, a well-known English player, not only has ability but great photographic charm, and certainly Griffith Jones should not be overlooked by Hollywood producers. Edmund Gwenn, whom we all knew and liked in Hollywood, excels as the dean."

Variety also gave the film kudos for high entertainment value in its review (February 2, 1938):

> "Robert Taylor brings back from Oxford an entertaining rah-rah film which is full of breathless quarter-mile dashes, heartbreaking boat race finishes and surefire box office sentiment. It is a draw picture for Taylor at a critical moment in his meteoric bid for fame. Score at the finish is Taylor, first; Oxford, second; Cambridge, third.
>
> "Picture is well-made and contains an amusing story of the kind told frequently in West Point, Annapolis, and dear old Siwash locales. Teamed to these sometimes hilarious adventures is a sentimental story which tells of Taylor's liking for Maureen O'Sullivan, whose brother is a rival in undergraduate affairs. Comes the moment when the brother faces disgrace and Taylor takes the rap. Looks as if he will be unable to stroke the crew in the annual pull against Cambridge, but Lionel Barrymore, father-publisher, arrives just in time to get at the truth of things.

"Cast is excellent throughout. Edmund Gwenn as the Dean of Cardinal College, one of the Oxford group, does a stand-out. Griffith Jones is the English boy, and gives a sincere and earnest performance. Miss O'Sullivan and her diction fit nicely into ensemble, and Vivien Leigh, as a college vamp, has looks and a way about her. Lionel Barrymore gives his customary good performance."

On February 17, 1938, Maureen O'Sullivan, Lionel Barrymore and Jack Conway, director of *A Yank at Oxford*, were the guests of Robert Taylor on the "Good News of 1938" radio program on KFI, and presented a funny skit to promote the movie. Also appearing on the show were Jack Benny and Fanny Brice, who enacted a love scene — with Mr. Benny doing a love scene, it had to have been hilarious.

The week that Maureen came back to America, she talked with Reine Davies who wrote the "Hollywood Parade" column in the *Los Angeles Examiner*, and it was obvious that being back in the land of her birth had a special meaning to her:

"On the day following the last scene for *A Yank at Oxford* at the Denham studio in London," said the Irish colleen, "I caught the mail boat for Dun Laoghaire. It was raining when we docked, but fans were standing there in the rain, smiling just the same, and they continued to wait while I autographed everything in sight.

"Nothing in Hollywood ever thrilled me quite as much as the sight of my parents and my old home at Saintsbury, Killiney. Everybody seemed ready to show me a royal good time, from the turkey dinner at the American legation in Dublin on Thanksgiving Day to the folk dancing at the 'Ceilí,' a delightful revival of the old Irish customs and traditions. I reveled in the old antique shops, the lace shops and the Irish countryside. My visit was all too short when MGM sent for me to return to Hollywood."

And indeed that was Maureen all her life when it came to her fans, she would greet them, talk with them, sign autographs to the point of exhaustion, and always have a smile. She was indomitable, and the appreciation of her adoring fans was reciprocated.

Years later, Maureen recalled the immense popularity of Robert Taylor when they arrived in London to make *A Yank at Oxford*: "There were a lot of reports in the newspapers that women were hiding under his bunk on the ship over, but I think Howard Strickling planted that one. The women were crazy about Robert and they called him, 'Robert TY-LER.' We had a country house near the studio in Denham, and the female fans would ride their bicycles down the street and call for 'Robert TY-LER' to come out. He was a very nice man, but not exciting really. You wouldn't pick him to be a movie star."

By this time in 1938, Maureen was expecting that she would not be asked to do another Tarzan picture. She expounded upon her feelings on this and other subjects in a lengthy interview with Lucie Neville of the *San Francisco Chronicle* entitled "No More 'Ooley-Ooley' for Maureen." (February 20, 1938)

"Tarzan will have to look for a new mate the next time he takes to the treetops because Maureen O'Sullivan is climbing steadily to a higher, more secure perch in movie-dom. No longer will she be cornered by crocodiles, terrorized by tigers or pursued by panthers. Three *Tarzan* pictures and three years in a phony jungle are enough for any girl, her studio has decided, especially for one as promising as the young Irish actress."

The article continued along the vein that Maureen was being rewarded for years of toil, and part of the studio's appreciation was the lead in *Port of Seven Seas*, intended for Luise Rainer, who fell sick and had to relinquish the role. (These things happened often, as Maureen herself lost a choice role because of illness in *Marie Antoinette,* and was replaced by Anita Louise.)

In an unofficial poll at the studio, Maureen was voted by 80 per cent as the most promising actress of this year. And she wasn't exactly working cheaply at $1750 per week on a long-term contract, earning more money than all but the top stars in Hollywood.

"I needed the experience," Maureen said philosophically about her numerous second-lead parts: "It was an apprenticeship, that's all. I feel as if this was rather like being rewarded for being good."

"As a matter of fact, I was crazy about the *Tarzan* pictures," admitted Maureen. "But they took too long. I was off the screen for the equivalent of three years. There was animal trouble, casting trouble, director, story and set trouble. Everything that could happen, happened. After all that time, they were released to a limited audience. And you don't advance much in your acting as an ape-man's wife."

Maureen also noted that she would have fun with the kids who lived on her block, who would think of her as Jane of the Jungle rather than an ordinary housewife.

"They'd go 'Oooley-ooley-ooley!' all over the neighborhood, and sometimes I'd answer them back. But when they saw me, I knew they were terribly disappointed because I wore ordinary clothes when they expected a brown leather apron and long hair.

"Children are so literal! I know I was, at least. I used to be awfully puzzled when I'd seen an actor die in a play, and when I went back to see it again, he'd be alive. I took some children to a Shirley Temple matinee during the holidays, and all over the theater they were clutching their mothers and boo-hooing, 'Mother! She's hurting Shirley!'

"Maybe I was too agreeable about going on with the *Tarzan* pictures," she continued. "If I'd had any sense, I probably would have refused after the first one. But playing stoogey parts hasn't done me any harm.

"When I worked with the Marx Brothers, I didn't have much to do but I learned valuable lessons about timing and how to get a laugh across. I think that hospital picture I made, *Between Two Women,* did me a lot of good with the studio and with the public. I was expecting more of *Anna Karenina* — my part looked so lovely in the script and I was so excited. But when it got on the screen, so much was cut. That's one drawback about playing with a really big star like Garbo — unless you're linked definitely with the star and are vitally necessary to the plot, your part can be cut to ribbons."

About her role in *Port of Seven Seas*, which co-starred Wallace Beery and Frank Morgan, Maureen noted that she had just completed her work on *A Yank At Oxford*:

"It was totally unexpected," said the actress. "I had just got back from London on Friday, and I started to work on Saturday. I wasn't even unpacked. I wasn't too sure about the part. I knew they wanted Rainer and that I was just second-best. So naturally, I was jittery. But John's so understanding — my husband's the director at Warner Brothers, so he knew exactly how I felt — and he saw that I had dinner in bed and my lights were out by 8 o'clock.

"John has been so good about my work," she continued, "and so understanding. Anybody will tell you I never had any serious ideas about a career until after I married. Most husbands expect their wives to settle down and run a house, and give little dinner parties occasionally, and all that. But John doesn't expect or want me to. Now I can concentrate on work — I do nothing except this," with a grand gesture towards the motion picture set.

It was also noted that one of her favorite haunts in her early years in Hollywood was the dance marathon at the Santa Monica skating rink, where various celebrities entertained on the behalf of prize money for the contestants. Lupe Velez donated $150 so that director George Cukor would sing 'Mammy,' and George Raft's agile tap dancing charmed the crowd. One night Maureen O'Sullivan sang an Irish ballad that delighted her fans and showed off a voice that was sweet and gentle.

The interview continued with a few comments about the actress and her husband of seventeen months, who often was less than gracious with the press. Maureen got her backside up and defended John Farrow whenever the subject came up of his aloof attitude with the ink-stained wretches of Hollywood, in the words of journalist Lucie Neville:

"Unquestionably she is extremely proud of her husband and resents any adverse criticism of him. This love-me-love-my-husband attitude is particularly noticeable during interviews, since her director husband is not markedly popular with the press."

The article concluded with the notes that they enjoyed spending time on their yacht; Farrow was a member of the Royal Irish Yacht Club and Maureen was learning to sail. The couple also spent what leisure time they had redecorating their newly-finished house — frequent guests included close friends Mr. and Mrs. John McCormack and author/humorist P. G. Wodehouse.

Although their lives were relatively peaceful, a riotous situation occurred when John had a beehive sent to the house one Saturday and Maureen and a maid removed the pasteboard carton before they realized what was inside. The bees swarmed all over the lower floor of the house and both women fled the premises until a man came out from an apiary and corralled the unwelcome visitors. That had to be a scene right out of an MGM comedy, albeit minus the Marx Brothers.

Port of Seven Seas was a big film for Maureen, a major role in which the actress received one of the strongest reviews of her career. *Variety* lauded her fine characterization of the French girl, Madelon:

"Maureen O'Sullivan is vastly beguiling as the soft-voiced, warm-eyed and openhearted girl. Hers is a tenderly luminous performance that fills out the emotional range of the role and gives the whole picture overwhelming plausibility. Even against the opaque character of the returned lover, her playing radiates conviction."

Originally cast to star as her French boyfriend Marius was James Stewart. In one sequence actually filmed, Madelon (Maureen) hears bad news about her lover (Stewart) and faints, striking her head against a cobblestone walk. Stewart was replaced after filming began by John Beal in the role of the lover Marius, and this scene was re-shot, of course, with Beal.

Maureen's other co-stars were Wallace Beery as Marius' father Cesar, and Frank Morgan as Panisse,

Maureen as the beguiling Madelon in *Port of Seven Seas*

an older man who is in love with the beautiful Madelon. Portraying her mother Honorine was the fine character actress Jessie Ralph, who had acted with Maureen in several other films. The cast also included Cora Witherspoon as Claudine, Etienne Girardot as Bruneau, and Henry Hull as Uncle Elzear.

The story begins in the seaport of Marseilles, France, where tavern owner Cesar argues constantly with his son Marius, especially over Panisse's infatuation with the beautiful Madelon (Maureen), who is deeply in love with Marius. The young man has a passion for the sea and signs up for a three-year voyage, informing his lover via a note because a final good-bye would break his heart. Madelon rushes to the docks to stop Marius, but faints as his ship is sailing away. Madelon doesn't try to stop Marius because she knows he loves the sea.

Maureen with John Beal and Wallace Beery in an emotional scene from *Port of Seven Seas*

One month later, a letter from Marius barely mentions Madelon, who is heartbroken. By this time she realizes that she is pregnant, and the father is out to sea. Panisse asks Honorine for the hand of Madelon, and promises a good life for her and the baby. Although she does not love Panisse, she agrees to marry him to give her child a father and a name.

Cesar is enraged with Panisse for "stealing" his grandchild, but he forgives his friend when he promises to make him the godfather. They agree to call the boy Cesar Marius Panisse. After the child is born, Panisse proves to be a good father and Madelon is relatively content in her life.

But one year later, on a day when Panisse has boarded a train for Paris on business, Marius returns and begs Madelon to take him back, swearing that he still loves her. When he later sees the child, Marius realizes that he is the father and asks Madelon to go away with him. Just then, Cesar arrives, and with great difficulty warns his son that the baby now belongs to Panisse, who is the legal husband of Madelon.

When Panisse returns to his home and sees Marius, he tells Madelon that she can have her freedom — but he is torn with remorse because he loves his baby son. Panisse then leaves to check on the baby, and Madelon and Cesar make Marius realize that Panisse is the true father.

Knowing that it would break the heart of Panisse to take the child away, Marius decides to return to the sea. He shakes the hand of Panisse and says good-bye to his father Cesar. The young man looks with longing at Madelon, and wonders what could have been. Madelon and Panisse are now alone with the baby, who is joyously sporting his first baby tooth.

The highlights of the *Variety* review of June 29, 1938 indicate that this film was one of the most superbly-acted productions of the decade, and that the principal players, Maureen, Frank Morgan, and Wallace Beery were at the highest levels of their respective careers:

"Genuine and touching drama ... tastefully produced, skillfully directed, and played with glowing intensity.

"Adapted from a play by Marcel Pagnol, *Port of Seven Seas* is merely a standard story with a locale of the Marseilles waterfront. Its underlying human values are sound, however, and are treated with rare sympathy and restraint. Result is an adult drama on an emotionally honest theme. It has occasional slow spots, but it never slobbers into pathos.

"Story is of the barest essentials and minimum of incident. But understanding and care have gone into the production. The characters are artfully drawn and each assumes a distinct individuality. The emotional scenes are likewise treated with admirable reticence and sincerity. James Whale's direction is knowing and deft.

"As the blustering, blundering, softhearted father of the boy, Wallace Beery is captivating. Similarly, Frank Morgan gives one of the most persuasive performances of his entire career. That is particularly evident in the scene in which the girl [Maureen] comes to see if he'll still marry her. Morgan's gentleness and quiet sincerity make the scene enormously stirring and invest the character with courage, stature and dignity.

"In that scene and in virtually every other one in the picture, Maureen O'Sullivan is vastly beguiling as the soft-voiced, warm-eyed and openhearted girl. Hers is a tenderly luminous performance that fills out the emotional range of the role and gives the whole picture overwhelming plausibility. Even against the opaque character of the returned lover, her playing radiates conviction."

Hold That Kiss was a top-notch romantic comedy with an impressive cast, and Maureen O'Sullivan as the rising star in the MGM stable was given the top billing. Her romantic co-star was Dennis O'Keefe, who had "Irish" written all over him. O'Keefe had that "boyish" look, and his character of Tommy Bradford is a charmer who sells travel packages and daydreams of visiting the exotic places that he describes to his clients.

Maureen was cast as June Evans, a young model with big aspirations, who has three goofy brothers in the personages of Mickey Rooney, Frank Albertson, and Phillip Terry. The sympathetic Mrs. Evans was played by the charming Fay Holden, who also portrayed Rooney's mother in the Andy Hardy pictures, and the superb character actress Jessie Ralph was Aunt Lucy. Rounding out the superior cast was the rotund George Barbier as an eccentric millionaire, and Edward S. Brophy, a very funny comedian who was a master of the double-take.

The story begins as Tommy Bradford (O'Keefe), a clerk at the Biltmore travel agency, and June Evans (Maureen), a model for the exclusive Maurice dress shop, bump into each other at the wedding reception of the daughter of wealthy J. Westley Piermont. She is delivering a dress and he is dropping off tickets for the honeymoon trip, but when they find themselves attracted to each other — well, the stories change somewhat. He claims to be a foreign correspondent, and she leads him to believe that she is an affluent society belle who leads a merry life-style.

When Tommy asks her for a date, she says maybe and does accept his phone number. That evening, June tells her mother of the young man she has met, but laments that he is out of her league because he is rich. Her brothers all come home for dinner, including: Chick (Rooney), a hot-shot clarinetist who is the leader of a jazz combo; Steve (Albertson), who works as a clerk at a betting parlor; and Ted (Phillip Terry), who is an usher at the local theater. When the brothers hear the story of the new love interest, Chick places a call to Tommy and then hands the phone to his embarrassed sister, who accepts his offer of a date that evening.

The couple decide to attend the Westminster dog show, and they run into Piermont, who has two dogs entered including a St. Bernard. The wealthy man is so convinced that his little Pomeranian is going to win, that he offers to give the St. Bernard to Tommy if he wins first prize. When the big dog wins, Piermont is true to his word and hands over the dog to Tommy, who in turn gives him to June, who reluctantly accepts and names him Blotto.

Meanwhile, Ma Evans and Aunt Lucy hatch a scheme to hold a dinner party at the apartment of her wealthy employer. They invite Tommy and June, while little brother Chick provides the entertainment with his jazz combo. Brother Steve helps to bring the food to the swank apartment, and feeling he has a surefire horse to win at the track, borrows Aunt Lucy's silverware from the drawer to use as collateral on a $25 loan. The money is acquired from Al (Edward S. Brophy), who just happens to be Tommy's roommate.

The party is quite a success, but when Lucy discovers the stolen silver, she frantically phones the police. Tommy's horse fails to pay off, and Al hocks the silver at a pawn shop; he is arrested and brought to the apartment. Aunt Lucy realizes that Steve is behind the stolen silver, and they convince the police that Al is just a harmless kleptomaniac.

Maureen with Dennis O'Keefe and Buck the St. Bernard in *Hold That Kiss*

Finally, the charade is too much for Tommy, who tells June that they live in two different worlds and it would never work. She thinks he is blowing her off — in reality each still believes the other to be rich. Aunt Lucy has recognized Tommy from the travel agency, and informs June of his deception. She goes to his place of work for a bit of revenge, embarrasses him, and then departs with a smile. Tommy sees her climb into the delivery van for Maurice's dress shop, and realizes she too has been less than honest. He goes to see Maurice and smugly asks that June model several expensive gowns, until she is completely exasperated at his audacity.

Leaving work, June asks her friend the van driver to give her a lift home. Tommy is hiding in the back of the van — he grabs June and explains the whole truth to her. They both agree to start fresh with no lies or exaggerations, and when he tries to kiss her, the St. Bernard is there to move in between them. But Tommy is persistent, and gets his kiss from June to seal the deal.

Maureen O'Sullivan was developing an excellent knack for comedy and had created her own "slow burn" — which she often used on her trio of childish brothers, as well as co-star O'Keefe, in numerous funny situations where only a look of reproval would do. She also used those large beautiful eyes to great effect, in scenes where she has exaggerated her status in life. They were just fibs, but the eyes told the story that she felt guilty, as she got in deeper and deeper with little hope of extricating herself from the quagmire of untruths.

The St. Bernard that June acquires also brings numerous laughs, as this huge dog now has to share the tiny apartment with her mother, three brothers, and herself. When Blotto needs a place to sleep the first night, he takes one of the beds and forces Chick and Ted to make do on the hard floor. And when June is miserable about her break-up with Tommy and runs to her bedroom to cry, it is Blotto who gently crawls onto the bed beside her to comfort her in her sorrow.

Hold That Kiss was really a gem of a romantic comedy, which was highlighted by the marvelous Jessie Ralph as Aunt Lucy, a street-wise old gal who is determined to help her niece (Maureen) land a man and get married. Mickey Rooney was on the verge of stardom and had already made his first Andy Hardy picture, *A Family Affair* (1937) with Lewis Stone and Fay Holden as his parents. Mickey was just plain teenage wild in this comedy, blasting away on his clarinet and driving his sister June crazy. Rooney was already displaying the immense energy that would make him a screen legend for many decades.

The critics and fans alike enjoyed this particular spin on the boy-meets-girl formula. Once again, MGM was laughing all the way to the bank. Maureen climbed one step higher up the ladder of success, and she was beginning to see the upper rungs through the haze and smoke of the Tarzan and Jane pictures that so far had dominated her career.

James Francis Crow of the *Hollywood Citizen News* lauded the fine performances, noting that the fans rocked with laughter at the preview (May 7, 1938):

> "*Hold That Kiss* might be described, somewhat optimistically, to be sure, as a million dollar picture — not from the standpoint of cost, but from the standpoint of profit. Unpretentiously budgeted, presented sans benefit of glamorous box office names, it is nevertheless aimed straight at the pocketbooks of the rank and file of the film fans, and it has the look of a surefire commercial success. In many ways comparable to the Judge Hardy and Jones Family series pictures, it excels these by virtue of better grades of writing, acting and direction. Last night's preview patrons greeted it joyously.
>
> "Dennis O'Keefe ... is definitely one of the assets of this new vehicle. Tall and slim, he is good-looking enough to take the hero's role, and he seems to have the priceless saving grace of a sound sense of humor.
>
> "The talented Maureen O'Sullivan has the feminine lead, Mickey Rooney exercises his scene-stealing proclivities as her young brother, Fay Holden is top-notch as her mother and Jessie Ralph the same as her aunt, and there are other effective performances by George Barbier, Frank Albertson, and Edward Brophy."

Three capsule reviews from the *Motion Picture Herald*, "What the Picture Did for Me" column, which were submitted each week by theater owners:

> *Hold That Kiss:* Dennis O'Keefe, Maureen O'Sullivan, Mickey Rooney — "The Irishers have it, in this one O'Keefe and O'Sullivan, and they make quite a team. Not forgetting Buck, the dog." — A. E. Hancock, Columbia Theatre, Columbia City, Ind. (July 23, 1938)
>
> *Hold That Kiss:* Dennis O'Keefe, Maureen O'Sullivan, Mickey Rooney — "Atta Boy, Mickey, you sure have some fans in this little town. They think you are just tops, and I think so myself. But talking about the picture, everyone was good. Jessie Ralph is swell in anything." — Ouida Stephano, Grove Theatre, Groveton, Texas. Small Town Patronage. (September 10, 1938)
>
> *Hold That Kiss:* Dennis O'Keefe, Maureen O'Sullivan, Mickey Rooney — "It just doesn't take a lot of money or stars to make a good picture and this proves it. One of the most entertaining pictures of the year and it will do business more on the second day. They even let you run it flat and don't even blind-check it." — Mayme P. Mussellman, Princess Theatre, Lincoln, Kansas. Small Town Patronage. (September 17, 1938)

A second romantic teaming of Maureen and Robert Taylor came about in *The Crowd Roars* (1938), one of the better boxing films of any era. But it went deeper than the criminal element that permeates this story — it was a wonderful Depression-era drama of two fathers that both make mistakes in dealing with their adult offspring, a romance that gathers momentum and finally comes to a head when Taylor takes a beating in the ring to save the life of Maureen, and finally justice for all as the good guys triumph and the bad guys take the fall.

Maureen was billed fourth as Sheila Carson, after Taylor and character actors Edward Arnold and Frank Morgan. She is not introduced until the forty-minute mark of the drama, and so the billing is really by order of appearance. There were many outstanding character performances in this picture, which included Lionel Stander as the wisecracking trainer, "Happy"; William Gargan as the washed-up boxer who dies in the ring in a fight with Tommy McCoy (Taylor); Nat Pendleton as the slick gangster "Pug" Walsh; and Leona Roberts as Tommy's mother, Laura.

Edward Arnold portrayed Sheila's father, the tough gambler who tries to protect her from the seedy boxing game. Morgan was Tommy McCoy's alcoholic father who gambles away every dime that his son earns in the boxing ring. When it seems he is beyond redemption, the old man commits a single heroic act that saves two lives.

There was also a superb performance by Gene Reynolds as Tommy the young boy; the lad goes on the road with his father to make money as a singer, as his old man plans for him to make the big money he never did in vaudeville. When a letter arrives with the sad news that Tommy's mother has died, the boy's pathos was so real as he sobs into his father's arms, theater patrons were probably reaching for their own handkerchiefs in commiseration.

The story begins as young Tommy McCoy is torn between two passions — singing in the church choir and fist fighting with other boys. He picks up a few dimes now and then singing in saloons to help out his mother, since his father Brian (Morgan) is a slacker who once was a small-timer in vaudeville. Tommy sings a beautiful Irish song at a boxing match for boys, and then takes on the winner at the urging of his father. When Tommy wins, pro boxer Johnny Martin (Gargan) offers to take the boy on tour and also teach him to box. Months pass and the old man drinks away Tommy's earnings instead of mailing the money back to Mrs. McCoy. A letter from Father Ryan informs Brian that his wife has died, and when the boy reads the letter he collapses in sorrow.

The years pass, and Tommy elevates to a young contender, while Martin is forced to retire. Brian is still wasting his son's money, drinking and gambling at the racetrack. Two hoods show up at the gym where Tommy (Taylor) and his trainer (Stander) are preparing for a big fight the coming Saturday. They demand $600 that Brian owes gambler Jim Cain (Arnold), and Tommy is enraged with his father for his utter lack of accountability for his actions.

Tommy goes to see the gambler and promises to pay after his weekend fight. Cain agrees rather amiably. When Tommy's opponent pulls out, he is replaced by Johnny Martin, who is making a comeback to support a new wife and child. Martin is over-the-hill, and Tommy decides to go easy on his old mentor and just box him one-handed — feigning an injury to his dynamite right hand.

One of Tommy's punches knocks Johnny to the mat, and the fight is over. The unconscious fighter is taken to the hospital, where Tommy meets Johnny's wife. Mrs. Martin doesn't blame Tommy, who hands her the entire purse for the bout. When the doctor gives them the bad news that Johnny is dead, they both are left in shock.

Meanwhile, Brian McCoy has sold Tommy's contract to Jim Cain to cover his gambling debts. The unsympathetic press has dubbed the young boxer, "Killer" McCoy. He is so upset he quits boxing, and he tells his old man to get out of his life. After a few months, Tommy goes to see Cain, and wants back in the fight game to make enough money to retire. Cain plans to promote him as a "lucky" one-punch fighter, so they can clean up on the long odds.

Cain sends Tommy to train at his country estate, which he owns under his real name of "Carson." Unexpectedly, Sheila Carson (Maureen) shows up on a weekend break from her fancy finishing school, and they hit if off almost immediately. Tommy realizes that Cain is using the phoney name to shield his daughter from his gambling racket, so he plays along. The two of them soon fall deeply in love, and Tommy promises to quit fighting after a few more big payoffs.

Tommy and Sheila continue meeting in the country, until one weekend Cain shows up and is surprised to find her new boyfriend is "Killer" McCoy. On the trip back to town, Cain warns Tommy not to see Sheila again, that she deserves better than a pug fighter from the slums. They resolve to settle the matter after the fight against Cigones, a top contender for the title.

Pug Walsh has bet a lot of money on the outcome, but discovers that Cain is secretly the manager of McCoy. He stands to lose a fortune if Tommy wins, so he kidnaps both Sheila and Brian McCoy on the day of the big fight. A note sent to Tommy reveals the threat that they both will die unless he fights until the eighth round, and then takes a dive. Cain also discovers that Sheila is missing — she and Tommy's father are being held by two of Walsh's thugs.

As the fight progresses, Tommy is taking a beating but knows he must last until the eighth round. At the hideout, Brian McCoy feigns a heart attack as they listen to the fight on the radio, and then grabs a gun from one of the hoods. Sheila hugs the old man for his bravery, and escapes to warn Tommy. The moment she leaves, there is a struggle for the gun and all three men are shot and die.

At the arena, Sheila is met by her father, who has blamed Tommy for her disappearance. She informs him that Pug Walsh was behind the kidnapping, and then rushes to ringside to alert Tommy that she is all right. Realizing his sweetheart is safe from harm, he pounds his opponent into a quick knockout in the eighth round. As Pug Walsh rises from his seat, the police are there to escort him to jail. Tommy tells the reporters at ringside that this is his last fight.

After all the trials and tribulations, Mr. Cain has warmed to Tommy and accepts him. Sheila and the ex-fighter exchange vows at the church where Tommy grew up, and are married.

Maureen O'Sullivan gave another of her fine performances as the whip-smart Sheila. In one scene with the young boxer Tommy, they are in a sailboat on a peaceful lake. They are discussing what they both want from life — he talks about success in the ring, money, all the good things in life.

Sheila asks with those stunning blue eyes, "What else do you want Tommy?" He looks at her and she repeats the same line with more emotion. By this time everyone knows what Tommy wants and he kisses her passionately, and there is no more doubt that they have fallen in love.

Maureen has a rather poignant scene where she talks about watching Tommy in his first fight and how she hated the brutality of two men beating each other senseless. She is also aware of the man who had died in the ring with Tommy, his former mentor Johnny Martin. Her passion in describing her hatred for what Tommy does truly comes from the heart, and it convinces Tommy — he promises to quit in a few fights before he becomes a broken ex-pug.

Maureen and Robert Taylor made a fine romantic couple, this time in *The Crowd Roars*

Maureen continued to be one of the few women who did both drama and comedy effectively, as most actresses settled into one niche or the other. In some pictures you'd find her doing great dramatic scenes with Garbo, Dressler, March, Shearer, and Beery, while in others she was in the middle of the Marx Brothers silliness, or chasing after crazy little brother Mickey Rooney.

This was a break-out film for Robert Taylor, who heretofore was looked upon as a "pretty boy" that didn't have the toughness to do "he-man" roles. *The Crowd Roars* changed that irrevocably, and Taylor gained countless fans who could now appreciate his new image — his career soared to towering heights as a virile, rugged leading man.

There was a bit of a funny situation which was reported by Sidney Skolsky of the *Hollywood Citizen News*, when he went to spectate the outdoor shooting of a scene for *The Crowd Roars*.

Maureen and Robert Taylor were filming a love scene on a large ranch far out in the Valley; they were leaning against a railing, and as far as you could see there was beautiful mountain greenery. And moving slowly across a hilltop on the next farm over was a man pushing a plow.

Director Richard Thorpe had Taylor and Miss O'Sullivan play the scene, but the sound man interrupted. He said: "That man up there on the hill is whistling a song and the mike picks it up. I can hear it distinctly."

Thorpe said: "That's all right, let it in. It'll be good atmosphere. Besides, this is a free country and we can't stop him from whistling on his own farm."

The actors started to do the scene again. The sound man interrupted, again. "Mr. Thorpe, we can't let him whistle that song in this picture. He's whistling 'Thanks for the Memory,' and that's a Paramount song."

It's unlikely that Bob Hope or Paramount would have minded, but the man was indeed asked to stop whistling until after the scene was completed.

Maureen was credited with being her usual beautiful self, and excellent in her scenes with Taylor, Arnold, Morgan, and Jane Wyman in one of her earliest roles as a bubble-headed classmate from finishing school. But this was Robert Taylor's film, and all the critics could talk about was his superb portrayal and how outstanding this drama really was.

The critics labeled *The Crowd Roars* a superior boxing drama, with the romance of Maureen and Taylor raising the picture above the level of typical fare. One particular capsule review from the *Motion Picture Herald* (September 17, 1938) did single out the outstanding work of the actress:

> "There is no question on this picture. It is highly dramatic and both Taylor and Miss O'Sullivan are great in their roles. This little lady is certainly coming along. She seems to take her roles in her stride. She has become deft and sure in the roles we have had her in lately. For a time she was not one of the 'Forgotten Men' but the 'Forgotten Woman,' until Metro picked her up and cast her in good roles. Not forgetting the unsung hero who always adds to any picture that he is in, Lionel Stander. And believe it or not, his name in a cast means something. He is a lot better than some of the palookas that have their name in lights." — A. E. Hancock, Columbia Theatre, Columbia City, Ind. General Patronage.

Variety (August 3, 1938)

> "The manly art of self-defense, otherwise known as the cauliflower industry, alias prizefighting, is a rough and tumble racket operated by big time gamblers with small time ethics, according to the film, *The Crowd Roars*, in which Robert Taylor leads with his left hand and registers satisfactorily at the

box-office. It's exciting melodrama with plenty of ring action, some plausible romance, and several corking good characterizations. Title refers, of course, to the shout of arena spectators when a knockout is near.

"Heart interest is centered in a love affair between Taylor and Maureen O'Sullivan. Frank Morgan creates something interesting out of the role of the pug's father, a drunkard and braggart. Edward Arnold is the conventional bookmaker and fight manager, who works successfully on the theory that the smartest gamblers are the biggest suckers."

Los Angeles Examiner Erskine Johnson (August 25, 1938)

"Robert Taylor's transition from a great lover into grimacing, fist-slinging 'Killer McCoy,' in a lusty drama of prize fighting is one of the most believable performances we've seen on the screen in years. Bloody and sweaty, Taylor punches his way through the picture in a manner that will win approval from fight game experts, and the male contingent, will not be distasteful to feminine fans unaccustomed to having their celluloid idols mussed up and mauled so thoroughly as is Taylor's fate in the picture.

"Taylor's amazing performance is exceeded only by the excellence of the picture itself. Played by a great cast of supporting stars and assorted pug uglies, *The Crowd Roars* is thrilling action interposed with heart warming drama and intense situations expertly directed by Richard Thorpe."

Motion Picture Herald "What the Picture Did For Me" (September 10, 1938)

The Crowd Roars: Robert Taylor, Maureen O'Sullivan, Frank Morgan, Lionel Stander — "A stand-out picture that will do business in any spot. A program picture plot built around an all star cast brings a bit of work that has the men as well as the women raving about Taylor, which is unusual. After this one Taylor can be counted on for big grosses his next time out." — Peter Panagos, Indiana and Sipe Theatre, Kokomo, Ind. General Patronage.

The Crowd Roars: Robert Taylor, Maureen O'Sullivan — "Here's a picture for any spot. Extended runs and give her gas. All the way a sweetheart of an American picture for all the family." — W. E. McPhee, Strand Theatre, Old Town, Maine. General Patronage.

Maureen's boss at MGM, Mr. Mayer, continued to push her toward stardom with alternating roles in dramas and comedies. She was rewarded for all of her hard work and superb reviews with top-billing in yet another romantic comedy, *Spring Madness* (1938), with co-star Lew Ayres and supported by Burgess Meredith, Ruth Hussey, Frank Albertson, and Sterling Holloway. This was an Ivy League picture which revolved around a group of college kids preparing to graduate. The big "spring dance" is the coming-out party for all the seniors who will soon embark on the challenges of real life, such as career, marriage, and children.

The funny stuff mostly comes from the supporting players as a bunch of wild and crazy college co-eds, while the real drama in the picture revolves around Maureen and Lew Ayres as young lovers who are faced with the very real possibility of splitting up immediately after the spring dance.

The story begins when Harvard senior Sam Thatcher (Ayres) and his roommate Lippencott (Meredith) are planning to go to Russia for a two-year sabbatical to study the culture, immediately after graduating. The big problem for Sam is that he has not yet told his girlfriend Alexandra Benson (Maureen), who is a student at the New England College for Women. Although the trip sounds like a grand adventure to Sam, the thought of leaving Alex behind is causing him to have second-thoughts and sleepless nights.

On an Easter week visit to Harvard, Alex invites her boyfriend Sam to the big Spring Dance at her school. Sam sees her off at the train station and tells her that he will try to make the dance, but does not give her a firm commitment. Shortly thereafter, "Lipp" receives word that the steamship is sailing for Russia two weeks early, to avoid a possible dock strike.

The coming weekend is the Spring Dance, and Sam decides to drive down to see Alex and tell her of his plans in person. Lippincott also shows up at the New England campus, knowing that Sam will need his moral support to tell Alex of his decision. All of Alex's friends are excited that they will finally meet the wonderful Sam, especially her best friend Kate (Ruth Hussey), and also Sally, Frances, and Mady.

When Sam does arrive, he has a heart-to-heart talk with Alex and explains that love and marriage should come later, after he has had his chance to see the world. Alex tries to be brave and understand his reasons, but beneath her facade she is shattered — she runs back to her dormitory and spends the evening sobbing while her friends commiserate.

Kate and the other girls scheme to get Sam and Lipp to miss their Monday boat, which would cancel the trip. They are friends with the local police chief, so they get the two Harvard lads arrested over a parking "misunderstanding."

They also arrange for the handsome college literature professor, Mr. Beckett (Truman Bradley), to be her "date" for the dance and to make Sam jealous. The boys are released just in time to go to the dance, and Sam heads for the women's dorm to have another talk with Alex.

Alex tells Sam that she is tired of all his good-bye speeches, and that he should just go. Just then Mr. Beckett arrives to pick up Alex, who is totally surprised but smart enough to play along! She exits arm-in-arm with the debonair Beckett, as Sam can only watch in dismay as his beautiful Alex strolls out of his life.

Later at the dance, Sam sees Alex dancing with the tall and dark Beckett, and can hardly contain his jealousy. He cuts in, and demands that the interloper stay away from "his girl." Sam finally admits to Alex that he too is head-over-heels in love and that the trip is off. They kiss passionately and all the girls cheer this felicitous outcome — even Lipp is happy.

At first glance, *Spring Madness* would appear to be a sweet little romantic comedy with an outstanding cast. In reality, it was a story within a story. The screwball comedy part is what happens whenever Maureen isn't in a scene; the supporting players are hilarious in the verbal sparring and byplay, in the age-old battle of the sexes running wild on a college campus.

When Maureen is on the screen, usually with Lew Ayres or Ruth Hussey (as her understanding best friend Kate), it's an intense drama of a young woman in love for the first time — and sadly, her heart is breaking. She's experiencing the pangs of love because her boyfriend is leaving to go on some sort of "guy" adventure, and telling her he won't be back for two years. She even asks flippantly if she can come along on the boat as some sort of cook's helper. The young woman Alex has some marvelous lines, such as "I'm tired of this face ... I've looked in the mirror too many times, and now I'm just tired of it." Another time she sounds world-weary when she tells her occasionally immature friends, "Sometimes I feel like I'm fifty years old, and you girls are all just acting like children."

Maureen O'Sullivan was so marvelous in her passion — if this wasn't just a "little" film she could have earned an Academy Award. She was Jennifer Jones in this picture, before Ms. Jones even came along. (She made her debut a year later in 1939.)

One moment she is intentionally giddy and light-minded, but there are tears in her eyes because her heart is breaking. In a subsequent scene, she passionately tells her lover she's had enough of his good-bye speeches, and now he really must leave. Now suddenly he is the one with pangs of doubt, realizing that he is leaving behind the best woman he'll ever find.

Maureen's acting was passionate in *Spring Madness*

Lew Ayres was a skillful actor, and their scenes together were special. Maureen performed some of the finest acting of her career to date, and the rest of the cast didn't let the production down either.

Burgess Meredith had an acting career that lasted over fifty years, and he was credible in almost everything he ever did. In this story, he was a wacky college guy who talks funny, acts even funnier, and goes around shooting photos of everyone's — well, backside. Ruth Hussey was sympathetic as the tall, cool brunette who is the best friend of Maureen's Alex, and the other gals who played her coterie of pals — Ann Morriss as Frances, Joyce Compton as Sally, and Jacqueline Wells as Mady — were all excellent in their roles. Truman Bradley as college professor Walter Beckett was convincing as the older man who moves in on Alex to make her boyfriend jealous, while Frank Albertson and Sterling Holloway rounded out the exceptional cast as two more goofy college cats who are crazy for girls and maybe just plain crazy.

The *New York Times* agreed with your author's assessment of this charming picture, calling it "irresistible" and nicknaming Maureen "the dependable" in a review of December 1, 1938:

> "Although a picture called *Spring Madness* may seem a trifle out of season, we counsel you to fling your winter garment of repentance at least temporarily into the fires rekindled by the Criterion Theatre.
>
> "The tragedy of young love, with a beautifully comic performance by Burgess Meredith, as a kind of anti-Cupid, to set it off, is not to be sneezed at even in the influenza season. And with Lew Ayres (the cinema's best unappreciated actor) as the victim of a sorority house matrimonial plot involving Maureen (the dependable) O'Sullivan, it is practically irresistible."

Variety saw this as a light comedy, without taking the time to see Maureen's fine performance in the dramatic scenes. They called her acting "capable," when in fact she was superb (November 16, 1938):

> "Carrying cast made up almost entirely of younger group of players, picture details romance of Harvard man Lew Ayres and Maureen O'Sullivan, student in nearby Women's College. Ayres is convincing in the lead, while Miss O'Sullivan capably portrays the girl who finally gets her man. Burgess Meredith and Joyce Compton, latter frivolous and cute blonde having a way with the boys, are best of supporting cast.
>
> "Rather light and fluffy comedy romance set in collegiate atmosphere, *Spring Madness* will fill the lower niche of duals in satisfactory fashion. It contains some diverting sequences that provoke laughs, but on the whole, shapes up as only mild entertainment."

By 1938, radio dramas and variety shows were becoming immensely popular, with American families sitting around in front of the old box radio, while the more affluent might own a beautiful console unit with a wood case. The Depression was easing up, and people were enjoying the wonderful — and free — entertainment that came over the airwaves every day and night.

Maureen started to become quite a popular radio actress as a variety show guest, and of course this was supplemental income that was hard to turn down. Her tremendous popularity as Jane in the Tarzan pictures and all the other MGM classics made her a fan favorite.

The "Good News of 1938" broadcasts were presented by Maxwell House on NBC radio in a one-hour format. The edition of February 17, 1938, was hosted by Robert Taylor, the rising MGM motion picture star. His guests for the show were Maureen O'Sullivan, Frank Morgan, Fanny Brice, Jack Benny, singer Allan Jones, and director Jack Conway, along with Meredith Wilson and his orchestra.

Maureen and Robert Taylor in *The Crowd Roars* ... off-screen they were good friends

Maureen's part of the program included a comedy routine involving the actress exchanging witty repartee with Robert Taylor, Jack Conway, and Jack Benny; also a dramatic presentation of *Epilogue to Love*, written by Dore Schary, was performed by Maureen and Robert Taylor. Her character is a blind girl named Mary who has learned to appreciate the talents that she does have.

The "Kraft Music Hall" was another one-hour NBC variety show that was hosted by Bing Crosby and Bob Burns. The guests on this program of March 3, 1938, were Maureen O'Sullivan and pianist Mischa Auer, who performed DeBussy as well as "My Sweet Baby," with Bing and Bob Burns on vocals. Maureen demonstrated examples of different Irish brogues, with the help of Bing, and together they sang the song, "If You're Irish." Among the many songs that Bing crooned this date, he stole "Thanks for the Memory" from his good pal Bob Hope.

On March 31, 1938, the "Good News of 1938" broadcast was again hosted by Robert Taylor, with guests which included Maureen O'Sullivan, Louis B. Mayer, Lionel Barrymore, Jack Conway, Una Merkel, Frank Morgan, and singer Connee Boswell.

MGM studio chief Louis B. Mayer addressed London (via shortwave), the audience, and British cast attending the *A Yank at Oxford* premiere at the Empire Theatre, while Maureen O'Sullivan, Jack Conway, Lionel Barrymore, and Robert Taylor also conveyed their messages and spoke to the audience. The one-hour program was filled with comedy routines and musical numbers. One of the songs was "I Can Dream, Can't I?" performed by Connee Boswell, a polio victim who recovered enough to continue her career as a singer.

The good news just kept coming on April 7, on the latest "Good News of 1938" broadcast, with guests Maureen O'Sullivan, Judy Garland, John Beal, Sam Levin, Fanny Brice, Frank Morgan, Hanley Stafford and Meredith Wilson. Among the entertainment, Maureen, Judy, and the others presented a humorous skit, "If Men Behaved in Barber Shops Like Women Do in Beauty Parlors."

Judy Garland was only fifteen years old at this time, and prior to her break-out role in *The Wizard of Oz*, she was considered as an up-and-comer with a beautiful voice. Eventually, she would be regarded as perhaps the most talented performer to ever sing, dance, and act in the motion picture business.

Next for Maureen O'Sullivan was the "Jergen's Woodbury Hollywood Playhouse" of April 17, 1938, presented on NBC and hosted by Tyrone Power. The talented actor and actress performed the dramatic play, *A Service of Love*.

The good folks at Maxwell House Coffee once again brought America another "Good News of 1938" broadcast on April 28, 1938, with guests Maureen O'Sullivan, heavyweight boxer Max Baer, Fanny Brice, Frank Morgan, Betty Jaynes, Douglas MacPhail, and Una Merkel.

Maureen's busy schedule included the "Kraft Music Hall" broadcast on July 28, 1938, a one-hour program on NBC, and also the "Jergen's Woodbury Hollywood Playhouse," in a dramatic presentation of *The Artists*, with the stars Maureen O'Sullivan and Charles Boyer on October 16, 1938.

There was a second appearance for Maureen on the "Kraft Music Hall," with guest stars Chester Morris, The Foursome Quartet, Claude Rains, and pianist Dalies Frantz on November 3, 1938. Chester Morris would soon become famous in a series of 1940s detective films in the character of "Boston Blackie," and decades later would star with Maureen in a popular stage play, *The Subject Was Roses* (1966).

On November 10, the "Good News of 1938" broadcast was hosted by Maureen's frequent co-star, Robert Young, and the guests included Maureen, Lionel Barrymore, Lew Ayres, George Murphy, Ruth Hussey, and Frank Morgan. Among the various musical numbers and comedy skits, Maureen O'Sullivan and Lew Ayres presented a dramatic re-enactment of the "gymnasium scene" from their recent film, *Spring Madness* (1938).

By the end of 1938, Maureen had starred in five motion pictures for the year, and appeared as one of the top guest stars on at least ten radio variety shows or dramatic programs. She became pregnant for the first time around September 1938. So it was quite a year for the young actress, still only twenty-seven years old, who was rising like cream to the top of the pitcher.

Besides her film and radio work, Maureen's face adorned the cover of many magazines during the 1930s. She was often interviewed by the press and various journalists, who found her cordial and receptive. Unlike some actors, male and female, Maureen always made herself available to speak to the press and was one of the most genial, and even funny, interview subjects of the Hollywood crowd.

CHAPTER FIFTEEN
"Maureen Becomes a Mother ... On-Screen and Real Life"

Maureen's co-star for *Let Us Live* was Henry Fonda, a rising star in Hollywood; 1939 also saw him in break-out roles in *Jesse James, Young Mr. Lincoln,* and *The Grapes of Wrath* (1940). Maureen received top billing in this crime drama, as she spends most of the picture attempting to track down the real killers while boyfriend Fonda anguishes on death row. She was loaned over to Columbia Pictures for the role of Mary Roberts, a spirited young woman desperately attempting to convince a flawed legal system that they have convicted two innocent men.

Ralph Bellamy portrayed the police detective who believes that an injustice has been done, and is relentless in tracking down the clues to beat the clock before the day of the execution. The screenplay was a collaboration of Allen Rivkin and Anthony Veiller, the latter perhaps best known for his screenplay for the 1946 *film noir* classic, *The Killers*.

The story begins at the café where Mary (Maureen) works as a waitress. Brick Tennant (Fonda), cab driver and fiancé, arrives to take her out for a date. That evening they peruse a small lot where the young couple hope to build a house someday; later that night they visit the Auto Show. Brick is ambitious and places an order for a second cab, so that he can double his taxi business. They also notice a police display of numerous guns and rifles, an arsenal confiscated from criminals.

Well past the midnight hour, Brick's old pal Joe (Alan Baxter) drops by his apartment, and Brick offers him a job driving the new cab. In the morning, Brick picks up Mary at her place and takes her to church; she is still mourning the recent passing of her mother and often prays at the church before work.

Meanwhile, fate is playing a bad hand for Brick and Joe. Unbeknownst to them, the gun display at the Auto Show was stolen, and three men held up a bank near the church and killed a guard. The bank robbers made their escape in a taxi, so all 120 cabbies in the city are questioned. When Brick and Joe are brought before a lineup of witnesses, they are inexplicably mis-identified — they merely resemble the true criminals.

Brick is sure that a trial will prove him innocent, and Mary is his witness — she was with him at the church when the crime took place. But the prosecutor claims that Mary may be trying to protect her boyfriend, and in fact that he was elsewhere while she was in the church praying. Although Brick and Joe are completely innocent, they are convicted of armed robbery and murder and subsequently sentenced to die in three weeks. At the prison, Brick's faith in justice is beginning to wane; as the judgment day approaches, he begins to crack despite Mary's insistence that she will find the truth before it is too late.

Mary enlists the aid of Lieutenant Everett (Bellamy), and she convinces him to continue the investigation because Brick is innocent. A second holdup results in another murder, and a series of clues points to the killers owning a special cab with a high-powered motor. The neighborhood kids, Mary's friends, uncover the "hot" cab and the owner is identified. Mary and Everett trail the three killers to a New York hotel, where after a shoot-out the men are arrested.

Back at the prison, it is only minutes before the condemned men will die. The hand of fate intervenes, and the governor pardons Brick and Joe as the final minutes are ticking away. The warden apologizes for the miscarriage of justice, and offers to shake Brick's hand. Angry and disillusioned, Brick refuses the handshake — he walks out of the prison with Mary to start a new life.

Maureen protects her man Henry Fonda

Let Us Live was a well-acted crime drama, and Maureen was called upon in several scenes to pour out her heart to try to convince someone, anyone — the witnesses, the prosecutor, the judge and jury — that she is telling the truth and that her boyfriend is not a killer, that he is innocent and this whole miscarriage of justice is a nightmare. Fortunately, the one person she does convince is the bulldog police lieutenant, Everett, portrayed expertly by Ralph Bellamy. Together they sort through various leads and dead ends, and when they run into opposition from the police chief and the prosecutor, they don't give up but continue the fight even when it appears to be impossible.

Frank Nugent of the *New York Times* loved this drama (March 30, 1939), calling it a borderline "great" film, and splitting credit between the director, the writers, and the three principals, Maureen, Fonda, and Bellamy:

> "*Let Us Live* is a taut and strongly played drama which Columbia presented at the Globe yesterday. Under the goad of John Brahm's forceful and eloquent direction, it explores its familiar theme with anything but contempt. Mr. Brahm is as alert as any director of Class B melodrama to his opportunities for swift and exciting action, to the inherent suspense in a death-house deadline when a clock is ticking away the swift last hours of an innocent man's life, to the frenzy of the condemned's sweetheart as she tries to convince official-dom that justice has not been done. But, instead of stopping there, Mr. Brahm has underscored his physical drama with the psychological. What, after all, must happen to a man who finds himself victimized by a legal machine which he always had regarded as his protector? That is the essence of Mr. Brahm's drama, the quality which raises it above the death-house thriller class and gives it dignity and maturity.
>
> "Although it is the film's direction that has made it good, if not great, Mr. Brahm must share his credit with Allen Rivkin and Anthony Veiller for a splendidly turned script, and to Henry Fonda, Maureen O'Sullivan, Ralph Bellamy, Alan Baxter and the others for the incisive performances all good directors seem able to extract from their players. *Let Us Live* is not exactly a novel theme, but it is news when so old a theme has been handled so well."

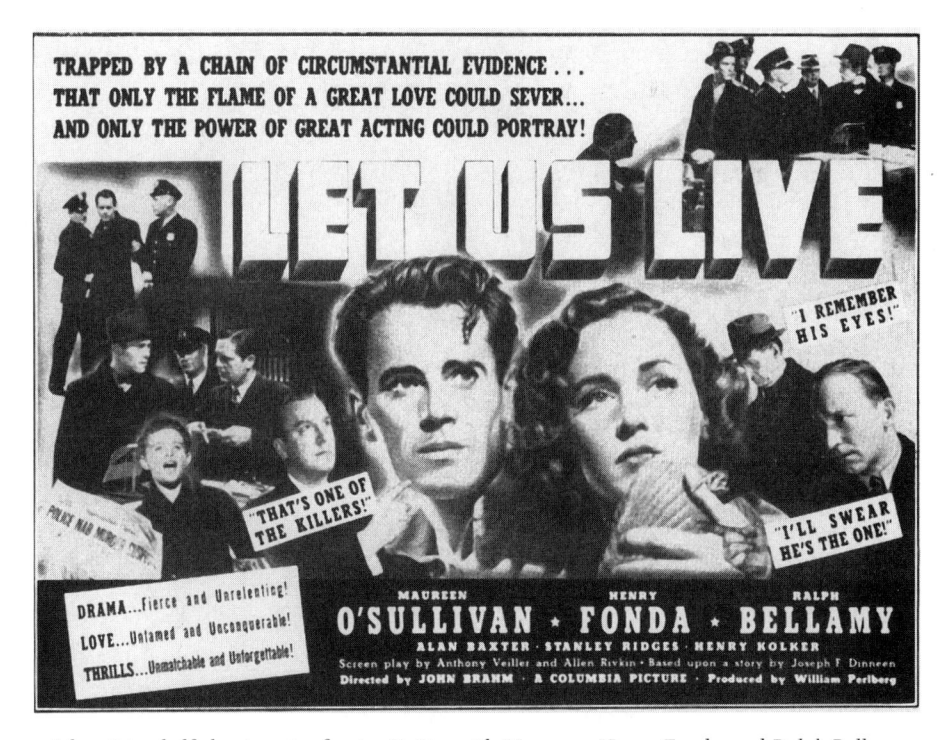

Advertising half-sheet poster for *Let Us Live* with Maureen, Henry Fonda, and Ralph Bellamy

When Metro-Goldwyn-Mayer began planning for the next Tarzan adventure, they definitely wanted Maureen in the story as Jane. She had other ideas, and felt that three films as the "wife of an ape-man," as she had put it, were enough. Several factors may have convinced her to do one more film, which would be called *Tarzan Finds A Son!* and would add the character of "Boy," an offspring for the jungle couple.

First and foremost might have been Maureen's loyalty to MGM and Louis B. Mayer, who may have convinced her that her great legion of fans would be terribly disappointed if she retired from the role. Movie-goers were accustomed to seeing the dynamic tandem of Weissmuller and O'Sullivan starring in each new episode of the Tarzan epics, and it would be a huge letdown without her. The depth of her character would be expanded in the new film, as she would now be the mother of a young son who needed her love, care, and guidance.

Maureen also ran into Edgar Rice Burroughs at a party in 1938, and she admitted to him that she had never read any of his novels. Mr. Burroughs' reply was to send her a complete autographed set of his works. The author of the Tarzan stories was a fond admirer of the young actress, and spent considerable time chatting with her on the sets of all the previous Tarzan films. Perhaps in part her friendship with Burroughs helped to convince her to continue in her role as Jane, at least one more time.

The new character of Boy was added to the jungle family, a miniature Tarzan who would also swing through the trees on vines, swim like a fish, have an affinity with the elephants and chimpanzees, and do the Tarzan yell.

When English-born actor Reginald Sheffield saw an ad in the *Hollywood Reporter* seeking the "All-American" boy, he knew his son would be perfect for the part. The elder Sheffield had appeared in Maureen's 1935 drama, *Cardinal Richelieu,* in a supporting role, and thus perhaps had an opportunity to stick his foot in the door in presenting his offspring to the bosses at MGM.

Seven-year-old Johnny had just finished working in the Broadway play, *On Borrowed Time,* in which he portrayed the grandson of star Dudley Digges. Johnny Sheffield weighed only four pounds at his premature birth, and lived in an incubator until he was ready to go home with his mother. He eventually grew to be as healthy as any boy, and only suffered the usual colds and childhood diseases.

Before the audition, Johnny attended the Karl Curtis swimming school in Beverly Hills to learn to swim, and he literally took to the water like a fish. Sheffield later was interviewed by the MGM hierarchy, by author Edgar Rice Burroughs, and by the star of the show, Johnny Weissmuller.

Weissmuller personally endorsed the selection of Sheffield as Boy, and gave his movie son swimming lessons during the production of their first film. Big John developed a strong affection for Little John (as he would be called), and they were very close during the decade that they filmed their eight Tarzan pictures together.

Johnny Sheffield was perfectly cast as Boy, and was indeed an athletic, miniature version of his mentor. The lad did most of his own stunt work and portrayed his role beyond the highest expectations. Weissmuller later stated with admiration that young Sheffield was "the greatest child athlete he had ever seen."

In 2006, Sheffield spoke with your author David Fury and recalled the chain of events in 1938 that resulted in him being chosen to co-star with Weissmuller and O'Sullivan in the first of many Tarzan screen adventures:

"Father read an article in the *Hollywood Reporter* which asked: 'Have you a young Tarzan in your backyard?' He thought he did and set up an interview. I was told there were more than 300 boys applying for the job of 'Boy.' Although I didn't know it at the time, the audition was to have two parts: first the 'Screen Test' and then the 'Swimming Test.' Had I known about the latter, I might have entered the former with a bit more trepidation.

"The screen test wasn't going to be too difficult as my acting training came in the theater, first on the west coast and then on the east coast, with my name 'up in lights' on Broadway in the play *On Borrowed Time*. I had 'paid my dues' as an actor and all that was involved was getting used to working before a camera and the crew rather than a theater audience. My father coached me for the screen test as he had done for the theater.

"Johnny Weissmuller liked me. It was decided that he should give me a swimming test as part of the selection process. Well, I could not swim a stroke at the time, but Big John said he would give me the test anyway! Someone 'up there' liked me! It was time to get in the water with Tarzan."

John Sheffield, who wrote the foreword for David Fury's biography of Johnny Weissmuller *Twice the Hero* (Artist's Press, 2000), also recalled more about the lovely lady who played his mother in the Tarzan movies, Maureen O'Sullivan:

"I remember thinking as Boy that I really had beautiful jungle parents. Big John had a great body and Maureen had a 'build' to go along with her inner beauty and lovely voice. My relationship with Maureen was as written in the script; she was Jane, my mother. That was our relationship. We didn't pal around or go places together off the set. Aside from morning and evening greetings, picture taking sessions, interviews, and an occasional lunch ours was a working relationship exactly as you saw it on the screen. She was Jane and I was her son, Boy. I would estimate that 97% of the time we spent together was working.

"She was kind and caring and never put me down. She was and is a professional actress and I knew she cared for me. She never tried to upstage me, or take advantage of me for personal advantage on the screen. She never took my light or in any way made it difficult for me to play my part. This made it easy for me and all I had to do was, show up, hit my mark, find my light, know my lines, and pay attention.

"Maureen has a lovely voice, a beautiful figure, and a wonderful carriage. Whether we were in the kitchen with Cheeta cooking eggs or in situations of great danger, I loved playing a scene with her. She was so sincere and real as Jane. Her delivery was so pure and direct — not to the camera, but to me — that I reacted as any boy would, and even though Boy was full of mischief and adventure I was compelled to obey Jane. That's how convincing Maureen O'Sullivan was as an actress. It had a lasting effect on me."

Maureen played the screen mother to Johnny Sheffield in *Tarzan Finds A Son!*

Johnny Weissmuller instructs Maureen in the fine art of swimming ... promotional photo shoot for the BVD swimming suit company (1931)

Above: Tarzan and His Mate ... filming a night scene with Maureen and Johnny
Below: A cliff-hanger with director Van Dyke and crew, *Tarzan, the Ape Man* (Maureen at far left, Neil Hamilton, and Woody Van Dyke in center of photo wearing cap)

Above: Maureen and co-stars Hamilton and Smith are joined by the midget and dwarf actors who portayed the pygmy warriors in *Tarzan, the Ape Man* (1932)
Below: Maureen with C. Aubrey Smith and Neil Hamilton, watching an action scene

Even in the jungle, Jane must look her best ... the make-up is applied for each and every scene. *Below:* The luggage rack of an automobile makes a nice make-up stand for Maureen.

Above: Maureen takes a break with Neil Hamilton and Paul Cavanagh ... *Tarzan and His Mate*

Below: Jane makes friends with one of the little people in *Tarzan Escapes* ... John Buckler is standing on the far right ... he would drown in a bizarre auto accident shortly before release of the film in November of 1936.

The animals were a big part of the fun of the Tarzan pictures ... Johnny and Maureen feeding a young zebra, while she cuddles two lion cubs and gets a big hug from Cheeta the chimpanzee

Above: Maureen and Johnny are feeding this baby elephant some treats
Below: Maureen and son Michael smile for the camera with one of the young chimpanzees

Above: Johnny shows off his strength ... Maureen mugs for the camera

Right: Maureen and Johnny are "framed" by this lighting unit ... there was always time for clowning and gag camera shots on the Tarzan sets.

Above: Maureen's boyfriend John Farrow visits the Tarzan set in 1933.
Below: Johnny with Benita Hume, Maureen, and John Farrow ... aboard Weissmuller's boat, the *Santa Guadalupe*, in 1935. They were taking a break from filming *Tarzan Escapes.*

Maureen and Johnny Weissmuller were the best of friends ...
Clockwise from above left: they appear to be stealing food, Tarzan stealing a kiss, sharing the Sunday comics, and Tarzan wooing Jane on a sunny afternoon

There were sexy photos and there were gag photos ... here's one of each

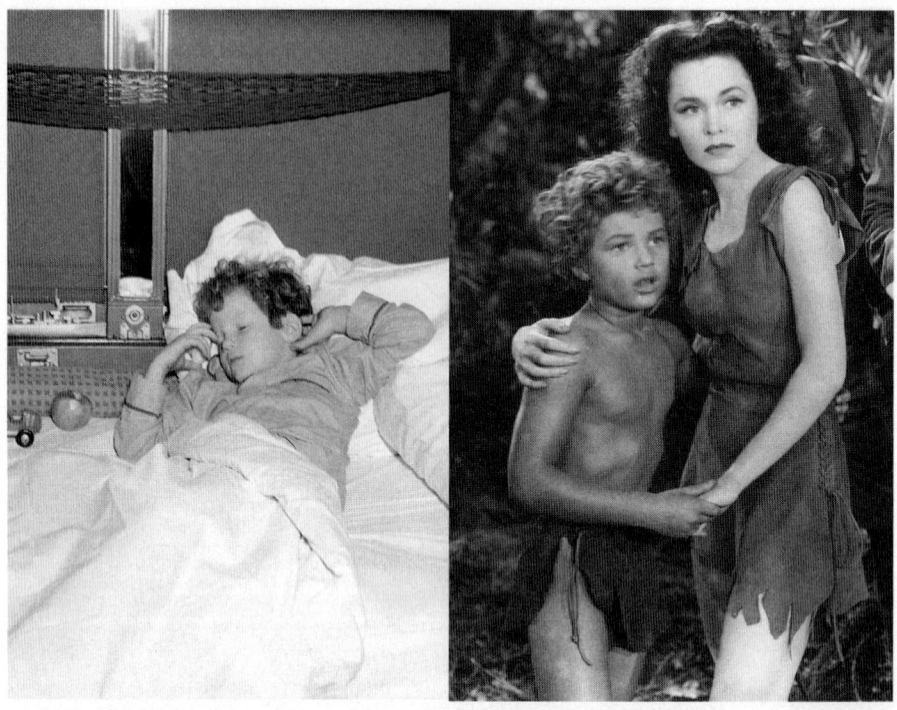

Above: Johnny Sheffield napped between takes ... facing jungle danger with his mother, Jane
Below: Maureen relaxed by knitting during the hours when she was not featured in a scene.

Above: Maureen and Johnny enjoyed playing checkers or gin rummy ... an MGM exec observes
Below: Another gag photo with Maureen, Johnny, and Cheeta the chimp

Above: Edgar Rice Burroughs presents Maureen with five loving cups, and her cup runneth over!

Left: Maureen is wearing a dress made from the Sunday Tarzan comics. Photo is signed: "To Mr. Burroughs, from his always affectionate frail-child Jane ... Maureen"

Author Edgar Rice Burroughs created the character of Tarzan, and sold the movie rights to MGM in 1931. Here a mighty elephant is the backdrop for this photograph with Maureen O'Sullivan and ERB, whom he affectionately called, "My perfect Jane!" This must have been a chilly day in Los Angeles, as Maureen is wearing a heavy coat.

This photograph shows why Maureen O'Sullivan and Johnny Weissmuller were the sexiest screen couple in America during the 1930s. A publicity still for *Tarzan, the Ape Man* (1932)

Tarzan Finds A Son! begins when a small plane with three passengers, Richard Lancing, his wife and their infant son, is traveling across East Africa bound for Capetown. The plane develops engine trouble, and the pilot warns them that they are going down. Lancing and his wife share a final kiss, and hold on tightly to the baby as the plane crashes in the jungle.

Jane and Tarzan find a baby in the jungle ... they become the adoptive parents of Boy

All the passengers are killed except the baby, whose crying draws the attention of the jungle animals. Shortly before the arrival of a Zambeli tribesman, Cheeta discovers the baby and carries him through the trees to the home of Tarzan. Jane is the first to realize that the baby is an orphan, and they are the only ones who can care for the child.

Tarzan, above Jane's protestations and laughter, names his adopted son, "Boy." As the years pass, the lad emulates his father, and becomes skilled in the ways of the jungle. Tarzan and Jane adore their son who is playful and sometimes mischievous.

One day a small safari arrives near the escarpment, led by Sir Thomas Lancing (Henry Stephenson) who is searching for the lost plane and his missing relatives. Also in the party are Austin Lancing and his wife (Ian Hunter, Frieda Inescort), who stand to inherit half of the Greystoke estate if they can confirm the death of their missing cousin. Their jungle guide is Sande (Henry Wilcoxon), who leads them to the plane but finds no evidence of any bodies.

An elephant wounded by gunshot informs Tarzan that there are intruders in the jungle, and he confiscates their rifles — later throwing them in the grotto. Jane arrives and tells Sir Thomas that the body of the woman is buried nearby, and that the bodies of the men were taken away by the hostile Zambelis, a cannibal tribe. When he asks about the infant, Jane lies and says that the child is buried with the mother.

The Lancings are satisfied that they can now claim the Greystoke estate, but Sir Thomas is not so sure. When he is introduced to Boy at the home of Tarzan and Jane, he sees the resemblance to his dead nephew and compels Jane to admit the truth. The unscrupulous Lancings form a plan to take the lad back to England, so they can control the estate as legal guardians. They convince Jane that Boy should return to his birth place to get a proper education.

Jane knows that her husband will never allow Boy to leave — with great guilt, she traps Tarzan in a deep grotto after he retrieves the safari guns. Sir Thomas realizes that Jane's cousins only intend harm to Boy, but before he can reveal the truth he is murdered by Lancing. Trekking through the hostile Zambeli country, the safari is captured, and one by one they are executed. Jane sees a crack in the barricade that only Boy could escape through, and she asks him to return to Tarzan for help.

A desperate Jane instructs her son Boy to run for Tarzan's help ... and not to look back

Jane courageously diverts the enemy, but she is wounded in the back by an enemy spear. Boy races through the jungle to the grotto, and with the help of the elephants, Tarzan is freed from the trap. Tarzan leads the charge of the elephant army, which tramples through the cannibal village and destroys it. Austin Lancing is killed, but Tarzan allows Sande and Mrs. Lancing to escape with their lives.

Tarzan is angry with Jane, because he feels that she has betrayed him. But when she collapses to the ground and he sees that she is bleeding, he begs her not to die. By now he realizes that Jane was tricked, and she tells Tarzan that her love is forever. Jane's wound is not fatal, and all is forgiven as the family returns to their own private world.

Filming began on January 9, 1939, and Maureen was already four months pregnant with her first child. Director Richard Thorpe was famous for his ability to work quickly and efficiently, and now these particular skills were paramount! Maureen's action scenes came first, since at this point she was not "showing" any signs of her impending motherhood. Towards the end of the shooting schedule, as her belly grew, she was photographed from above the waist, or holding various props to hide her pregnancy.

Since Maureen wanted her career to move in a new direction, it was decided that the character of Jane would be written out by ending her life with a Zambeli spear. After reading the original script, Edgar Rice Burroughs sent a strongly worded letter to MGM dated January 6, 1939, that killing off the character of Jane would be box-office poison, and that this was a mistake of the highest magnitude. A preview audience was shocked by the story ending with Jane's death, and voiced vigorous disapproval.

About this time the film's producers came to their senses, and used an alternate ending written by scriptwriter Cyril Hume in which Jane did indeed survive her spear wound. This final scene was shot after production was completed, and Maureen was photographed with Johnny holding her closely after she collapses to the ground.

When Tarzan discovers blood oozing from her back, he begins pleading with her not to die: "Jane not go ... Jane not die!" She smiles back at her mate, and since her wound is not fatal — she is now able to respond: "Yes, Darling ... everything's all right ... now."

Maureen has a beautiful smile on her face as she reassures Tarzan and he forgives her misguided betrayal. The ape-man's tears were genuine, and there wasn't a dry eye in the house as Tarzan gathered his love in his arms with grateful joy. Limited by the vocabulary that his Tarzan character was allowed to use, Weissmuller was nevertheless able to show strong emotion that welled up from his soul, and as Tarzan he continued to be a natural.

Johnny Sheffield joins them in the final scene as his parents ride Timba the elephant while he follows on the baby elephant, and a group of chimps are monkeying around on a third pachyderm in the rear. Like most of the later MGM Tarzan pictures, this was a typical happy ending.

The cast included veteran actor Henry Stephenson as Sir Thomas, who was superb as a man of principle. He is killed for warning Jane that the Lancings have put Boy's very existence in jeopardy with their insatiable greed. Ian Hunter as the duplicitous Austin Lancing, Frieda Inescort as his partner-in-crime, and Henry Wilcoxon as the shady safari guide also performed with excellence. Laraine Day, later a star, played a small role as Boy's natural mother who dies in the plane crash.

Tarzan Finds A Son! was released in June of 1939, after the movie-going public had waited almost three years for the genuine article of a Weissmuller and O'Sullivan Tarzan adventure. Movie fans certainly weren't disappointed, as the new picture was one of the very best of the long-running series.

The cost of production was less than one million dollars ($880,000), and it eventually brought in many times that sum. Audiences were also treated to a new process that produced an effective aqua hue to the film print, derived from mixing a sepia tone and a platinum tint; not Technicolor by any means, but it did give a more lifelike quality to the film texture.

Maureen O'Sullivan portrayed her role with the same depth and sensitivity that was now inherent in her persona of Jane. The scenes in which she struggles with her own conscience and must decide what's best for her son — and what's best for Tarzan — are extremely heartwarming. Maureen's character of Jane was a woman who was believable and courageous.

Her near-fatal confrontation with a hostile spear produced the touching, emotion-evoking reunion of Tarzan and Jane near the picture's conclusion. She was twenty-seven years old when this picture was produced, and with each passing year she continued to get more beautiful and gain new fans who appreciated her skills as an actress.

The critics were strongly enthusiastic about *Tarzan Finds A Son*, some even calling it the best of all the Tarzan pictures. And perhaps it was, with the marvelous addition of Johnny Sheffield as Boy, a story line that was new and exciting, and action that was non-stop.

Johnny and Maureen were both growing as actors, and as the years passed this picture would indeed prove to be one of the great classic adventures of the exciting 1930s decade.

Maureen gave her usual exceptional performance, and Carl Erskine of the *L. A. Examiner* labeled her work "first rate," while Carl Combs of the *Hollywood Citizen News* noted the Irish actress as "always appealing and courageous."

As usual, the reviews were all outstanding for Johnny, Maureen, and the new addition to the Tarzan family, Johnny Sheffield:

Hollywood Citizen News Carl Combs (May 27, 1939)

"There is only one man in the world authorized to call himself Tarzan. This, according to Edgar Rice Burroughs, the man who has the say because the mythical ape-man is a product of his literary imagination, is Johnny Weissmuller. For followers of cinema entertainment, and especially for the juniors, there could never be any other Tarzan other than Johnny Weissmuller, and it is a pleasure to report that, after a prolonged absence from screen activity, Johnny is back with his jungle cry, his animal friends, and a fresh assortment of African adventure.

"It is not impossible that *Tarzan Finds a Son* will even be more popular than preceding Tarzan pictures. It is expertly photographed, excitingly told, and, best of all, it introduces a third party to the Tarzan family. He is John Sheffield, tousle-topped youngster, whose emulation of his agile-limbed foster father is a source of constant delight. If nothing else does, his infectious boyish chuckle will win many a hardened movie goer, and scenes in which he bursts through the jungle foliage or romps with Tarzan underwater or scampers about with his jungle pets are scenes idyllic in their primitive lightheartedness.

"Maureen O'Sullivan, always appealing and courageous, continues as Tarzan's English-bred mate. In the picture she is prompted to give up their foster child, orphaned in a plane wreck, to his fortune-hunting relatives who have trekked into the jungle seeking the child and his dead parents, wealthy British peers.

"The picture was directed with good taste and with complete understanding of what a Tarzan movie ought to be by Richard Thorpe."

Los Angeles Examiner Erskine Johnson (June 21, 1939)

"Tarzan returned to town yesterday on the screens in the latest and probably best of the jungle series, *Tarzan Finds a Son*. If you crave excitement and thrills in your celluloids, it is a movie you shouldn't miss.

"Thrilling scenes as the story unwinds include Tarzan's rescue of the boy who is being charged by a rhinoceros, capture of Miss O'Sullivan and the boy by a tribe of vicious head hunters, and their rescue by Tarzan at the head of a herd of elephants, each ridden by a chimpanzee, who storm the stockade, battering the fence down and scattering the head hunters. Best scenes: Tarzan and the boy in a five-minute underwater swimming sequence, filmed at Silver Springs, Fla., the like of which you have never before seen on the screen.

"Johnny Weissmuller is his usual muscular self in the title role and the first time his meaningless grunts have been replaced by one syllable words such as boy, girl, and man. Young Sheffield turns in an amazingly good performance as Tarzan Junior, and even gives an imitation of Tarzan's yell. Miss O'Sullivan also turns in a first-rate performance."

During the months that she was filming her recent Tarzan picture, Maureen found the time to make a few radio appearances, including the "Chase and Sandborn" program on NBC radio. The January 29, 1939, broadcast featured a guest cast with Maureen O'Sullivan, Don Ameche, Nelson Eddy, Edgar Bergen and his dummy, Charlie McCarthy, and Dorothy Lamour, along with Ronald Armbruster and his orchestra.

The actress also made another appearance on the *Lux Radio Theatre*, in a CBS radio broadcast of *The Return of Peter Grimm* (February 13, 1939). Hosted by Cecil B. De Mille, the veteran producer would introduce his cast and mention each actor's current film work. This particular story had been written by DeMille, along with David Belasco, and the cast included Maureen O'Sullivan (Katherine), Lionel Barrymore (Peter Grimm), Peter Holden (William), Edward Arnold (Dr. McPherson), and Gavin Muir (Frederick).

Lionel Barrymore re-created his role of Peter Grimm from the 1937 motion picture of the same name. Maureen O'Sullivan portrayed Katherine Grimm, the devoted ward who reluctantly agrees to his dying wish that she marry his older nephew, Frederick, a charlatan who plans to strip his uncle's estate after his death. When Grimm does die, he comes back as a ghost to right the wrongs for which he is responsible. He is also there to guide his young nephew William, who is dying, to the land of the unknown which the child fears.

Alan Ladd was featured in the role of James, a young man who is secretly in love with Katherine, and doesn't even realize that she feels the same about him. At this time Ladd was still toiling in relative anonymity, but he would take Hollywood by storm after his break-out role in *This Gun for Hire* (1942), which shot him to stardom.

The next radio gig for Maureen was "Silver Theatre," in a production called *Dear Victim*, which was broadcast live from Columbia Square in Hollywood on February 26, 1939. Directed by Conrad Nagel, the cast featured Maureen O'Sullivan (Eileen O'Rourke), Herbert Marshall (Robert Desmond), Paula Winslowe (Mrs. McIntyre), and Eric Snowden (Bartley).

Maureen's character of Eileen O'Rourke is a smooth con-artist who falls in love with intended victim Herbert Marshall, who, unbeknownst to her, also makes his living by bilking the wealthy. This was certainly an unusual characterization for Maureen, who rarely had the opportunity to portray anyone who operated outside the law; in this case, a con-woman who meets her match.

The actress had worked with Basil Rathbone in two films in the past, and now the two were reunited in a "Kellogg Company" production called *Death Takes a Holiday*, broadcast on the NBC radio network on March 26, 1939. Others in the variety show included Groucho and Chico Marx, the Dolan Orchestra with the Foursome Quartet, along with Alexander Wollcott and John Carter (tenor).

While Maureen was temporarily away from the motion picture business in preparation for motherhood, her husband John Farrow was directing one of his better known films, *Five Came Back* (1939). This was the story of what happens to the passengers of an airliner that crash lands in the Amazon jungles; their lives are threatened by unfriendly natives that are planning an attack against the intruders. When the plane is finally repaired, only five can leave and the rest must stay behind to perish in the hostile jungle.

The stellar cast included C. Aubrey Smith, John Carradine, Elizabeth Risdon, Joseph Calleia, Kent Taylor, Chester Morris, Lucille Ball, Allen Jenkins, Patric Knowles, Wendy Barrie, and child actor Casey Johnson. John Farrow later directed a re-make of this picture called *Back from Eternity* (1956).

With another Tarzan picture wrapped up, it was time now for Maureen to concentrate on the more serious business of becoming a mother for the first time. Even she probably didn't foresee that she would eventually have six more children over the next dozen years, giving her and husband John Farrow one of the largest families in the Hollywood community.

On April 3, 1939, the mother-to-be was given a surprise baby shower by Carmelita Geraghty. Attending the party were Norma Shearer, Myrna Loy, Pat Paterson, and a few additional close friends from the acting trade.

Maureen's baby was due at the end of May, and her father Charles had planned to be in Los Angeles for the birth of his first grandchild. He was, however, unable to make the trip across the pond, but Mrs. O'Sullivan and Maureen's sister Sheila arrived to see her through the happy event.

On May 12, Harrison Carroll of the *Evening Herald Express* reported that Maureen wasn't the only O'Sullivan that had an interest in becoming a Hollywood movie star:

"It's touch and go whether Maureen O'Sullivan's sister, Sheila, ever gets back to Ireland to complete her course of training with the Abbey Players of Dublin. Two studios have offered screen tests to the youthful actress, who's one and one-half inches shorter than Maureen — and SO pretty.

"Her family, and especially Maureen, want her to go back and learn her trade in Ireland's top-flight repertory company, but the lure of Hollywood may outweigh them.

"Else, why is Sheila, who is slightly plump, dieting so faithfully to take off those pounds? Four of them have already come off — the hard way."

While young stars Jackie Cooper and Freddie Bartholomew were showing Sheila O'Sullivan the sights and sounds of town, Dorothy Manners (pinch hitting for Louella Parsons) noted the following on May 29 in her *Los Angeles Examiner* column:

"Sheila O'Sullivan, Maureen's 15-year-old sister who has been cutting her dramatic teeth with Ireland's Abbey Players, took a test Saturday that was so good MGM has signed her to a contract. What's even more interesting is that after a small role or two to help her gain camera experience, a part will be specially scripted into the next Tarzan picture for her. Well, Tarzan finds a son in his new picture with that very same title — so why not *Tarzan Gets a Sister-In-Law* when Sheila joins the cast?"

248 DAVID FURY

Maureen's big day came on May 30, 1939, when her son, Michael Damien Farrow, was born. Maureen's mother, sister Sheila, and new daddy John were at the hospital in support of the new mother and to see the newborn child. The middle name "Damien" was suggested by Farrow, who published a biography of Father Damien in 1937.

The following day Maureen gave a call to Louella Parsons, who had returned from vacation just in time to report the blessed event:

"The very first telephone call I received when I returned to my desk yesterday was from Maureen O'Sullivan. I couldn't believe my ears when I heard her voice telling me that her 24-hour-old-son, Michael Damien Farrow, was the most beautiful baby in the world and looked just like his pa. These women of today are amazing."

Maureen was ready for motherhood ... here she is with her screen baby from *Tarzan Finds A Son!*

CHAPTER SIXTEEN
"The Big War Changes Everything"

The summer of 1939 was the first extended "vacation" for Maureen in many years, as her studio had kept her constantly on the screen as one of Hollywood's busiest actresses. She had June, July, and most of August to spend with her new son and husband John, when he wasn't directing pictures. Life was good and the future looked as bright as the Northern Star for the Farrow-O'Sullivan clan.

The actress was soon ready to go back to work, however, and she sailed for England on August 21 to star in the MGM production of *Busman's Honeymoon* with Robert Montgomery. Sheila accompanied her older sister back to Ireland, and John Farrow and the baby would follow in six weeks time when he finished directing his current project. The plan called for Maureen to work on her film and the infant Michael to stay with her parents in Ireland.

Sheila had temporarily abandoned her hopes of becoming a Hollywood actress, and intended to return to Dublin's Abbey Players. The young actress had not been happy with her screen tests, and decided it was best to further hone her skills and perhaps try again at a later date. This pleased her parents, who did not want to give up another daughter to Hollywood, especially one as young as fifteen-year-old Sheila.

Maureen O'Sullivan was on the verge of becoming one of Hollywood's top stars, after a decade-long apprenticeship. She was getting more of the top roles, often star billing, and was considered by MGM to be their star of the future. By this time Norma Shearer was almost forty years old, and would retire by 1942. Greta Garbo, only thirty-four, would also retire after making *Two Faced Woman* (1941). Marie Dressler and Jean Harlow had succumbed to illness, the latter dying tragically at age twenty-six.

Maureen was destined to join other young actresses as top female leads such as Joan Fontaine and her sister Olivia De Havilland, Ida Lupino, Vivien Leigh, Katharine Hepburn, Greer Garson, and a select few others. Or was she? Perhaps fate had another plan.

Something happened in the waning months of 1939 that would not only change Maureen's life, but alter the entire course of history. It was worldwide, and in terms of eventual losses, it was cataclysmic. That event was World War II, and by August of 1939 the machinations of war were in an unstoppable forward mode. The actress would make five more films over the next two years, but when the U. S. became a full-fledged combat participant in 1941, she would retire and be off-screen until after the war's conclusion.

By the time she returned in 1948 in *The Big Clock*, she had lost her prime years as an actress — ages thirty to thirty-six. These lost years as a motion picture star could never be regained, but the loss was to her fans rather than to Maureen. She remained active and made her husband and family her number one priority — as well as contributing to the national war effort in every possible way that she could.

"Shortly after Michael was born war broke out," recalled Maureen. "The war shook us all out of blissful complacency. Before that we'd lived such charmed, insular existences that even through the Thirties no one talked about the Depression. The only sign I saw of it was a policeman crying outside a bank which had just been closed and was surrounded by a crowd of mournful looking people. That made a deep impression on me, but apart from that, the Depression seemed to go right over our heads like a cloud. I never heard it discussed once. Hollywood was a fantasy world in more ways than one. But it must be said that the industry did a lot for the war effort by producing some marvelous propaganda movies."

After arriving in London to begin filming *Busman's Honeymoon*, Maureen received a cable from MGM that she would be recalled to the United States if war broke out in Europe. On August 25, 1939, Harrison Carroll of the *Los Angeles Evening Herald Express* reported the following:

"As Europe speeds toward war, Hollywood film studios today are making frantic efforts to communicate with their stars who are traveling abroad.

"In a cable to Madeleine Carroll in Paris, Paramount urged the actress to return to America on the first boat. The blonde star has no camera commitments until October, when the picture *Safari* goes into production, but the studio fears for her safety.

"Other stars believed to be in France include Norma Shearer, Tyrone Power and wife Annabella, Edward G. Robinson, Gloria Stuart and her writer husband, Arthur Sheekman. Constance Bennett is supposed to be on the high seas.

"In London are Douglas Fairbanks, Robert Montgomery, and Maureen O'Sullivan. Just arrived there, Miss O'Sullivan cabled friends that only 96 passengers made the crossing on the Queen Mary. Sonja Henie is believed still to be in Norway.

"The critical situation abroad may cancel plans for many Hollywood celebrities to make appearances in London on October 8 at the benefit for the Cinematograph Trade Benevolent Fund. Deanna Durbin, Dick Powell, Mickey Rooney and the entire cast of the Hardy family pictures had expected to attend.

"Of the stars who have been planning trips to Europe, Barbara Stanwyck and Robert Taylor were among the few diehards today. They said they still intend to go."

Meanwhile, a week later on September 2, studio chief Louis B. Mayer was trying to contact Ben Goetz, who was in charge of the *Busman's Honeymoon* company in London, but the cable lines were severed. MGM had already instructed Goetz to get all Americans in their employ into a neutral airplane to carry them to an American boat; those stars included Robert Montgomery, director Richard Thorpe, and Maureen O'Sullivan, who was in Ireland with her family. Maureen's family home was near Dublin at Saintsbury, Killiney, an area that was believed to be out of range of an air-raid.

Within a week, Maureen along with Montgomery, his wife and two children, and director Thorpe were homeward bound, and the studio had canceled plans to film *Busman's Honeymoon* in England. By September 26, it was reported in the *Hollywood Citizen News* that all the principals were safely back in Tinseltown, having arrived a few days earlier.

Maureen was in London in the early days of the blackouts, and she later regaled the local Los Angeles reporters with a marvelous story. One day, the actress and her co-star Bob Montgomery and other members of the *Busman's Honeymoon* company were told to report downstairs at the hotel to receive air-raid instructions.

The head porter explained to them and the other guests that, in case of a night raid, they were to come downstairs and he would lead them across the street to a shelter.

One old lady was very much disturbed. "But, porter," she demanded, "what if it's raining?"

Without batting an eye, the porter replied, "In that case, madam, I shall find you an umbrella."

While Maureen was waiting to see if *Busman's Honeymoon* would be produced in the United States, her bosses at MGM decided instead to reassign her to another picture, which turned out to be *Pride and Prejudice*. Filming on this latter production would not begin until January 1940, so Maureen's infant son Michael and husband John had her undivided attention.

Meanwhile, the first week of November 1939, John Farrow took a flight to Vancouver to report to the Canadian naval reserve authorities. It wasn't confirmed that he would go into service at this point, but he had decided to volunteer. His current project as a director was the RKO re-make of *A Bill of Divorcement* (1940), with Maureen O'Hara and Adolphe Menjou in the roles originally filled in the 1932 classic version by Katharine Hepburn and John Barrymore.

To this point in his career, Farrow had directed sixteen films, mostly B-pictures, since splitting with MGM in 1937. His credits for Warner Brothers included *West of Shanghai* (1937) with Boris Karloff; *Men in Exile* (1937); *War Lord* (1937); *The Invisible Menace* (1938), again with Karloff; *She Loved a Fireman* (1938); *Little Miss Thoroughbred* (1938); and *Broadway Musketeers* (1938) all starring Ann Sheridan; and two Kay Francis vehicles, *My Bill* (1938) and *Women in the Wind* (1939).

Farrow had then moved over to RKO, where he continued to churn out "Bs" such as *Full Confession* (1939) with Victor McLaglen; *The Saint Strikes Back* (1939) with George Sanders; *Five Came Back* (1939), the previously mentioned plane crash melodrama with Chester Morris and Lucille Ball; *Reno* (1939) with Richard Dix; *Sorority House* (1939) with Anne Shirley and written by Dalton Trumbo; and *Married and in Love* (1940), a tale of love and infidelity. His final film before entering military service was *A Bill of Divorcement* (1940).

Farrow did indeed enter the Royal Canadian Navy in 1940 and was assigned the officer rank of commander. He eventually went to the Pacific Theater where he served until 1942, when he became gravely ill with typhus. At this time Farrow was released from duty and sent home to recuperate.

Maureen's brother Jack was already in the Irish military, and had served as an officer for several years by the time the war broke out. Lieutenant Jack O'Sullivan served with distinction in the North African campaign against Rommel. Later, he was transferred to the Paratroopers and was captured at Arnheim.

Although the United States was not yet involved with the war in Europe, as time passed it seemed to be an unavoidable event. Almost two years later, as a result of the attack on Pearl Harbor by the Japanese in December 1941, the inevitable would become reality.

The entire movie industry, centered in Hollywood, U.S.A., would be strongly behind the war effort for the next few years. Almost every star eventually became involved, from washing dishes at the Hollywood Canteen to traveling through war zones in Europe and the South Pacific entertaining the troops.

One such effort was represented by a humongous gala event at the Ambassador Hotel, where "stellar Hollywoodites and Los Angeles bluebookers turned out a thousand strong" for the Franco-British War Relief dinner and dance at the Cocoanut Grove on the evening of January 17, 1940.

Maureen O'Sullivan was part of the "most beautiful girls in the world" lineup of cigarette girls, which included a half-dozen or so of the most gorgeous women on planet earth.

This benefit was arranged under the supervision of Alan Mowbray, president of the British War Relief Association of Southern California; George

Fusenot, president of the French War Relief; Ronald Colman, Charles Boyer, and F. Stuart Rousel.

Ella Wickersham of the *Los Angeles Examiner* noted the following in her "Hollywood Parade" column the day after the event:

"Tops, of course, was the all-star chorus that came on to give lusty, if not so harmonious, renditions ... of the very Americanese, 'Swanee River' and 'The Man on the Flying Trapeze.' Included in this stellar chorus were Reggie Gardiner, Herbert Marshall, Ralph Forbes, Bill Powell, Dick Barthelmess, Alan Mowbray, Ronald Colman, Charles Boyer, Charles Laughton, Ian Hunter, Nigel Bruce, Robert Coote, and Laurence Olivier.

"Others on the priceless program were Bob Hope as master of ceremonies, Mickey Rooney, Judy Garland, Adolphe Menjou, Jan Kiepura, Mary Parker and Billy Daniels, Billy Lenhart and Kenny Brown, and the kilted pipers of Scottish Post No. 81, Canadian Legion.

"Earl Carroll's boast anent 'the most beautiful girls in the world' went into an eclipse when the cigarette girls came on. For in the eye-stunning lineup were Madeleine Carroll, Ann Sheridan, Elaine Shepard, Wendy Barrie, Joan Fontaine, Olympe Bradna, Maureen O'Sullivan, Ida Lupino, and Frances Robinson.

"And what a box-office these siren aides of Lady Nicotine stacked up for the worthy cause. For over the cellophane of their wares were other wrappers, adorned with French and British flags, and a space not only for their own prized autographs but also those of their customers. Clever, eh, what?

"Charles Boyer and Pat Paterson entertained for Tyrone Power and Annabella, Elsa Maxwell, Jan Kiepura, the Charlie Feldmans, Ida Lupino, Richard Gully, Charles Laughton, Enos Cobb, Paul Coze and Ann and Jack Warner.

"At Greer Garson's table were Benny Thau, the Louis B. Mayers, Eddie Mannix and Toni Lanier, and the Victor Savilles. Ronald Colman and Benita Hume's guests were Vivien Leigh and Laurence Olivier, Lee Russell and Herbert Marshall, Merle Oberon and the Frank Capras. In Lorayne and Alan Mowbray's party were Mayor and Mrs. Fletcher Bowron, Alice Faye, Louella Parsons and Dr. Harry Martin, and Dolores and Bob Hope.

"The newly-wedded Bill Powell and Diana Lewis were with Jessica and Dick Barthelmess and the Lewis Milestones. Other guests included Ouida and Basil Rathbone with the Nigel Bruces, Olivia de Havilland with Tim Durant and the Jules Steins, Deanna Durbin and Vaughn Paul, the C. Aubrey Smiths, Claudette Colbert and Dr. Joel Pressman, Marlene Dietrich, Ruth and Woody Van Dyke, the David Selznicks, Adolphe Menjou and Verree Teasdale, Anatole Litvak, and finally, sharing a table were the John Loders along with Maureen O'Sullivan and John Farrow."

The film industry marched along, and in January of 1940, Maureen began filming *Pride and Prejudice*, based on the classic novel by Jane Austen. The ensemble costume piece starred Laurence Olivier and Greer Garson, with Maureen as the second female lead and featuring Edmund Gwenn, Mary Boland, and Edna May Oliver in supporting roles. Olivier was fresh off the success of *Wuthering Heights* (1939) and *Rebecca* (1940), two of his greatest roles, while Garson, a British stage actress, was in just her second motion picture after her debut in *Remember* (1939).

Garson, like Maureen, was an Irish colleen who had to wait in line at MGM to find good roles because of the tough competition. In Michael Troyan's biography *The Life of Greer Garson*, he noted that Garson was one of many talented actresses at the studio:

"At Metro, well-regarded as 'The Women's Studio,' she was competing with the most formidable array of female talent in Hollywood. Besides Greta Garbo, Norma Shearer, Joan Crawford, and Myrna Loy, there were Katharine Hepburn, Lana Turner, Ann Sothern, Margaret Sullavan, and Maureen O'Sullivan. The studio may have had more stars than the heavens, but there did not seem to be enough good parts to go around."

In Jane Austen's novel, the two older sisters are Elizabeth and Jane, perhaps three years apart in age. In real life, Garson was indeed three years older than Maureen, and the two Irish beauties worked perfectly together in the roles of sisters who are extremely close and experiencing the pangs of love affairs that wander temporarily awry.

The two actresses had one lengthy scene together where they share their innermost feelings about their misadventures in love, and Greer and Maureen were both wonderfully convincing. Lizzie counsels Jane that things will work out in time, which buoys the hopes of the younger sister. Lizzie, however, has her self-doubts concerning her feelings for Darcy (Olivier), as her own situation seems to be hopelessly beyond repair.

The original 1940 filmed version of *Pride and Prejudice* began with an introductory foreword (later deleted from the final release), which sums up the essence of the times: "This is a story that takes place in the days when pride was a virtue and fashionable ... and prejudice the only defense of the spirited; when a kiss, however lightly given, meant a proposal of marriage; when young ladies were chaste and dutiful and had no careers except matrimony, and mothers pursued husbands for their daughters like baying hounds on the scent of a fox."

The story is set in early nineteenth century England in the rural village of Meryton, and revolves around the Bennet family: Mr. and Mrs. Bennet (Edmund Gwenn and Mary Boland), and their five lovely and very eligible daughters, Elizabeth (Greer Garson), Jane (Maureen O'Sullivan), Lydia (Ann

Rutherford), Kitty (Heather Angel), and Mary (Marsha Hunt). Mrs. Bennet lives in fear that her daughters will wind up as old maids, especially since a quirk in the language of the will bequeaths the family estate, Longburn, to a cousin, Mr. Collins (Melville Cooper), upon the ultimate death of Mr. Bennet.

Quite a stir is caused in town one day with the arrival of two wealthy bachelors, Mr. Darcy (Laurence Olivier) and Mr. Charles Bingley (Bruce Lester). They are accompanied by Bingley's sister Caroline (Frieda Inescort). Mrs. Bennet sees the possibilities of marrying off her two oldest daughters, Lizzie and Jane, and rushes home to her husband with the news. He has already taken the liberty of inviting the two gentlemen to a ball being held the coming weekend.

At the magnificent social event, Jane and Charles Bingley hit it off splendidly and dance the night away. Lizzie, however, finds Mr. Darcy to be rude and arrogant as he reveals his disregard and prejudice against the middle class, of which her family is a proud member. She even bluntly turns down his offer of a dance, which hurts his pride.

The family cousin, Collins, comes for a visit and asks Lizzie to marry him; she refuses of course, and he promptly marries her good friend Charlotte (Karen Morley). Later, both Darcy and Bingley leave Meryton for London, and Jane is heartbroken that the man she loves has left with apparently no plans to return. In reality, he was driven away by his sister Caroline, who insisted that he could do better than marry into the very ordinary Bennet family.

Lizzie visits Charlotte in London, and once again she runs into Mr. Darcy at the home of Lady Catherine de Bourgh (Edna May Oliver), his aunt, who is the very wealthy employer of Mr. Collins. Darcy is falling in love with Lizzie, and finally breaks down and asks her to marry him. She has feelings for him too, but his condescending attitude towards her family causes her to reject him in no uncertain terms. Darcy says the book is closed with the rejection, and he will never ask again.

When Lizzie returns to Meryton, she finds that her sister Lydia has run off with Wickham, an officer of the army. This of course disgraces the family, because they are not married. Mr. Bennet is combing the countryside trying to locate Lydia, without success, and the family is planning to move from Meryton to escape from the gossipy locals.

Jane and Lizzie have a long heartfelt talk about their shattered love lives. Lizzie confesses that Darcy had proposed to her, but that she regrettably turned him down. Jane admits that she is still heartbroken over the loss of Charles Bingley, and together they commiserate the sad state of the family affairs.

The mood brightens when Lydia and Wickham return to Meryton, happily married and wealthy as Wickham has come into an inheritance. This lifts the disgrace from the family, and the plan to move away is canceled.

Out of the blue comes a visit from Lady Catherine, who wishes to see Lizzie in private. Determined to discover if Lizzie is in love with her nephew Darcy, she warns her never to see him again or to even consider a proposal of marriage. She also informs Lizzie that it was Darcy who tracked down Wickham, and paid him enough money that he could afford to marry Lydia. Lizzie boldly announces that she will run her own life, for better or worse, and rings for the butler to help the unwanted guest out to her carriage.

Lady Catherine, feigning indignity, is secretly happy that her nephew is in love with such a fine and spirited woman. She tells Darcy so, who kisses his flustered aunt on the cheek. Darcy enters to confront Lizzie, confesses his undying love, and asks her to marry him. She says yes.

Meanwhile, Charles Bingley has returned to Jane and he too has asked her to marry him. Jane also accepts the marriage proposal, which brings great happiness to Mrs. Bennet — two of her daughters are now betrothed, and one is married. When it appears that Kitty and Mary also have prospective beaus, Mr. Bennet makes the wry comment to his wife, "Well, I guess that it is good that we didn't drown any of them when they were born."

Pride and Prejudice was originally scheduled to be produced in 1936 under the supervision of Irving Thalberg, with Norma Shearer and Clark Gable in the lead roles. Thalberg's death altered that plan, and when the film was eventually produced in 1940, the leads went to Olivier and Garson, who were good friends in real life and had worked together on the stage in London. Olivier, in the words of TCM host Robert Osborne, was "smitten" with Greer before meeting Vivien Leigh, whom he married in 1940.

When Maureen and Laurence Olivier ran into each other some decades later, they both were amazed that the film had remained a fan favorite for so many years, as Marsha Hunt (who portrayed Mary Bennet) recalled. "None of us had any idea the film would be so popular," said Hunt "Recently, Maureen O'Sullivan, who appears as my sister Jane, told me that when she met Olivier years later in England they expressed mutual surprise at the picture's success."

Olivier himself was clearly dissatisfied with his character of Mr. Darcy, and admitted as much in his autobiography. "I was very unhappy with the picture. It was difficult to make Darcy into anything more than an unattractive-looking prig, and darling Greer seemed to be all wrong as Elizabeth."

Indeed, Olivier's priggish character was mostly unlikable, but Greer Garson was marvelous and seemed to be the perfect choice to play the delightfully quirky and independent Lizzie Bennet, as noted by Bosley Crowther in the *New York Times:* "Greer Garson is Elizabeth — 'dear, beautiful Lizzie' — stepped right out of the book, or rather out of one's fondest imagination: poised, graceful, self-contained, witty, spasmodically stubborn, and as lovely as a woman can be."

Maureen, too, was perfectly cast as the lithesome Jane, the least flighty of the five Bennet sisters, and she is given the task of the serious acting scenes as the woman whose heart is easily broken but remains strong with the support of her older sister Lizzie. At twenty-eight years old, Maureen was never more beautiful, and she was as fine a dramatic actress as there was in Hollywood.

Fifty years later Maureen recalled her relationship with Greer Garson. "I hear from Greer all the time," said Maureen. "We became close friends on *Pride and Prejudice*. We had known each other before, but we really cemented it there. I was very fond of her. Now she was known at Metro-Goldwyn-Mayer as 'Career Greer' because she was very career-minded. She was very ambitious. So I was very surprised when she married Buddy Fogelson, and then just disappeared from the movie world. But they were very happy, and she took good care of him when he was ill for six months. And they settled in Dallas and had a ranch, and raised only white cattle."

Pride and Prejudice premiered at the Radio City Music Hall in New York on July 26, 1940, and played four weeks to enthusiastic crowds and exceptional reviews from the critics. On a final note about Mr. Olivier and Ms. Garson, during filming Harrison Carroll of the *Evening Herald Express* visited the set and reported the following short conversation with the great actor Olivier in his column of February 10, 1940:

"In a nearby sound stage at MGM, Vivien Leigh's next husband, Laurence Olivier, is working in *Pride and Prejudice*. At the moment, to be exact, he is looking on while Greer Garson, Maureen O'Sullivan, Karen Morley, Heather Angel, Ann Rutherford, Marsha Hunt, and a group of other players are dancing the polka.

'Did you ever work with Greer Garson in England?' we ask Olivier.

'Work with her?' says Olivier with a laugh. 'I invented Greer Garson.'

Mr. Carroll continued: "And while this turns out to be a slight exaggeration, it has a basis of truth. A number of years ago, in London, Olivier was about to direct and act in a play called 'The Golden Arrow.' Greer Garson, with a background of repertory experience, but still an unknown in London, was among those suggested for the leading feminine role. The producers of the play were in favor of getting a name actress, but the author and Olivier held out so staunchly for Greer that she got the part. The play was a flop, but it launched her on the road to stardom."

In a review dated July 10, 1940, *Variety* called *Pride and Prejudice* the perfect movie getaway for escapists seeking a view of the calmer days of the past:

> "Any novel which survives more than a century possesses unusual qualities, and *Pride and Prejudice* qualifies chiefly because of the characterization of Elizabeth Bennet (Greer Garson), eldest of the eligible sisters and a rather daring young woman with ideas of feminism far in advance of her contemporaries.

"There are some good performances. Mary Boland is a fluttering, clucking mother of a brood of young women whose aim is matrimony. Edna May Oliver, as the dominant Lady Catherine, comes on the scene late in the story and makes for some much-needed merriment. Melville Cooper does a good comedy bit and the Bennet sisters, as played by Maureen O'Sullivan, Ann Rutherford, Marsha Hunt and Heather Angel, provide charm and pulchritude.

"Laurence Olivier appears very unhappy in the role of Darcy, rich young bachelor, who is first spurned and then forgiven for his boorishness, conceit and bad manners.

"In the telling of the story, with its numerous lesser plots and complications, Robert Z. Leonard has found it's necessary in the direction to fill his screen with many characters, and the romance between Miss Garson and Olivier loses force and clarity.

"But for audiences that are clamoring for films far removed from present-day conflicts and problems, *Pride and Prejudice* fits perfectly into the formula. It is about people and life of an England of which only memories remain."

Almost immediately after the completion of *Pride and Prejudice*, Maureen was assigned to co-star with Robert Young in a Depression-era drama called *Sporting Blood*, about the sport of kings: horse racing. Also starring was the venerable Lewis Stone, taking a break from his recurring role as Judge Hardy. Stone was almost as well-known in that character as Maureen was recognized as Jane of the Tarzan pictures.

The story begins at a race track where Myles Vanders (Young) has great faith in his horse Skipper, and bets his last savings that his jockey will bring home a winner. When a crooked rival causes a track accident, Myles not only loses the race, but Skipper is injured in a fall. Although the horse will recover in three months time, Myles and his trainer Duffy (William Gargan) decide to retreat to the Vanders home in Virginia, a dilapidated old plantation that has been abandoned for twenty years.

When Myles was a boy, his father had run off with the wife of neighbor Davis Lockwood (Stone), and the lovers subsequently died in a tragic accident. This left hard feelings for both families, which still festered. Myles' mother passed away from her grief, and he was raised by an aunt.

Myles needs cash to live on until Skipper is ready to race in the Thomas Jefferson Handicap, but the local banker is a crony of Mr. Lockwood and refuses him a loan. Myles is furious and storms out to the Lockwood ranch to vent his frustration.

To placate the headstrong young man, Davis offers to loan him three thousand dollars until the big race. The collateral is the Vanders home, and Myles promises to leave forever in the event he should lose. Davis Lockwood plans to enter his own horse Prince in the race, and thus Myles has an added incentive to win.

While at the Lockwood home, Myles meets two beautiful young women, Linda (Maureen) and Joan (Lynne Carver), who are both aware of the bad blood between their father and the Vanders family. The girls, however, invite Myles to a party that evening where he proceeds to court Joan, realizing he could get revenge on Davis Lockwood with a marriage to one of his daughters.

Linda later visits Myles at his ranch, because she also has a love of horses and wants to see his thoroughbred, Skipper. They begin a friendship, and she is present when a favorite mare foals a colt, which has to be killed to save the mother. Linda begins to see that Myles, underneath his anger, is really a decent man who has always had hard luck.

Over dinner one night, Davis tells his daughters to stay away from Myles, warning that he is a bad penny just like his father. Linda defends Myles and tells her father that he was just a boy when this all started, and that he is now a hard-working man who deserves a break in life.

The bad luck continues at the Vanders ranch, where a fire destroys the barn and kills two favorite horses — Skipper is also injured. The fire was set by Jeff, the hired man of Davis Lockwood, who believes he is helping his employer. Now Skipper is out of the big race, and Myles also learns that Joan Lockwood has eloped with an old boyfriend, the wealthy Ted Milner.

Linda feels great compassion for Myles, and she offers to marry him. Myles is so full of self-pity that he couldn't love anyone, but he accepts the proposal, to get even with Davis Lockwood. Linda also brings over her prize mare Miss Richmond, a fast horse that they plan to enter in the race instead of the injured Skipper. When Myles brings Linda home, there is a fist fight between Myles and Duffy, who realizes that his friend is just using Linda.

As the day of the race approaches, Linda and Myles are becoming closer as they train Miss Richmond; with patience they overcome the filly's penchant to "pull up" rather than pass in a race. By now, Myles realizes what a rat he has been, and offers Linda the chance to leave. Believing that he will never love her, she packs and returns to her father who welcomes her home.

Duffy warns him to go after her before it is too late, but she is already gone. Myles realizes that if Miss Richmond wins the race and the $20,000 first prize, they will have enough money to have a decent life together.

On race day, Linda attends with her father, and spots her horse at the track. She realizes that Myles must be there as well. Linda tells her father that she doesn't care at all about Myles — but in fact she is still in love with him.

When the race begins, the Prince takes the lead and Miss Richmond is back in the field but making up ground quickly. At the final turn, Prince is ahead by a length and it is a two-horse race. As the finish line approaches, Miss Richmond surges ahead and wins the race by a neck!

After the race, Myles finds Linda and tells her that winning the race is meaningless unless she comes back to him. He confesses he loves her, and she admits the same. They kiss, the end.

Maureen and Robert Young made a dandy screen couple, and by this time he was rounding into a very solid dramatic lead. The duo had made five films together, and in each they were paired romantically. She had also made several pictures with Lewis Stone, usually cast as her father; in this story they have a very warm scene when she returns home after her breakup with Myles.

The family patriarch realizes that he had misjudged Myles and offers to go on her behalf to mend the bridges between the Lockwoods and the Vanders. She thanks him for his heartfelt offer, but realizes this must be worked out between the two of them. Lewis Stone was the perfect father figure, and more often than not — including his Judge Hardy portrayals — that was his role at MGM for two decades.

William Gargan, who had played a washed-up boxer in *The Crowd Roars*, was excellent as the best friend of Robert Young, and even punches him around once to knock some sense into him. Gargan had the few humorous scenes in the story, along with Tom Kennedy who played a track cop that always shows up at the wrong time. Clarence Muse was convincing as the old servant whose misguided loyalty to his boss causes a tragic fire that kills two horses.

Variety called the picture an "average programmer" with good performances from Young and Maureen O'Sullivan:

> "Robert Young does the best he can with a tough assignment in the lead, while Maureen O'Sullivan provides strength to her role as the headstrong daughter of Lewis Stone. Latter gives usual well-molded performance, while William Gargan catches many laughs as the trainer. Lynne Carver is an eyeful as the girl who toys with Young's affections."

Radio was pretty much of a fun gig for Maureen, and she enjoyed it greatly. She often got the opportunity to work with great actors with whom she had not crossed paths in the movie business. On March 3, 1940, Maureen starred in the "Gulf Screen Guild Theater" production of *Winter in Paris*, which was broadcast over the CBS radio network.

Maureen O'Sullivan portrayed Kathy, a foreign attaché who is of Russian and French heritage. Don Ameche portrayed the dashing American, Charles Mitchell Lewis. When she falls in love with her American counterpart (Ameche), this places them both in dangerous territory. Also in the cast was Warren William as the American embassy attaché.

In between movie assignments throughout her career, Maureen also did radio dramas and variety entertainment shows. Sometimes she would be working on one or two pictures at the same time, and then stop off at one of the radio networks and make a guest radio appearance in her "spare time."

CHAPTER SEVENTEEN
"John Farrow Goes to War ... Maureen Carries On"

After completing *Sporting Blood* in the spring of 1940, her 37th film for MGM over the past eight years, Maureen did the only thing she felt she could do: she opted out of her contract with Metro and moved to the Canadian military base at Halifax, Nova Scotia, to be with her husband. John Farrow was awaiting assignment overseas, and Maureen felt this was her way of supporting him and her country. He had given up his job as a director for a patriotic crusade, and now his wife had put her own career on hold for the same cause.

The United States wasn't at war yet, but her homeland of Ireland and the British Empire were fully engaged in fighting the German armies of Adolf Hitler. Not knowing how long she was going to be gone, Maureen sold the home she had shared with her husband in Beverly Hills. She had been through a war as a young child as well as the Irish Revolution, and she really didn't know if she would ever be going back to the United States.

While living in Canada, Maureen and John Farrow did a war bond short film in Montreal at the Associated Screen News Studios. During the war years, the actress made trailers and other short films to raise money through war bonds. Maureen also knitted to help pass the time, and it was an activity that she found enjoyable. "I've knitted and I've knitted," she noted with levity. "Why, we'd as soon think of leaving our shoes at home as leaving our knitting bags when we would go anywhere."

Maureen's "retirement" was short-lived, lasting only a few months. John shipped out, at which point the boredom commenced. When the call came from MGM in October of 1940 to take the romantic lead in *Maisie Was A Lady* (1941), Maureen jumped at the chance and headed for Hollywood.

The comedic lead was Ann Sothern, who would eventually star in ten of the "Maisie" series of films between 1939 and 1947. In between the two women, Lew Ayres played Maureen's alcoholic brother who eventually falls for Maisie. They make an odd couple, because he is a millionaire and she hasn't got two quarters to rub together.

The story begins at a carnival sideshow, where Maisie Ravier (Sothern) is employed as the amazing "headless" woman, a fake act that pays her $25 week for an eight-week run. When drunken playboy Bob Rawlston (Ayres) inadvertently exposes the fraud and causes Maisie to be fired, he tries to make it up to her by loaning her his expensive automobile to drive home to New York.

The Rawlston auto is recognized by the local police and she is arrested for car theft. At the trial, Bob admits that Maisie's story is true, and he apologizes profusely. The judge doesn't feel this is enough, and he orders Bob to provide a job for Maisie for eight weeks at a salary of $25 per week. The only job he has is as a maid at his mansion on fashionable Long Island; she accepts the position and forgives him. Maisie is amazed at the family home, which has expansive grounds, a swimming pool, and enough bedrooms for many guests.

This weekend is special, as Abby Rawlston (Maureen) is to announce her engagement and the house is full of her friends. The handsome boyfriend is Link Phillips (Edward Ashley), a selfish cad and undeserving of Abby.

Abby's father is a jet-setter who travels the world as his hobby. Instead of coming home for the engagement party, he sends his usual gift: expensive jewelry that Abby just stores away. Maisie makes friends with Abby and begins to see that she is a lonely woman whose only real friend is the family butler Walpole (C. Aubrey Smith). Walpole keeps a scrapbook on Abby's brother Bob from his college days, when he was a top student and earned many awards. Bob became an alcoholic after he came home one Christmas to announce his winning a fellowship, but everyone was gone and he was completely alone.

Maisie begins to see that most of Abby's guests are shallow, and the biggest phony of them all is Link, who makes a pass at Maisie in the hallway. When Link's old girlfriend, Diana, shows up at the party, she confronts Link for dropping her and instead opting to marry into the wealthy Rawlston family.

As the two are having a heated argument, Abby arrives to overhear everything and is shocked as the conversation unfolds. Diana produces a letter from Link wherein he informs Diana they can continue their affair after he is married to the wealthy young heiress. Now Abby sees the awful truth and runs from the room in despair. Diana slaps Link and tells him that his luck has run out — he soon departs.

Abby realizes that Link was only using her, and that her so-called friends were laughing behind her back. Maisie tries to comfort her, but Abby feels she has lost everything and is sobbing uncontrollably. She is so distraught that she takes an overdose of pills and is in a coma when she is discovered by Maisie on the bathroom floor.

Maisie angrily throws out all the guests, and calls for the family doctor. She then orders Bob to contact Abby's father "Cap" (Paul Cavanagh) to come home immediately, before it is too late. When Mr. Rawlston arrives, the doctor will not let him see Abby. She is in grave condition and has given up her fight for her life. Bob and his father discuss the situation, and they both seem resigned that they could have done nothing to foresee this result.

Maisie, overhearing the conversation, is enraged and tears into both men like an angry terrier. She chastises the father for never being home when his family needed him. Maisie tells Bob to stop being a drunk and be more supportive of Abby, who is his only sister and needs his love and friendship.

Bob and Cap go up to Abby's bedroom to be with her, hoping she will survive. When Abby awakens and sees them both by her bedside, concerned and holding her hands, she quickly recovers. Within a few days, she is happy and healthy and planning a long family vacation to Honolulu.

Abby is so grateful to Maisie that she offers her a new job as her companion, with a salary and status as a member of the household. As they prepare for the trip, Bob lets it slip that he is falling for Maisie, who is only too happy. But after talking with Walpole, Maisie realizes that she is just not right for Bob; she's poor, he's rich, and there's no way it would work. She hastily exits the house and joins a burlesque house as a dancer.

Bob spends weeks trying to track her down, and finally finds her at a vaudeville theater. He convinces Maisie that she has turned his life around and that they indeed can make a go of it. She accepts his offer of marriage and a kiss seals the deal.

The "Maisie" films were "B" pictures, but Maureen gave an "A" quality performance as a sweet woman who is about to make a bad mistake in marrying a real cad, well played by the suave Edward Ashley. Maureen gave a superb portrayal as a sensitive soul whose happiness, when shattered, causes her to fall so hard emotionally that she attempts suicide.

Maureen as Abby Rawlston in *Maisie Was A Lady*

Maureen's Abby Rawlston is a warm, compassionate woman who wants love in her life. However, with her father and brother elsewhere, she gets involved with a duplicitous Lothario. Fortunately, there is spunky Maisie to step in and foil the brute, who skulks out of the house after a wicked slap on the face administered by the old girlfriend (Joan Perry). It is also Maisie who gets Abby's family to realize how shallow their lives have become. And when they find the love they had suppressed, the three Rawlstons all gain strength to make a new and better life.

Ann Sothern as Maisie was a spitfire from Brooklyn who had to work for every dime, and didn't take any guff from anybody, rich or otherwise. The "Maisie" pictures were the second most popular comedy series of the times, trailing only the immensely successful "Andy Hardy" films. This was the first time that Maisie wound up with a boyfriend, albeit a drunken one. Lew Ayres made the most of a smallish part as a man who indeed does have character when he is sober.

C. Aubrey Smith had portrayed Maureen's father in the first Tarzan picture, and now a decade later he returned as her butler! Smith was a fine actor, and although pushing eighty he was still going strong. Also in a small role as a carnival barker was Joe Yule, Mickey Rooney's father, a former vaudevillian who did small character parts in many films.

Variety noted the merits of the film and actors (January 15, 1941):

"This is undoubtedly the best of the 'Maisie' series to date, and, with added marquee strength of Lew Ayres for lighting with Ann Sothern. Picture is a strong programmer that will catch many billtopping positions for profitable biz. Filled with elemental situations in both dramatic and comedy lines, it carries wide appeal for general audiences in the subsequents.

"Miss Sothern provides her usual fine characterization of the wisecracking showgirl to give upgrade impetus to popularity of Maisie with picture audiences. Ayres redeems a most unsympathetic role with his rejuvenation towards the finish. Maureen O'Sullivan does nicely in the spot of Ayres' sister, and C. Aubrey Smith provides his regular excellent portrayal as the head butler."

As was often done in the 1930s and 1940s, a radio version of the film was broadcast by the *Lux Radio Theater* on November 24, 1941, with the stars Ann Sothern, Maureen O'Sullivan, and Lew Ayres recreating their screen roles. As per usual, the show was hosted by Cecil B. DeMille, who was fond of Maureen and used her numerous times on the popular Lux radio program.

In the spring of 1941, Louis B. Mayer asked Maureen if she would consent to being Jane in two additional Tarzan films. They offered to sweeten the pot by making the setting of the second film New York City, where she would be able to wear the latest fashions instead of her usual ragged jungle shifts. To thoroughly consider her future as an actress, Maureen took her two-year-old son Michael on a three-week vacation to Bermuda, and returned on April 23, 1941. When asked about her husband, she told the press that Lieutenant Commander Farrow was on minesweeper duty in the South Pacific.

While Maureen was pondering this offer, screenwriter Cyril Hume was working on a script without the character of Jane, should the actress reject the studio's overtures. Hume's early outlines included a beautiful "glamour girl" hunting big game in Africa where she encounters Tarzan, who has a wounded heart after the death of his mate. Hume drafted a script which featured a femme fatale called "Sylvia Starke, International Glamour Girl No. 1." With the character of Jane eliminated, this would make Tarzan a bachelor and open to new romantic situations.

When Maureen accepted the proposal from the studio to do two more Tarzan films, the Cyril Hume story was tossed into the bin where all unused scripts go to die. At this point a disgruntled Hume asked to be relieved and Myles Connolly and Paul Gangelin were given the task of crafting the new jungle adventure. On June 14, 1941, with director Richard Thorpe behind the reins of the 10-week shooting schedule, Maureen and Johnny began filming the fifth episode of the series, this one entitled *Tarzan's Secret Treasure*.

The exceptional cast included Reginald Owen as the distinguished leader of the British scientific expedition, Professor Elliot; Owen had appeared in one of Maureen's early films, *Robbers' Roost* (1933), as her older brother. Tom Conway portrayed the true villain of the story, a callous man who very nearly causes the death of Tarzan. Conway, the brother of actor George Sanders, was well known during the 1940s as the "Falcon" in a highly successful series of detective thrillers.

Featured as a lovable Irishman who enjoyed his whiskey was Barry Fitzgerald, whose character of O'Doul developed a strong affection for and loyalty to Tarzan and his family. Fitzgerald appeared in many classic films during his career — usually as a warmhearted curmudgeon but sometimes in more powerful roles. He was one of the finest, and funniest, character actors in the business. Fitzgerald had many important roles in his career, including an Academy Award winning portrayal in *Going My Way* (1944) and other great films such as *Ebb Tide* (1937) and *The Naked City* (1948). Like Maureen O'Sullivan he was 100% Irish, and he jokes with Tarzan after their first handshake, "Mr. Tarzan, with a grip like that you must be at least part Irish."

Tarzan's Secret Treasure begins in the jungle paradise of Tarzan and Jane, as their son Boy joins his parents for a river swim. The lad discovers some gold nuggets that he brings to Jane, who explains the value of gold in the outside world she calls civilization. Tarzan tells of a hidden mountain of golden stone — gold that he calls worthless because it is meaningless to him.

Boy is fascinated by the tales of civilization, and runs away in the night to find out for himself. He comes across a village and makes friends with a native boy, Tumbo (Cordell Hickman), who becomes an orphan when his mother dies of jungle fever. Boy is blamed by the witch doctor and sentenced to die by fire. Fortuitously, an English safari arrives and saves Boy, but they are soon engaged in a fight for life against heavy odds.

Out of nowhere swings Tarzan, who has been tracking his lost son. The natives are scared away, and Boy recounts how his life was saved by the white men. Professor Elliot (Owen) explains that they are seeking the lost Vanusi tribe, and Tarzan offers to take them to their destination by his own secret shortcut. The others are Medford (Conway), Vandermeer (Philip Dorn), and a whiskey-drinking Irishman, O'Doul (Fitzgerald). Tarzan also takes young Tumbo, abandoned by his tribe, back home to Jane.

When Boy mentions his gold nuggets and the mountain of gold, Medford and Vandermeer are caught up with "gold fever." The two men plot to steal the gold, and ask Boy to show them where he found the gold nuggets. When Tarzan discovers they are after the gold, he orders them to leave the jungle and never return.

Maureen and Johnny Sheffield with the villainous tandem of Philip Dorn and Tom Conway

Meanwhile, Boy, O'Doul, and Professor Elliot are all infected with the jungle fever. Tarzan saves Boy and O'Doul with his own brand of jungle herb remedy, but Elliot dies when he is deprived of the medicine by Medford. While Tarzan is gone to get more herbs, Boy and Jane are kidnapped by Medford, who tells Tarzan they will be returned safely only if he reveals the location of the gold.

Upon finding the rich gold deposits, Medford back-shoots Tarzan, who falls to the bottom of a deep ravine — presumably dead. Jane and Boy are kept as hostages as the safari hastily departs through hostile Joconi territory. When they are captured, it appears all is lost — but in reality Tarzan still lives, and O'Doul and Tumbo manage to free him from the ravine.

The bound captives, including Jane and Boy, are being transported down the river via canoe, presumably to die by torture back at the village. From out of nowhere comes Tarzan's yell, and Jane and Boy have renewed hope. As Tarzan overturns the canoes one by one, the crocodiles devour the enemy.

Boy falls into the river and almost drowns, but Tarzan saves him in the nick of time. Medford and Vandermeer are not so fortunate — they are eaten by hungry crocodiles. Jane, too, falls into the river but Tarzan quickly pulls her to the safety of the shore, and the family is reunited. Mr. O'Doul is rewarded for his bravery with a heavy sack of gold and is sent home on the back of an elephant. Tumbo remains with his new family — Tarzan, Jane, and Boy.

One of the warmest scenes in any Tarzan picture was the one in which Johnny and Maureen as the jungle couple discuss their son Boy, and how easily he is impressed by the outsiders from civilization. Johnny's Tarzan feels these interlopers are mostly fools, with little comprehension of the values of the jungle people. "None of them have what we have," says Jane tenderly.

"Tarzan have Jane," replies the ape-man with conviction.

"Has it seemed a long time, Tarzan?" asks Jane romantically.

"Sun make one safari for Jane and Tarzan," answers Tarzan matter-of-factly.

"Oh Tarzan, a poet couldn't have said that more beautifully," responds Jane.

This was a lovely scene that was the hallmark of the MGM Tarzan movies: a true romantic relationship between Tarzan and Jane that often wasn't present in later Tarzan pictures. After a swim, there's more love talk as Tarzan and Jane lie together on the river bank and then kiss sensually.

In 1934, the Hays Office eliminated the sexy outfits of Maureen O'Sullivan and the eroticism of a nearly-naked jungle couple, unmarried lovers living in a virtual Garden of Eden.

But even in the later films there was always that deep-rooted bond between Tarzan and Jane, portrayed with such perfect screen chemistry by Johnny and Maureen. More than seventy years after the release of the initial MGM Tarzan pictures, Johnny Weissmuller and Maureen O'Sullivan are, to this day, symbols of a savage — yet romantic — relationship.

The photographs of Johnny and Maureen together from these early films are still published in magazines on a regular basis, because no amount of time passing could dull their appeal to the masses. The photographs are admittedly sexy, but they also convey that exceptional love affair that everyone would like to embrace just once in a lifetime.

Maureen had a very touching scene with Reginald Owen, who played the professor. The kindly man of science would rather rip out his own heart than cause any unhappiness to Jane and Tarzan by allowing a gold hunt by his unscrupulous partners. The actress has several other fine moments of acting in scenes with Johnny Sheffield as her wandering son, Boy, and also with Barry Fitzgerald, who develops such a deep affection for Jane and Tarzan that he risks his life to save them after they both fall into the dirty hands of the gold seekers.

Maureen with her jungle family ... the two Johnnys and Cheeta the chimp

Years later, Johnny Sheffield delved back into his memory banks and recalled some highlights of working with Johnny and Maureen on *Tarzan's Secret Treasure*.

"Swimming with Johnny Weissmuller was a real pleasure. There were some good shots of us there at the spring and some really good shots of us at the climax of the movie when Tarzan swam down river and rescued Jane and me from the Joconi. Big John was like a motor boat in the water. There is one cut during the rescue of me motoring along just like Tarzan that I really like."

In those beautiful underwater swimming scenes with Johnny Weissmuller and supposedly Maureen — the woman was, in actuality, Olympic swimmer Josephine McKim. Johnny could swim like a fish, literally, but this was not something that came naturally to Maureen. So the stunt girl did the beautiful underwater work, and the fans enjoyed the camera magic.

Bosley Crowther of the *New York Times* noted in his review of Christmas Day, 1941, that this Tarzan picture was all in good fun and adventure, like the previous editions:

> "God rest ye, merry gentlemen, let nothing you dismay ... *Tarzan's Secret Treasure* tells in truly comic-strip hyperbole of a shockingly outrageous attempt by a couple of greedy scientists to ravish the ape-man's paradise of its gold. And it concludes in the customary fashion with Tarzan conscripting his faithful friends, the beasts, to put the outsiders in their places and to save his African solitude for himself, his mate, and his youngster, who has grown to be quite a lad.
>
> "Don't let it throw you, Christmas revelers. It is all in the spirit of fun. And although there is nothing about it which would distinguish it from other Tarzan films — save the introduction of Barry Fitzgerald as a kindred soul in the wilds and the fact that Johnny Weissmuller has added a few words to his vocabulary — the animal scenes are amusing, especially those which star a chimpanzee, and the fanciful concept of the whole thing is, as usual, pleasantly lacking in guile."

When *Tarzan's Secret Treasure* was released to movie-going audiences at the Christmas holiday, 1941, the United States and Japan had engaged in war after the attack on Pearl Harbor, and truth be told, the Golden Age of Hollywood was over.

Weissmuller and Maureen had been portraying their characters of Tarzan and Jane for a full decade, and America had lost none of its love for the couple that brought exciting and romantic adventures to the screen for the price of a bowl of soup. He was a few pounds heavier than in his competitive days as a swimmer, but was still powerfully built and presented a commanding figure as the heroic Tarzan.

Maureen O'Sullivan at age thirty probably was at her peak in all the feminine ways — her character of Jane was still the quintessential match for Tarzan. But she was also a young mother now, and contemplating a larger family. It would only be a matter of time until she would be forced to give up the role of Jane and make her family her number one priority. A final portrayal in *Tarzan's New York Adventure* would be the swan song for Maureen as Jane.

The 1936 death of Irving Thalberg, MGM's boy wonder of the 1930s, had caused the studio to shift direction. Thalberg favored a literary foundation for many of the studio's great films, and the Tarzan adventures based on the works of Edgar Rice Burroughs were a stellar example.

However, the Tarzan series at MGM was beginning to wear thin after a full decade: the formula plots, the stock footage used repeatedly in each successive film, and the studio's waning interest signaled the coming end. Smaller budgets also resulted in the films becoming shorter in length, relegating them to the lower half of twin-bills at the theaters.

Seeking to give the Tarzan series a charge of energy and perhaps a modern look for Weissmuller and O'Sullivan, the scenario for the final MGM adventure was shifted to New York City. In this story, Tarzan and Jane travel together to recover their darling son, Boy, who is kidnaped by a ruthless white animal hunter and sold to a circus in *Tarzan's New York Adventure*.

This story is really one of the most heartwarming of the entire series, as Tarzan and Jane must travel halfway around the world to find their son (Johnny Sheffield), who has been stolen from his African home. At times this lovely little film brings tears to your eyes, as Tarzan fights for Boy in the courtroom against heartless lawyers, and also against insurmountable odds in the steel and concrete of an alien jungle called New York City.

Jane consoles Tarzan as they try to win custody of their son in a court of law

When Jane tells Tarzan that he must be willing to heed her advice and direction so that they can find Boy together, the jungle man promises to follow his mate to the ends of the earth to recover their son. With his loincloth left behind in the jungle, Weissmuller cuts an imposing figure in a 1940s double-breasted suit, which highlights his broad shoulders. Maureen O'Sullivan also looks stylish, clothed in the latest female fashions of the civilized world, her antelope-skin apparel left behind in the jungle.

Tarzan's New York Adventure begins as Tarzan, Jane, and Boy observe a plane that lands near the escarpment that guards their home. Tarzan knows this will mean trouble, and goes to meet the men to warn them to leave. Buck Rand (Charles Bickford) is in Africa to capture lions for the circus, and is accompanied by the amiable Mountford (Chill Wills) and the pilot, Jimmy Shields (Paul Kelly). Mountford and Shields are honest men and agree to Tarzan's terms to leave in the morning. Rand, on the other hand, is crooked and awaits the opportunity to get even with Tarzan.

The next morning, Boy and his trained elephants visit Rand's camp, and the three men are stupefied at the amazing tricks that the lad commands of his three pachyderms. Rand considers kidnapping Boy, but Shields warns him to forget it. Suddenly they are attacked by the deadly Joconi tribe. Boy calls out for help, and Tarzan and Jane are soon flying through the treetops to the rescue. When their support vine is severed, they both crash to the bottom of a wooded ravine. They survive, but a fire started by the Joconis threatens to roast them. Rand manages to convince Shields that he has seen Tarzan and Jane die, and thus they take Boy with them in the plane as they barely escape the spears of the Joconis.

Tarzan and Jane are able to climb from the ravine before the fire can burn them alive, but Cheeta warns them that the plane has taken Boy away. Jane cries out, "Tarzan, our whole world is gone ... whatever will we do?!"

Tarzan calmly responds with determination, "Tarzan find Boy!"

The commissioner in Nairobi informs them that the plane was bound for New York, and indeed a small boy was listed on the passenger manifest. They charter a plane, and are also outfitted in clothes of the civilized world.

Arriving in New York City, they track Jimmy Shields to the Club Moonbeam. Nightclub singer Connie Beach (Virginia Grey) informs them that Boy has been put to work in Colonel Sargent's circus on Long Island. When they arrive at the circus, Sargent pulls a gun on Tarzan and Boy is hidden away. Things are looking bad for Tarzan and Jane, until Jimmy Shields arrives with the police in the nick of time.

In order to get Boy back, Jane and Tarzan go to court the next morning. The judge is sympathetic, but the defense attorney tricks Jane into admitting that Boy was an orphan that they adopted after his parents were killed in a plane crash. Tarzan is so upset he starts a riot in the courtroom, and the judge orders a recess for the day.

Now, Jane tells Tarzan to get Boy back his own way — by the law of the jungle. Tarzan escapes the court building and jumps into a taxi, but halfway across the Brooklyn Bridge the police have him trapped. Risking a 200-foot drop, with Jane and Shields looking on, Tarzan dives to the river below.

Back at the circus, Mountford is determined to stop Sargent's plan to sell Boy to a circus in Rio de Janeiro. As Boy slips away, Mountford is shot in coldblood by Rand. Meanwhile, Jane, Connie, and Shields travel by taxi to the circus — Jane is confident that Tarzan will find a way to meet them there.

True to his oath, Tarzan arrives just as the kidnappers are retreating with Boy held hostage. When he is overpowered and caged by Rand's men, Tarzan calls the circus elephants to his aid — they bend the bars and free him. Leaping into the speeding getaway car, Tarzan saves Boy as Rand and Sargent are killed in a spectacular crash. Jane arrives and gathers her son in her arms. Once again, the family is reunited. Back in court, the judge is compassionate and awards Boy to Tarzan and Jane, who are anxious to return to their African home.

Tarzan's New York Adventure was a stark departure from the previous MGM Tarzan pictures, and for the most part a refreshing change of pace. Tarzan and Jane battling wits with lawyers and crooks in the concrete jungle of New York City contained an exciting new brand of action and adventure, and Tarzan's willingness to risk his own life for Boy was the ultimate display of courage.

A top-notch cast included: Charles Bickford as the unscrupulous lion trapper who kidnaps Boy; Paul Kelly as the compassionate pilot who aids Tarzan in finding his son; and Virginia Grey as the sexy torch singer, Connie Beach. Hollywood veteran Chill Wills portrayed the good guy who befriends Boy, and then pays the ultimate price for his loyalty to Tarzan and Jane.

Johnny Weissmuller did plenty of stunts in the picture, including the exciting studio scenes of Tarzan climbing on the exterior of a New York skyscraper, as well as location shots on the real Brooklyn Bridge. Johnny later recalled that they had to get permission from the city of New York to block off both ends of the bridge so they could film this scene. "It was easy to climb up there," said Johnny matter-of-factly. "I didn't do the dive because it was over 300 feet high."

Maureen as Jane observes with admiration when Tarzan makes this treacherous dive; only she believes that he will survive a dive from that height. Of course she knows that her husband is not just anyone, that Tarzan regularly does the impossible, and his mission is to recover Boy at all costs.

Perhaps the most classic scene from any Tarzan picture was used once again in *Tarzan's New York Adventure*. Johnny and Maureen reenact the famous "Me Tarzan, you Jane" scene on the veranda of their treehouse, as Jane confides to her mate, "You're my goodness, darling — my strength."

Tarzan responds to Jane's heartfelt admission and gently taps Jane's bosom and then his own, and says with tenderness, "Jane — Tarzan. Tarzan — Jane."

At this moment, Tarzan is aroused by passion and kisses Jane, then scoops up his mate and carries her away to a presumed romantic encounter — the scene fades leaving the rest to the collective imagination of the audience.

Johnny Sheffield remembered this particular film as his personal favorite of all the Tarzan pictures:

"Drama, suspense, comedy, excitement, education, adventure, and plot — this Tarzan has them all," noted Sheffield. "The others don't even come close! I still get excited watching this intercontinental adventure. It is a thrill looking up there and realizing I was part of it!

"What makes this Tarzan a 'classic' is the family-oriented plot and freedom of choice. Tarzan operates from emotion and principles, and acts through freedom of choice. He is not confined to the escarpment; he is bringing up his family there by choice. No one in their heart takes exception to Tarzan's motives.

"In a 'classic' there can be no unrest over the plot; the audience must be 100% behind the hero and 100% against the villain. Who can argue against a man fighting for the survival of his family?

Maureen looking stylish as her "family" takes a ride on the "El" in New York City

"Who can forget the courtroom scene when Tarzan and Jane see that the system won't get Boy back and they hold a 'family conference' right there in the courtroom to decide upon a family plan of action! 'Jane say, Tarzan go?' 'Yes, Tarzan,' she replies. Tarzan states, 'Tarzan get Boy back' and it's on! Cheeta cheers and Tarzan is 'out of there' with the 'City's Finest' right after him.

"He went along with civilization on a legal and political level until his instincts for family preservation required him to take direct action. We see that action explode as Tarzan swings over Manhattan and heads for Brooklyn! What could be more cosmopolitan than to dive off the Brooklyn Bridge? Is that a show stopper or what? If that doesn't stop your heart, you are already dead.

"*Tarzan's New York Adventure* involves the resourcefulness and humanity of Tarzan; family and responsibility as the nucleus for human growth and happiness; the vulnerability of the family to outside influences of evil. When circumstances compelled Tarzan to venture out across this world, he demonstrated his values by action and was willing to risk it all for his family. The movie clearly demonstrates family values."

Movie critic Harrison Carroll of the *Evening Herald Express* noted in his review that *Tarzan's New York Adventure* was the best of the recent Tarzan pictures and an exciting thrill-a-minute escapade (July 17, 1942):

"For what may be the last of its Tarzan pictures, MGM plays its ace-in-the-hole and brings the ape-man to civilization. The resulting film, *Tarzan's New York Adventure,* not only is the most exciting of the series (well, for a long time, anyway) but it is by far the funniest.

"It pits the jungle hero and his faithful mate against an unscrupulous circus man who kidnaps their son and carries him away to America to work under the big top as a boy animal trainer. Away from his jungles, Tarzan fares badly for a while. The law balks him from recovering his son. At this point, however, the ape-man gets mad, jumps out of a courtroom window, leads the police a merry chase up and down skyscrapers, dives off the Brooklyn Bridge, reaches the circus just as his boy is about to be spirited away to South America, and calling the menagerie elephants to his aid, saves the day in true jungle fashion.

"This gives you a small idea of the action that director Richard Thorpe has crowded into the picture. The comedy possibilities are exploited just as thoroughly, with first honors going to the chimpanzee which accompanies Tarzan and his mate to America, but with plenty of laughs stemming out of the ape-man's own reactions to the ways of the sophisticated world.

"All the familiar players do well in *Tarzan's New York Adventure* — Johnny Weissmuller, as the ape-man; Maureen O'Sullivan, as his mate; and little Johnny Sheffield, as their son. Unless you are an old grouch or too, too blase, you ought to find this picture quite a lark."

After releasing *Tarzan's New York Adventure* in July of 1942, MGM decided to get out of the Tarzan picture business. Sol Lesser had been after the Tarzan rights for the past decade, and secured several options from Edgar Rice Burroughs to make new Tarzan adventures in the coming years and release them through RKO Pictures. Johnny Weissmuller was part of the new deal, as was Johnny Sheffield; they both agreed to join Lesser in partnership to continue the legacy of Tarzan on screen.

About Johnny as Tarzan, Lesser later noted, "Weissmuller not only had the physique but he had that kind of face — sensual, animalistic, and good-looking — that gave the impression of jungle ... outdoor life. Undoubtedly, Johnny was the greatest of all Tarzans."

The producer also wanted Maureen to come aboard and be Jane in the new series, and on February 21, 1942, the following news item appeared in the *New York Times:*

"Contracts have been agreed upon by Sol Lesser, Johnny Weissmuller and Maureen O'Sullivan for the two players to continue their characterizations as Tarzan and Jane in a series of Tarzan films which Lesser will produce. Weissmuller and Miss O'Sullivan have been playing the parts at Metro for the last ten years, but Metro's rights to the Edgar Rice Burroughs stories have expired."

However, Maureen declined the offer as soon as she found out she was pregnant with her second son, Patrick, who would be born in November. As a minor consolation, MGM was kind enough to loan Lesser the talented chimpanzee who played Cheeta, to continue his characterization. It was unclear how many bananas Cheeta was paid for his work in the Tarzan pictures.

Lesser would keep after Maureen for two years, very politely asking her to once again don the ragged threads of Jane of the jungle. In fact, Lesser was so determined that the next two pictures, *Tarzan Triumphs* (1943), and *Tarzan's Desert Mystery* (1943) were produced without the character of Jane, who remained — in the story — back in England working as a nurse during the war. She would keep in touch with her husband and son via letters that Boy would read to Tarzan by the firelight each evening.

On December 3, 1943, Sol Lesser once again thought he had a deal to bring her back to star in the role of Jane, as noted in the *New York Times:*

"Maureen O'Sullivan, who has been off the screen for more than two years, will resume her role as Tarzan's mate, with Johnny Weissmuller, in the series produced by Sol Lesser for RKO. The first of the new group will be 'Tarzan and the Amazons,' which Kurt Neuman will direct. During Miss O'Sullivan's absence, the role was filled by Frances Gifford and Nancy Kelly."

Of course, Maureen did not sign with Lesser to star in any more Tarzan pictures. The most likely reason for turning down the film was that she became pregnant in the spring of 1944 with her daughter Mia, who would be born in February of 1945. Maureen had worked while pregnant before, but this time she decided against it.

When the deal fell through, Lesser reluctantly gave up and succeeded Maureen with Brenda Joyce for the 1945 entry, *Tarzan and the Amazons.* That she was replaced in the hearts and minds of her fans is unlikely — she would always remain the number one Jane to millions of movie fans.

In a 1982 interview, Maureen got her backside up a bit when the comment was made that perhaps she had very little to "bounce off of" as an actress while working in the Tarzan pictures.

"Well, that's not true. There was a great deal to bounce off of. I think people get confused about things. If you see the original *Tarzan, the Ape Man*, I was a wealthy, spoiled English girl going with her father on a safari, where she really wasn't wanted. She brought trunk-loads of beautiful clothes with her, which the poor natives had to carry through the jungle. She was very educated and all those things, and suddenly this man — Tarzan — picks her up and takes her away. She had never seen a man like that before — he'd never seen a woman at all. She teaches him to speak.

"It was written by Ivor Novello with a little looking over the shoulder by Noel Coward. He was there. Actually, they worked it out together. It was very sophisticated dialogue. It was the exciting thing of falling in love with the most primitive element of love and manhood, so I believed every word of it. Then, as we went on and on and on, people forgot the premise. They'd say, 'She's just a girl in the jungle.' Not so."

Maureen remained friends with Johnny Weissmuller and Johnny Sheffield, and she was very proud that her "jungle family" had continued success in the movies. The Tarzan role ended in 1948 for Johnny, but he became the star of a new series of "B" adventures as "Jungle Jim," and remained as popular as ever until his retirement in 1956. Sheffield made his last Tarzan picture in 1947, *Tarzan and the Huntress*, then starred in his own series of twelve jungle adventures as "Bomba, the Jungle Boy." In 1955, at age 24, Johnny Sheffield retired from the picture business, and went on to college and private business.

In recalling the eleven years that she spent under contract to MGM in 1992, Maureen had only good memories as she had changed from a child to a young woman with a growing family: "Metro-Goldwyn-Mayer was my family. I was young; I had just turned twenty when I came to MGM. I didn't know many people in California, so the studio was my family. I lost in a way connection with the outside world, in a sense. I wasn't aware of the Depression, can you imagine? Passed over my head like a cloud. Everyone seemed to live in Malibu, and on Sundays we would visit, and the only things we discussed were the films we were making. It was a world onto itself. And I would think if MGM had a fault, it was a fault really — they overprotected us. To the extent that when I left MGM a decade later, I couldn't do any of the practical things of life, because it was all done for you.

"I never had to take a driver's test. If I got a ticket, it was turned over to Whitey Hendry [MGM security chief]. If there was bad publicity, you took it up with Howard Strickling. Life was taken care of — and they spoiled us. Some of the players criticize MGM and say they don't have a good memory of the studio, but on the contrary, I feel they were loving, loving parents."

CHAPTER EIGHTEEN
"The War Years ... 1940 - 1945"

During the period of almost two years that John Farrow served in the Canadian Navy, Maureen went through some periods of loneliness as did all the wives back home. She would write long letters to friends and family, and some of her letters to journalist Gladys Hall were published in various magazines. The following is excerpted from one of Maureen's letters, expressing what she went through while John was temporarily out of her life. The letter was entitled "Sundays Are the Worst."

"I was sitting at the counter in a corner drugstore having an ice-cream soda one Sunday afternoon a few months after my husband went away to war. As I sat there, swizzling my straw around, so lonely I ached all over, a girl I knew slightly came in and sat next to me. Her husband was in the Navy, too. We had never exchanged more than a few casual remarks but, suddenly, we were talking like intimate friends.

"Sundays are the worst," I said. "John and I always called Sunday 'Our Day.' We went to church in the morning, came home and played with the baby. In the afternoon we sat by the fire or out in the garden, talked, read, had tea. The things you shared, the things which were habit, are the hardest to bear when you are alone.

"But I am in love with my husband. He is away, and in danger. No amount of glamour, fame, or riches can make that unbearable fact one bit more bearable for me. What does anything count when the one thing in the world you really care for is missing?

"I guess anyone in love must know this. As anyone knows that if you have a toothache the pain is just as bad when you are wearing a mink coat as when you put on a kitchen apron, whether you are talking to Charles Boyer or to a Fuller Brush man. A heartache is just as impartial, I have been afraid and I have been lonely. In that I am no different from many, many other American women today.

"Every time I see a headline in the paper I am afraid to look, my stomach turns over, I get so shaky I can't get out a nickel to buy the paper. Whenever I see a Western Union messenger coming up the path to my house my hands and feet turn to ice, I have all I can do to get to the front door. When there are weeks between letters from John, I know the awful feeling of that in-between time. It is like living in a hollow ring.

"Fear and loneliness are the two most unbearable emotions in the world. Especially if you have to live with them for any length of time. They have been my house-mates for more than two years now.

"I am afraid I was not a very heroic character at first. When the telegram came, almost three years ago, saying my husband was to sail from Halifax in ten days, the fact that I was working in a picture meant no more to me than it would to a girl working in a business office. I wanted only to go to him quickly, immediately. The studio was very kind and arranged for me to leave at once. I took a plane to Halifax.

"When John met me, late at night, looking very handsome in his uniform ... I burst into tears. (Why do they always look so heartbreakingly handsome in their uniforms?)

"We went to the hotel and talked all night. I tried, vainly, to find some consolation in the fact that we had eight days together before he would leave and perhaps I should never see him again. 'Never-see-him-again ... never-see-him-again' was the thought that kept hammering in my head, try as I would to put it to one side. But as each day slipped away, it felt more and more like a horrible dream from which I could not wake up.

"During those days I was no different from other young women who, like me, were experiencing this war-time parting for the first time. I did my full share of rushing frantically and futilely about asking people 'Do you think it is going to be all right? Quite safe, really, don't you think?' Naturally, they could not answer such questions. There are no answers.

"While we were together, the hours running away like minutes, I watched John eating his supper, clamping tobacco into his pipe-bowl, reading, propped up in bed, doing a dozen little everyday things and felt a special, urgent sense of gratitude for his immediate comfort and well-being. Now, I thought, here, this minute ... he is safe!

"Loving John as I do, and have always done, I nevertheless know that I never loved him quite like this. I think I learned then to appreciate today and to be less questioning about tomorrow.

"John sailed a few days before Christmas. The night before he left we had a Christmas dinner of chicken and champagne, put in a long distance phone call to the baby, exchanged presents and made believe, as best we could, that it was Christmas Eve at home. We said funny things, choked, pretended we were choking with laughter.

"It took me a long while to be able to look back on that night, not as something to be sick and sad about but as something to be grateful for because it was an experience more intimate than any other we shared.

"I began to realize that heightened moments such as these bring you closer to the one you love than years lived on a level plane. This is a kind of happiness — or is there a bigger word for it? In the morning, 'Cheer up, old girl,' he said — and was gone.

"I did not go down to see his ship sail, but unfortunately for me, I did see it pass from my hotel window. It was a cold, miserable day. The sea was gray and angry. The 180-foot converted warship, bound on its grim mission of submarine chasing and mine sweeping, looked to me as fragile as a child's dime-store toy.

"Fear really paralyzed me then. The fear that comes to all of us when they go away, on foot, on shipboard or in the air ... 'Destination Unknown.' I was soft. I couldn't take it. I spent the day being sick to my stomach.

"An officer's wife took pity on me. She said, 'My husband has been in the Navy for twenty-five years and nothing has happened yet.'

'Nothing has happened yet.'

"That was a tonic sentence. Every day and night since Johnny has been gone I have repeated it to myself, over and over again. It is wonderful how much it means to have a whole day go by, twenty-four hours, and still be able to say it. It was a gift to me, that sentence. I pass it on.

"I can't say that I never felt fear again, do not feel it now. But I do keep the thing decently covered and out of sight. To defeat anything, you must have a weapon stronger that the thing you are fighting. The captain's wife gave me the weapon of pride — pride in myself.

"Once the first violent nausea of fear had subsided, loneliness set in. During the interminable trip from Halifax to Hollywood, I went through the experience of concentrating on the scenery, and seeing nothing. People spoke to me, I answered them and had no idea what was said. I read a book from cover to cover without understanding one word of what was said.

"My life, when I got back, seemed suspended. Aimless. I was living in a hotel at the time. I thought, 'Why bother to get a house? Why unpack china, arrange books? I will wait until John comes back, then I will live properly again.'

"My little son, Michael, helped more than anything to bring me out of my apathy. Because a child is a happy creature he demands, and usually gets, some sort of gay response. There are the blessed routine demands. Whether you are having a doldrum or a drink, whether a letter has come, or not, the baby's hair must be cut, this is the day the baby visits his pediatrician, the baby has his bath at five o'clock.

"The things I had to do, with my hands and at the dictates of the clock, helped me to put the loneliness where I had put fear, out of sight and, at least occasionally, out of mind.

"I had, besides, to cut down expenses. My husband had, of course, given up his movie money when he joined the Navy. I realized that I must keep expenses within my earning capacity if Michael is to be protected against any eventuality. I found a charming little house which seemed to suit my altered needs. Instead of a couple, a personal maid, gardeners and a nurse, I have a cook and someone to take care of the baby. We had a swimming pool in the home we sold before John went in the Navy. Michael now has a canvas plunge in the garden. There is one car in the garage and I drive it myself. When I entertain, it is at buffet suppers where people help themselves.

"No great privations here, certainly, since anyone who can have a house, a car and a maid is over-privileged today. But everything is comparative, I have radically readjusted my way of living and in doing so, have found some real happiness. Now I feel that I am working shoulder to shoulder with John who, like all the men in the Service, has certainly readjusted his way of living and cannot, I remind myself with rather grim humour, indulge in the luxury of apathy.

"But once the readjustments were made, the practical problems worked out and a routine established, the loneliness came back, bleaker than before. I made stern efforts to snap out of it. I was grateful when I had a picture, but dreaded the long intervals between.

"I did Defense work, Red Cross work, served on committees, did benefits, I played tennis, rode, exercised violently so that I might sleep at night. Never very gregarious — John and the baby had been more than sufficient for me — I called my friends, forced myself to go out or have them in. In time I found that interests I had, at first stimulating, became real and warm. In sharing the problems with my friends I found that they, in turn, were sharing my burden with me.

"But being a war-time 'widow,' a bachelor girl, a single girl, presents some curious problems and, let us face it, temptations. One of the most insidious comes from the well-meaning individuals who advise you, 'You are wasting your youth. You ought to be going out more, having some fun. It is not fair to yourself, not fair to John, to stay alone so much. You are making yourself a peculiar character.'

"Some of the more outspoken come right out and say, 'You cannot live without sex, you know. My dear, the *glands* ...'

"But it is possible to live without sex and remain both healthy and sane. You can sit at home and concentrate on your right arm until it becomes an obsessional thing. But if you love your husband, you connect sex with him and besides, it seems to me a little weak when women whose husbands are fighting for freedom, deny they have the freedom to deny themselves.

"So I did not stay home any more than I could help. I did not go out on dates because my husband happens to be a man who would not understand at all if I should go out.

"Moreover, because I am in the pictures, whatever I do would be reported in the columns. No one perhaps would censure me for going out but it might make John look just a little silly and feel just a little uneasy.

"I solved my particular problem by becoming one of a group. Now I am accustomed to going to parties alone, and leaving them alone. Besides, and it is sad to say, I am no longer the only war-time 'widow' in Hollywood. Now, on Sunday afternoons, I often see Mary Fairbanks, Betty Montgomery, Mary Astor and others, having ice-cream sodas, buying magazines, trying to fill in time and drown out loneliness. We meet at parties, at Home Defense classes, at Red Cross meetings. In the present emergency, there is very little spare time, even for fear and loneliness. And I think we have found a sort of happiness (I know I have) — born of pride in what our men are doing and in the fact that we, too, can take life when it is not so soft and not so pleasant.

"If what I have written is of any importance, it is not because I am a valiant and conquering spirit, because I am not. I am, indeed, quite timid. I have often thought it frightfully amusing that I, of all the girls in Hollywood, should be chosen to play Tarzan's intrepid jungle wife in the Tarzan films.

"Before I had to face the problems we are all facing today I was sheltered, soft and spoiled. I was dependent on my husband for all my happiness. So that if I have come to quite cozy terms with the situation, it is safe to say that anyone can."

Eventually, Maureen would get her husband back from the war, in somewhat damaged condition as she would later describe. In the meantime, Lt. Commander Farrow was working on a book which was a history of the Papacy from the very beginning to the present day.

The volume was dedicated to Maureen, and said simply, "To my wife ..." In his short *Preface*, Farrow mentioned his inspirations for the book:

"It was the late and great Archbishop of Los Angeles, the Most Reverend John J. Cantwell, who suggested that this book be written. He thought, and I agreed, that a one-volume history of the 'August Dynasty' might well serve to introduce the uninitiated into an enjoyment of the unhurried delights of Pastor and the rest of the great company of scholars. But because of the war and other circumstances it was rather slow to take form. My notes and research books were carried in many strange places. I can remember when, on anti-submarine patrol, I would grope my way to the bridge in the cold dark hours of the early watch and receive the cheerful greeting, 'Well, have you finished another pope?' Throughout it all Archbishop Cantwell kept me fortified, both by letter and in person, with his encouragement. I salute his memory."

The 394-page volume entitled *Pageant of the Popes*, first published in 1942, covered every pope from St. Peter, who died in the year 67 A.D., through Pope Pius XII, who was chosen as head of the Roman Catholic Church in 1939.

Farrow had authored other books during the 1930s, including novels that were of quite a different nature. *The Bad One* was first published in 1930, and made into a motion picture the same year, starring Dolores del Rio and Edmund Lowe. This was a story of passion and lust set in Marseilles, with the heroine a Spanish bar girl named Lita.

In 1933 he wrote and published *Laughter Ends*, another novel of lusty men and women set in Tahiti, a favorite hideaway for Farrow. He also wrote a biography of Father Damien during a year when he lived on the island of Tahiti; this was published in 1937. Father Damien was a Roman Catholic missionary who helped lepers on the Hawaiian island of Molokai, until he, too, contracted the disease and subsequently died the grim death of a leper.

John Farrow was certainly an intelligent man, someone with a great imagination who was also a capable researcher. These are traits that contributed to his skills as a writer, and over the course of his life he also wrote or co-authored several movie screenplays. A few years after the war, he wrote a biography of Sir Thomas More, who was beheaded at the age of fifty-seven in 1535 after falling out of favor with the King of England. He also wrote and published a book of poems in the 1950s.

The obvious observation would be that Farrow was a man of diverse skills: a writer of both fiction and biography, and a motion picture director. His wartime occupation was a naval officer on a ship that swept the ocean bottoms for submarines and minefields in the North and South Atlantic. Back home, Maureen worried about her husband John. Eventually, he would get an early release, long before the war would actually conclude.

While John Farrow was away during the war, Maureen really had no intention of quitting her job as an actress. A navy man didn't make a great deal of money in those days, and she had a young son and plenty of expenses to cover.

But when she received a call from the War Department one day, saying that John would be coming home because he was seriously ill with the lingering effects of typhus, she knew she would have to devote her full attention to taking care of him. When she was asked by journalists why she stopped making films in 1942, she stated that it was the only thing she could do under the difficult circumstances.

"I quit to take care of my husband," said Maureen. "He was terribly ill. He had been discharged from the Navy — the Canadian Navy — and he was more or less expected to die. The doctors suggested that I put him in a hospital, but I couldn't do that. My husband is a very bad patient. He has to be doing something even when he is flat on his back.

"He knew, and I knew, that if he were put in a hospital with nothing to do he would die. It's a strange thing, but it was the offer of a job that saved his life. Paramount asked him to direct *Wake Island*, the story about the Marines who held out for so long against the Japanese.

"It was just the sort of script that appealed to my husband, and he jumped at the chance. The doctors, of course, all washed their hands of him but, you know, the minute he felt he was beginning to accomplish something, he began to perk up."

Farrow returned to civilian life sometime around January 1942, and *Wake Island* was filmed between April 17 and July 20 of the same year. The most obvious reason for choosing Farrow as the director was his recent military experience: he had been there and knew first-hand the realities of war. *Wake Island* was considered by film historians to be the first motion picture about World War II to deal with the grim experiences of battle, and was produced under the supervision of the War Department.

For thirteen years, Maureen O'Sullivan had been the girl-next-door that every man fell in love with — her co-stars in her films as well as the average Joe sitting in the theater seats with a box of popcorn. In forty-seven consecutive motion pictures she was a romantic lead — first or second.

There were plenty of movie roles offered to her during the war years, including *The Commandos*, that was to be directed by John Farrow, and the standing offer from Sol Lesser to reclaim her role of "Jane." She was pregnant with son Patrick through the summer and fall months of 1942, and charity work along with radio acting jobs kept her on the go. The same pattern would exist over the next few years, and she would be off-screen until 1948, when she would make her comeback in the *film noir* murder thriller, *The Big Clock*.

During the ensuing years Maureen stayed busy, not only having children but as a much-in-demand radio actress. She had done occasional radio between 1936 and 1940, but when her acting schedule began to lighten up in 1941, she began doing numerous radio programs to supplement the family income. Maureen was funny, she could do comedy, and she also put her marvelous dramatic talents to work in radio plays that usually had other top stars as cast members.

Maureen was able to do radio work through the war years even when she was pregnant, and there wasn't the large commitment of time that movie roles required. For a radio play, she would get a script and have a few weeks or so to learn her part; then on the day of the show, it was in and out in a few hours time. Rehearsals would be the week before the broadcast, and then it was on with the show. It is unknown exactly how many radio programs Maureen appeared on over a twenty-year period, because sometimes even a big star would "drop in" on a show and perform a role without any billing whatsoever.

There were many other stars during the 1940s and 1950s who also did radio dramas, recreating roles they performed in motion pictures or appearing as guests on variety shows. Some of the stars included Humphrey Bogart, Barbara Stanwyck, Errol Flynn, Joan Fontaine, the Barrymores, Mickey Rooney, Judy Garland, Bob Hope, Lena Horne, Burt Lancaster, Kirk Douglas, Maureen O'Hara, and Charles Laughton. Literally every big name actor and actress in the business did radio from time to time. William Conrad was one of the biggest radio stars and was the voice of Matt Dillon on radio's *Gunsmoke* for ten years; he also appeared on a few of Maureen's radio gigs. Conrad once told your author that he often worked on several hundred radio shows per year, and by the means of extrapolation, he estimated his booming voice graced perhaps 7,500 programs over his long radio career.

On July 17, 1941, Maureen was a guest on the "Bing Crosby Variety Show," with Warner Baxter, Vronsky and Babin (piano duo), and comedian Jerry Lester. The following month she was on the "Kraft Music Hall" (August 26, 1941), as well as another "Variety Show" on August 28 with Maureen and George Raft as the primary guests.

Maureen starred in the superb dramatic play, *Night Must Fall*, on October 24, 1941, on WABC, New York. The acclaimed British stage play had been done in a Hollywood screen version with Robert Montgomery, Rosalind Russell, and Dame May Whitty in 1937. This was a chilling mystery, with Maureen playing the role of a young woman who suddenly has to deal with a man she suspects of a grisly murder, a man who lives in her home as a boarder. When she herself is about to be the next victim, the police fortuitously arrive to arrest the pathological killer in the nick of time.

As part of her patriotic duties during the war years, Maureen was the guest on an "Army Camp Program" on August 30, 1941, which was broadcast stateside and to the troops overseas. On November 8, 1941, on NBC radio, Maureen narrated a program called "Lincoln Highway," and two weeks later did the CBS radio version of *Maisie Was A Lady*, hosted by Cecil B. De Mille and with her co-stars from the film, Ann Sothern and Lew Ayres.

On January 24, 1942, Maureen was one of dozens of big stars who volunteered time for "Hollywood's March of Dimes of the Air," a one-hour program with host Tommy Cook, a child actor, which was geared to promote Franklin D. Roosevelt's nationwide plea for contributions to help combat infantile paralysis.

Maureen's part of the program was a dramatic skit that focused on a wedding taking place in early 1942, whereby the principals secretly voice their doubts and fears concerning the wartime marriage. Maureen was Ann, James Cagney was her husband Bill West, and Lou Merrill was the minister. The idea was that marriage symbolized the "faith and the future" of America.

Also on the program was Bing Crosby singing "All God's People Shall Be Free"; a comic monologue by Bob Hope; a dramatic skit focusing on active participation for the good of all, with Claudette Colbert, Humphrey Bogart, and Janet Beecher; "The Things We Love" performed by Dennis Day; a comic skit on ventriloquism performed by Edgar Bergen and Charlie McCarthy; a comic routine "reporting on corn" in the various entertainment mediums, with Marlene Dietrich, Kay Kyser, and Tyrone Power; a comic skit with Fibber McGee and Molly; a monologue by Elliott Lewis (with orchestral accompaniment by Meredith Wilson); and a vocal rendition of "Ave Maria," performed by Deanna Durbin.

1942 photo of Maureen O'Sullivan ... she was thirty years old and in her prime

Orson Welles, actor, writer, director, was also a prominent name in radio, and his infamous 1938 Mercury Theater broadcast of *War of the Worlds* had caused a panic among radio listeners across America. On January 26, 1942, Maureen and John Barrymore were guests on "The Orson Welles Show" on the ABC radio network, which was sponsored by Lady Esther Cosmetics. Welles' company of actors included the mainstays of his famed Mercury Theater: Welles, Agnes Moorehead, Joseph Cotten, and Ray Collins.

On this date, Maureen, John Barrymore, Orson Welles and other members of his company performed *The Happy Hypocrite*. As the program began, Welles read his opening script:

"Good evening, this is Orson Welles ... (MUSIC) ... bringing you another radio show for Lady Esther. Our story tonight is a fable called *The Happy Hypocrite*. It was written by Max Beerbohm, a gentleman known by his devotees as 'the irrepressible Max.' With us tonight to play in the story is another gentleman who might also be called 'the irrepressible,' but only if we indulged in understatement. And since understatement isn't one of my vices, I ask you to imagine that I've pulled out my complete collection of epithets to welcome John Barrymore to our program. Having him here makes us all happy people, to say the least. And we're all the happier to add that Mercury is also graced with the comely presence of Miss Maureen O'Sullivan. This much being said, I think you'll agree that nothing remains but to get on with it. So here it is, ladies and gentlemen, *The Happy Hypocrite*."

After the broadcast, the original opening script read over the air by Welles was signed and inscribed to Maureen by both he and Barrymore.

Welles wrote, "With many, many thanks for a beautiful performance!" (signed) Orson Welles.

Barrymore wrote, "To a very lovely person and a divine actress — most sincerely" (signed) John Barrymore.

The actress had worked with Lionel Barrymore numerous times in films and radio dramas, and this was perhaps the first time, and probably the last time, she would work with the younger of the two Barrymore brothers. John would die five months later on May 29, 1942 at the age of sixty, from complications of cirrhosis of the liver.

During his last illness, Barrymore was asked if this was his final curtain call, and he responded in a typically droll manner, "Die? I should say not old fellow," quipped John. "No Barrymore would allow such a conventional thing to happen to him."

With many many thanks for a beautiful performance!

Orson (Welles)

OPENING

WELLES

Good evening, this is Orson Welles....

(MUSIC)

....bringing you another radio show for Lady Esther. Our story tonight is a fable called THE HAPPY HYPOCRITE. It was written by Max Beerbohm, a gentleman known by his devotees as "the irrepressible Max." With us tonight to play in the story is another gentleman who might also be called "the irrepressible," but only if we indulged in understatement. And since understatement isn't one of my vices, I ask you to imagine that I've pulled out my complete collection of epithets to welcome John Barrymore to our program. Having him here makes us all happy people, to say the least. And we're all the happier to add that Mercury is also graced with the comely presence of Miss Maureen O'Sullivan. This much being said, I think you'll agree that nothing remains but to get on with it. So here it is, ladies and gentlemen, THE HAPPY HYPOCRITE.

To a very lovely person — and a divine actress — best wishes of — John Barrymore

Orson Welles' radio introduction signed to Maureen by John Barrymore and Mr. Welles

Maureen had made three films with Mickey Rooney during the 1930s, and at this point he was literally the biggest star in Hollywood. Together they did the "Kraft Music Hall" on February 12, 1942, on NBC with additional guests Victor Mature and Igor Gorin.

In September of 1942, Maureen was visiting Victoria, British Columbia, with her husband John, when she landed in a hospital and was diagnosed with toxic dermatitis by her physicians. Her condition quickly improved, and Maureen, almost seven months pregnant, was able to go home to Hollywood after a brief hospital stay.

On November 27, 1942, Maureen and her husband John Farrow became the proud parents of their second son, Patrick Joseph. The Farrow children would be raised with the help of a governess, and there would be other domestic help that allowed both parents to continue their careers in the entertainment business. Without this added help, Maureen with seven eventual children would have been like the poor woman who lived in a shoe, pulling out her hair trying to feed, care, and manage a "full house."

John had rebounded well from his near-fatal illness and directed possibly his finest film, *Wake Island* in 1942. This patriotic drama had a superb cast which included Robert Preston, Brian Donlevy, William Bendix, Albert Dekker, and Rod Cameron. John Farrow was honored with his only Academy Award nomination for Best Director for *Wake Island*, and the film was also nominated for Best Picture, Best Original Screenplay, and Best Supporting Actor (William Bendix). It was also voted one of the ten best pictures of the year by *Film Daily*.

According to Minneapolis film historian Hank Brown, the scenes portrayed in *Wake Island* were extremely accurate and the patriotic motion picture was responsible for increasing enlistments almost tenfold. The audiences were so inspired by the bravery and sacrifice of the personnel depicted, the movie became the best recruitment weapon of the war to that point.

Farrow's work schedule was much lighter than it was before the war, directing only one or two pictures per year, perhaps as a concession to his health. He also directed *The Commandos Strike At Dawn* (1942), a war drama with Paul Muni; an adventure called *China* (1943) with Alan Ladd, William Bendix, and Loretta Young; the war propaganda picture *The Hitler Gang* (1944); and *You Came Along* (1945), with Robert Cummings traveling cross-country on a bond-selling tour.

With her new baby son Patrick barely six weeks old, Maureen performed on an ABC radio network "Variety Show" on January 8, 1943. The show also co-starred her good friend Groucho Marx. Also featured on the program was the Xavier Cugat Orchestra with songs from Lanny Ross and Georgia Gibbs, along with comedian Lew Lehr.

A few months later, she appeared on the "Cavalcade of America" program on June 28, 1943, in a wartime drama entitled, *Sky Nursemaid*. The cast included Maureen O'Sullivan as Nurse Jean Owens, Frank Readick as Sergeant Lou Stevens, and the classy Bea Benaderet in the role of Edna.

Maureen portrayed Lieutenant Jean Owens, the "sky nursemaid" whose deep compassion is mixed with nerves of steel — she is an inspiration to all she contacts in her line of work. She meets Sgt. Stevens, whose critically-ill younger brother is on board an air evacuation with Jean Owens in charge of the flight. The program focused on air evacuation between frontline and base hospitals.

A radio production of *Stage Door Canteen* was broadcast over ABC and to the troops on July 1, 1943, with guests that included Maureen O'Sullivan, fellow actor Edmund Gwenn, comedian Henny Youngman, and Bert Lytell, who was a leading man in the silent era. There was also a filmed version of *Stage Door Canteen* produced in 1943, with many of Hollywood's stars contributing their talents without compensation. Maureen was not in the movie, but Johnny Weissmuller was featured as a dishwasher doing his part for the patriotic cause.

Maureen next starred in the lead role on the ABC dramatic production of the *White Rose Murders* on July 6, 1943, and the following week performed for the troops on "Words With Music," which was a Department of War Information program broadcast to soldiers overseas (July 12, 1943). Miss O'Sullivan read her favorite Irish poetry, including pieces by William Butler Yeats, Padraic Colum, John Millington Synge, James Stevens, and Thomas Moore.

The "Hollywood Theatre of the Air" was an ambitious project that brought "big name" talent to NBC daytime radio, with a budget of up to $3,000 a week for the cast salaries. The show was sponsored by Proctor and Gamble, and the name was changed in October of 1943 to "Dreft Star Playhouse." The program adapted romantic dramas into 15-minute serial format, spread over five consecutive days.

Maureen O'Sullivan was the voice of American teacher Emmy Brown in *Hold Back the Dawn*, which was based on the novel by Ketti Frings and broadcast on the NBC radio network over August 30-September 3 and September 6-10, 1943.

This was the story of a former gigolo who flees Nazi-occupied Europe and makes it to Mexico, where he hopes to enter the United States but is stopped by the quota system. The man, Georges Iscovescu, plans to marry American Emmy Brown (Maureen), then divorce her and join his former lover, the very jealous Anita. But things get complicated when he begins to fall in love with Emmy, who is sweet and the most honest woman that Georges has ever known. (In the 1941 Paramount motion picture, the main characters were portrayed by Charles Boyer and Olivia de Havilland.)

The "Gulf Screen Guild Theater" production of *The Immortal Sergeant* was broadcast on the CBS radio network on November 22, 1943. The starring roles were filled by Maureen O'Sullivan and Franchot Tone, who were good friends and had portrayed lovers in two motion pictures from the 1930s.

When the holiday season arrived in 1943, Maureen was part of an all-star program "Variety: What's New?" that was broadcast on prime time Saturday night one week before Christmas. The guests included Don Ameche, Lena Horne, Maxie Rosenbloom, Carlos Ramirez, Hedda Hopper, Ruth Clifton, and Jack Douglas.

Cecil B. De Mille hosted the "Lux Radio Theatre" production of *The Constant Nymph*, broadcast on the CBS network on January 10, 1944. This was the story of Tessa Sanger (Maureen), a sensitive English woman who is secretly in love with frustrated composer Louis Dodd (Charles Boyer). Cast members were Alexis Smith, Walter Kingsford, and Pedro De Cordoba. *The Constant Nymph* was based on a 1924 novel by Margaret Kennedy, and filmed in 1943 with Joan Fontaine in the role of Tessa.

When a new version of *The Constant Nymph* was produced for "Front Line Theatre" and broadcast to the troops on Armed Forces Radio Service (March 20, 1944), there was a significant change: Maureen O'Sullivan sings in this version, whereas on the Lux broadcast, an unidentified vocalist sang in her place. Once again she co-starred with Charles Boyer, and during the intermission, Alan Roth and his Salon Orchestra performed the selection, "Lonesome Road."

Another "Lux Radio Theatre" production for CBS was hosted by Cecil B. De Mille, with the stars Maureen O'Sullivan and Charles Laughton in *This Land is Mine* (April 23, 1944). Maureen portrayed patriotic schoolteacher Louise Martin, who is worshiped from afar by timid co-worker Albert Lorrey (Laughton). The cast also included Regina Wallace as his dominating mother, along with Edgar Barrier, John McIntyre, and Howard McNeer.

"Everything for the Boys" were productions for American soldiers overseas, and the drama *Quality Street* was presented by NBC on May 23, 1944, with the stars Maureen O'Sullivan, Ronald Colman, and Agnes Moorehead. Based on J. M. Barrie's play, *Quality Street* featured Maureen as Phoebe Throssel, a young school teacher who feels that life is passing her by when she reaches her thirties. This prompts her to pose as her own niece Olivia, in order to recapture the essence of her youth. Phoebe is also secretly in love with soldier Valentine Brown (Colman), but he is unaware of her passion.

After the broadcast, Miss O'Sullivan and Mr. Colman conducted an informal chat via shortwave with two American servicemen stationed in Australia; this emphasized the purpose of the program, "Uniting the home-front and the battlefront overseas."

The chilling "Suspense" production of *The Black Shawl* was broadcast on CBS radio on July 27, 1944, written by R. R. Lewis and directed by William Spear. The drama starred Maureen O'Sullivan as Susan Appleby (in first person narration), along with Dame May Whitty (Mrs. Masters), Pat McGeehan, and Joseph Kearns. Maureen portrayed a woman who is a live-in companion to the mentally unbalanced Mrs. Masters. Dame May Whitty was a British stage actress who came to the United States to star in a screen version of *Night Must Fall* (1937), and loved Hollywood so much that she never left.

As Christmas 1944 approached, Maureen was very pregnant with her third child and was due in about six weeks. However, she was happy to star in the "Lux Radio Theatre" production of *Berkeley Square* on December 18 on the CBS radio network. Once again hosted by Cecil B. De Mille, the drama was based upon the Henry James novel, *The Sense of the Past*. The cast included Ronald Colman as Peter Standish and Maureen O'Sullivan as Helen Pettigrew.

The story begins in 1939, when American Peter Standish finds a diary of a distant relative who lived in the times of the Revolutionary War. Peter has a vision that he can travel back to the past, to the times of his ancestor. With the old diary as a guide, he believes he can recreate the same events that happened the week of September 3, 1784. When he arrives in Berkeley Square, London, on foot, he closes his eyes and the dream becomes reality.

When he meets Helen Pettigrew (Maureen) on her birthday, they both feel a strange and mutual attraction. Their paths continue to cross, and when they meet at Berkeley Square they have a long conversation as they begin to know each other more intimately. She wants to know of the future, because he has already been there. Suddenly, she is able to see the future through the eyes of Peter.

They both fall madly in love, and when they kiss they both know they must always be together. They are from different worlds, the past and the future. Helen tells him he must go back to his time, and gives him a wooden token that came from ancient Egypt. When he is back in September 1939, he breaks it off with his fiancée. His true love was Helen, who in truth died at the age of twenty-one — her tombstone lies in Berkeley Square.

At the end of the broadcast, after the customary commercials for Lux soap, Mr. DeMille chatted informally with Maureen and Roland Colman, and the threesome shared a few jokes.

On February 9, 1945, Maureen and husband John celebrated the birth of their first daughter, Maria de Lourdes Villiers Farrow at a Santa Monica hospital. Eventually the girl would be called "Mia," and as an adult would gain her own celebrity status as an actress of considerable talent.

The godparents were director George Cukor and Louella Parsons, both good friends of Maureen who would remain so for decades to come. Cukor was Jewish, but it didn't matter at all to the family. He was also a bachelor and never married, which made him a rather ideal godfather candidate: "George was our closest friend," recalled Maureen fondly. "He was a very responsible man, and we knew he would be caring, we knew he would be there. We were Catholic, but it wasn't an issue. George was just happy to do it; he felt close to the family."

At the christening ceremony, Maureen recalled a certain levity in the moment: "George was very funny. With his camera eye, he saw the gnarled hand of the archbishop with a big ring holding up this tiny baby. 'Wouldn't that be some shot for a camera?' he said.

"George was very perceptive. When Mia was born, she was a strong-willed child. Holding the tiny baby, George quipped, 'I think I'm carrying Eddie Mannix.'"

On April 12, 1945, President Franklin D. Roosevelt died at Warm Springs, Georgia. The word spread rapidly through the streets, and men and women stopped police officers and strangers on the street to get information. Everyone who could get to a radio did so, and waited for the news broadcast that would bring the official word.

In New York, Mayor LaGuardia appeared on WNYC radio to address the nation about the passing of the president, and called the event, "the greatest loss peace-loving people have suffered in the entire war." That evening the New York Philharmonic concert was cancelled, for only the second time in its history — the first being the evening after President Lincoln's assassination.

By Labor Day 1945, the separate wars in Europe and the South Pacific were finally concluded, with the United States and its Allies the victors after the long, agonizing conflicts against the armies of Germany and Japan. All across America there were celebrations, and eventually the soldiers came home. Many had died, while many more came home with physical and psychological trauma that would deeply affect the remainder of their lives.

The motion picture community had done its part during the war, with just about every celebrity volunteering their services to support and entertain the troops. The Hollywood Victory Committee was formed at the beginning of the war, and its purpose was to act as a clearing house for talent requests which poured into Hollywood from every part of the country.

Every star and player in the industry had pledged his or her services "for the duration." Membership in the committee included all Hollywood guilds, film, stage and radio actors, motion picture producers, radio and screen writers, screen directors and screen publicists.

Maureen O'Sullivan had also carried her share of the load, participating in War Bond short films and drives, and special radio broadcasts including the "March of Dimes," serving on committees, and various other acts of charity work and volunteering.

Johnny Weissmuller had worked with the War Department and instructed marines and soldiers who would be part of landing parties; they were shown proper technique to swim out from under gasoline that was burning on the surface of sea water. He also fought against the Nazis in *Tarzan Triumphs*, which had a strongly patriotic theme.

There were numerous charity projects orchestrated by the Hollywood Victory Committee, including FDR's diamond jubilee birthday ball attended by twenty-three picture personalities; the Navy relief fund show; several Red Cross broadcasts and benefits across the country; "Keep 'em Rolling" broadcasts for the office of emergency management; and foreign shortwave broadcasts, which featured Errol Flynn, May Robson, Cecil Kellaway, and Daphne Pollard.

National Red Cross broadcasts featured Marsha Hunt, Maxie Rosenbloom, Hedda Hopper, Lionel Barrymore, Henry Fonda, Gene Tierney, Edgar Kennedy, Roy Rogers, and Ralph Morgan. Tours for treasury defense bonds included two of America's beloved sweethearts, Dorothy Lamour and Ginger Rogers.

When Maureen O'Sullivan toured for War Relief, one of the actors on the tour was close friend Charles Laughton. She recalled that when he spoke out to the troops in one of his famed monologues, all the soldiers could hear him clearly: "Charles had such marvelous voice control: he could speak in a whisper and be heard a mile away, while I could shout and scream and still no one heard me."

Meanwhile, throughout the war, personal appearances at army camps were handled by Camp Shows, Inc., which were set up to increase troop morale by the War Department, the USO, the Citizens Committee for the Army and Navy, and the Hollywood groups.

Stars that made appearances in Camp Shows in the United States and in the war theaters included Joe E. Brown, Constance Moore, Linda Darnell, Reginald Gardiner, Ann Miller, Virginia O'Brien, Judy Garland, Mickey Rooney, Deanna Durbin, Jackie Cooper, Bob Hope, Betty Grable, Madeleine Carroll, the Ritz Brothers, the Andrews Sisters, Rosalind Russell, Myrna Loy, and numerous others.

Many actors volunteered for active duty and found themselves in the thick of the action, including James Stewart, who had perhaps the most illustrious military career of those actors who served in the war. By 1944, Stewart was assigned to a Liberator squadron that was deploying to England to join the Eighth Air Force. Stewart ascended the ranks to command his own squadron and flew twenty combat missions, including one to Berlin.

Others who served honorably in war zones included Clark Gable, Robert Montgomery, Sterling Hayden, Henry Fonda, Tyrone Power, Douglas Fairbanks, Jr., and Kirk Douglas. Burt Lancaster was a soldier who served in the Italian campaign during the war, but mostly worked as an entertainer.

Even Edgar Rice Burroughs, who was past sixty years old during the war years, served as a war correspondent. In his heart Burroughs was a patriot and an adventurer, and serving in this capacity during the war brought him close to the action.

Christmas week 1945, Maureen was a guest on "Request Performance" with Jeanette McDonald, Robert Walker, the Kay Thompson Singers, and Marta Wilkerson. The following day, December 22, Maureen again was featured on a "Request Performance" broadcast on the ABC radio network, and along with Robert Walker performed the Christmas play, *Gift of the Magi*.

By the end of the war, Maureen was ready to go back to work as a movie actress. However, she got pregnant once again in December 1945, and would have her fourth child the following year. On September 6, 1946, a son named John Charles was born to Maureen and her husband.

Meanwhile, John Farrow, Sr., continued on with his own career, and directed two films that were released in 1946: an adventure on the high seas, *Two Years Before the Mast*, with Alan Ladd, whose popularity was rising meteorically; and *California*, with Ray Milland as a wagon-master headed west and Barbara Stanwyck as the feisty gal by his side.

Farrow directed three films in 1947, including: *Easy Come, Easy Go*, a racetrack melodrama with Barry Fitzgerald, Diana Lynn, and Sonny Tufts; *Blaze of Noon*, a drama about the wide blue skies with Anne Baxter and William Holden as a U. S. mail pilot; and another action flick called *Calcutta*, with Alan Ladd and William Bendix avenging the murder of a close friend.

CHAPTER NINETEEN
"The Big Clock ... tick, tick, tick ... "

After an absence of almost six years from the big screen, finally, Maureen was ready and able to resume her motion picture career. On February 21, 1947, Thomas F. Brady announced the following in his *New York Times* column:

PARAMOUNT SIGNS MISS O'SULLIVAN

"Maureen O'Sullivan, absent from the screen since 1942, will resume her career next month as the leading woman in Paramount's *The Big Clock* with Ray Milland and Charles Laughton, the studio announced today. Miss O'Sullivan's last picture was *Tarzan's New York Adventure* in 1942, in which she played opposite Johnny Weissmuller's Tarzan; she had previously appeared in five other Tarzan films with Weissmuller.

"John Farrow, Miss O'Sullivan's husband, will direct *The Big Clock*, which was adapted to the screen by Jonathan Lattimer from a mystery novel by Kenneth Fearing."

Maureen wanted to make sure she got the part on her own ability, as she later recalled: "I returned to the screen in the Forties because my husband, John Farrow, wanted me to appear in several of his films. He didn't have the parts written with me in mind — in fact, with *The Big Clock,* I had to do a screen test because Paramount might not have wanted me for it, and they had the final say."

Milland was cast as George Stroud, a top investigative journalist and the editor of *Crimeways* magazine. Stroud works for the megalomaniacal Earl Janoth (Laughton), a man of power and wealth but so insecure that the only woman in his life is a paid mistress. Maureen portrayed Georgette Stroud, the loving wife whose patience is tested because her husband is always working, and George has promised her a lengthy vacation to rekindle the romance.

This was a perfect film for Maureen to make her comeback, because Charles Laughton and Ray Milland were good friends that she had known for years. In fact, the actress had worked with both gentlemen in *Payment Deferred* (1932). Milland was still a hot commodity after the critical acclaim of his Oscar-winning portrayal as an alcoholic who hits bottom in *The Lost Weekend* (1945). Laughton had also won an Academy Award for his superb acting in *The Private Life of Henry VIII* (1934).

The cast included George Macready as the sycophantic Steven Hagen, the right hand man to millionaire Janoth; Rita Johnson as Pauline York, the sexy blonde who plays games with all the men in her life; Elsa Lanchester, the real-life spouse of Laughton, portraying a kooky artist who recognizes the face of the murder suspect; and Henry Morgan as the creepy bodyguard who does most of Janoth's dirty work. Other familiar faces were Richard Webb, Dan Tobin, Harold Vermilyea, and Lloyd Corrigan. Also look for Noel Neill in the small role of a smart-mouthed elevator operator; she would earn her own fame as "Lois Lane" in the *Superman* television series of the 1950s.

The Big Clock begins at Janoth Publications in New York City, where the giant clock tower symbolizes the power and wealth of its owner, Earl Janoth (Laughton). *Crimeways* editor-in-chief George Stroud (Milland) has been promising his wife Georgette (Maureen) a honeymoon for the seven years since their marriage, and this evening they are booked on a train back to Virginia for a much-needed vacation. George takes a break from his daily duties to stop home and see his wife and young son, who are both disbelieving that this trip is really going to happen.

Back at work, George is confronted by Janoth who orders him to take a new assignment or be fired. Knowing that Georgette would disown him if he postponed their vacation, he angrily quits his job. George goes to a local bar to celebrate his unemployment, and runs into Janoth's mistress, Pauline York (Rita Johnson). She also has an axe to grind with Janoth, and is planning to expose him with a tell-all biography. Several drinks later, George realizes that he has missed his vacation train; Georgette and their son have left without him. Meanwhile, Georgette is worried about her husband, because she is unaware of his whereabouts.

The inebriated George and Pauline then visit Burt's Place, where the owner makes them a gift of a metal sundial with a green ribbon around it. They also stop by an antique shop where George outbids a woman for a Patterson painting of two hands; unbeknownst to him the other bidder is the painter herself, Louise Patterson (Elsa Lanchester).

George finally gets Pauline back to her apartment, and he falls asleep in a drunken stupor on the couch. A few hours later she wakes him and tells him to leave in a hurry, as she notices Janoth arrive in a taxi through her window. George grabs his painting but forgets the sundial; as he reaches the dark stairwell he sees his employer depart the elevator. Before he enters Pauline's apartment, Janoth detects someone by the stairs but cannot distinguish a face.

Inside the apartment, Pauline and Janoth have a heated argument, which accelerates into a shouting match and an exchange of vicious epithets. In his rage he grabs the heavy sundial and strikes Pauline, who falls dead on the carpet. In a state of shock, Janoth departs the building and walks several blocks to hail a cab — his destination is the home of Steven Hagen (Macready), to whom he admits that he just killed Pauline in a fit of madness. The wealthy publisher also warns that there may have been a witness, the man he saw in the shadows of the stairwell.

Hagen offers to clean up the mess, knowing he will have strong material to blackmail his boss should the need arise in the future. At Pauline's apartment, he grabs the murder weapon and later returns it secretly to Burt's Place. He also finds George's handkerchief in her purse, soaked with green liquor that had spilled on her dress.

Maureen with Ray Milland in the dark thriller, *The Big Clock*

George is unaware of the murder, and flies to join Georgette on their belated honeymoon. He is profusely apologetic, and when he tells her that he has quit his job, they both rejoice at the new freedom. Before they can even celebrate, George gets a call from Janoth asking for his help tracking a man he suspects is a criminal — Jefferson Randolph, last seen with a certain blonde in Burt's place where they got considerably drunk. George realizes that he is the man that Janoth is searching for, and tells him he'll return to handle the case. Georgette is disappointed, but he convinces her this is a matter of life or death.

Upon his return, George discovers that Pauline has been murdered, and the mythical Randolph is suspected of the crime. By this time George realizes that Janoth is the real murderer, and that this is all a smoke screen to draw attention elsewhere. He confronts Janoth and Hagen, who are covering the crime with a series of fabrications.

Janoth spearheads a crime team to track Randolph, while the antique dealer and Miss Patterson are brought to the Janoth Building to help identify the alleged murderer. The building is sealed off, and George is feeling claustrophobic like a rat in a trap.

Georgette arrives and George explains the whole sordid story — his wife reluctantly believes he is telling he truth. She offers to go track down the cab driver who is the true witness that Janoth is the killer. As the net tightens, George is trailed by Womack (Harry Morgan), the bodyguard of Janoth, into the clock tower. During a struggle a punch is thrown, and George narrowly escapes. When Womack follows in the elevator, George jams it between floors by wedging a letter opener in the door.

Georgette returns with the information that the cabbie has been paid off and is nowhere to be found. In Janoth's office, George offers enough evidence that Hagen is the killer, even though he suspects that Janoth committed the murder. Hagen begins to panic, and refuses to take the fall for his egocentric boss — he blurts out that Janoth is the real murderer and will swear to that in court.

Suddenly, Janoth pulls a gun and shoots Hagen in cold blood — George and Georgette are shocked as the murderer runs from the office. In hot pursuit is George, but Janoth has reached the elevator and fires a bullet wildly in his direction. He pulls open the door as George yells "Stop!" but he has already stepped into the empty elevator shaft — he plunges several floors to his death. The police are summoned, and George and Georgette are free to begin a new life.

Maureen O'Sullivan, actress but also spouse of the director, was excellent as Georgette Stroud, the wife who is really not all that understanding. She is upset that another vacation has been postponed, and she also suspects that George may have been involved with the murdered woman, Pauline York. Georgette had met Ms. York the day of the murder, when the sexy blonde model was having a drink with her husband at the Van Barth hotel. George claims total innocence, noting that he had just met the woman and she had started the conversation with him.

The character of Georgette is no Milquetoast, and even though she loves her husband, she warns him that an infidelity would be the breaking point for her. Finally, he is able to convince her that it is his demanding boss Janoth who is taking up all his time, not another woman.

Maureen and Milland had several fine dramatic scenes together, especially when she is trying to help him find the clues to prove he is not the murderer. George has his back against the wall, and his best ally is his loyal wife. This was a very serious role for Maureen; there are few smiles as she tries to help clear her husband of being a murder suspect.

Charles Laughton was brilliant in his role as Janoth, a man whose callous disrespect for just about everyone is tolerated because he has immense power. His publishing empire makes him an international figure, and his vast wealth contributes to his megalomaniacal perversion of what is real and what he himself sees as reality.

In *film noir* a man is usually ill-fated because of his involvement with a *femme fatale*, here in the person of the slinky Pauline. Her character is doomed because she has chosen to play a game with a man who finally reaches the breaking point and strikes her dead; now he too is destined to his own dark fate. In this picture the *anti-hero* is really George Stroud, but somehow he survives his involvement with the black-widow Pauline.

Ray Milland is in double trouble ... with co-stars Maureen O'Sullivan and Rita Johnson

Meanwhile, Janoth is the true evil in this story, and in the end he dies a most violent death; it is his retribution for the crime of murder and his willingness to place the blame on anyone other than himself. Simon Callow describes the character in his biography, *Charles Laughton: A Difficult Actor*:

"Laughton's Earl Janoth, the newspaper proprietor who murders his mistress, is an adroit creation, witty and vivid ... The performance is a technical tour-de-force of high-speed throwaway, comic and powerful at the same time.

The voice rarely rises in either pitch or volume — flick, flick, flick goes Janoth, even under extreme pressure. The scene of confrontation between Janoth and his mistress is the only eruption from Laughton, and even that is almost stylized: he plunges into a jealous reproach, puffing mechanically away at his cigarette, as she rounds on him, mocking his ugliness and undesirability. His lip begins to twitch — only his lip, as if it had a life of its own. When the lip can twitch no more, Janoth picks up a heavy object and hurls it across the room, killing his mistress. He stands just as impassively over her, upon which the scene cuts to him quite impassively and dryly confessing his crime to his assistant. Janoth has been demonstrated to us. We know nothing about how he feels, or why he is the way he is, but we know everything about what he is, and how he works — like a clock, as it happens, the image that dominates and unifies the whole film."

The Big Clock was undoubtedly Farrow's best work, due in part to the superb cast and a nail-biting story that kept movie audiences on the edge of their seats. The narration begins with a first-person flashback, with the opening sequence taking place in the clock-tower: George Stroud trying to figure out how his life went from being normal to nightmarish in only thirty-six hours. Suddenly he is a prime murder suspect, hunted in a ever-tightening net, and it gets worse when an order comes to "shoot to kill." Suddenly the mute bodyguard (Henry Morgan), has him cornered in the clock-tower and is ascending the spiral stair with his gun in hand. At this tense moment, time turns back to the previous morning, when Stroud was only hours away from embarking on a much-deserved vacation with his wife, Georgette.

The final sequence is a shocker — actually a double shocker. With the principals all gathered in Janoth's office, he pulls a gun and "Crack!" the weapon is fired and Hagen is shot dead. This was a stunning moment, and it gets even more sensational when the now-deranged Janoth runs from the office to the elevator to make his escape. This was the same elevator that Stroud had jammed, so there was in fact only a deadly air space behind the doors. After firing a shot towards his accuser, Janoth plummets to his death with a bloodcurdling scream.

This was a scene reminiscent of Hitchcock, as a very realistic looking body (dummy) falls vertically several floors to a fitting demise. Stroud's nightmare is finally over, and the murderer has paid the price of his crime. A further comment from author Simon Callow, noting the fine performances of the actors and the work of Farrow in *The Big Clock*:

"Directed by John Farrow, the reliable Australian director of any number of unremarkable films, it has a great elegance and flair in a style that might best be described as nearly *noir* — visually the film is dominated by the big clock itself, a massive tower within the Janoth building which would not seem out of place in Fritz Lang's *Metropolis*. The play of shadows is handled in a masterly way; while the plot with its inversions and convolutions (Ray Milland as a crime detective spends much of the film trying to track himself down, as does Laughton) presents an image of nightmarish reversals. Milland, Maureen O'Sullivan, and Henry Morgan as a psychopathic masseur are sharply focused."

Maureen later recalled working with Charles Laughton, who had a reputation as a temperamental actor when experiencing one of his darker moods: "One day Laughton came on the set and dramatically proclaimed that he could not work that day — that he was just not up to the scene which was one of the most dramatic in the movie. My husband, director John Farrow, very calmly said, in his own words, 'That's all right Charles, we will just cut this scene from the story.' After a little throat clearing Laughton recanted: 'Well, perhaps ... I can do it ... if I have a few minutes to 'gear' up to it.' Of course, Charles did the scene — and did it quite well."

Decades later, New York friend Hugh Hines asked Maureen how Elsa Lanchester felt about her husband Charles Laughton when he came out of the closet and admitted he was gay. "Well, Charles had his boyfriends and Elsa had her own coterie of young men as well," remarked Maureen with a smile.

The Big Clock was based on a clever story by Jonathan Latimer, and was later nominated for the Edgar Allan Poe Award for best mystery picture of 1948; nominations were submitted by a group of prominent American mystery writers. The critics thought highly of the film, including *Variety* (February 18, 1948):

> "Paramount has hit upon a top-speed formula and coupled it with a novel melodramatic twist to make *The Big Clock* one of the sure successes of the current year. What the doctor ordered is in this one — breathless pace after the first few feet, sharp plot convolutions, distinctly etched characterizations of the principles and a sock windup. It's the sort of film which will register from showcase to shooting gallery.
>
> "The device of a man being assigned to hunt himself down — a peculiar switch on the manhunt theme — is a fortuitous choice, used as it is here with cumulative effect. As Milland's technique, developed in less-personal probes, brings in clue after clue pointing to Milland himself, film takes on frenetic suspense. Each situation is adeptly handled to distill the maximum impact with a sock climax adroitly maneuvered. Solution is neatly tied at the windup.
>
> "Milland turns in a workmanlike job, polished to groove to the unrelenting speed of the plot. Laughton, unfortunately, overplays his hand so that his tycoon-sans-heart takes on the quality of parodying the real article. All supporting roles are excellently handled. Elsa Lanchester as a wacky portrait painter is particularly superb. She can tinge a screwball giggle with real humor and draw the most out of unpredictable doings. Henry Morgan is properly lethal as a hired thug and bodyguard. Maureen O'Sullivan performs smartly as Milland's much-jilted spouse. John Farrow's direction is top-flight, pushing the action along at the crisp pace required."

The *New York Times* called it a nearly "perfect" thriller, with the entire cast from top to bottom turning in outstanding portrayals (April 22, 1948):

> "*The Big Clock* ... is a dandy clue-chaser of the modern chromium-plated type, but it is also an entertainment which requires close attention from the start.
>
> "As the self-protection clue-collector, Ray Milland does a beautiful job of being a well-tailored smoothie and a desperate hunted man at the same time. Charles Laughton is characteristically odious as the sadistic publisher and George Macready is sleek as his henchman, while Maureen O'Sullivan is sweet as Ray's nice wife. Exceptional, however, are several people who play small but electric character roles: Elsa Lanchester as a crack-pot painter and Douglas Spencer as a barman, best of all. Miss Lanchester is truly delicious with her mad pace and her wild, eccentric laugh.
>
> "Indeed, some minor pedestal might be provided, too, for *The Big Clock*, a 17-jewel entertainment guaranteed to give a good — if not perfect — time."

It is interesting to note that when the picture was released in spring 1948, it played at the Paramount Theater, which was located in Times Square in New York City. Believe it or not, on the same bill at the same theater (and for the same admission), Duke Ellington and his Orchestra, along with Ella Fitzgerald, billed as "The First Lady of Song," were co-headliners along with *The Big Clock*. They were live and in-person, and for less than the price of a cheap dinner one saw the exciting motion picture and two of the living legends of the music business perform in concert.

Two capsule reviews in a *New York Times* ad offered the opinions of the two most famous of the Hollywood gossip columnists, Louella Parsons and Hedda Hopper.

Louella proclaimed, "My pick of the week is *The Big Clock*, a suspense thriller, exciting and delightful."

Ms. Hopper added, "It's Ray Milland's best performance since *The Lost Weekend*."

When Milland published a memoir in 1974 entitled *Wide-Eyed in Babylon*, he let it all hang out about his true feelings for the pair, both capable of making or breaking an actor or actress with the power of the pen.

"At that time [1948] there were two reigning queens in Hollywood, both female, each with a daily column in the two leading newspapers and a weekly radio show. They were pandered to and fawned upon to an incredible degree, and to all intents and purposes they ran the town.

"One of them was Louella Parsons, top columnist for Hollywood goings-on for the Hearst press and apparently a newspaperwoman from the year zero. By comparison with her rival she was rather kindly and seemingly vague, though with a mind like a bear trap. She never forgot a thing and, by the same token, never forgave anyone who crossed her. But she was never vicious.

"The other one was Hedda Hopper, top Hollywood columnist for the *Los Angeles Times* and an unmitigated bitch. She was venomous, vicious, a pathological liar, and quite stupid. She was a tall and rather handsome woman who at one time had been an actress on the New York stage but who never quite made it to the top row, I suspect because of her infinite capacity for making enemies, never friends. Wise Hollywood hostesses never invited columnists to their parties, because once you did you could never leave them off your list for future parties or they would crucify you."

Maureen and Milland did two radio versions of the motion picture, including the "Lux Radio Theatre" for the CBS radio network on November 22, 1948, and also a "Screen Director's Playhouse" production for NBC on July 8, 1949, which was sponsored by Pabst Brewing. This latter adaptation was introduced by John Farrow, and featured Ray Milland and Maureen in their starring roles, with the hard-edged voice of William Conrad stepping into the shoes of the Laughton character of the homicidal publisher. At the end of the drama, Ray Milland and Maureen joked with the director, Mr. Farrow: "I feel like my role is very similar to a doughnut," she said with a laugh. "I'm in the beginning and ending, but in the middle — nothing!"

Although Maureen had made a successful comeback in *The Big Clock*, she once again became pregnant in the spring of 1947 and would not act in another film for more than two years. By this time her brood included three boys and one girl; a second daughter, Prudence, was born on January 20, 1948, at St. Vincent's Hospital in Los Angeles. Another daughter, Stephanie Margarita, arrived less than sixteen months later on June 3, 1949, and the family had grown to six children.

Maureen was now thirty-eight years old, after celebrating her birthday two weeks before giving birth to her third daughter. With the steady expansion of the family, they needed a larger home as Maureen later recalled:

"After the Bel-Air house, we moved to a bigger one shaped like a horseshoe in Beverly Hills, and the nursery was on one side with its own little kitchen and our rooms and kitchen were on the other side. We only ever ate together on Sundays when John would cook spaghetti and we'd eat by the pool side. I wonder now if that was the right way to do things. Maybe the children should have been with us more.

"In Ireland, children were seen and not heard and although I thought that was going a bit too far, I didn't think children should necessarily always come first. My relationship with my mother hadn't been a particularly good one but it never occurred to me that it would be repeated with my own children because there was a big difference in the way I brought them up. I never criticized or undermined them. I just assumed they'd adore me because I was doing my very best, so why on earth shouldn't they?"

The Irish actress picked up her share of awards over her lifetime, and the previous year she and actor J. Carrol Naish were named 1947 winners of the annual St. Patrick Day awards by the Catholic Film and Radio Review. The awards, statues of St. Patrick and St. Brigid, were awarded to "an actor and actress of Irish heritage who manifest outstanding devotion to Irish ideals."

Maureen was also accorded a great honor in April 1948, when she was chosen "The Mother of the Year" by the Helping Hand organization in a luncheon held at the Beverly Hills Hotel. She of course was a very busy mother, and continued her work in radio during the long stretches when she was away from the movie sets. Meanwhile, husband John was able to direct two or three films per year to keep money coming in to the family coffers (which were strained by five hungry mouths, and counting).

John Farrow's next work as a director was *Beyond Glory* (1948), with Alan Ladd on trial at West Point and Donna Reed standing by her man; *Night Has a Thousand Eyes* (1948) featured Edward G. Robinson as a clairvoyant in an adaptation of the Cornell Woolrich novel; Ray Milland was once again superb in *Alias Nick Beal* (1949), as his character of the devil attempts to corrupt an honest politician, performed capably by Thomas Mitchell.

Farrow also directed *Red, Hot, and Blue* (1949) with Victor Mature and Betty Hutton, in a tale of crime and beautiful showgirls; and *Copper Canyon* (1950) again starring the versatile Ray Milland, this time in a western with Hedy Lamarr. Most directors had their favorite actors to work with, and for Farrow they were Alan Ladd, Ray Milland, William Bendix, and William Holden.

Meanwhile, John Farrow's better half, Maureen, brought in her salary with a steady diet of radio dramas, including the "Lux Radio Theatre" presentation of the classic *How Green Was My Valley* (March 31, 1947) on CBS radio. David Niven was Mr. Gruffydd, while Maureen was the voice of Angharad. Donald Crisp (Mr. Morgan) and Sara Allgood (Mrs. Morgan) played the same roles as in the 1941 film version.

Another popular radio broadcast of the day was the "Cavalcade of America," which was sponsored by Dupont on NBC radio. *The Doctor and the President* (April 21, 1947) starred Maureen as Eliza Waterhouse, a loyal wife whose doctor husband (Douglas Fairbanks, Jr.) advocates vaccination against smallpox despite public dissent, and who enlists the aid of President Jefferson (Bill Johnstone) to promote his beliefs to the American people. "This is Hollywood" on CBS radio presented the stirring drama, *The Adventuress* with the stars Maureen O'Sullivan and Richard Greene on Saturday, May 10, 1947.

During Christmas week, 1947, the Mutual network presented a special Christmas Rosary program, entitled "The Joyful Hour." The program consisted of music, prayers and a dramatization of the story of Christmas, with Ethel Barrymore and Pedro de Cordoba acting as narrators. Other stars that participated included Anne Blyth, MacDonald Carey, Perry Como, Jeanne Crain,

Bing Crosby, Dennis Day, Dick Haymes, Joan Leslie, Christopher Lynch, Roddy McDowell, Ricardo Montalban, the Mullen sisters, Maureen O'Hara, and Maureen O'Sullivan.

Maureen was a frequent guest star on the Mutual network broadcasts of "Family Theater," which was created by Father Patrick Peyton of the Holy Cross Fathers in an effort to promote family unity and prayer. During the ten-year run of the program it was virtually commercial free; during the normal commercial slots, there was a succinct appeal for family prayer in America.

Al Scalpone created the slogans that were used on each broadcast, "A world at prayer is a world at peace" and, most memorably, "The family that prays together stays together." A line from the poet Alfred Tennyson was used to open each broadcast: "More things are wrought by prayer than this world dreams of."

Father Peyton brought in James Stewart to introduce the first broadcast with Loretta Young and Don Ameche starring in the drama. Other outstanding actors also agreed to appear including Irene Dunne, Charles Boyer, and Ethel Barrymore.

Hollywood icons were used for the introductions, such as Edward G. Robinson introducing Pat O'Brien. Over the years, many of the greats of Hollywood appeared, including Gary Cooper, Gregory Peck, Shirley Temple, Jack Benny, Robert Mitchum, and Loretta Young, who starred in thirty of the 482 weekly dramas broadcast between February 13, 1947 and July 4, 1956. The show was free of religious dogma, and was one of the most popular weekly dramatic anthologies in radio history.

Maureen O'Sullivan appeared in at least twelve of the broadcasts, including *Once on a Golden Afternoon* with co-stars Natalie Wood and Tom Conway (June 10, 1948); *The Fountain of Youth* with John Dehner, Lurene Tuttle, and introduced by Don DeFore (August 10, 1949); *By Sun and Candlelight* with Gene Raymond and James Gleason (November 16, 1949); *20,000 Leagues Under the Sea* with Otto Kruger (August 23, 1950); *The Kid from Scratch Gravel* with Ted de Corscia (October 3, 1951); *The Heart Also Sees* with Jeanne Crain, Dale Robertson and Margaret Sheridan (October 15, 1952); *A Fine Wedding for Angelita* with J. Carroll Naish and Ricky Barra (October 28, 1953); *The Way of the Cross* with Jeff Chandler — Easter Program (April 14, 1954); *Every Good Boy Does Fine* with Maureen O'Sullivan and introduced by Jerry Lewis (May 18, 1955); *The Juggler of Our Lady* with Jack Haley and Paul Frees — Christmas Program (December 21, 1955); *Once Upon a Golden Afternoon* with Jeanne Bates (January 30, 1957); *Sylvia* with Jeanne Bates and hosted by Raymond Burr (August 28, 1957).

Maureen was a guest star on the "Catholic Charities Show" at least twice, including *A Question of Pianos* (April 18, 1948), also starring Bing Crosby, Bob Hope, Jimmy Durante, Ann Blyth, Gary and Lindsay Crosby; and a second appearance *Just in Case* (March 27, 1949) with guests Bing Crosby, Bob Hope, and Jimmy Durante. You will notice that on many of these radio broadcasts Maureen worked with Hope and Crosby, two of the greatest comedians of all-time. Sinatra had his "Rat Pack," while Maureen had Bob, Bing, and Durante, which wasn't too bad and made for some wonderful lifetime friendships.

The actress was also a guest several times on the "NBC University Theatre," a one-hour anthology with outstanding dramas such as *The Heart of Midlothian* (February 27, 1949), which was based on a novel by Sir Walter Scott. Maureen portrayed Jeannie Deans, a Scottish woman who is torn between her sisterly love and moral principle but sacrifices neither in the quest to save her younger sister from the gallows for killing her illegitimate child.

Also on "University Theatre" was the play *The Death of the Heart* (August 6, 1949) from Elizabeth Bowen's novel. Maureen O'Sullivan portrayed Porsche, an innocent young woman who "lives by her heart until her heart is broken by the experience of love." Co-starring were Dan O'Herlihy and Dennis Hoey.

A third appearance on "University Theatre" was *Precious Bane* (September 3, 1949), adapted from the novel by Mary Webb. Maureen O'Sullivan was cast as Prudence Sarne, a kindhearted country girl with a speech impediment who watches with regret as her brother Gideon's increasing greed destroys the lives of those they love. Co-starring were Dan O'Herlihy, Ralph Moody, and Rita Lynn.

Maureen also made a starring appearance with Ronald Colman in the CBS radio production of *Quality Street* on the "Hour of Stars" program, broadcast on November 6, 1949. Maureen was Phoebe Throssel and Colman was Dr. Valentine Brown, in a delightful comedy of errors based on a play by J. M. Barrie that originally opened in New York on November 11, 1901. (The 1937 motion picture had starred Katherine Hepburn and Franchot Tone.)

It is easy to see that although Maureen made only two motion pictures between 1943 and 1951, she still was plying her craft of acting. She appeared in at least forty radio dramas over this period of time, in addition to her heavy schedule as wife and mother.

Where Danger Lives (1950) was a family affair for Maureen and John Farrow, as she was billed fourth as Robert Mitchum's girlfriend, nurse Julie Dorn, and he was hired to direct. The other big name in the cast was Claude Rains, whose character gets murdered in record time.

This story of lust and murder was an RKO production, a studio that Howard Hughes had purchased in 1948. The big-name actor at RKO was rough-and-tumble Bob Mitchum, who starred in numerous *films noir* until the era of this genre ended around 1957. His female co-stars had included Ava Gardner, Jane Greer, and Jane Russell, but in this drama the femme fatale was Faith Domergue, a 25-year-old actress who had a sultry edginess about her.

She was the latest protégée of Hughes, a renowned womanizer, and had been involved with him — at some level — since she was fifteen years old (apparently with her parents' permission).

Farrow and Mitchum were both from the old Hollywood school of hard drinkers, and there were many more in the non-exclusive club to include John Wayne, Ray Milland, William Holden, John Barrymore, Errol Flynn, and Mark Hellinger. According to Mitchum biographer George Eels, the two men first considered working together over a drink:

"Mitchum and director John Farrow met quite by accident and embarked on a marathon drinking match. At one point Farrow said he would like to do a picture with Mitchum, and the actor responded that he would enjoy working with the director. During the next four hours they dreamed up a story, decided on Susan Hayward as the ideal leading woman, and assembled an entire package in their heads. Congratulating themselves on their accomplishment, they staggered to their cars. Next morning, a hung-over Farrow called to inquire whether Mitchum was serious about proceeding with their plans. Mitchum hedged. Eventually, each man revealed that he remembered nothing about the story they had spent the evening fantasizing. Nevertheless, Mitchum eventually spoke to the Phantom [Howard Hughes] and RKO took on *Where Danger Lives*, produced and directed by Farrow, with Mitchum, and Hughes's latest protege, Faith Domergue, in the leads."

According to Lee Server, in his Mitchum biography *Baby, I Don't Care*, Farrow wasn't exactly a saint and had a variety of vices:

"Johnny Farrow was the only director Bob had ever met who could outdrink him. The good-looking, blond, former Australian seaman ... was known as a mean, ruthless son of a bitch by everyone who knew him, except for the coteries of Roman Catholic priests with whom he spent much time in pious and arcane discussions of Church doctrine and ecumenical history. Mitchum, like everyone else, had a difficult time equating the roistering philanderer he knew with the man who wrote devotional biographies of the saints and of Father Damien, 'the leper priest.'"

Although Farrow was a tough, no-nonsense director, Mitchum was even tougher and didn't take any guff from anyone, directors included. One particular scene in *Where Danger Lives*, Mitchum must tumble down a shabby hotel staircase in a barely conscious state, suffering from a head wound and delirium. After Mitchum performed the dangerous stunt himself, Farrow shouted out, "Cut! Okay, let's do it again!" Bob shot him his dirtiest look and replied in a strong two-word epithet, and walked off the set (probably to have a drink).

Mitchum's longtime personal secretary, Reva Frederick, noted that John Farrow's reputation as a philanderer was justified and well-earned:

"He was a professional Catholic, Farrow," said Ms. Frederick. "Always surrounded by nuns and priests. But his private life was entirely different. He cast the extras — the women — almost entirely with women he wanted for his own amusement, girls he would make at his command." (From the Mitchum biography, *Baby, I Don't Care*, by Lee Server.)

Where Danger Lives begins at a San Francisco hospital, where Dr. Jeff Cameron (Mitchum) works mostly with children infected by polio. He is assisted by his nurse Julie (Maureen), who is also his fiancée. After a long shift, well past the midnight hour, he is called to attend to a beautiful woman who has attempted suicide. When she wakes up, he is holding a white rose that is intended for Julie, but the unidentified woman assumes it is for her. The woman checks herself out of the hospital using a phony name, but leaves Dr. Cameron a note asking him to come the next evening to her sea-cliff home — she signs it "Margo."

Jeff is attracted to the woman and is intrigued by her mystery — he breaks a date with Julie and goes to see Margo to satisfy his curiosity. Before long they are having a torrid affair, but she tells him she is going away with her wealthy father, Frederick Lannington. Jeff gets drunk and goes to see Lannington (Claude Rains) — he is shocked to discover that her "father" is in actuality her husband.

Lannington is aware that Margo is having an affair, and when an argument between the three turns heated, Jeff is struck on the head with a fireplace iron. Jeff pushes Lannington, and the older man falls and strikes his head, knocking him unconscious. Jeff is staggered by the blow, and dunks his head under the bathroom faucet to revive himself. When he returns, Lannington is dead, and Jeff realizes that he could be charged with murder. (Jeff is unaware that Margo actually murdered her husband by suffocating him with a pillow while he was out of the room.)

Jeff is no longer thinking clearly, and reluctantly agrees with Margo's plan to travel to Mexico to start a new life together. He is suffering the early symptoms of a concussion, and is aware that he could die without rest. Before long, the police discover the murder and are trailing them across Arizona where they plan to cross the border at Nogales. Along the way, they trade cars and also sell her jewelry for cash to bribe their way past the border guards.

While waiting at a sleazy hotel for the van that will transport them over the border, Margo reveals that she has stolen huge sums from her late husband and stashed them in a bank in Mexico City. She also admits that she had smothered her husband, and that Jeff had nothing to do with his death. By now Jeff realizes that Margo is mentally ill, and tells her to go without him because his right leg is going numb from the concussion. When he passes out from delirium, she tries to smother him with a pillow, leaving him for dead.

When Jeff revives he stumbles down the hotel staircase to the street, where he sees Margo in the back of the van. As he staggers toward her, she begins shouting psychotically and shoots him with her pistol. The police are nearby, and shoot Margo. In her dying words, perhaps for the love of Jeff, she admits she killed her husband without his help.

Later, Jeff is recovering at a hospital, when he asks his doctor if he could arrange to have some flowers sent to his old girlfriend. The doctor meets a woman out in the hallway, Julie, and hands her the order for one white rose — she now realizes Jeff is still in love with her. Asking if he is allowed visitors, the doctor tells her, "Just one — you." Julie smiles warmly and enters the room to rekindle the flame.

As dark as this story is, filled with murder, avarice, rage, greed, deception, with bad breaks going against the Mitchum character at every turn — it ends on this upbeat note of the reunion of former lovers. Maureen was as beautiful as ever in this scene, and her genuine warmth makes you realize that Jeff was truly fortunate to survive his ordeal with the *femme fatale* (the seductive Faith Domergue), and be reunited with his true love, Julie the faithful nurse.

Maureen was teamed up with most of the big stars of the 1930s and 1940s eventually, either on screen or radio dramas, and now she could add Mitchum to her memory book. He was one of the giants of the screen and a truly fine gentleman, despite his own reputation of being a womanizer, hard-drinker, and even a street brawler.

Maureen's screen time was quite short in this picture, a few minutes at the beginning and then the closing scene. Also getting the short shift was Claude Rains, who was a major star in his own right but had only the one scene. He is the murder victim after the contentious argument with the drunken Mitchum and his cheating wife, who was plotting his demise and just waiting for the perfect dupe to come along.

This was the second and final time Maureen would act in a picture directed by her husband John Farrow. Considering her limited screen time, she probably told her spouse: "Honey, thanks but I'll find my own film roles from now on." Seriously, what this film could have used was more O'Sullivan and Claude Rains and less faith — Domergue, that is. But with Howard Hughes pulling the strings like a puppeteer, that wasn't the end result.

Maureen recalled that she and John were on the short list of people on this planet who actually socialized with the eccentric Mr. Hughes, a.k.a. "The Phantom," before the days when he became a total recluse:

"Yes, I have actually *seen* Howard Hughes," said Maureen with an emphasis on the word 'seen.' "He was never on the lot when we were making *Where Danger Lives* at RKO, but he used to have dinner with us occasionally. He was a great friend of John's. I didn't find him odd — that was before he was odd,

I suppose. He was a rather good-looking, shy man, not all that exciting apparently. What I mean is that he was not witty nor did he say anything that I can remember. He was very conservatively dressed and quite nice. People always said how hard it was to get Howard on the phone, but John always got through."

This film was unusual because only two stars really mattered — Mitchum because he was the box-office draw and Domergue, because this was her official film debut — Mr. Hughes was intent on making her a star. Miss Domergue was described in a *Hollywood Reporter* review as a "beauty with a good figure, a fascinating voice and decided flare for sultry roles."

Faith Domergue was a competent actress, as sultry types go, but never came even close to the motion picture stardom that Hughes had planned for her. *Where Danger Lives* was one of her better films, due at least in part to the power of her co-star, Robert Mitchum.

The reviews were relatively weak, despite Mitchum's strong performance. Maureen O'Sullivan, in a minuscule role, had no opportunity to make a significant contribution to the final product:

> *Variety* (June 1950): "*Where Danger Lives* is just a fair mystery melodrama. Good exploitation angles and Robert Mitchum's name will help its grossing chances in some situations, but the overall outlook is spotty. Story is a highly contrived, never credible chase melodrama that puts the principals in seemingly impossible situations. Other than Mitchum and Miss Domergue, footage gives little length to the supporting players and Rains has only one sequence at the start of the action. Miss O'Sullivan's role is colorless and short. John Farrow's direction fails to hold the footage together. He does, however, punch some suspense into several of the scenes."

On March 1, 1950, Maureen made an appearance on "This Is Your Life," which was hosted by Ralph Edwards and sponsored by Phillip Morris cigarettes. This was a "live" broadcast; each week from 1947 through 1961, first on radio and then later on television, Edwards interviewed famous people and talked about their lives, hopes, and dreams. Other guests included Ila Olrich Hope, Belle Kennedy, Ken Murray, Velma Wayne Dawson, and (from an earlier broadcast) W. C. Fields.

Where Danger Lives was released in July of 1950, and by the end of October Maureen was pregnant once again. Mr. and Mrs. John Farrow already had six children, and when Theresa came into the world on July 22, 1951, the household was finally complete. The fourth daughter in the family was born at Maureen's favorite hospital, St. Vincent's, and would later be known as "Tisa."

By this time, the seven Farrow children made for one of the largest families in Hollywood. By 1965, however, Maureen had to share the record with fellow actress Jeanne Crain, who had her seventh child with husband Paul Brinkman that year. Maureen and Jeanne were friends, and had acted together in at least one radio drama.

CHAPTER TWENTY
"The 1950's ... Baby Boom Generation"

Back in 1949, understanding the power of owning your own independent production company, and realizing the dearth of genuine family films, Maureen decided to strike out in that direction. Observing the success of actors who were now producing their own films, she was making serious plans to do the same, as noted in *The New York Times* on October 26, 1949:

"Maureen O'Sullivan is organizing her own independent motion-picture company, which, she said today, would be incorporated as a California concern in the next few weeks.

"Miss O'Sullivan, who is the wife of John Farrow, director, expects to specialize in the making of features with what she called "family themes" and which deal with the problems of the average home and the raising of children. Two stories, she said, are now under consideration for filming."

For whatever reasons, most likely financial, these grandiose plans fell through. The big name actors, like Burt Lancaster and John Wayne, were able to raise the money when they produced their own pictures. They had huge drawing power at the box office, and financial backers were willing to take the risks.

Vast wealth was something that Maureen and John Farrow did not have, but they were certainly not poor. They lived in a beautiful home on Beverly Drive, and owned a beach house at Malibu. The couple also had seven children by 1952, which created myriad financial challenges. And they both had to keep working to pay the proverbial "piper."

They jointly did some magazine and newspaper print ads for "Rheingold Beer" in 1952 showing them playing chess together, and Maureen did some additional ads for Rheingold by herself. She proclaimed: "But I don't have to tell you that Rheingold has no peer among beers. If you're a true New Yorker, you know it's the largest-selling beer in town — you've made it so. Millions of people agree — it's always beer as beer *should* taste!"

Maureen appeared in ads for Jergens lotion holding her new baby in 1950, and she also did magazine ads in the 1950s for Camel cigarettes, with a caption that supposedly quoted her words: "Camels taste so good and rich — and I'm glad they're so truly mild!"

Maureen also did print ads for Pan American airlines in 1954 which featured a photograph of her and all seven of her youngsters. Maureen and her kids were all climbing a loading stair to board a Pan Am airliner, and the caption announced: "Pan American sure knows how to run an airline! I'm flying to Ireland this year and I'm taking my seven children because it's so quick and easy to take them by clipper."

Beginning in 1952, after her seventh child was born, Maureen worked quite steadily in films and television for the next seven years. Her first top-billed role in a decade came in just the type of "family" film that she wanted to make; it was called *Bonzo Goes to College*, with a supporting cast that included Edmund Gwenn, Charles Drake, Gigi Perreau, and Gene Lockhart.

The previous year, a very successful film had been made called *Bedtime for Bonzo* (1951), which starred Diana Lynn and Ronald Reagan, who would later become President of the United States. In the earlier film, Reagan portrayed a professor who uses Bonzo for an experiment to prove that it is possible to teach even a monkey the difference between right and wrong.

The sequel, *Bonzo Goes to College*, begins at a carnival where Bonzo earns money by correctly answering questions posed by customers. A couple of hucksters, Lefty and Wilbur, pose a trick question which Bonzo fails to answer, and the chimp's trainer chastises him for losing their money. Bonzo's feelings are hurt, and he sneaks a ride on a truck and arrives at Pawlton College, where football coach "Pop" Drew (Gwenn) is desperately searching for a quarterback for his team.

Pop lives with his daughter Marion (Maureen) and her husband Malcolm (Drake), along with their daughter Betsy (Perreau), who is feeling dejected because she doesn't have any friends. Pop hopes to cheer up his granddaughter, and hides a new bike in her bedroom. Meanwhile, Bonzo has climbed the trellis to her room and she finds the chimp, thinking this is her surprise gift from Gramps.

Before long, Marion and Malcolm discover the mix-up, but after the pleadings of Betsy, they agree to let her keep Bonzo as a pet. Eventually, Betsy brings Bonzo to see one of Pop's football practices, and the chimp stuns everyone by his ability to throw a football like a champion quarterback. After passing his college entrance exams with straight "A's," Bonzo is appointed as the team's quarterback just in time for the big championship game.

The two crooks Lefty and Wilbur have heard about the game, and kidnap Bonzo so they can win big money by betting against Pawlton College. They replace Bonzo with an incompetent chimp named Pam, who indeed is losing the game while Bonzo mopes in a motel room. Bonzo slips out at halftime and makes it to the stadium in time to enter the game and catch the winning touchdown.

The happy days of the 1930s ...

Right: Maureen and John Farrow pose for the camera while strolling down the avenue ... actually it appears to be a railroad track.

Above: This was Maureen's favorite photo of her and husband John

Maureen and John Farrow returning from a trip to Ireland, around 1936

Wedding day photo of Maureen ... she married John Farrow on September 12, 1936

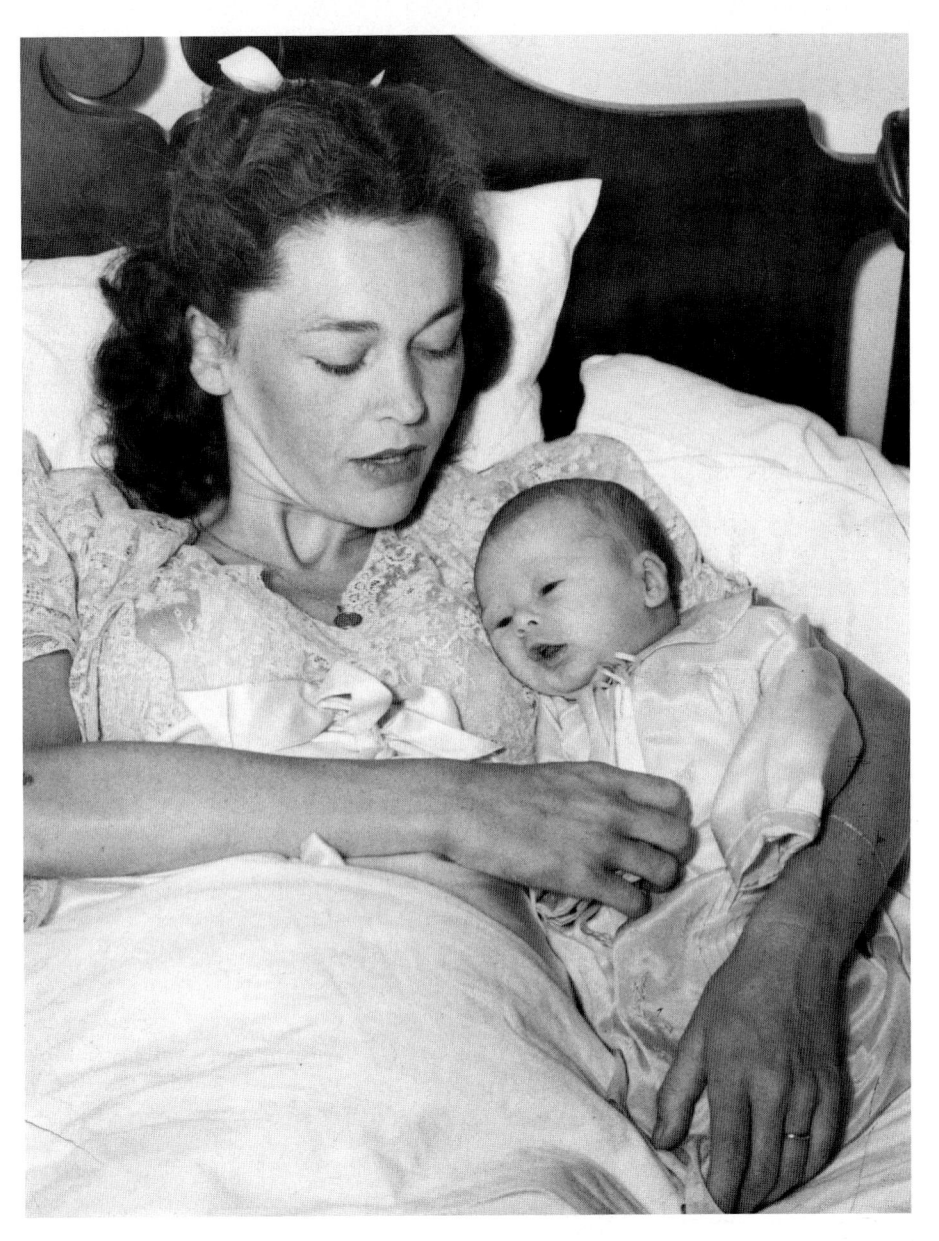

Michael Damien Farrow was born on May 30, 1939 ... he was the first of seven children

Above: Maureen's family home in Ireland at Saintsbury, Killiney during a 1938 visit
Below: Maureen with her husband, Commander Farrow … after his enlistment in 1940

Maureen and two-year-old Michael sharing coffee and doughnuts in an airport, 1941

Above: 1949 family photo ... John, Maureen, and five children

Below: 1951 family photo ... Maureen and John with all seven children

Betsy races to congratulate Bonzo, as Marion, Pop, and everyone gathers around the now-famous chimp. When a talent scout arrives with a contract to play pro football, Bonzo instead chooses to remain with Betsy and the Drews, because he is now part of the "family."

Bonzo Goes to College was the type of family film that Walt Disney produced, and although this was a Universal-International production, the results were the same. It was great family fun, and was literally a barrel of laughs.

This was certainly not a demanding role for Maureen, as *Variety* would note, but she was quite excellent as the understanding mother who makes room for a chimpanzee named Bonzo in her home. The actress had worked with chimpanzees in the Tarzan films, and they always gave her trouble. No mention here how she got along with Bonzo II, who starred in this film, but we could assume that there were no serious incidents.

Maureen starred in this family film with Edmund Gwenn and Bonzo the chimp

Edmund Gwenn portrayed Maureen's father, "Pop" Drew — two old friends from the good old days at MGM in the 1930s. They had worked together in three films, including *Pride and Prejudice* (1940), when he had also portrayed her father. Gwenn almost always played lovable old curmudgeons, and had won an Academy Award for his memorable role in *Miracle on 34th Street* (1947).

Gigi Perreau did a fine job as the young lady who makes friends with Bonzo, and encourages his many talents such as throwing a football. Maureen was the mom of the family, and the two actresses would have a similar mother-daughter relationship in the 1958 film, *Wild Heritage*. Charles Drake portrayed Maureen's husband, the easygoing college professor. His long career in Hollywood included roles as fathers and brothers, occasional villains, and almost always as a second lead or character actor.

Variety's review of September 1952 lauded the comedy as a humorous family film that was expected to do well at the box-office:

> "Universal has another bright prospect for the family trade in *Bonzo Goes to College* — sequel to last year's *Bedtime for Bonzo*, and should be successful in all situations. Broad comedy is run off slickly to cover the plot holes and sustain the general merriment of the theme. Script doesn't make too many demands of the human cast but Gigi Perreau and Edmund Gwenn easily take top honors as the youngster and her grandfather, making each a warm, credible character. Maureen O'Sullivan and Charles Drake are okay as the parents, with Gene Lockhart doing another good job as the kid's other grandfather."

Television was the new medium, and would gradually replace radio as an outlet for dramatic and comedic programming. By 1950, it was certainly grabbing its share of fans, who could now see what they had only been hearing for decades. Perhaps Maureen's earliest television work was as the hostess of "The Children's Hour" (1951), an independently produced one-hour program aimed at youngsters. Her first dramatic credit came on the weekly anthology, "Hollywood Opening Night," in *The Lucky Coin*, directed by Richard Irving. This melodrama was broadcast on December 1, 1952, and Maureen co-starred with Wendell Corey. Maureen would continue to intersperse television roles with her film work throughout the 1950s.

Maureen was still an occasional guest on radio, and on August 26, 1952 she appeared on "Mr. Jones Rediscovers America" on the CBS radio network. Other guests included actor George Murphy and baseball legend Joe DiMaggio, who retired from the Yankees after the 1951 season. DiMaggio was no stranger to the world of Hollywood, and later married Marilyn Monroe in 1954.

Maureen's next motion picture was *All I Desire* (1953), a starring melodrama for Barbara Stanwyck with Richard Carlson and Ms. O'Sullivan in supporting roles. Carlson was the ex-husband who is haunted by the memory of his former wife, and Maureen portrayed the local drama teacher Sara Harper who carries a torch for the high school principal, Henry Murdoch.

The balance of the cast included a number of young actors and actresses who would be recognizable today because they were television stars of the era. Billy Gray played young Ted, and he had the role of "Bud" in "Father Knows Best"; Guy Williams would go on to star in the Disney adventure series, "Zorro";

Richard Long would later play one of Stanwyck's sons on "The Big Valley"; Stuart Whitman would have a long career as a movie star; Lyle Bettger had countless roles as villain types for several decades; Marcia Henderson and Lori Nelson as the two daughters were familiar young actresses of the 1950s.

The story begins in the year 1910, when vaudeville actress Naomi Murdoch (Stanwyck) receives a letter from her daughter Lily, asking her to attend her senior play in which she is starring. Naomi departed ten years before, leaving her husband Henry (Carlson) and three children, Joyce, Lily, and Ted to fend on their own. She decides to return to the small Wisconsin town to see the play, but puts on a false front that she is a successful Shakespearean actress.

When Naomi returns Lily is delighted to see her, but daughter Joyce is angry that she has invaded their peaceful family life. Ted had never known his mother and is open-minded, but Henry is shocked that his estranged wife has returned after all these years. This is all fodder for small-town gossip, of which there is plenty in Riverside. Also anxious to see Naomi again is Dutch Heinemann (Bettger), who was having an affair with Naomi before she left town.

The local drama teacher, Sara Harper (Maureen) is in love with Henry, but she knows that he has never gotten over the heartbreak of his former wife's desertion. When Naomi returns, Sara can see that her love for Henry will continue to be unrequited, because he is still in love with the woman that he married. Sara even encourages Naomi to stay and return to her husband, because she loves Henry and feels this would be the best situation for him and the children.

Naomi begins to realize that she still loves Henry, and misses her children greatly. She meets Dutch on the backwoods riding trail, and he wants to rekindle their affair. When she rebuffs his pass, his rifle falls and accidentally shoots him. Ted is nearby and together with his mother they get Dutch to the doctor. The wound is serious, but he will survive.

From his hospital bed Dutch tells Naomi he wants no part of her anymore, that she deserves to be with her weak husband, Henry. But Henry is not weak, he has become strong and tells Naomi he loves her and wants her back. They decide to reunite, and the Murdoch family is together again.

Stanwyck looked good at age forty-six, but it was never her looks that made her a star; it was that husky voice along with her timing and the ability to turn on emotion from deep inside. Barbara was one of the great actresses, but like Maureen she never won an Academy Award even though she was certainly deserving.

Barbara later said of her goals as an actress: "Put me in the last fifteen minutes of a picture and I don't care what happened before. I don't even care if I was IN the rest of the damned thing — I'll take it in those fifteen minutes."

About her role in *All I Desire*, Barbara Stanwyck said, "I'm playing the type of part I've played many times — a bad woman trying to make up for past mistakes. But I like gutsy roles. Namby-pambies have no interest for me. I'd rather not act at all than do a Pollyanna. I've got to play human beings. I think I understand the motives of the bad women I play."

Maureen said that she noticed that Stanwyck was somewhat icy with her, and she couldn't understand why. Perhaps it had something to do with the fact that her husband John had directed the western adventure *California* (1946) with Stanwyck and Ray Milland. Farrow had a way of rubbing people the wrong way, especially actors under his command, and maybe he had pushed the wrong buttons on Ms. Stanwyck. Pure conjecture of course, but here is what Maureen said of working with Barbara:

"I did not have a very big part in *All I Desire*," said Maureen. "It was just something I did to keep my hand in. I don't recall finding the director, Douglas Sirk, very sympathetic, nor did I find *her* sympathetic. Barbara Stanwyck, I mean. She was always so popular and everybody adored her, but I found her a cold person, and she was the only actress in my working experience who ever went home leaving me to do the close-ups with the script-girl, which I thought was most unprofessional. I was quite surprised. There, that's the only unkind thing that's ever been said about Barbara Stanwyck!"

The actress had one extended sequence with Stanwyck which is a very warm scene, and it is Maureen's best moment to shine in this picture. In a private meeting, Sara asks Naomi to give a dramatic reading at that evening's graduation ceremony, on a night when her daughter Lily will graduate from high school. Sara admits that she is in love with Henry Murdoch but that she wants what's best for him, and that she is willing to give him up. It is a noble gesture by Sara, who realizes that she lost Henry the moment Naomi came back to town. Maureen was very convincing in this scene, and as *Variety* would note, she made the most of her character and her limited screen time.

It wasn't a great role for Maureen, but then again this wasn't a great film by any means. It was enjoyable, mainly because of the women stars Barbara, Maureen, and the two young actresses, Marcia Henderson and Lori Nelson. Maureen looked attractive yet conservative in her role as a school teacher; Stanwyck on the other hand was dolled up to look glamorous because she portrayed a flashy vaudeville actress. Richard Carlson and Lyle Bettger were just passable, but young Billy Gray as Ted was excellent as a boy who grew up without his mother, and now he must deal with feelings he has never known.

Variety said of the picture in its review of June 1953:

> "The Ross Hunter production and Douglas Sirk's direction pull all stops to make the picture a 79-minute excursion into sentimentality. With help of Miss Stanwyck's performance, the soap-operish tear-jerking is palatable. Carlson plays the stiff-necked husband character straight to make it acceptable. Lyle

Bettger is sadly misused as the former lover. Neither writing nor direction establish the character properly to make it an understandable heavy. Maureen O'Sullivan does what she can with the role of a school teacher hopelessly in love with Carlson."

Mission Over Korea was one of the more authentic war films from the 1950s, and was produced in February of 1953, a few months before the Korean War actually ended in July of that year. Part of the reason the film was so realistic was that producer Robert Cohn used a considerable portion of the 85,000 feet of location footage that was shot by a camera crew near the Korean front lines. The action is almost non-stop, as it details the lives of two reconnaissance pilots who are constantly in and around heavy action on both the ground and in the air.

The two pilots were played by John Hodiak, the older veteran, and John Derek, the young flyer with a wild streak that often got him into trouble. Maureen O'Sullivan portrayed Nancy Slocum, the spouse of Captain George Slocum — she lives at the military base in Japan with their two children. The fourth major star in the picture was Audrey Totter, a no-nonsense nurse who works at the South Korean base where the men are stationed.

The story begins in June 1950, at an American Army base in Kimpo, South Korea. Cpt. George Slocum (Hodiak) receives orders that he can return to Japan briefly to see his wife Nancy (Maureen) and his two kids. Slocum is the pilot of an L-5 single-engine surveyor plane, and when he arrives in Japan he is "buzzed" by another L-5 pilot who has mistaken him for his brother.

The young pilot is Lt. Pete Barker (Derek) who has been assigned to Kimpo Army base, and will be joining Cpt. Slocum when he returns. Barker has a brother, Jerry, who is also a pilot and works with Slocum back at Kimpo. Pete meets Army nurse Kate (Totter), and they discover they have a mutual attraction but she puts the brakes on the fast flyer.

George surprises his wife Nancy at home, and she is swept into his arms as they embrace. As the wife of a career Army pilot, she is constantly worried about her husband. George and Nancy have two children, a boy and a girl, and they are very much in love. They have just a few short days to rekindle their romance — it is cut short when George receives orders to return to his base in South Korea. Nancy and the children are there at the plane to see her husband off, and she is introduced to Pete Barker, who is also leaving. The planes take to the air, and Nancy waves good-bye to her husband. She worries that she will never see him again.

As the two pilots approach the airstrip, they are shocked at the vision — Kimbo has been bombed and now is in ruins. George and Pete land their planes and discover that Jerry Barker is seriously wounded. When they are attacked by local Korean sympathizers, Jerry is killed. They are able to escape, and when they leave they take with them Clancy, a Korean boy who is the camp mascot.

In his grief over his brother's death, Pete wants to fight the whole enemy army. He even has the mechanic Swenson mount a bazooka on his plane so that he can attack rather than just observe. On the next mission, Pete tries to blow up an enemy tank but instead is shot down himself. He survives, and manages to avoid being captured.

Back at the base, Cpt. Slocum is ordered to airlift much-needed medical supplies to a nearby battalion that is under attack, and he takes a nervous Swenson with him. After completing the mission, George returns to discover Pete walking into camp with an escort of Korean soldiers. Despite the fact that Pete does dangerous things, George admires his courage and they become friends over the course of completing several missions together.

One night their base is attacked by enemy soldiers, and George suffers a serious chest wound. Pete loads George into his plane to get him to an Army hospital, and when he arrives Kate is there to administer a transfusion and get Slocum into surgery. Later than night Kate tells Pete that George didn't make it. Back in Japan, his wife Nancy is informed that her husband has died bravely in combat.

Pete is ordered to fly a mission to photograph key bridges, and he takes Sgt. Maxie Steiner with him. They are successful and they also spot an enemy tank brigade through the battle smoke. With the aid of a powerful new radio, they pass the location to a fighter squadron that destroys the tanks. Meanwhile, Pete has been shot in the arm and is bleeding profusely, unable to hold the controls. Steiner has literally no pilot training, but manages to fly the plane back to base. They crash land but survive, and they live to fight another day.

The women in *Mission Over Korea*, Maureen and Audrey Totter, played important roles as the loving wife and the dedicated nurse, respectively. This was a serious war picture, and the gals were limited in screen time as the battle dramas took top priority. Maureen was now forty-one years old, still beautiful, but she was approaching middle age. There was added character in her face, and the days of being cast for her beauty alone were over. Most of her future roles would be as wife and mother.

Maureen and John Hodiak as her husband have a few warm scenes together after they are reunited. They are obviously very much in love, and they are victims themselves of war. When Cpt. Slocum is killed, the wife is left without her husband, and the children have lost their father.

This picture contained exciting battle scenes, but it also showed the compassion of war and the collateral damage when soldiers are killed and families suddenly lose their loved ones.

John Hodiak was a respected leading man in a variety of roles in the 1940s and 1950s. He was especially excellent in his role as a world-weary pilot who would rather be with his wife and children, but realizes his duty as a soldier comes first. Hodiak was thirty-nine years old when this picture was filmed, and he would die of a sudden heart attack just two years later in 1955. Hodiak was married to Anne Baxter, who starred in the John Farrow film, *Blaze of Noon* (1947).

John Derek also was credible as the headstrong young flyer who takes up his own vendetta against the enemy when his brother is killed. Derek had numerous starring roles in the 1950s, but he is better known for the three beautiful actresses that he later married: Ursula Andress, Linda Evans, and Bo Derek.

There was also a strong supporting cast in this war picture, with at least three familiar faces even if you might not know their names: Harvey Lembeck and Richard Erdman as the two ground mechanics, Maxie and Swenson, who are pals of George Slocum; and Rex Reason, the handsome second lead who portrayed the commanding officer, Major Hacker. There is one very warm scene where an African-American soldier (Richard Bowers) sings the song "Forgive Me" as his fellow soldiers listen and dream of loved ones back home.

Maureen began doing numerous dramatic television shows in 1953, because really good movie roles were becoming tougher to find. The younger actresses were getting all the best roles — women in their thirties like Ava Gardner, Grace Kelly, Jean Simmons, Susan Hayward, Virginia Mayo, and Rhonda Fleming. And thus television was a welcome medium for older actresses and actors to ply their trade.

Ms. O'Sullivan was a desirable actress for these types of roles, and she did at least five dramatic performances in 1953 alone. One of the popular anthologies of the day was a program sponsored by the Ford Motor Company, which lasted for five seasons. Maureen made two appearances this calendar year on "Ford Theater," including: *They Also Serve*, with John Hodiak; and *The Trestle*, with Phillip Carey and Tim Considine.

The "Schlitz Playhouse of Stars" was broadcast every Friday night for eight seasons with plays and stories from Somerset Maugham, Ernest Hemingway, Noel Coward, and Ellery Queen. Guest stars included David Niven, Helen Hayes, James Dean, Raymond Burr, Gene Kelly, Agnes Moorehead, Rosalind Russell, Anthony Quinn, Vincent Price, and Maureen O'Sullivan, who starred with Jerome Cowan and Skip Homeier in the drama, *Parents' Weekend*.

Maureen had made many appearances on the "Lux Radio Theater" in its heyday, and she also became a guest star on "The Lux Video Theater," a dramatic anthology which aired from 1950-1957 and was broadcast live from

New York in its early years. Maureen co-starred with Ronald Reagan in the drama, *Message in a Bottle*, which was written by Gerald Holland and directed by Richard Goode. The guest cast also included George Macready and George Pembroke.

Another of the outstanding television dramas of the day was "Four Star Playhouse," which was on the air for four seasons beginning in 1953. The CBS production had four big-name stars that rotated from week-to-week: Dick Powell, David Niven, Charles Boyer and Ida Lupino. And the guest casts each week included many fine actors and actresses who were well-known from the motion pictures.

Maureen was the guest star in *The Gift*, which aired on Christmas Eve, 1953, and her co-star was Charles Boyer. Not only was there an outstanding cast that included Dan Tobin, Ann Doran, and Virginia Christine, but the episode was directed by one of the great directors, Robert Aldrich, who was in the early stages of his career.

The actress was good friends with Boyer, and his wife Pat Paterson was her best friend. Maureen and Charles had acted together in radio dramas in the past. Now they portrayed a middle-aged couple, husband and wife, who are in love with each other but dealing with a difficult family issue.

This story takes place at Christmas, the time of year when businessman Carl Baxter (Boyer) becomes moody and antagonistic because his estranged son Michael chose to be a geologist and is virtually out of his life. His kindly wife Minna (Maureen) hopes that he will forget the rift between them, because she misses the warm Christmas days of the past.

When George discovers that his wife secretly goes out each Christmas and purchases toys and gifts for poor children, he realizes what a mean "Scrooge" he has been. He buys a tree with ornaments, and several gifts for his wife. And when he tells her that he has forgiven his son, it is a happy Christmas indeed for the Baxters.

Additional radio programs that Maureen did around this time included "The Bob Hope Show" the week of February 2-6, 1953. This NBC radio production was presented by General Foods, and Miss O'Sullivan was Bob Hope's daytime guest for the week. Maureen and Bob had done many radio shows together in the past, especially during the war years when the broadcasts went to the troops overseas.

Maureen was a guest on the premiere of a new NBC radio broadcast called "Ask Hollywood," which aired on October 4, 1953. Dave Garroway was a popular talk-show host and had a two-hour NBC radio program in the 1950s called "Sunday With Garroway." His guests on May 9, 1954 included Maureen O'Sullivan, poet Ogden Nash, Dr. Lillian Gillbreth, actor MacDonald Carey, and Rabbi David De Sola Pool.

Maureen did not act in any films in 1954, mainly because daughter Mia contracted polio, a dreaded childhood disease that crippled thousands of children every year. Polio had been around for the better part of a century, with no cause or cure in sight. In the summer of 1952 alone nearly 58,000 Americans, mostly children, contracted the disease in a massive outbreak.

Mia began feeling the effects of the disease around her ninth birthday in February of 1954. Shortly thereafter, the child was taken by her parents to Los Angeles General Hospital, which had a ward for contagious diseases.

After a spinal tap, it was confirmed that Mia indeed was one of the unfortunate children infected with polio and it would be necessary to place her under quarantine. Her belongings and clothes were burned when she was confined to the hospital; with six brothers and sisters at home, every precaution had to be taken.

Maureen and John were upbeat with Mia, telling her she would recover in a short time and be able to come home to her family. Visiting time was only twenty minutes long, three times a week, and that was through a glass pane at the end of her hospital room. Obviously this was a difficult time for the parents and the whole Farrow family. Mia was as thin as a stick to begin with, and sometimes even the strongest of children wound up crippled or worse after contracting polio.

The ward contained children and some adults, many of them in iron lungs. Some of the weaker children succumbed to the disease and died. Mia was one of the lucky ones who underwent all the treatments including the iron lung and survived, suffering only minor long-term effects. She was able to return to school in September of 1954, only half-days at first until she regained her strength around Christmas.

The savior who found a miracle cure for polio after years of research was Jonas Salk, and an announcement was made in April of 1955 that an effective polio vaccine had been developed. Salk was born in 1914 in East Harlem on 106th Street, and was a toddler when the horrific 1916 epidemic had struck New York City. Back then the disease was called "Infantile Paralysis" and there were over 9,000 cases reported with a stunning 2,448 deaths the summer of 1916.

Living through this terrible outbreak of the disease as a child had a profound effect on Salk, who worked from 1947 through 1952 with his fellow researchers developing the vaccine. After considerable testing, including vaccinating children who had already contracted the disease, by 1955 an effective vaccine was finally ready for nationwide use. The scourge of polio would be defeated at last and the number of cases decreased dramatically each year; by 1961 only 1,312 American children contracted polio, which was a 98 percent improvement over the epidemic of 1952.

Maureen did have two films in release in 1954, although they had been produced earlier in 1953. The first drama was called *Duffy of San Quentin*, and the second, a sequel, was entitled *The Steel Cage*. Both films were based on the real-life story of Clinton T. Duffy, who took over as warden of San Quentin prison in 1940 and was responsible for cleaning up one of the most corrupt penal systems in the country.

At San Quentin prison in California, bookkeeper Clinton Duffy (Paul Kelly) is asked to take over as warden temporarily while a replacement is hired. With the encouragement of his wife Gladys (Maureen), Duffy takes his job seriously and begins implementing changes for the betterment of the prisoners, including: healthier food, the abolition of solitary confinement in the "dungeon," and the elimination of the "stool pigeon" system, where fellow inmates ratted each other out in exchange for favors from the guards.

Duffy also gets rid of the crooked captain of the guards, Pierson (Horace McMahon), who is responsible for much of the corruption at the prison. One of the prisoners, "Romeo" Harper (Louis Hayward), is considered a troublemaker but in actuality was imprisoned by false evidence planted by prosecutor Wynant (George Macready).

Gladys takes charge of finding a qualified nurse to take over the prison hospital, which presently offers little in medical care. The woman she hires, Anne Halsey (Joanne Dru), slowly wins the trust and respect of the men after a rocky start. Romeo begins to fall in love with her, and she has feelings for him as well. When Wynant is also sentenced to prison, he admits his crimes against Romeo, who is therefore acquitted in a new trial. Romeo and Anne then get married, and Warden Duffy with Gladys by his side stay on to run the prison.

Variety reviewed *Duffy of San Quentin* in February of 1954, and called it an average programmer:

> "Paul Kelly appears as Duffy and Maureen O'Sullivan as his understanding wife. He is competent as far as script and direction permit, as are Miss O'Sullivan, Louis Hayward, the bitter railroaded prisoner, and Joanne Dru, the beautiful nurse with whom Hayward falls in love."

In *The Steel Cage*, both Paul Kelly and Maureen reprised their roles as Duffy and his wife, Gladys. This second prison drama was actually three separate vignettes, and Maureen appeared in only the first segment, a light comedy, entitled "The Chef." The story begins as prison chef Louis (Walter Slezak) is about to be paroled, which dismays fellow convict Billy Brenner, a gourmet who loves the delicious cooking of Louis.

On the outside, Louis gets a job at a high-class restaurant, where his girlfriend Marie is also employed as a waitress. Unbeknownst to Louis, Brenner has arranged for a bogus customer to repeatedly disparage his meals, which angers Louis. When he finally loses his temper, Louis gets in a fight with the dupe and winds up being arrested and losing his parole.

Gladys (Maureen), the warden's wife, smells a rat and investigates the disturbance at the restaurant which has cost her friend Louis his freedom. She discovers that the so-called "customer" was in reality an ex-con and confidence man named Gilbert Lee, alias "Phil the Hook."

Gladys informs her husband, Warden Duffy, of the whole scheme designed to get Louis back so he would once again be the prison chef. After the warden gets all the facts, he reinstates Louis' parole and "Phil the Hook" takes his place inside the prison walls.

Variety noted in its October 1954 review of *The Steel Cage* that the episode entitled "The Chef," with Walter Slezak, Paul Kelly, and Maureen O'Sullivan, was "the best of the trio." Maureen had previously worked with Kelly in *Tarzan's New York Adventure* (1942), as the pilot Jimmy Shields who befriends Tarzan and Jane and helps them recover their kidnapped son.

The second story, "The Hostages," concerned an attempted prison break and the subsequent violence and bloodshed; John Ireland, Laurence Tierney, and Lyle Talbot were the featured players. The third story, "The Face," starred Kenneth Tobey as a convicted murderer and atheist who finds God while restoring the mural of "The Last Supper" at the prison. The prison chaplain (Arthur Franz) attempts to save his soul, but Steinberg (Tobey) is killed when caught in the cross-fire of a prison break.

In 1954, a whole new generation of movie fans, and lots of the older ones too, were treated to the thrill of seeing the original Tarzan adventures, *Tarzan, the Ape Man*, and *Tarzan Escapes*, in theaters across the country. These two classics, with Johnny and Maureen as Tarzan and Jane, were re-released to great success and the adulation of the fans.

It was rare for any film to be re-released, with exceptions like *Gone with the Wind* and *The Wizard of Oz*. However, these exciting Tarzan films proved to be immensely popular a second time around. Younger movie fans were enthralled at the beauty of Maureen O'Sullivan in her prime years as Jane of the jungle, and seeing Weissmuller at his most virile as the ape-man.

By 1957, most of the Tarzan pictures began showing up on network television, and as each decade would pass, Maureen would make new fans who discovered her films playing on late-night TV. By the 1980s, new generations of movie fans were treated to the six MGM Tarzan films on videocassette, and eventually the DVD format.

In 1997, American Movie Classics showed the entire series of Tarzan films, and once again Maureen and Johnny found a mixture of young and older fans who found their adventures enthralling.

324 ♃ DAVID FURY

So when Maureen at times said she regretted the Tarzan pictures for various reasons, it was usually done with a wink and a nod. In the next moment she would admit how much fun she had doing the adventures with Johnny Weissmuller. Maureen also realized that her greatest acclaim and enduring fame came from her character of Jane.

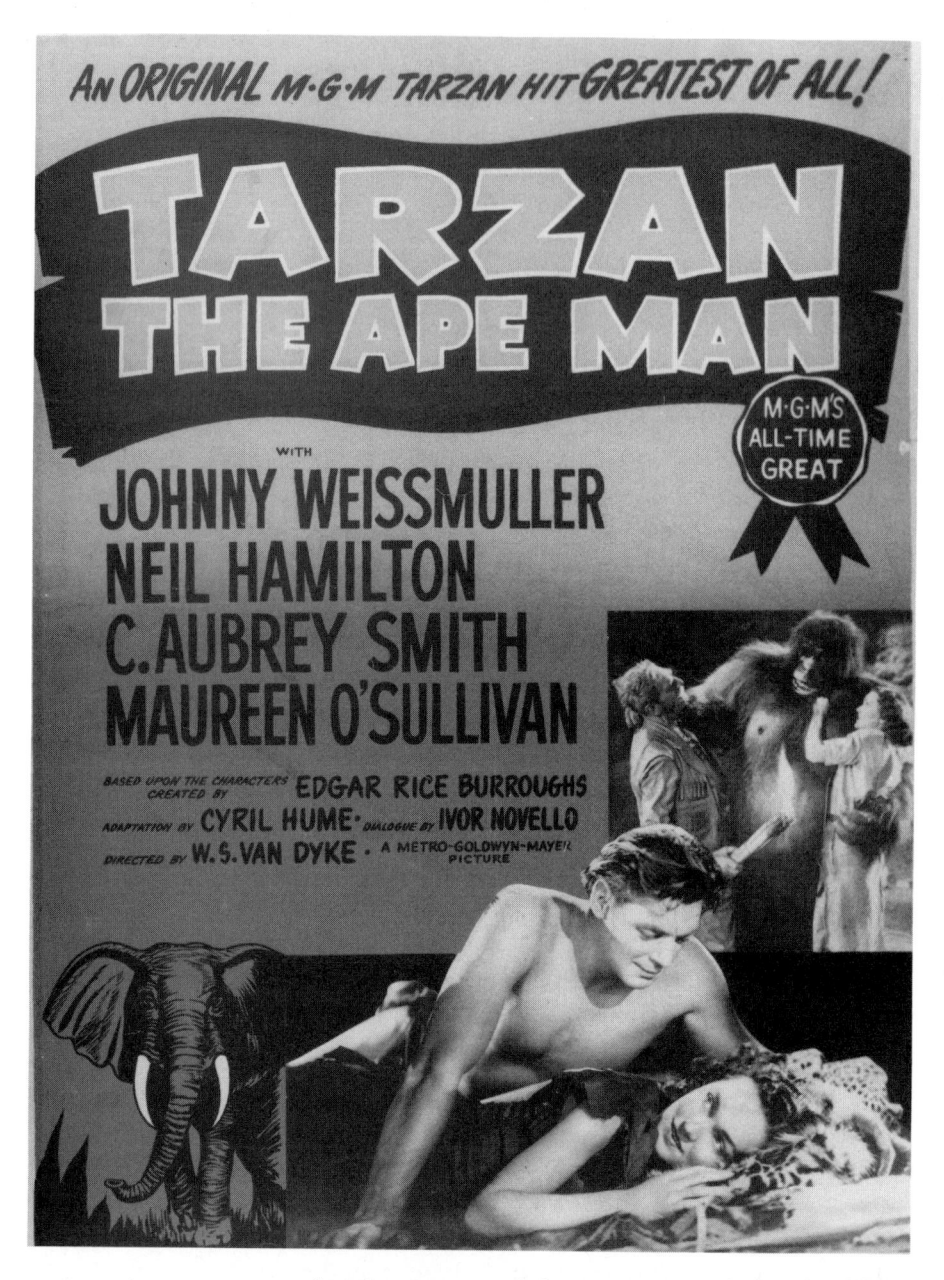

Tarzan, the Ape Man was re-released in 1954 ... a whole new generation of movie fans fell in love with Maureen O'Sullivan and Johnny Weissmuller in their characters of Tarzan and Jane

CHAPTER TWENTY-ONE
"The Redoubtable Mr. Farrow"

Meanwhile, back at the ranch, John Farrow followed up his work at RKO in *Where Danger Lives* with another Mitchum vehicle called *His Kind of Woman* (1951), also starring the Howard Hughes bombshell and protégée Jane Russell.

Russell, in her 1985 autobiography, noted that Robert Mitchum was concerned that this would be another venture with the Hughes negative magic touch to it. In other words, all the good projects were bypassed and the bad projects were the ones Hughes wanted to do:

"Mitch wanted very much to do something good," said Ms. Russell, "and he was afraid we weren't going to get the chance because there wasn't anyone very talented running the studio."

"Mitch was right. When we got the script for *His Kind of Woman*, it was just another man meets woman story with a little intrigue thrown in. It was a shame, because that man was a good actor and deserved better. He could memorize pages in just minutes. John Farrow, the director, a bright man who had an evil sense of humor, and Vincent Price, a brighter man, with a delicious sense of humor, made up the group ... I don't remember too much about the picture, but the people are with me yet. I fell in love with both Vinnie and Mitch."

Farrow's next picture was *Submarine Command* (1951) with William Holden as an officer trying to make the adjustment to peacetime after the war was over. Holden, a notorious drinker, commented about this particular picture: "It's a funny thing, I don't remember a thing about making *Submarine Command*. I was drunk through the whole picture. The only thing I remember is when Don Taylor and I jumped off a ship and swam to a submarine. We did it as a joke on the director, John Farrow, who thought the stunt was being done by doubles."

The post Civil-war western *Ride Vaquero!* (1953) starred Robert Taylor and Ava Gardner when she was at the peak of her beauty. Charles Higham, in his biography, *Ava*, noted that the actress found Farrow almost intolerable:

"She [Ava Gardner] disliked the director, the late John Farrow, because of his sadistic treatment of the horses. Farrow, husband of Maureen O'Sullivan, was a rough Australian who used to fly to Los Angeles on Saturdays, fly back the next morning with an armful of call girls to carouse and fornicate all through the Sabbath, then turn up on the set on Mondays with a hangover, cursing at everyone."

Mia Farrow, in her 1997 autobiography *What Falls Away*, recalled that her father did indeed have a terrible temper when angered, and that there also were cracks in the marriage of Farrow and her mother, Maureen O'Sullivan:

"When I was about ten, I got hopping mad and called the nanny a fat bastard and ran away to the Wonder Bread factory, across the Santa Monica tracks. I hid out there for a while, and when it got dark, I came home. My father was waiting, and he whacked me clear across the room. He had an almighty temper. When I was six or seven, my brothers and I put together the filthiest poem we could think of — we even got it to rhyme. Only somehow my mother got hold of it. She said, 'You just wait till your father gets home,' which was the scariest thing imaginable. After a long, hellish wait, he sent for me. I had to hang on to the big beige chair, and I thought he'd break my back with his walking stick. Jesus. He was something.

"He slept in a different bedroom from my mother, which had its own private entrance. Mom says she had that put in during his affair with Ava Gardner in 1953, while they were filming *Ride, Vaquero!* 'I thought I'd be so annoyed if I heard him coming in in the middle of the night,' she explains."

A relationship between Farrow and Ava Gardner — and she knew many men in her life — must have occurred prior to the filming of *Ride, Vaquero!* Ava had married Frank Sinatra on November 7, 1951, and he even came to the set for two weeks to keep his wife company in the summer of 1952. Ms. Gardner makes no mention whatsoever of Farrow in her 1990 autobiography, *Ava: My Story*.

Maureen obviously was aware of the numerous affairs of her husband, but like many women she chose to overlook it for the sake of her children. Maureen had mentioned John's "private entrance" as early as 1938, in an interview in which she said this was installed in their home so that he could "return late after a night out with the boys."

In some of her interviews after her marriage Maureen said she was angry with Farrow that he wasn't faithful to her during their courting days of the 1930s. How long he was faithful to her after they were married in 1936 would be pure speculation. Almost every source that mentions John Farrow also notes that he was a philanderer, even his daughter Mia Farrow.

Ms. Farrow comments in her 1997 memoir that she wasn't aware of her father's wayward ways, with the one exception:

"I didn't know about all the women then. Except for Ava Gardner. When I came into his office at the studio I caught a glimpse, a flash, a tear in the fabric, just a little slit, quick, close it back up. He was very handsome —

everybody said so. After he died, women used to come up to me and they'd look at me a certain way and I knew what they were going to say: *I knew your father.* I never knew what to reply, or what expression to wear."

It's hard to say exactly why Maureen stayed with John Farrow considering his unfaithful habits. Perhaps he was the type of fellow who kept asking for one more chance; and she would give it to him. Before they were married Maureen said of Farrow: "I can't live with him, and I can't live without him." Apparently this was still the case in the 1950s when his many affairs were obvious to everyone including his wife. She had taken a vow, "Till death do us part ..." Clearly, Maureen was determined to keep her family together and hold true to that vow even if it meant a compromise in the marriage contract.

John Farrow continued to direct two films per year and the next was *Botany Bay* (1953). This sea drama had Alan Ladd aboard a convict ship bound for Australia, while James Mason was the vicious captain. *Plunder of the Sun* (1953) featured rugged Glenn Ford on a treasure hunt down Mexico way. Author Ronald L. Davis in his John Wayne biography noted the relationship between Farrow and Ford was contentious, which included many tense arguments during production:

"Initially, Glenn Ford had been scheduled to play the title role in *Hondo,* which would have fulfilled the actor's two-picture agreement with Wayne-Fellows Productions. But Ford had disliked working with the often callous John Farrow on *Plunder of the Sun,* and since Farrow was slated to direct *Hondo,* the star backed out. Rather than delay production, Duke stepped into the role after James Edward Grant had revised the script."

Consequently, *Hondo* (1953), from a Louis L'Amour western novel, became a John Wayne starring role, with Farrow directing. Geraldine Page was the female star in this picture, and she recalled sitting around in the intense heat of Carmago, Mexico, and listening to the political conversations of the Duke, Ward Bond, and John Farrow.

"John Wayne would talk so sensibly," said Ms. Page, "but that Mr. Farrow was very much a Machiavellian sort of syllogist ... and Ward Bond was just an oversimplifying bully.

"It seemed to me that John ... would wander out towards something that made sense to me — but that Farrow, in his clever way, would take what John said and weave it back into this pattern of what horrified me."

A Bullet Is Waiting (1954) was another Farrow western with Rory Calhoun and Jean Simmons, and after that it was back working for John Wayne — star and producer — in *The Sea Chase* (1955). This story had the Duke as a German ship captain involved with Lana Turner in an adventure of the high seas. There was immediate trouble on the set between Farrow and Lana Turner, as described in the 1988 biography of John Wayne by his wife Pilar:

"When Duke's co-star, Lana Turner, flew to the islands, she found she'd been booked into a single room at the Kona Inn. To make matters worse, her room adjoined Farrow's — a director noted for dramatic flirtations with his leading ladies. Turner was furious. She interpreted the arrangement as another example of the 'casting couch' state of mind so prevalent in Hollywood at the time.

"Farrow wanted a charming female companion on location. It probably never dawned on him that Turner might be hostile to sleeping arrangements that had been made without her consent. The idea that she involve herself with Farrow was preposterous in any case. She'd just married actor Lex Barker, and he planned to join her as soon as he could."

Reportedly, Farrow tried to fire Lana Turner a few days into production because she repeatedly missed her morning call. The Duke interceded and got Farrow and Turner to kiss and make up — figuratively speaking — and the film was eventually completed by the end of the year.

In the middle of production, newly-divorced John Wayne was ready to marry Pilar, and the ceremony took place in Hawaii on November 1, 1954, during a break from filming *The Sea Chase*. The bride was given away by John Farrow, while Francis Brown was the best man, and Mary St. John, Wayne's secretary, was the matron of honor. Lana Turner and her husband, Lex Barker, were in attendance. (Barker, interestingly, had taken over for Weissmuller in 1949 as Tarzan when Johnny retired from the role.)

While Maureen didn't make any films during 1954 or 1955, she did do a large volume of television work after Mia recovered from her bout with polio. She was the host of a syndicated program called "Irish Heritage" in 1954. Maureen, of course, was born and raised in Ireland, and she would often say, "If there's any magic in my soul, it comes from Ireland."

Maureen was once again a guest on "Ford Theatre" in the episode, *Daughter of Mine*, a romantic drama concerning a well-bred girl and a boy from the other side of the tracks. Maureen and Pat O'Brien played the parents with Margaret O'Brien and Richard Jaeckel as the young couple. The actress also starred in the "Lux Video Theatre" production of *September Tide*, from a story of modern-day England by Daphne Du Maurier, with Maureen and John Sutton, and hosted by James Mason.

1955 guest roles included "Fireside Theatre," a popular NBC drama in which Maureen co-starred with John Howard and Peter Reynolds in *Brian*. Next was "Climax Theatre" on CBS, *The Great Impersonation*, a teleplay of an E. Phillips Oppenheim story. Maureen O'Sullivan portrayed Lady Dominey, Michael Rennie was Lord Dominey, and Zsa Zsa Gabor was the Princess Stephanie. "Casablanca" on ABC was hosted by Gig Young, and the episode was called *Labor Camp Dispute*. The cast included Maureen O'Sullivan as Helen,

Charles McGraw as Rick, and William Hopper as Randall. Hopper was the son of Hollywood columnist Hedda Hopper, and he was well-known as Paul Drake on *Perry Mason*.

Maureen next played herself in a "Climax Theatre" production of *The Louella Parsons Story* on CBS. More dramatic roles for the actress in 1956 included "The Whistler" in the episode *Trademark*, and also "Star Stage," with the rather intriguing title of *Scandal on Deepside*.

Maureen portrayed a lady haunted by the ghost of her departed, but still devoted, maid in the "Matinee Theatre" production of *Ladies' Maid's Bell*. She starred in "Dupont Theatre" (Cavalcade of America) in an ABC Christmas drama called *The Blessed Midnight*, about a woman involved with a motherless and penniless Bronx waif (Danny Richards, Jr.). She also appeared in a second 1956 Christmas drama on "Lux Video Theatre" called *Michael and Mary*, from a story by A. A. Milne and hosted by Gordon McRae. (Mary Pickford did a version of *Michael and Mary* on her own dramatic radio series in 1934.)

In addition to her motion picture work in 1957, Maureen starred in ABC's "Crossroads Theatre," in a drama called *The Man Who Walked on Water*, with William Prince. A return to "Climax Theatre" saw the actress in *Let It Be Me*, a story about the recording industry with Eddie Albert, Charles Ruggles, Steve Forrest, along with singers Jill Corey and Johnny Desmond.

Perhaps the best dramatic series of the 1950s was "Playhouse 90," which offered "live" productions as well as filmed versions between 1956 and 1961 on CBS. "Playhouse 90" became the standard against which all other dramatic anthologies were judged. A drama written by Rod Serling, *Requiem for a Heavyweight*, was critically acclaimed and swept the 1956 Emmys, winning six awards including best direction, best teleplay, and best actor Jack Palance. Continued excellence became the standard and future productions such as *The Miracle Worker, The Comedian, The Helen Morgan Story*, and *Judgment at Nuremberg* represented the very best dramatic television of the era.

Maureen O'Sullivan and Joseph Cotten were chosen to star in the "Playhouse 90" production, *Edge of Innocence*, which aired on October 31, 1957. This outstanding 90-minute drama featured a prominent director in Arthur Hiller and respected writer in Berne Giler, along with a top-notch cast. Other cast members included Teresa Wright, Lorne Greene, DeForest Kelley, and Beverly Garland. This was the story of an unscrupulous criminal lawyer who falls in love with a wealthy widow from a socially prominent family, and subsequently becomes a suspect in her brother's disappearance and murder.

In the summer of 1956, Maureen was signed for the western, *The Tall T* (1957), with legendary actor Randolph Scott. Randy portrayed Pat Brennan, a career cowboy who recently purchased his own small spread after years as ramrod on a huge ranch, "The Tall T."

This of course was where the film's title came from, which was based on an Elmore Leonard novelette published in *Argosy Magazine* in 1955. Director Budd Boetticher told author Robert Nott why he chose Maureen and other cast members for their roles:

"I liked Maureen from the *Tarzan* films on and I needed a girl that wasn't glamourous. She was the kind that nobody's going to marry. And John Hubbard was a friend of mine, and I wanted a weak actor to play that guy because he was a bum. Henry Silva I just loved. He came down to play the part, and he had never seen a horse up close before, and he put the wrong foot in the stirrup! *[Laughs]* But, he rode fairly well, I thought.

"Nobody knows how to finish pictures today. We did. When Randy says to her, 'Come on now, it's gonna be a nice day,' you think to yourself, 'God, I hope so!' "

Maureen O'Sullivan hadn't made a western picture since 1933, when she co-starred with George O'Brien in *Robbers' Roost*. She later said she loved doing this picture and working with Scott, who had started out in pictures the same time as Maureen. By this time, at age 58, he was one of the biggest names in Hollywood. The seven films he made with director Budd Boetticher in the 1950s, including *The Tall T*, were perhaps his best work and cemented his place in screen history as arguably the best — and most believable — screen cowboy of them all. John Wayne was larger than life, Burt Lancaster did all of his own stunts, Gary Cooper always died with his boots on, and Randy Scott portrayed the "man alone against great odds" better than anyone. You always knew that somehow he would survive, save the heroine (in this case Maureen), and find a way to bring retribution against the forces of evil.

The balance of the cast included Richard Boone as the ringleader of the vicious trio of killers, Frank Usher, who finds a companion to talk to in the weather-beaten cowboy, Pat Brennan (Randy Scott). The latter has some intellectual savvy and Usher hopes that maybe he will understand his motives for becoming a criminal, not just view him as a killer.

Boone could portray a heroic type, as he did in his TV series *Have Gun, Will Travel*, but when called upon to be a villain he was superb. His character of Usher is intelligent, and the wheels are always spinning in his brain; he keeps both Brennan and the woman Doretta alive because he finds them useful. The cowboy skins an antelope that has been killed for meat, while she cooks the meals and also is the meal ticket. When her wealthy father pays her ransom, Usher figures to be a wealthy man. Although only implied, you assume that Usher will tie up all the loose ends later and double-cross his partners; he's too smart to share that much money with a couple of yahoos who came from dirt and will surely wind up in hell. Henry Silva as "Chink" was chilling as the cold-blooded killer, and the crusty stage driver was well-played by Arthur Hunnicutt.

The story begins as rancher Pat Brennan (Scott) stops at the stage relay station run by Hank Parker to water his horse and visit with young Jeff, Hank's son. Pat promises to bring the lad back a bag of candy, when he returns from his mission of buying a seed bull from his former employer, Tenvoorde, who operates the Tall T ranch.

Pat buys the candy in town and also is introduced to Doretta Mims (Maureen), who has just married her father's bookkeeper Willard (John Hubbard) that very morning. They have hired a private coach to take them to Bixby for their honeymoon, and the driver is Ed Rintoon (Arthur Hunnicutt), a cantankerous coot who has little respect for Mims and the fact that he married the unglamorous Doretta for her father's money.

At the Tenvoorde ranch Pat plans to buy the bull, but his former boss offers to let him have the bull if he can ride him — if he loses Pat has to give up his horse. Not the luckiest guy, Pat is thrown from the bull and lands in a water trough. He trudges away from the Tall T with only his saddle and figures to borrow a horse from Hank at the relay station.

Along the trail Pat hitches a ride with Rintoon's coach, over the objection of Mims — but not Doretta, who is embarrassed at her new husband's rudeness. When they reach the relay station, it is eerily deserted and Hank and Jeff are nowhere in sight. An armed man steps out from the barn and orders them to drop their guns. The leader, Frank Usher (Boone), is flanked by two young gunslingers, Chink (Silva), and Billy Jack (Homeier).

Pat complies, but Rintoon reaches for his shotgun and is shot dead by Chink, a man who takes pleasure in killing. When Pat discovers that Hank and his son have been murdered and dumped into the well, he realizes just how remorseless these men really are. Pat also understands that these ruthless men will kill all of them eventually, when a whim strikes their fancy.

Mims tries to bargain for his life by telling Usher that his wealthy wife Doretta would be worth a fifty-thousand dollar ransom from her father. Usher agrees and sends Mims and Billy Jack to arrange the deal by handing a note to a passer-by for delivery to Doretta's father, a wealthy copper magnate.

While waiting for the pay-off, they regroup at the gang's hideout in the hills, where Pat and Doretta are sequestered in a shallow cave. The deal is struck and the duplicitous Usher offers to let Mims ride away with his freedom. The craven coward gallops out of camp, but before he is out of range he is shot dead by Chink.

By this time, Pat and Doretta begin to see the courage in each other — despite the difficult circumstances they are falling in love. She admits she didn't love her husband, but married him because of her loneliness. Pat warns her that they must keep their eyes open, and be ready to act to save their lives when the time is right.

The next morning, Usher rides out of camp to collect the ransom, and Pat uses psychology on Chink to make him think that his partner plans a double-cross with the money. Chink rides out to safeguard the cash, and Pat tells Doretta to unbutton her blouse and lure Billy Jack into the cave. When he grabs the woman, Pat rushes in and the two men struggle over the gun — which discharges into the neck of Billy Jack and kills him.

The sound of gunfire brings Chink back to camp, and by now Pat and Doretta are both armed with guns and hiding in the rocks. Chink takes cover in the cave, and Pat tells Doretta to fire six shots slowly at the cave opening. Chink thinks that the shooter is Pat and now he must reload, but when he steps from the cave Pat shouts out his name and then guns down the man who murdered his friends.

Pat and Doretta now await the return of Usher, who rides into camp and discovers his cohorts are both dead. Pat gets the drop on him, and orders him to lower his weapon and the saddlebag of money. Usher has his own plan, and reminds Pat that he could have had them both killed earlier but spared them. Usher tells Pat he is going to ride out of camp and never return, figuring that Pat will never shoot him in the back.

Usher mounts his horse and rides from camp, but when he reaches the cover of the ridge he pulls his rifle and gallops full-steam back towards Pat, guns blazing, intent on killing his adversary and regaining the cash. Pat is ready and returns fire and Usher is shot in the face — he falls to the ground screaming in pain, and then dies a deserved death.

The dragon is slain, and Pat tosses aside his rifle. Doretta looks into the eyes of the man who has won her heart, and they walk away arm and arm into the future.

Maureen O'Sullivan commented in 1974 how much she enjoyed working with cowboy legend Randolph Scott: "Of my later films, I loved doing *The Tall T*. It was *fun* making it, *and* I had my own way for once: I did it without makeup and I had this long red hair. It was all shot at the foot of the High Sierras, and we used to ride a lot and take long walks, and of course, once out of town our star, Randy Scott, was mobbed — he was a big hero. I thought Budd [Boetticher] was a great director, and I liked the story. I always enjoyed making Westerns ... except that the men looked a bit scruffy!"

Of course, although Maureen is treated like a "plain Jane" in the picture, no make-up or frills, she was still beautiful with her long red hair and trim figure. There was also a veiled sexuality about her character that the right man would notice, which in this film was Mr. Scott. As the confirmed bachelor cowpoke, he falls for her, and they make passionate love when they are confined in a small cave that later turns into a love nest.

Maureen and Randolph Scott were doomed lovers who survived in *The Tall T*

The recently widowed woman wakes up Brennan (Scott) in the middle of the night, and apologizes for her display of grief that morning when her husband was killed. He responds with understanding, but adds, "Right now you need to stay alive more than you need somebody."

She says, "I can't help the way I feel ..." When he asks her if she loved her husband, she responds that she did — but he calls her a liar and says, "You never loved your husband, Mrs. Mims, did you? And you knew that he didn't love you, not for one minute did you believe that."

In a touching speech Maureen says, "Do you know what it's like to be alone, in a camp full of roughneck miners? A father who holds a quiet hatred for you because you're not the son he's always wanted ... Yes, I married Willard Mims ... because I couldn't stand being alone any more! (with great emotion ...)

"I knew he didn't love me, but I didn't care — I thought I'd make him love me. And by the time that he'd asked me to marry him, I'd lied to myself inside for so long that I believed it was me he cared for ... and not the money ... and now this."

Scott responds, "So what have you lost save for a little pride? Afraid you can't get another man, is that it? Afraid what people might say? Even if Willard did marry you for the money, at least he married you. He married you, he was your first and last chance so you grabbed it."

At this point Maureen is burning with anger and tries to plant a vicious slap on his face, which he catches and holds her arm in a tense position ... as if the slap could still come. They are staring at each other as they become more aroused, and then he grabs her behind the neck and pulls her down so she is across his lap, his hand still clutching her hair so she can only gasp and must listen to his words.

"You think no one will have you because you bite your lip and hang your head ... but let me tell you something! You're as much woman as any of 'em! A lot more than most, but you gotta realize if you don't think anything of yourself, how do you expect anyone else to?"

She shakes her head and cries out because she has never known such passion and her eyes are of full of tears, and he says, "Don't say you can't, cause you can. You can't always sit back and wait for something to happen ... sometimes you gotta walk up ... and TAKE what you want!"

By this time Maureen's bosom is heaving and she is gasping, and they kiss feverishly as the scene fades to darkness. This was a scene where you knew that the kiss was just a prelude, there was too much lust between them that had to be resolved. Maureen was so sensuous in this scene, and she was just what Randy Scott had described: "You're as much woman as any of 'em! A lot more than most ... "

Maureen is incredibly beautiful in the candle lighting, despite the fact she was purportedly a plain woman. Movie fans could see that she was stunning, and her honest confession and her sensuality were really getting to Randy Scott. When he grabs her around the neck and pulls her down to the ground, this movie became much more than just another cowboy picture. It became a classic, and this was literally one of Maureen's best scenes of her movie career.

In a review from *American Cinematheque*, *The Tall T* is described as:

"Tense, sexually ambiguous story of rancher Randolph Scott kidnapped by killer Richard Boone (in a career-making performance) and his gun-happy henchmen. Brilliantly scripted by Burt Kennedy (based on an Elmore Leonard story), *The Tall T* switches effortlessly from folksy humor to tragic violence, leaving the viewer literally breathless."

In the *Variety* review of April 1957, *The Tall T* received high marks and Maureen is singled out for her exceptional performance:

"There's a wealth of suspense in the Burt Kennedy screenplay based on a story by Elmore Leonard. From a quiet start the yarn acquires a momentum which explodes in a sock climax. Modest and unassuming, Scott is a rancher who's been seized by a trio of killers led by Richard Boone.

"Also captured are newlyweds Maureen O'Sullivan and John Hubbard. Originally the outlaws planned a stage robbery, but are urged privately by the craven Hubbard to hold his heiress-wife for ransom in the hope that this move might save his skin. For the gang has already slain a stage relay man, his small son, and stage driver Arthur Hunnicutt.

"Under Budd Boetticher's direction the story develops slowly, but relentlessly, toward the action-packed finale. Scott impresses as the strong, silent type who ultimately vanquishes his captors.

"Miss O'Sullivan registers nicely as the heiress who wins Scott after the outlaws slay her traitorous husband. Boone is crisply proficient as the sometimes remorseful outlaw leader. His psychopathic henchmen are capably delineated by Skip Homeier and Henry Silva."

Another review in *The Great Western Pictures* by James Robert Parish and Michael R. Pitts recognizes the characterization by Maureen as outstanding:

"*The Tall T* is a compact little feature which interpolates beautifully the characters' interplay with fetching Western backgrounds (especially the contrast between lush settings and the arid desert arena). An interesting aspect of this feature is the character of timid, plain Doretta [Maureen O'Sullivan], whose husband has married her for her money. As she works with Pat, she blossoms into an individual, a sexually attractive female very much worth having. (At one point in the narrative, she successfully seduces outlaw Billy Jack.) At the finale, it is no surprise that Pat and Doretta have fallen in love."

Maureen's next starring role, and her last motion picture for several years, was another excellent western called *Wild Heritage* (1958) with co-star Will Rogers, Jr. Maureen had made two films with his father, Will Rogers, Sr., back in the 1930s when she was employed by Fox Film. Even though Rogers was top-billed in this current film, he actually had just a supporting role.

Maureen is the star of this picture from beginning to end as the matriarch of a frontier family that travels west by covered wagon. Her character of Emma Breslin was strong and capable, and she had to have these qualities because her husband Jake is killed early in the story.

Oldest son Dirk was portrayed by Rod McKuen, who would go on to a long and very successful career as a singer-songwriter and poet. The other three Breslin children were played by Gigi Perreau as "Missouri," Gary Grey as Hugh, and George Winslow as Talbot.

Eleven-year-old child actor George "Foghorn" Winslow earned his nickname because he possessed a basso-profundo voice that made him stand out in all of his film roles. He was also a fine actor but made only a dozen films before retiring, including *Gentlemen Prefer Blondes* (1953) with Marilyn Monroe, and *Artists and Models* (1955) with Dean Martin and Jerry Lewis. The lad was excellent in *Wild Heritage* as the youngest son who is more levelheaded than his older siblings, and in fact comes up with viable solutions to various sticky problems. For example, when their wagon wheel breaks and they appear to be stranded, he suggests making a skid to temporarily replace the wheel — it worked perfectly.

The supporting cast included Jeanette Nolan as the head of another family heading west that becomes entwined in the lives of the Breslins. Nolan was a wonderful character actress who was in countless motion pictures and television roles. The headstrong brother and sister of the Bascomb family were portrayed by a young Troy Donahue as Jesse and Judy Meredith as the tomboy, Callie. In the course of things, the young adults of both families become involved, first as rivals, then friends, and finally they begin to pair up in couples to marry.

The story begins in 1875 when Easterners Jake (Paul Birch) and Emma Breslin (Maureen) and their four children head west to claim some land for a farm. It is a difficult trip by covered wagon, but Jake's strong character and sense of humor keeps the family in a good mood and on an even keel. Jake has a dream that the west is the land of opportunity where they can put down roots and have room to breathe.

At the settlement town near their claim in Topknot, Jake accidentally bumps a man at the saloon and a fight erupts. Jake foolishly is armed with an old pistol, and Jud and his partner Arn, two vicious cattle rustlers, kill Jake in cold blood. Emma is devastated at the sudden death of her husband, but a local lawyer, Judge Copeland (Will Rogers) helps the family bury Jake and convinces them to build their new life here rather than returning to the east.

After they find a beautiful piece of land in the valley, they begin building a cabin and planting a vegetable garden. Emma makes friends with Janice Bascomb (Nolan) and her husband Bolivar, but Jesse and Callie are always fighting with her four children, Dirk, Hugh, Missouri, and Talbot. Tragically, Mr. Bascomb is crushed by a horse and dies.

When a small bunch of cowboys passes through pushing a large herd of cattle, Dirk and Hugh make friends with the leader, Rusty, and two of his men, Chaco and Brazos. The boys tell Rusty how they plan to settle the score some day with Jud and Arn, the two men who killed their father. Rusty is sympathetic, and shows them how to wear a handgun and the art of shooting.

Meanwhile, Jud and Arn have seen the herd and make plans to rustle the cattle. At dawn the next morning the rustler gang attacks. Dirk and Hugh help to defend the herd, but Brazos is killed. In his dying words, he gives his two fine handguns to Dirk and Hugh. Rusty has lost all of the herd except 100 cows, which he gives to the Breslins so they can start their own cattle ranch. He heads back to Texas, empty-handed but not bitter.

When the boys return, they discover that Emma and Missouri have come down with the fever — they rush to the Bascomb farm for help. Janice and Callie tend to the women, who recover in a few days. Dirk and Hugh have decided to share the herd with the Bascombs, because the families are becoming inseparable. When they discover that Arn and Jud are planning to steal their small herd, they take turns on guard each night.

One late night, Arn and Jud shoot Callie while she guards the cattle, and rustle off the herd. Fortunately, Callie is only wounded. Emma and Janice tend to her health until she is past the danger point. The three angry young men, Dirk, Hugh, and Jesse, ride purposefully to the settlement looking for the men who shot Callie.

When Emma discovers that her sons are armed and looking for the killers of her husband, she jumps in the wagon and races for town — praying that she is not too late. The three young men find Jud and Arn at the saloon, and when they step out in the street a gunfight is imminent. The experienced gunmen easily out-draw the young challengers — Jesse is wounded in the arm and Hugh's gun is shot from his hand.

Just as Jud and Arn are about to finish the job, little Talbot strolls across the street and tosses a loaded gun to Hugh, and together the Breslin brothers gun down their father's killers. Emma arrives in a wagon just in time to realize

Maureen O'Sullivan (far left) as pioneer woman Emma Breslin in *Wild Heritage*

her sons are safe and alive, and the blood feud is over. Judge Copeland assures them that their land claim is now settled, and he also has his eye on Emma, who is a fine figure of a woman indeed.

Maureen as the pioneer woman Emma Breslin, with salt and pepper hair and a cotton dress, was as beautiful as ever with her stunning blue eyes and warm smile. She had developed over the past decade as an actress with great depth, and the only unfortunate thing was there just weren't enough good roles to go around.

This was a fine western melodrama, with a fair share of action, adventure, romance, and touching pathos. When the father of the family is killed, it is an unexpected turn of events. But it does create a situation where the Breslin family, with Maureen leading the way, must fight against the odds in the untamed west.

Will Rogers, Jr., as Judge Copeland, gradually reveals his attraction for the widow Emma Breslin (Maureen), and she sees the strength in him that would be a good influence on her brood of four children. By the end of the story, he is ready to pop the question. *Wild Heritage* is a western that deals explicitly with deaths common during these pioneer times, but it was also wholesome entertainment that could be enjoyed by the whole family. There was also some beautiful scenery captured in the splendor of CinemaScope and Eastmancolor. Interestingly, this was only the second film of Maureen's career that was photographed in color, following the recent *The Tall T*.

While Maureen was busy with her own career, John Farrow took a job as a screenwriter and in 1956 earned his only Academy Award, sharing the Oscar with James Poe and S. J. Perelman for the screenplay of *Around the World in 80 Days* (1956), which also won for Best Picture. Farrow had previously co-authored screenplays for other motion pictures, including: *The Invisible Menace* (1937), *Reno* (1939), and *Night Has a Thousand Eyes* (1948).

Farrow was also a poet, and in 1955 published *Seven Poems in Pattern*, a book twenty-five pages in length with a collection of his best work — seven poems including "Mass At Westminster," "Ever Mystery," "The Glorious Once," "Hear Me," "Thoughts by the Surf," "Anchor Watch," and "A Letter from His Commanding Officer," which was written during World War II.

Directing jobs were getting scarce for Farrow and *Back from Eternity* (1956) was a re-make of his 1939 film, *Five Came Back*. This second film wasn't as good as the original, but did have a decent cast including Rod Steiger, Gene Barry, Robert Ryan, and Anita Ekberg. Farrow then produced and directed *The Unholy Wife* (1957), with blonde bombshell Diana Dors in a plot with Tom Tryon to kill her husband, capably played by Rod Steiger.

John Farrow's next film was an adventure on the high seas, *John Paul Jones* (1959), filmed in England in 1958. Maureen was in London with John, and also with them were sons Johnny and Patrick, and daughters Mia, Prudy, Steffi, and Tisa. John Charles Farrow, their eleven-year-old son, made his film debut as the Scottish emigrant boy, John Paul (before he added Jones to his name). Patrick and Mia also had small cameos in the picture. Remaining at home was their oldest son Michael, who didn't want to leave his friends and the life of a California teenager for several months abroad.

The family lived in Madrid at the Castellana Hilton Hotel upon arrival, and later moved to Benidorm, a small village on the southern coast of Spain. Maureen and the kids lived in a rented house in the town, while Farrow isolated himself in a hotel.

John Paul Jones had an outstanding cast which included Robert Stack as the title character, along with Charles Coburn, Macdonald Carey, Marisa Pavan, Peter Cushing, Bruce Cabot, and even Bette Davis made a guest appearance as Catherine the Great. This was an excellent role for Stack, a handsome leading man who had been in movies since 1939. By the following fall, Stack would star in *The Untouchables* as crime buster Eliot Ness, and would become one of the most popular television heroes in America.

The sea and naval battle scenes were photographed on location near the small Spanish town of Denia, as a trio of eighteenth-century frigates battled it out in front of camera crews in a natural harbor halfway between Alicante and Valencia on the Mediterranean coast. At the conclusion of filming, the family took part in a week-long festival that was celebrated each year by the local citizens of Denia.

When the film was "in the can," Maureen and the children went to Ireland for a vacation near the Wicklow Mountains, where everyone could ride horses and visit with relatives on the O'Sullivan side of the family. Farrow went to London to edit the film, and Maureen and the kids followed later. There they lived at the Park Lane Hotel, and all six of the children were sent to school to keep pace with their classmates back in Los Angeles. The younger girls Tisa and Steffi attended a day school in London, Prudy and Mia went to a convent boarding school in Surrey, and the boys Patrick and Johnny enrolled at a school in Bournemouth.

Meanwhile, back in California, Michael was taking flying lessons and enjoying the life of a young man on his own for the first time. On October 28, 1958, nineteen-year-old Michael Farrow was killed in a small plane crash over the San Fernando Valley in California. Michael, who had a student flying certificate, and David H. Johnson, 21, an instructor at an airport in nearby Pocoma, were in a small craft that collided with one piloted by Donald W. Preneville, 39, of Glendale.

The authorities notified the next of kin of the three victims, including Maureen and John in London. It was an accident that stunned the whole family, as the death of a teenager is an unforeseen tragedy. Suddenly, they had to cope with the realization that they would never see Michael again. He was the oldest, first born, and everyone had their own private thoughts on this sad day.

Maureen and John made arrangements to fly back to the United States, to attend the funeral of their son Michael Damien Farrow. Maureen later recalled that director George Cukor, a close family friend, was there to meet them in Los Angeles: making arrangements for the funeral, offering his heartfelt condolences, and following a Jewish tradition, bringing food to the post-funeral gathering.

After the funeral, John returned to finish post-production on *John Paul Jones*, and Maureen rejoined the family in London. They left the unhappy memories of the Park Lane Hotel for a quaint English house on Swan Walk in Chelsea.

For various reasons, this motion picture turned out to be the last directing job of Farrow's career. Certainly the death of his son brought him great sorrow, and perhaps contributed to his early retirement at age fifty-four. Farrow had always been a drinking man, and it wouldn't take a doctor to diagnose him as being an alcoholic. The death of his son turned up the volume on his melancholia, and he became increasingly consumed with the premise of his own death.

The relationship between Maureen and John was more strained than ever, as daughter Mia Farrow, age thirteen at the time, described in her 1997 memoir:

"Tensions between my parents had escalated. Their demons were driving them apart, and in their grief they found no solace in each other.

"My father was drinking heavily. One evening, in an awful rage, he began shouting, and he chased my mother with a long knife through the ground-floor rooms of the house. I froze at the foot of the stairs until at last, knife in hand, he careened out into the night. My mother and I watched the door and after a time we made hot chocolate. But still I was shaking, so she put me into her own big bed saying that when Dad returned he'd find me there and surely then he'd soften because he loved me so. Then she climbed the stairs to the safety of my little attic room, while I propped myself up in bed, with my face right under the light, and waited."

John Farrow, at one time talented and sociable, had become a dangerous threat to everyone that he was close to, especially his wife. Booze was his escape from reality, but his alcoholism was tearing up the family.

During the 1930s when Farrow was courting Maureen, she was deeply in love with him and thought him to be the most wonderful man in the world. In the 1940s, after his war service, she respected him for his talents and together they built a very large family. As the decade of the 1950s faded to the end, the loving part of their marriage was over. Their relationship was merely a shell, and the happiness of the past was a far distant memory.

CHAPTER TWENTY-TWO
"Aftermath of a Tragedy"

For reasons of her own, Maureen O'Sullivan retired from the screen once again in 1959. By the fall of the year the family had returned to California, although Mia stayed on at the convent school in Surrey to continue her education. Maureen found a more affordable residence on North Roxbury Drive, a smaller house that didn't compare with the beautiful home on Beverly Drive they had lived in for years. Life had changed, and circumstances dictated their current situation.

At first glance it seems odd that she would quit acting in motion pictures at this time, especially since her recent screen portrayals in *The Tall T* and *Wild Heritage* were her best in years. She was also very much in demand for television roles, and in truth, Maureen loved her career as an actress. Undoubtedly she wanted to work, but emotionally she was not yet ready.

Maureen was still mourning the death of her son, which she took very hard. It is an old axiom that parents do not wish to outlive their children, and in this case Michael was nineteen years old and had his whole life ahead of him.

These things happen to ordinary people and also to celebrities; death makes no distinction by wealth or social status. Johnny Weissmuller's daughter Heidi died in 1962 in a car crash, at nineteen, the same age as Michael Farrow; Buster Crabbe's daughter Sande died in 1957 of anorexia; Dean Martin's son Dean Paul died in a plane crash in 1987; Paul Newman's son Scott died of a drug overdose in 1978; Mary Tyler Moore's son Richard died of an accidental gunshot wound in 1980. These tragic deaths happen all the time, and in every case they are devastating to the families. The loss of their oldest son was equally devastating to Maureen and her husband John. And their marriage, certainly one of the longest in Hollywood, was now in a hellish state.

John Farrow was unemployed, and his personal problems were exacerbated because he couldn't find any viable work as writer or director. He was realizing his own mortality, and feeling more bitter with his unfulfilled existence. Each day he would read the obituaries, shaking his head and muttering "gone" each time he saw the name of an old acquaintance who had passed.

The only friends who visited him were the Jesuit priests, and they would sit and discuss religious scripture and dogma until the wee hours of the morning, all the while drinking straight scotch whiskey. Discussions would become arguments, and the glasses would be filled again.

It was summer 1960 when fifteen-year-old Mia returned from her schooling in England. She later depicted her father's demeanor as "morose, difficult, and demanding." Maureen did the best she could with the current situation and took up painting, setting up an easel and spending her days in the sunny alcove of her upstairs bedroom — away from John. He would spend his time in his downstairs bedroom, contemplating his own death, his mental and physical health spiraling downward.

Sometimes Mia would listen in on these marathon conversations between her father and the Jesuits, and then head for her bedroom. Mia Farrow later described the state of things at this time in her memoir, *What Falls Away:*

"When I grew tired I crept upstairs past my mother's dark room, where she lay weeping.

"It was impossible for me to communicate in any important sense with either of my parents, however much I longed to. A feeling of failure slowly settled around me. My brothers and sisters were now in trouble too. We had been through too much, too separately; and now in the isolation our grief imposed on us, we could not reach each other."

Acting would eventually become Maureen's savior, but it would be on the stage and not the silver screen. Part of the reason for her departure from Hollywood was simply that age was catching up with all the actresses of the Golden Age of Hollywood. The careers of Bette Davis, Joan Crawford, Barbara Stanwyck, Myrna Loy, and even Katherine Hepburn were reaching the fading point. Bette Davis went so far as to place a full-page ad in the Hollywood trade papers when her career began skidding in the 1950s:

"MOTHER OF THREE; divorcee; American. Twenty years experience as an actress in motion pictures. Mobile still and more affable than rumor would have it. Wants steady employment in Hollywood. References upon request."

The same could be said for all of the female stars of the 1930s, including Maureen. Only one of this group took weekly television seriously as an option and that was Stanwyck, who had a successful TV drama for several years called *The Big Valley*. Most of these actresses kept acting, although in smaller roles, character parts, and television films when they became popular in the 1960s.

The great male actors, despite growing older, maintained their star status. Instead of fading away, they simply dropped dead — most long before their time. Legendary stars Clark Gable and Gary Cooper, both born at the turn of the century in 1901, died in 1960 and 1961 respectively, still in their prime. Jeff Chandler also died in 1961 at age forty-three, after a botched operation on his back. Dick Powell died in 1963 at age fifty-nine, while John Wayne survived cancer in the 1960s to live another decade. The balance of the giant stars from the 1930s were either dead, fading away to character parts, or simply retired like Cary Grant, Robert Montgomery, and William Powell.

By the spring of 1961, Maureen began considering a return to acting. That fall she appeared on dramatic television for the first time since 1957 when she starred in "Alcoa Premiere," a weekly anthology hosted by Fred Astaire. This one-hour melodrama, directed by John Newland, was entitled *Moment of Decision*, and aired on November 7, 1961. The story revolved around a famous magician who bets on his life and almost loses, with Astaire, Maureen and Harry Townes in the starring roles. Astaire portrayed Alex Berringer, with Maureen as Elizabeth Lozier and Townes as her husband Hugh.

Much like "Playhouse 90" had been, "Alcoa Premiere" on CBS represented top quality dramatic presentations. Great stars such as Charlton Heston, Ray Milland, Richard Kiley, Cliff Robertson, Dana Andrews, Robert Redford, Diana Hyland, Elizabeth Montgomery, Carol Lynley, Suzanne Pleshette, and Maureen O'Sullivan were complemented by well-known writers such as Ray Bradbury and directors that included John Ford. The show lasted for just two seasons, but it wasn't for a lack of stars or a dedication to excellence.

This one television appearance returned her to acting, but of greater importance for Maureen was a visit from her close friend Pat O'Brien in the fall of 1961. The Irish legend, a longtime friend of the family, convinced her to give the "legitimate" stage a try. The actress had thirty years of experience working in front of a camera, but her "live" acting had been limited to radio and some television dramas. These scenarios weren't quite the same as getting up in front of a paying audience with the knowledge you must get it right the first time. Maureen had a wonderful memory and could memorize entire scripts, so she finally agreed that she would give it a shot if the right play came along.

O'Brien knew of an opportunity at the Drury Lane Theater in Chicago that was casting for a play called *Roomful of Roses*, and he thought Maureen would be ideal in the role of Nancy Fallon. It turned out she was perfect for the part, and the actress and the play were a success beginning the week of October 1, 1961. Plays at this Chicago landmark theater usually ran for eight weeks after a two-week rehearsal.

The Drury Lane was a famous venue that was run by Tony DeSantis beginning in 1951. Both he and the theater were still going strong decades later into the 1990s. It was a classy establishment that brought in big stars such as Ginger Rogers, Douglas Fairbanks, Jr., Claudette Colbert, David Janssen, George Hamilton, Shelley Winters, Gene Barry, and Chuck Connors.

Roomful of Roses was written by Edith Sommer and had originally opened at the Playhouse Theatre on Broadway in 1955, with Patricia Neal in the role of Nancy. The play takes place at the home of Nancy and Jay Fallon in Midlothian, Illinois during the month of September.

Nancy (Maureen) and Jay (John Himes) have a seven-year-old son Larry, but she hasn't seen her fifteen-year-old daughter Bridget in eight years, after a messy divorce from her ex-husband Carl in which he won custody of the girl.

Now, the teenager is coming for a three-week visit while her father gets remarried. Nancy is excited to become reacquainted with her daughter, but they start out practically as strangers. They have exactly three weeks to become mother and daughter once again, and neither realizes that is precisely what each party desires.

The character of Nancy, as described by the author, was "a vital, attractive woman in her middle thirties [Maureen was fifty]. Her nature is warm and generous and, like many who are capable of an impulsive grand gesture, she is incapable of foreseeing the consequences."

After the successful run of *Roomful of Roses*, a confident Maureen landed the female lead in a comedy written by Sumner Arthur Long that toured on the summer circuit in 1962, under the name *Cradle and All*. Stops along the way included Westport, Connecticut, and Falmouth, Massachusetts.

Starring opposite Maureen was Paul Ford, who played her husband. Ford was a well-known stage actor, but is probably best remembered as the harried colonel on the Sgt. Bilko television series, *You'll Never Get Rich,* with Phil Silvers.

The main characters were Maureen as Edith Lambert; her husband Harry (Ford), who owns a lumber company; son-in-law Charlie (Orson Bean), and daughter Kate (Fran Sharon), both freeloaders who live with Harry and Edith. Neither are terribly ambitious.

The basic premise involved a warmhearted woman of middle-age (Maureen) who becomes pregnant, and her cantankerous husband cannot accept the fact that he is going to be a father at his age. He already has a married daughter that he would love to get out of the house, along with his lazy son-in-law, and now his wife kindly informs him that they going to be parents once again. All of the action of the play takes place in the living room of the Lambert home in Calverton, Massachusetts, over a period of a few days during the summer.

Director George Abbott saw the independent production and agreed to bring it to Broadway that fall with the revised title, *Never Too Late*. A preview performance was given at the Playhouse on November 20, to benefit the Homemaker Service of the Children's Aid Society.

The Sumner Long comedy officially opened at The Playhouse on Broadway on November 27, 1962, and it became a smash hit. The critics were exuberant and Howard Taubman of *The New York Times*, in his review of November 28, 1962, noted the hilarity of Long's comedy and the outstanding portrayals of Paul Ford and Maureen O'Sullivan, whom he called "sweet and adorable."

> "If you have wondered what Broadway has needed all along to dispel gloom and spread joy, *Never Too Late* has the answer. It's Paul Ford as the romantic lead. By normal stage standards Ford does not cut a romantic figure. As Harry Lambert, the mature father-to-be, he knits his brows in a permanent

scowl, looks out of his blue eyes belligerently on a hostile world, curls the lines around his mouth in fixed distaste and braces his portly figure vainly to withstand his family's persistent lack of understanding and consideration.

"Harry Lambert is in constant full cry, and he has endless outrages to complain about. He has a married daughter who is too indolent to breakfast before lunch. He has a son-in-law who speaks as if someone were twanging his vocal cords and holding his nose, who insipidly calls him Dad and who works for him and lives with him. He has a sweet, faithful wife who attends to endless chores without a murmur, but at an age when a woman should know better, she finds herself pregnant.

"*Never Too Late* is floated on little more than its one comic idea. But Mr. Long keeps it bubbling along merrily a healthy percentage of the time—at least 75 per cent, at a reasonable estimate. He has a capacious armory of bright lines. Some are richly in character, and many others sound fine when uttered somberly or painfully by Mr. Ford or twanged by Orson Bean as his son-in-law.

"Maureen O'Sullivan as Harry's patient, if surprising, wife is sweet and adorable, and let's wish her and Harry the son they want to name John Fitzgerald. Fran Sharon is pert as Harry's daughter, and John Alexander is helpful as the Mayor, Harry's neighbor.

"Mr. Abbott knows how to keep this sort of farce capering. There are some fine bits of business, no doubt of his devising. Mr. Bean, trying out a bathtub waiting to be removed from the living room to the new bathroom, twangs cheerfully when he discovers that he as well as the baby fits into it. Mr. Ford and Mr. Bean tote the tub up a stairway in a divertingly managed feat of awkward strength.

"It is true, *Never Too Late* flags now and then. Do you expect to laugh all the time? Look at the miseries it has wished on Paul Ford by making him a sort of romantic lead."

Maureen O'Sullivan was soon the toast of the town, and probably not in her wildest dreams did she imagine things would work out this well. The classy actress from Hollywood's Golden Age had reinvented herself and had a hit Broadway play on her hands. It might have been somewhat ironic that Maureen, a mother of seven who was still having children at age forty, was now playing a woman in her forties who finds herself pregnant by surprise. It was perfect casting; if anyone understood motherhood and mid-life pregnancy it was she.

Maureen had a suite at the Algonquin, a famous hotel on West 44th Street and just a short cab ride to The Playhouse, which was located at West 48th Street near Broadway. By Christmas, her daughter Mia joined her in New York, after completing some further schooling in London. Mia was seventeen years old now, and was thinking about going to medical school to become a doctor.

It was a happy time for Maureen. Her director George Abbott would often escort his leading lady out for a late supper after the show. Kirk Douglas, starring in *One Flew Over the Cuckoo's Nest* on Broadway, would treat Maureen and Mia to dinner on occasion to celebrate the success both plays were enjoying. She stayed out late and loved it, sleeping in and then ordering room service before going to the theater for the night's performance.

Maureen with daughter Mia in late 1962 ... enjoying the Broadway success of *Never Too Late*

It was all the glitz and glamor of Broadway success, and Maureen was showered in affection by the fans that had adored her for decades as a movie star. Many friends and acquaintances would attend the play, and then visit her dressing room after the show to congratulate her. There were flowers, cards, telegrams and gifts. They would attend clubs and parties into the wee hours, for this was New York where one could enjoy the nightlife all night without batting an eye. Mia was along for the ride, for her mother was a celebrity enjoying a wave of success and fame. *Never Too Late* had the look of a long-runner, so Maureen gave up her suite at the Algonquin Hotel and found an apartment for herself and Mia in early 1963.

Back in Beverly Hills, John Farrow lived with the other children at the house at 809 N. Roxbury. Maureen was the sole bread winner now, and she would send money home to pay expenses. Husband and wife in name only, their phone calls were sporadic and usually concerned the shortage of money. Maureen knew better than to be sucked into his vortex of despair, and would only speak to John when it was absolutely necessary. Mia noted about this period of separation between her parents, "Her paychecks were not enough, and their phone calls were brief and bitter."

And then a phone call came one morning for Maureen with the news: her husband had died late in the evening on Sunday, January 27, 1963, of a massive heart attack. John's body was discovered by Tisa, and Maureen lamented the circumstances when she said "for an eleven-year-old girl this was a tremendous shock." John's hand was on the receiver, as if he were attempting to make a telephone call. Maureen later confided to a friend, "I'll never know if he was trying to call for help or calling one of his women."

The actress flew back to Los Angeles for the funeral, and once again her close friend George Cukor handled much of the arrangements and also was a pallbearer. Maureen later reflected on her emotions after the death of her husband:

"It all seemed so terribly unreal. A moment before I'd been drunk with the euphoria of a big Broadway hit, and the next moment I was a lonely widow unable to live without tranquilizers. The only thing to do was get out there and keep working."

This was the end of twenty-six years of marriage between Maureen and John Farrow. In most respects the marriage had been over for years, but now it was official. She was a widow with six children to feed, clothe, and raise all on her own.

Death brought an end to John Farrow's tortured existence. Alcohol abuse had addled his brain and changed him from someone whom Maureen loved to a completely different person. Alcoholics are often portrayed in the movies as lovable types like W. C. Fields, or even William Powell — whose "Thin Man" character drank martinis like they were water. His character was glib, his antics while inebriated were cute and completely acceptable.

In real life, alcoholics are rarely anonymous and often bring misery to everyone in their lives. The final decade of Farrow's life represent the ugly years in the Maureen O'Sullivan story. These had been unhappy times for Maureen, but at last they were over. She could recall the good years, and later in life she took the high road always when speaking of Farrow, and said that for the most part their marriage was successful. She insisted on remembering the best, and refused to dwell on the negative. There was no choice now but to move on, and luckily she had a wonderful acting job waiting for her on the Great White Way.

A lifetime later, Maureen was able to reflect on those difficult days when she had to deal with the deaths of her son Michael and her husband John:

"The strange thing is that I never cried when I heard that John had died and I haven't to this day. It doesn't mean that I don't feel the loss acutely.

"Grief comes out in other ways than just crying, and when my eldest son, Michael, was killed in a mid-air plane crash at the age of nineteen when he was training for the Marine Corps, I couldn't cry at all — just as I couldn't cry when my father or John died.

"But each death is like something dying inside you forever and that feeling of unremitting loss never goes away. These deaths and losses are at the back of my mind all the time. I've come to the conclusion that some things are just too big to cry about.

"I've never been able to cry much and I don't know why. Maybe those nannies had something to do with it, because at a very young age I learned that crying wasn't going to get me anywhere. The only time I remember crying properly was when I started at boarding school and then I'd cry myself to sleep every night with the thought of those years of solitude ahead of me.

"I'm not a crier by nature, and I know other people who are like me. Hope makes me cry — and happy endings."

Back in New York, Maureen was given a week off from the play to get her emotions together, and Paul Ford joked to ease the tension: "What are you complaining about? At least you've had a week off."

Her first performance back was rocky, but director George Abbott knew that she would be all right. After a few shows she was back in top form, and the play went on for more than two years as a big hit. Eventually, Maureen found a large apartment in New York so the whole family could join her, and the house in Los Angeles was sold.

The actress later noted the friendships made during the run of *Never Too Late* were some of the closest of her life, and also that New York became her home after so many years of living in Beverly Hills:

"I got very close to the cast in *Never Too Late*," said Maureen. "We were great friends and would always socialize together. But I was very naive because I'd never done a play before and I thought it would go on for ever and ever. I certainly didn't expect such a terrible feeling of loss when it finally closed after two years.

"It was one of the few times in my life that I cried and cried, because suddenly it hit me that everyone else had a life to go back to whereas I had nothing. John was dead, California was over and the only thing to do was get on out there and look for another job."

When the play did close after its successful New York run, Maureen went to England and took over for Joan Bennett at the Royal, Nottingham, in *Never Too Late* during Ms. Bennett's temporary indisposition. Maureen later toured with the play, giving fans across America an opportunity to see her live and in person. Beginning in February of 1965, Maureen starred with Arthur Godfrey in a national tour of *Never Too Late* which began at the Palm Beach Playhouse in Florida. She also made an appearance on Godfrey's daily radio program on February 3 of that year to promote the tour of the play. And even that wasn't the end, because next was a motion picture of Sumner Long's vastly popular stage play.

Maureen at age 52 ... as lovely as ever in *Never Too Late* on the Broadway stage

The movie version of *Never Too Late* (1965) co-starred Maureen and Paul Ford in their respective roles as Edith and Harry Lambert. The balance of the cast were Hollywood actors who replaced the lesser known Broadway actors. Connie Stevens and Jim Hutton stepped in as Kate and Charlie, while Jane Wyatt, Henry Jones, and Lloyd Nolan filled the other lead characters. Directing was Bud Yorkin, and the producer was Norman Lear, the master of comedy.

The story takes place in New England where Harry Lambert (Ford) owns a lumber company. His loving wife Edith (Maureen) puts up with his cantankerous ways, and he is devoted to her. Also living with them are his daughter Kate (Stevens) and her husband Charlie (Hutton), who are freeloading off the parents. Harry would love to see them out on their own.

Edith is suffering from chronic fatigue and goes to see her doctor, where she is informed that the only thing wrong is that she is pregnant. At first shocked, she then celebrates by going on a shopping spree and comes home with a new outfit and hairstyle. Harry, always the cheapskate, chastises her for spending money until he learns of the pregnancy. The whole family is stunned by the announcement and Harry, close to sixty, feels that he cannot deal with the prospect of starting all over.

With Edith preparing for the new baby, Kate is forced to do all the housework because Harry refuses to hire a maid. She counters her father's stubborn streak by attempting to have her own baby, but she only succeeds in wearing husband Charlie down so much he is too tired to do anything else including go to his job at the lumber yard.

Harry and Charlie are frustrated husbands, and get drunk as skunks. They also insult Mayor Crane (Nolan), who defeated Harry in the last election. Crane is so angry that he reneges on a contract to buy lumber from Harry for the town's new stadium.

Edith feels that Harry doesn't love her or the new baby, and leaves him. She goes to Boston, where Harry tracks her down and professes his love and admits he is happy to be a new father again and promises to make everything right. Meanwhile, Charlie has apologized to Crane and regained the lumber contract, and he and Kate are planning to build their own home. Now that Harry and Edith have reconciled, they make a fresh start by going on a second honeymoon.

The filmed version of *Never Too Late* was Maureen's first motion picture since 1958, and she was playing a woman around the age of forty or so. She was fifty-four years old, but she easily passed for a woman ten years younger. Her figure was trim as always, and *Variety* noted that Maureen "looks great and handles light comedy with a warm, gracious flair." The actress had been absent from the screen for seven years, and the *Variety* review of October 27, 1965, proclaimed that it had been much too long:

"*Never Too Late* is excellent film comedy which shapes as a money picture. Outstanding direction and acting give full life to this well-expanded legiter about an approaching-menopause wife who becomes pregnant to the chagrin of hubby, spoiled-brat daughter, and free-loading son-in-law. Comedy ranges from sophisticated to near-slapstick, all handled in top form.

"Sumner Arthur Long adapted his play which though essentially a one-joke affair he has filled out with exterior sequences which enhance, rather than pad. While the result is a family pie, it's not a pollyanna potpourri of fluff. There's some meaty dialog for adults.

"Paul Ford and Maureen O'Sullivan are smartly re-teamed in their Broadway roles of small town Massachusetts parents, settled in middle age habits until wife's increasing fatigue is diagnosed as pregnancy. Miss O'Sullivan has long been absent from the screen, and older audiences will only recall her in 'Tarzan' pix and a few plush-mounted Metro oldies. She looks great and handles light comedy with a warm, gracious flair.

"Yorkin's direction is top-notch whether the action is in the kitchen, parlor, bedroom, street or bar, sites of solid vignettes set the right tone."

Indeed, Maureen was the best thing that happened to this screen version of *Never Too Late*. Paul Ford was a touch too hammy, while Connie Stevens and Jim Hutton were over the top as the young couple living with the parents.

Maureen stole every scene that she was in, and was simply amazing as Edith. When she is walking with a sprightly step down the sidewalk after realizing that she is going to be a mother once again, it is a classic moment. She later dips into the beauty parlor for a modern hairstyle, and also buys a new dress that is more with the current times. Edith wants to escape from her image as a stuffy housewife, because now she is going to be a "young" mother — 25 years after the birth of her daughter.

And when her husband seems to be embarrassed at his impending fatherhood, Edith Lambert feels rejected and bolts in her car for Boston to think things over. When Harry arrives and begs for her forgiveness, she talks him into staying in Boston for a second honeymoon. He readily agrees, extremely relieved to have his wife back after thinking he had lost her.

There was one position that Maureen took in 1964 that just plain didn't work out. "The Today Show" was looking for a female co-anchor to share the desk with Hugh Downs and Jack Lescoulie. When she was first offered the job by producer Al Morgan, she turned it down because she was enjoying the successful run of *Never Too Late*. Morgan persisted, and eventually Maureen agreed to do the show just on Mondays until the end of the play in May, and then join the cast of "Today" on a full-time basis.

"It will be something very new in my entertainment career and I'm quite excited," said Maureen. "I don't mind having to get up early for 'Today.' I used to get up at 4:30 or 5 a.m., to go on movie location."

At the time, Maureen thought it would be a nice steady income for her family and an easy gig. The problems, plural, included the fact that she was NOT a morning person, and had to get up very early to get ready for the show. Maureen really loved to sleep late, read the papers, and relax and eat her breakfast. And since they weren't going to move the show to an afternoon slot, this became an untenable situation.

The final thing that grated on her was that she was a big star with a Broadway show, and she was interviewing people that were — well, not big stars. Some of the guests were her contemporaries, but many were people she had never met and she didn't know what to say to them. In the end, it just didn't work out, and Maureen left the show as graciously as possible after six months.

She did describe her position as the 'Today girl' as "asinine," and gave her reasons for leaving the show: "It's not enough to sit there and smile every day with nothing to do ... the show is simply no place for a woman."

Maureen decided to stick with stage work, which would keep her immensely busy over the next two decades. Proving she hadn't lost her sense of humor over the "Today" debacle, Maureen appeared with comedians Tom Poston and Orson Bean on the quiz show, "Stump the Stars," on August 3, 1964. Bean, of course, was one of her co-stars from *Never Too Late*. This show had been on for more than a decade as a summer replacement, and was hosted by Mike Stokey under various titles including "Celebrity Charades" and "Pantomime Quiz." Regular panel members over the years included Hans Conreid, Sebastian Cabot, and Stubby Kaye.

The actress also appeared on one episode of "Ben Casey" in January of 1965, her first dramatic television since 1961. The show was entitled *A Boy is Standing Outside the Door*, and Maureen portrayed Irene Crain. This was the most successful doctor show of the decade, starring Vince Edwards as Dr. Ben Casey and Sam Jaffe as Dr. David Zorba, with Franchot Tone as Dr. Daniel Freeland. Tone and Maureen were old friends going back to the early 1930s, and made a few movies together back in the day. Other guest stars on this episode were William Marshall, Susan Flannery, and Elsa Lanchester, the wife of the late Charles Laughton.

In November of 1965, Maureen was a celebrity auctioneer to raise money for the Dag Hammarskjold Memorial, which was a pedestrian bridge on 47th Street between First and Second Avenues in New York. Maureen auctioned off a Fiat automobile, and other items included a pillowcase that Beatle Paul McCartney had slept on, a beagle hound named Bess, a dress worn by Barbara Streisand, Gene Kelly's dancing shoes, various artwork, and a box of cigars autographed by Maureen O'Sullivan.

CHAPTER TWENTY-THREE
"The Affairs of an Older Actress"

Shortly after the death of her husband, Maureen began acclimating herself to the life of a single woman. This was an entirely different world than when she was a bachelor girl in Hollywood during the 1930s. Back then everything was taken care of for her down to the last detail by Metro-Goldwyn-Mayer, and she had received the star treatment.

Now in 1963, living in New York, she was a 51-year-old widow with six children. Patrick was the oldest at age twenty, and Tisa the youngest at age eleven. She was currently a Broadway star in the successful play *Never Too Late*, but all the little details of life were now her concern to handle without a partner to lean upon for support and guidance.

The apartment Maureen eventually found was located on Central Park West, on the eleventh floor overlooking Central Park. It was a classic old building, built around the turn of the century, with high vaulted ceilings at least ten feet tall. The whole apartment had a solid, dependable feel to it, with all the original floors, moldings and wall panels. Maureen would live in this apartment for the next twenty years, and she was quite grateful that she always had this safe haven to call her home.

There were nine large rooms including a huge kitchen with a butcher-block table that seated ten people. The ancient dumbwaiter in the larder wall was in disrepair, but when the building was first erected it had been a conduit from the basement kitchens which sent meals upward to the tenants. Maureen's bedroom had a black wrought-iron screen that divided her room, with an ivy plant that clung to the twisted slats. The other space was her office, a place to read, study her scripts, and meditate.

The apartment was large enough that it would accommodate all of her children, considering the older ones were striking out on their own. Mia married in 1966 and Patrick wed his sweetheart Susan the same year, which left Johnny, Prudy, Steffi, and Tisa still under the guidance of the family matriarch.

Eventually all of Maureen's children would leave the nest, marry, and have families of their own. After her divorce from second husband André Previn in the late 1970s, Mia Farrow and her children lived with her mother at the spacious apartment once again.

The more than two-year run of *Never Too Late* ended after 1007 performances, and Maureen had no intention of taking a break. She was in demand as an actress, and was getting multiple offers to star in various productions. The trick was to pick a good play, with a talented director and cast.

Her next work was in *Two Dozen Red Roses,* a comedy staged at the Pheasant Run Playhouse in St. Charles, Illinois (beginning the week of November 1, 1964). The three-act comedy was written by Kenneth Horne from an Italian play by Aldo de Benedetti, and was directed by David Morrison.

Two Dozen Red Roses starred Maureen O'Sullivan as Lindsay Verani and Bill Morey as her husband Alberto. The story is set in Rome, and takes place in the living room of the Veranis' house. The other characters are Tomasso (Lew Prentiss) as their best friend who is caught in the middle when they are both thinking of having an affair; Rosina (Corinne Carr), the Veranis' young maid; and Bernardo (Jerry McDaniel), the handsome florist who is the lover of Rosina.

Maureen's character of Lindsay Verani is described by the author as "a very handsome and attractive woman of forty — mercurial, impulsive and charming — though not always the soul of logic." (In the original 1949 play Mrs. Verani's name is Marina.)

The basic premise is that a married woman of forty (Maureen), decides to take a two-week vacation by herself because her marriage has lost its excitement. She feels that the attentions of other men might make her feel like a vibrant woman once again.

Her husband is hurt that she needs time away from him, and decides to spice up his own life by sending two dozen roses to a beautiful countess — whom he has never even seen — as his own form of "dalliance." When his wife Lindsay receives the roses by mistake with the anonymous card, the situations start to get sticky and interesting.

In 1965, Maureen began a national tour of *The Subject Was Roses,* a postwar drama by Frank Gilroy. This play concerns the emotional upheavals of an Irish family in the Bronx, and takes place in May of 1946. Gilroy noted his story was autobiographical to a certain degree, because he had come from an Irish family who had lived in the Bronx. It is a drama of a couple who are happy to have their soldier son home from the war, when many sons did not return. There are just three characters, and the events unfold over a two-day period. The director was Ula Grosbard, the personal choice of the author, Mr. Gilroy.

The principal players are Nettie Cleary (Maureen), her husband John (Chester Morris), and their son Timmy (Walter McGinn). The setting is the Cleary apartment, where a party the previous evening had welcomed Timmy home after the war. John and Nettie converse often about family matters, but rarely argue; now that Timmy is home their conversations are most often about him and what he will do now that he is a civilian. They are still in love, despite being married for over twenty-five years.

Father and son get along, but problems arise when Timmy wants to do his own thinking and strike his own path. John feels the mother and son are always siding together, and therefore he, more often than not, is the third wheel.

The young man drinks more than he should, every day, morning and night. Old wounds begin to fester, arguments erupt. Nettie is angry with her husband and leaves the apartment, disappearing for more than twelve hours. Both John and Timmy are worried about her, but both realize she needs some time to clear her head. When Nettie returns, she says she sat through several showings at the local movie theater. She thought matters over, and now everything is fine.

Timmy discovered a lot in the two days he had been home. He learned how his father met his mother, from both points of memory. He no longer blames either one for the things that were wrong; he is wise enough now to know that there is no blame to place. He also tells his parents he is getting his own apartment immediately so he can live his own life. They are both satisfied that this is a good decision.

The Subject Was Roses had originally opened on Broadway on May 25, 1964, with a cast of Jack Albertson, Irene Dailey, and Martin Sheen. The play was a winner of the Pulitzer Prize, Drama Critics Circle, and Tony awards.

When the play went on a national tour in September of 1965, Maureen, Morris, and McGinn took over the lead roles for the next two years including stops in Westport, CT, Millburn, NJ, San Carlos, CA, W. Covina, CA, Paramus, NJ, Chicago, Atlanta, Palm Beach, and a return engagement on Broadway at Henry Miller's Theater in February of 1966. The play closed in 1967 after 834 performances, which was a pretty good run considering the advance sale for opening night in 1964 (with the original cast) was $162. It is interesting to note that the standby for Walter McGinn was Dustin Hoffman.

Maureen's stage work continued to keep her feeling alive, and being the eternal optimist, she hoped romance would re-enter her life when the time was right. Her work and her children kept the still-youthful widow extremely busy, but deep in her heart she wanted to find a man to fill the romantic void. The actress had many male friends in the acting trade, and for a period she dated Van Heflin. The talented actor had many outstanding roles in his career, including the cop in *The Prowler* (1951), the farmer in *Shane* (1953), and the courageous deputy in *3:10 to Yuma* (1957).

Maureen was looking for that once-in-a-lifetime love that would bring her true happiness, and after a few years of playing the single girl she set about to find a lasting relationship: "Children don't take the place of a husband. Many women — and I'm one of them — need both. I'd like to find a strong, wonderful, brilliant man who'd be everything to me and consider me everything to him."

When her daughter Mia, age 21, began her relationship with 50-year-old Frank Sinatra in 1966, rumors persisted that they would soon marry. Maureen responded to the press about the age difference and joked, "Mr. Sinatra? Marry Mia? It would make better sense if he would marry *me*!"

However, Maureen was supportive of her daughter's eventual decision to marry Sinatra, and made the formal announcement to the press on July 13, 1966. The actress said she was "delighted" about the impending nuptials and added, "Frank is a wonderful person and I know they will be very happy."

When the marriage became reality six days later, Maureen could only sit back and hope it would work out in the long run. There were no members of either family at the ceremony, but Red Skelton was in the wedding party.

Of course, it's well-known and highly publicized that the union between Sinatra and Mia Farrow was rather short-lived. The popular singer-actor had his lawyer file separation papers in November of 1967, and the divorce became final in 1968.

One person who was hoping the relationship would work out was Frank's teenaged daughter Tina. She noted several decades later in her memoir, *My Father's Daughter,* that Mia had many admirable qualities and that she also had a very wonderful mother in Maureen: "It wasn't hard to see how Dad could have fallen in love with her," said Tina Sinatra of Mia. "As a bonus, my father got a dream mother-in-law: Maureen O'Sullivan, one of the world's warmest and most gracious people."

Maureen could hardly keep up with all the stage work she was offered over the next few years, and the money was pretty good. In one of her letters to George Cukor, she noted that her salary for her current play was $2000 per week plus an apartment and a car. Her tone was that of happiness and excitement, and she was obviously enjoying her continued success on the stage.

Next came a play by Robert Soderberg called *The Five-Oh-Seven* (aka *The Wednesday Problem*) which was staged at the Royal Poinciana Playhouse in Palm Beach in March, 1967. Maureen starred as Marian Plummer. This Florida theater was owned by Frank J. Hale, and the entire 10-week run of the 845-seat house was sold out before opening night in January.

The Five-Oh-Seven was one of several plays that were to be staged during the winter season, that also included: Nord Riley's farce *The Armored Dove,* starring Joan Fontaine and Tom Ewell; Lonnie Coleman's *A Warm Body,* with Dina Merrill and Kevin McCarthy; and William F. Brown's *The Girl in the Freudian Slip,* with Alan Young and Marjorie Lord.

Hardly taking a pause to catch her breath, Maureen returned to Broadway at the Plymouth Theatre for *Keep It in the Family,* a rather dark drama that was produced by David Merrick. Opening night was September 27, 1967, which followed a two-week preview at the Colonial in Boston. The play was written by Bill Naughton, who had recent successes in *All in Good Time* and *Alfie*. Patrick McGee, acclaimed as the Marquis de Sade in *Marat/Sade* the previous year, was cast as the iron-fisted father of the Brady family, and Maureen was his gentle wife, Daisy. Others in the cast included Marian Hailey as Florence Brady, Sudie Bond as Betsy Jane, Jeff Siggins as Billy Brady, Burt Brinckernoff as Michael Brady, and Karen Black as Hilda Brady.

Clive Barnes, in his *New York Times* review of September 28, noted that the play was not your average Broadway fare: "We are asked to believe in a monster — a suburban Barrett of a small-town Wimpole Street who rules his family with a whim of iron. He lives by the books — the Good Book and the cash book. His wife is made to render accounts, his children, who live in mortal dread of him, cannot smoke or read *Esquire*, and are expected to be punctual in their weekly contributions from their pay envelopes.

"As Mr. Magee's wife, Maureen O'Sullivan, the family's nurse and umpire, had a lovable graciousness that, while jarring with the more realistic conventions of Mr. Magee, was attractive in its own right. I liked also Burt Brinkerhoff as the gutsy but chicken-scared elder son. So there it is — a very mixed play perhaps but with pleasure as well as disappointment in the mixture. It is a cut above average and more worth seeing than most Broadway drama."

A month later, Clive Barnes once again had more good things to say about the acting of Ms. O'Sullivan: "Other good performances have enlivened our dramatic evenings. I'm thinking of Maureen O'Sullivan, Bert Brinckerhoff and, wrong-headed but magnificent, Patrick Magee in *Keep It in the Family*, Burl Ives in *Dr. Cook's Garden*, Alfred Drake in *Song of the Grasshopper*, William Redfield in *A Minor Adjustment*, Sandy Dennis and William Daniels in *Daphne in Cottage D*."

In mid-October, Maureen attended a party at the Rainbow Room on the 65th floor of the RCA Building to pay homage to Marlene Dietrich, who had just made her Broadway debut at age 62 at the Lunt-Fontanne Theatre. When Maureen arrived, career autograph seekers David Starr and Celia Gordon called out to the famed actress: "Oh, there's Maureen O'Sullivan. Hi, Maureen. Oh, she's gorgeous."

Other stars attending the party for Dietrich were Joan Fontaine, Tallulah Bankhead, Michael Cacoyannis and Irene Papas, Burt Bacharach and his wife Angie Dickinson, Dionne Warwick, Sybil Burton, Alexander Cohen and his wife, and others close to the actress.

You Know I Can't Hear You When the Water's Running consisted of four one-act plays, written by Robert Anderson (who was married to Teresa Wright). The original Broadway production opened on March 13, 1967, with a cast of Martin Balsam, George Grizzard, and Eileen Heckart. When the show moved to the Coconut Grove Playhouse in Miami, Florida (June 27, 1967, to June 2, 1968), the cast members were Maureen O'Sullivan, José Ferrer, and Ben Piazza.

The four vignettes were entitled *The Shock of Recognition, The Footsteps of Doves, I'll Be Home for Christmas,* and *I'm Herbert.* This was an evening of comedy, and the first story is about a playwright who wants to experiment with male nudity on Broadway.

The *New York Times* noted the following on October 20, 1967, extolling the outstanding array of talent in the Florida entertainment arena:

"The Coconut Grove Playhouse is enjoying one of its best seasons with José Ferrer and Maureen O'Sullivan in *You Know I Can't Hear You When the Water's Running.* Plays scheduled to follow it are *Lock Up Your Daughters,* the English musical, with Cyril Ritchard; *There's a Girl in My Soup,* with Van Johnson; a pre-Broadway tryout of David Merrick's new play, *Is the Real You Really You?,* and *Call Me Madam* with Ethel Merman."

Meanwhile, Frank Sinatra was at the Fontainebleau Hotel for a six-week run, and Jack Benny was performing at the Hilton Plaza; Diahann Carroll and Woody Allen were next on the schedule. Buddy Hackett opened at the Diplomat for two weeks, followed by Victor Borge, and then Allen and Rossi. At the Eden Roc, Sergio Franchi and Della Reese were performing in two different rooms, and others booked there were Don Rickles, John Davidson, Diana Ross and the Supremes, Earl Grant, and Belle Earth. Phyllis Diller opened at the Deauville, with The Temptations and then Phil Ford and Mimi Hines to follow. Now that is an impressive list of talent, all at one time, and somewhere other than New York.

Maureen next teamed up with Sam Levene in *Don't Drink the Water,* a comedy written by Woody Allen. Their characters of Walter and Marian Hollander were filled in the original Broadway production (1966) by Lou Jacobi and Kay Medford, and later in a film version (1969) by Jackie Gleason and Estelle Parsons.

The premise of the play concerns a New Jersey caterer (Levene) and his quirky wife (Maureen), and their funny situations while on vacation with their daughter in the Iron Curtain country of "Vulgaria." The basic plot was pretty thin: a family of three are thought to be spies, they are imprisoned, and they try to escape. The two veteran actors toured with the play over the summer of 1968, including stops in New Hampshire, Long Island, upstate New York, and Charlotte, Virginia.

The stage was now her life, and she relished every moment of the acting and travel. When she was semi-retired some thirty years later, Maureen looked back on the decade of the 1960s: "I especially loved touring and sometimes I would take my youngest child, Tisa, with me. It was something new and exciting as well as being a wonderful way to see America. It was also fun meeting up with people from my days in Hollywood who were doing the same thing.

"I was happy when I was working, but in between jobs I was often unhappy. I discovered how lonely you can be, even when you have your children around you. And going through the Sixties was a turbulent time for everyone. The children were all shattered by their father's death, but they kept it to themselves, and I'm not sure how they coped exactly. We didn't talk about it much, just got on with our lives as best we could. But it can't have been easy losing a parent and being uprooted from your home all at the same time."

In the summer of 1969, Maureen landed a starring role as Mrs. Baker in *Butterflies Are Free*, a comedy by Leonard Gershe. Co-starring was Keir Dullea as her blind son Don Baker, who moves into his first apartment in Greenwich Village. In defiance of his mother, Don insists on standing on his own two feet, and subsequently falls in love with Jill (Blythe Danner), the girl who occupies the adjoining apartment. According to author Leonard Gershe, the character of Jill in the play was inspired by his friend, Mia Farrow.

Butterflies Are Free previewed at the Cherry County Playhouse in Michigan on August 12, then moved to Falmouth Playhouse in Massachusetts, and then Westport Country Playhouse in Connecticut the final week of the month. Scheduled for a fall premiere at the Booth Theater on Broadway, the *New York Times* ran a marvelous photo of Maureen and Keir Dullea that announced: "*Butterflies Are Free* — Keir Dullea will be a blind young man making his way on his own, Maureen O'Sullivan his possessive mother, in the Leonard Gershe play which Milton Katselas is directing for an October premiere at the Booth."

Unfortunately, something happened between the preview run that ended in September and the scheduled Broadway opening in late October. Maureen was unable to take the role as planned, probably due to illness, and was replaced by stage veteran Eileen Heckart.

The Front Page, a farcical comedy written by Ben Hecht and Charles MacArthur, was staged at the Ethel Barrymore Theatre in New York. The production opened Saturday, October 15, 1969, and closed February 28, 1970, after 159 performances. The play was written in 1928 and first opened on Broadway that same year at the Times Square Theatre. It was also a 1931 motion picture with Pat O'Brien, Mae Clark, and Effie Ellsler in the role of Mrs. Grant.

This 1970 edition of the play starred Bert Convy as court reporter Hildy Johnson, Kendall March as his fiancée Peggy Grant, and Maureen O'Sullivan as her mother, Mrs. Amelia Grant. Robert Ryan also had a lead role as Hildy's boss, the tough newspaper editor, Walter Grant. The story takes place at the Press Room of the Chicago Criminal Courts Building, where a hanging is scheduled to take place the next morning.

When the condemned man escapes, a manhunt takes most of the court reporters across the city. After the man surrenders himself to Hildy Johnson, Mrs. Grant becomes a frightened witness and is temporarily kidnapped to keep her out of the way. Mrs. Grant is a middle-aged woman who is anything but happy with her daughter Peggy's choice of a prospective husband.

Other prominent cast members included Will Gregory, Conrad Janis, Val Avery, Peggy Cass, John McGiver, and Harold J. Kennedy, who also directed the production.

When the play originally opened on October 18, 1969, Helen Hayes portrayed the character of Mrs. Grant. On December 1, 1969, Molly Picon supplanted Miss Hayes, and on January 5, 1970, Maureen O'Sullivan replaced Picon for the balance of the run. Paul Ford also was a replacement in the role of the mayor.

Charley's Aunt is a classic English farce by Brandon Thomas and was first performed on the London stage in 1892, where it ran for four years at the Royalty Theatre. At one point, the play was running simultaneously in 48 theaters in 22 languages, including Esperanto, Chinese, Zulu, and Afrikaans. This current version was staged in the English language at the Brooks Atkinson Theatre on Broadway and opened on July 4, 1970.

There are rather hilarious complications when an Oxford College student impersonates his friend Charley's aunt, rather unwillingly, and the real aunt subsequently arrives upon the scene. Television star Louis Nye portrayed the impersonator, Lord Fancourt Babberly, who looked to be one of the oldest students in the history of college. The cast also included Michael Goodwin as Jack Chesney, Melville Cooper as Brassett, Rex Thompson as Charles Wykeham, and the director was Harold Stone.

Maureen's character, Donna Lucia d'Alvadorez, is the wealthy widow of a Brazilian millionaire and her only relative, nephew Charley, is a student at Oxford. She enters the story halfway through the second act, forcing the impersonator, Lord Fancourt, to exit, stage left.

The author described the character of Donna Lucia as "a well-preserved, beautiful, kindly woman of middle age, with a young face, but grey hair. She has a keen sense of humor, and is capable of taking charge of any situation. She is not at all sentimental, but has a deep feeling of real sentiment in her nature. She is dressed in an afternoon summer dress with a matching coat, hat and gloves, and carries several visiting cards in her purse-bag."

Reviewed by Clive Barnes of the *New York Times* after opening night, there was reason for optimism that the play would have a good run.

"It is a cheerful, sweet, funny and harmless play. It does have a certain innocence, even a certain uncomplicated logic.

"I liked very much the cool graciousness of Maureen O'Sullivan as Donna Lucia d'Alvadorez, Charley's real aunt. Melville Cooper's basset-hound expression as the scout, Brassett, and Martyn Green's flustered gentility as Col. Sir Francis Chesney had a definite authenticity.

"Mr. Stone has done his best, Mr. Nye and the others have done their best, but the show does look a little cheap, a little like an attempt to turn a fast buck. I doubt whether it will succeed at that commercial level. Yet there are decent enough things in it."

Proving that Broadway can be cold and ruthless, the play suffered from a lack of attendance and was killed after only nine performances. Maureen packed her bags, figuratively, and moved on to the next play.

One of the reasons why Maureen continued to work so hard was simply that she truly needed the money. All of her children had reached adulthood, but some were still living at home and she had plenty of expenses. Of course she loved her work as an actress, and it did provide a good income when she was working. In those days there were no residuals for actors from the countless classic films in which she starred from the 1930s. The "Tarzan" pictures alone should have made her a wealthy woman, but that injustice was a fact of life for all actors of that era.

Her burden, so to speak, was eased somewhat when two of her daughters got married the second week of September, 1970. On the 11[th,] Mia Farrow married André Previn in London, at the Rosslyn Hill Unitarian Church in the borough of Hampstead. At the time, Mr. Previn was the principal conductor of the London Symphony Orchestra. The maid of honor was Mia's younger sister Stephanie, and the best man was her fiancé, Jim Kronen. Mr. Previn's mother and Maureen were the only other guests present.

Two days later, on the 13th, Stephanie Farrow married Jim Kronen, an American artist. The ceremony took place at a country church in Leigh, a small village 20 miles south of London. In attendance were Mia and new husband André Previn, who played wedding music on the church organ. The proud mother, Maureen, was also present to experience the joy of witnessing two of her daughters walk down the aisle and say their vows. The grandchildren were also beginning to pile up for the family matriarch, the latest being twin sons that had been born in February to Mia and André Previn.

In 1970, Maureen and Johnny Weissmuller were reunited in the all-star comedy, *The Phynx*. It was their first motion picture together since 1942 in *Tarzan's New York Adventure*. Weissmuller attempted to describe the thin plot: "I read the script," said Johnny with a laugh, "but it didn't help much. All I know is, 35 celebrities are abducted to Albania. Some beatniks are involved in the rescue. It was frantic, and fun!"

The *Motion Picture Guide* said of the farcical drama:

"A disappointing all-star extravaganza with a silly plot that must have been sold to the assembled cast by one of the greatest con-men of all time."

Maureen and Johnny were among many old-time celebrities in this one, including Ed Sullivan, Xavier Cugat, Joe Louis, former Bowery Boys Leo Gorcey and Huntz Hall, Guy Lombardo, Andy Devine, Dick Clark, Dorothy Lamour, Jay Silverheels, ventriloquist Edgar Bergen and his dummy Charlie McCarthy, Ruby Keeler, Butterfly McQueen, Pat O'Brien, Rudy Vallee, Martha Raye, Richard Prior, and Joan Blondell.

This was also an opportunity for Maureen and Johnny Weissmuller to get together socially for the first time in years, one evening after shooting their scenes for *The Phynx*. Maureen, Johnny, and his wife Maria dined at the luxurious Scandia Restaurant, which was located at 9040 Sunset Boulevard in Beverly Hills. Kenneth and Teddy Hansen, a brother and sister-in-law team, founded the Scandia in 1946, serving Scandinavian cuisine.

Also present at the dinner was Maria's daughter Lisa; Weissmuller legally adopted her in 1971. Lisa's real father had been killed in WWII, so Johnny wanted to give her his name.

The restaurant was famous for its dish "The Oskar" which was named after a Swedish King. It was veal with bearnaise sauce, asparagus and crab legs. The foursome undoubtedly had the house specialty, along with Maureen's favorite, champagne, to toast the evening's festivities.

This dinner was probably the last face-to-face social meeting of Johnny and Maureen, as she was living in New York and he was living in Florida and then later in Las Vegas.

Lisa, who met Maureen for the first and only time, said it was a thrill to meet the woman who had portrayed Jane in Johnny's Tarzan films: "Maureen O'Sullivan was well-mannered and very much the lady. She was just plain classy and very beautiful."

Maureen and Johnny also got together for a photo shoot for the cover of the April 1970 issue of *Esquire* magazine, a beautiful color portrait of the couple thirty-five years after their heyday as Tarzan and Jane. The title of the article: "Tarzan and Other Heroes Come Back Once More."

Over the years, Johnny and Maureen were on the cover of hundreds of magazines worldwide, most often as their famous characters of Tarzan and Jane. Now a handsome middle-aged couple, this was their final portrait together.

In the summer of 1971, Maureen starred along with Cyril Ritchard in the Samuel Taylor comedy, *The Pleasure of His Company*. The actress portrayed Kate Dougherty, whose daughter Jessica is making plans for her impending marriage. The comedy in two acts takes place in the Dougherty home high on a hill in San Francisco, overlooking the Golden Gate Bridge.

The author described the character of Kate as "handsome and self-possessed." The preparations for the wedding become a state of chaos when her ex-husband Biddeford Poole arrives for the wedding and promptly moves in with Kate, her husband Jim, and daughter Jessica.

Ritchard recreated his Broadway role of "Pogo" Poole, a globe-trotting adventurer who rarely visits his daughter but nonetheless Jessica adores him madly. She has romanticized him as the perfect father who has finally returned home to his family. Kate's current husband Jim becomes quite jealous when he finds Poole romancing his wife, and he almost breaks his neck falling down when he sees Poole steal a kiss from Kate when she isn't looking.

Kate is not foolish enough to fall for the charm of her ex-husband, but she does react emotionally: "We're high on a hill in San Francisco, and it's a thousand and eighty years later, and I'm wind-blown every day of my life! Don't you turn it on for me, Pogo Poole! I'm an elderly, overweight clubwoman, and I like it, I like it, I like it!"

But it is Jessica that he is really after, as Poole manages to break up her impending nuptials and convince her to come with him on a year-long tour of the world. Kate is helpless to break the spell of Jessica's father, and in the end she realizes that getting to know her father in this way won't be a bad thing after all. And Jessica promises to marry her fiancé Roger in one year when she returns from her magic adventure.

Veteran actor Cyril Ritchard had starred in the original 1958 play at the Longacre Theatre, and also staged the production. His most famous role was as Captain Hook in the Broadway musical Peter Pan with Mary Martin. The villainous Hook was his signature role, winning Ritchard a Tony Award in 1955. More than a decade later, Ritchard and Maureen O'Sullivan delighted theater patrons with their own charming version of *The Pleasure of His Company* at several stops along the New England theater circuit.

Just to give one an idea of the acting talent that graced these summer playhouses, also starring on various stages in 1971 on the New England circuit were: Faye Dunaway, Mickey Rooney, Douglas Fairbanks, Jr., Jean Stapleton, Linda Lavin, Sheila MacRae, Sandy Dennis, Bernadette Peters, Leonard Nimoy, Hume Cronyn, Eli Wallach, Anne Jackson, Barbara Britton, and many other household names. Maureen worked this summer circuit for many years, whenever she wasn't hooked up with a Broadway play. The money was good, and the acting company was even better.

Other off-Broadway theater that Maureen starred in during the 1960s and 1970s included: *Barefoot in the Park* by Neil Simon, in the role of the mother-in-law, Ethyl Banks; *Heartbreak House* by George Bernard Shaw; *The Little Foxes* by Lillian Hellman; *Hay Fever*, performed by the Seattle Repertory Theatre with Maureen O'Sullivan as the Guest Artist (1970-71 season); *Butterflies Are Free*, in Denver, Colorado (1972); and *The Price* with co-star Howard Duff, which played at the Falmouth Playhouse during the 1973 summer circuit.

Maureen O'Sullivan received top billing, along with Tony Tanner, in *No Sex, Please, We're British*, which opened at the Ritz Theatre on Broadway on February 20, 1973, following a string of previews. The two-act comedy was written by Anthony Marriott and Alistair Foot, and was directed by Christopher Hewett. The action takes place in an apartment above a sub-branch of the National United Bank in Royal Windsor, England, on a Monday in June.

The cast included Maureen O'Sullivan as Eleanor Hunter, Tony Tanner as Brian Runicles, Stephen Collins as Peter Hunter, J. J. Lewis as Frances, along with Ronald Drake, John Clarkson, Leon Shaw, Jill Tanner, Robert Jundelin, and Jennifer Richards.

Maureen O'Sullivan with Tony Tanner in the ribald Broadway comedy *No Sex Please, We're British*

The story begins when Eleanor (Maureen) makes a surprise visit to her son Peter (Collins) and his wife Frances (Lewis) at their apartment. He is the manager of the bank directly below the apartment, and they are quite astonished to find out that Eleanor seems to be planning a lengthy visit of indefinite duration.

When Peter is wrongly delivered a package of pornographic photographs, he asks his friend Brian (Tanner) to get rid of the package. When Brian throws it in the Thames River, the police find the photos floating near a local college and are searching for someone they call the "Phantom Pornographer."

Next they receive a package of "blue" films and a large parcel of dirty books, and they are stunned at the onslaught of unwanted pornography from an unknown source.

Meanwhile, Eleanor remains oblivious to all these strange doings, and even finds herself a gentleman caller in Leslie Bromhead, a friend of the family. Mr. Needham arrives looking for Bromhead, and is offered the spare room to spend the night. When two young prostitutes show up and begin entertaining Needham, who is groggy from a sleeping pill, the situations become bawdy with sexual comedy.

No Sex, Please, We're British did not please Walter Kerr of the *New York Times*, who said in his review of March 4, 1973:

"Farce doesn't have to be plausible, of course. But it shouldn't be so gratuitously simple-minded — or, for that matter, so visually prosaic — that our strongest urge is to climb up on the stage and relieve those poor dithering people of the package ourselves. Anything to help them simmer down."

Mr. Kerr did note that the lead actress from Ireland did the best she could with the role, under rather trying circumstances:

"Maureen O'Sullivan, as a starchy and intruding mother-in-law, looks very well in the pleasant colors costumer Jeffrey B. Moss has washed over her, and is prepared to bestow a certain grace upon the proceedings; the part, however, does not return the compliment."

During the summer of 1974, Maureen did a lengthy interview with Kingsley Canham while she was starring in *No Sex, Please, We're British* before British audiences in London's West End. She was asked what it was like to be involved with so many films while working for MGM in the 1930s, and at times acting in three different films simultaneously:

"Perhaps I would shoot some Tarzan scenes in the morning," recalled Maureen, "then go on to *The Barretts of Wimpole Street* in the afternoon, and then some small film like *The Bishop Misbehaves* in the evening. But always they were shooting those Tarzan films, so I would have no idea how long each one took. I enjoyed changing from one film to another because I found that in motion pictures you have to have your own mental continuity anyway, as they are not shot in sequence. So it didn't make any difference really what I did in the morning or what I did in the afternoon.

"MGM's class or standard was largely due to Cedric Gibbons' influence on the sets and decor; his high standards were matched by Douglas Shearer's recording and the other departments. Of course, they had these marvelous writers under contract and Irving Thalberg was wise enough to use their talents. Very few of the producers were intellectuals *per se*, but they were so devoted to their work — that was all they cared about. The whole colony was orientated to work, and it was the substance of all conversation. It was a small world like that."

In late 1972, Maureen attended a dinner party in New York, and one of the other guests was actor Robert Ryan, whose wife Jessica had died of cancer in May of that year. Maureen and Ryan had leading roles in *The Front Page*, and their paths had crossed numerous times over the years.

Their casual friendship of the past was re-ignited at the dinner party, and they soon became a couple seen about town at the Broadway shows and restaurants. They hit it off so well that before long the relationship turned serious.

Ryan had a long career in the movies in lead and supporting roles, but he actually preferred the legitimate stage. As an actor he had many strong portrayals, and could play a brave heart or a duplicitous villain with equal aplomb.

Robert Walsten noted that she was good for him, and helped to lift him from the depression caused by the loss of his wife: "Maureen was wonderful for Robert because she was warm, sensible, Irish, and she understood his dark moods and how to cope with them."

Another friend, Albert Hackett, observed about the relationship between Maureen and Ryan: "Maureen fell madly in love with Robert, and I think they were going to be married. But Robert wanted to wait a respectable period of time after Jessica died before getting married."

An important factor for both to consider was that Ryan had been diagnosed with cancer of the lymph glands, which had been in remission since his initial diagnosis and treatment in late 1970. Ryan had been a heavy smoker all his life, and even his doctors told him it was too late to quit. Realizing the prospect of a short life expectancy, Ryan probably thought it unwise to marry and then leave Maureen a widow shortly thereafter.

In the spring of 1973, Ryan completed *Executive Action* (1973) with Burt Lancaster, who was a close friend of the actor. This turned out to be Ryan's last film, and by the end of June he had become a very sick man. On July 3, Ryan was admitted to Roosevelt Hospital in New York, complaining of a persistent and severe back pain.

Maureen was with him at his bedside for the next several days, when the doctors told her and the actor's three adult children that his cancer had returned and had spread to his lungs. By the evening of July 11, Ryan's condition had worsened and his lungs hemorrhaged, causing his death by suffocation. Maureen had faithfully stayed by his side to the very end of his life.

In the mid-1970s, Maureen found a little house in Rutland, Vermont, on Killington Avenue that was kitty-corner to the home of her son Patrick Farrow and his wife Susan. She described the house in a letter to George Cukor as "over 100 years old, and will be very special when it is fixed up." Maureen loved little houses, and would take one over a mansion any day. They were cute and comfortable, and the upkeep and maintenance were manageable.

Maureen also described her state of mind to her dear friend George when she said: "It's strange, I have found being alone far from the ideal situation in life. But, being buffeted around by the winds so to speak, is in the end rewarding. When I was married, I really did not know *what* I thought or felt because John's thoughts were so much a part of my daily living. And then one gets courage not to be afraid of what one is — whether it be good or bad. I suppose these are the rewards of getting older.

"Your letter, dear George, gave me an added dose of courage to be — perhaps the Maureen that lay hiding. You gave me a great, great lift!

"Very much love and how do I say I appreciate you being there all my adult life." (signed) Maureen

While most of Maureen's work during the 1970s was on the legitimate stage, she did act in the occasional made-for-TV movie, including *The Crooked Hearts*, which aired in November of 1972 on the ABC network. Based on the novel *Lonelyheart 4122* by Colin Watson, this was the story of a charming widow (Rosalind Russell), who joins a lonely hearts club to meet a man, who turns out to be the equally charming Douglas Fairbanks, Jr. Also in the cast were Michael Murphy, Dick Van Patten, and Penny Marshall.

Maureen's character was Lillian Stanton, the proprietress of the introductions service. Ross Martin was policeman Daniel Shane, who begins investigating the disappearance of two women who had been members of the lonely hearts club. The police begin the probe with Lillian Stanton, who appears to be an honest woman running a legitimate enterprise.

Rosalind Russell portrayed Laurita Dorsey, on the outside a prim middle-aged woman who purports to considerable affluence, but in reality she is a whiskey-drinking, cheroot-smoking con-woman who bilks wealthy bachelors. Fairbanks, meanwhile, was cast as Rex Willoughby, a suave fortune hunter who is capable of murder. When two women go missing, the police begin following Miss Dorsey in hopes of unraveling the mystery and also safeguarding her life. It turns into a deadly game of cat-and-mouse, as Miss Dorsey and Willoughby attempt to con each other, and neither is what they allege to be.

The Crooked Hearts turned out to be the last film role for Rosalind Russell, who died four years later at age sixty-eight. She had been a major star in the 1930s and 1940s, and both she and Maureen had been rivals for the same man, Robert Young, in *West Point of the Air* (1935). Her autobiography, *Life is a Banquet*, was published posthumously in 1977, and one of her more notable quotes about her profession was: "Acting is standing up naked and turning around very slowly."

A review in the *New York Times* by Howard Thompson said the telefilm was likeable, and that Maureen looked like a million (dollars, that is):

"A 90-minute exercise called *The Crooked Hearts*, in which Rosalind Russell and Douglas Fairbanks, Jr. try to charm each other out of money, is pleasant but wears exceedingly thin.

"The strangers have met through a place called Handclasp House (the funniest touch in the show), a kind of super-refined correspondence file presided over by Maureen O'Sullivan. Added to this, two detectives look in from time to time to remind us that a killer is loose and undoubtedly stalking Miss Russell.

"Finally, after much placid meandering, the whole thing is yanked taut by a vicious showdown the sleuths should have scented long before. Some viewers probably would settle for outright comedy minus the clanky hanky-panky, with Miss Russell simply being her rakish, lah-de-dah self. This lady's not for murder, she's for winks. And so, at this point, is Mr. Fairbanks, with his vintage courtliness.

"Miss O'Sullivan, looking like a million, Ross Martin, Michael Murphy and Kent Smith all do well in supporting roles, under Jay Sandrich's smooth direction of an equally smooth script by A. J. Russell. But better a short breeze than a long-winded teaser."

In October of 1976, Maureen had a starring role in the ABC television drama, *The Great Houdinis*, a screen biography of the famed magician of the early 20th century. Harry Houdini, portrayed by Paul Michael Glaser, was the greatest escape artist and illusionist the world ever knew and had an amazing career from his breakthrough in 1899 until his untimely death in 1926. At the beginning of his career he was a huge vaudeville star, later crossed the Atlantic to become an even bigger star in Europe, and went on to become a hero of the silent screen performing his amazing array of tricks and illusions for movie audiences.

Martin Beck discovered Houdini in a beer garden in St. Paul, Minnesota, and his handcuff escapes were just the beginning of almost three decades of public adulation for the man and his amazing magic. His escapes became more daring and mystifying and he became known as "The King of the Handcuffs" and "The Celebrated Police Baffler." In 1908, he introduced the famous milk can escape, and he reminded his audiences that "failure meant a drowning death." Also in his repertory were the extremely dangerous "manacled bridge jumps," as huge crowds gathered to see their hero escape unscathed from a possible watery death. And perhaps his most elaborate stunt of them all was the "Chinese Water Torture Cell Escape," which brought him his greatest notoriety and added to his fame as the world's most amazing escape artist.

The telefilm covered his early years of failure, his marriage to Beth (Sally Struthers) in 1894, and his lifelong devotion to his mother (Ruth Gordon).

Miss Gordon was nominated for an Emmy Award for her performance as Houdini's mother, Cecelia Weiss.

Maureen O'Sullivan portrayed Lady Doyle, who was the wife of Sir Arthur Conan Doyle (Peter Cushing), the author of the immensely popular Sherlock Holmes mysteries. Houdini and Sir Arthur became close friends during one of his early tours of England. But their friendship later became strained over the issue of Spiritualism: Sir Arthur and his wife were firm believers while Houdini considered it to be purely a fraud.

In an effort to prove to his friend that Spiritualism was real and that one really could communicate with the dead, Sir Arthur had his wife Lady Doyle (Maureen) conduct a seance with Houdini's departed mother, who had died in 1913. During the seance she went into a trance and wrote down a message which she claimed had come from the spirit of Cecelia Weiss, his dead mother. Houdini claimed that Lady Doyle's seance and the message were a hoax, which caused a severe rift in the friendship between the two men. In 1926, on his death bed, Houdini told his wife Beth that he would one day himself speak to her from the other world.

The Great Houdinis was written and directed by Melville Shavelson, and the cast also included Vivian Vance, Adrienne Barbeau, Bill Bixby, Nina Foch, Wilfrid Hyde-White, Geoffrey Lewis, and Jack Carter.

On Sunday, May 2, 1976, Maureen joined in a gala tribute at the Schubert Theatre, with well over 100 of the biggest names in Broadway. The evening was called, *George Abbott ... A Celebration,* and honored the director's 63 years as a Broadway producer, director, playwright, and actor. Mr. Abbott had been Maureen's director in her great Broadway success, *Never Too Late,* and they were close friends.

A partial list of guests saluting their esteemed colleague, in alphabetical order, included: Richard Adler, Christine Andreas, Desi Arnaz, Elizabeth Ashley, Alexandra Borrie, David James Carroll, Tim Cassidy, Betty Comden, Donald Corriea, Howard Da Silva, Fredd Ebb, Ed Evanko, Joey Faye, Arlene Francis, Martin Gabel, Jack Gilford, Ben Grauer, Adolph Green, June Havoc, Will Holt, Del Horstman, George S. Irving, Anne Jackson, John Kander, Maria Karnilova, Garson Kanin, Sam Levene, Shirley MacLaine, Liza Minnelli, Sono Osato, Maureen O'Sullivan, Julian Patrick, Eddie Phillips, Barry Preston, Harold Prince, Jerome Robbins, Donald Saddler, Alan Sanderson, Stanley Simmonds, Roy Smith, Tim Smith, Jean Stapleton, Maureen Stapleton, Jule Styne, David Thome, Eli Wallach, and Walter Willison.

Sabrina Fair by Samuel Taylor was first presented at the National Theatre in New York in 1953, with a cast that included Cathleen Nesbitt as Maude Larrabee, Joseph Cotten as Linus, and Margaret Sullavan as Sabrina.

During a one-year run at the Arlington Park Theatre, Arlington Heights, Illinois (June 1, 1976-May 31, 1977), Maureen O'Sullivan assumed the role of Maude Larrabee with a cast that included Martin Milner, Sylvia Sidney, Heather MacRae, Robert Urich, Richard Bowler, Marie Brady, and Barrie Moss. (Maureen did a lot of summer plays with Golden Age actress Sylvia Sydney — they used to "compete" to see who could get the best roles.)

The character of Maude Larrabee, as described by the author, is "a woman of grace and charm and determination. She has been a reigning beauty all her life, and at fifty-eight gives no sign of abdicating. She is fair and blue-eyed, bright and quizzical, and her smile is a devastatingly effective mingling of laughter and rue. She is slender and small-waisted and erect, with a bearing and walk that make her seem taller than she is. She has a way of speaking with a wide-eyed candor and directness that makes every remark of hers important beyond its meaning."

The story takes place at the Larrabee home on the North Shore of Long Island where Maude lives with her husband. They have two adult sons, Linus and David, who visit often. The family chauffeur, Fairchild, goes to meet his daughter Sabrina at the train station. She is returning to New York that afternoon after working five years in Paris. Sabrina left home as a shy girl and returned as a beautiful woman of the world, and David and Linus both find her incredibly desirable. But of course she also has a wealthy French boyfriend who wants to marry her, and thus things begin to get complicated.

Maureen also starred in *Ladies of the Corridor* in the summer of 1977, along with Barbara Britton and Lilia Skala. The 1953 play by Dorothy Parker was directed by William E. Hunt at the Tappan Zee Playhouse in Nyack, Rockland County, New York. The Tappan Zee was built on South Broadway in 1903, when Nyack was a quaint Victorian village — in its early years it was known as the Broadway Theater. The 750-seat theater had been dark for two seasons, but sprung to new life when the local government approved a $20,000 restoration loan, which touched off round-the-clock activity to prepare the theater for the five-week season.

A few years later, in January of 1980, Maureen hosted a party at the Rockland Lake Manor to help raise the $150,000 necessary to complete the refurbishment of the Tappan Zee. At that time, the Playhouse Preservation Association was trying to obtain landmark status for the red-brick, neo-classical building which had been a vaudeville theater and a silent-movie house during its early years of operation.

Motion picture retrospectives featuring films from the 1930s-1950s increased in popularity during the 1960s, and several of Maureen's classic MGM pictures were often part of these film revivals held at various venues. Of course the Tarzan pictures were re-released in the 1950s, a rarity for any film, but revivals continue to the present day. For example, the New York Museum of

Modern Art ran the first three Tarzan adventures in a Films for Children program in July of 1974; and a summer retrospective at the Regency Theater in New York included *Tarzan and His Mate* (1934), and the MGM classic, *The Thin Man* (1934). Other films that would pop up at various conventions and revivals included *David Copperfield* (1935), *A Day at the Races* (1937), *Pride and Prejudice* (1940), and all six of the O'Sullivan-Weissmuller Tarzan pictures.

In September of 1977, Johnny Weissmuller was scheduled to be the main guest at the Nostalgia Convention, a four-day event staged over Labor Day weekend at the Americana Hotel in New York. The former Olympic champion and movie Tarzan was immensely popular whenever he appeared in public, and literally traveled around the world promoting swimming as a goodwill ambassador for the sport and for the Swimming Hall of Fame in Ft. Lauderdale, Florida. Some of the convention highlights included continuous showings of many classic films, and newsreels from the 1939 World's Fair, in which Weissmuller and Eleanor Holm starred in Billy Rose's Aquacade.

This would be an opportunity for Maureen and her former co-star to have dinner and catch up on old times. Sadly, Johnny never made it to New York after suffering a stroke the week before in Los Angeles. This was virtually the end of Weissmuller's public life, as the stroke diminished his health and vitality and made him a recluse for his remaining years. After recuperating in the Motion Picture Hospital for a period of two years, he retired to Acapulco.

Johnny Weissmuller spent the rest of his days with his wife Maria, reading letters from his legion of faithful fans and basking in the sun until his death in 1984. During those last few years, Maureen often called Maria and asked about Johnny's health. On occasion, he would take the telephone and listen to the greeting and kind words of his former co-star and lifetime close friend. Because of the stroke Johnny had difficulty speaking, but hearing Maureen's gentle voice brought him great joy.

The Glass Menagerie is one of the most famous of Tennessee Williams' stage plays, and also has been filmed several times for motion pictures and television. Maureen O'Sullivan starred as Amanda Wingfield at the Music Hall in Cohoes, New York, during a five-month run from October 29, 1977 through March 19, 1978. Laura was played by Elaine Hausman, with Peter Webster as Tom, and the gentleman caller, Jim O'Connor, was Robert Bacigalupi.

The story takes place in St. Louis during the Depression, and Tom Wingfield recalls his youth while living with his mother, Amanda, and his slightly crippled sister, Laura. Tom is a sensitive young man who lives vicariously through the exciting adventures of the movies, but yearns to give up his menial job for his own life of adventure, perhaps as a merchant seaman.

Amanda often lives in the past, recalling her youth as a southern belle who had many gentleman callers. Amanda insists that Tom bring home for dinner a "gentleman caller" to meet Laura, a withdrawn, delicate young woman who is extremely self-conscious of her handicap. Tom brings home his co-worker Jim O'Connor, who coincidentally knew Laura from high school, and they strike up a fast friendship that Laura mistakes as romance. When Jim reveals that he is already engaged, Laura is devastated, but her mother insists that the future is still bright with the hope that things will work out. Tom, guilt-ridden over his failure to help his sister break out of her shell, joins the merchant marines to lead his own life.

Maureen O'Sullivan was excellent in her portrayal, and Tennessee Williams described the character of Amanda as "a little woman of great but confused vitality clinging frantically to another time and place. There is much to admire in Amanda, and as much to love and pity as there is to laugh at. Certainly she has endurance and a kind of heroism, and though her foolishness makes her unwittingly cruel at times, there is tenderness in her slight person."

Other great actresses who have portrayed Amanda Wingfield include Gertrude Lawrence in the 1950 motion picture with Jane Wyman, Arthur Kennedy and Kirk Douglas; Katherine Hepburn in a 1973 television version; and Joanne Woodward in a 1987 telefilm that was directed by her husband, Paul Newman. In the original 1945 stage production at the Playhouse on Broadway, Laurette Taylor played the role of Amanda Wingfield.

On the last day of April, 1978, Maureen and dozens of famous actresses, as well as a few actors, showed up at the Lincoln Center to pay tribute to George Cukor, who directed numerous classic films and was known as a director who brought the best out of the women in his pictures. Maureen had her own special relationship with Mr. Cukor, and they were lifelong friends.

Among the two-thousand guests present was his favorite female star, the reclusive Katharine Hepburn, who made a total of ten films with the director. Also in the audience to salute Mr. Cukor were the stars of some of his biggest pictures, including Angela Lansbury, *Gaslight* (1944); Ruth Gordon, *Two Faced Woman* (1941); Joan Bennett, *Little Women* (1933); Joan Fontaine, *The Women* (1939); and Shelley Winters, *A Double Life* (1947). Also attending as guests were several other female stars who never made a Cukor film but were close to the director, such as Gloria Swanson, Ruth Warrick, Dorothy Loudon, and Kitty Carlisle Hart.

Cukor admitted that *Little Women*, with Katharine Hepburn, Joan Bennett, Frances Dee, Jean Parker, and Edna May Oliver was his favorite film. Some of his other classic films included *Dinner at Eight* (1933), *Camille* (1936), *The Philadelphia Story* (1940), *Adam's Rib* (1949), *Born Yesterday* (1950), *A Star Is Born* (1954), *My Fair Lady* (1964), and *David Copperfield* (1935), the only film that Maureen O'Sullivan did for the legendary director.

The actress recalled that the praise she had received for doing the child bride's death scene in *David Copperfield* was not due to any great histrionics on her part, but the result of Mr. Cukor's unique directing gimmicks: "They raved about my agonized look and the tears in my eyes," she laughed, "but it was all because George was twisting my feet off-camera. I couldn't get it right."

Cukor, of course, was Mia's godfather, and Maureen recalled that he never forgot things like the children's baptisms, birthdays, first communions and graduations. "I'm surprised he had time to direct pictures," she joked. "He spent more time at the Good Shepherd Church, than he did at the studio."

During the years after John Farrow's death, the two would often dine together when she was visiting or working in California: "He had such exquisite taste. He always did things right, wonderful service, superb silver. I didn't like to talk about my work," noted Maureen. "It was just personal. George would always talk about the children. 'You have such perspective on your children,' he would say with a gleam in his eye, but then the whole issue made him laugh."

George Bernard Shaw's classic five-act romance, *Pygmalion*, was staged by the Center Theatre Group at the Ahmanson Theatre in Los Angeles between September 29, 1978 and June 2, 1979. The cast included Maureen O'Sullivan as Mrs. Higgins, Robert Stephens as Professor Higgins, Roberta Maxwell as Eliza, William Roerick as Col. Pickering, and Milo O'Shea as Mr. Doolittle. Completed in 1913, it is the story of an uneducated flower girl named Eliza Doolittle who goes to the esteemed Professor Henry Higgins and asks him to give her lessons in proper English and diction so she can move up in the world and work in a flower shop.

Seeing a challenge and the ironic humor in the situation, Higgins accepts Eliza as his student and also makes a bet with his friend Pickering that he can change this unwashed street-child into a sophisticated lady who could pass as a duchess within six months. As the experiment progresses, Eliza proves to be a fast study and within a few months her language, diction, and manners are vastly improved. Both Higgins and Pickering are developing a fondness for the girl, although neither will admit they have any emotional attachment.

At this point the Professor brings Eliza to visit his mother, Mrs. Higgins (Maureen), who sees the beautiful transformation and the emergence of a sensitive girl who has a heart of gold. Eliza realizes she has an ally in Mrs. Higgins, who sympathizes with the fact that she is seen as an experiment by her son who doesn't see the inner beauty and genuine character of his subject.

On graduation day, so to speak, Eliza passes all the tests with flying colors: a garden party, a dinner party, and an opera. No one even suspected that she was formerly a common guttersnipe, and Higgins is all full of himself with his triumph. With the experiment over, Eliza sarcastically asks if she can keep her new clothes and has an angry exchange with Professor Higgins.

In the middle of the night she disappears and goes to the home of Mrs. Higgins, her friend and sympathizer. When the Professor finds her there, he is distraught but won't admit to the fact that he has fallen for Eliza and rants and rages to cover his own emotional inadequacies. Mrs. Higgins orchestrates the situation to show off Eliza as the true gem that she is: a one-in-a-million girl now without the rough edges. Other guests at her home at the moment include Col. Pickering, and Eliza's father, Mr. Doolittle, who is about to be married.

When the Professor and Eliza are temporarily alone, they have a long animated conversation about how each has feelings, but they will be fine without each other. Both are crying out to be loved, but neither will say as much. When it is time to leave for Mr. Doolittle's wedding, the Professor tells her that he expects to see her soon, and she responds that she will never see him again. Mrs. Higgins takes Eliza in her carriage to the wedding, while the self-satisfied Professor remains by himself. Mrs. Higgins knows in her heart that they have fallen in love with each other, and despite their hardheaded personalities, they will eventually work things out.

When *Pygmalion* opened in Los Angeles, George Cukor sent Maureen a bouquet of flowers and a card wishing her the best in her new play. Maureen wrote back to her lifelong friend at the first opportunity:

"Dearest George, thank you for the lovely flowers and dear, dear note on opening night. I remember when I opened on Broadway in 'Never Too Late,' the courage you gave me then — the first flowers were from you.

"The play is going well and reviews, etc., are good. I greatly would like to invite you to see it, but I'm afraid I might be like Katharine Hepburn, who told me she goes to pieces when you are out front! Do you think?

"Perhaps not. I'm getting more secure. I hope you had a marvelous — and I know interesting trip — I hope to see you before I go. If 'Pygmalion' doesn't go to New York, I leave here next day for Lake Forest, Michigan where I will do 'Morning's at Seven' by Paul Osborn, with a good & lighthearted director in Vivian Matalon — lovely to work with. The tension created by John Dexter was so great, one could be electrocuted — but he was nice to me and more relaxed when we got to the theater. It is a lovely production [*Pygmalion*] — sets, clothes, & director!

"Lots of Love & Thanks dear George ..."

(signed) Maureen

Mandy's Grandmother was a one-hour CBS "Young People's Special" which starred Maureen O'Sullivan as the grandmother, Amy Levitan as Mandy, Kathryn Walker as Mandy's mother, and Philip Carlson as the father. *Mandy's Grandmother* was nominated for a 1979 Oscar for "Best Short Film, Live

Action" and was directed and produced by Andrew Sugerman. The basic premise of the story was that Mandy's grandmother (Maureen) visits her in America for the first time, and the family goes through a difficult period adjusting to grandma's presence.

The amazing and diverse array of acting projects continued for Maureen when she starred in the United Methodist Communications production of *One Who Was There* (1979), portraying Mary Magdalene. It is the story of a woman who witnessed the arrest and crucifixion of Jesus, and her difficult journey in the year A.D. 64 traveling from Jerusalem to her home in Galilee.

At this juncture of her life she is lonely and disillusioned, and haunted by the memory of the death of Jesus. Recalling the day of the crucifixion, she spoke the words: "We screamed, his mother and I ... no one heard. The men were not even there."

She recalls helping the women anoint the body of Jesus for burial, and on the following morning she returned to the unguarded cave with Peter and John. The cave was open, and the body of Jesus was gone. After everyone had left and she was alone, Mary saw Jesus one last time and he spoke with her.

The passing of the years had left Mary Magdalene haunted by her memories and her faith was shaken. The recent murder of Peter in Rome had left her empty inside, and her spiritual strength was eroded and overshadowed by despair.

But during her journey through the desert, accompanied only by a donkey, she meets several new friends who believe in Jesus and are spreading the word of his life and times. Her heart is touched by this new generation of believers who invite her into their home, to celebrate a baby's birth and to break bread with them. Mary Magdalene's heart is lightened by meeting these new friends, but still she is determined that she must return home to Galilee.

Before her journey is complete, she has realized that she has not lost her faith and that there is still work to be done. She turns the donkey around and they head back to Jerusalem, as Mary Magdalene returns to serve the only God in which she truly believes.

This was a project that was near and dear to the heart of Maureen O'Sullivan, who was a strong believer in the Christian faith. Joining her in the cast was her daughter Tisa Farrow, who portrayed the young Mary Magdalene in several flashback scenes. Also in the cast were Gregory Abels, Victor Arnold, Robert Dryden, and Hugh Moffat.

The story was written by Suzy Loftis and Donald Hughes, who also served as director. Much of the production was filmed in Israel, and Maureen had her work cut out for her in scenes where she is plodding along in the desert keeping pace with her donkey. Maureen had several poignant scenes and short soliloquies that construct the story and set up the flashback sequences. The actress at age 68 was still beautiful, proving that true beauty is timeless.

On November 18, 1979, the Theater Hall of Fame enshrined 51 Broadway artists at a gala celebration at the Uris Theater, and Maureen O'Sullivan was one of the 300 guests invited to salute the inductees. Among the artists honored were Harold Arlen, Shirley Booth, Henry Fonda, Katharine Hepburn, Lotte Lenya, Jerome Robbins, Tennessee Williams, Jason Robards, Boris Aronson, Rex Harrison, Arthur Miller, William Saroyan, Julie Harris, Jessica Tandy, and Hume Cronyn.

Maureen also accepted the award on the behalf of Henry Fonda, her co-star in the 1939 crime drama *Let Us Live*. They had been friends for decades, and had crossed paths many times in Hollywood and also on the Broadway theater circuit. Joseph Papp and Arlene Francis presided over the awards ceremony, which was held for the first time since 1973 — a hiatus attributed to a lack of money — and it brought the honor roll at the Theater Hall of Fame to a total of 183.

The famous actress was pretty much of a soft touch when it came to any benefit that helped to restore, resurrect, or save old theaters from the wrecking ball. A benefit for St. Malachy's Church, the New York theater-district church popularly known as the Actors' Chapel, was held on May 27, 1980 at the Sheraton Center Imperial Ballroom, 52nd Street and Seventh Avenue.

The dinner, dance, and show package featured such personalities as Maureen O'Sullivan, Ray Bolger, Dorothy Loudon, Helen Hayes, Bill Boggs, Nancy Marchand, Chita Rivera, Celeste Holm, John Kander and Fred Ebb, Maxine Sullivan, Debbie Allen, Danielle Brisbois, Marianne Tatum, Kay Armen, Frank McHugh, Ted Hook, and Vincent Sardi. Proceeds of the gala event were earmarked for the church's outreach program, which included a luncheon program for the elderly, a hypertension clinic, a Times Square clean-up program, and a community theater.

Maureen did win an award of her own in November of 1980, but it was of a completely different nature than an acting accolade. Maureen was given the Catholic Interracial Council's 1980 Hoey award as "a distinguished Catholic who has worked to combat racial and religious bigotry and discrimination in our society." The ceremony was held during a benefit at the Shubert Theater on West 44th Street, with actor Tony Randall as the master of ceremonies.

The actress was also starring on Broadway at the time, and when Thanksgiving arrived she was doing a matinee performance of *Morning's at Seven* at the Lyceum Theatre. Later in the day she told reporters that this would be "a perfect Thanksgiving — perfect because when I get home, everything will be ready." The turkey dinner, she said, was being prepared by her son, Patrick Farrow, who was also celebrating his 28th birthday, and his wife, Susan. Other family members who were expected to be present included Maureen's daughters Stephanie, Prudence, and Tisa. Also home for the holiday were daughter Mia and most of her children, who shared the huge apartment with Maureen.

CHAPTER TWENTY-FOUR
"Maureen Meets Her Match: James Cushing"

In 1980, Maureen attended an art exhibition of her son Patrick's work at a gallery in Rutland, Vermont. Patrick Farrow created various pieces of artwork in the medium of fine-crafted metal, including a replica of a nuclear-powered submarine that was scaled down to approximately three-feet in length. This was one of Patrick's first creations, and was considered a brilliant piece with every detail in replication of the original. Everything on the inside and the outside of the miniature submarine mirrored the original; if you opened a door, you'd see the corresponding room. All the portholes, doors, decks, gunnery, controls, and towers were perfectly replicated by skillful craftsmanship.

Another piece that Patrick built was a galleon, an 18th century Spanish sailing ship complete with all the masts, rigging and sails. Patrick had spent part of the summer of 1958 in Spain watching his father direct the picture *John Paul Jones* (1959), which featured numerous ocean battle scenes with three 18th century sailing warships locked in combat. Perhaps his inspiration for his nautical artwork had been viewing and sailing upon the actual ships that summer from his past.

On the occasion of the exhibit, Maureen was accompanied by actor Gary Merrill. They were currently working together in the Broadway production *Morning's At Seven*, which was being staged at the Lyceum Theatre.

Someone who was particularly interested in Patrick's submarine was a businessman from New York, James Cushing, a collector of various hand-crafted artwork. He also noticed Maureen as perhaps the most beautiful woman he had ever seen, and wondered to himself if he had any chance with the famous actress who was currently single. He had seen her movies throughout the years, and like most other men, he had a crush on the Irish beauty.

Now here she was at Patrick Farrow's art exhibit, and Jim Cushing was interested in two things: the miniature submarine and the mother of the artist. The gallery owner introduced Jim Cushing to Maureen O'Sullivan, and as they say in the movies, this was the start of something big.

Maureen later recalled that first meeting with her future husband:

"I immediately liked him and tried to find out more about him but all anyone would tell me was that he was a film buff, had his own construction business, and spent a lot of the time either at church or in charity meetings. 'Lord, how dreary!' I thought."

Jim Cushing did indeed purchase the submarine, which he thought was an outstanding piece and for which he paid a commensurate price. Also, through Patrick, he became better acquainted with Maureen and asked her to join him one day at the Saratoga race track in upstate New York, where his family had owned a box for decades. The box had been his father's, and then it was passed on down to Jim. Maureen enjoyed watching horse racing, but she wasn't much of a gambler and only made $2 bets.

The Cushing box was filled that day with various friends and everyone later went out to dinner. Maureen recalled that now she began seeing the "real" Jim Cushing — in an environment where he could relax and be himself:

"I realized that he wasn't dreary at all but, in fact, very interesting and knowledgeable. He did indeed know a lot about films but he wasn't a bore. Nor was he unbearably earnest."

The Saratoga racing season ran only from the last week of July through Labor Day, and thus Jim had a limited time frame to make his move. He asked Maureen to join him again at the track, and she said she would meet him at Saratoga. Jim made a bold gesture and asked if he could pick her up — Maureen said yes, and that made it an "official" date. And now, in the vernacular of the race track, they were off and running!

When Jim subsequently offered Maureen the use of his condo in Phoenix for a winter vacation, she responded that it would be fun only if he were there to show her the sights: "I had found him interesting and attractive from the start but when we were alone together in Arizona I fell completely and utterly in love with him and he did with me. That's the way it's been ever since."

Maureen O'Sullivan and Jim Cushing pretty much became a couple at that point, and to call them soul mates would be a true statement of their love and affection for each other. The qualities that Jim admired in Maureen were her personality, charm, wit, warmth, and her beauty. At age sixty-nine she looked much younger, and she was still one of the most beautiful women in the world. Jim was nine years younger than Maureen, but the age difference was never a consideration. She was young at heart and had plenty of energy, and Jim did his best to keep up with her.

"Jim is my best friend," said Maureen sincerely. "He's a wonderful man. I don't know what I'd do without him. Of course he gets a bit sour every now and again but we never argue."

Jim Cushing was a native New Yorker, born in Schenectady on July 1, 1920, to parents James Edward Cushing, Sr., and Mary Beatrice Sweeney. His only sibling was a sister, Mary Elizabeth (Beth). Jim's last two years of high school were at a private school in Connecticut, where one of his instructors, Paul Child, taught him art, etching, and jujitsu. Paul Child later married a woman who would become the world-famous chef, Julia Child.

Sometime after the turn of the century, Jim's father worked on the Panama Canal for four years, returned to New York briefly to marry his sweetheart, and then brought her back to Panama with him until the Canal was completed. In 1913, he used his experience in explosives to start his own business, Cushing Stone Company, which in time became very lucrative and allowed him to provide well for his wife and two children.

After high school, Cushing went to Nichols College in Massachusetts for a business education, and graduated in 1942. By this time the world was at war, and Jim signed up with the U. S. Army. Initially, he was assigned as a military policeman in New York City, where it was his job to keep off-duty soldiers from getting into serious trouble before they shipped out. Jim recalled that his time served in New York as an MP was the "most fun" that he had during his tour of duty. Later he transferred to the combat engineers, and by early 1945 the young serviceman arrived in Germany for the final months of the war in Europe. The primary objective of his unit was to rebuild bridges; as the Germans retreated, they would blow up their own bridges rather than leave them intact for the Allied forces to cross.

After serving 42 months with Uncle Sam, at the war's conclusion, Jim went into business with his father. Eventually, he took over the family stone enterprise and soon expanded into other construction-related ventures. He was a successful businessman, and made considerable money in his life. As life progressed, Jim would come to own three homes simultaneously: the Cushing family homestead in Schenectady near the Mohawk country club; a four-bedroom Yankee Barn in Grantham, New Hampshire; and later a condo in Phoenix to escape the harsh New England winters.

Although he was a bachelor, it was a rather unique situation. Cushing had raised his sister's three children, Cindy, Willard, and Jim, after his sister Beth and her husband both died. Cushing, who was the godfather to his sister's children, took over the responsibility of being father, mother, and uncle all rolled into one.

Cindy Amerson recalled the circumstances to your author in 2006: "My parents died when I was sixteen years old. They were very ill for a long time. I have two younger brothers, James and Willard. Uncle Jim was my godfather. He adopted all of us and we went to live with him. He dropped everything for us. He also had to run the family business as his dad died right after my mom and dad. If it weren't for him, I don't know where I'd be right now. He's been quite the dad to us all! He got me to come to Arizona for college because he loved it and was buying a home here."

As the love affair deepened between Maureen and Jim, she sold her little house in Rutland and also gave her New York apartment to her daughter Mia. By this time Maureen's oldest daughter was divorced from second husband

André Previn, and in addition to their three birth children Mia had begun adopting several orphans. So she was very happy and appreciative of getting the apartment on Central Park West for herself and her large family.

By the summer of 1983, Jim and Maureen had been together for three years, and he popped the question. Maureen said "yes" and the wedding date was set for August. They decided on a small private wedding to be held at Siena College, where Jim was a member of the board and also a close friend of Father Hugh Hines, the board president. (Siena is a Franciscan liberal arts college located in the suburbs of Albany, New York.)

They were married on August 23, 1983 by Father Hines, with close friends Albert and Jane Gorman as the best man and matron of honor, respectively. For the honeymoon they spent the night at the Woodstock Inn in the Vermont countryside, which was about 35 miles from their home in New Hampshire. The Gormans hosted a luncheon for Jim and Maureen, along with Father Hines, at a private club in Albany.

Wedding day photo of Jim and Maureen, with Albert and Jane Gorman

Before they were married, the couple had decided that the wedding should be either very large, because of the large families and many friends, or very small. They chose the latter because it seemed to be the right fit for the situation.

In the spring of 2006, Jim Cushing spoke with your author David Fury about his relationship with Maureen and their years together:

"We enjoyed going to the theater, Broadway shows, and then out to dinner," remarked Cushing. "Sometimes we'd leave after the first act, if the play wasn't that great ... one time it was a Neil Simon play, so you can never tell what will be good by the author. After the show we'd usually go to dinner at a little French restaurant on 57th Street that we loved ... it's a shame it's closed now. Sometimes we'd meet John and June Springer there for dinner ... he was Maureen's publicist and they were both good friends of ours.

"Maureen loved to dance, ballroom dancing. She took pleasure in walking anywhere, and swimming sometimes in our pool in Schenectady. My wife was an avid reader, both fiction and nonfiction, and one thing she really LOVED was sleeping late, often till noon. I would go out to breakfast with friends, and then come home and she would have made some brunch and would eat it in bed. Most people don't know that Maureen also wrote short stories that were published in magazines in the 1960s and 1970s, including one that was called 'The Umbrella.'

"She really enjoyed driving and had an Oldsmobile, late 1970s model, and one day we were traveling in separate cars. I started ahead of her and pulled over to the side of the road and stood by my car, assuming she would see me and pull over. When I saw her approach, she didn't slow down at all and just barreled on by me!

"I tried to catch up with her and didn't succeed, and I returned home and waited for her. Somehow Maureen got lost and was almost out of gas, and she fortunately located a highway patrol office and stopped in there for assistance.

"This very nice female officer went and got some gas for her car, and then followed her until she got back to the right road for Schenectady. I was worried sick and figured the worst had happened, but it turned out to be nothing at all. We did have a good laugh about her blowing right by without even seeing me as I frantically waved my arms in vain!

"Maureen loved doing summer stock and in 1986 was offered a part in *Barbarians* at the Williamstown Summer Festival; she also did *Love Letters* there in 1994. We'd often stay with Dr. Bill Everett, who was the board president, and his wife Genater. If their house was full we'd stay at the Hotel Orchards.

"In the early years, Nikos was the artistic director, and he was later succeeded by Peter Hunt, who became a good friend to both Maureen and myself. There were usually two plays going, one on the main stage and another on the smaller stage.

"We enjoyed going to Williamstown every year for their summer season, which was located at Williams College in Massachusetts. On those two occasions Maureen acted on stage, the other times we were there as guests just to enjoy the wonderful plays they put on each summer. There was an amazing level of talent there and other small theaters across the country — sometimes the plays were better than what you could see on Broadway."

Maureen also decided to learn to cook after she had known Jim a few years, and eventually she did indeed get the knack of the culinary arts: "When I got married to Jim I decided that finally it was time to teach myself to cook," noted the actress. "It was all trial and error to start with and I experimented with some very ambitious recipes.

"When Mia and I used to share the flat in New York we would cook by Zen. We'd put a steak in the oven and wouldn't take it out until one of us said, 'I feel it's cooked now,' then the other would say, 'Yes, I feel it's cooked, too.' We put ourselves in the position of the steak and we were always right."

About his wife's cooking skills, husband Jim Cushing said of Maureen: "She was a good cook without ever claiming to be one."

Throughout the years that Jim was "courting" Maureen, she stayed busy on the stage with several productions that ran anywhere from a few weeks to almost two years. When they first met she was on stage in the critically acclaimed *Morning's at Seven*. It had been almost seven years since she had been in a major play on Broadway, even though she had worked steadily in regional theater productions.

There was quite a buzz along the Great White Way that Maureen was returning to Broadway, as reported by Carol Lawson in her "News of the Theater" column of November 21, 1979:

"Maureen O'Sullivan, who has not appeared on Broadway since 1973 — in the short-lived *No Sex, Please, We're British* — is talking about returning this winter in a revival of Paul Osborn's comedy *Morning's at Seven*. She acted in the play last summer in Lake Forest, Ill., and the production sparked interest in bringing *Morning's at Seven* back to New York.

"Although Miss O'Sullivan is talking about doing the show, her words for publication are guarded. 'The contracts aren't signed yet,' she said. 'I'm so superstitious. This is a delightful play, and I hope and pray that it goes through. I think we'll go into rehearsal in February.'"

The original production of *Morning's at Seven* opened on Broadway on December 1, 1939, and played only 44 performances despite respectable reviews. It was directed by Joshua Logan and had a distinguished cast that included Dorothy Gish and Enid Markey, the actress who created the role of "Jane" in the first Tarzan picture in 1918.

Maureen was hoping that her return to Broadway would create something of a mother-daughter act, because her daughter, Mia Farrow, was starring in *Romantic Comedy* at the Barrymore Theatre at that current time. "Won't that be nice?" quipped Maureen. "Anything can happen in the theater — and does. That's why we love it so much. Mia and I hope to do a play together next, but I'm not free to talk about it yet."

Morning's at Seven turned out to be a much bigger success than anyone's wildest dreams, and was somewhat of a tribute to writer Paul Osborn's undying belief in his own work. Osborn, who was at opening night with his wife Millicent, waited more than forty years for this play to be recognized as an outstanding literary work. Maureen became good friends with Millicent Osborn, and they stayed in touch over the years. When Paul Osborn died in 1988, Maureen and husband Jim attended the memorial service for the writer.

Morning's at Seven opened on April 10, 1980, at the Lyceum Theatre on Broadway and concluded to thunderous applause. The story revolves around four sisters who have lived in a small mid-western town their entire lives, and now in the year 1922, they are all in their mid-60s to early-70s. Two of the sisters, Cora (Teresa Wright) and Ida (Nancy Marchand), live next door to each other with their husbands. Cora is married to Thor Swanson (Maurice Copeland), and Ida is married to Carl Bolton (Richard Hamilton).

Nancy Marchand, Elizabeth Wilson, Maureen, and Teresa Wright in *Morning's at Seven*

Down the street resides a third sister Esther (Maureen), who lives with her husband David Crampton (Gary Merrill). She is known as Esty, and is the oldest at age 72 and most petite of the sisters.

The Boltons have a 40-year-old son Homer (David Rounds) who lives with them, and he in turn has a 39-year-old girlfriend, Myrtle (Lois de Banzie) to whom he is secretly engaged. The fourth sister, Aaronetta (Elizabeth Wilson) has always lived with Cora and Thor, and she has never married. Aaronetta is called Arry by the family members.

Although this premise may sound dull at first glance, *Morning's at Seven* was really a comedy of the highest order, and brought heartfelt laughter and even tears to the audiences. Some of the funny situations included one of the husbands, Carl, who has spells that put the entire family into a state of trauma. These aren't fainting spells, but when he begins bemoaning his fate, that he has wasted his life by not taking the correct "fork in the road" and becoming a dentist, he places his head against the wall and, in a small house, everyone has to walk around him. When he is 20 minutes late one evening, Ida wants the river dragged for his body — only there is no river in this small town.

Esty's husband David is a control freak who wants to monitor her every movement, and she must sneak out in order to visit with her family. When he strolls down one day and catches his wife with her sisters, he declares that now she is a "free agent" and can do whatever she pleases with her life. He also tells her that they will "split" their house, with she taking the upper floor with the bathroom, and he will live in the lower level. Esty doesn't know what to make of this, but she and her sisters all agree that David is losing it and perhaps needs to be committed to an institution.

A more serious situation arises when Arry writes a letter confessing to her sister Cora that she once had a romantic tryst with her husband Thor, just the one time when she was seventeen and Cora was sick in the hospital. There are moments of hilarity when the letter falls into other hands, and various sisters are chasing each other from house to house to reclaim the letter.

Even though Homer has been going out with Myrtle for twelve years, this occasion is the first time he has brought her home to meet all of his family members, including his eccentric aunts and uncles. Homer and Myrtle announce they are to be married, but no one can believe it. When the engagement is called off, it is because Carl decides to move down the street to live with David — Homer feels he must stay at home and care for his mother Ida.

When the last big announcement is made that Myrtle is pregnant, the marriage is back on, even though no one can believe that bland Homer really had it in him. It turns out he was just shy, but now has a real life planned with his new bride. When Esty hands the incriminating letter to Cora to read, despite the protestations of Arry, all the family secrets are out in the open.

Cora asks Arry to move out, so she and Thor can have their final years together. Arry soon finds a new home with Ida and Carl, who are more than happy to have her come live with them.

Above: Maureen and Paul Ford had a big hit and a two-year run on Broadway in *Never Too Late* ... the play was later produced as a motion picture (1965).

Left: Maureen with Chester Morris and Walter McGinn. The trio starred in *The Subject Was Roses* in a national tour, 1964-65.

Above: The entire cast of *Morning's at Seven*, which won the 1980 Tony Award for Best Revival ... Maureen is at the far right, seated
Below: Maureen as Mrs. Higgins with Robert Stephens in *Pygmalion* (1979)

Maureen and Jim's wedding day, August 23, 1983 …

Maureen says "I do" and Jim kisses his new bride

Above: Maureen with Ione Skye in a sci-fi thriller, *Stranded* (1987)
Below: Publicity photo for *Hannah and Her Sisters* (1986)

Above: Close friend Father Hugh Hines presided over the wedding of Jim and Maureen in 1983
Below: Jim, Kathleen Turner, and Maureen at the Broadway premiere of *Cat on a Hot Tin Roof*

Above: The whole town of Boyle, Ireland turned out in 1988 to greet Maureen and dedicate this plaque ... which was placed on the building on Main Street where she was born on May 17, 1911

Below: Town officials congratulate Maureen on her special day

Above: Hal Roach, age 99, and Meredith Harless toast their good friend on her special day at the Walk of Fame party in 1991
Below: Maureen with son Patrick Farrow and his daughter, Theresa. The actress is holding the plaque which is a replica of her star on Hollywood Boulevard, placed directly next to Johnny Weissmuller's star.

Above: Jim and Maureen in the kitchen of their Phoenix home ... 1998

Below: Maureen and Jim are smiling despite being caught in the rain on the day of her Walk of Fame ceremony in Hollywood ... February 27, 1991

By this time David has realized he was a fool to give his loving wife an ultimatum. He apologizes to Esty and admits that they have had a good life. When David asks his wife if she ever felt the years were wasted, Esty responds warmly, "No, David. But, you see, I always had you."

The reviews for *Morning's at Seven* were outstanding, and Walter Kerr of the *New York Times* said in his column of April 11, 1980:

"This seems to me a perfect production of uniquely shaped play, merry and mellow and just possibly a bit mad."

About Maureen, pushing age 69 but still vibrant with eyes that enchanted even without the advantage of a motion picture close-up, Mr. Kerr noted:

"Fourth sister: Maureen O'Sullivan, declaring herself 72 with her everlastingly pretty smile and sneaking by to see her kinfolk though husband Gary Merrill has forbidden her to. Mr. Merrill finds his in-laws spectacularly unintelligent, and, wearing his most genial grin, tells them so to their faces. In fact, he threatens, if his wife keeps on seeing them he's going to split up his house and seal her off on the second floor. Naturally, she continues to see them; otherwise we wouldn't have those knowing eyes to look at or her well-remembered, faintly frog-like voice to listen to. And, naturally, she gets caught, a situation which at least solves her identity problem. 'I know where I'm at,' she instantly and cheerfully announces, 'I'm on the second floor.'"

Frank Rich, in his *New York Times* column of August 8, 1980, called *Morning's at Seven* the best play in town, and considering that this was Broadway, that was quite a compliment:

"I must confess that, for me, both the best play and the best musical in town are old shows. *Morning's at Seven*, the 1939 Paul Osborn comedy at the Lyceum, not only holds up well, it also looks more modern than such contemporary message plays as *Home* and *Children of a Lesser God*. Though Mr. Osborn's subjects are loneliness and death, he doesn't lecture the audience; his serious concerns fly in on the wings of offbeat laughter. The central characters, four elderly sisters in a 1920's Midwestern town, could not be in the hands of better actresses: Nancy Marchand, Maureen O'Sullivan, Teresa Wright and Elizabeth Wilson."

Anna Quindlen of the *New York Times* noted on April 20, 1980, that the four women stars of the play were in reality as close as any real-life siblings:

"We really are like sisters, I swear to God," laughed Teresa Wright. "Sometimes I really think we are."

"So, apparently, do the audiences for *Morning's at Seven*," wrote Miss Quindlen, "the play in which the four actresses star. The revival of Paul Osborn's 1939 comedy about four aging sisters and their family relationships scored an overwhelming critical success when it opened last week. Downstairs, at the Lyceum, on the bulletin board, are reviews that pronounce the production, directed by Vivian Matalon, 'superb,' 'enchanting,' 'wonderful,' 'a triumph.'"

Elizabeth Wilson, who portrayed Arry, added that the marvelous collaboration was a result of the caring attitude of the entire ensemble cast:

"It's the nature of good work. It's the nature of this play. It's the nature of Vivian and Paul."

Maureen chipped in with her own two cents worth: "And its in our own natures. There's not a stinker in the whole bunch."

Anna Quindlen added the comment that "Miss O'Sullivan punctuated her words with the melting smile that may be one of the great legacies of the motion pictures of the 30s and 40s."

The veteran actress also noted that when she went to meet with Mr. Matalon about the role of oldest sister Esther, he convinced her that she was perfect for the part:

"He said, 'Don't you know you *are* Esty? You see things a little off.' And he was right," said Maureen. "I feel perfectly comfortable with Esty. She's childish in a way but also very smart. And I love the play." She also added that she couldn't have been any happier at this moment, "Now I'm just floating."

One more tidbit from Walter Kerr of the *Times* explains why this play was special, and not your common Broadway fare that was soon forgotten:

> "*Morning's at Seven* ... the acting and staging and writing are all so funny and perceptive and emotionally gratifying. But the director, Vivian Matalon, has done one more thing, and I think it's quite original and not the same old last year's thing.
>
> "By 10:30 we've unraveled almost all of three families' tangles, in part most touchingly, in part hilariously. But Maureen O'Sullivan and Gary Merrill, as the most intelligent and most firmly estranged of the couples, haven't thrashed matters out yet. Miss O'Sullivan may be wearing a contented smile, but her smile doesn't indicate a compromise. Mr. Merrill may have a wicked grin on his face, but he hasn't given in or given up. They are now about to talk. Maybe.
>
> "But it's the end of Paul Osborn's play and, if the production were an ordinary one, the curtain would probably be lowered gently as they stare at each other across the lawn. Not here, not now. Just as we're waiting to hear the first syllable exchanged between them, Mr. Matalon slams down every last one of his lights, pitching the stage into a staggering darkness."

When it came time to hand out the Tony Awards for 1980, *Morning's at Seven* scored big, winning the Tony for "Best Revival of a Play," "Best Director" (Vivian Matalon), and "Featured Actor" (David Rounds). The Tony Awards were founded in 1947 as a memorial to Antoinette Perry, who headed the American Theater Wing during World War II. Even though they didn't win a Tony, Frank Rich said of the four women stars on the night of the awards: "Nancy Marchand, Elizabeth Wilson, Teresa Wright, Maureen O'Sullivan are the theatrical family of one's dreams in *Morning's at Seven*."

. The prestigious "Drama Desk" awards came out in June of 1980, and a Special Drama Desk award for "Ensemble" acting went to Maureen O'Sullivan,

Nancy Marchand, Elizabeth Wilson, and Teresa Wright as the four sisters of *Morning's at Seven*. Also winning was Vivian Matalon for "Best Director" and Lois de Banzie for "Outstanding Featured Actress" for her portrayal of the prosaic Myrtle.

Morning's at Seven continued into 1981 playing before enthusiastic audiences. In February of that year Kate Reid replaced Nancy Marchand in the role of Ida Bolton — the production didn't miss a beat, and happily marched onward. By the summer of 1981, the cast was vastly different, with only Maureen remaining (and Kate Reid), and now joined by Carmen Mathews, Nancy Kulp, and Sheppherd Strudwick replacing original cast members.

When the play finally shut down later that year, it still had another life in the form of an A&E/CBS video production that played on the Showtime network in September of 1982. Once again directed by Vivian Matalon, the cast included original members Maureen O'Sullivan as Esty, Elizabeth Wilson as Arry, Teresa Wright as Cora, Maurice Copeland as Thor, along with Kate Reid as Ida, King Donovan as Carl, Robert Moberly as Homer, Charlotte Moore as Myrtle, and Russell Nype as Maureen's stage husband, David Crampton.

One additional accolade for Maureen came from the 1983 Cable Ace Awards, when she was nominated for "Best Actress in a Theatrical Program" for her marvelous portrayal of Esty Crampton. After the final votes were tallied, Maureen was a bridesmaid, losing out to Julie Christie in the filmed version of the Terrence Rattigan play, *Separate Tables*.

On April 18, 1983, Maureen was the host to a gala party at the Century Café on W. 43rd Street, to benefit the New Amsterdam Theater Company, an organization dedicated to the preservation and performance of old musicals. The benefit followed a performance of the vintage musical *Rosalie*, by George Gershwin and Sigmund Romberg. Two of the stars of the show, Dina Merrill and Cliff Robertson, also joined Maureen at the benefit. The evening's entertainment included several Gershwin tunes from the show performed by pianist Steve Ross and singer Paula Laurence, and the Gay Men's Chorus Chamber Choir.

Another summer stock play that Maureen did was *Outward Bound* at the Playhouse in Ogunquit, Maine, in July of 1983. Maureen co-starred with Tammy Grimes, John Ireland, David McCullum, Keir Dullea, and Tyrone Power, Jr. On closing night Tammy Grimes gave a pearl necklace to Maureen that Jim Cushing said left her "dumbstruck" at the generosity of the gift.

Gradually around 1983, Maureen began finding most of her work away from the stage, initially in various television roles and then her big comeback in motion pictures in 1986. *All My Children,* set in the fictional East Coast suburb Pine Valley, arrived on the soap scene in 1970, and Susan Lucci as

Erica Kane has out-survived a string of husbands since that time. Maureen joined the cast in April of 1983 as Olive Whalen, and her character, as the soaps are inclined to do, was eliminated a few weeks later.

The actress found the daytime soaps to her liking, and in the fall of 1984 she joined the cast of the CBS soap opera, *The Guiding Light*. The long-running daytime stalwart had come on the air in 1952, and was still going strong well into the 21st century. *The Guiding Light* was set in the fictional city of Springfield, and the drama revolved around the complex and often convoluted lives of the Bauer, Spaulding, Lewis, Marler, and Cooper families.

When Maureen joined the cast as Miss Emma Witherspoon, she was scheduled to be killed off after a few weeks. She joked to her friends at the time, "Things are going well with the show, so I won't be taking the poison pill for a while yet."

The character given the assignment of killing Miss Witherspoon was the evil Susan Piper, portrayed by Carrie Nye. "I played a murdering, thieving, bad-to-the-bone person," recalled Nye in 1985. "I poisoned Maureen O'Sullivan, and that's like killing Bambi's mother. I thought I'd get death threats ..."

Too Scared to Scream (1985), a made-for-TV murder mystery was originally filmed in 1982 under the title *The Doorman*. Longtime television cop Mike Connors starred as Lt. Dinardo, who teams up with female undercover officer Kate (Anne Archer) to solve a series of bizarre murders in a Manhattan luxury brownstone. British leading man Ian McShane portrayed Hardwick, a Shakespeare-quoting doorman who is the prime suspect.

Maureen probably felt right at home, as she had lived in a Manhattan apartment building just off Central Park for the past twenty years. She played the role of Inez Hardwick, the invalid mother of the suspect, who doesn't even realize that her rather strange son is being tracked by the police.

Maureen O'Sullivan received an Honorary Degree from Siena College in New York on May 22, 1983, and one of the guests to honor Maureen on this date was California governor George Deukmejian, who had been elected to office a few months earlier in the year. Deukmejian was a 1949 Siena graduate himself, and came to honor Maureen and the other honorary graduates on this date.

Maureen and the "Duke" were on opposite sides of the political fence, and she was concerned that they might get into a political brouhaha. But he was very nice to her and they got along quite well. Maureen had never attended a day of college in her life, but she was thrilled to be honored for her sixty-three years of dedication to the acting trade and her many years of education at the "school of hard knocks."

Honorary degree from Siena ... Father Hines (left), Maureen, George Deukmejian (far right)

Jim Cushing retired in 1985 and sold his business so he could relax and enjoy life with his wife. They traveled some, and Maureen acted in occasional plays, movies and TV shows. They would visit her six adult children and the grandkids whenever they could. Maureen told the youngsters, "Call me Grandma Maggie," after the moniker that Johnny Weissmuller had given her when they first met in 1931. Some years Jim would book a table at the Hanover Inn near Dartmouth for Thanksgiving, and they would be joined by Patrick and Susan and their kids. On occasion there were those special family gatherings that included her other children Prudence, Stephanie, Theresa, Mia, and John, and lots of grandchildren as well:

"My children are my greatest joy and I'm very, very proud of them," said Maureen. "Every one of them, without exception, is a very remarkable human being — kind, talented, imaginative and intelligent.

"The real way to bind children to you is to let them go," said the mother of seven. "Clutching is no good; it simply makes them determined to be rid of you. But once they're free, they surprisingly want to come back to you as friends."

Maureen kept in constant touch with her family, as Jim told *People Magazine* in 1986: "There isn't a period in any given week when they don't check in with each other."

The actress agreed, with a smile on her face when she retorted, "Yeah, probably just making sure I'm not becoming a boozy old broad!" She also noted that her fairy tale life was still in full bloom, and she posed the question, "Do you think I'm a Pollyanna?" Maureen always looked at life with an optimistic viewpoint, and she revealed as much when she said, "I still have the feeling that anything can happen. Look, I got him," reaching over to squeeze the hand of her husband Jim.

"I feel there are all kinds of new things I haven't done before," proclaimed Maureen. She also noted that she wanted to try as many different types of roles as possible, because as she put it, "grandmothers are boring."

In January of 1985, Maureen O'Sullivan joined many of her fellow stars from the 1930s in saluting Myrna Loy at Carnegie Hall, a tribute sponsored by the Academy of Motion Picture Arts and Sciences. Lauren Bacall appeared as master of ceremonies, and some of the other guests included Lillian Gish, Lena Horne, Joseph L. Mankiewicz, Burt Reynolds, Sylvia Sidney, Robert Mitchum, Sidney Lumet, Teresa Wright, Maureen Stapleton, and Tony Randall.

Miss Bacall noted that she admired Miss Loy "as a person, an actress and a face, but also as a woman aware of what went on in the country and world. She's not a frivolous human being. And she's a great wit, which I'm a sucker for." Miss Loy watched the proceedings from a seat in the auditorium's first tier; at age 79 she looked frail but glamorous in a spangled gown.

Maureen was one of the guests who spoke of her long friendship with Myrna Loy, back to the days when they worked for Fox Film and made a picture together called *Skyline* (1931), with Myrna out of type as a blonde bombshell. They also co-starred in *The Thin Man* (1934), along with William Powell, in the film that launched Miss Loy to stardom. The actress was never nominated for an Academy Award, putting her in the same luckless category as Maureen O'Sullivan. Nevertheless, the two veteran stars were two of the finest actresses to ever grace the silver screen.

In June of the same year, Maureen and several other big name stars appeared in a staged reading of Strindberg's *Playing with Fire* and Chekhov's *Bear* at the Promenade Theater, located at 76th and Broadway. The readings were directed by Susan Flakes, and other members in the stellar cast included Glenn Close, Anthony Herrera, Raul Julia, Lily Knight, and William Roerick.

*B*arbarians was staged at the Williamstown Theatre and ran from June 26 through July 5, 1986. The Maxim Gorky three-act play was directed by Nikos Psacharaopoulos, who spent thirty-three years at Williamstown and also directed at other high-profile venues including Broadway. The native of Greece urged everyone, including the press, to just call him "Nikos." When he died in 1989, he had transformed Williamstown from a college summer stock program into a nationally known theater. Many well-known actresses and actors would return each year to work for Nikos, including Maureen O'Sullivan.

Maureen's character in *Barbarians* was Tatyana Bogayevskaya, described by the author as "a gentlewoman of property and Lydia's aunt, age 55." Other main characters included Ann Reinking as Lydia, William Swetland as the Mayor, Christian Clemenson as Grisha, Stephanie Zimbalist as Katya, Richard Thomas as Dr. Makharov, James Naughton as Tsyganov, and Daniel Hugh Kelly as Cherkoon.

The story takes place in a small provincial Russian town in the early 1900s, where the railroad is being built through the previously peaceful countryside. There is a great deal of discussion amongst the people about this project, and the engineers who are designing the railroad are the "barbarians" of the title. The lovers are very passionate, so much so that anything can happen. There are love triangles, crimes of passion, and unforeseen deaths.

In the final scene, Maureen's character of Tatyana hears a loud crack in the next room where her daughter Lydia and several people are congregated, and she says, "What was that noise? I was about to go up to bed."

When she is told that the woman Nadiezhda has shot herself right in front of several people including her husband, amidst the panic and despair, she responds: "Silly woman. I'd never have thought ... not her." And then the final curtain ends the play.

In 1986, Maureen made a guest appearance on the *Miss USA Pageant*, in which she recited the famous poem by Emma Lazarus "The New Colossus," which was speaking of New York City of 1883. The general populace might not be familiar with the first dozen lines or so of the short poem, but the last few lines are well-known to most Americans who have studied patriotism:

> *Give me your tired, your poor, your huddled masses yearning to be free*
> *The wretched refuse of your teeming shore*
> *Send these, the homeless, tempest-tossed to me*
> *I lift my lamp beside the golden door!*

The winner of the 1986 *Miss USA Pageant*, by the way, was Miss Texas, Christy Fichtner. The first runner-up was Halle Berry, Miss Ohio, who went on to become an acclaimed actress by the 1990s and eventually won the Best Actress Oscar for her fine portrayal in *Monster's Ball* (2001).

On May 18, 1987, the day after her own 76th birthday, Maureen participated in the gala celebration on ABC television entitled "Happy Birthday Hollywood." Staged at the gigantic Shrine Auditorium in Los Angeles, Liza

Minnelli kicked off the evening's entertainment with an opening "Happy Birthday" number that recounted a story of "chutzpah and pluck, heartache and luck."

There was plenty of musical entertainment during the three-hour prime time extravaganza, and most of the stars had only to walk out on stage and be introduced to the thundering applause of the audience. The evening benefitted the Motion Picture and Television Country House and Hospital in Woodland Hills, a cause that was near and dear to Maureen's heart.

Just a few of the big stars that attended included Burt Lancaster, Charlton Heston, Bernadette Peters, Sammy Davis, Jr., Robert Wagner, James Coburn, Carol Burnett, Burt Reynolds, and a number of old-time actresses including Lillian Gish, Ruby Keeler, Luise Ranier, Ginger Rogers, Esther Williams, Jane Powell, and the star of the Tarzan pictures, Maureen O'Sullivan.

One event that Maureen and Jim really enjoyed was the Annual American Cinema Awards, which were hosted by David Gest each winter at the Beverly Hilton Hotel in Beverly Hills. They were invited every year, and they were able to attend nine times between 1983 and the mid-1990s. This annual event was a private affair that raised money for a foundation that benefitted various charities including the Motion Picture Hospital in Woodland Hills, California.

Many of the greatest living stars of Hollywood would attend, and just some of the guests included Robert Mitchum and his wife Dorothy, Douglas Fairbanks, Jr., Lauren Bacall, Joseph and Patricia Cotten, Shirley Temple Black and her husband, Wendy Hiller, Ricardo Montalban and his wife, Cab Calloway and spouse, Elisha Cook, Jr., Alida Valli, Gloria DeHaven, Milton and Ruth Berle, June Havoc, Joel and Frances Dee McCrea, Jane Greer, Patty Andrews, Rosemary Clooney, Kirk and Anne Douglas, Robert and Vera Goulet, Paul Henreid, Audrey Hepburn, Ruby Keeler, Janet Leigh, Sophia Loren, Virginia Mayo, Dorothy McGuire, Cesar Romero, Elizabeth Taylor, Teresa Wright, Jane Wyman, Jon Voight, Burgess Meredith, Lionel Stander, Claudette Colbert, Maureen O'Sullivan and her husband James Cushing.

Also attending were numerous former child stars such as Roddy McDowell, Spanky McFarland, Freddie Bartholomew, Jackie Cooper, and Johnny Sheffield. There were always special honored guests, and at the 1988 shindig, for example, actors Gene Kelly and Shirley Temple were honored for "Distinguished Achievement in Film." Hosting the event that year were Leslie Caron and Robert Wagner, and besides the banquet there were film clips from the movies of Kelly and Temple and musical presentations that enlivened the night. Good food and drinks complemented the warm conversations between friends and the events of the evening.

Towards the end of the show, Robert Wagner got up and introduced all the celebrities one by one with the spotlight on each. This was the part of the night that everyone loved, and with all the applause it took 45 minutes to complete the introductions.

The 1993 event was very special for Maureen because it was her first reunion with Johnny Sheffield in many years. Back in the days when she was making Tarzan pictures for MGM, child actor Sheffield portrayed her son "Boy" in three classic films beginning with *Tarzan Finds A Son!* (1939), and followed by *Tarzan's Secret Treasure* (1941), and *Tarzan's New York Adventure* (1942).

Maureen and her husband Jim were assigned to sit at a table with Milton and Ruth Berle, Gloria DeHaven, and Spanky McFarland, along with Johnny and Patty Sheffield. In 1999, Johnny Sheffield spoke with David Fury and recalled this memorable reunion:

"The last time I saw Maureen personally was February 15, 1993, while attending the American Cinema Awards charity banquet in Hollywood. I was talking with Uncle Milty (Milton Berle), who was seated across from me, when I felt a hand on my shoulder and heard a voice say, 'Hello, Boy, how are you?'

"That voice, Maureen's voice, took me back 51 years. Before I turned around to look, I could see all of my jungle family in my mind. Tarzan, Jane, Cheetah, Bulie, Leo, and myself all together in our escarpment paradise. What a moment. In the course of the evening, Maureen confided in me that in spite of all the roles she had played in her life, she now felt fortunate to have played Jane with Johnny Weissmuller in the Tarzan series and fortunate the Tarzan series became a classic and that she was reconciled to that fact.

"Maureen was a working actress all her life and played many roles, but she will be remembered for 'All Time' for her role of Jane in the Tarzan adventures. I love and remember her as my Jungle Mother and all that that means to me."

Patty Sheffield also recalled to the author on one of his visits to the Sheffield home, "Maureen O'Sullivan was petite and very beautiful. I remember how tiny she was as well as how soft her voice, gentle as a soft Irish breeze. John was especially happy over the reunion as he was very fond of Maureen. Also her husband Jim was easy to visit with as he was in the paving business and for John and me, who are also in the trades, it is nice to meet people of like backgrounds."

Maureen and Jim always enjoyed these annual fund-raising events, and also the parties that Roddy McDowell would hold the same weekend. The American Cinema Awards banquet was always on a Saturday night, and Roddy's parties were either Friday night or Sunday afternoon. These parties were more informal, so everyone could just relax and enjoy the company of many old friends.

Quite often Maureen and Jim would take the opportunity while in Los Angeles to visit old friends who were living at the Motion Picture and Television Country Home and Hospital in Woodland Hills. Many older actors and actresses lived there in old age or poor health, including Johnny Weissmuller for almost two years after his 1977 stroke. They would visit with anyone who Maureen knew from the old days, including Howard Ephrom, a friend from New York.

Whenever she recalled her old friend Johnny Weissmuller, Maureen always spoke fondly of her co-star in the Tarzan pictures. It was a sad day for her when he died on January 20, 1984, in Acapulco, where he had lived the final years of his life.

When the actress did a lengthy interview in 1990 for the MGM documentary, *When the Lion Roars*, her eyes welled with tears when speaking of her dear friend, and she admitted, "I loved Johnny. We remained friends 'til the end."

Shortly after his death, Maureen phoned Maria Weissmuller, Johnny's spouse since 1963, with her condolences. Maureen was married to Jim Cushing by this time, and they resided at their Union Street home in Schenectady. Maria asked Maureen to write a remembrance of Johnny from his days as Tarzan on the silver screen, perhaps to be used as his eulogy at his Los Angeles memorial service. Maureen wrote several pages, and included this short note:

"Dearest Maria: Here are my memories of Johnny. I hope it is O.K. and that you get it on time. I just phoned you and will call tomorrow. Love to you and Lisa." (signed) Maureen

The lengthy dissertation was entitled: "What was Johnny Weissmuller really like?" In her own words Maureen continued with her own history of the MGM Tarzan years with Johnny:

"The legend of 'Tarzan' never seems to die. I get fan mail — photos of Johnny and me from our 'Tarzan' days. Sometimes they are autographed by Johnny — sometimes not. A note is enclosed with the ever-present question 'What was Johnny Weissmuller really like?' Well, I can't write an essay on Johnny every time, so I write 'Johnny was a wonderful person — and now that he is gone, he is a great loss to those of us who loved him.' And I add, 'He is a loss to the world.'

"So, what was Johnny Weissmuller really like? Apart from my husband and children, I have spent more time with Johnny than with anyone else in my life. But how was I to know that, on the bright California morning that we first met?

"We walked to the set where shooting was already in progress. A section of jungle had been created on the back lot, and for the first time I saw Johnny Weissmuller.

"Sunlight fell through the trees turning to gold a figure that looked to me like a Greek statue — perfect in its proportions. His hair glinted gold in the dappled sun. The action of the scene sounds insignificant. It wasn't. As cameras turned, he rested his foot on the body of a lion that lay before him, a spear piercing the [stuffed] animal's side. With a grace more beautiful than any dancer I have ever seen, he slowly lifted the spear from the animal's body in an arc, before lowering it to his side. 'Cut' called Van Dyke. I was silent as though I had just watched a beautiful ballet — or seen a wonderful painting — I had.

"Johnny came over to where we stood. 'Meet your leading lady,' said our producer. Johnny held out his hand and said, 'Hi Maggie.' He smiled and added, 'Good luck!' I almost looked over my shoulder. Who was Maggie? I had never been called that before. So Maggie it was, and Maggie I remained through a lot of years of friendship.

"I soon found out that this Golden God was a big kid — and that he loved to joke and tease. Johnny was never-ending in his search for fun — inventive too. When my birthday came around I was presented with a huge cake. The crew and cast gathered around while I blew out the candles and made a wish. As I stuck the knife in the cake the whole thing blew up in a stream of fireworks. However, a smaller cake was there for compensation.

"I became so wary of Johnny's jokes that this really rebounded on me. We were working on a particularly pretty set. Wild birds and friendly animals wandered at will. Suddenly I felt a sharp pain in the calf of my leg. 'I'm not going to let Johnny see this is hurting me!' I thought. The pain became excruciating and looking down I saw that a Cockatoo had embedded its beak in my leg — and having a curved beak it could break loose. It was flapping its wings and seemed as frightened as I was. The trainer came and cut the flesh away from the rounded beak. I was laid up with a tetanus shot for a week and still have my scar to show for it.

"Johnny had an uncanny gift with animals. They all loved him and Johnny was totally without fear. I have a funny picture in my mind of Johnny, Boy, Cheeta and myself in a scene together. I am on one side of Johnny, Cheeta on the other. A rope is tied around Cheeta's leg and held tightly off-camera by the trainer so that the ape cannot get at me! I have seen Johnny playfully wrestling with lions that were thought to be not quite tame, cuffing them as they would their baby cubs.

"I have often been asked if Tarzan and Jane carried their romance off-screen. No, we didn't. Johnny was at heart a simple soul. He loved the idea of a home, so he liked being married. In every one of the films we did together he had a different wife. None of them made him happy until he married Maria, who was with him 'through health and in sickness' until the day he died. Maria was the best thing, he told me the last time I saw him, that had happened in his life.

"Johnny's life off-screen must have been pretty hectic with all these wives coming and going, but it never affected our jungle world. There we were the ideal couple. We had our little treetop home; Jane did the housekeeping while Tarzan cared for the necessities of their lives. The animals were their friends. The rivers their playgrounds. And always and above all, they loved each other. I sometimes thought people could learn much from the simple story of Tarzan and Jane.

"So now to the final question that I am asked so often, 'What were those times really like?' I say they were happy days — wonderful days, the most wonderful part was being with Johnny who I never saw angry, or depressed or even slightly 'out-of-sorts.' Johnny, who did not seem to know — no matter what, the meaning of unhappiness. I pray that it was always so."

Johnny and Maureen were the best of friends ... from Day 1 until his death in 1984

CHAPTER TWENTY-FIVE
"Busy Actress, Happy Lady"

After an absence of twenty-one years from the big screen, Maureen returned in *Hannah and Her Sisters*. This 1986 film featured her daughter Mia Farrow, along with a talented ensemble cast that included Michael Caine, Barbara Hershey, Diane Wiest, Max Von Sydow, Sam Waterston, Carrie Fisher, Lloyd Nolan, and Woody Allen, who also wrote and directed the script.

Not only was Maureen extremely happy with the outstanding reviews garnered by the film, but it gave her the opportunity to work — for the very first time — with her daughter Mia Farrow in a motion picture. And since the film was photographed in New York, her beloved Manhattan, it was a pleasure for her to ply her trade and also remain close to home.

Hannah and Her Sisters is set in New York City, and the family dinner scenes were actually filmed in Maureen's former Manhattan apartment that was then occupied by Mia and her children. The story is a series of vignettes of a family with its own set of problems, hardly unique, but the situations alternate between tense, poignant, and hilarious. The characters are all deeply flawed, which makes them immensely human.

Three sisters are at the center of the story, including Hannah (Mia Farrow), Lee (Barbara Hershey), and Holly (Diane Weiss). The parents are Maureen and Lloyd Nolan as Norma and Evan, former actors who never quite hit the big time. Caine is Hannah's husband Elliot, Woody Allen is her ex-husband Mickey Sachs, Von Sydow is Lee's live-in lover Frederick, Fisher is close family friend April, and Waterston is an architect who romances both Holly and April.

The story takes place over several years, and the entire family always gathers at Hannah's for the Thanksgiving feast. They eat, drink, and discuss familial matters and problems — they are a large family that seems to genuinely enjoy each other's company. They have their share of arguments and misunderstandings, but rarely are any hard feelings held over.

Always at these dinners Norma sings old love songs while Evan plays the piano — in their younger days they were well-known on stage and screen. Sometimes Norma has a few too many drinks, and she and Evan argue — usually he claims she was flirting with some younger man. But they love each other greatly and these are just minor blips in a lifelong love affair.

Hannah is the talented one in the family, an actress and a mother. Norma and Evan favor her over sisters Holly and Lee — both women are unemployed and each has a rocky relationship history. Her ex-husband Mickey is a television producer who is suicidal because he thinks he has a brain tumor. When he discovers he does not, he spends the rest of the story searching for the meaning of life.

Like many families, even though they love each other, passions sometimes overflow into treacheries. The worst breach is the fact that Hannah's husband Elliot is secretly in love with her sister Lee, and when she admits to the same they begin having an affair. While the guilt-ridden Elliot is having secret days with Lee, Hannah notices that her husband has changed and she wonders out loud if he still loves her. Eventually Lee meets someone else, and Elliot gratefully resumes his devotion to Hannah.

Holly, after borrowing some money from Hannah, writes a screenplay and shows it to Mickey Sachs. He thinks the story shows merit and she quickly becomes a successful writer. Unexpectedly, they fall for each other, marry and have a child. Lee also has a wonderful new man in her life, and her affair with Elliot is ancient history. When Thanksgiving comes around again, they are one big happy family and any discords of the past are long forgotten.

Hannah and Her Sisters was a successful return to the big screen for the actress, and over the next few years she would make several motion pictures and television films. One of the main reasons Maureen had avoided Hollywood was that she wanted to live in New York, and working on the stage had afforded her that opportunity. Of course she had also traveled extensively, as many of her plays were road shows with extended runs.

When filming first began, Maureen and Woody butted heads over her character, who was described in Allen's script as "a boozy old broad with a filthy mouth." Maureen saw Norma in a more sympathetic light than her director: "She was pretty much of a bitch, but she's a zippy old gal, and I got to like her," said the actress with a laugh. "I don't mean to sound conceited, but I think Woody ended up liking her too." Maureen also admitted that she and Woody argued and at times tempers flared, but the end result was a masterpiece: "Woody is around quite a bit, and I yell and scream; these four-letter words have a way of slipping out."

In the picture she is teamed with Lloyd Nolan as her husband, a veteran actor she had known for many years. He had also appeared in the screen version of her big Broadway hit, *Never Too Late*. In an early scene the couple are seated at the piano and performing a duet of "Bewitched, Bothered, and Bewildered" for the whole family. They both sounded in fine voice as they crooned this old classic love song.

At one of the subsequent Thanksgiving dinners, Evan (Nolan) is seated at the piano and he tells a story of Norma (Maureen) being so beautiful in their heyday, that men would drive their cars right up on the sidewalk when they saw her walking down the street. Norma responds with a laugh and says, "Well, a slight exaggeration ... but only slight!"

Maureen has one marvelous scene with Lloyd Nolan and Mia, who comes by her parents' apartment after her mother has had a few drinks too many and engages in a loud argument with her husband. Hannah calms them both down, gets some coffee into her mother, and the scene concludes with Nolan playing a beautiful old tune on the piano, while gazing lovingly at this wife and daughter. This was a marvelous encore performance for Lloyd Nolan, the classy veteran actor who died at age eighty-three shortly after filming concluded.

Maureen with Lloyd Nolan ... their performances were royal in *Hannah and Her Sisters*

The critics were unanimous in calling this an outstanding film, as well as applauding the return of Maureen O'Sullivan to the big screen. A representative review came in *Films in Review* of May 1986, as Kenneth M. Chanko noted the following:

> "In one magnificent film Woody Allen has fully rounded and refined his art. The performances are uniformly flawless and the material is so well conceived that characters with a mere five to seven minutes of total screen time make tremendous impressions."

The *Los Angeles Times* review of February 7, 1986 by Sheila Benson noted:

> "Perfection is boring, but boring is the very last word to describe *Hannah and Her Sisters*, which just may be a perfect movie. Mellow, beautiful, rich and brimming with love, *Hannah* is the best Woody Allen yet and, quite simply, a great film ... His cast is absolutely splendid, although it must be said that he's loaded the dice in the women's favor."

David Denby of *New York* (February 10, 1986) called *Hannah and Her Sisters* "a great film, the richest and most complex of Woody's creations, and also the most fluent." Denby also described the relationship of the film's two elder stars, who both delivered magnificent performances:

> "Like some warring pair in a Bergman film, Hannah's parents (Maureen O'Sullivan, Farrow's real-life mother, and the late Lloyd Nolan) are held together by a mysterious compound of friendship and loathing. They are both retired musical-comedy players of the second rank, and after a vicious argument (the same vicious argument they've been having for 50 years), Lloyd Nolan sits at the piano and sings — the only act that can draw his wife back to him. And at that moment, Mia Farrow turns away from both of them and toward the camera, her eyes filled with relief. For Woody Allen, she is the spirit of reconciliation and love; she holds things together."

Rex Reed of the *New York Post* also had high praise:

> "If you are still in touch with your own heart, or feel the need to share it with people you love you'd be mad to miss it. *Hannah and Her Sisters* is a work of astonishing wisdom and maturity that embraces life in all its crazy, contradictory emotional contexts touching — instructing, and uplifting the lives of all who see it."

And the venerable critic Vincent Canby of the *New York Times* expressed that Maureen's work in this film was perhaps the finest of her career:

> "*Hannah and Her Sisters* is so much of a piece — a movie in which all aspects of the production fit together with such ease and seeming effortlessness — that I'm afraid the initial reviews couldn't do justice to each of the individual performances. This is especially true of the contributions by Mr. Nolan, whose last screen role this was, and Miss O'Sullivan, who has starred in dozens of films over the decades, including the 'Tarzan' movies with Johnny Weissmuller and the elegant *Pride and Prejudice*. In all that time, however, she's never had five minutes on the screen to equal her work here."

Canby also noted at Oscar time that Maureen's "remarkable" performance was as good as any actress who would be nominated that year:

> "As much as I admire Miss Wiest, I can't understand how she could be nominated without nominations also going to her 'Hannah' co-supporting stars (if that's what they are), Mia Farrow and Barbara Hershey. And if Miss Wiest is to be classified as a supporting actress instead of a star of 'Hannah,' what would you call the remarkable Maureen O'Sullivan in the same film — a *supporting* supporting actress?"

Hannah and Her Sisters was nominated for several Academy Awards including Best Picture, and brought home winners in Diane Wiest (Supporting

Actress), Michael Caine (Supporting Actor), and Woody Allen (Best Screenplay written directly for the screen).

When director Francis Coppola wanted an older actress to play Kathleen Turner's grandmother in *Peggy Sue Got Married* (1986), the first person he thought of was Maureen O'Sullivan. Coppola called her agent and arranged a meeting, where he was planning to offer her the role.

Maureen and her husband Jim went to the appointed rendezvous, and he recalled she had certain trepidations that she might not be right for the part. They sat down at a table and Coppula slid a cigarette lighter across the table to her — on it was inscribed "Alias Nick Beal" (a 1949 film that had been directed by her first husband, John Farrow).

Mr. Coppula explained to Maureen that he was a big fan of hers and that he wanted her for the role of the kindly grandmother. Eventually Maureen's case of the jitters subsided, and when they left the meeting husband Jim said to her, "You've got the role." And she was quite happy about landing the part, as she realized that at age seventy-five it was difficult to land a significant role in a major film with a top-notch cast and director. The picture turned out to be a major success, and Kathleen Turner was nominated for Best Actress at Oscar time.

The story revolves around Peggy Sue Bodell (Kathleen Turner), a divorced middle-aged woman with two grown children who is preparing to attend her 25-year high school reunion. Her ex-husband Charlie (Nicolas Cage) sells electronics and his skirt-chasing of younger women recently led to their divorce. Peggy's daughter Beth (Helen Hunt) helps her get ready for the big night, and Peggy is dressed in a gorgeous 1950's party dress that will definitely make her the belle of the ball.

Upon arrival, Peggy is still the most beautiful girl in her class, and all of her old friends are there including Charlie. When she is chosen "Queen of the Ball," her head is spinning and she falls to the stage in a faint. After she awakens, she is back in her senior year a few days before graduation, but she has total memory of the future. Everyone is there, her parents, her younger sister, her friends, and of course Charlie.

Peggy recalls fainting at the reunion, and thinks she is dreaming, or perhaps even dead. When she finally realizes she has truly "time-traveled" back to her senior year, she is determined not to make the same mistakes again. The biggest mistake of them all was marrying Charlie, and she vows to break up with him and not get pregnant on her approaching eighteenth birthday (as she did the first time around).

One of the things that Peggy wants to do is visit her grandparents, who in the future have passed away. She travels by bus up to the old family cabin, where she is warmly welcomed by her grandfather Barney (Leon Ames) and grandmother Lizzie (Maureen O'Sullivan). Peggy tells them the story of her returning to the past, and they believe her. In fact, her grandfather offers to take her to his lodge meeting, where one of their secret ceremonies held by the lodge brothers might possibly send her back to the future.

When the lights dim and then come back on, Peggy Sue is gone. However, it was only Charlie who kidnapped her and takes her out to the greenhouse to tell her one last time how much he loves her. When he gives her a present for her birthday, the locket that will ultimately contain the photos of their two children, Peggy Sue gives in and makes love to Charlie. Her head begins spinning again, and when she awakens she is in the hospital where she was taken after she collapsed at the reunion ball. Charlie is there with her, and tells her that she had fainted because of a heart problem but now she was going to be fine.

She comments on how old and tired he looks, and he admits that he has been sitting with her at the hospital for days. When he asks for one more chance to make their marriage work, she invites him to dinner on Sunday with the children. Charlie embraces Peggy Sue and weeps with happiness that perhaps he can win back the woman he has always loved.

For Maureen O'Sullivan, even though she has only one three-minute scene, this was a very warm part and her character was rich with sentimentality. Her partner in the scene, Leon Ames who played Barney, had also been in the movies since the 1930s and was the perfect complement as a wise old gentleman who doesn't have a mean bone in his body.

When the scene begins, Peggy Sue is with her grandparents in the sitting room, with a roaring blaze in the fireplace. The conversation drifts to the subject of dreams, and how real they can be sometimes. Peggy Sue had dreamed that her grandmother had died, but the older woman told her she wasn't afraid to die and even knew when it was going to happen.

Peggy Sue begins telling them her whole story of fainting and returning to the past, and when she is done her grandmother says, "If you believe it darling, then I believe. Being young is just as confusing as being old. The things that happened to me fifty years ago ... are more on my mind that the things that happened today."

When Peggy Sue laments that she is remembering the future, her grandmother once again advises her, "Right now you're just browsing through time. Choose the things you'll be proud of, things that last."

Peggy Sue admits that she is most proud of her children, Scott and Beth, and misses them so much. She tells her grandmother that her beautiful daughter Beth is named after her grandmother, and the older woman is overjoyed and says as they warmly embrace, "Oh, sweetheart, thank you."

(This was a poignant scene for Maureen, done in close-up with her beautiful blue eyes shimmering ... a touching moment that can bring tears to your eyes if you are not careful.)

There's one more brief scene where grandma Lizzie sends the two of them off to the lodge meeting, and that is the extent of Maureen's role in this film. But it was so well done that most critics mentioned her contribution in their reviews.

Movie fans and journalists alike loved this charming comedy, and it was deemed a strong comeback effort for Coppola. He was famed for his *Godfather* trilogy which won a slew of Academy Awards for the first two films, but this was arguably his best work in the past decade.

Rex Reed of the *New York Post* extolled the virtues of *Peggy Sue Got Married* in his review of October 6, 1986:

> "The movie has magic and charm in abundance, but what Coppola and his scriptwriters, Jerry Leichtling and Arlene Sarner, are saying is: 'Be selective in life. Hold on to the things that matter, the experiences of lasting value.' Peggy Sue learns the choices she made are not so bad after all. The message is deeply moving.
>
> "Through the range of emotional power of Kathleen Turner, it is immensely touching to see her visit her grandparents' farm again ... It's great to see classy veterans like Leon Ames and Maureen O'Sullivan as Peggy Sue's loving grandparents, and even the younger actors seem regenerated by the material.
>
> "To be honest, I'm not sure I can assess the impact of *Peggy Sue Got Married* rationally. I saw much of it through an avalanche of tears. At a time when I leave a lot of movies feeling nothing, that is gushing but genuine praise indeed."

The *Los Angeles Times* review of October 8, 1986 by Sheila Benson hits the nail right on the head when she comments:

> "You go to *Peggy Sue Got Married* expecting '60s nostalgia, 'a blast from the past,' Buddy Holly and lime-green leisure suits. You get all that, but nothing prepares you for the rush of real emotion the film generates, for its poignance, its reassurance or its high of pure pleasure.
>
> " 'If you could go back, knowing what you know now ...' is as reliable a premise as it is intriguing. What would you change? Would you marry him again? Have that sexual fling? Set your feet in the same ruts? Or hold back, with the knowledge of the social revolution to come?
>
> "Francis Coppola takes that premise, dusts it off, looks at it both seriously and unseriously, and gives it back to us as a rueful love story and a deeply stirring appreciation of the past.
>
> "The acting is grand. Turner, in between her character's two ages, bites into the role with a bravura that makes us want to forget the differences and be carried by her own, wild-eyed wonder at her predicament. And her rush of feeling (as she visits her grandparents, Leon Ames, Maureen O'Sullivan) is contagious."

Films in Review notes that the acting is first rate, even if there are a few holes in the screenplay (January 1987, Pat Anderson):

> "Barbara Harris and Don Murray are convincing as Peggy Sue's Norman Rockwell-like parents, and the seasoned performers Maureen O'Sullivan and Leon Ames handle well the characters of Peggy Sue's grandparents. Kathleen Turner, who has already proved herself in light comedy, does a fine job."

Walter Goodman of the *New York Times* commented that the scenes with Maureen and Leon Ames, along with Miss Turner, were the best in the picture:

> "The most touching scenes in Francis Coppola's *Peggy Sue Got Married* come when 45-year-old Peggy Sue, finding herself 25 years back in time, visits her grandparents. The old folks are played by Leon Ames and Maureen O'Sullivan with a kind of distracted affection, the way grandparents are often seen by kids, doting yet somewhat unconnected. But Peggy Sue is no longer a kid ... her meeting in middle age with the grandparents she loved as a girl is poignant."

After having major supporting roles in two immensely popular films, Maureen was anxious to continue her motion picture resurgence. The next project that came her way was *Stranded* (1987), a family drama that takes a twist into science fiction when a small band of aliens make an unplanned visit to a small southern town.

The story begins when Grace Clark (Maureen) and her granddaughter Deirdre (Ione Skye) have a minor disagreement over a young man that Grace wants to invite over for dinner. Apparently, the young man is no longer on Deirdre's "A" list. Deirdre has lived with Grace ever since her parents were killed in a car accident a year ago.

That evening, Deirdre goes out for a cigarette, and she beholds a powerful blue aura in the sky that appears to descend and land nearby. She runs inside the house to see if her grandmother is all right, and both women become scared when they hear sounds in the house. Grace grabs her shotgun and prepares to defend herself and Deirdre.

Their fear becomes fright when they discover that a family of aliens has taken refuge in their home. They eventually discover through a mind-meld that this is the royal family from a distant galaxy, and that their planet has been destroyed. The king, queen, and prince are guarded by a warrior armed with a laser gun, and they also have a pet (of some sort) that Grace nicknames "Jester." They're actually beautiful creatures, and when Grace first sees them she says to Deirdre, "They almost look like angels."

When two neighbors stop by the house and notice the front door open, the younger man enters brandishing a revolver and shoots the queen when he is startled by their strange appearance. The alien warrior blasts the attacker dead with a deadly laser, and the young man's father, Burdett, races away in a frenzy to get help. Grace tries to help the queen, but she is mortally wounded.

By the time sheriff McMahon (Joe Morton) arrives with his police force, one of his deputies is already dead after confronting the alien warrior. The sheriff not only has to deal with this tense situation, but Vernon Burdett is intent on killing the aliens with a loaded rifle. He eventually gets into a shouting match with the sheriff, taunting him with racial slurs. The sheriff is cool and collected, and has Burdett escorted off the premises.

Meanwhile in the house, Grace and Deirdre are safe and unharmed and have made friends with the aliens. They are told that they are being hunted by an assassin who is intent on killing the last of the royal family. Sheriff Morton bravely enters the house to speak with Grace who explains to him the life-and-death situation of the alien beings. The sheriff is seeking a peaceful resolution, but also realizes he has two dead local citizens as well.

Morton is wounded by Burdett, who shoots him from ambush and also kills the king with a rifle shot. The volatile warrior lasers him as retribution — the murderer lies dead as well. The sheriff makes it to the house, where Grace helps to bandage his gunshot wound.

When the assassin arrives disguised as a female government agent, she vaporizes the alien warrior. Suddenly it appears that all is lost, but Grace walks up from behind and blasts the assassin with her shotgun. Deirdre says her good-byes to the prince, and along with Jester they depart in the space vehicle. The sheriff survives his wounds, and Grace and Deirdre spend the following day talking to the media about their strange experience in an otherwise quiet southern town.

Maureen had "special star" billing in this picture, but her role as the feisty grandmother was easily the star of the story. She's raising a teenager whose parents have been killed, and when her home is invaded by aliens, she doesn't panic but befriends them and tries to help them survive their terrible ordeal. In the end, Grace uses her shotgun to bravely eliminate the final threat to her new alien friends.

Joe Morton was excellent as the beleaguered sheriff who not only has to deal with the life-and-death state of affairs, but also the local redneck citizens who hinder the investigation and nearly cause his death. Ione Skye was fine as the teenaged Deirdre, who has compassion for the aliens and develops an affection for the young prince. And Brendan Hughes as the prince did well with a role where he had to emote without speaking the English language whatsoever.

Janet Maslin of the *New York Times* panned the film, but saved her one positive comment for Maureen O'Sullivan, saying her talents were wasted in this venture:

> "Science fiction is almost never as lifeless as *Stranded* ... it unfolds at a snail's pace and manages to be uneventful all the way through. The creatures look as if they've had terrible past experiences with hairstyling mousse, and

one of them likes the teenage girl enough to stick around for a good-bye kiss. Even for those who believe love is where you find it, this is going too far.

"Humans in the cast include Joe Morton as the solemn sheriff, Ione Skye as the ingenue and Maureen O'Sullivan as the elderly lady who's much classier than this material deserves. None of them is photographed to good advantage, since virtually the entire film takes place in the dark."

Maureen had become good friends with director Peter Hunt at the Williamstown Film Festival, and when he offered her a guest role as Dorothy Richardson on the CBS police drama, *Legwork*, she was happy to accept. The one-hour episode, "All This and a Gold Card, Too," was directed by Hunt and aired on October 31, 1987. It was also a convenient gig for Maureen, as the show was filmed on location in New York City.

Margaret Colin starred as Claire McCarron, a former Manhattan district attorney who is now solving crimes as a private detective. Patrick James Clark was her brother, Lt. Fred McCarron of N.Y.P.D., and Frances McDormand portrayed Willie Pipal, Claire's contact in the D.A.'s office. The talented McDormand was at the beginning of her career, and would later become a motion picture star. She would eventually win the Best Actress Oscar for her portrayal of the pregnant female police chief in the Coen brothers' dark comedy, *Fargo* (1996).

After the success of *Hannah and Her Sisters*, Woody Allen wanted to team Mia Farrow and Maureen in another film, an offbeat drama entitled *September* (1987). The original cast had Miss Farrow as the daughter, Maureen as the mother, along with Dianne Wiest, Denholm Elliot (as the physicist-husband), and Charles Durning (as the neighbor). In this original version, Christopher Walken was the writer, but he was later replaced by Sam Shepard. After ten weeks of hard work by everyone, *September* was finished. Well, not quite.

After viewing the edited film, Woody Allen decided to re-write and re-shoot the whole picture. This was a big problem, as many of the original cast members were not available because of other work commitments. Maureen was hospitalized with pneumonia, and had to be replaced by character actress Elaine Stritch. Shepherd and Durning were both involved with long-standing projects, and could not continue with the re-shoot. Denholm Elliot switched roles and became the neighbor; Jack Warden was brought in to be the physicist; and Sam Waterston supplanted Shepard as the aspiring writer.

After Maureen was replaced by Elaine Stritch, Woody Allen compared the two actresses in the role and said each had given a strong, yet different, performance:

"Maureen, because she's older, was more vulnerable where Elaine was more in charge. But both were good and that's why this could be played on stage in different ways."

The River Pirates (1988) was based on the novel, *Good Old Boy: A Delta Boyhood*, and Maureen was cast in the supporting role of Aunt Sue Harper. Other adult roles included Richard Farnsworth as Percy, Dixie King-Wade as Mamie, along with Caryn West and Richard Council as the parents of Willie. Filmed on location in Natchez, Mississippi, the story takes place in 1944 in the imaginary town of Yazoo as the United States is embroiled in the war.

The real stars of this "coming-of-age" drama were the children, most of them between ten and twelve years old. Ryan Francis had the lead role of Willie, a lad whose best older friend Bobby Lee has gone off to fight the Nazis. Other child actors included Gennie James as Rivers, Doug Emerson as "Spit" McGee, Devin Ratray as Bubba, Kevin Joseph as Henjie, Ben Wylie as Billy, Dule Hill as Robert E. Lee, and Jordan Marder as Buster.

The youngsters have more than their share of childhood fun and adventure, including a haunted house where a scary old hag lives; a seven-foot legendary creature called the Yazoo; another group of older boys who are intent on beating them up; and a gang of river pirates that are robbing houses and graves in the town until Willie, Rivers, and the boys discover them hiding in the old mansion with their stolen loot.

The coming-of-age portion of the story involves serious questions that Willie poses to his grandfather Percy, including why his young friend Robert must go to a separate school for black children, while the white children have their own school. Willie finds this unfair, and his grandfather explains that perhaps this situation will change in more enlightened times.

Willie also discovers his first feelings of love, for Rivers, who has a lovely singing voice and can run with the boys as well as anyone. When word arrives from the Army that Bobby Lee has been killed in the war, Willie has a difficult time accepting this loss and refuses to attend the funeral. During the service, however, he arrives and plays taps on his trumpet for his fallen friend.

Maureen's role of Aunt Sue was interesting, as she was a charming southern belle who never married and lived with her sister Mamie (Wade) and her husband Percy (Farnsworth). Her character is slightly touched by age, and she often recalls her younger days when she had many beaux competing for her attention.

Her best scene is where Willie plays a little prank on his Aunt Sue and telephones the house from the general store, pretending to be quiz show host Bert Parks. The mischievous lad tells his excited aunt that if she answers three questions correctly, she can win one-thousand dollars on his "Break the Bank" radio program.

Aunt Sue can hardly contain her joy as she answers the first two questions, but when she misses the difficult third question — even with the help of her brother-in-law Percy — the harmless prank is over and Aunt Sue is only mildly disappointed. This was a cute scene, and the Irish actress did surprisingly well with a southern accent. Maureen also received "Special Guest Star" billing that was befitting her status as a Hollywood legend.

Maureen had worked with Kathleen Turner in *Peggy Sue Got Married* (1987), and when she learned that Ms. Turner was going to star in a Broadway production of *Cat on a Hot Tin Roof*, with Howard Davies as the director, she and husband Jim decided to take the plunge and make an investment. They contacted Fran and Barry Weissler who were producing the show, and they were happy to welcome them as associate producers.

This was something they had never done, because Maureen had wanted solely to be an actress. But once the decision was made, they put their heart and soul into the matter and really enjoyed seeing the project come to fruition. Kathleen Turner was delighted that Maureen and Jim had come on board.

Cat on a Hot Tin Roof opened on Broadway on March 21, 1990 and ran for 149 performances until it closed on August 1, 1990. Maureen and Jim attended the gala Broadway premiere at the Eugene O'Neill Theatre, after nine off-Broadway preview performances. The Tennessee Williams play had originally been produced on Broadway in 1955, starring Barbara Bel Geddes in the role of Maggie and Elia Kazan as the director. Meanwhile, the 1958 classic motion picture was directed by Richard Brooks, with Paul Newman as Brick, Elizabeth Taylor as Maggie, Burl Ives as Big Daddy, and Judith Anderson as Big Momma.

In this current stage production, Kathleen Turner portrayed Maggie, Daniel Hugh Kelly played Brick, while Charles Durning and Polly Holliday were cast as Big Daddy and Big Momma, respectively. The reviews were strong, and the *New York Times* called Kathleen Turner "radiant," while Durning's character of Big Daddy was "a cracker-barrel Lear and Falstaff in one."

The three lead actors of Turner, Durning, and Holliday were all nominated for 1990 Tony Awards, with Durning's fine portrayal of Big Daddy winning in the category of Best Featured Actor in a Play. The producers, including the Weisslers along with Maureen and Jim Cushing, were nominated for a 1990 Drama Desk Award in the category of Outstanding Revival of a Play.

On February 27, 1991, Maureen received her long-overdue star on the Hollywood Walk of Fame. The guests included Ann Rutherford, Cesar Romero, Hal Roach, Janet Leigh, Roddy McDowell, Meredith Harless, Maureen's son Patrick and his daughter Theresa Tucker, Jim Cushing and his daughter Cindy Amerson. Most of the actors from the past were gone — the big stars that had worked with Maureen in her 1930's MGM films. Ann Rutherford spoke of her fondness for Maureen, who had played her sister in the classic *Pride and Prejudice* (1940). Cesar Romero recalled that they were lovers in *Cardinal Richelieu* (1935), and Maureen remembered that Romero had given her one of her first serious screen kisses.

Maureen's star on Hollywood Boulevard is located right next to that of Johnny Weissmuller. It was a rainy day in Los Angeles, the first day it had rained in weeks, and of course the umbrellas were out. The honorary mayor of Hollywood, Johnny Grant, presided over the event and also slipped and fell on the wet sidewalk. Mr. Grant picked himself up and carried on, with only his pride slightly damaged. The banquet celebrating Maureen's big day was held at the Beverly Wilshire Hotel, where Maureen shared a few memories and thanked everyone for attending.

Maureen gets her Walk of Fame star in 1991, surrounded by friends and husband Jim Cushing

The Beverly Wilshire was the favorite hotel for Jim and Maureen, and the couple would stay there whenever they were in Los Angeles. From the hotel they would often walk the three blocks to Maureen's former home on Beverly Drive, where she had lived with John Farrow and her children during the 1940s and 1950s. They never went up to the house, but Maureen would linger for a few minutes and walk once through the neighborhood with Jim, and then they would stroll back to the hotel.

Back in the day, the venerable producer Hal Roach lived right next door to Maureen's family, and Hal and his wife also had four daughters that were the same ages as the Farrow girls — Mia, Steffi, Prudy, and Tisa.

Jim Cushing recalled that Pat Paterson, wife of Charles Boyer, was Maureen's closest friend from her Beverly Hills years. Mrs. Boyer was being treated for cancer in 1978, but succumbed to the disease. Two days later, Charles Boyer killed himself with a gun at their home. They had been married for 44 years, and the actor felt his life was no longer worth living without his life partner.

In the fall of 1991, Maureen made a guest appearance in the short-lived light crime drama *Pros and Cons*, which did have a strong cast that included Richard Crenna, James Earl Jones, and Madge Sinclair. Crenna portrayed L.A. private detective Mitch O'Hannon, James Earl Jones was his new partner Gabriel Bird, and Madge Sinclair was Josephine Austin.

This particular episode was directed by Jerry Thorpe, the son of long-time MGM director Richard Thorpe. The elder Thorpe was the man who directed more of Maureen's films than any other director. Maureen later recalled that she enjoyed working with Richard Crenna a great deal, and thought him to be a very talented man.

Maureen also appeared in the television movie, *With Murder in Mind* (1992), which starred Elizabeth Montgomery, Robert Foxworth, and Howard Rollins, Jr. The film was based on a factual story about Buffalo, N.Y. real estate agent Gayle Wolfer (Montgomery) who is shot and left for dead by one of her clients (Rollins). The heinous crime came about after she realized the man is the one who had killed her policeman husband.

The woman is physically and emotionally scarred from the incident, but nevertheless is determined to find her attacker. One day while at a county fair she recognizes her assailant, and is shocked to discover that he is a deputy sheriff. No one believes Gayle at first because the man is such an upstanding citizen, but the case eventually goes to trial.

Maureen was cast in the supporting role of Aunt Mildred. Howard Rollins, Jr. was the duplicitous Samuel Carver, and Robert Foxworth as Bob Sprague helped to unravel the mystery. Foxworth would marry Elizabeth Montgomery in 1993 after a long relationship together.

The TNT production of *The Habitation of Dragons* (1992) was based on the 1988 Horton Foote play. Maureen O'Sullivan was part of an ensemble cast in this Depression-era drama that takes place in 1935 in Harrison, Texas.

It is the story of the Tollivar family, which has more than its share of bad luck and family dysfunction. Leonard Tollivar (Frederic Forrest) and his brother George (Brad Davis) are both lawyers, but only Leonard is successful.

George has taken a break from law and is working as a clerk in a department store. Their mother Leonora (Jean Stapleton) is a widow, and their older cousin Miss Helen (Maureen) lives nearby and is a close family member.

Leonard is married to Margaret (Hallie Foote), and they have two young sons, Horace and Leonard, Jr. Margaret is having an affair with local resident Wally Smith (Elias Koteas), who is employed by her husband. Her brother Billy Dalton is also a lawyer and is running for county attorney, and his chief opposition comes from George Tollivar, who plans a return to law practice. Long-lost uncle Virgil (Pat Hingle) arrives for a visit, completely broke, and suffers a heart attack upon his arrival.

All the bad luck for this family had begun years ago, when Horace McMahon committed suicide with a shotgun. This was covered up when Leonard hid his father's suicide note, but all the family members secretly suspected the death was by his own hand. In the ensuing years, the rivalry between brothers Leonard and George had simmered, but finally boiled over when they had a huge argument over the family farm that was owned jointly by both of them.

Tensions begin to rise when Leonard discovers that his wife is having an affair with Wally, and he confronts her. She admits to the affair, and asks for a divorce. The same day, however, horrific news is brought to Leonard that his two young sons have both drowned in the river, while they were being watched by Wally, who had taken the boys swimming.

Things go from bad to worse when Margaret suffers a nervous breakdown after the death of her sons, and Leonard also falls into a deep depression after the funeral. More tragedy occurs when Margaret's brother Billy shoots and kills the man she was having an affair with, Wally Smith. After Billy is convicted of killing Wally, he receives a suspended sentence and leaves town.

Leonard has a difficult time forgiving his wife Margaret for her affair, but when he catches her on the verge of suicide, he relents and they agree to reconcile. By this time George has married, become a father, and has been elected county attorney; he is now the successful brother with a wife, child, and career. Leonora was relieved to see her two sons acting once again as brothers. All the tragedy now seems to be behind them.

Miss O'Sullivan had a supporting role in this rather somber television play, and capably performed most of her scenes with Pat Hingle as another family elder, Virgil. Her character of Helen remained on the edges of all these heartaches, attending the funerals, conversing with Virgil about the hot summer weather and reminiscing about the past. She once again used a southern accent, and emoted convincingly as a relative who commiserates with the pain of her extended family.

There is so much tragedy in this household that only near the end of the story does there appear a ray of hope that the worst is behind them. Jean

Stapleton was excellent as Leonora, and her fine dramatic acting was a far cry from her comedic role as Edith Bunker on *All in the Family*. Frederic Forrest and Brad Davis were both convincing as brothers who have fences to mend, and Hallie Foote was reminiful of Vivien Leigh as a southern belle whose nervous breakdown leaves her contemplating suicide over her guilt complex.

Maureen's years at MGM had been the centerpiece of her career, ten years of enduring fame that were spotlighted by the six Tarzan films she made with Johnny Weissmuller. In March of 1992, Turner Network Television presented a six-hour documentary over three nights entitled, "MGM: When the Lion Roars." John O'Connor of the *New York Times* devoted his column to the program and the history of the studio (March 20, 1992):

> "Lavish and shamelessly self-serving, entitled 'MGM: When the Lion Roars' is a just about perfect match of subject and treatment — the biography of what is called without much exaggeration 'the greatest motion-picture studio the world has ever known.'
>
> "Life in front of and behind the cameras is recalled by everyone from Maureen O'Sullivan (Jane to Johnny Weissmuller's Tarzan) to Sam Marx, veteran story editor at MGM.
>
> "The real point is that the old MGM lure still works. One peek into this fabulous dream factory, and you'll be hooked. As the Master of Ceremonies might loudly proclaim: Lights! Camera! Magic!"

Maureen talked with the folks at TNT for 90 minutes, but it was her memories of making the Tarzan pictures that they found most fascinating:

"They tried different things to make Jane look pretty sexy," recalled the actress. "And first off they had the idea of having Jane wearing no bra — no brassiere at all — and she would always be covered with a branch, and they tried that and it didn't work. So then, they made a costume and it wasn't that bad at all. There was a little leather bra and a loincloth with thongs on the side. But it started such a furor, that the letters just came in. So it added up to thousands of women who were objecting to my costume. And I think that was one of the things that started the Legion of Decency.

"Now in those days," continued Maureen, "they took those things very seriously, the public did. Do you know I was offered land in San Francisco, I was offered all kinds of places where I could go in my shame — to hide from the cruel public who were ready to throw stones at me. It's funny you know — we were unreal people and yet we were real."

When Maureen was asked to briefly highlight what the studio had meant to her then, and now, she recalled those years with heartfelt sincerity: "Metro-Goldwyn-Mayer meant a great deal to me. When we went to a preview when the lion came on the screen, even before the film, people would applaud. Metro had a real magic of its own, power, and prestige — I'm very proud to have been a part of that."

When asked about Louis B. Mayer, Maureen responded: "I think of Metro-Goldwyn-Mayer as being a family. And I think of Mr. Mayer as the patriarch. And then there were very powerful 'uncles' around the lot, the producers, like Thalberg and David Selznick. But he was the head honcho. He would walk across the lot, followed by the producers, the writers, and Howard Strickling. He was like a great swan with all the little ducklings and swans following behind him. I always felt like I should curtsy as he went by. He had power, and he also had an innate showmanship.

"He only sent for me once, and it really was funny. I had been bad about writing home, like a lot of kids. So I suppose my father wrote to Mr. Mayer and said 'Please see that my daughter writes home more frequently.'

"So I got a call to go to Mr. Mayer's office, and I walked in and Ida said, 'Mr. Mayer will see you now,' and I walked smack dab into a bust of Napoleon. I looked around for Mr. Mayer, and you have to make this long walk over to the desk, and by that time I was all shook up. And he said, 'Maureen, you've not been a very good daughter. You're not writing home enough. I have two good daughters,' and he showed me photographs of his daughters Irene and Edie. 'They're not like you — you're not writing home as you should.' (Maureen added the comment, with a giggle, "Isn't that divine?")

"He also said to me, 'We are your new family here in Hollywood, but I hear you don't want to do this next picture. Don't you trust your family?' I had just done 'Tarzan' and I didn't want to do a western with George O'Brien.

"Mr. Mayer said to me, 'We are your family, we tell you what to do.' And I did it, of course."

In 1994, Maureen made what was probably her last television portrayal in *Hart to Hart: Home Is Where the Hart Is*. The popular television series of the 1980s starring Robert Wagner and Stephanie Powers had continued in a succession of made-for-TV films in the 1990s.

Maureen portrayed octogenarian Eleanor Biddlecomb, a respected teacher and writer who literally owns the town of Kingman's Ferry. This sleepy hamlet has numerous dark secrets and the older woman knows every last one of them. One evening, Eleanor travels to a mysterious clandestine meeting. Inexplicably, the brakes on her car fail, the vehicle skids violently, and she is killed.

Subsequently, Jonathan and Jennifer Hart travel to Kingman's Ferry to attend the funeral of Jennifer's beloved mentor, Eleanor. Suspecting foul play, the husband-and-wife detectives launch an investigation that reveals that the small town's idyllic facade hides an undercurrent of deception.

A trail of mysterious clues leads the Harts to long-hidden secrets about the town that were directly tied to Eleanor's untimely "accident." When Jonathan and Jennifer begin uncovering the town's dirty laundry, they are perilously close to becoming the next victims.

Other prominent characters included Roddy McDowall as a duplicitous lawyer, Howard Keel as a swaggering businessman, Alan Young as a crazy-like-a-fox local, and Mitchell Ryan as the police chief. Lionel Stander, who had appeared in *The Crowd Roars* (1938) with Maureen and Robert Taylor, portrayed the Harts' right-hand man, Max.

In January of that year Maureen and Jim attended a 70th birthday celebration for Andy Anselmo at the Roundabout Theater Company. Anselmo was a singer who appeared on Broadway, in nightclubs, on television and radio programs — however his greatest fame came as a vocal teacher to the stars. Many of his famous clients came this evening to honor Anselmo, including Maureen, Geraldine Fitzgerald, Liza Minnelli, Mary Tyler Moore, Mandy Patinkin, Joanne Woodward, Julie Harris, Billy Stritch, and Jo Loesser. Some came to sing, and others such as Maureen came to speak to the audience about their friendship with Anselmo.

Maureen became a student of Anselmo because when she gravitated to the stage in the 1960s, she needed to increase the strength of her voice to project to the audience. Anselmo was a great teacher and also a friend and confidante to his students. Geraldine Fitzgerald made the comment of Anselmo, "The quality that he has and that all great teachers share is that he never makes negative remarks to his pupils. Whatever you try will be respected and you feel you can take risks."

Also in 1994, Maureen returned to the stage at Williamstown to perform *Love Letters* by A. R. Gurney. The play ran on the main stage from August 16 to August 28, 1994, and featured several acting couples on different nights performing the two-person dramatic recital.

Maureen was teamed with stage actor John Randolph, and other couples included Eli Wallach and his wife Anne Jackson. On the night that Maureen took the stage, her husband Jim attended with Mia Farrow as their guest.

Some of the other male stars included Richard Benjamin, Stephen Collins, Christopher Reeve, James Naughton, Richard Thomas, and James Whitmore. They were paired off with actresses Karen Allen, Jane Curtin, Celeste Holm, Mary Tyler Moore, Paula Prentiss, and Elaine Stritch.

Love Letters traces the lifelong correspondence of straight-laced lawyer Andrew Makepeace Ladd III and full-of-life artist Melissa Gardner. It is the story of their bittersweet relationship told in the words of their letters, some of which is clear and some left unsaid. They first meet when they are children in the year 1937, when Andy is a guest at Melissa's birthday party.

The set is simply a table and two chairs where the two actors sit, looking at the audience rather than each other. There is no rehearsal, no lines to memorize, and the entire play is read aloud by the two actors. He wears a dark grey suit, while she wears a simple, expensive-looking dress. The only props are a water decanter and two glasses.

Author A. R. Gurney notes of his play, "In performance, the piece would seem to work best if the actors didn't look at each other until the end, when Melissa might watch Andy as he reads his final letter. They *listen* eagerly to each other along the way, however, much as we might listen to an urgent voice on a one-way radio, coming from far, far way."

About her own life and her relationship with her husband Jim, Maureen admitted in 1994 that these were indeed her golden years: "My life is very peaceful. We have a lovely house here in the country and another in New Hampshire.

"We spend our winters in Phoenix. Between the packing and unpacking and visiting our children and grandchildren, I have plenty of interesting things to do. It's the payoff time for my life."

Jim and Maureen were both very fond of Siena College, which is located in Loudenville, New York, and Jim served on the board for several years. Their home on Union Street in Schenectady, which was situated on three and a half acres of land, was eventually donated to Siena. Also a series of dormitories at the college were renamed "Cushing Village" in 1995, and Maureen and Jim attended the dedication ceremony.

One particular event that was special for Maureen and Jim was "A Night Under the Stars," a musical spectacular that benefitted the Michael Bolton Foundation. The evening of music was held on June 25, 1995, at the Westin Bonaventure Hotel at the outdoor plaza theater.

Maureen and Jim Cushing were saluted as Foundation Humanitarians, and there was an all-star lineup of entertainment. Petula Clark sang several of her biggest hits, and other guests included Ann Miller, Helen Reddy, Ed Ames, Gene Barry, Michael McDonald, Deniece Williams, Glenn Yarbrough, Little Anthony and the Imperials, and Michael Bolton. Once again this event was produced and directed by David Gest, and there was also a special 80th birthday celebration for actress Ruth Warrick.

After Maureen's kind act of writing the foreword for your author's Tarzan history, *Kings of the Jungle* (McFarland, 1994), the Edgar Rice Burroughs fan club was anxious to have the actress famed as Jane at one of their annual conventions. In September of 1995, Maureen attended for the very first time the Burroughs Bibliophiles shindig which that year was held in Rutland, Vermont, not far from her New Hampshire home. An invitation was extended to Maureen and her husband Jim Cushing, requesting her presence as an honored guest for the Labor Day convention.

One of the attendees was Jerry Spannraft of Chicago, who recalled Maureen's visit to the convention (called the Dum Dum, named after the powwow of the great apes in the Tarzan novels of Edgar Rice Burroughs):

"Early in the year, it was rumored that Maureen O'Sullivan would be at the Dum Dum," said Spannraft. "Later information noted that she would not be able to attend due to a schedule conflict. About two o'clock on Saturday afternoon, someone announced that Maureen had arrived in front of the hotel, along with her husband James Cushing. We all rushed out to welcome her, and I got my first glimpse of the former 'Jane.'

"When she walked into the dealer's room, I was standing next to her. She stopped at the doorway and said: 'Oh my — I never knew anything like this existed.'

"When she saw the numerous photos, posters, lobby cards, and books relating to her and Johnny Weissmuller, she remarked, 'Johnny would be so happy.'

"She fondly recalled her co-star in six Tarzan pictures with a succinct statement, 'He was a wonderful man.'

"A table and chair were brought out for her so she could sign items for the group. Maureen respectfully signed photos for all the attendees at the convention, with a warm smile for everyone. We then closed down the line, and Ms. O'Sullivan went out to her car with her husband.

"As a group we thanked her for coming, and of course took numerous photographs when she was presented with a floral bouquet and fruit basket. Maureen waved good-bye and departed in the automobile.

"She was a wonderful lady — very classy and so polite."

Mike Conran was another Tarzan fan who recalled the delight of meeting Maureen at the convention: "A highlight of the 1995 Dum Dum was the personal appearance of Maureen O'Sullivan, the only 'true' Jane in the Tarzan movies.

"Maureen entered the hotel to the applause of a grateful group of Edgar Rice Burroughs fans. She was presented with a dozen roses, as George McWhorter welcomed Maureen and expressed the group's delight at her attendance."

Laurence Dunn of England remembered: "When Maureen arrived at the convention hotel, George McWhorter turned to her and with a wave of his hand said, 'These are all your fans.' To which Maureen replied, 'They can't be — they're too young!'

"After Maureen left, there was such a buzz in the air that we had finally met the definitive Jane."

When it was time for Maureen's visit to conclude, McWhorter, the editor of the Burroughs Bulletin and the curator at the Burroughs museum at the University of Louisville, recalled a lasting and indelible final memory:

"We were leaving the huckster room at the Dum Dum when Ms. O'Sullivan remarked, 'Everybody has been giving me photos and posters; I feel like a thief.'

"I blurted out, 'No! The only thing you have stolen is our hearts.' She turned and gave me the sweetest smile I've ever seen on a human face."

In 1996, Maureen sat down with the folks at Turner Classic Movies and talked about her life in the picture business over a one-hour interview. The actress was always happy to talk about her career — she was knowledgeable, articulate, and her memory was still sharp at age 85.

She started at the very beginning in Ireland, when she was chosen to make *Song O' My Heart* with John McCormack. When the interviewer mentioned that Americans probably wouldn't know who McCormack was in this day, she seemed shocked: "Really? Oh, I think music fans and opera fans would know who he was even today. He was Ireland's greatest tenor. Getting him for a film was a big, big thing."

Maureen mentioned that her first residence after she arrived in 1929 was a hotel room she shared with her mother: "I brought my mother with me to Hollywood, and they put us in this perfectly AWFUL apartment, and there was only one bed in the alcove. My mother insisted I take the bed: 'You're going to be working darling, you'll need your rest.' So there was what they called a Murphy bed, you opened the door in the wall and then pulled the bed down. So my mother and I pulled down the Murphy bed and it was loose — and the bed ran all over the room and smashed the window." Maureen was giggling now at the humor of this anecdote, as she continued.

"By this time my mother was so upset she said she needed a drink. I said to her, 'Mummy, what do we know about Prohibition?' Well in Ireland it was treated as a joke, so I said, 'All right, I'll go out and get you a bottle of gin.' So I went to the drug store and I asked for a bottle of Gilbert's gin, and they said 'What?' I said, 'Well, any brand of gin will do if you don't have that brand.'

"And they said they'd have me arrested, that there was a policeman right outside. And there was. I guess he saw I was innocent, and he let me go. But it was all so strange to me. I had a miserable time, to tell you the truth; there wasn't much glamor.

"After my mother returned to Ireland, they put me in a room at the Studio Club with three other girls. They wore my stockings and they wore my clothes, and they talked all night when I wanted to sleep. It was just wild. And I thought, 'How am I going to get out of this dreadful place?' And there was only one telephone on our floor, and one evening I overheard my roommate in a conversation with a man: 'Okay, you S.O.B.', said the girl, 'if you don't pay my room rent I'm going to tell your wife what happened on the train!' (Maureen was laughing quite hardily by this time!)

"I laughed and slapped my hands and said, 'I'm out of here!' I went to the studio head the next day and said, very pious: 'I can't live in such an immoral place," practically cracking with laughter inside. So they moved me into a house and gave me a chaperone — she was a cousin of George M. Cohan.

"And I was seeing Oscar Levant at that time, and the studio said, 'Oh, you can't go out with that piano pounder.' And Dixie Lee was also under contract to Fox, and she was seeing Bing Crosby, and they said to her, 'Oh, you can't go out with that groaner!' So society was limited, according to the studios.

"And it was that year that I met John Farrow, who had a wild reputation, I have to say — he was young, why not. The studio said I couldn't go out with him — he was a writer at Fox at the time. Naturally, he was the person I wanted to go out with the most. So on my birthday he came to take me out in this lovely big blue car, a chauffeur, and flowers — he knew how to do things. And Aggie, my chaperone — she adored him, thought he was wonderful, and she encouraged our dates. I began to have a good time from then on. But the first year was, really — hellish."

Maureen also mentioned Lew Ayres and Russell Gleason as young men she knew from the studio, and they would take her out to see *All Quiet on the Western Front* (1930), a film in which they had starred. She said she got a little tired of seeing the same film repeatedly, but they were so proud of it that she humored them.

When Maureen spoke of Norma Shearer, the great actress who was married to Irving Thalberg, she noted that she was very much a perfectionist: "I was very fond of Norma and we became quite good friends — I liked her very much. She played a part like you would practice a violin — she'd keep on and on and she'd do it over and over — 'til you wanted to go crazy. Then she'd say, 'Let's do it again, maybe I can do it better.'"

Maureen had a small role with Norma and Clark Gable in *Strange Interlude* (1932), but they became close during the filming of *The Barretts of Wimpole Street* (1934). "Every afternoon after we became friends, she'd invite me to her bungalow for an eggnog. And after two eggnogs, director Sidney Franklin would say with a smile, 'Why don't you two go home for the day, and come back tomorrow.'

"Norma was very dear, and she came to my home for lunch one day and she wanted to use the bathroom. When I brought her a fresh towel, she was drying her hands on the shower curtain. And when I asked her why she was doing that, she said 'Oh, I don't like to get the towels dirty.' She was very sweet that way."

When asked about Wallace Beery, Maureen said that he was a difficult actor to work with who never learned his lines at home — instead waiting till the day of the shoot and flubbing his long speeches over and over. She related an anecdote that Robert Ryan had told her, that when the actor was making a western with Burt Lancaster called *The Professionals* (1966), a small plane flew too low and ruined the scene. Burt said, "Well, that was probably Wally Beery flying that plane." It was a joke of course, but if someone screwed something up on a movie set you could always blame it on the late Mr. Beery, who died in 1949.

Maureen mentioned that she seldom saw any of her films when they were made, because she was simply too busy. Her MGM contract called for a salary of $250 a week in the early days, but they docked your pay if you only worked three days in a week. For Maureen, that rarely happened because she was often working on two or even three films at a time. "Sometimes we'd even work on Sundays, before the Actor's Guild — I saw very few of my films until later years when they came on television. And even then, when I came on the screen — I'd shut off the set. I don't like to look at myself," she admitted with her broad Irish smile.

Maureen recalled that in the beginning of their screen relationship, William Powell didn't really like Myrna Loy, and that it was later that they became friends. When asked if Powell were as charming in real life as he was in the movies, Maureen noted, "He was more charming, he was very witty. He was an amazing wit, you'd enjoy him at a dinner party — he didn't need to be given the lines to say."

The legendary Greta Garbo was the star of the film *Anna Karenina* (1935), and Maureen was assigned to play the younger sister, Kitty. It was a small role, and she went to the producer David O. Selznick and admitted, "David, I really don't want the part, it's so small." But Selznick told her, "It's better to have a small role in a great film, than to be the star of a B-picture."

Maureen described her first meeting with Garbo, and admitted she was stunned by her beauty: "She came on the set and she looked like a goddess, she really did. Of course I was intimidated by her — she was almost unreal, even to people at MGM. I'd never even seen her. I was introduced to her and she said, 'I'm very happy that you are playing Kitty.'"

Maureen did the voice in her best Garbo accent, and said the actress was really quite friendly and asked her about the current gossip around the studio. "They never tell me anything around here," lamented Greta. When Maureen mentioned that Margaret Sullavan was making a film called *The Good Fairy* on the next set, Miss Garbo joked, "A film called *The Good Fairy*? What kind of a film is that!"

The subject jumped to the creepy thriller, *The Devil-Doll* (1936), directed by Tod Browning. "It's a fascinating film," said Maureen, "and was way ahead of its time in terms of filming and special effects. Browning was a strange man, he didn't tell you much, didn't talk much — he was a little strange-looking. He was my neighbor in Malibu at the time — but once he came home and went into his house, you never saw him at all. He'd close the door, that was it. He was a very mysterious man. But *Devil-Doll* was a wonderful film."

Commenting on F. Scott Fitzgerald, who wrote some scenes for *A Yank at Oxford* (1938), Maureen said warmly, "I liked him very much. He came out to my home in Malibu to meet me — he was going to write all the scenes for me and Bob Taylor. We had a mint julep and he was interesting because as a young girl in Ireland I had read some of his works. I had just missed the 'Jazz Era' by a couple of years, so I was fascinated to meet him. He was either the oldest young man I'd ever seen, or the youngest old man. He was nice-looking, but he looked like he had lived life. We got along very well."

The question was posed "Of which of your films are you most proud?" After some thought, Maureen mentioned *The Barretts of Wimpole Street* as one of her best pictures. Then, perhaps surprisingly, she admitted that her role of Jane meant a great deal to her: "Speaking of the Tarzan films, I got awfully sick of it for a while. But now as the years go by, I'm happy. I've become rather possessive about Jane after all these years. Maybe not so strange. My son said the other day that they, my children, were all glad that I had been the original Jane. I feel I should be proud of being Jane, because they remain classics to this day. Back then I wanted to be the great actress and do other things, but now I'm happy."

Maureen was asked about her hugely successful play, *Never Too Late*, which they decided to film as a motion picture in 1964. And they were talking about casting Rosalind Russell in the lead role that Ms. O'Sullivan had made famous on Broadway. Maureen got rather upset about this development, as she revealed: "I thought, no I want to do it. So I came to California, and I asked to see the producers, and I said, 'I should play the film.' I persuaded them — I did it myself. So when I got back to New York, my agent said, 'How the hell did you get the film?' And I said, 'I got it by myself — sheer gall!' Bud Yorkin, the director was very nice — he put up with me."

Maureen recalled working with various animals in the Tarzan pictures, and said she got along fine with Jackie the lion. However, the mighty beast made her rather nervous in one particular scene: "Jackie was tame, he was a lovely lion! But I didn't like the idea of him walking behind me in a long dolly shot. I wouldn't have minded walking behind him, so I could see what he was doing."

One of the stories from her MGM days was quite funny, concerning the chimpanzees that worked in the Tarzan films. "I got along with Cheeta at first, the young chimps were very sweet. They're nice till they're about three years old — and then do they get mean. And there were two men in the cast, Neil Hamilton and Paul Cavanagh, and they'd been bitten by this monkey. And I laughed at them and called them sissies, until the chimp bit me! And they were delighted. But I didn't get along with the monkeys after that at all.

"There was one chimp who used to come on the set in blue jeans, and a little shirt and tie sometimes, and it was very cute. The monkey trainer was a woman named Emma. And one day the chimp bit Emma, and the men went to her rescue. But she said, 'No, stay back — I'll fix this little monster.' So they rolled on the floor and fought, and finally the trainer won. I guess she didn't bite Emma anymore, just me."

The famous elephant stampede scene turned into a real stampede, but she held her ground on her pachyderm while the guys bolted and ran: "That was scary. I was on top of my elephant, who was very tame, and we were filming on the back lot. Suddenly, something must have frightened the elephants, about a dozen of them, and they trumpeted and stamped their feet, and it was a terrifying feeling. The actors on other elephants jumped off and ran — but I stuck with my elephant, and it was all right. She got me through the stampede. Neil Hamilton was on one elephant, he was off like a flash! I laughed at him, but he did the wise thing."

When asked if Jane had a yell like Tarzan, Maureen recalled with a little smile, "Yes she did, but I can't do it. It was done by the sound department. Nice yell. A call, rather. Let's call it a call instead of a yell."

Maureen celebrated her birthday on May 17, 1998, in the company of husband Jim, at Vincent's restaurant in Phoenix. This was Maureen's favorite eating establishment at their winter retreat in Arizona, and the cuisine was dubbed by the owner-chef, "southwestern French." Having been born in Ireland in 1911, this was her 87th birthday. There were many cards from family, friends, and her loyal fans, and she enjoyed a few glasses of her favorite champagne as Jim offered a toast to his wife on her special day.

Maureen and husband Jim were a happy loving couple ... you can see it in their eyes

Shortly after her birthday, Maureen did a lengthy interview with Tom Weaver of *Classic Images* magazine, and the subject for the umpteenth time was her role as Jane in the Tarzan pictures. Despite the fact that she had covered the same ground many times, Maureen was always gracious and generous with her answers when doing an interview about her past.

Once again asked about Johnny Weissmuller, Maureen responded with that warm smile that meant it was coming from the heart: "Oh, Johnny was wonderful, I really loved him like a brother. He was a big kid. He was fun. He was just what he looked like. He loved to laugh. He had no pretensions whatsoever about being a champion swimmer or any of those awards that he had won — national and worldwide awards. He had no feeling about that. He was just like anybody else, like a prop man or like one of the electricians. He was just a real nice guy. And good friend. I was very fond of Johnny."

In the spring of 1998, Maureen was having some health problems which she decided to address before returning to her New Hampshire home for the summer and fall months. After a complete physical, it was discovered that her carotid arteries on either side of her neck needed to be "cleaned out" because they were becoming clogged with plaque.

In consultation with her Phoenix doctors and her husband Jim, it was decided that they would do one side of her neck and the other side as soon as feasible. In mid-June Maureen entered Scottsdale Memorial Hospital in suburban Phoenix for the procedure.

The first surgery went fine and Maureen was recovering as expected at the hospital. She was even joking with her husband Jim that they should have a little party with the nurses because she was feeling so chipper.

After talking with her doctors, the second surgery was scheduled immediately to take care of the other side of her neck. Unfortunately, although the procedure went fine the recovery did not go well. The second surgery proved to be too taxing on her system, and she began to fade on Monday, June 22. As family members gathered around her bedside, Maureen died of heart failure late that evening. With Maureen when she died was her husband Jim, daughter Tisa, stepdaughter Cindy and her husband Claude Amerson. Prudence arrived later.

The passing of Maureen O'Sullivan was a tragic event for movie fans all over the world. One of her few remaining contemporaries from the Golden Age of Hollywood was old friend Bob Hope, who said, "The world has lost a lovely leading lady."

Father Hugh Hines, who had presided over the marriage ceremony of Maureen and Jim Cushing in 1983, offered these reflections to your author in the spring of 2006:

"Maureen's funeral was in the Siena College Chapel. While it was private, there were a good number of people present. Her children, of course, all her grandchildren, and friends of Maureen and Jim. I presided at the mass. Mia gave a beautiful reflection about her mother at the mass. I remember Mia saying that one of her first recollections of her mother was 'My Mother is so pretty!' And Maureen certainly was both externally, but even more internally. Maureen is buried in the Cushing plot in the Holy Redeemer Cemetery in Schenectady, New York."

Father Hines offered a few more memories, which he called "rambling remembrances:"

"After her marriage she still appeared in several movies and at least one soap opera, I think, *The Guiding Light*. I remember I asked her how long she would be in it and she added rather lightly, 'Oh I am poisoned in five weeks.' My mother and some of her friends were fans of both Maureen and the soaps so I clued them in on what was going to happen. A few weeks later Maureen said that her performance received a lot of favorable attention so she said, 'Tell your mother that I won't be drinking my fatal cup of tea for a few more weeks.'

"One evening the Cushings invited me out to dinner and we met at their home in Schenectady, and Maureen said we were not going out; she was cooking something at home. I was thinking 'movie and stage actresses don't cook' and said something to the effect, 'I didn't know you could cook,' and she looked at me, one eyebrow raised, and said, 'Father, I've had seven children, one doesn't have seven children and not know how to cook.' It was a very tasty meal."

Maureen corresponded regularly over the years with a handful of friends and some faithful fans, including your author David Fury. In the decades past she was capable of writing long, many pages long, letters to close friends such as George Cukor. She would pour her heart out if things were going well, rambling along in a happy mood talking about a little house that she was fixing up or the successes of her children.

Jim Cushing fondly recalled their Sunday routine, when they were home in either New Hampshire or Phoenix. After Maureen would rise around eleven in the morning, Jim would pull out a stack of letters from fans and say, "Okay, let's do this many today." And he would have maybe 20 or 30 letters and large envelopes containing photographs of the actress from her films, especially the Tarzan pictures.

Maureen would playfully groan, and then laugh and say, "Okay, let's get to it!" After they got started reading the letters it got to be kind of fun. She would sign the photos and signature cards, and Jim would put them in the stamped envelopes to go to the post office on Monday.

Over the years, Maureen O'Sullivan received tens of thousands of fan letters, and signed her autograph on photos and in person — one could estimate well over one-hundred thousand times. She preserved her popularity with generations of movie fans not only because of her timeless role as Jane in the Tarzan pictures, but because of that innate friendliness towards her huge legion of fans. Maureen maintained a willingness to keep in touch with fans and always signed autographs.

Ms. O'Sullivan was damn good at what she did, which is why she remained a star for more than a half-century. She also had a healthy respect for her occupation as an actress. Even though she never took any acting classes, Maureen ultimately developed her own style that worked on stage and the silver screen as well. She became a very fine actress who outlasted just about every one of her contemporaries from the Golden Age: "I didn't pretend to be an actress. I just tried to be natural, the best I could."

A statement that she made in 1982 when she was appearing in *Morning's At Seven* on stage, summed up her long career: "I always used to say, when I was a young girl, that I'd rather be a good character actress and go on forever than be a star." In reality, she was a star in her prime and like all quality actresses, she made the transition to character parts in her later years. But when you saw her name on the opening credits of a film presentation, silver screen or television, you knew you were in for a treat.

Maureen and Jim Cushing were together for almost twenty years, and they were extremely happy years for both. Career-wise, this was an exceptional run for the actress as well, as she stayed busy on the legitimate stage and made a successful comeback the last decade of her life on the big screen. Jim stated it best when he said about his wife:

"Maureen thought of herself as an actress, God bless her — until her dying day."

Motion Picture Filmography

1. SONG O' MY HEART • 1930 Fox Film Corp.
Cast: John McCormack *(Sean O'Carolan)*, Alice Joyce *(Mary O'Brien)*, **Maureen O'Sullivan** *(Eileen O'Brien)*, Tommy Clifford *(Tad O'Brien)*, J. M. Kerrigan *(Peter Conlon)*, John Garrick *(Fergus O'Donnell)*, Edwin Schneider *(Vincent Glennon)*, J. Farrell McDonald *(Joe Rafferty)*, Effie Ellsler *(Mona)*, Emily Fitzroy *(Aunt Elizabeth)*, Adres De Segurola *(Guido)*, Edward Martindel *(Fullerton)*. **Credits:** *Directed by* Frank Borzage; *Story,* Tom Barry; *Adaptation,* Sonya Levien; *Art Director,* Harry Oliver; *Photography,* Chester Lyons; *Grandeur Camera,* J. O. Taylor; *Editorial Supervision,* John Stone; *Film Editor,* Jack Murray; *Costumes,* Sophie Wachner; *Asst. Director,* Lew Borzage. *Running time:* 90 minutes. *Release date:* March 11, 1930

2. SO THIS IS LONDON • 1930 Fox Film Corp.
Cast: Will Rogers *(Hiram Draper)*, Irene Rich *(Mrs. Hiram Draper)*, Frank Albertson *(Junior Draper)*, **Maureen O'Sullivan** *(Elinor Worthing)*, Lumsden Hare *(Lord Percy Worthing)*, Mary Forbes *(Lady Worthing)*, Bramwell Fletcher *(Alfred Honeycutt)*, Dorothy Christy *(Lady Amy Ducksworth)*, Ellen Woodston *(nurse)*, Martha Lee Sparks *(little girl)*. **Credits:** *Directed by* John Blystone; *Scenarist,* Sonya Levien; *Adapt-Dialogue,* Owen Davis; *Camera,* Charles G. Clarke; *Sets,* Jack Schulze; *Film Editor,* Jack Dennis; *Music and Lyrics,* James F. Hanley, Joseph McCarthy; *Sound Engineer,* Frank MacKenzie; *Asst. Director,* Jasper Blystone; *Costumes,* Sophie Wachner. *Running time:* 92 minutes. *Release date:* May 23, 1930

3. JUST IMAGINE • 1930 Fox Film Corp.
Cast: El Brendel *(Single O)*, **Maureen O'Sullivan** *(LN-18)*, John Garrick *(J-21)*, Marjorie White *(D-6)*, Frank Albertson *(RT-42)*, Hobart Bosworth *(Z-4)*, Kenneth Thomson *(MT-3)*, Wilfred Lucas *(X-10)*, Mischa Auer *(B-36)*, Joyzelle *(Loo Loo/ Boo Boo)*, Ivan Linow *(Loko/Bobo)*. **Credits:** *Directed by* David Butler; *Story-Dialogue by* B. G. De Sylva, Lew Brown, Ray Henderson; *Art Director,* Stephen Goosson, Ralph Hammeras; *Photography,* Ernest Palmer; *Film Editor,* Irene Morra; *Songs:* "The Drinking Song," "The Romance of Elmer Stremingway," "Never, Never Wed," "There's Something About an Old-Fashioned Girl," "Mothers Ought To Tell Their Daughters," "I Am the Words, You Are the Melody," "Dance of Victory," "Never Swat a Fly" by B. G. De Sylva, Lew Brown, Ray Henderson; *Music Director,* Arthur Kay; *Dance Director,* Seymour Felix; *Recording Engineer,* Joseph E. Aiken; *Asst. Director,* Ad Schaumer; *Costume Design,* Dorothy Tree, Alice O'Neill. *Running time:* 108 minutes. *Release date:* November 23, 1930

4. THE PRINCESS AND THE PLUMBER • 1930 Fox Film Corp.
Cast: Charles Farrell *(Charlie Peters)*, **Maureen O'Sullivan** *(Princess Louise)*, H. B. Warner *(Prince Conrad of Daritzia)*, Joseph Cawthorn *(Merkll)*, Bert Roach *(Albert Bowers)*, Lucien Prival *(Baron von Kemper)*, Murray Kinnell *(Worthing)*, Louise Closser Hale *(Miss Eden)*, Arnold Lucy. **Credits:** *Directed by* Alexander Korda; *Story,* Alice Duer Miller; *Screenplay-Dialogue,* Howard J. Green; *Photography,* L. William O'Connell, Dave Ragin; *Art Director,* Stephen Goosson; *Film Editor,* Margaret V. Clancey; *Music Director,* Arthur Kay; *Recording Engineer,* Arthur L. von Kirbach; *Asst. Director,* Ewing Scott; *Costumes,* Sophie Wachner; *Assoc. Producer,* Al Rockett. *Running time:* 72 minutes. *Release date:* December 21, 1930

5. A CONNECTICUT YANKEE • 1931 Fox Film Corp.
Cast: Will Rogers *(Hank Martin, also known as Sir Boss)*, William Farnum *(King Arthur/inventor)*, **Maureen O'Sullivan** *(Alisande/girl in mansion)*, Myrna Loy *(Queen Morgan le Fay/seductive woman in mansion)*, Frank Albertson *(Clarence/Emile le Poulet)*, Brandon Hurst *(Sagramor/servant in mansion)*, Mitchell Harris *(Merlin/doctor)*, Ward Bond *(queen's knight)*. **Credits:** *Directed by* David Butler; *Adaptation and dialogue,* William Conselman; *Photography,* Ernest Palmer; *Special Effects,* Fred Sersen and Ralph Hammeras; *Settings,* William Darling; *Film Editor,* Irene Morra. *Asst. Director,* Ad Schaumer; *Costumes,* Sophie Wachner; *Sound Recording,* Joseph E. Aiken. Based on the novel *A Connecticut Yankee in King Arthur's Court* by Mark Twain (New York, 1889). *Running time:* 96 minutes. *Release date:* April 5, 1931

6. SKYLINE • 1931 Fox Film Corp.
Cast: Thomas Meighan *(Gordon A. McClellan)*, Hardie Albright *(John Breen)*, **Maureen O'Sullivan** *(Kathleen Kearny)*, Myrna Loy *(Paula Lambert)*, Stanley Fields *(Captain Breen)*, Jack Kennedy *(Mike Kearny)*, Robert McWade *(Judge Scott)*, Donald Dillaway *(Gerry Gaige)*, Alice Ward *(Mrs. Kearny)*, Dorothy Peterson *(Rose Breen)*.**Credits:** *Directed by* Sam Taylor; *Associate Producer,* John W. Considine, Jr.; *Story-Dialogue,* Kenyon Nicholson and Dudley Nichols; *Art Director,* Duncan Cramer; *Photography,* John Mescall; *Musical Score,* George Lipschultz; *Sound Recording,* W. W. Lindsay, Jr; *Costumes,* Dolly Tree. Based on the novel *East Side, West Side* by Felix Riesenberg (New York, 1927). *Running time:* 68 minutes. *Release date:* October 3, 1931

7. THE BIG SHOT • 1931 RKO Pathe Pictures, Inc.
Cast: Eddie Quillan *(Ray Smith)*, **Maureen O'Sullivan** *(Doris Thompson)*, Mary Nolan *(Fay Turner)*, Roscoe Ates *(Rusty)*, Belle Bennett *(Mrs. Isabel Thompson)*, Arthur Stone *(Old Timer)*, Louis John Bartels *(Mr. Howell)*, Otis Harlan *("Doc" Teasley)*, William Eugene *(Jack Spencer)*, Edward McWade *(Uncle Ira)*, Harvey Clark *(Mr. Hartman)*, A. S. Byron *(Mr. Potts)*, Charles Thurston *(town marshal)*. **Credits:** *Directed by* Ralph F. Murphy; *Associate Producer,* Harry Joe Brown; *Story,* George Dromgold and Hal Conklin; *Screenplay and Dialogue,* Earl Baldwin and Joseph Fields; *Photography,* Arthur Miller; *Art Director,* Carroll Clark; *Film Editor,* Charles Craft; *Costumes,* Gwen Wakeling; *Music Director,* Arthur Lange; *Sound Engineer,* Earl A. Wolcott. *Running time:* 66 minutes. *Release date:* December 18, 1931

8. THE SILVER LINING • 1932 Atlantic Pictures Corp.
Cast: Maureen O'Sullivan *(Joyce Moore [also known as Mary Kane])*, Betty Compson *(Kate Flynn)*, John Warburton *(Larry Clark)*, Montagu Love *(Michael Moore)*, Mary Doran *(Doris Lee)*, Cornelius Keefe *(Jerry)*, Martha Mattox *(Matron)*, Wally Albright *(Bobby O'Brien)*, Grace Valentine *(Mrs. O'Brien)*, John Holland *(Tommy)*, J. Frank Glendon *(Judge)*, Jane Kerr *(Matron)*, Mildred Golden *(Ella Preston)*, Marion Stokes *(Edna Joyce)*, Helen Gibson *(Dorothy Dent)*. **Credits:** *Directed by* Alan Crosland; *Producer,* Emil Jensen; *Story,* Hal Conklin; *Adaptation and Dialogue,* Gertrude Orr; *Cinematography,* Robert Planck; *Art Director,* Jack Schultze; *Film Editor,* Doris Drought; *Musical Score,* Lee Zahler; *Sound Engineer,* L. E. Tope; *Production Manager,* George Bertholon. *Running time:* 75 minutes. *Release date:* April 16, 1932. Previewed in November 1931 as *Thirty Days* also known as *The Big House for Girls.*

Maureen was paid $300 to star in this 1931 drama shortly before signing with MGM. Her character of Joyce Moore lands in jail for 30 days in a case of mistaken identity ... but it turns her life around for the better.

9. TARZAN, THE APE MAN • 1932 M-G-M
Cast: Johnny Weissmuller *(Tarzan)*, **Maureen O'Sullivan** *(Jane Parker)* Neil Hamilton *(Harry Holt)*, C. Aubrey Smith *(James Parker)*, Doris Lloyd *(Mrs. Cutten)*, Forrester Harvey *(Beamish)*, Ivory Williams *(Riano)* **Credits:** *Directed by* W. S. Van Dyke; *Produced by* Bernard H. Hyman; *Adaptation by* Cyril Hume; *Dialogue by* Ivor Novello; *Photography by* Harold Rosson and Clyde de Vinna; *Film Editors,* Ben Lewis and Tom Held; *Recording Director,* Douglas Shearer; *Art Director,* Cedric Gibbons; *Production Manager,* Joseph J. Cohn; *Animal Supervision,* George Emerson, Bert Nelson, Louis Roth, Louis Goebel; *Photographic Effects,* Warren Newcombe; *Additional Cinematography,* William Snyder; *Opening Theme,* "Voodoo Dance" by George Richelavie, *Arranged by* Fritz Stahlberg, P. A. Marquardt. *Based upon the characters created by* Edgar Rice Burroughs. *Running time:* 99 minutes. *Release date:* March 1932

10. THE INFORMATION KID • 1932 Universal Pictures
Cast: Tom Brown *(Marty Black)*, James Gleason *(Silk Henley)*, **Maureen O'Sullivan** *(Sally)*, Andy Devine *(Information Kid)*, Mickey Rooney *(Midge)*, Borton Churchill *(chairman of committee)*, Morgan Wallace *("Cueball" Kelly)*. **Credits:** *Directed by* Kurt Neumann; *Producer,* Carl Laemmle, Jr.; *Screenplay,* Earle Snell; *Story,* Gerald Beaumont and Charles Logue; *Cinematography,* Arthur Edeson; *Art Director,* Stanley Fleischer; *Film Editor,* Philip Cahn; *Sound,* Robert Pritchard. *Running time:* 71 minutes. *Release date:* May 28, 1932

11. STRANGE INTERLUDE • 1932 M-G-M
Cast: Norma Shearer *(Nina Leeds [Evans])*, Clark Gable *(Dr. Ned Darrell)*, Alexander Kirkland *(Sam Evans)*, Ralph Morgan *(Charlie Marsden)*, Robert Young *(Gordon)*, **Maureen O'Sullivan** *(Madeleine)*, May Robson *(Mrs. Evans)*, Henry B. Walthall *(Professor Leeds)*, Mary Alden *(maid)*, Tad Alexander *(Gordon, as a child)*. **Credits:** *Directed by* Robert Z. Leonard; *Dialogue and Continuity*, Bess Meredyth and C. Gardner Sullivan; *Photography*, Lee Garmes; *Art Director*, Cedric Gibbons; *Film Editor*, Margaret Booth; *Gowns*, Adrian; *Recording Director*, Douglas Shearer. Based on the play *Strange Interlude* by Eugene O'Neill (New York, 1928). *Running time:* 110 minutes. *Release date:* July 15, 1932

12. SKYSCRAPER SOULS • 1932 M-G-M
Cast: Warren William *(David Dwight)*, **Maureen O'Sullivan** *(Lynn Harding)*, Anita Page *(Jenny)*, Verree Teasdale *(Sarah Dennis)*, Norman Foster *(Tom Shepherd)*, Gregory Ratoff *(Vinmont)*, George Barbier *(Norton)*, Jean Hersholt *(Jake)*, Wallace Ford *(Slim)*, Hedda Hopper *(Ella Dwight)*, Helen Coburn *(Myra)*, John Marston *(Bill)*, Purnell B. Pratt *(Brewster)*, Arnold Lucy *(Hamilton)*, Edward Brophy *(man in elevator)*, Billy Gilbert *(ticket agent)*, Tom Kennedy *(masseur)*. **Credits:** *Directed by* Edgar Selwyn; *Dialogue and Continuity*, Elmer Harris; *Adaptation*, C. Gardner Sullivan; *Photography*, William Daniels; *Art Director*, Cedric Gibbons; *Film Editor*, Tom Held; *Recording Director*, Douglas Shearer; *Song*, "Metropolitan March" by Emil Frey. Based on the novel *Skyscraper* by Faith Baldwin (New York, 1931). *Running time:* 99 minutes. *Release date:* August 4, 1932

13. OKAY, AMERICA • 1932 Universal Pictures
Cast: Lew Ayres *(Larry Wayne)*, **Maureen O'Sullivan** *(Sheila Barton)*, Louis Calhern *("Mileaway" Russell)*, Edward Arnold *("Duke" Morgan)*, Walter Catlett *(City editor "Lucille")*, Allan Dinehart *(Roger Jones)*, Henry Armetta *(Sam)*, Charles Dow Clark *("Obituary")*, Emerson Tracy *(Jerry Robbins)*, Marjorie Gateson *(Mrs. Herbert Wright)*, Frank Sheridan *(police commissioner)*, Rollo Lloyd *(Joe Morton)*, Margaret Lindsay *(Ruth Drake)*, Gilbert Emery *(John Drake)*, Virginia Howell *(Mrs. John Drake)*, Berton Churchill *(Jacob Baron)*, Ruth Lyons *(Phyllis Martin)*, Frank Darien *(O'Toole)*. **Credits:** *Directed by* Tay Garnett; *Producer*, Carl Laemmle, Jr.; *Original Story and Screenplay*, William Anthony McGuire;. *Photography*, Arthur Miller; *Editor*, Ted Kent; *Sound*, Jess Moulin. *Running time:* 80 minutes. *Release date:* September 8, 1932

14. PAYMENT DEFERRED • 1932 M-G-M
Cast: Charles Laughton *(William Marble)*, **Maureen O'Sullivan** *(Winnie Marble)*, Dorothy Peterson *(Annie Marble)*, Verree Teasdale *(Mme. Collins)*, Ray Milland *(James Medland)*, Billy Bevan *(Hammond)*, Halliwell Hobbes *(prospective tenant)*, William Stack *(the doctor)*. **Credits:** *Directed by* Lothar Mendes; *Screenplay*, Ernest Vajda and Claudine West; *Photography*, Merritt B. Gerstad; *Art Director*, Cedric Gibbons; *Film Editor*, Frank Sullivan; *Recording Director*, Douglas Shearer. Based on the play *Payment Deferred* by Jeffrey F. Dell and the novel by E.M. Forster (London, 1926). *Running time:* 80 minutes. *Release date:* November 7, 1932

15. ROBBERS' ROOST • 1933 Fox Film Corp.
Cast: George O'Brien *(Jim Wall)*, **Maureen O'Sullivan** *(Helen Herrick)*, Walter McGrail *(Brad)*, Maude Eburne *(Aunt Ellen)*, Reginald Owen *(Cecil Herrick)*, William Pawley *(Hank Hays)*, Clifford Stanley *(Happy Jack)*, Robert Greig *(Tulliver)*, Doris Lloyd *(Prossie)*, Gilbert Holmes *(Briggs)*, Frank Rice *(Daniels)*, William Nestell *(Mac)*, Vinegar Roan *(Smoky Slocum)*, Ted Oliver *(Latimer)*, Fred Toones *(Ferryboat driver)*, Frank McGrath *(Mexican)*.**Credits:** *Directed by* Louis King; *Screenplay*, Dudley Nichols; *Photography*, George Schneiderman; *Art Director*, Joseph Wright; *Sound Recording*, Bernard Freericks; *Wardrobe*, David Cox; *Musical Director*, George Lipschultz. *Songs:* "Listen to the Lambs" and "Shout All Over Heaven," spirituals "Cowboy's Heaven" and "I Adore You (Yo te adoro)," *words and music by* Val Burton and Will Jason. Based on the novel *Robbers' Roost* by Zane Grey (New York, 1932). *Running time:* 64 minutes. *Release date:* February 1933

16. THE COHENS AND KELLYS IN TROUBLE • 1933 Universal Pictures
Cast: George Sidney *(Nathan Cohen)*, Charles Murray *(Captain Patrick Kelly)*, **Maureen O'Sullivan** *(Molly Kelly)*, Frank Albertson *(Bob Graham)*, Andy Devine *(Andy Anderson)*, Jobyna Howland *(Queenie Truelove)*, Maude Fulton *(Fern)*, Henry Armetta *(Captain Silva)*, Maurice Black *(Nick)*, Arthur Hoyt *(Boswell)*, Max Davidson *(Larsen)*, Herbert Corthell *(panhandler)*, Olive Cooper *(Swedish stewardess)*, Willie Fong *(Ah Chung)*, Don Brody *(Chauffeur)*, Ed Le Saint *(freighter captain)*, Jack Raymond. **Credits:** *Directed by* George Stevens; *Producer*, Carl Laemmle, Jr.; *Screenplay*, Albert Austin and Fred Guiol; *Story*, Homer Croy and Vernon Smith; *Photography*, Len Powers; *Art Director*, Stanley Fleischer; *Film Editor*, Robert Carlisle. *Running time:* 69 minutes. *Release date:* March 1933

17. TUGBOAT ANNIE • 1933 M-G-M
Cast: Marie Dressler *(Annie Brennan)*, Wallace Beery *(Terry Brennan)*, Robert Young *(Alec Brennan)*, **Maureen O'Sullivan** *(Pat Severn)*, Willard Robertson *(Red Severn)*, Tammany Young *(Shifless)*, Frankie Darro *(Alec, as a child)*. Jack Pennick *(Pete)*, Paul Hurst *(Sam)*, Willie Fung *(Chow)*. **Credits:** *Directed by* Mervyn LeRoy; *Associate Producer*, Harry Rapf; *Adaptation*, Zeida Sears and Eve Greene; *Photography*, Gregg Toland; *Art Director*, Merrill Pye; *Film Editor*, Blanche Sewell; *Interior Decoration*, Edwin B. Willis; *Recording Director*, Douglas Shearer. Based on the "Tugboat Annie" short stories by Norman Reilly Raine in *The Saturday Evening Post*. *Running time:* 87 minutes. *Release date:* August 1933

18. STAGE MOTHER • 1933 M-G-M
Cast: Alice Brady *(Kitty Lorraine)*, **Maureen O'Sullivan** *(Shirley Lorraine)*, Franchot Tone *(Warren Foster)*, Phillips Holmes *(Lord Aylesworth)*, Ted Healy *(Ralph Martin)*, Russell Hardie *(Fred Lorraine)*, C. Henry Gordon *(Ricco)*, Alan Edwards *(Dexter)*, Ben Alexander *(Francis Nolan)*, Larry Fine *(store customer)*, Snowflake *(porter)*, Harry Holman *(Rumley)*. Credits: *Directed by* Charles Brabin; *Screenplay,* John Meehan and Bradford Ropes; *Photography,* George Folsey; *Art Director,* Stanwood Rogers; *Film Editor,* Frank Hull; *Interior Decoration,* Edwin B. Willis; *Gowns,* Adrian; *Orchestra Conductor,* Lou Silvers; *Dance Director,* Albertina Rasch; *Recording Director,* Douglas Shearer; *Songs:* "Beautiful Girl" and "I'm Dancing on a Rainbow," *words and music by* Nacio Herb Brown and Arthur Freed; "Any Little Girl That's a Nice Little Girl Is the Right Little Girl for Me," *words and music by* Fred Fisher. Based on the novel *Stage Mother* by Bradford Ropes (New York, 1933). *Running time:* 85 minutes. *Release date:* September 1933

19. TARZAN AND HIS MATE • 1934 M-G-M
Cast: Johnny Weissmuller *(Tarzan)*, **Maureen O'Sullivan** *(Jane)*, Neil Hamilton *(Harry Holt)*, Paul Cavanagh *(Martin Arlington)*, Forrester Harvey *(Beamish)*, Nathan Curry *(Saidi)*, William Stack *(Tom Pierce)*, Desmond Roberts *(Henry Van Ness)*, Paul Porcasi *(Monsieur Feronde)*, Yola D'Avril *(Madame Feronde)*; Everett Brown *(native bearer)* Credits: *Directed by* Cedric Gibbons (uncredited direction by Jack Conway); *Produced by* Bernard H. Hyman; *Screenplay by* James Kevin McGuinness; *Adaptation by* Howard Emmett Rogers and Leon Gordon; *Photographed by* Charles G. Clarke and Clyde de Vinna; *Film Editor,* Tom Held; *Recording Director,* Douglas Shearer; *Art Director,* Arnold Gillespie; *Production Manager,* Joseph J. Cohn; *Second Unit Directors,* James McKay, Erroll Taggart, Nick Grinde; *Animal Supervision,* George Emerson, Bert Nelson, Louis Roth, Louis Goebel; *Special Effects,* James Basevi; *Art Effects,* Warren Newcombe; *Photographic Effects,* Irving Ries; *Sound Effects,* T. B. Hoffman, James Graham, Mike Steinore; *Opening Theme,* "Voodoo Dance" by George Richelavie, *Arranged by* Fritz Stahlberg, P.A. Marquardt; *Closing Theme,* "My Tender One" by Dr. William Axt. *Based upon the characters created by* Edgar Rice Burroughs. *Running time:* 116 minutes at preview, 95 minutes in general release. *Release date:* April 1934

20. THE THIN MAN • 1934 M-G-M
Cast: William Powell *(Nick Charles)*; Myrna Loy *(Nora Charles)*; **Maureen O'Sullivan** *(Dorothy Wynant)*; Nat Pendleton *(Lieutenant John Guild)*; Minna Gombell *(Mimi Wynant)*; Porter Hall *(McCauley)*; Henry Wadsworth *(Tommy)*; William Henry *(Gilbert Wynant)*; Harold Huber *(Nunheim)*; Cesar Romero *(Chris Jorgenson)*; Natalie Moorhead *(Julia Wolf)*; Edward Brophy *(Joe Morelli)*; Clay Clement *(Quinn)*; Thomas Jackson *(reporter)*; Walter Long *(Stutsy Burke)*; Bert Roach *(Foster)*; Ben Taggart *(police captain)*. Credits: *Directed by* W. S. Van Dyke II; *Producer,* Hunt Stromberg; *Screenplay,* Albert Hackett, Frances Goodrich; *Assistant Director,* Les Selander; *Photography,* James Wong Howe; *Art Directors,* Cedric Gibbons, David Townsend; *Editor,* Robert J. Kern. Based on the novel *The Thin Man* by Dashiell Hammett. *Running time:* 91 minutes. *Release date:* July 1934

21. HIDE-OUT • 1934 M-G-M
Cast: Robert Montgomery *(Lucky Wilson)*, **Maureen O'Sullivan** *(Pauline Miller)*, Edward Arnold *(Lieutenant MacCarthy)*, Elizabeth Patterson *(Ma Miller)*, Whitford Kane *(Pa Miller)*, Mickey Rooney *(Willie)*, C. Henry Gordon *(Tony Berrelli)*, Muriel Evans *(Babe)*, Edward Brophy *(Brill)*, Henry Armetta *(Louis Shuman)*, Herman Bing *(Jake Lillie)*, Louise Henry *(Millie)*, Harold Huber *(Dr. Warner)*, Roberta Gale *(hat check girl)*, Virginia Verrill *(singer on* "All I Do Is Dream of You"*)*, Ruth and Lester *(dancers in adagio dance)*. Credits: *Directed by* W. S. Van Dyke II; *Producer,* Hunt Stromberg; *Screenplay,* Frances Goodrich and Albert Hackett; *Story,* Mauri Grashin; *Photography,* Ray June and Sidney Wagner; *Art director,* Cedric Gibbons; *Art Director Associates,* David Townsend and Edwin B. Willis; *Film Editor,* Basil Wrangell; *Recording Director,* Douglas Shearer; *Wardrobe,* Dolly Tree; *Musical Score,* Dr. William Axt; *dance numbers staged by* Arthur Appell and Chester Hale; *Songs:* "The Dream Was So Beautiful" and "All I Do Is Dream of You," *words by* Arthur Freed, *music by* Nacio Herb Brown. *Running time:* 82 minutes. *Release date:* August 1934

22. THE BARRETTS OF WIMPOLE STREET • 1934 M-G-M
Cast: Norma Shearer *(Elizabeth Barrett)*, Fredric March *(Robert Browning)*, Charles Laughton *(Edward Barrett)*, **Maureen O'Sullivan** *(Henrietta Barrett)*, Katharine Alexander *(Anabel Barrett)*, Ralph Forbes *(Captain Surtees Cook)*, Marion Clayton *(Bella Hedley)*, Ian Wolfe *(Harry Sevan)*, Ferdinand Munier *(Dr. Chambers)*, Una O'Connor *(Wilson)*, Leo G. Carroll *(Dr. Ford-Waterlow)*, Vernon Downing *(Octavius Barrett)*, Neville Clark *(Charles Barrett)*, Matthew Smith *(George Barrett)*, Robert Carlton *(Alfred Barrett)*, Allan Conrad *(Henry Barrett)*, Peter Hobbes *(Septimus Barrett)*, Lowden Adams *(butler)*. Credits: *Directed by* Sidney Franklin; *Produced by* Irving G. Thalberg; *Screenplay,* Ernest Vajda, Claudine West and Donald Ogden Stewart; *Photography,* William Daniels; *Art Director,* Cedric Gibbons; *Art Director Associates,* Harry McAfee and Edwin B. Willis; *Film editor,* Margaret Booth; *Gowns,* Adrian; *Recording Director,* Douglas Shearer; *Musical Score,* Herbert Stothart. Based on the play *The Barretts of Wimpole Street* by Rudolf Besier (London, 1930). *Running time:* 111 minutes. *Release date:* September 1934

23. DAVID COPPERFIELD • 1935 M-G-M
Cast: W. C. Fields, *(Wilkins Micawber)*; Lionel Barrymore, *(Mr. Peggotty)*; **Maureen O'Sullivan**, *(Dora Spenlow)*; Madge Evans, *(Agnes Wickfield)*; Edna May Oliver *(Aunt Betsey Trotwood)*; Lewis Stone, *(Mr. Wickfield)*; Frank Lawton *(David the adult)*; Freddie Bartholomew, *(David the child)*; Elizabeth Allan, *(Mrs. Clara Copperfield)*; Roland Young, *(Uriah Heep)*; Basil Rathbone, *(Mr. Murdstone)*; Jessie Ralph, *(Nurse Peggotty)*; Jean Cadell, *(Mrs. Micawber)*; Violet Kemble Cooper, *(Jane Murdstone)*; Elsa Lanchester, *(Clickett)*; Lennox Pawle, *(Mr. Dick)*; Una O'Connor,

(Mrs. Gummidge); John Buckler, *(Ham)*; Hugh Williams, *(Steerforth)*; with Ivan Simpson, Hugh Walpole, Mabel Colcord, Herbert Mundin, Fay Chaldecott, Florine McKinney, Marilyn Knowlden, Harry Beresford, Renee Gadd, Arthur Treacher. **Credits:** *Directed by* George Cukor; *Produced by* David O. Selznick; *Assistant Director,* Joseph Newman; *Adaptation,* Hugh Walpole; *Screenplay,* Howard Estabrook; *Photography,* Oliver T. Marsh; *Art Director,* Cedric Gibbons; *Wardrobe,* Dolly Tree; *Music,* Herbert Stothart; *Film Editor,* Robert J. Kern; *Recording Director,* Douglas Shearer. *Based on the novel by* Charles Dickens. *Running time:* 133 minutes. *Release date:* January 18, 1935

24. WEST POINT OF THE AIR • 1935 M-G-M

Cast: Wallace Beery *("Big Mike" Stone)*, Robert Young *("Little Mike" Stone)*, Lewis Stone *(General Carter),* **Maureen O'Sullivan** *(his daughter "Skip"),* Russell Hardie *(her brother Phil),* Rosalind Russell *(Dare Marshall),* James Gleason *(Joe "Bags"),* Henry Wadsworth *(Lieut. Pettis),* Robert Taylor *(Jaskarelli),* Robert Livingston *(Pippinger),* Frank Conroy *(Captain Cannon),* G. Pat Collins *(Lieutenant Kelly),* Ronnie Cosby *("Mike" as a boy),* Bobbie Caldwell *("Phil" as a boy),* Marilyn Spinner *("Skip" as a girl).* **Credits:** *Directed by* Richard Rosson; *Producer,* Monta Bell; *Screenplay,* Frank Wead and Arthur J. Beckhard; *Original Story,* James K. McGuinness and John Monk Saunders; *Photography,* Clyde DeVinna; *Aerial Photography,* Charles A. Marshall and Elmer Dyer; *Art Director,* Cedric Gibbons; *Art Director Associate,* Howard H. Campbell; *Film Editor,* Frank Sullivan; *Wardrobe,* Dolly Tree; *Synchronized Score,* Charles Maxwell; *Recording Director,* Douglas Shearer. *Running time:* 88 minutes. *Release date:* March, 1935

25. CARDINAL RICHELIEU • 1935 M-G-M

Cast: George Arliss *(Cardinal Richelieu),* **Maureen O'Sullivan** *(Lenore),* Edward Arnold *(Louis XIII),* Cesar Romero *(Andre de Pons),* Douglass Dumbrille *(Baradas),* Francis Lister *(Gaston),* Halliwell Hobbes *(Father Joseph),* Violet Kemble Cooper *(Queen Marie),* Katharine Alexander *(Queen Anne),* Robert Harrigan *(Fontrailles),* Joseph Tozer *(De Bussy),* Lumsden Hare *(Gustavus Adolphus, King of Sweden),* Russell Hicks *(Le Moyne),* Keith Kenneth *(Duke D'Epernon),* Murray Kinnell *(Duke of Lorraine),* Herbert Bunston *(Duke of Normandy),* Guv Bellis *(Duke of Buckingham),* Boyd Irwin *(Austrian Prime Minister),* Leonard Mudie *(Olivares),* Reginald Sheffield *(Richelieu's outrider).* **Credits:** *Directed by* Rowland V. Lee; *Associate Producers,* William Goetz and Raymond Griffith; *Asst. Director,* Ben Silvey; *Screenplay,* Maude Howell; *Adaptation,* Cameron Rogers; *Dialogue,* W. P. Lipscomb; *Photography,* Peverell Marley; *Art Director,* Richard Day; *Film Editor,* Sherman Todd; *Costumes,* Omar Kiam; *Sound,* Vinton Vernon and Roger Heman; *Music Director,* Alfred Newman. Based on the play *Richelieu* by Sir Edward Bulwer-Lytton (London, 1839). *Running time:* 82 minutes. *Release date:* April 18, 1935

26. THE FLAME WITHIN • 1935 M-G-M

Cast: Ann Harding *(Dr. Mary White),* Herbert Marshall *(Dr. Gordon Phillips),* **Maureen O'Sullivan** *(Lillian Belton),* Louis Hayward *(Jack Kerry),* Henry Stephenson *(Dr. Jock Frazier),* Margaret Seddon *(Mrs. Grenfell),* George Russell *(Mr. Rigby),* Eily Malyon *(Murdock),* Claudelle Kaye *(Nurse Carter),* Sam Hayes *(Radio announcer).* **Credits:** *Directed and Produced by* Edmund Goulding; *Asst. Director,* Dolph Zimmer; *Screenplay,* Edmund Goulding; *Photography,* James Wong Howe; *Art Director,* Cedric Gibbons; *Art Director Associates,* William A. Horning and Edwin B. Willis; *Film Editor,* Blanche Sewell; *Recording Director,* Douglas Shearer; *Wardrobe,* Dolly Tree; *Orchestra Conductor,* Victor Baravalle; *Music composed by* Jerome Kern. *Running time:* 75 minutes. *Release date:* May, 1935

27. WOMAN WANTED • 1935 M-G-M

Cast: Maureen O'Sullivan *(Ann Gray),* Joel McCrea *(Tony Baxter),* Lewis Stone *(District Attorney Martin),* Louis Calhern *(Smiley),* Edgar Kennedy *(Sweeney),* Adrienne Ames *(Betty Randolph),* Robert Grieg *(Peedles),* Noel Madison *(Joe Metz),* Granville Bates *(Casey),* William B. Davidson *(Collins),* Richard Powell *(Lee),* Erville Alderson *(constable),* Gertrude Short *(Gertie),* Stanley Andrews *(foreman of jury),* Bob Murphy *(dissenter),* John Dilson, Phil Tead, Marg G. Bradley, Hector V. Sarno *(jurors),* Gayne Whitman *(attorney),* Margaret Bloodgood *(matron).* **Credits:** *Directed by* George B. Seitz;. *Screenplay,* Leonard Fields and Dave Silverstein; *Photography,* Charles Clarke; *Art Director,* Cedric Gibbons; *Art Director Associates,* Joseph Wright and Edwin B. Willis; *Film Editor,* Ben Lewis; *Wardrobe,* Dolly Tree; *Musical Score,* Dr. William Axt; *Recording Director,* Douglas Shearer; Based on the story or play *Get That Girl* by Wilson Collison (publication unknown). *Running time:* 70 minutes. *Release date:* July, 1935

28. ANNA KARENINA • 1935 M-G-M

Cast: Greta Garbo *(Anna Karenina),* Fredric March *(Count Vronsky),* Freddie Bartholomew *(Sergei),* **Maureen O'Sullivan** *(Kitty),* May Robson *(Countess Vronsky),* Basil Rathbone *(Alexei Karenin),* Reginald Owen *(Stiva),* Reginald Denny *(Yashvin),* Phoebe Foster *(Dolly),* Gyles Isham *(Konstantin Levin),* Joan Marsh *(Lily),* Ethel Griffies *(Mme. Kartasoff),* Harry Beresford *(Matve),* Sarah Padden *(governess),* Cora Sue Collins *(Tania),* Mary Forbes *(Princess Sorokina),* Joe E. Tozer *(butler),* Guy D'Ennery *(tutor),* Buster Phelps *(Grisha),* Sidney Bracy *(Vronsky's valet),* Harry Allen *(Cord),* Ella Ethridge *(Anna's maid).* **Credits:** *Directed by* Clarence Brown; *Produced by* David O. Selznick; *Screenplay,* Clemence Dane and Salka Viertel; *Dialogue Adaptation,* S. N. Behrman; *Photography,* William Daniels; *Art Director,* Cedric Gibbons; *Art Director Associates,* Frederic Hope and Edwin B. Willis; *Film Editor,* Robert J. Kern; *Musical Score,* Herbert Stothart; *Vocal and Choral,* Russian Symphony Choir; *Ballet staged by* Margarete Wallmann; *Mazurka staged by* Chester Hale; *Recording Director,* Douglas Shearer; *Consultant,* Count Andrey Tolstoy; Music selections from the ballet *Eugene Onegin* by Peter Ilyich Tchaikovsky. Based on the novel *Anna Karenina* by Leo Tolstoy (Moscow, 1876). *Running time:* 93 minutes. *Release date:* August 30, 1935 (New York premiere)

29. THE BISHOP MISBEHAVES • 1935 M-G-M
Cast: Edmund Gwenn *(James, Bishop of Broadminster)*, **Maureen O'Sullivan** *(Hester Grantham)*, Lucile Watson *(Lady Emily)*, Reginald Owen *(Guy Waller)*, Dudley Digges *("Red")*, Norman Foster *(Donald Meadows)*, Lilian Bond *(Mrs. Millie Waller)*, Melville Cooper *(Collins, the chauffeur)*, Robert Greig *(Rosalind)*, Charles McNaughton *("Frenchy")*, Etienne Girardot *(Brooke the butler)*, Ivan Simpson *(Mr. Grantham)*, Lumsden Hare *(Constable)*. **Credits:** *Directed by* E. A. Dupont; *Screenplay,* Leon Gordon; *Photography,* James Van Trees; *Art Director,* Cedric Gibbons; *Art Director Associates,* Harry McAfee and Edwin B. Willis; *Film Editor,* James E. Newcom; *Wardrobe,* Dolly Tree; *Musical score,* Edward Ward; *Recording Director,* Douglas Shearer. Based on the play *The Bishop Misbehaves* by Frederick Jackson (New York, 1935). *Running time:* 86 minutes. *Release date:* September 1935

30. THE VOICE OF BUGLE ANN • 1936 M-G-M
Cast: Lionel Barrymore *(Springfield Davis)*, **Maureen O'Sullivan** *(Camden Terry)*, Eric Linden *(Benjy Davis)*, Dudley Digges *(Jacob Terry)*, Spring Byington *(Ma Davis)*, Charley Grapewin *(Cal Royster)*, Henry Wadsworth *(Bake Royster)*, William Newell *(Mr. Tanner)*, James Macklin *(Del Royster)*, Jonathan Hale *(D.A.)*, Frederick Burton *(warden)*, James Marcus *(Ed Armstrong)*, Clayton Drew *(Mr. Lancy)*, William Moore *(Pettigrew's boy)*, Guy Sar *(Mr. Pettigrew)*, Ben Hall *(Gabe)*, Sidney Bracy *(clerk)*, Lew Kelly *(sheriff)*, Burr Caruth *(judge)*, Louis Mason *(defense attorney)*, Lillian Drew *(Mrs. Lancy)*, Marie Layton *(Mrs. Pettigrew)*. **Credits:** *Directed by* Richard Thorpe; *Producer,* John W. Considine Jr.; *Screenplay,* Harvey Gates and Samuel Hoffenstein; *Photography,* Ernest Haller; *Art Director,* Cedric Gibbons; *Art Director Associates,* Stan Rogers and Edwin B. Willis; *Film Editor,* George Boemler; *Wardrobe,* Dolly Tree; *Recording Director,* Douglas Shearer; *Music Score,* Rudolph Kopp. Based on the novel *The Voice of Bugle Ann* by MacKinlay Kantor (New York, 1935). *Running time:* 70 minutes. *Release date:* February 1936

31. THE DEVIL-DOLL • 1936 M-G-M
Cast: Lionel Barrymore *(Paul Lavond [aka Madame Mandelip])*, **Maureen O'Sullivan** *(Lorraine Lavond)*, Frank Lawton *(Toto)*, Rafaela Ottiano *(Malita)*, Robert Greig *(Coulvet)*, Lucy Beaumont *(Mme. Lavond)*, Henry B. Walthall *(Marcel)*, Grace Ford *(Lachna)*, Pedro de Cordoba *(Matin)*, Arthur Hohl *(Radin)*, Juanita Quigley *(Marguerite Coulvet)*, Claire du Brey *(Mme. Coulvet)*, Rollo Lloyd *(detective)*, E. Allyn Warren *(commissioner)*, Billy Gilbert *(butler)*. **Credits:** *Directed by* Tod Browning; *Producer,* Edward J. Mannix; *Screenplay,* Garrett Fort, Guy Endore and Erich Von Stroheim; *Story,* Tod Browning; *Photographer,* Leonard Smith; *Art Director,* Cedric Gibbons; *Art Director Associates,* Stan Rogers and Edwin B. Willis; *Film Editor,* Fredrick Y. Smith; *Wardrobe,* Dolly Tree; *Recording Director,* Douglas Shearer; *Apache dance,* Val Raset; *Music Score,* Franz Waxman. Based on the novel *Burn, Witch, Burn!* by Abraham Merritt (New York, 1933). *Running time:* 79 minutes. *Release date:* July 1936

32. TARZAN ESCAPES • 1936 M-G-M
Cast: Johnny Weissmuller *(Tarzan)*, **Maureen O'Sullivan** *(Jane)*, John Buckler *(Captain Fry)*, Benita Hume *(Rita Parker)*, William Henry *(Eric Parker)*, Herbert Mundin *(Herbert Henry Rawlins)*, E. E. Clive *(Masters)*, Darby Jones *(Bomba)*, Monte Montague *(riverboat captain)*. **Credits:** *Directed by* Richard Thorpe; *Associate Producer,* Sam Zimbalist; *Screenplay by* Cyril Hume; *Based upon the characters created by* Edgar Rice Burroughs; *Recording Director,* Douglas Shearer; *Art Director,* Elmer Sheeley; *Photographed by* Leonard Smith; *Film Editor,* W. Donn Hayes; *Set Decorations,* Edwin B. Willis; *Special Effects Director,* A. Arnold Gillespie; *Photographic Effects,* Thomas Tutwiler; *Art Effects,* Warren Newcombe; *Opening Theme,* "Cannibal Carnival" by Sol Levy; *Closing Theme,* "My Tender One" by Dr. William Axt. *Running time:* 95 minutes. *Release date:* November 1936

33. A DAY AT THE RACES • 1937 M-G-M
Cast: Groucho Marx *(Dr. Hugo Z. Hackenbush)*, Chico Marx *(Tony)*, Harpo Marx *(Stuffy)*, Allan Jones *(Gil Stewart)*, **Maureen O'Sullivan** *(Judy Standish)*, Margaret Dumont *(Mrs. Upjohn)*, Leonard Ceeley *(Whitmore)*, Douglas Dumbrille *(Morgan)*, Esther Muir *(Cokey Flo)*, Sig Rumann *(Dr. Steinberg)*, Robert Middlemass *(sheriff)*, Vivien Fay *(ballet dancer)*, Ivie Anderson *(swing dancer)*, Frankie Darro *(Morgan's jockey)*. **Credits:** *Produced by* Irving Thalberg and Lawrence Weingarten; *Directed by* Sam Wood; *Screenplay,* Robert Pirosh, George Seaton and George Oppenheimer; *Original Story,* Robert Pirosh, George Seaton; *Photography,* Joseph Ruttenberg; *Art Director,* Cedric Gibbons; *Art Director Associates,* Stan Rogers and Edwin B. Willis; *Film Editor,* Frank E. Hull; *Wardrobe,* Dolly Tree; *Recording Director,* Douglas Shearer; *Music Director,* Franz Waxman; *Music presentation,* Merrill Pye; *Musical arrangements,* Roger Edens; *Choral and orchestral arrangements,* Leo Arnaud; *Orchestra,* George Bassman and Paul Marquardt; *Music numbers staged by* Dave Gould. *Songs:* "On Blue Venetian Waters," "A Message from the Man in the Moon," "Tomorrow Is Another Day" and "All God's Children Got Rhythm," *music by* Bronislau Kaper and Walter Jurmann, *lyrics by* Gus Kahn. *Running time: 109 minutes. Release date:* June 11, 1937

34. THE EMPEROR'S CANDLESTICKS • 1937 M-G-M
Cast: William Powell *(Baron Stephan Wolensky)*, Luise Rainer *(Countess Olga Mironova)*, Robert Young *(Grand Duke Peter)*, **Maureen O'Sullivan** *(Maria Orlech)*, Frank Morgan *(Colonel Baron Suroff)*, Henry Stephenson *(Prince Johan)*, Douglas Dumbrille *(Korum)*, Charles Waldron *(Doctor Malchor)*, Frank Reicher *(Pavloff)*, Bernadene Hayes *(Mitzi)*, Donald Kirke *(Anton)*, Ian Wolf *(Leon)*, Barnett Parker *(Albert)*, Bert Roach *(porter)*, Paul Porcasi *(Santuzzi)*, E. E. Clive *(auctioneer)*, Emma Dunn *(housekeeper)*, Frank Conroy *(Colonel Radoff)*, Spencer Charters *(usher)*, Theodore von Eltz *(adjutant)*, Mitchell Lewis *(plainclothesman)*, Egon Brecher *(chief of police)*, Erville Alderson *(conductor)*,

Clarence H. Wilson *(station-master)*, Rollo Lloyd *(jailer)*, Maude Turner Gordon *(concierge)*, Lionel Pape *(sugar daddy)*, William Stack *(Czar)*. **Credits:** *Directed by* George Fitzmaurice; *Producer,* John W. Considine, Jr.; *Screenplay,* Monckton Hoffe, Harold Goldman; *Photography,* Harold Rosson; *Montage,* Slavko Vorkapich; *Art Director,* Cedric Gibbons; *Art Director Associates,* Daniel Cathcart and Edwin B. Willis; *Film Editor,* Conrad A. Nervig; *Gowns,* Adrian; *Recording Director,* Douglas Shearer; *Musical Score,* Franz Waxman. Based on the novel T*he Emperor's Candlesticks* by Baroness Orczy (London, 1899). *Running time:* 89 minutes. *Release date:* July 1937

35. BETWEEN TWO WOMEN • 1937 M-G-M

Cast: Franchot Tone *(Dr. Allen Meighan)*, **Maureen O'Sullivan** *(Claire Donahue)*, Virginia Bruce *(Patricia Sloan)*, Leonard Penn *(Dr. Tony Wolcott)*, Cliff Edwards *(Snoopy)*, Janet Beecher *(Miss Pringle)*, Charley Grapewin *(Dr. Webster)*, Helen Troy *(Sally)*, Grace Ford *(Nurse Howley)*, June Clayworth *(Eleanor)*, Edward Norris *(Dr. Barili)*, Anthony Mace *(Tom Donahue)*, Hugh Marlowe *(priest)*, Bud Flanagan *(Patricia's friend)*. **Credits:** *Directed by* George B. Seitz; *Screenplay,* Frederick Stephani and Marion Parsonnet; *Original story,* Erich von Stroheim; *Photography,* John Seitz; *Art Director,* Cedric Gibbons; *Art Director Associates,* Stan Rogers and Edwin B. Willis; *Film Editor,* W. Donn Hayes; *Recording Director,* Douglas Shearer; *Gowns,* Adrian; *Musical score,* Dr. William Axt. *Running time:* 89 minutes. *Released:* July 1937

36. MY DEAR MISS ALDRICH • 1937 M-G-M

Cast: Edna May Oliver *(Mrs. Lou Atherton)*, **Maureen O'Sullivan** *(Martha Aldrich)*, Walter Pidgeon *(Ken Morley)*, Rita Johnson *(Ellen Warfield)*, Janet Beecher *(Mrs. Sinclair)*, Paul Harvey *(Mr. Sinclair)*, Charles Waldron *(Mr. Warfield)*, Walter Kingsford *(Mr. Talbot)*, Roger Converse *(Ted Martin)*, Guinn Williams *(the "bouncer")*, Leonid Kinskey *(a waiter)*, Brent Sargent *(Gregory Stone)*, J. Farrell MacDonald *("Doc" Howe)*, Robert Greig *(the major domo)*, Harry Tyler *(taxi driver James Joseph McElarney)*, Lya Lys *(The Queen)]*.**Credits:** *Directed by* George B. Seitz; *Original Story and Screenplay,* Herman J. Mankiewicz; *Photography,* Charles Lawton, Jr; *Art Director,* Cedric Gibbons; *Art Director Associates,* Randall Duell and Edwin B. Willis; *Film Editor,* William S. Gray; *Wardrobe,* Dolly Tree; *Recording Director,* Douglas Shearer; *Musical Score,* David Snell. *Running time*: 73 minutes. *Release date:* September 1937

37. A YANK AT OXFORD • 1938 M-G-M

Cast: Robert Taylor *(Lee Sheridan)*, Lionel Barrymore *(Dan Sheridan)*, **Maureen O'Sullivan** *(Molly Beaumont)*, Vivien Leigh *(Elsa Craddock)*, Edmund Gwenn *(Dean of Cardinal)*, Griffith Jones *(Paul Beaumont)*, C. V. France *(Dean Snodgrass)*, Edward Rigby *(Scatters)*, Morton Selten *(Cecil Davidson, Esq.)*, Claude Gillingwater *(Ben Dalton)*, Tully Marshall *(Cephas)*, Walter Kingsford *(Dean Williams)*, Robert Coote *(Wavertree)*, Peter Croft *(Ramsey)*, Noel Hewlett *(Tom Craddock)*, Edmund Breon *(Captain Wavertree)*, Harlan Briggs *(printer)*, Doodles Weaver *(Bill)*. **Credits:** *Directed by* Jack Conway; *Producer,* Michael Balcon; *Screenplay,* Malcolm Stuart Boylan, Walter Ferris and George Oppenheimer; *Original story,* Leon Gordon, Sidney Gilliatt and Michael Hogan; *Based on an idea by* John Monk Saunders; *Contributors to screen construction,* Frank Wead and F. Scott Fitzgerald; *Photography,* Harold Rosson; *Art Director,* L. P. Williams; *Film Editor,* Charles Frend; *Supervising Film Editor,* Margaret Booth; *Recording Directors,* A.W. Watkins and C. C. Stevens; *Costumes,* Rene Hubert; *Musical Score,* Hubert Bath and Edward Ward. *Running time:* 103 minutes. *Release date:* February 1938

38. PORT OF SEVEN SEAS • 1938 M-G-M

Cast: Wallace Beery *(Cesar)*, Frank Morgan *(Panisse)*, **Maureen O'Sullivan** *(Madelon)*, John Beal *(Marias)*, Jessie Ralph *(Honorine)*, Cora Witherspoon *(Claudine)*, Etienne Girardot *(Bruneau)*, E. Allyn Warren *(Captain Escartefigue)*, Henry Hull *(Uncle Elzear)*, Robert Spindola *(boy)*, Doris Lloyd *(customer)*, Paul Panzer *(postman)*, Jerry Colonna *(Arab rug seller)*, Fred Malatesta *(bird seller)*, Moy Ming *(Chinese peddler)*, George Humbert *(organ grinder)*. **Credits:** *Directed by* James Whale; *Producer,* Henry Henigson*; Screenplay,* Preston Sturges; *Photographer,* Karl Freund; *Montage Effects,* Slavko Vorkapich; *Art Director,* Cedric Gibbons; *Art Director Associates,* Gabriel Scognamillo and Edwin B. Willis; *Film Editor,* Frederick Y. Smith; *Wardrobe,* Dolly Tree; *Recording Director,* Douglas Shearer; *Music Score,* Franz Waxman. Based on the play *Fanny* by Marcel Pagnol (Paris, Dec. 1931). *Running time*: 81 minutes. *Release date:* June 1938

39. HOLD THAT KISS • 1938 M-G-M

Cast: Maureen O'Sullivan *(Jane Evans)*, Dennis O'Keefe *(Tommy Bradford)*, Mickey Rooney *(Chick Evans)*, George Barbier *(Mr. J. Westley Piermont)*, Jessie Ralph *(Aunt Lucy)*, Edward S. Brophy *(Al)*, Fay Holden *(Mrs. Evans)*, Frank Albertson *(Steve Evans)*, Phillip Terry *(Ted Evans)*, Ruth Hussey *(Nadine)*, Barnett Parker *(Maurice)*, Buck the dog *(Blotto)*. **Credits:** *Directed by* Edwin L. Marin; *Producer,* John W. Considine, Jr.; *Original story and screenplay,* Stanley Rauh; *Photography,* George Folsey; *Art Director,* Cedric Gibbons; *Art Director Associates,* John Detlie, Edwin B. Willis; *Film Editor,* Ben Lewis; *Wardrobe,* Dolly Tree; *Recording Director,* Douglas Shearer; *Musical Score,* Edward Ward. *Running time*: 79 minutes. *Release date:* May 1938

40. THE CROWD ROARS • 1938 M-G-M

Cast: Robert Taylor *(Tommy McCoy)*, Edward Arnold *(Jim Cain)*, Frank Morgan *(Brian McCoy)*, **Maureen O'Sullivan** *(Sheila Carson)*, William Gargan *(Johnny Martin)*, Lionel Stander *("Happy" Lane)*, Jane Wyman *(Vivian)*, Nat Pendleton *("Pug" Walsh)*, Charles D. Brown *(Bill Thorne)*, Gene Reynolds *(Tommy as a boy)*, Donald Barry *(Pete)*, Donald Douglas *(Murray)*, Isabel Jewell *(Mrs. Martin)*, J. Farrell MacDonald *(Father Ryan)*, Leona Roberts *(Laura McCoy)*. **Credits:** *Directed by* Richard Thorpe; *Producer,* Sam Zimbalist; *Screenplay,* Thomas Lennon, George Bruce, George Oppenheimer; *Photography,* John Seitz; *Montage Effects,* Slavko Vorkapich; *Art Director,* Cedric Gibbons; *Art Director*

Associates, Eddie Imazu and Edwin B. Willis; *Film Editor,* Conrad A. Nervig; *Wardrobe,* Dolly Tree; *Recording Director,* Douglas Shearer; *Musical Score,* Edward Ward. *Running time:* 92 minutes. *Release date:* August 1938

41. SPRING MADNESS • 1938 M-G-M

Cast: Maureen O'Sullivan *(Alexandra Benson),* Lew Ayres *(Sam Thatcher),* Ruth Hussey *(Kate McKim),* Burgess Meredith *(Lippencott),* Ann Morriss *(Frances),* Joyce Compton *(Sally Prescott),* Jacqueline Wells *(Mady Platt),* Frank Albertson *(Hat Hatton),* Truman Bradley *(Walter Beckett),* Marjorie Gateson *(Miss Ritchie),* Renie Riano *(Mildred),* Sterling Holloway *(Buck),* Dick Baldwin *(Doc),* J. M. Kerrigan *(Maloney),* Thurston Hall *(Mr. Platt),* Louis Jean Heydt *(Paul Phillips),* Harry Tyler *(taxi driver),* Spencer Charters *(police chief),* Willie Best *(porter).* **Credits:** *Directed by* S. Sylvan Simon; *Associate Producer and Screenplay,* Edward Chodorov; *Photography,* Joseph Ruttenberg; *Art Director,* Cedric Gibbons; *Art Director Associate,* Stan Rogers; *Film Editor,* Conrad A. Nervig; *Set Decorations,* Edwin B. Willis; *Wardrobe,* Dolly Tree; *Recording Director,* Douglas Shearer; *Musical Score,* Dr. William Axt. Based on the play *Spring Dance* by Philip Barry (New York, 1936), adapted from an original play by Eleanor Golden and Eloise Barragon. *Running time:* 67 minutes. *Release date:* November 1938

42. LET US LIVE • 1939 M-G-M

Cast: Maureen O'Sullivan *(Mary Roberts),* Henry Fonda *("Brick" Tennant),* Ralph Bellamy *(Lieutenant Everett),* Alan Baxter *(Joe Linden),* Stanley Ridges *(District attorney),* Henry Kolker *(Chief of police),* Peter Lynn *(Joe Taylor),* George Douglas *(Ed Walsh),* Philip Trent *(Frank Burke),* Martin Spellman *(Jimmy Dugan),* Charles Trowbridge *(Judge).* **Credits:** *Directed by* John Brahm; *Producer,* William Perlberg; *Screenplay,* Anthony Veiller and Allen Rivkin; *Story,* Joseph F. Dinneen; *Photography,* Lucien Ballard; *Art Director,* Lionel Banks; *Film Editor,* Al Clark; *Gowns,* Kalloch; *Sound,* George Cooper and Percy Townsend; *Music Director,* M. W. Stoloff; *Music,* Karol Rathaus. *Running time:* 68 minutes. *Release date:* February 1939

43. TARZAN FINDS A SON • 1939 M-G-M

Cast: Johnny Weissmuller *(Tarzan),* **Maureen O'Sullivan** *(Jane),* Johnny Sheffield *(Boy),* Ian Hunter *(Austin Lancing),* Henry Stephenson *(Sir Thomas Lancing),* Frieda Inescort *(Mrs. Austin Lancing),* Henry Wilcoxon *(Mr. Sande),* Laraine Day *(Mrs. Richard Lancing),* Morton Lowry *(Richard Lancing),* Gavin Muir *(pilot),* Uriah Banks *(Mooloo).* **Credits:** *Directed by* Richard Thorpe; *Produced by* Sam Zimbalist; *Screenplay by* Cyril Hume; *Based on the characters created by* Edgar Rice Burroughs; *Recording Director,* Douglas Shearer; *Art Director,* Cedric Gibbons; *Associate,* Urie McCleary; *Photographed by* Leonard Smith; *Film Editors,* Frank Sullivan and Gene Ruggiero; *Special Effects,* A. Arnold Gillespie, Warren Newcombe, Max Fabian; *Animal Trainer,* George Emerson; *Asst. Director,* Dolph Zimmer; *Musical Director,* David Snell; *Music by* Sol Levy and Dr. William Axt. *Running time:* 95 minutes. *Release date:* June 1939

44. PRIDE AND PREJUDICE • 1940 M-G-M

Cast: Greer Garson *(Elizabeth Bennet),* Laurence Olivier *(Mr. Darcy),* **Maureen O'Sullivan** *(Jane Bennet),* Mary Boland *(Mrs. Bennet),* Edna May Oliver *(Lady Catherine de Bourgh),* Ann Rutherford *(Lydia Bennet),* Frieda Inescort *(Miss Caroline Bingley),* Edmund Gwenn *(Mr. Bennet),* Karen Morley *(Mrs. Charlotte Collins),* Heather Angel *(Kitty Bennet),* Marsha Hunt *(Mary Bennet),* Bruce Lester *(Mr. Charles Bingley),* Edward Ashley *(Mr. George Wickham),* Melville Cooper *(Mr. Collins),* Marten Lament *(Mr. Denny),* E. E. Clive *(Sir William Lucas),* May Beatty *(Mrs. Phillips),* Marjorie Wood *(Lady Lucas),* Gia Kent *(Anne de Bourgh),* Louis Payne *(Mr. Phillips),* Gerald Oliver-Smith *(Fitz William),* Hugh Greenwood *(Canon Stubbs),* Vernon Downing *(Captain Carter),* Claud Allister *(Mr. Beck).* **Credits:** *Directed by* Robert Z. Leonard; *Producer,* Hunt Stromberg; *Screenplay by* Aldous Huxley and Jane Murfin; *Director of photography,* Karl Freund; *Art Director,* Cedric Gibbons; *Art Director associate,* Paul Groesse; *Supervising Film Editor,* Robert J. Kern; *Set Decorations,* Edwin B. Willis; *Gowns,* Adrian; *Men's Costumes,* Gile Steele; *Recording Director,* Douglas Shearer; *Dance Director,* Ernst Matray; *Technical Advisor,* George Richelavie; *Hair,* Sydney Guilaroff; *Makeup,* Jack Dawn; *Musical Score,* Herbert Stothart. Based on the novel *Pride and Prejudice* by Jane Austen (London, 1813), and the play by Helen Jerome (New York, 1935). *Running time:* 117 minutes. *Release date:* July 1940

45. SPORTING BLOOD • 1940 M-G-M

Cast: Robert Young *(Myles Vanders),* **Maureen O'Sullivan** *(Linda Lockwood),* Lewis Stone *(Davis Lockwood),* William Gargan *(Duffy),* Lynne Carver *(Joan Lockwood),* Clarence Muse *(Jeff),* Lloyd Corrigan *(Otis Winfield),* George H. Reed *(Stonewall),* Tom Kennedy *(Grantly),* Russell Hicks *("Sneak" O'Brien),* George Lessey *(banker Cobb),* William Tannen *(Ted Milner),* Helene Millard *(Martha Winfield),* Allen Wood *(jockey),* Eugene Jackson *(Sam),* Etta McDaniel *(Chloe),* Shirley Deane *(Mrs. Plunket),* Donald Dillaway *(Mr. Plunket),* Alfred Hall *(horse owner),* Nels Nelson *(jockey).* **Credits:** *Directed by* S. Sylvan Simon; *Producer,* Albert E. Levoy; *Screenplay,* Lawrence Hazard, Albert Mannheimer and Dorothy Yost; *Original story,* Grace Norton; *Photography,* Sidney Wagner; *Art Director,* Cedric Gibbons; *Art Director Associate,* Stan Rogers; *Film Editor,* Frank Sullivan; *Set Decorations,* Edwin B. Willis; *Wardrobe,* Dolly Tree; *Recording Director,* Douglas Shearer; *Musical Score,* Franz Waxman. *Running time:* 85 minutes. *Release date:* July 1940

46. MAISIE WAS A LADY • 1941 M-G-M

Cast: Ann Sothern *(Maisie),* Lew Ayres *(Bob Rawlston),* **Maureen O'Sullivan** *(Abby Rawlston),* C. Aubrey Smith *(Walpole),* Edward Ashley *(Link Phillips),* Joan Perry *(Diana Webley),* Paul Cavanagh *(Cap Rawlston),* William Wright *(judge)*, Edgar Dearing *(cop)*, Charles D. Brown *(doctor)*. Joe Yule *(barker)*, Hans Conreid *(guest)*, Hillary Brooke *(guest)*. **Credits:** *Directed by* Edwin L. Marin; *Producer,* J. Walter Ruben; *Screenplay,* Betty Reinhardt, Mary C. McCall, Jr.; *Original story,* Reinhardt and Myles Connolly; *Photography,* Charles Lawton; *Film Editor,* Frederick Y. Smith; *Art Director,* Cedric Gibbons; *Art Director Associate,* Stan Rogers; *Set Decorations,* Edwin B. Willis; *Wardrobe,* Dolly Tree; *Recording Director,* Douglas Shearer; *Musical Score,* David Snell. Based on the character created by Wilson Collinson. *Running time:* 78 minutes. *Release date:* January, 1941

47. TARZAN'S SECRET TREASURE • 1941 M-G-M

Cast: Johnny Weissmuller *(Tarzan)*, **Maureen O'Sullivan** *(Jane)*, Johnny Sheffield *(Boy)*, Reginald Owen *(Professor Elliot)*, Barry Fitzgerald *(O'Doul)*, Tom Conway *(Medford)*, Philip Dorn *(Vandermeer)*, Cordell Hickman *(Tumbo)*, Everett Brown *(Joconi chief)*, Martin Wilkins *(headman)* **Credits:** *Directed by* Richard Thorpe; *Produced by* B. P. Fineman; *Screenplay by* Myles Connolly and Paul Gangelin; *Based upon the characters created by* Edgar Rice Burroughs; *Photography,* Clyde de Vinna; *Recording Director,* Douglas Shearer; *Art Director,* Cedric Gibbons; *Set Decorations,* Edwin B. Willis; *Film Editor,* Gene Ruggiero; *Special Effects,* Warren Newcombe; *Assistant Director,* Gilbert Kurland; *Musical Score,* David Snell; *Music by* Sol Levy and Dr. William Axt. *Running time:* 81 minutes. *Release date:* December 1941

48. TARZAN'S NEW YORK ADVENTURE • 1942 M-G-M

Cast: Johnny Weissmuller *(Tarzan)*, **Maureen O'Sullivan** *(Jane)*, Johnny Sheffield *(Boy)*, Virginia Grey *(Connie Beach)*, Charles Bickford *(Buck Rand)*, Paul Kelly *(Jimmy Shields)*, Chill Wills *(Mountford)*, Cy Kendall *(Sargent)*, Russell Hicks *(Judge Abbotson)*, Howard Hickman *(Blake Norton)*, Charles Lane *(Beaton)*, Elmo Lincoln *(roustabout)*. **Credits:** *Directed by* Richard Thorpe; *Produced by* Frederick Stephani; *Screenplay by* William R. Lipman and Myles Connolly; *Story,* Myles Connolly; *Based upon the characters created by* Edgar Rice Burroughs; *Photography,* Sidney Wagner; *Recording Director,* Douglas Shearer; *Art Director,* Cedric Gibbons; *Set Decorations,* Edwin B. Willis; *Film Editor,* Gene Ruggiero; *Special Effects,* Arnold Gillespie, Warren Newcombe; *Opening Theme,* "Cannibal Carnival" *by* Sol Levy; *Musical Score,* David Snell. *Running time:* 71 minutes. *Release date:* August 1942

49. THE BIG CLOCK • 1948 Paramount Pictures, Inc.

Cast: Ray Milland *(George Stroud)*, Charles Laughton *(Earl Janoth)*, **Maureen O'Sullivan** *(Georgette Stroud)*, George Macready *(Steve Hagen)*, Rita Johnson *(Pauline York)*, Elsa Lanchester *(Louise Patterson)*, Harold Vermilyea *(Don Klausmeyer)*, Dan Tobin *(Roy Cordette)*, Henry [Harry] Morgan *(Womack)*, Richard Webb *(Nat Sperling)*, Elaine Riley *(Lily Gold)*, Luis Van Rooten *(Edwin Orlin)*, Lloyd Corrigan *(McKinley)*, Frank Orth *(Burt)*, Margaret Field *(second secretary)*, Phillip Van Zandt *(Sidney Kislav)*, Henri Letondal *(antique dealer)*, Douglas Spencer *(Bert Finch)*, B. G. Norman *(George, Jr.)*, Noel Neill *(elevator operator)*. **Credits:** *Directed by* John Farrow; *Production,* Richard Maibaum; *Screenplay,* Jonathan Latimer; *Director of Photography,* John F. Seitz; *Art Directors,* Hans Dreier, Roland Anderson, Albert Nozaki; *Editor Supervisor,* Eda Warren; *Set Decorations,* Sam Comer, Ross Dowd; *Costumes,* Edith Head; *Music score,* Victor Young; *Sound,* Hugo Grenzbach,Gene Garvin; *Special Photography Effects,* Gordon Jennings; *Process Photography,* Farciot Edouart; *Makeup Supervisor,* Wally Westmore. Based on the novel *The Big Clock* by Kenneth Fearing (New York, 1946). *Running time:* 95 minutes. *Release date:* April 9, 1948

50. WHERE DANGER LIVES • 1950 RKO Radio Pictures

Cast: Robert Mitchum *(Dr. Jeff Cameron)*, Faith Domergue *(Margo)*, Claude Rains *(Mr. Lannington)*, **Maureen O'Sullivan** *(Julie Dorn)*, Charles Kemper *(police chief)*, Ralph Dumke *(Klauber)*, Billy House *(Mr. Bogardus)*, Harry Shannon *(Dr. Maynard)*, Philip Van Zandt *(Milo DeLong)*, Jack Kelly *(Dr. Mullenbach)*, Lillian West *(Mrs. Bogardus)*. **Credits:** *Directed by* John Farrow; *Production,* Irving Cummings, Irwin Allen; *Screenplay,* Charles Bennett; *Story,* Leo Rosten; *Director of Photography,* Nicholas Musuraca; *Art Directors,* Albert S. D'Agustino, Ralph Berger; *Film Editor,* Eda Warren; *Set Decorations,* Darrell Silvera, John Sturteyant; *Sound,* John Tribby, Clem Portman; *Makeup artist,* Mel Berns; *Hairstylist,* Larry Germain; *Music Director,* C. Bakaleinikoff; *Music,* Roy Webb. *Running time:* 84 minutes. *Release date:* July 8, 1950

51. BONZO GOES TO COLLEGE • 1952 Universal-International Pictures

Cast: Maureen O'Sullivan *(Marion Drew)*, Charles Drake *(Malcolm Drew)*, Edmund Gwenn *("Pop" Drew)*, Gigi Perreau *(Betsy Drew)*, Gene Lockhart *(Clarence B. Gateson)*, Irene Ryan *(Nancy)*, Guy Williams *(Ronald Calkins)*, John Miljan (Wilbur Crane), David Janssen *(Jack)*, Jerry Paris *(Lefty Edwards)*, Frank Nelson *(Dick)*, Richard Garrick *(Judge Simpkins)*, Bonzo II *(Bonzo)*. **Credits:** *Directed by* Frederick de Cordova; *Production,* Ted Richmond; *Assistant Director,* Jesse Hibbs; *Screenplay,* Leo Lieberman, Jack Henley; *Story,* Leo Leiberman; *Director of Photography,* Carl Guthrie; *Art Directors,* Bernard Herzbrun, Hilyard Brown; *Film Editor,* Ted Kent; *Set Decorations,* Russell A. Gausman, Ruby Levitt; *Gowns,* Bill Thomas; *Sound,* Leslie I. Carey, Corson Jowett; *Hairstylist,* Joan St. Oegger; *Makeup,* Bud Westmore; *Music,* Frank Skinner. Based on the character created by Raphael David Blau and Ted Berkman. *Running time:* 78 minutes. *Release date:* September 1952

52. ALL I DESIRE • 1953 Universal-International Pictures

Cast: Barbara Stanwyck *(Naomi Murdoch)*, Richard Carlson *(Henry Murdoch)*, **Maureen O'Sullivan** *(Sara Harper)*, Lyle Bettger *(Dutch Heinemann)*, Marcia Henderson *(Joyce Murdoch)*, Lori Nelson *(Lily Murdoch)*, Richard Long *(Russ Underwood)*, Billy Gray *(Ted Murdoch)*, Lotte Stein *(Lena Engstrom)*, Dayton Lummis *(Col. Underwood)*, Fred

Nurney *(Peterson)*, Guy Williams *(Philip)*, Stuart Whitman *(Dick)*, Thomas E. Jackson *(Dr. Tomlin)*. **Credits**: *Directed by* Douglas Sirk; *Production,* Ross Hunter; *Assistant Director,* Joseph E. Kenny; *Screenplay,* James Gunn, Robert Blees; *Adaptation,* Gina Kaus; *Director of Photography,* Carl Guthrie; *Art Directors,* Bernard Herzbrun, Alexander Golitzen; *Film Editor,* Milton Carruth; *Set Decorations,* Russell A. Gausman, Julia Heron; *Costumes,* Rosemary Odell; *Sound,* Leslie I. Carey, Robert Pritchard, Robert Beauregard; *Dance Director,* Kenny Williams; *Hairstylist,* Joan St. Oegger; *Makeup,* Bud Westmore; *Music Director,* Joseph Gershenson. *Song:* "All I Desire," *words and music by* David Lieberman. Based on the novel *Stopover* by Carol Brink (London, 1951). *Running time:* 79 minutes. *Release date:* July 1953.

53. MISSION OVER KOREA • 1953 Columbia Pictures

Cast: John Hodiak *(Cpt. George Slocum)*, John Derek *(Lt. Pete Barker)*, Audrey Totter *(Kate)*, **Maureen O'Sullivan** *(Nancy Slocum)*, Harvey Lembeck *(Sgt. Maxie Steiner)*, Richard Erdman *(Cpl. Swenson)*, William Chun *(Clancy)*, Rex Reason *(Major Hacker)*, Richard Bowers *(singing soldier)*, Todd Karns *(Lt. Jerry Barker)*, Al Choi *(Major Kung)*. **Credits**: *Directed by* Fred F. Sears; *Production,* Robert Cohn; *Asst. Director,* James Nicholson; *Screenplay,* Jesse L. Lasky, Jr., Eugene Ling, Martin M. Goldsmith *(based on a story by* Richard Tregaskis); *Director of Photography,* Sam Leavitt; *Film Editor,* Henry Batista; *Art Director,* George Brooks, *Set Decorations,* Frank Tuttle; *Sound Engineer,* George Cooper; *Music Director,* Mischa Balaleinikoff; *Song:* "Forgive Me," *words by* Benedict Mayers, *music by* Raymond Mattori; *Technical Advisor,* Cpt. Paul F. Hopkins. *Running time:* 86 minutes. *Release date:* August 1953

54. DUFFY OF SAN QUENTIN • 1954 Swarttz-Doniger Productions

Cast: Louis Hayward *(Edward "Romeo" Harper)*, Joanne Dru *(Anne Halsey)*, Paul Kelly *(Warden Clinton T. Duffy)*, **Maureen O'Sullivan** *(Gladys Duffy)*, George Macready *(Winant)*, Horace McMahon *(Pierson)*, Irving Bacon *(Doc)*, Joel Fluellen *(Bill)*, Joseph Turkel *(Frank)*, Jonathan Hale *(Boyd)*, Michael McHale *(Pinto)*, Marshall Bradford *(Lowell)*, DeForest Kelley *(detective)*, Sandy Aaronson *(guard)*, Peter Brocco *(Nealy)*. **Credits:** *Directed by* Walter Doniger; *Screenplay,* Doniger; *Story,* Swarttz, Doniger; *Director of Photography,* John Alton; *Art Director,* Daniel Hall; *Supervisor Editor,* Chester Schaeffer; *Editor,* Edward Sampson; *Set Decorations,* Fay Babcock; *Wardrobe,* Jerry Bos; *Sound,* Frank Webster, Jr.; *Special Effects,* Ray Mercer; *Makeup,* Curly Batson; *Hairdresser,* Edith Keon; *Music,* Paul Dunlap. *Based on the serial story* "San Quentin Is My Home" *by* Clinton T. Duffy, *The Saturday Evening Post* (Mar-May 1950). *Running time:* 78 minutes. *Release date:* March 1954

55. THE STEEL CAGE • 1954 Phoenix Films, Inc.

Cast: Paul Kelly *(Warden Clinton T. Duffy)*, **Maureen O'Sullivan** *(Gladys Duffy)*, "The Chef": Walter Slezak *(Louis)*, "The Hostages": John Ireland *(Al)*, Lawrence Tierney *(Chet Harmon)*, "The Face": Kenneth Tobey *(Steinberg)*, Arthur Franz *(Father Harvey)*. With Alan Mowbray, *(Gilbert Lee)*, George E. Stone *(Solly)*, Lyle Talbot *(Square)*, Elizabeth Fraser *(Marie)*, Stanley Andrews *(prison official)*, Morris Ankrum *(Garvey)*, Don Beddoe *(Ferness)*, Robert Bice *(prisoner)*, George Chandler *(Shorty)*, Ned Glass *(Pete, the guard)*, Herb Jacobs *(prisoner)*, Henry Kulky *(George)*, Charles Nolte *(Frank)*, Gene Roth *(Billy Brenner)*, James Seay *(Doctor)*, Charles Tannen *(patient)*, Ben Welden *(Mike)*. **Credits:** *Directed by* Walter Doniger; *Screenplay contributors,* Berman Swarttz, Walter Doniger, Oliver Crawford, Guy Trosper, Scott Littleton; *Photography,* John Alton, Joseph Biroc; *Art Director,* Daniel Hall; *Editors,* Chester Schaeffer, Everett Dodd; *Wardrobe,* Jerry Bos; *Sound,* Frank Webster, Sr., Ben Winkler; *Effects,* Ray Mercer; *Makeup,* Curly Batson; Based on *The San Quentin Story* by Clinton T. Duffy and Dean Jennings (New York, 1950). *Running time:* 80 minutes. *Release date:* November 1954

56. THE TALL T • 1957 Scott-Brown Production/Columbia Pictures

Cast: Randolph Scott *(Pat Brennan)*, Richard Boone *(Frank Usher)*, **Maureen O'Sullivan** *(Doretta Mims)*, Arthur Hunnicutt *(Ed Rintoon)*, Skip Homeier *(Billy Jack)*, Henry Silva *(Chink)*, John Hubbard *(Willard Mims)*, Robert Burton *(Tenvoorde)*, Robert Anderson *(Jace)*, Fred E. Sherman *(Hank Parker)*, Chris Olsen *(Jeff Parker)*. **Credits:** *Directed by* Budd Boetticher; *Produced by* Harry Joe Brown and Randolph Scott; *Screenplay,* Burt Kennedy; *Asst. Director,* Sam Nelson; *Director of Photography,* Charles Lawton Jr.; *Art Director,* George Brooks; *Film Editor,* Al Clark; *Set Decorations,* Frank Tuttle; *Sound,* Ferol Redd; *Music Composer and Conductor,* Heinz Roemheld. Based on the Elmore Leonard novelette, *The Captive* (1955). *Running time:* 78 minutes. *Release date:* April 1, 1957 (Technicolor)

57. WILD HERITAGE • 1958 Universal-International Pictures

Cast: Will Rogers, Jr. *(Judge Copeland)*, **Maureen O'Sullivan** *(Emma Breslin)*, Rod McKuen *(Dirk Breslin)*, Casey Tibbs *(Rusty)*, Troy Donahue *(Jesse Bascomb)*, Judy Meredith *(Callie Bascomb)*, Gigi Perreau *(Missouri Breslin)*, George 'Foghorn' Winslow *(Talbot Breslin)*, Gary Gray *(Hugh Breslin)*, Jeanette Nolan *(Ma Bascomb)*, Paul Birch *(Jake Breslin)*, John Beradino *(Arn)*, Phil Harvey *(Jud)*, Lawrence Dobkin *(Josh Burrage)*, Stephen Ellsworth *(Bolivar Bascomb)*, Ingrid Goude *(Hilda Jansen)*, Christopher Dark *(Brazos)*, Guy Wilkerson *(Chaco)*. **Credits:** *Directed by* Charles Haas; *Production,* John E. Horton; *Asst. Director,* Sam Schneider; *Screenplay,* Paul King, Joseph Stone; *Story,* Steve Frazee; *Director of Photography,* Philip Lathrop; *Art Directors,* Alexander Golitzen, Robert Boyle; *Film Editor,* Edward Mann; *Set Decorations,* Russell A. Gausman, John P. Austin; *Costumes,* Martin Haack; *Sound,* Leslie I. Carey, Donald Cunliffe; *Makeup,* Bud Westmore; *Music Supervisor,* Joseph Gershenson. *Song:* "When Johnny Comes Marching Home," *words and music by* Louis Lambert. *Running time:* 78 minutes. *Release date:* August, 1958. (CinemaScope, Eastmancolor)

58. NEVER TOO LATE • 1965 Warner Bros. Pictures
Cast: Paul Ford *(Harry Lambert)*, **Maureen O'Sullivan** *(Edith Lambert)*, Jim Hutton *(Charlie Clinton)*, Connie Stevens *(Kate Clinton)*, Jane Wyatt *(Grace Kimbrough)*, Henry Jones *(Dr. James Kimbrough)*, Lloyd Nolan *(Mayor Crane)*. Credits: *Directed by* Bud Yorkin; *Producer,* Norman Lear; *Screenplay,* Sumner Arthur Long; *Director of Photography,* Philip Lathrop; *Art Director,* Edward Carrere; *Set Decorations,* Ralph S. Hurst; *Film Editor,* William Ziegler; *Sound,* Everett Hughes; *Costume Design,* Sheila O'Brian; *Makeup,* Gordon Bau; *Hairstylist,* Jean Burt Reilly; *Music,* David Rose. *Title Song:* Jay Livingston, Ray Evans, David Rose. *Sung by* Vic Damone. Based on the play by Sumner Arthur Long, *Never Too Late* (New York, 1962). *Running time:* 105 minutes. *Release date:* November 4, 1965. (New York premiere, December 25, 1965)

59. PHYNX, THE • 1970 Cinema Organization/Warner Brothers
Cast: A. Michael Miller, Ray Chippeway, Dennis Larden, Lonny Stevens *(The Phynx)*, Lou Antonio *(Corrigan)*, Mike Kellen *(Bogey)*, Michael Ansara *(Col. Rostinov)*, George Tobias *(Markevitch)*, Joan Blondell *(Ruby)*, Martha Raye *(Foxy)*, Larry Hankin *(Philbaby)*, Teddy Eccles *(Wee Johnny)*, Pat McCormack, Barbara Noonan, Sally Ann Struthers, Rich Little, Sue Bernard, Ann Morrell, Sherry Miles, Patty Andrews, Busby Berkeley, Xavier Cugat, Fritz Feld, John Hart, Ruby Keeler, Joe Louis, Marilyn Maxwell, Harold Sakata, Ed Sullivan, Rona Barrett, James Brown, Cass Daley, Leo Gorcey, Louis Hayward, Patsy Kelly, Guy Lombardo, Butterfly McQueen, Richard Pryor, Col. Harland Sanders, Rudy Vallee, Edgar Bergen and Charlie McCarthy, Dick Clark, Andy Devine, Huntz Hall, George Jessel, Dorothy Lamour, Trini Lopez, Pat O'Brien, Jay Silverheels, Clint Walker, **Maureen O'Sullivan**, Johnny Weissmuller *(cameos)*. Credits: *Directed by* Lee H. Katzin; *Produced by* Bob Booker, George Foster; *Written by* Stan Cornyn; *Photographed by* Michel Hugo; *Editor,* Dann Cahn; *Production Designer,* Stan Jolley; *Set Decorator,* Ralph S. Hunt; *Costumes,* Donfeld; *Music and Lyrics by* Mike Stoller, Jerry Leiber. *Running time:* 91 minutes

60. THAT'S ENTERTAINMENT, PART II • 1976 MGM/UA
Cast: Fred Astaire, Gene Kelly, Judy Garland, Mickey Rooney, Bing Crosby, Robert Taylor, Greer Garson, Clark Gable, Kathryn Grayson, Leslie Caron, Jeanette MacDonald, Nelson Eddy, Doris Day, Ann Miller, Ann Sothern, Frank Sinatra, Jimmy Durante, Eleanor Powell, John Barrymore, Louis Armstrong, Joan Crawford, Ronald Colman, Elizabeth Taylor, William Powell, Jean Harlow, Melvyn Douglas, Greta Garbo, Esther Williams, Ethyl Waters, W.C. Fields, Bud Abbott, Lou Costello, Jack Benny, Stan Laurel, Oliver Hardy, The Marx Brothers, Nanette Fabray, Lena Horne, Debbie Reynolds, Ginger Rogers, Bobby Van, Dinah Shore, Cyd Charisse, Donald O'Connor, Grace Kelly, Marge and Gower Champion, Betty Hutton, Howard Keel, Lassie, Spencer Tracy, Katharine Hepburn, **Maureen O'Sullivan**, Johnny Weissmuller. Credits: *New sequences directed by* Gene Kelly; *Produced by* Saul Chaplin and David Melnick; *Narration by* Leonard Gershe; *Music by* Nelson Riddle; *Photography,* George Folsey; *Editors,* Rod Friedgan and David Blewitt. *Running time:* 133 minutes

61. HANNAH AND HER SISTERS • 1986 Orion Pictures Corporation
Cast: Woody Allen *(Mickey Sachs)*, Michael Caine *(Elliot)*, Mia Farrow*(Hannah)*, Barbara Hershey *(Lee)*, **Maureen O'Sullivan** *(Norma)*, Lloyd Nolan *(Evan)*, Max von Sydow *(Frederick)*, Dianne Wiest *(Holly)*, Carrie Fisher *(April)*, Sam Waterston *(David)*, Daniel Stern *(Dusty)*, Tony Roberts *(Mickey's ex-partner)*, Lewis Black *(Paul)*, Julia Louis-Dreyfus *(Mary)*, Christian Clemenson *(Larry)*, Julie Kavner *(Gail)*, J. T. Walsh *(Ed Smythe)*, John Turturro *(writer)*, Bobby Short *(himself)*. Credits: *Written and Directed by* Woody Allen; *Producer,* Robert Greenhut; *Director of Photography,* Carlo Di Palma; *Editor,* Susan E. Morse; *Sound,* Les Lazarowitz; *Sound Editor,* Jack Fitzstephens, *Production Designer,* Stuart Wurtzel; *Set Decorator,* Carol Joffe; *Set Dresser,* David Weinman; *Costumes,* Jeffrey Kurland; *Make-up,* Fern Buchner. *Running time:* 107 minutes. *Release date:* February 1986

62. PEGGY SUE GOT MARRIED • 1986 Tri-Star/Delphi IV and V Productions
Cast: Kathleen Turner *(Peggy Sue Bodell)*, Nicolas Cage *(Charlie Bodell)*, **Maureen O'Sullivan** *(Elizabeth Alvorg)*, Leon Ames *(Barney Alvorg)*, Helen Hunt *(Beth Bodell)*, Barry Miller *(Richard Norvik)*, Catherine Hicks *(Carol Heath)*, Joan Allen *(Maddy Nagle)*, Kevin J. O'Connor *(Michael Fuzsimmons)*, Jim Carrey *(Walter Getz)*, Lisa Jane Persky *(Delores Dodge)*, Lucinda Jenney *(Rosalie Testa)*, Wil Shriner *(Arthur Nagle)*, Barbara Harris *(Evelyn Kelcher)*, Don Murray *(Jack Kelcher)*, Sofia Coppola *(Nancy Kelcher)*, John Carradine *(Leo)*. Credits: *Directed by* Francis Coppola; *Producer,* Paul R. Gurian. *Screenplay,* Jerry Leichtling and Ariene Sarner; *Photography,* Jordan Cronenweth; *Editor,* Barry Malkin; *Music Editor,* George Craig; *Sound,* Richard Bryce Goodman; *Sound Editor,* Michael Kirchberger; *Production Designer,* Dean Tavoularis; *Art Director,* Alex Tavoularis; *Set Designer,* Roger Dietz; *Set Decorator,* Marvin March; *Special Effects,* Larry Cavanaugh; *Choreographer,* Toni Basil; *Costumes,* Theadora Van Runkle; *Make-up,* E. Thomas Case; *Music,* John Barry. *Running time:* 105 minutes. *Release date:* October 1986

63. STRANDED • 1987
Cast: Ione Skye *(Deirdre)*, Joe Morton *(Sheriff McMahon)*, **Maureen O'Sullivan** *(Grace Clark)*, Susan Barnes *(Helen Anderson)*, Cameron Dye *(Lt. Scott)*, Michael Greene *(Vernon Burdett)*, Brendan Hughes *(Prince)*, Gary Swanson *(Sergeant)*, Spice Williams *(Warrior)*, Flea *(Jester)*, Dennis Vero *(Sir)*, Florence Schauffler *(Queen)*. Credits: *Director,* Tex Fuller; *Screenplay,* Alan Castle; *Photography,* Robert Brinkmann; *Art Director,* Donna Stamps-Scherer; *Set Decorations,* Lisette Thomas; *Film Editor,* Steven E. Rivkin; *Wardrobe, Hair, Make-up,* Daniel Paredes; *Sound,* Peter Bentley; *Special Effects,* Allen L. Hall, Peter Kuran; *Production Manager,* Mare Cantin; *Music,* Stacy Widelitz. *Running time:* 81 minutes.

Television Films

64. THE CROOKED HEARTS • 1972 ABC/Lorimar Productions
Cast: Rosalind Russell *(Laurita Dorsey)*, Douglas Fairbanks, Jr. *(Rex Willoughby)*, **Maureen O'Sullivan** *(Lillian Stanton)*, Ross Martin *(Sergeant Daniel Shane)*, Michael Murphy *(Frank Adamic)*, Kent Smith *(James Simpson)*, Dick Van Patten *(Edward—Desk Clerk)*, Patrick Campbell, *(Taxi Driver)*, Liam Dunn *(writer)*, Penny Marshall *(waitress)*, Kenneth Tobey *(fisherman)*, Bill Zuckert *(security guard)*. **Credits:** *Directed by* Jay Sandrich; *Executive Producer,* Lee Rich; *Producer,* Allen S. Epstein; *Teleplay,* A. J. Russell; *Photography,* Joseph Biroc; *Editor,* Gene Fowler, Jr.; *Art Director,* Jan Scott; *Music,* Billy Goldenberg. Based on the novel *Lonelyheart 4122* by Colin Watson (New York 1967). *Running time:* 90 minutes. *Airdate:* November 8, 1972

65. THE GREAT HOUDINI • 1976 ABC Circle Films
Cast: Paul Michael Glaser *(Harry Houdini [Erich Weiss])*, Sally Struthers *(Bess Houdini)*, Ruth Gordon *(Cecilia Weiss)*, **Maureen O'Sullivan** *(Lady Doyle)*, Peter Cushing *(Arthur Conan Doyle)*, Vivian Vance *(Minnie)*, Adrienne Barbeau *(Daisy White)*, Bill Bixby *(Rev. Arthur Ford)*, Jack Carter *(Theo Weiss)*, Nina Foch *(Reverend LeVeyne)*, Wilfrid Hyde-White *(Melville)*, Clive Revill *(Slater)*, Geoffrey Lewis *(Dr. Crandon)*, Barbara Rhoades *(Margery)*, Marilyn Brodnick *(Dorothy Weiss)*. **Credits:** *Written and Directed by* Melville Shavelson; *Photography,* Arch R. Dalzell; *Editor,* John M. Woodcock; *Production Designer,* Tracy Bousman; *Technical Advisor,* Harry Blackstone, Jr.; *Music,* Peter Matz. *Running time:* 100 minutes. *Airdate:* October 8, 1976

66. TOO SCARED TO SCREAM • 1985 Movie Store Productions
Cast: Mike Connors *(Lt. Dinardo)*, Anne Archer *(Kate)*, Leon Isaac Kennedy *(Frank)*, Ian McShane *(Hardwick)*, Ruth Ford *(Irma)*, John Heard *(Lab Technician)*, Carrie Nye *(Graziella)*, and Special Guest Star **Maureen O'Sullivan** *(Inez Hardwick, mother)*. **Credits:** *Directed by* Tony Lo Bianco; *Producer,* Mike Connors; *Screenplay,* Neal Barbera & Glenn Leopold; *Photography,* Larry Pizer; *Editors,* Ed Beyer & Michael Economou; *Production Designer,* Lilly Kilvert; *Music,* George Garvarentz. *Running time:* 104 minutes

67. THE RIVER PIRATES • 1988 Disney Channel/PBS/Wonderworks
Cast: Richard Farnsworth *(Percy)*, Ryan Francis *(Willie)*, Gennie James *(Rivers)*, Doug Emerson *("Spit" McGee)*, Devin Ratray *(Bubba)*, Kevin Joseph *(Henjie)*, Ben Wylie *(Billy)*, Dule' Hill *(Robert E. Lee)*, Jordan Marder *(Buster)*, Dixie King-Wade *(Mamie)*, Caryn West *(Mrs. Morris)*, Richard Council *(Mr. Morris)*, Anne Ramsey *("The Hag")*, and Special Guest Star **Maureen O'Sullivan** *(Aunt Sue)*. **Credits:** *Produced and Directed by* Tom G. Robertson; *Screenplay,* Paul W. Cooper; *Editor,* Craig Tyree; *Production Designer,* Edward Gianfrancesco; *Director of Photography,* Hie Agopian; *Costume Design,* Jeanette Oleska; *Make-up and Hair,* Catherin Mahlin; *Sound,* Will Gethin-Jones; *Original Music,* Elliot Sokolov; *Narrated by* Ralph Waite. Based on the novel *Good Old Boy: A Delta Boyhood* by Willie Morris. *Running time:* 108 minutes

68. WITH MURDER IN MIND • 1992 CBS Television (aka *With Savage Intent*)
Cast: Elizabeth Montgomery *(Gayle Wolfer)*, Robert Foxworth *(Bob Sprague)*, Howard Rollins Jr. *(Brian Furman/Samuel Carver)*, **Maureen O'Sullivan** *(Aunt Mildred)*, Lee Richardson *(John Condon)*, Paul McCrane *(Tim Franczyk)*, Danton Stone *(Benny Lazara)*, Tom Mardirosian *(Capt. Bob Browning)*, Jude Ciccolella *(Conrad Marley)*, Ronny Cox *(McLaughlin)*, Mary Ann Hagen *(Susan Claridge)*, Adam LeFevre *(Roger McBain)*, Kevin O'Rourke *(Ted Sloan)*, Seret Scott *(Sarah Bendix)*, Tom Even *(Judge Kubiniec)*, Joan Riordan *(Audrey Moore)*. **Credits:** *Directed by* Michael Tuchner; *Producer,* Robert Huddleston; *Teleplay,* Daniel Freudenberger; *Photography,* William Wages; *Editor,* David Campling; *Production Designer,* Patricia Van Ryker; *Music,* Misha Segal. *Running time:* 100 minutes. *Airdate:* May 12, 1992

69. THE HABITATION OF DRAGONS • 1992 Turner Pictures
Cast: Frederic Forrest *(Leonard Tollivar)*, Jean Stapleton *(Leonora Tollivar)*, Brad Davis *(George Tollivar)*, Hallie Foote *(Margaret Tollivar)*, **Maureen O'Sullivan** *(Miss Helen Taylor)*, Pat Hingle *(Uncle Virgil)*, Elias Koteas *(Wally Smith)*, Joanna Miles *(Evelyn Sparks)*, Roberts Blossom *(Charlie)*, Hawthorne Jones *(Lonny Johnson)*, Horton Foote, Jr. *(Billy Dalton)*, Lucinda Jenney *(Bernice Dalton)*, Blake Stokes *(Horace Tollivar)*, Chris Lane *(Leonard Tollivar, Jr.)*, David Smith *(Lester Whyte)*. **Credits:** *Directed by* Michael Lindsay-Hogg; *Executive Producer,* Michael Brandman; *Producer,* Donald P. Borchers; *Teleplay,* Horton Foote *(based on his play)*; *Photography,* Paul Laufer; *Editor,* Claudia Finkle; *Production Designer,* Vaughan Edwards; *Music,* David Shire. *Running time:* 94 minutes

70. HART TO HART: Home Is Where The Hart Is • 1994 NBC/Columbia
Cast: Robert Wagner *(Jonathan Hart)*, Stefanie Powers *(Jennifer Hart)*, **Maureen O'Sullivan** *(Eleanor Biddlecomb)*, Lionel Stander *(Max)*, Alan Young *(Charley Loomis)*, Howard Keel *(Captain Jack)*, Tracey Ellis *(Claire Stinson)*, Roddy McDowall *(Jeremy Sennet)*, Jack Kruschen *(Mayor Trout)*, Mitchell Ryan *(Chief Carson)*, Brian Cousins *(Eldon)*, Brian Patrick Clark *(Brock)*, Jeanna Michaels *(Abby Stinson)*. **Credits:** *Directed by* Peter Hunt; *Executive Producers,* Robert A. Papazian, James G Hirsch, Robert Wagner; *Producers,* Stefanie Powers, James Polster; *Teleplay,* Lawrence Hertzog; *Based on characters created by* Sidney Sheldon; *Photography,* Roy H. Wagner; *Editor,* Andrew Cohen; *Production Designer,* Peter M. Wooley; *Music,* Arthur B. Rubinstein. *Running time:* 100 minutes. *Airdate:* February 18, 1994

Radio Appearances

1. Hollywood Hotel (June 19, 1936) CBS (1 Hour)
Guests: Maureen O'Sullivan, Lionel Barrymore, Frances Langford, Anne Jamison, Igor Gorin. Credits: Hosted by Louella Parsons and Dick Powell; directed by George Mack Garrett; orchestra conducted by Raymond Paige.
2. Lux Radio Theatre "Captain Applejack" (Oct. 19, 1936) CBS (1 Hour)
Cast: Maureen O'Sullivan, Frank Morgan, Akim Tamiroff, Zita Johann.
Hosted by Cecil B. DeMille.
3. Good News of 1938 (Feb. 17, 1938) Presented by Maxwell House NBC
Hosted by Robert Taylor; announcer, Ted Pearson. Guests (in order of appearance): Frank Morgan, Fanny Brice, Hanley Stafford, Jack Benny, Allan Jones, Maureen O'Sullivan, Jack Conway.
4. Kraft Music Hall (March 3, 1938) Features Bing Crosby, Bob Burns NBC
Guests: Maureen O'Sullivan and Mischa Auer.
5. Good News of 1938 (March 31, 1938) Maxwell House NBC (1 Hour)
Hosted by Robert Taylor; announcer, Ted Pearson. Guests: Maureen O'Sullivan, Connee Boswell, Fanny Brice, Hanley Stafford, Louis B. Mayer, Lionel Barrymore, Jack Conway, Gilbert Russell, Una Merkel, Frank Morgan.
6. Good News of 1938 (April 7, 1938) Maxwell House NBC (1 Hour)
Guests: Maureen O'Sullivan, Judy Garland, John Beal, Sam Levin, Fanny Brice, Frank Morgan, Hanley Stafford and Meredith Wilson.
7. Jergen's Woodbury Hollywood Playhouse "A Service of Love" (April 17, 1938) NBC
Hosted by Tyrone Power. Cast: Maureen O'Sullivan and Tyrone Power.
8. Good News of 1938 (April 28, 1938) Maxwell House NBC (1 Hour)
Guests: Maureen O'Sullivan, Max Baer, Fanny Brice, Frank Morgan, Betty Jaynes, Douglas MacPhail, Una Merkel, others.
9. Kraft Music Hall (July 28, 1938) NBC (1 Hour)
Guests: Maureen O'Sullivan, others
10. Jergen's Woodbury Hollywood Playhouse "The Artists" (Oct. 16, 1938) NBC
Cast: Maureen O'Sullivan and Charles Boyer.
11. Kraft Music Hall (November 3, 1938) NBC (1 Hour)
Guests: Maureen O'Sullivan, Chester Morris, The Foursome Quartet, Claude Rains, Dalies Frantz (piano).
12. Good News of 1939 (Nov. 10, 1938) Maxwell House NBC (1 Hour)
Hosted by Robert Young. Guests: Maureen O'Sullivan, Lionel Barrymore, Lew Ayres, George Murphy, Ruth Hussey, Fanny Brice, Hanley Stafford, Frank Morgan, Douglas McPhail and Meredith Wilson.
13. Chase and Sandborn (Charlie McCarthy) (January 29, 1939) NBC
Guests: Maureen O'Sullivan, Don Ameche, Nelson Eddy, Edgar Bergen, Dorothy Lamour and Ronald Armbruster (orchestra leader).
14. Lux Radio Theatre "The Return of Peter Grimm" (Feb. 13, 1939) CBS (1 Hour) Hosted by Cecil B. De Mille. Cast: Maureen O'Sullivan *(Katherine)*, Lionel Barrymore *(Peter Grimm)*, Peter Holden *(William)*, Edward Arnold *(Dr. McPherson)*, Alan Ladd *(James)*, Gavin Muir *(Frederick)*.
15. Silver Theatre "Dear Victim" (February 26, 1939) (30 minutes)
Cast: Maureen O'Sullivan *(Eileen O'Rourke)*, Herbert Marshall *(Robert Desmond)*, Paula Winslowe *(Mrs. McIntyre)*, Eric Snowden *(Bartley)*, Joe Kearns *(Herr Muller/banker)*. Credits: Directed by Conrad Nagel; orchestra, Felix Mills; written by Grover Jones and True Boardman; announcer, John Conte.
16. Kellogg Company: The Circle "Death Takes a Holiday" (March 26, 1939)
Cast: Maureen O'Sullivan and Basil Rathbone. Variety guests: Groucho and Chico Marx, Dolan Orchestra/Foursome Quartet, Alexander Wollcott, John Carter. NBC
17. Gulf Screen Guild Theater "Winter in Paris" (March 3, 1940) CBS
Cast: Maureen O'Sullivan *(Kathy)*, Don Ameche *(Charles Mitchell Lewis)*, Warren William *(George Connley, American Embassy Attache)*. Credits: Hosted by Roger Pryor; story, Steve Fisher; music, The Gulf Orchestra.

18. Hecker Productions "Lincoln Highway" (April 5, 1941) NBC
Cast: Maureen O'Sullivan, others
19. Bing Crosby Variety Show (July 17, 1941) NBC (1 hour)
Guests: Maureen O'Sullivan, Warner Baxter, Vronsky and Babin, Jerry Lester
20. Kraft Music Hall (August 26, 1941) NBC
Guests: Maureen O'Sullivan, others
21. Variety Show (August 28, 1941) NBC (1 hour)
Guests: Maureen O'Sullivan, George Raft, others
22. Dramatic Radio "Night Must Fall" (Oct. 24, 1941) WABC (30 minutes)
Cast: Maureen O'Sullivan, others
23. Lux Radio Theatre "Maisie Was A Lady" (November 24, 1941) CBS
Cast: Maureen O'Sullivan *(Abby Rawlston)*, Ann Sothern *(Maisie Ravier)*, Lew Ayres *(Bob Rawlston)*, Henry Stephenson *(Walpole)*, Tory Charlton *(Diana)*, Lloyd Davis *(Cap)*, Grif Barnett *(Judge)*, Gene O'Donnell *(Link)*. Hosted by Cecil B. De Mille; announcer, Melville Ruick.
24. Hollywood's March of Dimes of the Air (January 24, 1942) NBC
Guests (in order of appearance): Bing Crosby, Bob Hope, Irene Dunne, The Merry Macks, Claudette Colbert, Humphrey Bogart, Janet Beecher, Dennis Day, Edgar Bergen, Marlene Dietrich, Kay Kyser, Tyrone Power, James Cagney, Maureen O'Sullivan, Lou Merrill, Fibber McGee and Molly, Elliot Lewis, Meredith Wilson, Deanna Durbin. Credits: Written and produced by Arch Obler; host, Tommy Cook; orchestra, Gordon Jenkins.
25. The Orson Welles Show "The Happy Hypocrite" (Jan. 26, 1942) WABC
Cast: Maureen O'Sullivan, John Barrymore, Orson Welles, Agnes Moorehead, Joseph Cotten, Ray Collins. Sponsored by Lady Esther Cosmetics.
26. Kraft Music Hall (February 12, 1942) NBC (1 hour)
Guests: Maureen O'Sullivan, Mickey Rooney, Victor Mature, Igor Gorin.
27. Variety Show (January 8, 1943) WABC (45 minutes)
Guests: Maureen O'Sullivan, Groucho Marx, Lew Lehr, Cugat Orchestra, Lanny Ross, Georgia Gibbs, songs.
28. Cavalcade of America "Sky Nursemaid" (June 28, 1943) NBC (30 minutes)
Cast: Maureen O'Sullivan *(Nurse Jean Owens)*, Frank Readick *(Sargent Lou Stevens)*, Bea Benaderet *(Edna)*. Credits: Written by Sue Taylor White; musical score, Donald Vorhee. Sponsored by Dupont.
29. Variety Program "Stage Door Canteen" (July 1, 1943) WABC (30 minutes)
Guests: Maureen O'Sullivan, Bert Lytell, Edmund Gwenn, Henny Youngman.
30. Dramatic Radio "White Rose Murders" (July 6, 1943) WABC (30 minutes)
Cast: Maureen O'Sullivan, others
31. Words With Music Dept. of War Information (July 12, 1943) (30 minutes)
Guest: Maureen O'Sullivan reads her favorite Irish poetry to soldiers abroad. Works include pieces by William Butler Yeats, Padraic Colum, John Millington Synge, James Stevens and Thomas Moore. Organist: Milton Charles.
32. Hollywood Theatre of the Air "Hold Back the Dawn" NBC
(August 30-September 3 and September 6-10, 1943)
Dreft Star Playhouse 15-minute serial format sponsored by Proctor and Gamble.
Cast: Maureen O'Sullivan, others
33. Gulf Screen Guild Theater "The Immortal Sargent" (Nov. 22, 1943) CBS
Cast: Maureen O'Sullivan and Franchot Tone.
34. Variety Program: "What's New?" December 18, 1943 (1 hour)
Guests: Don Ameche, Maureen O'Sullivan, Lena Horne, Maxie Rosenbloom, Carlos Ramirez, Hedda Hopper, Ruth Clifton, Jack Douglas.
35. Lux Radio Theatre "The Constant Nymph" (January 10, 1944) CBS
Cast: Charles Boyer *(Louis Dodd, composer)*, Maureen O'Sullivan *(Tessa Sanger)*, Alexis Smith *(Florence Crighton)*, Walter Kingsford *(Charles)*, Pedro De Cordoba *(Sanger)*. Hosted by Cecil B. De Mille.
36. Front Line Theatre "The Constant Nymph" (March 20, 1944)
(Screen Guild Theater/Armed Forces Radio Service)
Cast: Charles Boyer *(Louis Dodd)*, Maureen O'Sullivan *(Tessa Sanger)*, Geraldine Fitzgerald *(Florence Crighton)*. Intermission Music: Alan Roth and His Salon Orchestra perform "Lonesome Road."
(Maureen O'Sullivan sings in this production; on the previous Lux broadcast, an unidentified female vocalist performed in her place.)
37. Lux Radio Theatre "This Land is Mine" (April 23, 1944) CBS
Cast: Charles Laughton *(Albert Lorrey)*, Maureen O'Sullivan *(Louise Martin)*, Edgar Barrier *(Major von Keller)*, Regina Wallace *(Albert's mother)*, Dennis Green *(George Lambert)*, Ralph Lewis *(Paul Martin)*, Cliff Clark *(Professor Sorrell)*, Douglas Wood *(the mayor)*, John McIntyre, Charles Seal, Norman Field, Tyler McVay, Howard McNeer. Hosted by Cecil B. De Mille; orchestra conductor, Louis Silvers; announcer, John M. Kennedy.

38. Everything For The Boys "Quality Street" (May 23, 1944) NBC
Cast: Ronald Colman *(Valentine Brown)*, Maureen O'Sullivan *(Phoebe Throssel)*, Agnes Moorehead *(Susan Throssel)*. Credits: Adapted from J. M. Barrie's play, "Quality Street by Arch Obler; announcer, Frank Martin; music by Gordon Jenkins. (Presented by Electric Autolite Co.)
39. Suspense "The Black Shawl" (July 27, 1944) CBS (30 minutes)
Cast: Maureen O'Sullivan *(Susan Appleby)*, Dame May Whitty *(Mrs. Masters)*, Pat McGeehan, Joseph Kearns. Credits: Produced and directed by William Spear; written by R. R. Lewis. (Presented by Roma Wines)
40. Lux Radio Theatre "Berkeley Square" (Dec. 18, 1944) CBS (1 hour)
Cast: Ronald Colman *(Peter Standish)*, Maureen O'Sullivan *(Helen Pettigrew)*, Dorothy Lovatt, Charles Seal, Gloria Gordon, Leslie Dennison, Claire Vadera, Jacqueline DeWitt, Colin Campbell, Eric Snowden, Norman Field, Gwenn Delano. Credits: Hosted by Cecil B. De Mille; based upon the Henry James novel, *The Sense of the Past*; music, Lou Silvers; announcer, John M. Kennedy.
41. Request Performance "Gift of the Magi"(Dec. 23, 1945) WABC (30 minutes)
Cast: Maureen O'Sullivan and Robert Walker
42. Lux Radio Theatre "How Green Was My Valley" (March 31, 1947) CBS
Cast: David Niven *(Mr. Gruffydd)*, Maureen O'Sullivan *(Angharad)*, Donald Crisp *(Mr. Morgan)*, Sara Allgood *(Mrs. Morgan)*.
43. Cavalcade of America "The Doctor and the President" (April 21, 1947) NBC
Cast: Douglas Fairbanks, Jr. *(Benjamin Waterhouse)*, Maureen O'Sullivan *(Eliza Waterhouse)*, George Zucco *(Uncle)*, Henry Blair *(Danny)*, Bill Johnstone *(Thomas Jefferson)*. Credits: Written by Robert Wallston; music by Robert Armbruster; announcer, John Easton. (Sponsored by Dupont)
44. This is Hollywood "The Adventuress" (May 10, 1947) CBS
Cast: Maureen O'Sullivan and Richard Greene
45. Christmas Rosary Program "The Joyful Hour" (Dec. 20, 1947) Mutual
The program consisted of music, prayers and a dramatization of the story of Christmas, with Ethel Barrymore and Pedro de Cordoba acting as narrators.
Guest stars: (in alphabetical order) Anne Blyth, MacDonald Carey, Perry Como, Jeanne Crain, Bing Crosby, Dennis Day, Dick Haymes, Joan Leslie, Christopher Lynch, Roddy McDowell, Ricardo Montalban, the Mullen sisters, Maureen O'Hara and Maureen O'Sullivan.
46. Catholic Charities Show "A Question of Pianos" (April 18, 1948) NBC
Guests: Maureen O'Sullivan, Bing Crosby, Bob Hope, Jimmy Durante, Ann Blyth, Gary and Lindsay Crosby.
47. Family Theatre "Once Upon a Golden Afternoon" (June 10, 1948) Mutual
Cast: Maureen O'Sullivan, Tom Conway, Natalie Wood.
48. Lux Radio Theatre "The Big Clock" (November 22, 1948) CBS
Cast: Maureen O'Sullivan *(Georgette Stroud)*, Ray Milland *(George Stroud)*. Hosted and produced by William Keighley.
49. NBC University Theatre "The Heart of Midlothian" (Feb. 27, 1949)
Cast: Maureen O'Sullivan *(Jeannie Deans)*, Ina Ronsley *(Effie Deans)*, Phillip Friend *(Jordie Robertson)*, Raymond Lawrence *(David Deans)*, Whitfield Conner *(the Bailey)*, Ben Wright *(Reuben Butler)*, George Pembroke *(the Jailer)*, Doris Lloyd *(The Queen)*. Credits: Directed by Andrew C. Love; adapted by Frederick Schlicht and Ernest Canoy from the novel by Sir Walter Scott; announcer, Don Stanley; music by Dr. Albert Harris.
50. Catholic Charities Show "Just in Case" (March 27, 1949) NBC
Guests: Maureen O'Sullivan, Bing Crosby, Bob Hope, Jimmy Durante.
51. Screen Director's Playhouse "The Big Clock" (July 8, 1949) NBC
Cast: Maureen O'Sullivan *(Georgette Stroud)*, Ray Milland *(George Stroud)*, William Conrad *(Earl Janoth)*, Larry Dobkin. Credits: Dramatic direction, Bill Karne; introduced by John Farrow; adapted by Richard Alan Simmons (from a novel by Kenneth Fearing); music conducted and composed by Henry Russell; announcer, James Wallington. Sponsored by Pabst Brewing Co.
52. NBC University Theatre "The Death of the Heart" (Aug. 6, 1949) (1 Hour)
Cast: Maureen O'Sullivan *(Porsche)*, Dan O'Herlihy, Ramsey Hill, Monte Maquette, Norma Vardon, Donald Morrison, Dennis Hoey, Queenie Leonard.
Credits: Directed by Andrew C. Love; adapted by Richard E. Davis from Elizabeth Bowen's *The Death of the Heart*; music by Albert Harris; announcer, Don Stanley.
53. Family Theatre "The Fountain of Youth" (Aug. 10, 1949) Mutual
Cast: Maureen O'Sullivan, John Dehner, Lurene Tuttle. Hosted by Don DeFore.
54. NBC University Theatre "Precious Bane" (September 3, 1949) (1 Hour)
Cast: Maureen O'Sullivan *(Prudence Sarne)*, Dan O'Herlihy *(Gideon Sarne)*, Joseph Granby, Ralph Moody, Ramsey Hill, Earl Keene, Rolfe Sedan, Rita Lynn. Credits: Adapted from the novel *Precious Bane* by Mary Webb.
55. Hour of Stars "Quality Street" (November 6, 1949) CBS
Cast: Maureen O'Sullivan and Ronald Colman

56. Family Theatre "By Sun and Candlelight" (Nov. 16, 1949) Mutual
Cast: Maureen O'Sullivan, James Gleason, Gene Raymond.
57. This Is Your Life (March 1, 1950) NBC (30 minutes)
Special guests: (in order of appearance) Ila Olrich Hope, Maureen O'Sullivan, Belle Kennedy, Ken Murray, Velma Wayne Dawson, and (from an earlier broadcast) W.C. Fields. Credits: Hosted by Ralph Edwards; original music, Alexander Lazlow; announcer, Art Ballinger.
58. Family Theatre "20,000 Leagues Under the Sea" (Aug. 23, 1950) Mutual
Cast: Maureen O'Sullivan hostess, Otto Krueger.
59. Mr. Jones Rediscovers America (August 26, 1952) CBS
Guests: Maureen O'Sullivan, Joe DiMaggio, and George Murphy.
60. Family Theatre "The Kid from Scratch Gravel (October 3, 1951) Mutual
Cast: Maureen O'Sullivan, Ted de Corscia.
61. Family Theatre "The Heart Also Sees" (October 15, 1952) Mutual
Cast: Maureen O'Sullivan hostess, Jeanne Crain, Dale Robertson, Margaret Sheridan.
62. The Bob Hope Show (Feb. 2-6, 1953) NBC Presented by General Foods.
Guest cast: Maureen O'Sullivan was Bob Hope's daytime guest for the week.
63. Ask Hollywood "Premiere" (October 4, 1953) NBC
Guest: Maureen O'Sullivan.
64. Family Theatre "A Fine Wedding for Angelita" (Oct. 28, 1953) Mutual
Cast: Maureen O'Sullivan, J. Carroll Naish, Ricky Barra.
65. Family Theatre "The Way of the Cross" (April 14, 1954) Mutual
Cast: Maureen O'Sullivan and Jeff Chandler. Easter Program (30 minutes)
66. Sunday with Garroway (May 9, 1954) NBC (2 Hours)
Guests: Maureen O'Sullivan, Patrick J. Kelly, Ogden Nash, Dr. Lillian Gillbreth, MacDonald Carey, Rabbi David De Sola Pool. Hosted by Dave Garroway.
67. Family Theatre "Every Good Boy Does Fine" (May 5, 1955) Mutual
Cast: Maureen O'Sullivan *(Mrs. Gregg)*, others. Hosted by Jerry Lewis; announcer, Tony La Frano; music composed and conducted by Harry Zimmerman.
68. Family Theatre "The Juggler of Our Lady" (December 21, 1955) Mutual
Cast: Maureen O'Sullivan *(Narrator)*, Jack Haley *(Barnaby, the Juggler)*, Paul Frees, Victor Rodman, Ralph Moody, Herb Ellis. Credits: Written and directed by Robert Hugh O'Sullivan; music composed and conducted by Harry Zimmerman; announcer, Tony Le Frano. Christmas Program.
69. Family Theatre "Once upon a Golden Afternoon" (Jan. 30, 1957) Mutual
Cast: Maureen O'Sullivan, Jean Bates.
70. Family Theatre "Sylvia" (August 28, 1957) Mutual (30 minutes)
Cast: Maureen O'Sullivan, Jean Bates, Vic Perrin, Kathy Johnson, Richard Beals.
Credits: Directed by John T. Kelley; written by R. Powers Savage. Hosted by Raymond Burr.

Note: **Maureen O'Sullivan** was a guest on numerous radio programs in the 1960s and 1970s to promote her stage appearances.

Television Appearances

1. **The Children's Hour** (1951) Maureen O'Sullivan, Host
2. **Hollywood Opening Night** "The Lucky Coin" (December 1, 1952)
Cast: Maureen O'Sullivan, Wendell Corey.
Credits: Directed by Richard Irving.
3. **Ford Television Theatre** "They Also Serve" (January 1, 1953) NBC
Cast: Maureen O'Sullivan, John Hodiak.
4. **Schlitz Playhouse of Stars** "Parent's Weekend" (March 20, 1953) CBS
Cast: Maureen O'Sullivan, Jerome Cowan, Skip Homeier.
5. **Ford Television Theatre** "The Trestle" (June 11, 1953) NBC
Cast: Maureen O'Sullivan, Phillip Carey, Tim Considine.
6. **Lux Video Theatre** "Message in a Bottle" (September 3, 1953) CBS
Cast: Ronald Reagan, Maureen O'Sullivan, George Macready, George Pembroke.
Credits: Directed by Richard Goode, written by Gerald Holland.
7. **Four Star Playhouse** "The Gift" (December 24, 1953) CBS
Cast: Charles Boyer *(Carl Baxter)*, Maureen O'Sullivan *(Minna Baxter)*, Dan Tobin *(George Lennox)*, Joan Camden, Ann Doran, Virginia Christine.
Credits: Directed by Robert Aldrich; screenplay by John and Gwen Bagni (from a story by Amory Hare); produced by Charles Boyer.
8. **Irish Heritage** (1954) Maureen O'Sullivan, Host
9. **Ford Television Theatre** "Daughter of Mine" (October 7, 1954) NBC
Cast: Maureen O'Sullivan, Pat O'Brien, Margaret O'Brien, Richard Jaeckel, Tol Avery
10. **Lux Video Theatre** "September Tide" (October 28, 1954) NBC
Cast: Maureen O'Sullivan, John Sutton.
Credits: Hosted by James Mason; from a story by Daphne Du Maurier.
11. **Fireside Theatre** "Brian" (February 2, 1955) NBC
Cast: Maureen O'Sullivan, John Howard, Peter Reynolds.
12. **Climax Theatre** "The Great Impersonation" (March 10, 1955) CBS
Cast: Maureen O'Sullivan *(Lady Dominey)*, Michael Rennie *(Lord Dominey/Major General von Ragestein)*, Zsa Zsa Gabor *(Princess Stephanie)*.
Credits: Hosted by Bill Lundigan; teleplay of an E. Phillips Oppenheim story.
13. **Casablanca** "Labor Camp Dispute" (November 8, 1955) ABC
Cast: Maureen O'Sullivan *(Helen)*, Charles McGraw *(Rick)*, William Hopper *(Wilson Randall)*, Don Randolph *(Captain Rudolph)*. Hosted by Gig Young.
14. **Climax Theatre** "The Louella Parsons Story" (3-8-56) CBS
Cast: Maureen O'Sullivan (as herself)
15. **The Whistler** "Trademark" (March 18, 1956)
Cast: Maureen O'Sullivan
16. **Star Stage** "Scandal on Deepside" (March 30, 1956)
Cast: Maureen O'Sullivan
17. **Matinee Theatre** "Ladies' Maid's Bell" (September 4, 1956)
Cast: Maureen O'Sullivan
18. **Cavalcade of America** "The Blessed Midnight" (Dec. 18, 1956) ABC
Cast: Maureen O'Sullivan, Danny Richards Jr., David Saber, Frances Bavier, Carole Wells, Virginia Gregg
19. **Lux Video Theatre** "Michael and Mary" (December 27, 1956) NBC
Cast: Maureen O'Sullivan
Credits: Hosted by Gordon McRae; story by A.A. Milne.

20. Crossroads "The Man Who Walked on Water" (January 4, 1957) ABC
Cast: Maureen O'Sullivan and William Prince

21. Climax Theatre "Let It Be Me" (March 21, 1957) CBS
Cast: Maureen O'Sullivan *(Miriam)*, Eddie Albert *(Barney)*, Charles Ruggles *(Dan)*, Steve Forrest *(Pete)*, Jill Corey, Johnny Desmond.
Credits: Story by Eileen and Robert Mason Pollock; hosted by Bill Lundigan and Mary Costa.

22. Playhouse 90 "Edge of Innocence" (October 31, 1957) CBS
Cast: Maureen O'Sullivan *(Julia Williams)*, Teresa Wright *(Carol Morton)*, Joseph Gotten *(Robert Rainey)*, Lorne Greene *(Lowell Williams)*, Beverly Garland *(Gay Sherman)*, Dan Barton *(Jay Pauling)*, DeForest Kelley
Credits: Directed by Arthur Hiller; Story by Berne Giler. (90 minutes)

23. Alcoa Premiere "Moment of Decision" (November 7, 1961) CBS
Cast: Fred Astaire *(Alex Berringer)*, Maureen O'Sullivan *(Elizabeth Lozier)*, Harry Townes *(Hugh Lozier)*, Katherine Henryk *(Molly)*, Connie Gilchrist *(Emma)*, Oliver McGowan *(Dr. Lockridge)*, Cathleen Cordell *(Mrs. Lockridge)*.
Credits: Directed by John Newland; script by Larry Marcus, Peter Tewksbury, James Leighton; hosted by Fred Astaire.

24. The Today Show (1964)
Cast: Maureen O'Sullivan co-anchor NBC

25. Candid Camera (1964) Maureen O'Sullivan (guest)

26. Stump the Stars (August 3, 1964.)
Guest cast: Maureen O'Sullivan, Tom Poston, Orson Bean, Hans Conreid, Sebastian Cabot, Stubby Kaye; hosted by Mike Stokey.

27. Ben Casey "A Boy is Standing Outside the Door" (January 4, 1965) ABC
Cast: Maureen O'Sullivan, William Marshall, Susan Flannery, Elsa Lanchester, Vince Edwards *(Dr. Ben Casey)*, Sam Jaffe *(Dr. David Zorba)*, Franchot Tone *(Dr. Daniel Freeland)*.

28. What's My Line? (14 November 1965)
Cast: Maureen O'Sullivan playing "Mystery Guest"

29. One Who Was There (1979) United Methodist Communications
Cast: Maureen O'Sullivan *(Mary Magdalene)*, Gregory Abels, Victor Arnold, Robert Dryden, Hugh Moffat, Tisa Farrow.
Credits: Directed by Donald Hughes; written by Suzy Loftis, Hughes. (37 minutes)

30. Mandy's Grandmother (April 4, 1980) CBS
Cast: Maureen O'Sullivan *(Grandmother)*, Amy Levitan *(Mandy)*, Kathryn Walker *(Mother)*, Philip Carlson *(Father)*, Yvette Deas *(Sharon)*, Rosetta Le Noire *(librarian)*, Christopher Erickson *(Paulie)*.
Credits: Produced and directed by Andrew Sugerman. (60 Minutes)

31. Morning's at Seven (September, 1982) A&E/CBS
Cast: Maureen O'Sullivan *(Esty)*, Kate Reid *(Ida)*, Elizabeth Wilson *(Arry)*, Teresa Wright *(Cora)*, Maurice Copeland *(Thor)*, King Donovan *(Carl)*, Robert Moberly *(Homer)*, Charlotte Moore *(Myrtle)*, Russell Nype *(David)*.
Credits: Directed by Vivian Matalon; written by Paul Osborn.

32. All My Children (April 21, 1983-May 10, 1983) ABC
Guest cast: Maureen O'Sullivan as Olive Whalen

33. Guiding Light (Fall, 1984) CBS
Guest cast: Maureen O'Sullivan as Miss Emma Witherspoon

34. Miss USA Pageant (1986) Cameo
Guest cast: Miss O'Sullivan recites "The New Colossus"

35. Happy Birthday Hollywood (1987) Cameo
Guest cast: Maureen O'Sullivan, many others

36. Legwork "All This and a Gold Card, Too" (October 31, 1987) CBS
Cast: Margaret Colin *(Claire)*, Maureen O'Sullivan *(Dorothy Richardson)*, Frances McDormand *(Willie)*, Patrick James Clarke *(Fred)*, William Bogert *(Klopf)*, Francois Gitoday *(Jimmy)*, Philip Bosco *(Dawson)*, Thomas Gibson *(Robbie Richardson)*, Brad O'Hare *(Peter Richardson)*.
Credits: Directed by Peter Hunt; teleplay by Frank Abatemarco and Deborah R. Baron.

37. Pros and Cons (1991) ABC
Cast: Richard Crenna *(Mitch O'Hannon)*, James Earl Jones *(Gabriel Bird)*, Madge Sinclair *(Josephine Austin)*, Maureen O'Sullivan *(guest star)*.
Credits: Directed by Jerry Thorpe; story by Tom Chehak.

Stage Appearances

1. ***A Roomful of Roses*** — Drury Lane Theatre, Chicago (opened the week of October 1, 1961)
Cast: Maureen O'Sullivan *(Nancy Fallon)*, John Himes *(Jay Fallon)*, Stephen Herbst *(Larry Fallon)*, Jeanette Leahy *(Grace Hewitt)*, Sue Kiss *(Jane Hewitt)*, Harry James *(Dick Hewitt)*, Nicki Pierce *(Bridget MacGowan)*, Richard Dix *(Carl MacGowan)*, Jane Sindt *(Wilhelmina)*.
Credits: Directed by Vernon Schwartz; written by Edith Sommer; produced by Carl Stohn, Jr.

2. ***Never Too Late*** — The Playhouse, New York (November 27, 1962 — 1007 performances)
Cast: Maureen O'Sullivan *(Edith Lambert)*, Paul Ford *(Harry Lambert)*, Orson Bean *(Charlie)*, Fran Sharon *(Kate)*, Leona Maricle *(Grace Kimbrough)*, House Jameson *(Dr. James Kimbrough)*, Wallace Engelhardt *(Mr. Foley)*, John Alexander *(Mayor Crane)*, Ed Griffith *(policeman)*.
Credits: Directed by George Abbott; produced by Elliot Martin and Daniel Hollywood; written by Sumner Arthur Long; setting and lighting by William and Jean Eckart.
(See text for more information on *Never Too Late*.)

3. ***Two Dozen Red Roses*** — Pheasant Run Playhouse, St. Charles, Illinois (opened the week of Nov. 1, 1964)
Cast: Maureen O'Sullivan *(Lindsay Verani)*, Bill Morey *(Alberto Verani)*, Jerry McDaniel *(Bernardo)*, Corinne Carr *(Rosina)*, Lew Prentiss *(Tomasso Savelli)*.
Credits: Directed and designed by David Morrison; produced by Carl Strohn, Jr.; written by Kenneth Horne; adapted from the Italian play by Aldo de Benedetti.

4. ***The Subject Was Roses*** — National tour (began August, 1965 including an engagement on Broadway at Henry Miller's Theater in February of 1966; closed May 21, 1967 after 834 total performances)
Cast: Maureen O'Sullivan *(Nettie Cleary)*, Chester Morris *(John Cleary)*, Walter McGinn *(Timmy Cleary)*.
Credits: Directed by Ulu Grosbard; written by Frank D. Gilroy; scenery, Edgar Lansbury; lighting, Jules Fisher; costumes, Donald Foote.

5. ***The 5.07*** — Royal Poinciana Playhouse, Palm Beach, Fla. (March, 1967)
Cast: Maureen O'Sullivan *(Marian Plummer)*.
Credits: Written by Robert Soderberg.

6. ***Keep It in the Family*** — Plymouth Theatre, Broadway, New York, N.Y. (September 27, 1967); two week preview run at The Colonial in Boston, Mass. (opened September 11, 1967).
Cast: Maureen O'Sullivan *(Daisy Brady)*, Patrick Magee *(Frank Brady)*, Marian Hailey *(Florence Brady)*, Sudie Bond *(Betsy Jane)*, Jeff Siggins *(Billy Brady)*, Burt Brinckernoff *(Michael Brady)*, Karen Black *(Hilda Brady)*, Tom Atkins *(Arthur)*.
Credits: Presented by David Merrick; written by Bill Naughton; staging, Allen Davis; setting, Lloyd Burlingame; costumes, Mary McKinley.

7. ***You Know I Can't Hear You When the Water's Running*** — Coconut Grove Playhouse, Miami, Florida (June 27, 1967 to June 2, 1968).
Cast: Maureen O'Sullivan, Jose Ferrer and Ben Piazza.
Credits: Written by Robert Anderson; directors included Hal Halvorsen, Billy Matthews, Danny Simon, Joey Faye, Robert Linden, Anthony Perkins, Malcolm Black, Robert Moore, Richard Altman.

8. ***Don't Drink the Water*** — Touring company summer 1968, including stops in New Hampshire, Long Island, NY, upstate New York, and Charlotte, Virginia.
Cast: Maureen O'Sullivan and Sam Levene.
Credits: Written by Woody Allen.

9. ***Butterflies Are Free*** — Previewed August- September 1969 at the Cherry County Playhouse in Michigan, also Falmouth Playhouse, Massachusetts, and Westport Country Playhouse in Connecticut.
Cast: Keir Dullea *(Don Baker)*, Maureen O'Sullivan *(Mrs. Baker)*, Blythe Danner *(Jill)*. (Note: For the Broadway opening in October, Maureen was replaced by Eileen Heckart, due to Ms. O'Sullivan's illness.)
Credits: Written by Leonard Gershe.

10. ***The Front Page*** — Ethel Barrymore Theatre, Broadway, New York (opened October 15, 1969, closed February 28, 1970 — 159 performances)
Cast: Bert Convy *(Hildy Johnson)*, Kendall March *(Peggy Grant)*, Maureen O'Sullivan *(Mrs. Grant)*, Robert Ryan *(Walter Burns)*, John McGiver *(The Mayor)*, Patrick Desmond *(Earl Williams)*, Will Gregory *(Wilson)*, Robert Milli *(Endicott)*, James Flavin *(Murphy)*, Ed Riley *(McCue)*, Bob Larkin *(Schwartz)*, Conrad Janis *(Kruger)*, Harold J. Kennedy *(Bensinger)*, Walter Flanagan *(Woodenshoes Eichorn)*, Val Avery *(Diamond Louis)*, Charles White *(Sheriff Hartman)*, Dody Goodman *(Jenny)*, Peggy Cass *(Mollie Malloy)*, Bernie West *(Mr. Pincus)*.
(Maureen O'Sullivan assumed the role of Mrs. Grant on January 5, 1970. She was preceded in the role by Helen Hayes and Molly Picon.)
Credits: Directed by Harold J. Kennedy; written by Ben Hecht and Charles MacArthur; designed and lighted by Will Steven Armstrong; costumes, Sara Brook.

11. ***Charley's Aunt*** — Brooks Atkinson Theatre (opened July 4, 1970)
Cast: Maureen O'Sullivan *(Donna Lucia d'Aladorez)*, Michael Goodwin *(Jack Chesney)*, Melville Cooper *(Brassett)*, Rex Thopson *(Charles Wykeham)*, Louis Nye *(Lord Fancourt Babberley)*, Lynn Milgrim *(Amy Spettigue)*, Andra Akers *(Kitty Verdun)*, Martyn Green *(Col. Sir Francis Chesney)*, Eric Berry *(Stephen Spettigue)*, Bruce Blaine *(Brassett's assistant)*, Elizabeth Swain *(Ela Delahay)*.
Credits: Directed by Harold Stone; written by Brandon Thomas; settings by Robert T. Williams; lighting by F. Mitchell Dana; costumes, Richard Anderson.

12. ***Hay Fever*** — Seattle Repertory Theatre, Seattle, Washington (1970-71 season)
Guest Artist: Maureen O'Sullivan.

13. ***The Pleasure of His Company*** — Touring company (summer 1971)
Cast: Maureen O'Sullivan *(Kate Dougherty)*, Cyril Ritchard *("Pogo" Poole)*.
Credits: Written by Samuel Taylor.

14. ***Butterflies Are Free*** — (Denver, Colorado 1972)
Cast: Brandon De Wilde *(Don Baker)*, Maureen O'Sullivan *(Mrs. Baker)*.
Credits: Written by Leonard Gershe.

15. ***No Sex, Please, We're British*** — Ritz Theatre (February 20, 1973)
Cast: Maureen O'Sullivan *(Eleanor Hunter)*, Stephen Collins *(Peter Hunter)*, J. J. Lewis *(Frances Hunter)*, Tony Tanner *(Brian Runicles)*, Ronald Drake *(Leslie Bromhead)*, John Clarkson *(Superintendent Paul)*, Leon Shaw *(Mr. Needleham)*, Jill Tanner *(Susan)*, Jennifer Richards *(Barbara)*.
Credits: Directed by Christopher Hewett; written by Anthony Marriott and Alistair Foot; setting by Helen Pond and Herbert Senn; lighting by John Harvey.

16. ***The Price*** — Falmouth Playhouse (summer 1973)
Cast: Maureen O'Sullivan and Howard Duff.

17. ***Sabrina Fair*** — Arlington Park Theatre, Arlington Heights, Ill. (June 1, 1976-May 31, 1977)
Cast: Maureen O'Sullivan *(Maude Larrabee)*, Martin Milner, Sylvia Sidney, Heather MacRae, Robert Urich, Richard Bowler, Marie Brady and Barrie Moss.
Credits: Directed by Harold J. Kennedy; written by Samuel Taylor; technical director, William Fosser; props, Sandy Lewis; sets and lighting, William B. Fosser.

18. ***Ladies of the Corridor*** — Tappan Zee Playhouse in Nyack, N.Y. (1977)
Cast: Maureen O'Sullivan, Barbara Britton and Lilia Skala.
Credits: Directed by William E. Hunt; written by Dorothy Parker.

19. ***The Glass Menagerie*** — Cohoes Music Hall, Cohoes, N.Y. (Oct. 29, 1977-March 19, 1978)
Cast: Maureen O'Sullivan *(Amanda Wingfield)*, Elaine Hausman *(Laura Wingfield)*, Peter Webster *(Tom Wingfield)*, Robert Bacigalupi *(Jim O'Connor)*.
Credits: Written by Tennessee Williams; executive director, Louis J. Ambrosio; technical director, David Fletcher; props, Paula Gouras; lighting, Toni Golden; costumes, Bob Wojewwodski; Dona Granata; sets, Michael Anania.

20. ***Pygmalion*** — Ahmanson Theatre, Los Angeles, CA (Sept. 29, 1978-June 2, 1979)
Cast: Maureen O'Sullivan *(Mrs. Higgins)*, Robert Stephens *(Professor Higgins)*, Roberta Maxwell *(Eliza)*, Milo O'Shea *(Doolittle)*, William Roerick *(Col. Pickering)*, Neva Patterson *(Mrs. Eynsford Hill)*, Margaret Hilton *(Mrs. Pearce)*, Dale Hodges *(Clara)*, James David Cromar *(Freddy)*, Rosemary Lord *(parlour maid)*.
Credits: Written by George Bernard Shaw; direction, John Dexter; sets and costumes, Jocelyn Herbert and Andrew Sanders; lighting, Andy Phillips.

21. ***Morning's at Seven*** — Lyceum Theatre (Opened April 12, 1980)
Cast: Maureen O'Sullivan *(Esther Crampton)*, Teresa Wright *(Cora Swanson)*, Maurice Copeland *(Theodore Swanson)*, Elizabeth Wilson *(Aaronetta Gibbs)*, Nancy Marchand *(Ida Bolton)*, Richard Hamilton *(Carl Bolton)*, David Rounds *(Homer Bolton)*, Lois de Banzie *(Myrtle Brown)*, Gary Merrill *(David Crampton)*.
Credits: Directed by Vivian Matalon; written by Paul Osborn; presented by Elizabeth I. McCann, Nelle Nugent and Ray Larsen; setting, William Ritman; costumes, Linda Fisher; lighting, Richard Nelson.

22. *Barbarians* — Williamstown Theatre, Williamstown, Mass. (June 26-July 5, 1986)
Cast: Maureen O'Sullivan *(Tatyana Bogayevskaya)*, William Swetland *(Redozubov "Vassily" the Mayor)*, Christian Clemenson *(Grisha, his son)*, Stephanie Zimbalist *(Katya, his daughter)*, Louis Beachner *(Pavlin)*, Richard Thomas *(Dr. Makharov)*, Daniel Davis *(Mavrisky)*, Margaret Klenck *(Nadiezdha, his wife)*, Joe Ponazecki *(Chief of Police)*, Ann Reinking *(Lydia)*, Robert Clohessy *(Arkhip Pritykin)*, Barbara Eda-Young *(Pelageya, his wife)*, James Naughton *(Sergei Tsyganov)*, Daniel Hugh Kelly *(Yegor Cherkoon)*, Laila Robins *(Anna, his wife)*, Apollo Dukakis *(a beggar)*.
Credits: Directed by Nikos Psacharaopoulos; written by Maxim Gorky; translated by Kitty Hunter-Blair, Jeremy Brooks and Michael Weller; settings and costumes, Santo Loquasto; lighting, William Armstrong.
23. *Love Letters* — Williamstown Theatre, Main Stage (August 16-28, 1994)
Cast: Maureen O'Sullivan *(Melissa Gardner)*, John Randolph *(Andrew Makepeace Ladd III)*. Others performing the same roles on different dates included: Eli Wallach with Anne Jackson, Richard Benjamin, Stephen Collins, Christopher Reeve, James Naughton, Richard Thomas, James Whitmore, Karen Allen, Jane Curtin, Celeste Holm, Mary Tyler Moore, Paula Prentiss, Elaine Stritch.
Credits: Written by A.R. Gurney.

Other off-Broadway theater that Maureen O'Sullivan starred in during the 1960s and 1970s included:
24. — *Barefoot in the Park* by Neil Simon (in the role of the mother-in-law, Ethyl Banks)
25. — *Heartbreak House* by George Bernard Shaw
26. — *The Little Foxes* by Lillian Hellman

Maureen and Chester Morris from *The Subject Was Roses, national tour 1966-67*

An original portrait by Thomas Yeates

Acknowledgments

There are many people to thank in accomplishing this project, which turned out to be rather massive in terms of the amount of research and the final size of the volume. I'll try to mention everyone, but if I forget someone it is not an intentional slight.

First of all I would like to thank Jim Cushing, Maureen's husband since 1983, for his support of this biography. I sincerely appreciate your efforts, including personal memories of your wife and the many photographs you provided. Of course we cannot forget Maureen herself, who was a long-distance friend to me and wrote the foreword to my 1994 book, *Kings of the Jungle*. Thank you Maureen, and I hope this biography bespeaks my admiration and affection for you. Many thanks to Johnny Sheffield for his memories of his screen mother, Jane, who influenced his life greatly when he was just a "Boy."

Next I must thank my editor, Carolin Kopplin, for her many hours of dedicated work over the eighteen months of researching and writing this book. Carolin is dedicated, tireless, and often times, brilliant. Carolin splits her time between her home in Munich, and London. She is devoted to the theatre.

Many thanks to my final proofreader, Annie Margis, of Long Beach, California. She took the necessary time to smooth away some rough edges, and find the little flaws and spelling mistakes. Annie is an author, editor, and the president of the California Writers Club of Long Beach.

My family and friends have always been supportive of my writing projects, and I could not make it through the difficult times without them. Special friends who were there through thick and thin include: Rudy Sigmund, Hank Brown, Jason and Judith Dene (Maureen's grandson and granddaughter-in-law), George McWhorter, Martin Smiddy, Frank Westwood, Ralph Brown, Mike Conran, Jerry Spannraft, Bill Morse, Jim Larson, Gene Kerr, Martin Smiddy, Roger Skrenes, Danton Burroughs, Patty Sheffield, Lisa Weissmuller, Ed Gallagher, Hilary Costello, Carol Furry, Joni Kreuser, and Maggi Brooks.

A gracious tip of the hat to artist Thomas Yeates for his original drawing of Maureen O'Sullivan. My gratitude to Stacey Behlmer at the Margaret Herrick Library, Academy of Motion Picture Arts and Sciences, and her husband Rudy Behlmer for his extensive research on the MGM Tarzan pictures in the 1980s. Also huge thanks to the librarians in Hennepin County, Minnesota, for countless hours of effort and research to aid this project.

Photographic Credits

My sincere gratitude goes to the contributors of photographs in this volume, including:

> Maureen O'Sullivan
> Jim Cushing
> Judith Dene
> Ralph Brown
> Danton Burroughs and Edgar Rice Burroughs, Inc.
> George McWhorter and the Burroughs Bibliophiles
> Frank Westwood and the Edgar Rice Burroughs Society
> Martin Smiddy
> Jerry Spannraft
> Gene Kerr
> Rudy Sigmund
> (all other photos are from your author's collection)

Many thanks to the motion picture studios and the photographers who captured the beauty of Maureen O'Sullivan from 1929 to 1994, including: Metro-Goldwyn-Mayer, Columbia Pictures, Universal, etc.

Bibliography

Books and Reference Volumes
Ardagh, John "Ireland and the Irish" Hamish Hamilton, London 1994
Billups, Connie "Maureen O'Sullivan: A Bio-Bibliography" Greenwood Press 1990
Callow, Simon "Charles Laughton: A Difficult Actor" Grove Press 1987
Crow, Jefferson Brim "Randolph Scott: The Gentleman from Virginia" Wind River 1987
Curtis, James "W.C. Fields: A Biography" Alfred A. Knopf 2003
Davis, Ronald L. "Duke: The Life and Image of John Wayne" University of Oklahoma Press 1998
Dagneau, Gilles "Ava Gardner" Gremese 2002
Drazin, Charles "Korda: Britain's Only Movie Mogul" Sidgwick & Jackson, London 2002
Dunning, John "The Encyclopedia of Old-time Radio" Oxford University Press 1998
Edwards, Anne "Vivien Leigh" Simon and Schuster 1977
Eels, George "Robert Mitchum" Franklin Watts, New York 1984
Farrow, Mia "What Falls Away" Doubleday 1997
Flamini, Roland "Thalberg: The Last Tycoon and the World of M-G-M" Crown 1994
Gardner, Ava "Ava: My Story" Bantam Books, New York 1990
Golway, Terry "For the Cause of Liberty: A Thousand Years of Ireland's Heroes" S & S 2004
Graham, Sheila "The Garden of Allah" Crown Publishers, New York 1970
Gronowicz, Antoni "Garbo: Her Story" Simon and Schuster 1990
Hamann, G.D. "Maureen O'Sullivan in the '30's" Filming Today Press, Hollywood
Hannsberry, Karen Burroughs "Bad Boys: The Actors of Film Noir" McFarland 2003
Higham, Charles "Ava" W. H. Allen London 1975
Kanfer, Stefan "Groucho: The Life and Times of Julius Henry Marx" Alfred A. Knopf 2000
Lambert, Gavin "Norma Shearer" Alfred A. Knopf 1990
Ledbetter, Gordon T. "John McCormack: The Great Irish Tenor" Charles Scribner's Sons 1977
Levy, Emanuel "George Cukor: Master of Elegance" William Morrow and Co. New York 1994
Lanchester, Elsa "Elsa Lanchester: Herself" St. Martin's Press 1983
Linet, Beverly "Ladd: The Life, The Legend, The Legacy of Alan Ladd" Arbor House 1979
Louvish, Simon "Monkey Business: The Lives and Legends of the Marx Brothers" St. Martin's 2000
Milland, Ray "Wide-Eyed in Babylon" William Morrow & Co. 1974
Mitchell, Glenn "The Marx Brothers Encyclopedia" Reynolds & Hearn LTD 2003
Marx, Groucho and Anobile, Richard "The Marx Brothers Scrapbook" Darien House 1973
Nott, Robert "Films of Randolph Scott" McFarland & Co. 2004
Parish, J. R. and Bowers, R. L. "MGM Stock Company: The Golden Era" Arlington House 1973
Parish, James Robert and Michael R. Pitts "The Great Western Pictures" Scarecrow Press 1976
Quirk, Laurence J. "The Complete Films of William Powell" Citadel Press 1986
Ragan, David "Who's Who in Hollywood" Arlington House 1976
Roberts, Randy and Olson, James S. "John Wayne: American" Simon & Schuster 1995
Robyns, Gwen "Vivien Leigh: Light of a Star" A.S. Barnes 1970
Rogers, Will "The Autobiography of Will Rogers" Edited by Donald Day Aeonian Press
Rogers, Will "The Will Rogers Scrapbook" Edited by Bryan B. Sterling Bonanza Books 1980
Russell, Jane "Jane Russell: An Autobiography" Franklin Watts, New York 1985
Russell, Rosalind "Life Is A Banquet" (with Chris Chase) Random House, NY 1977

Schatz, Thomas "The Genius of the System" Pantheon Books, New York 1988
Server, Lee "Robert Mitchum: Baby I Don't Care" St. Martin's Press 2001
Strachan, Hew "The First World War" Viking/Penguin, New York 2003
Swenson, Karen "Greta Garbo: A Life Apart" Lisa Drew/Scribner 1997
Thomas, Bob "Golden Boy: The Untold Story of William Holden" St. Martin's Press 1983
Thomson, David "The New Biographical Dictionary of Film" Alfred A. Knopf, New York 2004
Michael Troyan, "A Rose for Mrs. Miniver: The Life of Greer Garson" U. Press of Kentucky 1999
Walker, Alexander "Vivien: The Life of Vivien Leigh" Weidenfeld & Nicolson 1987
Wayne, Jane Ellen "Ava's Men: The Private Life of Ava Gardner" St. Martin's Press 1990
Wayne, Pilar with Thorleifson, Alex "My Life with the Duke" PaperJacks 1988
"Biographical Encyclopedia & Who's Who in the American Theatre" James H. Heineman 1966
"Who's Who in the Theatre" (Edited by Ian Herbert) Pitman, London 1977

Magazine and Newspaper Articles
Behlmer, Rudy "Tarzan, Hollywood's Greatest Jungle Hero"
    American Cinematographer (January and February, 1987)
Canham, Kingsley "Interview with Maureen O'Sullivan" *Focus on Film,* (No. 18, Summer 1974)
Carstairs, John Paddy "There's No Stopping Maureen O'Sullivan" *Film Pictorial* (Aug. 3, 1935)
Chrisman, J. Eugene "Maureen Escapes from the Jungle" *Hollywood Magazine* (Nov. 1934)
Donnell, Dorothy "I Don't Want a Hollywood Marriage" *Motion Picture* (October 1934)
Esquire "Tarzan and other Heroes Come Back Once More" (April 1970, cover photo)
Evans, Harry "Tarzan and His Mate" *The Family Circle* (May 25, 1934)
Galligan, David "Maureen O'Sullivan, Mama Mia" *Hollywood Studio Magazine* (Aug. 1981)
Gallagher, John "Maureen O'Sullivan, Star of the Silver Screen" *Irish America* (Feb. 1989)
Grafton, Samuel "Some People Have to Grow Up Twice" *Good Housekeeping* (January 1955)
Henderson, Kathy "Talking with Maureen O'Sullivan" *Redbook* (September 1987)
Historical New York Times, numerous reviews and articles, 1929 - 1998
Hutchings, David "Maureen O'Sullivan Finds Her Star Reborn ..." *People Weekly* (April 14, 1986)
O'Sullivan, Maureen *Hello Magazine* (four parts, July 23, July 30, August 6, August 13, 1994)
O'Sullivan, Maureen "The Umbrella" *Ladies' Home Journal* (January 1970)
    Short story written by Maureen O'Sullivan
Weaver, Tom and Nielsen, Ray *Films of the Golden Age* "Our Favorite Jane" (Summer 2000)

Private Letters
Cukor, George "Letters to Mr. Cukor from Maureen O'Sullivan"
    Source: George Cukor file, Margaret Herrick Library
Hall, Gladys "Letters from Maureen O'Sullivan to Gladys Hall" 1936, 1938, 1940
    Source: Gladys Hall file, Margaret Herrick Library

Video Interviews
MGM interview with Maureen O'Sullivan, for "When the Lion Roars" April 1990
Turner Network interview with Maureen O'Sullivan, September 9, 1996

Personal Interviews
    Maureen O'Sullivan (with David Fury) 1992
    James Cushing (with David Fury) 2006
    Johnny Sheffield (with David Fury) 2000, 2006

Index

A

A Connecticut Yankee 44, 45
A Day at the Races 185, 188, 190
A Yank At Oxford 209
Abbott, George 345, 369
Albertson, Frank 37, 40, 91, 220, 228
Albright, Hardie 48
"Alcoa Premiere" *343*
All I Desire 314
"All My Children" 387
Allen, Woody 358, 397, 406
Ameche, Don 260
Ames, Leon 401
Anna Karenina 155
Annual American Cinema Awards 392
Arliss, George 143
Arnold, Edward 78, 121, 143, 223
Astaire, Fred 343
Austen, Jane 254
Ayres, Lew 79, 228, 261

B

Bankhead, Tallulah 182
Barbarians 391
Barker, Lex 328
Barretts of Wimpole Street, The 127
Barrymore, John 286
Barrymore, Lionel 135, 166, 209 246, 286
Bartholomew, Freddie 135, 155
Beal, John 217
Beery, Wallace 96, 140, 217, 418
Bellamy, Ralph 235
"Ben Casey" 352
Between Two Women 203
Bickford, Charles 271, 272
Big Clock, The 295
Big Shot, The 51
Bishop Misbehaves, The 161
Boetticher, Budd 330, 335
Boleslawski, Richard 153

Bonzo Goes to College 312
Boone, Richard 330
Borzage, Frank 11, 13, 28, 33
Boyer, Charles 277, 320, 410
Boyle, Ireland 15
Brady, Alice 100
Brendel, El 40
Browning, Tod 172, 419
Bruce, Virginia 202
Buckler, John 174, 179
Bull, Clarence 109
Burroughs, Edgar Rice 55, 104, 111, 238, 243, 294
Burroughs, Hulbert (Hully) 104
Burroughs, John Coleman (Jack) 104
Busman's Honeymoon 250
Butterflies Are Free 359

C

Charley's Aunt 360
Cage, Nicolas 401
Cagney, James 284
Calhern, Louis 78, 151
Camel cigarettes 39
Cardinal Richelieu 143
Carlson, Richard 314
Cat on a Hot Tin Roof 408
Cavanagh, Paul 106
Chevalier, Maurice 131
Cigarette cards 40
Clifford, Tommy 12-13, 28-29, 32, 35
Cocoanut Grove nightclub 77
Codona, Alfredo 62, 113
Cohens and Kellys in Trouble, The 91
Conlon, Tom 54
Connaught Rangers 16
Convent of the Sacred Heart 23-27
Conway, Jack 105
Conway, Tom 265
Coppola, Francis 401
County Roscommon, Ireland 15
Crabbe, Buster 77

Cradle and All 344
Crawford, Joan 71, 86, 181
Crooked Hearts, The 367
Crosby, Bing 233, 284
Crowd Roars, The 223
Cukor, George 138, 292, 340, 347, 366, 372, 374, 423
Curry, Nathan 107
Cushing, James (Jim) 377-382, 389, 392-394, 408-410, 415, 421-424

D

Dag Hammarskjold Memorial 352
David Copperfield 135
Davies, Marian 87
DeMille, Cecil B. 188
Depression, 1930s 49
Derek, John 317
DeSantis, Tony 343
Deukmejian, George 388
Devil Doll, The 169
Devine, Andy 91
Dietrich, Marlene 357
DiMaggio, Joe 314
Domergue, Faith 306
Don't Drink the Water 358
Douglas, Kirk 345
Downs, Hugh 351
Drake, Charles 312
Dressler, Marie 96
Dru, Joanne 322
Drury Lane Theater 343
Dublin Horse Show 11, 28
Duffy of San Quentin 322
Dullea, Keir 359
Dumbrille, Douglas 143, 199
Dumont, Margaret 190
Dunn, James 73, 85
Durante, Jimmy 181

E

"Edge of Innocence" 329
Edwards, Vince 352
Ellington, Duke 302
Emperor's Candlesticks, The 202

F

Fairbanks, Douglas, Jr.. 86, 367
Farnsworth, Richard 407
Farrell, Charles 42, 181
Farrow, John Charles (son) 294, 339
Farrow, John Villiers 66, 86, 93, 103, 121, 135, 139, 165, 169, 182, 185, 189, 196, 208, 246, 249, 251, 261, 277, 282, 294, 295, 306, 311, 325-327, 338, 340-341, 346-347, 418
Farrow, Mia (daughter) 291, 321, 326, 339, 340, 342, 356, 361, 397
Farrow, Michael Damien (son) 248, 340
Farrow, Patrick (son) 339, 366, 376-377
Farrow, Prudence (daughter) 303
Farrow, Stephanie (daughter) 303, 361
Farrow, Theresa (daughter) 310
Fast Companions 69
Feist, Felix 55
Fields, W. C. 135, 138, 181
Fitzgerald, Barry 265
Fitzgerald, Ella 302
Fitzgerald, F. Scott 419
Five-Oh-Seven, The 356
Flame Within, The 146
Flying Codonas 113
Fonda, Henry 235
Ford, Glenn 327
Ford, Paul 344
Foster, Norman 74, 162
"Four Star Playhouse" 320
Fox Films 29-35
Fox Studio Club 35
Fox, William 30, 35
Foxworth, Robert 410
Fraser, Mary Lovatt (mother) 16
Front Page, The 359

G

Gable, Clark 24, 71, 181, 418
Garbo, Greta 155, 181, 419
Garden of Allah Hotel 181
Gardner, Ava 326
Gargan, William 224, 258
Garland, Judy 233
Garrick, John 40

Garson, Greer 254, 257
Gaynor, Janet 39, 42, 181
Gibbons, Cedric 105
"Gift, The" 320
Girardot, Etienne 218
Glass Menagerie, The 371
Gleason, James 69
Godfrey, Arthur 349
Gorky, Maxim 390
Goulding, Edmund 146
Graham, Sheila 182
Grauman's Chinese Theater 33, 103
Gray, Billy 314
Great Houdinis, The 368
Grey, Virginia 271, 272
Grieg, Robert 151, 162
Gronowicz, Antoni 161
"Guiding Light, The" 388
Gwenn, Edmund 161, 209, 254, 312

H

Habitation of Dragons, The 410
Hall, Gladys 182, 189, 277
Hamilton, Neil 60, 105, 106
Hammett, Dashiell 117
Hannah and Her Sisters 397-401
"Happy Hypocrite, The" 286
Hardie, Russell 100, 140
Harding, Ann 146
Harlow, Jean 67, 118, 197
Hart to Hart: Home Is Where the Hart Is 413
Hays Office 129
Hayward, Louis 146
Hearst, William Randolph 87
Heflin, Van 355
Hepburn, Katharine 372
Hide-Out 121
Hines, Father Hugh 301, 380, 422
Hingle, Pat 411
Hodiak, John 317
Hold That Kiss 220
Holden, Fay 220
Holloway, Sterling 228
Hoover, Herbert 29
Hope, Bob 227, 422
Hopper, Hedda 74
Houdini, Harry 368

Howard, Leslie 67, 72
Howe, James Wong 118
Hughes, Howard 306, 309
Hull, Henry 218
Hume, Cyril 173, 243, 264
Hunt, Peter 406
Hussey, Ruth 228
Hutton, Jim 350

I

Irish America 14

J

Jaffe, Sam 352
John Paul Jones 338, 377
Johnson, Rita 296
Jones, Allan 190
Just Imagine 40

K

Keep It in the Family 356
Kelly, Paul 271-272, 322
Killiney, Ireland 21, 28
Knockvicar, Ireland 17
Korda, Alexander 42

L

Ladd, Alan 246
Ladies of the Corridor 370
Laemmle, Carl, Jr. 86
Lancaster, Burt 311, 366
Lanchester, Elsa 131, 135, 296, 352
LaRocque, Rod 105
Laughton, Charles 80, 128, 138, 295
Lawton, Frank 135, 172
Lear, Norman 350
"Legwork" 406
Leigh, Vivien 24, 27, 209
Leitzel, Lillian 62
LeRoy, Mervyn 96
Lescoulie, Jack 351
Lesser, Sol 111, 274
Let Us Live 235
Levene, Sam 358
Long, Sumner Arthur 344, 351
Love Letters 414

Loy, Myrna 45, 49, 117, 247, 390
Lusitania (ship) 18
"Lux Radio Theatre" 188, 264-290

M

Mission over Korea 317
Macready, George 296, 322
Magdalene, Mary 375
Maisie Was A Lady 261
Mandy's Grandmother 374
Mannix, Eddie 172
March, Fredric 127, 155
Marchand, Nancy 383
Marshall, Herbert 146
Marx Brothers 181, 185-190
Marx, Groucho 194, 288
Matalon, Vivian 387
Mayer, Louis B. 67, 88, 146, 149, 207-209, 238, 264
McCormack, John 11, 28, 30, 33, 189
McCrea, Joel 151
McDormand, Frances 406
McGinn, Walter 354
McKim, Josephine 111
McKuen, Rod 335
Meighan, Thomas 47
Mendes, Lothar 84
Meredith, Burgess 228
Merrill, Gary 377, 383
Metro-Goldwyn-Mayer 54, 117, 146, 188
"MGM: When the Lion Roars" 412
Milland, Ray 80, 295, 302
Miss USA Pageant 391
Mitchum, Robert 306, 325
Monroe, Marilyn 314
Montgomery, Elizabeth 410
Montgomery, Robert 121, 249
Morgan, Frank 199, 202, 217, 223
Morgan, Ralph 71
Morgan, Henry 296
Morning's at Seven 376- 382, 386, 424
Morris, Chester 234, 354
Morton, Joe 405
Mundin, Herbert 173, 179
Murray, Charles 91
My Dear Miss Aldrich 205

N

Never Too Late 344, 346, 348- 353, 420
No Sex, Please, We're British 364
Nolan, Jeanette 336
Nolan, Lloyd 350, 397

O

O'Brien, George 88
O'Brien, Pat 343
O'Connor, Una 129, 135
Okay America 77
O'Keefe, Dennis 220
Oliver, Edna May 135, 205, 254
Olivier, Laurence 24, 27, 254, 256
Olympics of 1932 70
On Borrowed Time 238
One Who Was There 375
O'Neill, Eugene 71
Osborn, Paul 382
O'Sullivan, Charles Joseph (father) 14-18, 133, 185, 188
O'Sullivan, Elizabeth (sister) 17, 134
O'Sullivan, Lt. Jack (brother) 17, 189, 252
O'Sullivan, Mary (mother) 14, 20, 35
O'Sullivan, Patricia (sister) 17, 134
O'Sullivan, Sheila (sister) 17, 134, 247
Ottiano, Rafaela 172
Outward Bound 387
Owen, Reginald 88, 162, 265

P

Port of Seven Seas 217
Page, Geraldine 327
Paramount Pictures 301
Parsons, Louella 43, 96, 104, 121, 138, 172, 213, 248, 292
Paterson, Pat 247, 320, 410
Payment Deferred 80
Peggy Sue Got Married 401-404
Perreau, Gigi 312, 335
Peyton, Father Patrick 305
Pidgeon, Walter 205
Pierce, James 104
"Playhouse 90" 329
Pleasure of His Company, The 362
Powell, William 45, 117, 181, 199

Powers, Stephanie 413
Previn, André 361
Pride and Prejudice 254
Princess and the Plumber, The 42
Production Code (of 1934) 177
"Pros and Cons" 410
Psacharaopoulos, Nikos 390
Pygmalion 373

Q

Quillan, Eddie 51

R

Rainer, Luise 199
Rains, Claude 306
Ralph, Jessie 218, 220
Rathbone, Basil 135, 155, 246
Reagan, Ronald 312, 320
Ritchard, Cyril 362
River Pirates, The 407
Robbers' Roost 88
Rogers, Rena 11
Rogers, Will 36, 44, 45
Rogers, Will, Jr. 335, 338
Rollins, Howard, Jr. 410
Romero, Cesar 143
Roomful of Roses 343
Rooney, Mickey 69, 121, 220, 287
Roosevelt, Franklin Delano 29
Russell, Jane 325
Russell, Rosalind 140, 367
Rutherford, Ann 254
Ryan, Robert 359, 366, 418

S

Sabrina Fair 369
Saintsbury, Killiney 21
Scott, Randolph 329, 332
Seitz, George B. 153
Selznick, David O. 135, 155
September 406
Shearer, Norma 71, 127, 247, 418
Sheffield, Johnny 238, 268, 270, 392
Sheffield, Patty 393
Sheffield, Reginald 143, 238
Sidney, George 91

Siena College 388, 415
Silver Lining, The 53
Sinatra, Frank 356
Skye, Ione 404
Skyline 45-47
Skyscraper Souls 74
Slezak, Walter 323
Smith, C. Aubrey 60, 264
So This Is London 36
Sommer, Edith 343
Song O' My Heart 29, 31, 32, 33, 35
Sothern, Ann 261
Sporting Blood 258
Spring Madness 228
Stack, Robert 339
Stage Mother 100-101
Stander, Lionel 224, 414
Stanwyck, Barbara 314
Steel Cage, The 322
Stephenson, Henry 146, 199, 244
Stevens, Connie 350
Stewart, James 168, 217, 293
Stone, Lewis 135, 140, 151, 258
Stranded 404-406
Strange Interlude 71
Stritch, Elaine 406
Subject Was Roses, The 354

T

Tall T, The 329, 334
Tanner, Tony 364
Tarzan and His Mate 86, 103-116, 177
Tarzan Escapes 165, 173-180, 323
Tarzan Finds A Son! 238-245
Tarzan, the Ape Man 56-66, 323
Tarzan's New York Adventure 270-274
Tarzan's Secret Treasure 264-269
Taylor, Robert 140, 207, 209, 223
Teasdale, Verree 75
Thalberg, Irving 54, 67, 130, 186
Thin Man, The 117
Thirty Days 68
"This Is Your Life" 310
Thorpe, Richard 153, 173, 227, 243, 265
"Today Show, The" 351
Tolstoy, Leo 155
Tone, Franchot 100, 202, 352

Too Scared to Scream 388
Totter, Audrey 317
Trader Horn 58
Tugboat Annie 96
Turner Classic Movies 417
Turner, Kathleen 401, 408
Turner, Lana 328
Twain, Mark 46
Two Dozen Red Roses 354

V

Van Dyke, Woody 55, 60, 118, 121
Velez, Lupe 66
Voice of Bugle Ann, The 166
von Stroheim, Erich 203

W

Where Danger Lives 306-307
Wagner, Robert 413
Wake Island 283
Walker, Jimmy 29
Waxman, Franz 172
Wayne, John 327
Weissmuller, Johnny 40, 55, 77, 105, 109, 140, 164, 182, 238, 267, 274, 293, 324, 341, 361, 371, 394, 412, 422
Welles, Orson 286
West Point of the Air 140
Wilcoxon, Henry 244
Wild Heritage 335
William, Warren 74, 260
Williamstown Film Festival 406
Wills, Chill 271
Wilson, Elizabeth 384
Winchell, Walter 78
With Murder in Mind 410
Wodehouse, P. G. 189
Woman Wanted 151
Wood, Sam 190
World War I 17
World War II 249
Wright, Teresa 383
Wyatt, Jane 350

Y

Yeaman, Elizabeth 111, 121, 207
Yorkin, Bud 350
You Know I Can't Hear You When the Water's Running 357
Young, Loretta 186
Young, Robert 71, 96, 140, 199, 258
Yule, Joe 264

Z

Zanuck, Darryl 163